From MIGRANTS
to CITIZENS

From MIGRANTS *to* CITIZENS

Membership in a Changing World

T. Alexander Aleinikoff

Douglas Klusmeyer

editors

CARNEGIE ENDOWMENT FOR INTERNATIONAL PEACE
Washington, D.C.

From Migrants to Citizens: Membership in a Changing World
may be ordered from:
BROOKINGS INSTITUTION PRESS
1775 Massachusetts Avenue, N.W.
Washington, D.C. 20036
Tel. 1-800-275-1447 or (202) 797-6258
Fax: (202) 797-6004
www.brook.edu

Library of Congress Cataloging-in-Publication data

From migrants to citizens: membership in a changing world / T. Alexander Aleinikoff
and Douglas Klusmeyer.
p. cm.
Includes bibliographical references and index.
ISBN 0-87003-159-7 (paper)
1. Citizenship. 2. Emigration and immigration law. I. Klusmeyer, Douglas B., 1957–
II. Aleinikoff, Thomas Alexander, 1952–
K3224.F76 2000   00-008408
323.6—dc21   CIP

9 8 7 6 5 4 3 2 1

The paper used in this publication meets minimum requirements of the American
National Standard for Information Sciences—Permanence of Paper for Printed
Library Materials: ANSI Z39.48-1984.

Typeset in
Times Roman

Composition by
AlphaWebTech
Mechanicsville, Maryland

Printed by
R. R. Donnelly and Sons
Harrisonburg, Virginia

Contents

**Part Two. Citizenship in the Aftermath of Major
Political Transformations**

**Part Three. Dual and Supranational Citizenship:
Limits to Transnationalism**

Part Four. Ethnic Republics? Citizenship in Israel and Japan

Conclusion

Foreword

STATES THAT HAVE witnessed high levels of immigration or emigration in recent years are facing new, difficult questions about citizenship policies. When
and how should citizenship be extended to new immigrants? How should continuing links that immigrants increasingly maintain with their homelands be
recognized? Should dual nationality be embraced, tolerated, or discouraged?
Which rights and opportunities should be limited to citizens; which should also
be made available to immigrants? Policy makers, advocates, and scholars
around the globe are focusing ever-mounting attention on such questions.

Two years ago, the International Migration Policy Program of the Carnegie
Endowment for International Peace established the Comparative Citizenship
Project to examine the extent to which citizenship policies can and ought to aid
the integration of immigrants into receiving states. The research collected thus
far points to three general policy conclusions. First, the long-term viability of
societies in the next century is far more contingent upon solving the immigration puzzle, and particularly the immigration-integration nexus, than was apparent until very recently. Second, success in solving or resolving this puzzle
demands that a nation's political, intellectual, and financial investments in immigration issues reflect a more appropriate balance between policies on admission and citizenship. Third, in order to understand better such critical concepts
as "integration," "membership," and "citizenship," it is essential that the
broader social context be kept in view. Citizenship issues are particularly sensi-

ix

tive because they blur the lines that have traditionally distinguished foreign and domestic policy domains.

The goal of the Comparative Citizenship Project is to investigate citizenship policies in multiple contexts, to clarify the central issues in the policy debates, and to propose effective ways to address these issues. This present collection of essays represents the first of three volumes from this project. The collection contains a carefully developed set of case studies that analyzes policy trends in emergent and developed liberal-democratic states. The cases were selected to provide a wide-ranging comparative basis to identify points of divergence and convergence in citizenship policy trends. Building upon this work, the next volume will analyze the comparative implications of these trends and general issues of citizenship that cut across the individual case examples. The final volume will propose specific, concrete policy solutions to address these issues.

Modern liberal-democratic principles provide the general normative framework for this project, but both the content and the application of such principles are always open to critical differences in interpretation. No single or universal model of living together successfully as members of a community exists. Each state's nation-building mythology, history, and institutions help to define the route it will take toward achieving the fuller integration of those within its borders. But the principles of tolerance, inclusion, and equality suggest a set of common standards fundamental to any notion of liberal-democratic citizenship.

The Ford Foundation and the Luso-American Development Foundation have generously supported this project.

JESSICA T. MATHEWS
President
Carnegie Endowment for
International Peace

Acknowledgments

THE INTERNATIONAL MIGRATION POLICY PROGRAM originally commissioned the essays collected here for a conference held during June 1998 at Airlie House in Warrenton, Virginia. Unless otherwise noted, the authors of the essays have translated extracts from their original languages into English. Together with an excerpted version of the introduction, the essays authored by Lowell W. Barrington, Donald Galloway, Ayelet Shachar, and Gianni Zappalà and Stephen Castles were published as a special symposium in *Georgetown Immigration Law Journal,* 13. 2 (1999). In preparing this volume, Allison Baker, Maria Dostoinova, Marissa Hughes, and Hilary Chantal Kivitz provided valuable research assistance. We would also like to express our appreciation to Yasmin Santiago, who coordinated planning for the conference and has contributed considerably to the overall success of this project. With great deftness and patience, Carmen Cook copyedited the entire manuscript. Finally, we are pleased to acknowledge our debt to the Ford Foundation for its generous support of this project from its inception. We are especially grateful to Taryn Higashi and Mary McClymont for their support and encouragement.

D.B.K.
T.A.A.

Introduction

DOUGLAS KLUSMEYER

DURING THE PAST DECADE, citizenship has become a salient issue for policy makers, scholars, immigrants, and the public at large. It has emerged as a chronic source of controversy in long-running debates over access to welfare benefits, criteria for naturalization, the legitimacy of plural nationality, and the accommodation of multicultural diversity. One major reason for this growing interest in citizenship matters has been the increasing scale and pace of international migration in a world organized geopolitically around the membership boundaries of nation-states. The citizenry of a nation-state or even of a supranational body such as the European Union is a membership association whose collective identity presupposes drawing lines between the included and the excluded.

The realities of global migration have forced all states to rethink not only their policies of admission, but also their allocation of rights, burdens, and benefits to citizens and other residents. The admission of immigrants with cultural heritages and historical experiences different from those of their host societies inevitably changes the fabric of these societies and requires a complex process of mutual adaptation. For states committed to the liberal-democratic ideal of the rule of law, this process must honor basic principles of human rights as set forth

The author would like to express his gratitude for comments on earlier drafts of this essay to T. Alexander Aleinikoff, Miriam Feldblum, Chikako Kashiwazaki, and Anne Rodsick.

in domestic constitutions and in international treaty instruments. No consensus exists over how these rights are to be understood or implemented, but they nonetheless provide the language through which differences must be negotiated.

This book arose out of the Comparative Citizenship Project of the Carnegie Endowment's International Migration Policy Program. The overarching purpose of this project is to investigate and evaluate how different citizenship policies have been used to promote social cohesion in modern liberal-democratic states that have experienced large-scale immigration. To meet this purpose also requires examining those policies that have (unwittingly or not) most fostered the marginalization and exclusion of immigrant minorities within their host societies. Citizenship policy is, of course, only one factor that affects the opportunities of immigrants and their successful incorporation into their host societies, but it can be a highly significant one both as an indicator of a host society's commitment to facilitating inclusion and as a means of securing the status of newcomers. Failure to define transparent and fair membership rules risks creating different (and almost by definition unequal) classes of membership, with significant potential to undermine social cohesion.

As part of this project, the International Migration Policy Program commissioned the authors of these articles to analyze trends in each country's citizenship policies, examine the special challenges to and features of these policies, and provide a common basis for comparative evaluation. The authors of these studies were asked to examine a common set of issues in the development of the legal rules (judicial, legislative, or administrative) that govern citizenship policy, such as rules concerning the acquisition of citizenship, the rights of aliens, the issue of plural citizenship-nationality, and general strategies employed to enhance social cohesion. The essays show that any concrete understanding of these rules must situate them within the distinct historical contexts of the particular countries addressed. Choices among citizenship rules are usually shaped more by historical experience, existing cultural norms, and expedient political calculations than by deduction from abstract principle or compelling reasons of logical consistency.

The kind of comparative perspective offered here makes it possible to rethink long-held policy assumptions, to identify policy alternatives, and to assess the costs and benefits of these alternatives. Moreover, although citizenship matters fall formally under the legal jurisdiction of individual states, the policies of one state may have significant implications for the citizenship laws and legal status of aliens of other states—for example, with respect to plural nationality. In today's global migration system, the line between domestic and international spheres is becoming increasingly blurred.

This volume of essays is divided into four sections with a brief separate introduction of each section. The first section focuses on three so-called classic lands of immigration: Australia, Canada, and the United States. This designation reflects, in part, the historical reality that the overwhelming majority of their populations are immigrants or the descendents of immigrants and, in part, the dominant national self-understandings of these countries. They have welcomed immigrants as a source of economic growth and demographic expansion, but their histories are also replete with policies of discrimination and restriction based on race, ethnicity, and gender. Since the end of the Second World War, Australia and Canada have experimented most boldly with policies that promote inclusion through the positive recognition of multicultural differences. During this same period, the United States has opened its admissions policies to immigrants from all points of the globe, which has dramatically enhanced its polyethnic diversity. Nevertheless, the United States has (at least formally on the federal level) always taken a laissez-faire approach to the problem of promoting the inclusion of immigrants amid rising multicultural differences.

The second section comprises essays on three sets of "emerging" states: the Baltic states, the Russian Federation, and South Africa. We have grouped them together under the rubric "emerging" because they have all been undergoing radical transformations over the past decade in a quest to develop stable liberal democracies in new circumstances. For these states, immigration has posed a much more complex and difficult challenge than for the classic lands of immigration discussed in the first section, because the risks of fragmentation and disorder are more grave and immediate. In the classic lands of immigration, for example, the issue of plural citizenship can usually be safely treated as a minor concern that does not now directly threaten national solidarity or security—whatever public controversies this issue may periodically incite. By contrast, the recent achievement of independence by the Baltic states and the presence of a sizable Russian minority in each of them makes the potential problem of divided loyalties and conflicting duties that holding plural citizenships may raise seem much more palpable to many. All three of these studies demonstrate not only the importance of membership questions in defining the character of liberal-democratic orders, but also the crucial context that the structure of a particular civil society gives to the meaning of any membership status. Can a shared civic commitment to liberal-democratic norms provide a basis for bridging differences of race, ethnicity, and culture? That question is a major challenge that anyone sharing this commitment must address.

The third section focuses on Israel and Japan. This classification brings to the fore the strong ethnic dimension of these states' dominant national self-understandings, but the presence of this dimension is scarcely unique to these states. Perceived shared bonds of ethnicity and race inform (to greater or lesser degrees) nearly every country's national self-understanding, and differences in such perceptions have long been a potent source of conflict within countries as well as across officially drawn national borders.

Israel qualifies as much as any state to be included as a classic land of immigration. Its existence and development have depended upon immigration, but immigration targeted toward a specific, ascriptively defined group of immigrants to forge a national homeland. Israel's Law of Return makes this goal explicit, but it also raises troubling questions about the status of other groups in Israeli society. By contrast, post–Second World War Japan has never recruited (or permitted) immigrants to settle on a large scale. The economic dimension of the international migration system is driven as much by the need to fill domestic labor market niches as by the desire of immigrants seeking better opportunities. The post–Second World War Japanese economy has not relied heavily on the importation of foreign labor, in part, perhaps, because of its interest in preserving a perceived national homogeneity among its people. Since the 1980s, however, a popular belief has emerged among many Japanese that their country has been experiencing immigration for the first time. This belief demonstrates how easily past patterns of labor importation can be forgotten, because during its Imperial period Japan did permit entrance of large numbers of Koreans as colonial migrants and as conscripted foreign labor toward the end of the Second World War.

The fourth section, National and Supranational Identities, contains essays on the European Union and Mexico. The European Union (EU) has often been held out as the prime example of a newly emergent supranational body that binds together a collection of member national states within an international framework. Is the EU the harbinger of a trend toward new forms of transnational membership that will supercede the importance of citizenship within particular nation-states, or is it little more than a device to reduce market barriers to the flows of labor, trade, and capital? No one now can answer this question definitively, but the recognition of a common EU citizenship illustrates how issues of national membership are becoming inseparably tied to larger regional and international contexts.

The North American Free Trade Agreement (NAFTA), entered into by Canada, Mexico, and the United States, may be the first step toward a broader institutional and political integration among these states, but at this stage it is no more than a commercial arrangement designed to liberalize the flows of trade and capital. As a major sending country to the United States, Mexico has an understandable interest in the welfare of its emigrants there. The Mexican government's recent change in its nationality law to facilitate the acquisition of U.S.

citizenship without sacrificing Mexican nationality suggests further how transnational linkages among such regional partners are growing.

To highlight points of comparison among these country studies, this introduction will focus on two central issues in the acquisition of citizenship. As this introduction seeks to show, however, these issues are inseparable from broader policy concerns over citizenship and the promotion of social cohesion among liberal-democratic states.

Acquisition of Citizenship through Birth or Descent

The essays assembled in this volume all grapple with the most fundamental questions of citizenship: how individuals acquire it and what rights attach to it. To answer these questions requires first stipulating the criteria that determine eligibility for citizenship, the processes through which it is obtained, and the requirements that govern its acquisition. The vast majority of individuals acquire citizenship through three primary means: by birth on the soil of the sovereign's territory (the principle of *jus soli*), by descent according to blood kinship (the principle of *jus sanguinis*), and by naturalization through formalized legal procedures. Citizenship may also be obtained through marriage, adoption, or other specialized circumstances.

Modern states often employ some variation of all three of the primary means to satisfy different purposes. Even those states that have adopted the principle of *jus soli* in its broadest form have still recognized a need to combine it with elements of *jus sanguinis*. The children of U.S. citizens born outside of its territory, for example, receive their parents' citizenship by virtue of descent. Those who acquire U.S. citizenship in this manner cannot transmit it to their children through *jus sanguinis* unless they have previously established residence in the United States. Stipulating residence as a criterion for the acquisition of citizenship reflects a larger issue over the degree and substance of the connections that should be necessary between a polity and its citizenry. The residence requirement is a connections test designed to prevent the transmission of citizenship across generations to descendents who have no substantial tie with the United States.

Australia, another traditional country of immigration, also limits the transmission of citizenship by descent to children born outside its territory to those who have at least one parent who had acquired Australian citizenship other than by descent or who had resided in Australia for at least two years prior to registration of the child at an Australian consulate as an Australian citizen. Canadian citizens can transfer their citizenship to children born outside its territory, but where the parent has acquired citizenship in this manner the child may lose his or her Canadian citizenship if the child fails to register with Canadian authorities before the age of twenty-eight.

Not all states apply this kind of connections test. South African citizens, for example, may transmit this status to their children born outside the Republic for generations. There are no apparent residency requirements or cutoff provisions. The open-ended nature of such acquisition rules may affect only a small minority of South African citizens, but these rules ask us to consider how the relationship between a polity and its citizens should be understood. By contrast, naturalized Mexican citizens may forfeit their Mexican citizenship if they reside outside of Mexico for more than five years.

As the studies in this volume show, the state's choice of means for acquiring citizenship has important consequences in promoting the inclusion or exclusion of persons and groups within a polity. In his evocative contribution to this book, Donald Galloway elucidates the core issues that any liberal-democratic society must face in making citizenship policy. The most fundamental issue turns on the question "Who belongs?" As Galloway's discussion of Canadian citizenship makes clear, there is no simple way to answer this question. He points out that throughout the twentieth century two competing visions have driven debate over these matters among Canadians, and among many outside of Canada. The first, which he labels "collectivist" or "nationalist," has emphasized the role of citizenship as a tool for promoting social cohesion and preserving common traditions. Proponents of this vision have argued for the importance of enhancing a distinctive shared national identity that links the citizenry together as a community and enables citizens to participate in a common way of life. This vision highlights a central dimension of citizenship as a means by which societies "regenerate" themselves through the inclusion of new members, whether by birth or migration, while maintaining connections with their historical pasts.

A second competing vision, which emphasizes equal respect for individual dignity and the right of persons to pursue their own private ends, has deep roots in modern Western liberal thought. This vision, as Galloway argues, has become integral to conceptions of political membership where the principle of subjecthood, based on a bond of subservient allegiance, has given way to one of citizenship, based on a notion of sharing in sovereignty. Any principle of justice that grounds the vesting of rights as an entitlement of individual personhood necessarily implies a universalism of this criterion; that is, it should apply equally to all persons irrespective of their particular membership status. But such rights can only be effectively guaranteed and exercised within distinct, political bodies of which the individual is a recognized member.

Galloway's observation that questions of citizenship are always inextricably bound to larger issues of sovereignty, national identity, the framework of political order, and individual liberties is surely correct. The salience of all these issues to citizenship policy is abundantly evident in the ten other essays in this symposium. Like Galloway's, these essays demonstrate the importance of examining a state's citizenship policies against its particular historical context rather than as a mere matter of general legal principles or theoretical deduction.

Lowell Barrington addresses the particular challenges facing the Baltic states. After regaining their independence, these states have had to balance a strong interest in reconstituting their national unity around an ethnic model of nationhood against the need as self-proclaimed liberal-democratic states to respect the rights of minorities who entered during the era of Soviet annexation. In contrast to traditional countries of immigration such as Australia, Canada, and the United States, which have been guided by a positive valuation of immigration as necessary for desired demographic and economic growth, the Baltic states have had to adjust to the legacy of immigration during the period of Soviet domination. The Baltic states have chosen to emphasize an ethnic understanding of nationhood, which assumes that shared ties of culture, ancestry, and historical destiny are fundamental to the definition of collective identity. Their interrupted status as independent states heightens the significance of ancestry and historical precedent as a criterion for citizenship acquisition.

In examining the implications of an ethnic understanding of social membership, however, Barrington cautions against drawing too simple an equation between an ethnic understanding of the nation and an exclusivist citizenship policy aimed at minorities of a different ethnic character. Such a reductionist equation obscures other important factors that shape citizenship policy, notably the role of choice exercised by policy makers in deciding among policies. As a case in point, Barrington highlights the different approaches toward citizenship adopted by Lithuania and Latvia. The political elites of both countries, he observes, perceive their countries in highly ethnic terms, but Lithuania's citizenship policy has been notably more inclusive than Latvia's. Despite their ethnic understanding of national identity, Lithuania's leaders have by this account displayed a genuine commitment to the promotion of "inter-ethnic harmony" and to the legitimacy of minority claims to membership in the Lithuanian nation.

Lithuania took the key step toward a broadly inclusive citizenship policy just before its independence from the Soviet Union. A 1989 citizenship law, for example, granted automatic citizenship to all permanent residents who had been born in Lithuania or with a parent or grandparent who had been born there. This law, Barrington observes, was "strongly based on the principle of *jus soli*. . . ."

After regaining independence, the Lithuanian government in 1991 tightened citizenship acquisition requirements, but it did not revoke citizenship from those persons who had received it during the Soviet annexation.

Since regaining their independence, all three Baltic states have emphasized to varying degrees *jus sanguinis* as the basis for acquiring citizenship. The Lithuanian Parliament, for example, in 1991 enacted a new law that rescinded the right to automatic citizenship of all permanent residents. It restricted this right to persons who had either been citizens before 1940 (and their descendents) or had been lawful permanent residents from 1919 to 1940. Yet, the Parliament did not revoke citizenship from those persons who had received it during the annexation era. It also provided for the restoration of Lithuanian citizenship to individuals who had been Lithuanian citizens during the annexation period but who now resided in another state.

As Barrington notes, the danger that an emphasis on descent over place of birth or residence could have strong exclusionary effects on minorities in the political system has been exemplified in Latvia. After independence, the Latvian government recognized citizenship only of those individuals (and their descendents) who had held citizenship before annexation. It further refused to enact any provisions for naturalization. As a result, most minorities have been ineligible to vote in elections for either local or national offices.

These former soviet bloc countries seek to address issues of citizenship within their own carefully defined borders on a national level. On a broader level, as George Ginsburgs demonstrates, the Russian Federation as the successor to the Soviet Union has had to meet even larger challenges in developing a common citizenship policy acceptable to all its member states. One of these challenges, notes Ginsburgs, lies in the unique historical legacy of Soviet membership imposed from above. The Russian Federation's policy, for example, proceeds from the premise that, ideally, the shared citizenship of the parents should be the decisive factor in determining the citizenship of their children. That is, parental lineage is a more important criterion than place of birth. In accordance with international legal norms that disfavor statelessness, however, the Russian Federation also grants citizenship to children born within its territory whose parents were citizens of other republics that once formed part of the Soviet Union and where current member republics have declined to confer their own citizenship.

In this way, the Russian Federation seeks to fill the gap for children denied citizenship within member republics. By contrast, the European Union offers no provisions to confer EU citizenship to children born within its territory who have not acquired the citizenship of a member state. The conferral of EU citizenship depends entirely on an individual's status as a citizen of a member state, irrespective of differences among member states in their citizenship acquisition policies.

In the case of both the Russian Federation and the European Union, their citizenship acquisition policies reflect ambiguities in the past and present political and legal relationships of member states to the polity as a whole. In both instances, member states remain jealous of their sovereignty within their broader supranational frameworks. Ginsburgs persuasively argues that preserving a unitary federation-wide citizenship with primacy over member-state citizenship is key to maintaining the institutional integrity of the Russian Federation. He leaves open the question of whether the Russian Federation will be able to withstand challenges from member states seeking greater control over their own citizenship policies.

Marco Martiniello discusses similar challenges to the supranational integrity of the new European Union citizenship. He points to the great irony that just when a supranational "European citizenship" has finally been codified through the Maastricht and Amsterdam Treaties, EU member states may now cling ever more insistently to controlling their own national citizenship policies as one of the few areas remaining to them to exercise their own autonomous sovereignty. Where one might think that the recent creation of a common European currency was a decisive step in the promotion of European unity, such a transfer of authority may impel member states to attach even more significance to national citizenship as a symbol of national sovereignty.

By contrast, federal citizenship in the U.S. has, at least since the Civil War, had clear primacy over member-state citizenships. The postwar constitutional amendments adopted during the Reconstruction era determined for the first time that constitutionally protected rights were equally binding on state governments as well as on the federal government. In contrast to the EU and the Russian Federation, the fact that member states are not the loci of separate national self-understandings considerably bolsters the primacy and unitary character of U.S. federal citizenship.

This is not the case in the EU, where many Europeans regard their particular national citizenships as primary, a feeling that has discouraged their exercise of EU citizenship rights. Martiniello offers several additional explanations for the limited practice of EU citizenship rights. The first is a lack of publicly disseminated information regarding how these rights can be exercised. The second concerns delays in the effective implementation of these rights. The third is the relative insignificance of these rights to the overwhelming majority of European citizens who reside within their own national states. EU citizens, for example, have the right to vote and stand for elections to the European Parliament, but this body is the weakest EU political institution, so voting may seem to involve more trouble than it is worth.

The creation of a common EU citizenship "from above," Martiniello observes, has formalized three levels of basic membership, ranked according to different menus of civil, socioeconomic, and political rights that members possess. Citizens of EU states residing within their national state's borders have the fullest menu of these rights. EU citizens living in member states other than their own are entitled to a more abbreviated menu of rights, such as the right to vote in local and European elections but not the right to vote in the national elections of their state of residence. Citizens of nonmember states have the fewest rights. Long-term residents may enjoy important civil and socioeconomic rights, but few political rights. They cannot obtain EU citizenship directly, but only through first obtaining citizenship in a member state, subject to that state's particular naturalization requirements.

This "triangular" structure of EU membership, Martiniello argues, may further marginalize resident aliens, especially if the notion of a shared, singular European cultural identity is promoted at the expense of a respect for multicultural diversity. This respect should rest not simply on a commitment to fundamental human rights, but also on the recognition of the reality of Europe's deeply multicultural past and present. As Martiniello points out, however, the issue of cultural diversity has never figured prominently on the agenda of EU leaders and is often obscured by the problem of accommodating the particularist national self-understandings of the member states.

Martiniello sees the best hope for forging greater unity within the EU through the construction of citizenship "from below," involving coalitions of individuals with interests and institutional ties that cut across national borders. He contends that the low voter turnout for European national elections may be an indication of an active public resistance (rather than mere apathy) to the way that EU citizenship has been imposed from above and its failure to address the needs of average citizens. From this perspective, the continuing institutional weakness of the EU Parliament as an instrument of transnational, popular political representation appears to be a major missed opportunity to enhance a deeper public identification with the EU as a common home through shared participation in self-governance. The effects of this weakness on voter turnout also underscore the importance of situating any analysis of citizenship rights within the institutional contexts in which these rights are implemented and exercised. The right to vote does not mean much if the representative body for which one is voting has little effective power or voice. As Martiniello argues, individuals' perceptions of citizenship rights are just as important as the formal political and socioeconomic intentions of the governments granting those rights.

Perceptions of citizenship also figure strongly in Ayelet Shachar's examination of the citizenship policies of Israel, a state founded on a highly ethnic conception of nationhood. This conception, rooted in nineteenth-century Romantic nationalist ideology, recognizes Israel as the homeland of the Jewish people; but Israel must share this homeland with its Arab minorities. The Law of Return is the centerpiece of Israeli citizenship policy. It automatically grants every Jewish immigrant full and equal citizenship immediately upon arrival. As Shachar explains, this law rests on a diasporic conception of Jews around the globe as one national people, a membership bond that existed before the creation of the modern Israeli State. Israel has received a vast flow of immigrants since the enactment of this law. From the beginning, the open-ended nature of this invitation to Jews worldwide to resettle in Israel has sparked considerable and recurrent debate over the question of "who is a Jew" with entitlement to citizenship. Rival religious and secular understandings of Jewishness have driven much of this debate, but shifts in the predominant source countries of Jewish immigrants have also contributed to it.

Massive numbers of Russian Jews entered Israel from 1989 to 1993, for example. They enjoyed an automatic entitlement to citizenship, although their ties with Judaism and the State of Israel had hitherto been minimal. Their sheer number and cultural foreignness injected fresh energy into the debate among the Israeli public over who should be entitled to return.

This debate rests on the fact that the Law of Return invests a deeply ascriptive character into the heart of Israeli citizenship policy. Such ascriptive tendencies are especially apparent when contrasted with the government's long denial of citizenship to Arab refugees who had been residents of the area before the state was formed. Shachar uses the example of Russian Jewish immigrants to illustrate that ascriptive categories, such as "Jewishness," are always open to competing definitions that may fall across a broad spectrum. Giving Jewish immigrants a privileged entitlement of such magnitude can only reinforce the perception of Arabs as no better than second-class citizens.

Another essay addressing the importance of perceptions of citizenship is that by Jonathan Klaaren. He has produced an incisive analysis of South African citizenship policy and its reception by certain population groups. From its first citizenship law of 1949 to its Bantu Homelands Citizenship Act of 1970 to its Restoration Citizenship Act of 1986, South Africa's legislation illustrates dramatically how citizenship and nationality status can be manipulated to reinforce a caste hierarchy within a putative liberal-democratic republic. The 1949 law established the first "common" citizenship for South Africans applicable to both the white minority and the black majority. As Klaaren explains, however, citizenship did not automatically confer the right to vote. That right was restricted on racial grounds. The Bantu Homelands Act of 1970 introduced a distinction between homelands citizenship, to which all blacks were assigned, and a common South African nationality. Initially, homeland citizenship and South African citizenship remained tied, but when the South African government began granting homeland independence, those homeland citizens lost both their South African citizenship and nationality. This tactic created gradients of membership rights that effectively barred the black majority from the exercise of popular sovereignty in the South African Republic. The Restoration Citizenship Act of 1986 made a partial step toward restoring citizenship to homeland blacks, but it applied only to those who held permanent residence in South Africa.

Against this background, Klaaren devotes the bulk of his analysis to the legislative history and policy implications of the South African Citizenship Act of 1995. The act restored a single, common citizenship regime for South Africans, but it did not repeal the separate citizenship laws of the independent homelands nor address effectively the reality of large numbers of migrants who have been entering the country as temporary workers. Despite the stated intent to eradicate the effects of apartheid legislation, the actual results of this act have been fairly modest. Where one might have expected that a common ideal of citizenship built around a shared allegiance to republican principles might provide a source of civic unity amid great cultural and social diversity, this ideal has yet to come to the fore in South Africa.

A strong political understanding of citizenship as a consensual bond of allegiance has also not yet emerged in Japan. Chikako Kashiwazaki's essay provides one of the most thorough surveys of Japanese citizenship policy and law available in English. As Kashiwazaki notes, Japan bases its citizenship acquisition law on a strictly applied principle of *jus sanguinis*, but she argues against simple explanations that attribute the use of this principle to an ethnically narrow national self-understanding. She contends that a *jus sanguinis* system can be as inclusive as a *jus soli* system, and would have little practical effect depending upon a number of variables including the strictness of naturalization rules. Like Barrington, Kashiwazaki also warns against invoking broad national character arguments that are too often grounded on popular stereotypes and exaggerate the relative "uniqueness" of particular countries within the global migration economy. To situate Japan's place within this economy, she has developed a richly comparative framework. One point of comparison rests on sources of economic growth. In contrast to many European states after the Second World War, Kashiwazaki points out, Japan did not import large numbers of foreign workers to sustain its economic growth. She reports that foreign residents currently compose only 1.2 percent of the Japanese population, so Japan has not had to face the problem of immigrant incorporation on nearly the same scale as many EU states.

In explaining Japan's reliance on a strict *jus sanguinis* system, Kashiwazaki traces its introduction back to the codified nationality laws of 1899. She points out that the policy makers were influenced by European models of citizenship acquisition. Moreover, the *jus sanguinis* system, she observes, proved "compatible with previous legal practices, in particular the family registration system that had been used to define the subject population."

Like Barrington, Kashiwazaki emphasizes the important role that international bodies and treaty instruments can play in constructively influencing domestic policy. After Japan ratified the International Covenant on Civil and Political Rights in 1979 and the United Nations Covenant relating to the Status of Refugees in 1981, for example, the government amended important discriminatory provisions in its citizenship policy that had been directed against foreign residents.

The issue of plural nationality has recently become a source of controversy in the United States in response to Mexico's 1997 amendment of its nationality law. This controversy vividly illustrates again why citizenship, though recognized as a subject of domestic jurisdiction, can implicate larger international concerns. The amended law permits Mexicans who acquired their nationality at birth on Mexican territory to acquire additional nationalities without forsaking their original Mexican nationality. In his essay on Mexican nationality, Manuel Becerra Ramírez argues that this legal change occurred in reaction to perceived discrimination against Mexicans in the United States. Through this change, the Mexican government sought to encourage Mexicans residing in the United States to obtain the fullest range of political and civic rights through the acquisition of U.S. citizenship by removing the potential loss of Mexican nationality as a deterrent to naturalizing in the United States. By this change, the Mexican government hoped to minimize a difficult choice often faced by immigrants between severing a fundamental relationship with their homeland and taking full advantage of the opportunities and legal protections in a new host society.

The amended nationality law rests on a carefully drawn distinction between *nationality,* understood as a state membership affiliation, and *citizenship,* a status that confers specific political rights such as voting in Mexican elections. In the acquisition of Mexican nationality, Mexico applies a mixed system of *jus soli* and *jus sanguinis*. Persons born on Mexican territory acquire Mexican nationality and, as nationals, are automatically entitled to Mexican citizenship at the age of eighteen. The conferral of Mexican nationality to a child born in Mexico is not contingent on the nationality of the child's parents. At the same time, the child of a Mexican national, who was born in Mexico, is also automatically entitled to Mexican nationality if the child is born outside of Mexican territory. This entitlement applies irrespective of the parents' existing location of residence.

Acquisition of Citizenship through Naturalization

Most of the authors of these essays also address the specific laws and ideologies governing the processes of naturalization. Naturalization is not only an important mode through which citizenship is acquired, but also one of the few in which volitional choice is involved in its acquisition both on the part of prospective new citizens and on the part of states conferring it. The motives of individuals seeking to naturalize may be highly instrumental or deeply patriotic, but whatever their reasons they are choosing to enter the most privileged form of shared belonging that liberal-democratic polities bestow. In determining criteria and procedures for naturalization, states, too, are making choices regarding the desired character of new citizens, their terms of allegiance, and the future shape of their populations. Because so much is at stake in such choices, naturalization policies are often subject to considerable controversy by affected groups and interests.

The rules governing naturalization vary widely among states, but all recognize these rules as important tools of inclusion and exclusion. The states with the most inclusive policies discussed in this volume are the three so-called classic lands of immigration: Australia, Canada, and the United States. All three have similar requirements. Prospective new citizens must be lawful permanent residents for several years prior to applying, possess good moral character (for example, have no major criminal convictions), demonstrate an adequate knowledge of their new country's history and civics, and have a basic command of the language. All three states also require an oath of loyalty. In the United States, new citizens taking the oath must swear exclusive loyalty to the United States and explicitly renounce all former loyalties to other sovereigns. Canada and Australia demand a much less exclusive expression of allegiance. Their pledges do not require a renunciation of other loyalties or a profession of sole loyalty to the country.

Israel has developed naturalization requirements substantively similar to those of the United States, Canada, and Australia for those ineligible for citizenship under the Law of Return. Israel also requires prospective citizens in naturalizing to renounce prior citizenships, but its loyalty oath specifies swearing neither primary nor exclusive allegiance to the State of Israel. On the simplest level, Arabs and Jews born in Israel enjoy the same right to acquire citizenship through *jus sanguinis*. All children whose parents are Israeli citizens automatically acquire it. As Shachar shows, however, the actual picture is considerably more complicated than this straightforward rule would suggest. The hundreds of thousands of Arabs who fled the area during the 1948 war that followed the establishment of the Israeli State, but who did not return almost immediately after the war ended, lost their entitlement to automatic citizenship. Many of these individuals eventually did return during the 1950s to settle permanently, but they often found meeting citizenship eligibility requirements extremely difficult. Since most did not have citizenship elsewhere, they became stateless. The Israeli government did not squarely address their plight until 1980. At that time, the government conferred citizenship retroactively on these Arab residents and, in turn, granted automatic citizenship to their children.

Although Israel's formal naturalization requirements are not notably more restrictive than those of Australia, Canada, or the United States, its requirements stand in sharp contrast to the automatic and immediate conferral of citizenship granted to Jewish immigrants under the Law of Return. Israel, however, is hardly the only liberal-democratic state that has distinguished among classes of immigrants in its naturalization policies. T. Alexander Aleinikoff points out that the United States' original citizenship law specifically restricted naturalization to whites and that the last of such racial restrictions was not removed until 1952. During the 1920s and the 1930s, Australia also denied citizenship on racial grounds. After the Second World War, it still adhered to an ethnic _model of nationhood as a member of the larger British national family.

Discriminatory citizenship policies based on racial and ethnic categories are endemic in the histories of many Western democratic states, even in such classic lands of immigration as Australia. The essay by Gianni Zappalà and Stephen Castles is particularly instructive in this regard. The authors examine the post–Second World War Australian experience with immigration and naturalization, as Australia has moved from an exclusivist "White Australia" policy to an active promotion of multicultural diversity. Beginning after the war, Australia launched a major and successful effort to recruit immigrants. Millions came to settle. The government viewed the acquisition of citizenship as essential to their integration into Australian society, but naturalization rates remained low throughout the 1950s and 1960s. This low rate was often attributed to a lack of loyalty, but this perception missed the depth of the issues involved. As Zappalà and Castles observe, "there was little understanding that the complexity of the regulations, poor English language ability, and having to renounce one's country of birth made citizenship an unattractive option for many immigrants. . . ."

The government gradually introduced measures to reduce administrative complexity, lower fees, and simplify procedures, but this proved insufficient to boost naturalization rates significantly. By the end of the 1960s, the government finally began to realize that discrimination against immigrants and the failure to take their needs into account was a major deterrent that discouraged migrants from seeking to become Australian citizens. To make newcomers feel welcome as Australians would require a new understanding of what it meant to be Australian, an understanding that could accommodate the immigrants' own distinct interests and heritages. Toward this end, the government eliminated from its citizenship law special privileges and exemptions for British immigrants that had, at least symbolically, reflected Australia's self-understanding as ethnically British. As the government began to address deeper structural problems in the 1970s, naturalization rates rose. By 1991, Zappalà and Castles report, "70 percent of eligible overseas-born residents were Australian citizens."

Despite such achievements, government support for multicultural citizenship programs has seriously eroded since the mid-1990s. The long-term consequences of this decline remain unclear. Such reversals in the direction of public policy are not uncommon among states trying to absorb larger numbers of newcomers. But the postwar history that Zappalà and Castles so deftly analyze suggests that any prolonged retreat will simply produce greater divisions.

In contrast to Australia, the United States does not actively promote immigrant integration as official policy. This lack of policy may be one important reason why 6 or 7 million residents, despite their eligibility, have not elected to naturalize. In his essay, Aleinikoff points to other reasons deterring naturalization. He discusses the relatively few differences in rights and benefits that distinguish citizenship status from permanent resident status, the broad provision of *jus soli* that does not require parents to be citizens in order for their children to acquire citizenship, the knowledge of history and language needed to satisfy naturalization requirements, and the exclusivity of the oath of allegiance given in the naturalization process.

Nonetheless, Aleinikoff observes, naturalization rates have risen dramatically in recent years. He attributes this rise to a mix of incentives that are primarily negative. The Immigration and Naturalization Service, for example, introduced a requirement that all permanent residents must obtain a new resident alien card but, at the same time, made it known that the financial costs of such a card would be only slightly less than the costs charged for naturalization. Perhaps the most powerful of these negative incentives, which appeared to punish alien residency while rewarding naturalization (however unintentionally), included anti-immigrant campaigns and debates in the 1990s suggesting that previously available access to significant rights and benefits might be taken away from aliens.

One possible lesson to draw from this story is that negative incentives, such as expanding the differences in the rights and benefits enjoyed by citizens and aliens, is an effective tool to promote naturalization. As Aleinikoff points out, plausible normative arguments can be made that citizens are entitled to a broader array of fundamental rights and benefits than are aliens. It is difficult, however, to see how these kinds of incentives deepen any form of affective loyalty that new citizens 3would feel to their host polity; instead, they may cheapen the symbolic value of citizenship as bond of consensual allegiance. Moreover, as Aleinikoff argues, lawful members of a society who are not citizens, but are no less active participants in and contributors to it, also have a strong claim to that society's benefits and protections. Aleinikoff contends that the key distinction to be drawn between the membership status of citizens and that of long-term lawfully resident aliens should turn on political rights, that is, the rights to hold elective office and to vote in national elections. From this perspective, the hallmark of liberal-democratic citizenship involves belonging to a sovereign community whose people collectively exercise self-governance.

In contrast to the United States' and Australia's naturalization policy, the Baltic states have had to adjust to the reality of immigrants admitted under Soviet-imposed regimes. As Barrington notes, Lithuania and (to a somewhat lesser extent) Estonia have adopted the most inclusive naturalization policies. The naturalization requirements in Lithuania's 1991 citizenship law stipulated that applicants must pass a written and oral language test, have resided permanently in Lithuania for ten years, demonstrate sufficient familiarity with the Lithuanian Constitution, relinquish prior citizenships, and make a nonexclusive loyalty declaration.

For its part, Estonia's 1992 citizenship law made applicants eligible for naturalization after two years of permanent residence (amended to five years in 1995), although the term of residence would be counted only after March 30, 1992. The law also required a test of language competence in Estonian. This language requirement has posed a considerable barrier to prospective applicants for naturalization, however, because the Estonian language is exceptionally difficult to learn and governmental provisions for language courses have been inadequate. As a result, naturalization rates have remained low.

Barrington contrasts these two sets of inclusive naturalization policies with the much more restrictive policies of Latvia. After achieving independence, the Latvian government refused to recognize or adopt a naturalization law until after the elections for the first Latvian Parliament in 1993. Latvia's citizenship acquisition policy effectively barred most non-ethnic Latvians (between 700,000 and 800,000 persons) from participating in the elections for this Parliament, and, therefore, from participating in the subsequent drafting of citizenship legislation. The 1993 citizenship law that this Parliament enacted reflected its members' intent to avoid any rapid large-scale naturalizations and, perhaps, to encourage the exodus of non-Latvian minorities. For instance, it imposed restrictions on eligibility for naturalization according to age and place of birth, and it stipulated other naturalization requirements regarding terms of residence, language competence, and official registration that made naturalization difficult. The citizenship law proved effective as a tool of exclusion. "Of the 140,000 residents who were eligible to apply by 1998," Barrington reports, "only approximately 10,000 had applied, and only 7,477 had become citizens. . . ."

Although Estonia's citizenship policies have been more exclusive than Lithuania's, they might have been far more so but for the influence that international bodies were able to exercise on Estonian political leaders. Barrington emphasizes the critical role that such organizations as the Council of Europe played in pushing the Estonian government toward more inclusive citizenship policies. He shows that the effectiveness of these bodies in influencing governmental policies cannot rely on moral suasion alone. Instead, such influence must include concrete incentives ranging from offers of increased trade and direct financial assistance to stipulating conditions of membership in regional political organizations. His analysis demonstrates that despite the fact that citizenship has traditionally been considered an exclusive domain of domestic law, states may still be held accountable to international norms. As the Estonian example makes clear, the force of international accountability may be at best modest, but it can still provide an important check on the worst excesses of ethnic chauvinism.

The question of naturalization policy has also been a problem for Japan. Despite the fact that naturalization rates have been rising during the 1990s, Kashiwazaki observes that Japan's naturalization requirements have remained strict. These requirements include the provision of extensive supporting documents by applicants and an expectation of full assimilation. Yet, even long-term foreign residents who meet these requirements have no guaranteed right to acquire Japanese citizenship. The combination of a strict *jus sanguinis* system with a restrictive naturalization policy has had predictable consequences. First- and second-generation Korean residents, Kashiwazaki reports, have largely resisted acquiring Japanese citizenship out of a sense that this would betray their national as well as cultural identity as Koreans. Their children born in Japan have no automatic entitlement to citizenship, although they may attend Japanese schools, speak fluent Japanese, and have had no substantive contact with their Korean "homeland." This very lack of contact, however, may now be bolstering the younger generation's willingness to acquire Japanese citizenship through naturalization, because they are less likely to look upon it as forsaking their own distinct cultural heritage.

In the protection of the rights of permanent resident aliens, Kashiwazaki identifies a recent trend toward gradual expansion that is similar to the earlier experience of many EU countries. "Throughout the 1970s," she observes, "the residential status of long-term resident aliens remained insecure." Long-term resident aliens also suffered from discrimination in their access to social services, such as health care. In the 1980s and 1990s, however, the Japanese government has begun to address these problems in a serious fashion. This trend found in both Japan and in many EU member states would seem to confirm Aleinikoff's model of lawful permanent settlement as the emerging standard among liberal-democratic states in the treatment of alien rights.

Where Japan has sought to restrict immigration rigidly, Mexico has had to deal with the reality of continuing immigration across its southern border. Mexico's naturalization requirements are similar to those of other countries that receive large numbers of immigrants. The average foreign resident seeking to naturalize must have lived in Mexico for five years, speak the national language, and demonstrate knowledge of the country's history and culture. Like the United States, Mexico also insists that naturalization applicants renounce any additional nationality. In light of the recent amendment of its nationality law explicitly recognizing the legitimate status of plural nationality, this renunciation requirement may seem paradoxical, but it reflects the different perspectives many states apply to their nationals who have settled abroad and to those newcomers who have immigrated.

Conclusion

The final chapter, by Miriam Feldblum, takes a broader look at the comparative citizenship trends highlighted across the different country and regional reports. Based on the data and analyses of the previous chapters, Feldblum examines the different ways in which states are increasingly organizing the allocation and distribution of formal nationality access, dual nationality, naturalization as well as other membership rights, benefits, and obligations. As demonstrated by each of the authors, immigrants in the countries under review experience different "rations" of membership across policy domains, both in terms of their legal standing and substantive claims. In fact, the country and region reports point to differentiated distributions of citizenship both within and across polities. Feldblum argues that these patterns are significant because they underscore the continuing efforts by states to manage the allocation of membership rights, benefits, and obligations to immigrants. The chapter is divided into the three sections. The first section discusses the qualified extension of access to formal citizenship and dual nationality, while the second section focuses on the extent to which states have differentiated immigrants' access to membership rights. Feldblum contrasts the qualifying of rights and benefits to foreigners (including access to social services and nationality) with—in the area of immigration control—the rise of claims-making and participation both for and by immigrants in these same policy domains. Finally, Feldblum concludes that increasing levels of governance—local, national, and beyond the national state—are now engaged in the allocation of citizenship.

These articles demonstrate how far citizenship studies have advanced since T. H. Marshall published his classic work *Citizenship and Social Class*.[1] Two of the major assumptions shaping his work have become untenable. First, Marshall treated the state as a bounded polity in which the issue of admitting new members and their eventual incorporation into their host society never arose. Second, he could write confidently of a common culture that all members of a polity would share without ever examining the terms of this common culture or addressing the challenges posed by the reality of cultural diversity.

In discussing both the incorporation of newcomers into their host societies and the issue of cultural diversity, terms such as *assimilation* and *integration* are often used without any clear specification of their concrete meaning or of the public policy purposes they are intended to serve. This lack of specificity is especially problematic for two reasons. First, no agreement exists over the definition of these terms. Second, and relatedly, the meaning of these terms will inevitably look different from the perspective of the host society than from that of newcomers. Moreover, significant normative questions are at issue regarding how such terms should be understood in the context of modern liberal-democratic principles. Both assimilation and integration can too easily imply a largely one-sided process in which newcomers adapt themselves to the structures of life and dominant culture of their host societies. It may be appropriate to reframe the issue, not as integration or assimilation, but as creating conditions that advance equal opportunity through which all members of a society can choose their own avenues of participation and thereby find common ground with other members. By this view, a central criterion for determining the allocation of rights, benefits, and burdens among members would be the degree to which they either impede or facilitate equal participation.

The articles published here demonstrate vividly why such issues have become central to citizenship policy and the difficulties that different states have

---

1. Republished in Marshall and Bottomore, 1992.

experienced in grappling with them. These authors offer deeply informed and insightful guides to the specific developments in citizenship policy, even as they bring out the larger questions that such policies are increasingly being forced to address.

References

Marshall, T. H., and Tom Bottomore 1992. *Citizenship and Social Class.* London: Pluto Press.

PART ONE

Citizenship in Countries
of Immigration

CHAPTER ONE

Introduction

DAVID A. MARTIN

THE NATIONS COVERED in the next chapters make a natural grouping: three states that traditionally identify themselves proudly as countries of immigration. Several striking similarities in the citizenship policies and practices of Australia, Canada, and the United States emerge from the following pages. If these policies were clear inheritances from a common British colonial past, the overlap might be unremarkable. But many of them do not trace to earlier British practice, and in any case the path to independence followed by the United States, through revolutionary violence long before the others showed signs of trying to separate even in mild ways, diverges so sharply from that of the other two that one suspects something deeper is reflected in the coincidences. Perhaps certain citizenship policies have simply proved to make sense, over decades of practice and experience, for large, generally successful, polyethnic nations that are, at least by the late 1990s, accustomed to accommodating large and diverse influxes of foreigners each year. Some of the chief similarities follow:

CITIZENSHIP AT BIRTH.   All follow a strong form of *jus soli*, assuring citizenship at birth to persons born in the territory, even if the parents are foreigners. Canada and the United States do so whatever the status of the parents (excepting only diplomats), while Australia, which used to be as expansive, trimmed its rule in 1986 to recognize the child's citizenship only if one parent is a citizen or permanent resident. But even the 1986 reform contains a pragmatic bow to the realities of imperfect immigration control, for a child born in Australia to illegal migrants becomes an Australian citizen on his or her tenth birthday if resident since birth. Australia, like its two sister immigration countries, thereby avoids the problems associated with disaffected second- and third-generation noncitizen immigrants that have appeared in some European countries that know not the *jus soli*. All three countries also recognize *jus sanguinis* but join in policies designed to avoid transmitting their nationality indefinitely once a family has lost significant connection to the society. They use different variants of requirements for periods of parental residence on national soil before the birth, or the child's residence before a specified age if he or she wishes to retain citizenship, or both.

DEPORTATION AND CITIZEN CHILDREN.   All three countries have wrestled with the issue of deporting the unlawfully present parents of citizen children, and all have decisions approving the practice, even though it means, de facto, that the citizen children will leave with the parents. This outcome is sometimes viewed as excessively harsh by European commentators. But the unanimity of practice by the three immigration countries on this point suggests that such a rule may be an inescapable concomitant of expansive *jus soli* rules, lest mere fertility provide an easy loophole in normal immigration controls.

NATURALIZATION.   All three countries offer naturalization on fairly easy terms to foreign residents who want to acquire it. The list of specific requirements is lengthy in each country, but each winds up with strikingly similar provisions, despite variations in details and waiver possibilities. Lengthy specifications help minimize official discretion, which seems to be part of the plan, for naturalization is encouraged and is meant to be predictably accessible for those contemplating the choice. The basic requirements are (1) an application; (2) a minimum age of eighteen (before that age, naturalization is generally derivative upon naturalization of the parent); (3) prior lawful admission as a permanent resident; (4) a stated residence period, which could be seen as a probationary stage or as a time for acculturation, ranging from two to five years; (5) a requirement of familiarity with the new country's language; (6) a knowledge requirement, generally quite similar among the three, although the exact content is specified somewhat differently in the statutes: for Australia and Canada, acquaintance with the responsibilities and privileges of citizenship, and for the United States, knowledge of the fundamentals of U.S. history and the principles and form of its government; and (7) an oath of allegiance. In this age that trumpets multiculturalism, these commonalities describe polities that still insist, in a carefully measured way, on elements of a shared culture to be learned by aspiring members. The elements consist primarily of language and some degree of shared understanding about how governments operate and ought to operate—that is, in service of a sovereign citizenry. That Canada's language requirement offers two choices, English or French, reflects that country's unique membership challenge, but even there bilingualism has not eroded to an indifference that would tolerate self-selected multilingualism on the part of new members.

Only the United States still includes in its oath language renouncing other allegiances. Moreover, only the United States, perhaps reflecting its history as a country "dedicated to a proposition," in Abraham Lincoln's words, requires a specific finding of "attach[ment] to the principles of the Constitution." In modern practice, however, attachment is not a significant hurdle for applicants. Australia and the United States expressly require also a finding of good moral character—which primarily serves to screen out those who have committed crimes during their probationary period. Canada does not include such a specification, but it does disqualify from naturalization those who are under a deportation order, and perhaps this latter provision serves, in practice, to bar those with serious criminal records.

Debates Over Dual Nationality

These states have all migrated from the early twentieth-century consensus, reflected in the 1930 Hague Convention, that was hostile to dual nationality, but all have changed course at various times, still wrestle with the issue, and remain far from a settled consensus on the matter. Canada is the most explicitly tolerant of dual citizenship, requiring no renunciation of other allegiances at the time of naturalization and not treating naturalization elsewhere as an event that triggers loss of Canadian citizenship. But a 1994 official commission, discussed here by Galloway, urged limiting dual nationality and expressed concern about those who treat citizenship as a mere "insurance policy." The United States still requires renunciation by naturalizing citizens, but it is decreasingly serious about enforcing that part of the oath. Earlier U.S. laws treating naturalization elsewhere as an automatic expatriating act were greatly limited by Supreme Court interpretations of the U.S. Constitution and eventually were amended to conform. Now U.S. citizenship is lost on such an occasion only if the citizen specifically intends to relinquish it when acquiring another. Australian practice, as Zappalà and Castles note, is the opposite of that of the United States. Naturalized Australian citizens may retain their earlier allegiances, but Australians who naturalize elsewhere lose their original nationality. As in Canada, 1994 also produced an Australian commission report urging reforms, but in this case in the direction of greater acceptance of dual nationality. Political calculations made the government unwilling, under two different parties, to proceed with the recommendation. The United States has witnessed no comparable official recommendation, but the Aleinikoff chapter gives evidence of the growing chorus of commentators calling for greater acceptance of dual nationality, as well as persistent voices of resistance. Congress has made no serious moves toward changing the statutes in this direction. Elite opinion in each of these countries appears somewhat distant from popular opinion, which remains more skeptical about the risks associated with divided loyalties. Whether this divergence reflects a lack of enlightenment by the public in a global era or instead a failure by elites to take seriously the ordinary citizen's valuing of loyalty, sacrifice, and commitment is not clear.

These debates over dual nationality may reflect a deeper insecurity or confusion that is surprisingly present for each of these nations. On any world scale of political, economic, and social achievement, these countries are spectacular success stories. No doubt that is part of why they remain popular countries of immigration; people want to partake of those successes. But each worries that while people are eager to come as immigrants, they are not joining as citizens in sufficient number—or if the numbers are high, that people are doing so for instrumental or selfish reasons rather than as an expression of real commitment. This fear has been voiced in the United States, especially since amendments in 1996 greatly restricted the public assistance available to legal immigrants. As Aleinikoff recounts, that change had the predictable effect of greatly spurring naturalization, but some of the authors of the restriction then complained that the naturalization backlogs grew for the wrong reasons. A similar debate occurred in Canada, but, remarkably, in the more sedate judicial precincts of a court case challenging the reservation of certain public service jobs for Canadian citizens. As Galloway describes *Lavoie v. Canada,* two noted political theorists battled it out as expert witnesses over whether such a policy could be sustained as a valid incentive to naturalize. Peter Schuck supported such an approach (and the court ultimately agreed), but Joseph Carens asked whether naturalization is validly induced by such parochial considerations. The three chapters therefore provide much food for thought on these questions: What are the wrong reasons to naturalize? Why do such successful societies manifest this concern? And just what are the right reasons?

To an important extent, this anxiety reflects the general success of what Aleinikoff calls the "lawful settlement as membership" model. Each of these three societies has chosen to treat lawful permanent residents, for nearly all purposes, on a par with citizens. Such residents have long enjoyed ample legal protections—probably expanded in recent times through both statutory changes and adherence to international human rights treaties; nearly full access to the job market (saving only some public service jobs); free mobility; and wide social and economic opportunities. (The chapters do not deny lingering effects of discrimination, but apparently these are types of discrimination not perceived as easily remedied through naturalization.) In that context, many immigrants see little to be gained from changing citizenship. This fact may reveal a lamentable decline in the level and importance of political debate and engagement, because political rights are the main benefit denied to noncitizens. But in any case, the dissatisfaction or concern about the quantity and quality of naturalization decisions is visible throughout all three chapters.

The foundation of that social concern is this fact (and it is reflected as well in the ongoing debates over dual nationality): a significant portion of each country's populace hungers for citizenship to signify more than a mere alliance of convenience. Various nouns appear in the chapters' narratives, or in manifold quotes from official commissions, parliamentary debates, or court decisions, to describe the desired quality: cohesion, unity, commitment, belonging, identifying with the nation, making citizenship more meaningful, "resacrilization" of citizenship, loyalty, sacrifice, solidarity—or "mateship and a fair go," in the captivating idiom of the Australians. Galloway is skeptical of this hunger and concerned that it may result in policies that override individual rights and equal respect of persons, whereas Aleinikoff and Zappalà and Castles seem prepared to find more merit in the impulse. Perhaps it should not be surprising that these would crop up as concerns for multiethnic societies in a decade when other states are coming apart at their ethnic seams. Whatever the source, many of the participants in these societies' debates sense, without fully articulating the reasons, that the institution of citizenship contributes significantly to the glue that helps polyethnic societies find some measure of unity.

A New Metaphor

In the meantime, inspired by the threefold modeling provided in two of the chapters (and the multifold typologies offered in the third), I close by attempting a similar contribution. It is nothing so ambitious as a set of models—merely a set of metaphors that may help capture some of what these societies now seek. Zappalà and Castles describe three ideal-typical models of incorporation of immigrants: *differential exclusion*, whereby immigrants are incorporated in specialized ways, for example, as guest workers in the economic life of the country, but still denied access to other arenas; *assimilation,* whereby immigrants are asked to undertake a one-sided process of adaptation; and *pluralism,* which entails equal rights in all spheres of society but retention of cultural diversity.

The three countries treated in this section have no real truck with the first model—or at least they no longer do. But the other two gave rise to metaphors that have often been used in the debate. Assimilation of course calls to mind Zangwill's famous *melting pot,* from which a single unified alloy emerges although the starting materials may be highly diverse.[1] This metaphor was strikingly popular in the United States through the early part of the twentieth century, but it fell out of favor in the latter half, as ethnic groups came to decry enforced uniformity, insisted on retaining elements of their own cultures, and won support from wide segments of society. Thus the melting pot came to be replaced by the pluralists' or multiculturalists' image, the *salad bowl,* whose diverse ingredients remain highly distinguishable.[2] They each retain their own identity. The anxieties about commitment, loyalty, or solidarity that linger in these three multicultural countries, however, suggest the limits of that metaphor. The ingredients of a salad do not really cohere. All they share is the same physical bowl and, perhaps, the same thin layer of dressing.

A third metaphor is available, the *stir-fry.*[3] Appropriately enough, this dish is a foreign import to U.S. shores, a seasoned mix of vegetables and meat or seafood typically stirred together in a wok over an open flame. The image better reflects the heat generated in the process of immigration and mutual adaptation. But more important is what happens to the ingredients. They do not lose their distinctiveness; this is no melting pot. You can always tell the broccoli from the chicken, and even from the green peppers or the cauliflower. But the ingredients cannot remain wholly unchanged either. A well-cooked stir-fry subtly changes the constituent parts and makes them part of a unified single dish. Moreover, the flavor of the whole changes, incrementally, as new ingredients are added. Adaptation is not one-sided.

The challenge for all three of the countries in this section is to make such diversity-with-unity work. The elusive and multidimensional concept of citizenship is bound to play a key role.

---

1. Zangwill, 1916.

2. See D'Innocenzo and Sirefman, 1992.

3. This image was first suggested to me by a 1992 cartoon drawn by Dirk Locher of the *Chicago Tribune* (reprinted in University of Maryland, 1994, p. 3). It portrays an elementary school classroom whose blackboard announces the day's subject: "American History and Racial Relationships." A child stands at his desk reciting to a frowning teacher: "My father says we aren't a melting pot anymore, we're stir fried." The cartoon seems critical of the idea, but on reflection the image strikes me as richer than the artist may have realized.

References

D'Innocenzo, Michael, and Josef P. Sirefman, eds. 1992. *Immigration and Ethnicity: American Society—"Melting Pot" or "Salad Bowl?"* Westport, Conn.: Greenwood Press.

University of Maryland. 1994. *Report from the Institute for Philosophy & Public Policy*, vol. 14, number 1/2.

Zangwill, Israel. 1916. *The Melting-Pot: Drama in Four Acts.* New York: Arno Press.

CHAPTER TWO

Citizenship and Immigration in Australia

GIANNI ZAPPALÀ
STEPHEN CASTLES

If . . . copies of an Australian Citizenship Act which made sense were distributed we might all come to feel and better understand the value of our citizenship. Better still if we could at the same time have . . . copies of a Constitution that in its broad outline did describe the nature of our federal polity in terms all could understand.

Sir Ninian Stephen, former governor-general of Australia, 1993

AS A NATION-STATE, Australia is a fairly recent creation. The history of modern Australia goes back to 1788, when the first British colonists arrived. In 1901, Australia became a self-governing entity through Federation and the adoption of a constitution. This step, however, did not mean full independence, since Australia remained a dominion within the British Empire and followed the economic and foreign policy interests of the "Mother Country" without question—even into two world wars. Nor did Federation create the Australian citizen, since the Constitution did not mention citizenship and Australians were to remain British subjects until 1949. Even then, despite the introduction of its own citizenship, Australia continued to lack some of the trappings of nation-

This paper draws largely on work done for the research project "Intercultural Relations, Identity and Citizenship: A Comparative Study of Australia, France, and Germany." We acknowledge funding from the Volkswagen Foundation and the Australian Research Council. We thank Colleen Mitchell, Ellie Vasta, and Luke McNamara.

hood: for instance, a foreign monarch is still head of state. Unlike most modern countries, therefore, it is impossible to state precisely when the nation-state was born (if indeed, it has been fully). Australia Day, the 26th of January, commemorates the arrival of the First Fleet (bearing convicts and soldiers) in Sydney Cove, rather than an act of creating nationhood, and is referred to bitterly by Indigenous Australians as "Invasion Day."

Similar contradictions are to be found in the development of the Australian people. The Aboriginal and Torres Strait Islander peoples (the "Indigenous Australians") were decimated, dispossessed, and marginalized by white settlement:[1] their numbers fell from an estimated 500,000 in 1788 to just 67,000 in 1901.[2] The white settlers of the nineteenth century brought ethnic and class conflicts with them from Britain: the struggles between the English and the Irish affected Australian politics into the twentieth century, while immigration became an issue of class conflict, with employers wanting cheap "coolie labor," and unions demanding immigration control and wages "fit for white men." Chinese and other non-European immigrants encountered considerable racism. By the time of Federation, Australians saw themselves as a new "branch of the British race," who would create an egalitarian society while maintaining their British links. The White Australia Policy was considered vital for national survival.[3] Until World War II, Australia continued to develop its identity as a white society based on British culture and heritage. Yet after 1945, Australia embarked on a mass immigration policy, designed to strengthen the nation demographically and economically. Table 2-1 shows how Australia's population has changed in the past half-century.

Against the intentions of its architects, this immigration program was to transform Australia into one of the most culturally diverse countries in the world.[4] The aim was to bring in mainly British immigrants, but the source areas became increasingly diversified: eastern and northern Europe in the late 1940s, southern Europe in the 1950s and 1960s, and then—with the collapse of the White Australia Policy—Asia in the 1980s and 1990s. Table 2-2 shows how Australia's immigrant population has changed since 1971. While the numbers of immigrants from the United Kingdom and Ireland have remained fairly constant, some of the older European immigrant groups have declined (for exam-

1. See, for example, Reynolds, 1987.
2. See Galligan and Chesterman, 1997, pp. 45, 59. The 1901 figure should be taken with caution, as Aborigines were not counted in the census, and the various states had differing definitions on who should be considered an Aborigine.
3. See, for example, McQueen, 1975.
4. See Castles et al., 1992, p. 1.

Table 2-1. *Population of Australia, 1947–1996*
Units as indicated

Census year	Total population	Overseas-born population	Overseas-born as percentage of total
1947	7,579,385	744,187	9.8
1954	8,986,530	1,286,466	14.3
1961	10,508,186	1,778,780	16.9
1971	12,755,638	2,579,318	20.2
1976	13,548,448	2,718,318	20.1
1981	14,576,330	3,003,834	20.6
1986	15,602,163	3,247,301	20.8
1991	16,407,045	3,689,128	22.5
1996	17,892,418	3,908,213	21.8

Source: Australian Bureau of Statistics, various years, *Census of Population and Housing-Australian Families and Households*, Canberra, Australian Bureau of Statistics (on file with authors).

ple, from Italy and Greece), while the "other Europe" category has grown. The big increases, however, are in Asia-born and New Zealand–born immigrants.

Today, 22 percent of the Australian population is overseas-born, and a further 20 percent are children of immigrants (the highest immigrant proportion of any developed country except Israel).[5] Thus, about 7.3 million of the 17.9 million people living in Australia in 1996 were either immigrants or their children. Settlers have come from more than 100 countries; Australians can have any skin color, speak a vast range of languages, adhere to any of the world's religions, and follow a great variety of cultural practices.

For the purpose of studying ethnicity in Australia, it is useful to separate English-speaking background (ESB) and non-English-speaking background (NESB) immigrants. About 2.5 million members of the Australian population in 1996 were immigrants from NESB countries. If we add the second generation, about 4.8 million people, or a quarter of the Australian population, were of NESB origin. Another indicator of ethnicity is language: the 1996 census showed that nearly 3 million people spoke a language other than English at home. The most common were Italian (376,000 speakers), Greek (270,000), Cantonese (202,000), Arabic (178,000), Vietnamese (146,000), German (99,000), Mandarin (92,000), Spanish (91,000), and Macedonian (71,000).[6]

An important factor in considering relations between different ethnic groups is their relative size. Apart from the Italians (1.4 percent of the total population),

5. See Australian Bureau of Statistics, July 1997.
6. See Australia, Department of Immigration and Multicultural Affairs, 1997, *Immigration Update*.

Table 2-2.   *Immigrant Population of Australia by Birthplace*
Thousands

Place of birth	1971	1981	1991	1996
Europe	2,197	2,233	2,300	2,217
United Kingdom and Ireland	1,088	1,133	1,175	1,124
Italy	290	276	255	238
Former Yugoslavia	130	149	161	. . .
Greece	160	147	136	127
Germany	111	111	115	110
Other Europe	418	418	457	618
Asia (with Middle East)	167	372	822	1,007
New Zealand	81	177	276	291
Africa	62	90	132	147
America	56	96	147	151
Other and not stated	18	36	75	95
Total	2,591	3,005	3,751	3,908

Source: Australian Bureau of Statistics, various years, *Census of Population and Housing-Australian Families and Households*, Canberra, Australian Bureau of Statistics (on file with authors).

no first-generation NESB group makes up more than 1 percent of Australia's population. By contrast, in some European countries certain ethnic groups are large enough to constitute substantial minorities, for example, the 2 million Turks in Germany, or the million-plus people of Algerian origin in France. The Australian people today consist of an Anglo-Australian majority and a large number of relatively small minority groups.

These peculiarities of Australian history are significant in that they have been influential in the formation of a model of the nation-state and of citizenship different from both the Western European and the U.S. models. Unlike European countries, it is difficult for Australians today to appeal to a sense of shared ethnic heritage, since the population has such diverse origins. Until the 1960s, official policy was to base national identity on British heritage and to deal with diversity through assimilation. Easy access to naturalization was part of this model: the waiting period was reduced from an initial five years to just two by 1984.[7] Absorbing newcomers into the dominant Anglo-Australian culture and identity was also crucial. It was the failure of this attempt to maintain cultural homogeneity—demonstrated through language maintenance and the formation of ethnic communities—that led to the abandonment of assimilation policy and the introduction of multiculturalism in the 1970s. Ethnic belonging clearly could no longer provide an adequate basis for membership in an increasingly diverse country.

7. See Australia, 1984, Australian Citizenship Amendment Act, § 11.

But Australia cannot easily adopt the model of civic belonging developed by other immigration countries, like the United States. Australia lacks the historical events that would symbolize its autonomy and uniqueness. There is no act of national liberation like the American Revolution, and no document laying down what it means to be an Australian analogous to the U.S. Constitution and Bill of Rights. What is belonging to be based upon, if neither ethnicity nor shared historical experience provides a core notion of "imagined community"? Although Australia, like the United States, treats the act of naturalization of immigrants as a public rite of passage, few Australians could give a clear idea of what it means to be a citizen, beyond the right to a passport and the duty to vote (which is compulsory in federal and state elections).

Citizenship and its legal and constitutional basis, however, are issues of public debate in Australia—perhaps more so today than at any time since 1901. There are a number of reasons for this:

—1. The impending centenary of Federation, which many people see as an opportunity to review the Constitution and possibly modify it to enshrine modern conceptions of citizenship;

—2. The debate about whether Australia should sever the connection with the British monarchy and become a republic. A Constitutional Convention in February 1998 decided on a formula for change. However, this was rejected by a Referendum in November 1999, confirming the status quo.

—3. Uncertainty about the position of Indigenous Australians within the society and polity. A referendum held in 1967 was a powerful assertion of the political will to bring about inclusion of Indigenous Australians, yet their continuing social and economic marginalization, together with recent conflicts about land rights, cast doubt on their full possession of substantive citizenship;

—4. Recent measures to subject new immigrants to waiting periods (currently of two years) for eligibility to a range of welfare benefits have undermined the principle of equal treatment of all legally admitted permanent residents. As in the United States, this trend toward greater differentiation between the rights of citizens and resident noncitizens marks a major shift in policy;

—5. Current debates on national identity have again raised the issue of whether rules on naturalization and dual citizenship should be changed to more clearly define the meaning of citizenship.

In this paper we will examine the meaning of citizenship in Australia and discuss some of the current tendencies toward change. We will start by looking at the mixture of *jus soli* and *jus sanguinis* that determines formal belonging as a citizen. In this context, we will discuss the position of Australia's Indigenous Australians. Then we will examine rules for naturalization, and how these have evolved in response to attempts to manage mass immigration since 1945. We will discuss dual citizenship, a trend that is on the increase in Australia as in many other countries. Australian practice on dual citizenship is in important respects the exact opposite of the U.S. model. This topic, too, is marked by intense public debate, especially with regard to the political rights of dual citizens. We further discuss differences in rights between citizens and noncitizens. We will review some of the current public debates on citizenship and finally discuss models of citizenship and where Australia fits in international comparison.

Who Are Citizens of Australia?

The present conception and practice of Australian citizenship can only be understood against Australia's past background and development as part of the British Empire and then Commonwealth. Although some see the 1901 Federation of what were then colonies into the Commonwealth of Australia as the official beginning of nationhood, the Constitution that enacted that union had very little—if anything—to say about issues such as who is a citizen of Australia, and what their rights as well as duties and obligations are or should be.[8] One reason for this reticence was that the framers associated the term "citizen" with republicanism, and the status of British subject was seen as more appropriate to the Crown's position of center and protector of British colonies, dominions, and possessions.[9] A second reason was that the delegates at the constitutional conventions thought that if the word *citizen* appeared in the Constitution, it would create confusion about whether it referred to being a citizen of the states or of the Commonwealth.[10] Perhaps most important, the status of British subject did not imply that its holders necessarily held the types of rights associated with citizenship. Indigenous Australians and non-European immigrants from British colonies (for example, India, parts of China, and the New Hebrides) were British subjects, but Australia's founding fathers did not want to give them equal rights. Leaving the definition of rights to parliamentary statutes made it easier to discriminate against "inferior races."[11] That is why Australia has no document stating the rights of citizens, like the U.S. Bill of Rights or the French Declaration of the Rights of Man.[12]

8. The Constitution does make reference to citizenship of a foreign power in section 44(i). We return to this in Dual Citizenship *infra*.

9. See Chesterman and Galligan, 1997, pp. 2–3; see also Galligan and Chesterman, 1997, p. 57.

10. See Galligan and Chesterman, 1997, p. 57.

11. See Galligan and Chesterman, 1997, p. 57.

12. See Galligan and Chesterman, 1997, p. 57.

The end of World War II saw a greater desire on the part of Dominions, such as Australia, for policies that reflected more local needs and concerns (economic as well as political), though still within the Imperial-Commonwealth framework.[13] A 1947 Commonwealth-wide conference therefore agreed that each Commonwealth country would enact its own legislation governing citizenship but would also continue to confer an additional status of British subject. In the same year that Britain enacted its British Nationality Act[14] (which created a separate citizenship for Britain and its colonies), Australia passed the Nationality and Citizenship Act, 1948.[15] So it was not until 1949 that "Australian citizens" came into being, although this status was in addition to the general status of British subject that they still held. Yet, what the difference between being an Australian citizen, as opposed to a British subject, involved was not clear to either the population or those who administered the act. Despite the 1948 act, citizenship continued to be seen in cultural and ethnic terms (that is, British), rather than in terms of rights and responsibilities. As Jordens argued:

This culturally normative conception of citizenship was clearly reflected in the definition of "alien" embodied in the Act. A nation's understanding of itself is revealed by the categories of people it regards as foreign, alien and "other." From 1948 to 1987 Australia's citizenship legislation defined an alien as "a person who does not have the status of British subject and is not an Irish citizen or a protected person." The image of Australians enshrined in the Act, therefore, was that of an Anglo-Celtic people.[16]

The conception of citizenship during this period led to positive discrimination in favor of British immigrants, and obstacles against non-British immigrants. Non-British immigrants, for instance, were only eligible for citizenship after having been resident in Australia for five years and two years after making a "Declaration of Intention to Apply for Naturalization." Furthermore, they had to renounce any previous allegiances at public naturalization ceremonies. In contrast, British immigrants could apply for citizenship after only one year in Australia. Non-British immigrants, or "aliens," had limited property rights, only partial access to income protection, and no voting rights.[17] British immigrants (even noncitizens) faced none of these restrictions. They could claim age, invalid, and widows' pensions (restricted to British subjects only);[18] had

13. See, generally, Zappalà, 1994, p. 5.
14. Great Britain, 1948, British Nationality Act.
15. Australia, 1948, Nationality and Citizenship Act (later called the Australian Citizenship Act, 1948).
16. Jordens, August 1991, p. 1.
17. Jordens, August 1991, p. 1.
18. See Jordens, 1995, p. 92.

access to public housing (also restricted to British subjects);[19] and had the right to vote (even if they had not been naturalized).[20] It should not be surprising, therefore, that many British immigrants did not take up Australian citizenship, as for all intents and purposes their rights were the same as native Australians.

Although Australia's formal rules of citizenship had been and were based on the principle of *jus soli*, behind these rules lay an ethno-blood notion of the "national family" that made Australia similar to countries whose citizenship laws were based on *jus sanguinis*.[21] This fact was reflected in the title of the principal act itself, placing both "Nationality" and "Citizenship" side by side ("Nationality" was only removed from the title in 1973). This conception of citizenship had detrimental consequences for a nation that was embarking on one of the world's largest migration programs. Conceived in a period when the expectation was that there would be ten British immigrants for every one non-British immigrant, it may have had some justification. But as immigrants increasingly came from non-British origins, they had to show that they "belonged" to the "national family," which was British. Being an Australian citizen therefore was not distinct from being a British subject. The postwar immigration program made Australia one of the most multiethnic states in the world. Imposing a notion of "belonging" to some sort of preexisting British nation became increasingly tenuous.[22]

The changes that had occurred in Australian society since the postwar migration program began to receive serious recognition with the election of the Australian Labor Party (ALP) government, led by Prime Minister Whitlam in 1972. This period saw the beginning of the policy of multiculturalism that would be supported by all major political parties until 1996.[23] Reflecting these changes, several important amendments were made to the laws and, as a consequence, the conceptions governing citizenship in Australia, the impact of which was an official "shedding of the nexus between nationality and citizenship."[24] By the 1990s, despite a reticence to officially accept dual citizenship,[25] the changes to citizenship "completed a long evolution from a formal official recognition of multiculturalism to an almost nationality-neutral Act."[26] The massive non-British immigration that Australia experienced has been at the root of

19. See Jordens, 1995, pp. 64–65.
20. See Jordens, 1995, p. 52.
21. See, generally, Davidson, 1997.
22. See Davidson, 1997.
23. At the election that was held on March 2, 1996, the ALP lost government after thirteen years in office. A new government was formed by a coalition of the two main conservative parties, the Liberal Party and the National Party, under the prime ministership of John Howard. Throughout this paper the terms *Coalition* or *Coalition government* are used to refer to this political grouping.
24. See Davidson, 1997, p. 88.
25. See discussion *infra* Dual Citizenship.
26. Davidson, 1997, p. 119.

a "long process of legislative, administrative, and eventually cultural change."[27] Australia is shifting away from a culturally bound notion of citizenship toward a civic one, permitting equality of rights for all Australians, irrespective of their origins. Citizenship is based not on ethnicity or culture, but on the principle of territoriality, that is, residence on the territory of the Australian state.

The Situation of Indigenous Australians

When did Aboriginal and Torres Strait Islander people become citizens? The answer depends on whether one uses a purely legal definition of citizenship, or whether one takes a broader definition based on T. H. Marshall's idea of citizenship as the status of "full membership of a community" that confers civil, political, and social rights.[28] In legal terms, Indigenous Australians were subjects of the British Crown before Federation in 1901, and remained so afterwards. They became Australian citizens in 1949 (through the Nationality and Citizenship Act, 1948). But just as subjecthood had not conferred rights, citizenship after 1949 was an "empty shell," because Indigenous Australians continued to be excluded from most of the rights and duties of Australian citizens.[29] The 1967 referendum is generally seen as the act of recognition of formal citizenship rights for Indigenous Australians, although even then many forms of legal discrimination remained. It did little, however, to achieve actual equality of enjoyment of rights, whether civil, political, or social, for Aborigines. A prominent Indigenous leader, Mick Dodson (formerly federal Aboriginal and Torres Strait Islander social justice commissioner) concludes: "In practice, Aboriginal and Torres Strait Islanders did not, and still do not, exercise and enjoy basic citizenship rights."[30]

The colonization of Australia was justified by the legal doctrine of *terra nullius*, according to which the land was not possessed by anyone before arrival of the British. Indigenous rules on land use were not seen as constituting legal tenure. Thus, the Aborigines were legally invisible. Since they did exist and resisted British seizure of the land, however, the colonists waged a war of extermination against them, which lasted into the twentieth century. By the time of Federation, the remaining Aborigines were dispossessed and marginalized. The authorities of the various colonies appointed "protectors" and set up reservations to house the "dying race."[31] Indigenous Australians were in no position to claim their rights, even if the status of subject had conferred any on them.[32] In

---

27. See Jordens, 1995, p. 1.
28. See, generally, Marshall, 1964, p. 65.
29. See Galligan and Chesterman, 1997, p. 58.
30. Dodson, 1997, p. 57.
31. Davidson, 1997, p. 193.
32. See Davidson, 1997, Chapter 6.

fact, the Australian Constitution[33] expressly excluded Aborigines from the special race power[34] that gave the Commonwealth the right to make laws for people of other races. This power was designed to allow regulation of the situation of Chinese, Pacific Islanders, and so on, while Aboriginal affairs were left to the states. The Constitution also excluded Aborigines from being counted in the census,[35] because the census was mainly designed to count the number of electors in each state, and Aborigines were not supposed to vote.[36]

Although Aborigines had been by law (though not usually in practice) allowed to vote in all states except Queensland and Western Australia, they were denied the right to vote at the federal level through the Commonwealth Franchise Act, 1902.[37] This act also stripped them of the right to vote in state elections.[38] This act was just one of many discriminatory measures in every area of Australian society that made Indigenous Australians into an impoverished, oppressed, and excluded minority.[39] As it became apparent in the early twentieth century that Indigenous Australians were not dying out, but indeed increasing in numbers, a new policy of assimilation was introduced. This policy involved a range of measures designed to destroy Aboriginal culture. The cruelest practice was that of forcibly taking away children (especially those of mixed parentage) from Aboriginal parents.[40] This continued into the 1960s, as the recent inquiry into the "Stolen Generations" has documented.[41]

Becoming Australian citizens in 1949 changed little for Indigenous Australians, not even giving a general right to vote. The Commonwealth Electoral Act, 1962,[42] finally gave Indigenous Australians the right to vote,[43] but unlike other Australians, enrollment and voting were not compulsory. It was not until 1983 that the rules were changed so that Indigenous Australians had the same voting obligations as other citizens.[44] The 1967 referendum did not, as is often stated, confer citizenship on Indigenous Australians. In fact, it simply changed the two references to Aborigines in the Constitution, giving the Commonwealth the right to make laws for all Indigenous Australians, and including them in fu-

33. Section 9 of the Commonwealth of Australia Constitution Act, 1900, promulgated the Australian Constitution.
34. See Australian Constitution, 1900, ch. I, pt. 5, § 51, ¶ 26.
35. Australian Constitution, 1900, ch. VII, § 127 (repealed 1967).
36. See Galligan and Chesterman, 1997, p. 45.
37. Australia, 1902, Commonwealth Franchise Act.
38. See Rubenstein, 1995, pp. 503, 519.
39. See, for example, Markus, 1987; Reynolds, 1987; Rowley, 1970.
40. See Davidson, 1997.
41. See Human Rights and Equal Opportunities Commission, 1997.
42. Australia, 1962, Commonwealth Electoral Act.
43. See Australia, 1962, Commonwealth Electoral Act, § 2 (removing the prohibition contained in earlier versions of the legislation).
44. See Jordens, 1995, pp. 11–12.

ture population censuses. The referendum had enormous symbolic significance, however: it represented a major shift in public attitudes toward Indigenous Australians, with most people now seeing them as Australians who should have equal rights. This change was partly a result of many years of political activity by Indigenous organizations and white people who supported them, leading up to a successful campaign to mobilize public opinion before the referendum.[45]

Yet, formal membership for Indigenous Australians did not in itself overcome white racism, nor the disastrous social effects of two centuries of oppression. The passage of the Racial Discrimination Act, 1975[46] (which was necessary because of Australia's ratification of the International Convention on the Elimination of All Forms of Racial Discrimination)[47] was an important milestone because it did give an avenue for redress for some types of discrimination. Yet, even today, indicators such as labor market position, educational attainment, health conditions, life expectancy, and political participation reveal that Indigenous Australians are not full citizens.[48] Important changes in the 1990s have made new approaches vital. The High Court's 1992 decision in *Mabo v. Queensland*[49] overthrew the colonial legal doctrine of *terra nullius*, which led to pressure, especially from mining and farming interests, for legislation to regulate land ownership. The result was the Native Title Act, 1993,[50] which set out to define the rights of Indigenous Australians to the land, and to establish mechanisms to implement these rights. This assertion of the rights of Indigenous Australians is deeply threatening to many Australians, including groups with considerable economic and political power.[51]

Present Rules of Citizenship Acquisition

As noted earlier, citizenship (with some minor exceptions) is not a concern of the Constitution. For instance, a constitutional commission recommended in 1988 that section 51 of the Constitution, enumerating the Commonwealth Parliament's heads of power, be modified to give the Federal Parliament power to make laws with respect to nationality and citizenship.[52] Such a separate "citizenship power" would give Parliament a stronger constitutional basis for legislation in this area. The key piece of federal legislation that affects citizenship in

45. See Davidson, 1997, Chapter 6.
46. Australia, 1975, Racial Discrimination Act.
47. See, generally, International Convention on the Elimination of All Forms of Racial Discrimination, opened for signature March 7, 1966, 660 U.N.T.S. 212.
48. See Peterson and Sanders, 1998. This publication examines all these particular issues.
49. *Mabo v. Queensland* (no. 2) (1992) 175 C.L.R. 1.
50. See Australia, 1993, Native Title Act.
51. See Dodson, 1997, p. 58.
52. See Rubenstein, 1995, p. 506.

Australia is the Australian Citizenship Act, 1948,[53] which has been described by a former governor-general of Australia as a "masterpiece of legislative incoherence."[54] Although the act has undergone several amendments since 1948, the most recent changes to the act concerning who is an Australian were made in 1986. The Citizenship Act provides for the acquisition of Australian citizenship through four main ways: birth, adoption, descent, and by grant.

JUS SOLI. Acquisition of citizenship by birth is dealt with in section 10 of the Australian Citizenship Act, 1948.[55] In general, a person born in Australia on or after August 20, 1986, will be an Australian citizen if (a) one of their parents was at the time of their birth an Australian citizen or permanent resident; or (b) they have been ordinarily resident in Australia for a ten-year period from the time of their birth.[56] The 1986 decision to limit the *jus soli* principle was the result of the case of *Kioa v. West*,[57] where it had been argued that the child of the parents who were subject to a deportation order was an Australian citizen and was therefore entitled to natural justice.[58] Even though the court did not support this argument, the government saw fit to amend the legislation to avoid any future challenges by illegal immigrants who had had children while in Australia.

Children born on Australian soil of illegal immigrants are therefore not Australian citizens. But the law does allow children born in Australia on or after August 20, 1986, to become Australian citizens on their tenth birthday, if they did not become citizens at birth and have been resident in Australia for the ten years since their birth.[59] This still does not alter the parents' rights either to citizenship or to remain in Australia if they were or are illegal noncitizens. In general, people born in Australia between January 26, 1949, and August 19, 1986, are Australian citizens, while those born before January 26, 1949 (that is, those who were British subjects), are also Australian citizens.[60]

53. Australian Citizenship Act, 1948 (originally called the Nationality and Citizenship Act). Other federal acts that also relate to citizenship issues are the Migration Act, 1958; the Public Service Act, 1922; and the Electoral Act, 1918, aspects of which are discussed below.
54. Stephen, 1993, p. 9.
55. Australian Citizenship Act, 1948.
56. See Australian Citizenship Act, 1948, § 10(2)(a)-(b).
57. *Kioa v. West* (1985) 159 C.L.R. 550.
58. See Rubenstein, 1995, p. 507.
59. See Australian Citizenship Act, 1948, § 10(2)(b).
60. This policy includes a person born in Australia (including territories) before January 26, 1949, who would have been an Australian citizen if the Citizenship Act had been in force at their birth; a person born in the Territory of New Guinea before January 26, 1949; a person naturalized in Australia before January 26, 1949; a person who before January 26, 1949, had been ordinarily resident in Australia or the Territory of New Guinea, or partly in Australia and the Territory of New Guinea for at least five years; a person born outside Australia and the Territory of New Guinea before January 26, 1949, who enters Australia and whose father falls within the above rules; a woman, who, before January 26, 1949, had been married to a person who becomes or would have

JUS SANGUINUS.   Section 10B of the act provides that people born outside Australia are Australian citizens where the following conditions are satisfied: (a) their name is registered at an Australian consulate within eighteen years of their birth, and at least one of their parents was at the time of their birth an Australian citizen who had acquired that citizenship other than by descent; or (b) at least one of their parents was at the time of their birth an Australian citizen who had acquired that citizenship by descent and before registration was present in Australia for a period or periods amounting to not less than two years.[61]

Citizenship by adoption is possible if the adoptee has been lawfully adopted by an Australian citizen or by two persons one of whom is an Australian citizen and was a permanent resident in Australia at the time of adoption.[62]

Citizenship by Naturalization

Apart from citizenship by birth, citizenship by naturalization (or grant) is the most important and discussed mode of citizenship acquisition in Australia. Acquisition of Australian citizenship by naturalization or grant is contained in section 13 of the Australian Citizenship Act, 1948,[63] and gives the minister for immigration discretion to grant citizenship to people who satisfy all the following at the time they apply for citizenship: (1) they are permanent residents;[64] (2) they have reached the age of eighteen;[65] (3) they understand the nature of the application;[66] (4) they have been present in Australia as a permanent resident for a period totalling not less than one year during a period of two years immediately preceding the date that the application was lodged;[67] (5) they have been present as a permanent resident in Australia for a period or periods to not less than two years during a period of five years immediately preceding the date that the application was lodged;[68] (6) they are of good character;[69] (7) they possess a basic

---

become an Australian citizen and who had entered Australia before January 26, 1949; and illegitimate children born outside Australia in a British Commonwealth country or the Republic of Ireland before January 26, 1949, whose mother at the time of their birth was a British subject ordinarily resident in Australia or the Territory of New Guinea.

61. See Australian Citizenship Act, 1948, § 10B. This act excludes those who were present as prohibited immigrants, prohibited noncitizens, illegal entrants, or those in breach of a law of a prescribed Territory (that is, Norfolk Island or the Territory of Cocos Islands).

62. See Australian Citizenship Act, 1948, § 10A(a)-(b).

63. See Australian Citizenship Act, 1948, § 13.

64. See Australian Citizenship Act, 1948, § 13(1)(a).

65. See Australian Citizenship Act, 1948, § 13(1)(b).

66. See Australian Citizenship Act, 1948, § 13(1)(c).

67. See Australian Citizenship Act, 1948, § 13(1)(d).

68. See Australian Citizenship Act, 1948, § 13(1)(e).

69. See Australian Citizenship Act, 1948, § 13(1)(f).

knowledge of English;[70] and (8) they have an adequate knowledge of the responsibilities and privileges of Australian citizenship.[71] Finally, the act also states that if granted citizenship, the person would be likely to reside in Australia or maintain a close and continuing association with Australia.[72]

Brief Historical Overview

The procedures governing naturalization have undergone several significant changes especially in response to the postwar migration program. The first nationwide Naturalization Act was passed in 1903.[73] This act deemed those people already naturalized in the colonies as being naturalized in the Commonwealth and those who were naturalized in the United Kingdom or had been resident in Australia for two years were allowed to naturalize. This act continued the previous discriminatory policies of the colonies by also excluding Asians and blacks from naturalization provisions.[74] The Commonwealth Nationality Act, 1920,[75] which was superseded by the Nationality and Citizenship Act, 1948,[76] made a distinction between native-born and naturalized Australians and aliens, and was the first act to describe non-Australian citizens as "aliens." The Nationality and Citizenship Act, 1948, stated the main conditions that had to be met in order for "aliens" to naturalize as Australian citizens. It is not coincidental that the first act that created an "Australian citizenship" came into being at the same time that Australia embarked on its massive postwar migration program that would see the influx of millions of "aliens." The intention was that these "aliens" would be turned into "New Australian" citizens and assimilate to the existing cultural norms. The Department of Immigration was, and continues to be, responsible for administering citizenship and naturalization matters.

Although immigrants were encouraged to become Australian citizens, many did not do so,[77] which caused several government inquiries and campaigns to encourage citizenship take-up among immigrants.[78] The lack of take-up (a term

70. See Australian Citizenship Act, 1948, § 13(1)(g). This requirement does not apply to those aged fifty years or more, or whose ability is affected by a physical or intellectual impairment.

71. See Australian Citizenship Act, 1948, § 13(1)(h). This requirement does not apply to those aged sixty years or more, or whose understanding is affected by a physical or intellectual impairment.

72. See Australian Citizenship Act, 1948, § 13(1)(j).

73. See Australia, 1903, Naturalization Act; see, also, Davidson, 1997, p. 60.

74. See Davidson, 1997, p. 60.

75. Australia, 1920, Commonwealth Nationality Act.

76. Australia, 1948, Nationality and Citizenship Act.

77. See Jordens, 1997, p. 181.

78. See Jordens, 1997, p. 175.

used for encouraging immigrants to obtain citizenship) was seen primarily as the result of a lack of loyalty on the part of immigrants, a failure to take up their side of the "bargain."[79] There was little understanding that the complexity of the regulations, poor English-language ability,[80] and having to renounce one's country of birth[81] made citizenship an unattractive option for many immigrants from NESB. Furthermore, many could not understand why they had to take an oath of allegiance to a foreign monarch in order to become "Australian" citizens.[82]

In order to increase citizenship rates, various amendments were made to the 1948 act. In 1955, the need for the "Declaration of Intent" was removed and the fee for naturalization certificates was reduced, then abolished in 1959.[83] Despite evidence that suggested that the requirement of renunciation of immigrants' former nationality was a key factor in low citizenship take-up rates, in 1966 the government incorporated the renunciation into the Oath of Allegiance to the Queen.[84] It was also in 1966 that the restriction of age, invalid, and widows' pensions to British subjects only was removed.[85] In 1967, in the context of Australia's involvement in the Vietnam War, conscription for aliens was introduced, giving them a major responsibility of citizenship whether they wanted to become naturalized or not.[86] Yet, throughout the 1960s, only just over half of all eligible aliens had applied for citizenship.[87] Government leaders and opinion makers were still concerned that many immigrants lacked commitment to Australia.[88]

It had become obvious that low naturalization rates had perhaps less to do with administrative complexity (although their gradual easing and simplifying did help) and more to do with the failure of assimilationist policy. As Jordens argued, "By the late 1960s the Government and the bureaucracy were beginning to [recognize] that the reluctance of migrants to accept Australian citizenship was often caused by systemic discrimination and the inability of Australian institutions and services to respond to their needs."[89] This realization meant that changes to the act after this period altered the terms of how citizenship was con-

---

79. See Jordens, 1997, p. 181.
80. See Jordens, 1997, p. 178.
81. See Jordens, 1997.
82. See Jordens, 1997, p. 174.
83. See Jordens, 1997, p. 177.
84. See Jordens, 1997, p. 179.
85. See Jordens, 1997, p. 186.
86. See Jordens, 1997, p. 175.
87. See Jordens, 1997, p. 183.
88. See Jordens, 1997, p. 181.
89. Jordens, August 1991, p. 8.

ceptualized in more significant ways. Symbolic changes were also introduced. After 1964, for example, the heading of the Australian passport was changed from "British Subject" to "Australian" (although the words "British passport" still appeared under the Australian coat of arms).[90] Moreover, in 1969, the initial five-year waiting period for naturalization was reduced to three, but only for aliens who could read and write English.[91] The wording of the act was also changed to read that an Australian citizen had the "status" of a British subject, rather than stating that an Australian citizen was a British subject.[92] "Henceforth it was sufficient to state that a person was an Australian citizen without the addition of 'British subject.'"[93] It was not until 1973, however, that substantial changes to the 1948 act began in earnest.[94]

The privileged status of British immigrants was also abolished in 1973, with both British and other immigrants required to reside in Australia for three years before they could apply for citizenship.[95] British immigrants were now also required to take the oath or affirm their allegiance to become citizens of Australia, although it was only in 1984 that British immigrants who now came to Australia no longer had automatic voting rights.[96] Further changes to the act were made in 1984, 1986, and 1994, including a further reduction in the residence requirement from three to two years, and replacing the allegiance to the British monarch with allegiance to Australia and its people. In brief, these changes continued to simplify and ease the process for immigrants to become citizens, and also reflected the realization that "Australia was no longer simply British."[97] Indeed, some have argued that naturalization procedures in Australia are now some of the most liberal in the world:

> From a country of [*jus*] *soli* which . . . had erred in practice towards the [*jus*] *sanguinis,* Australia became a country of [*jus*] *soli* whose rules about naturalization were so open and policies so apt for the [globalization] of the twenty-first century that . . . they were being proposed as models for the rest of the world.[98]

90. See Davidson, 1997, p. 88.
91. See Davidson, 1997, p. 88.
92. See Davidson, 1997, p. 88.
93. Davidson, 1997, p. 88.
94. See Davidson, 1997, p. 88.
95. See Davidson, 1997, p. 88.
96. See Davidson, 1997, p. 88.
97. Davidson, 1997, p. 89.
98. Davidson, 1997, p. 87; see, also, Castles, 1992, "The Australian Model," p. 549.

The post-1973 changes had the desired effect in that citizenship take-up rates increased from their low levels in the pre-1973 period.[99] In 1991, 70 percent of eligible overseas-born residents were Australian citizens.[100] The highest rates of naturalization of immigrants in Australia for at least ten years (more than 95 percent) are shown by people from Greece, Lebanon, Poland, Vietnam, and the Philippines. The lowest rates (less than 50 percent) are found among people from the United Kingdom and New Zealand.[101] Several factors are involved in why different groups may have different citizenship rates, for instance, length of residence and type of migration (refugees being more likely to take up citizenship as soon as they are eligible in order not to remain stateless). In 1996, there were 15.89 million Australian citizens living in Australia and an estimated additional 1 million people who would be entitled to become citizens if they so wished. In 1996–1997, the number of people granted citizenship was 108,266, with the major countries of former citizenship in that year being (in rank order) Britain, China, New Zealand, former Yugoslavia, Vietnam, and the Philippines.[102]

Settlement Policy: From Assimilation to Multiculturalism

The changing rules and practices concerning naturalization must be seen in the context of changes in the policies of social incorporation of immigrants over the past fifty years. The assimilationist policies in operation from the 1940s to the 1960s embodied a concept of what it meant to be an Australian citizen quite different from that of the later policy of multiculturalism. Yet, assimilationism and multiculturalism did share common features: both policy makers and the general public always expected most immigrants (whether from Britain or elsewhere) to stay permanently and become citizens. Under assimilationism, however, the dominant view was that the newcomers had to give up their original languages and cultures and embrace Anglo-Australian culture and behavioral patterns if they were to be accepted as part of the national community. Later, in the multicultural period, the official view (albeit one that was always contested by some) was that immigrants had a right to maintain their languages and cultures, and form ethnic communities. This practice was consistent with being Australian, as long as there was an overriding commitment to certain core val-

99. See Davidson, 1997, p. 107.
100. See Davidson, 1997, p. 107 (citing the 1991 Census Matrix table CSC6171).
101. Australian Bureau of Statistics, 1993, p. 19.
102. Australia, Department of Immigration and Multicultural Affairs, 1998.

ues and behavioral norms. Accordingly, educational and social policies concerned with incorporation of immigrants differed in the two periods.[103]

In Australia, the tradition of government involvement in managing immigration and settlement goes back to the early colonial period. This background led to the establishment of a specific Federal Department of Immigration dedicated to planning and promoting mass immigration in 1945. The department recruited immigrants overseas, organized travel, and set up special "on-arrival" services, such as migrant hostels, assistance in finding employment, and basic English courses. What developed was a two-class system of immigration in which British migrants, and many other northern Europeans as well, were given assisted passages, could bring their families at once, and had full labor-market and civil rights upon arrival. Those from eastern and southern Europe were less likely to get an assisted passage, had no automatic right to family reunion, were frequently directed into undesirable jobs (generally in factories or construction), and were generally treated as inferior.[104] But there was a third, invisible, class: those who were not admitted at all. The White Australia Policy still kept out all nonwhites and was applied so zealously that even the Asian wives of Australian soldiers who had served overseas were excluded.

In these early years, cultural difference was seen as a threat to national unity. Immigrants were expected to quickly assimilate into Australian society by living and working among Australians, and by learning English. Special measures for immigrants were seen as detrimental to assimilation, so newcomers received little help in dealing with settlement difficulties, or problems of linguistic or cultural difference. The Department of Immigration did help establish and fund voluntary Good Neighbor Councils, designed to assist assimilation at the local level. There were also New Settlers' Leagues and annual Citizenship Conventions (held from 1950 to 1970). Such bodies initially focused mainly on the needs of British immigrants, although they also made efforts to persuade non-British immigrants to naturalize and assimilate.[105]

The main mechanism of assimilation for non-British immigrants was seen in becoming an Australian citizen, which was marked by formal ceremonies and the swearing of an oath of allegiance. As stated at the 1957 Citizenship Convention, an application for citizenship by a NESB immigrant was "placing the seal on his membership of our community and upon his intention to identify himself permanently with us."[106] As Davidson points out, this "communitarian logic" of

---

103. See, generally, Davidson, 1997.
104. See Collins, 1997, pp. 23–24.
105. See, generally, Jakubowicz, 1989, p. 1035; Jordens, 1997.
106. Davidson, 1997, p. 169 (citing Digest of the Australian Citizenship Convention, 1957).

belonging was based on the idea of "one people" based on British traditions for Australia.[107] As already noted, low naturalization rates were seen as problematic; yet, they reflected the reality that NESB immigrants were not being economically and socially assimilated, but rather were being incorporated into segmented labor and housing markets. Migrant workers, both male and female, became heavily concentrated in the expanding manufacturing industries of Melbourne, Sydney, and Adelaide. By the 1960s, observers were speaking of a "southern European occupational ghetto."[108] Researchers found that many immigrants were living in isolation and poverty, and many children were failing at school because of lack of language courses and remedial teaching.[109] In response, a number of special services were established, including immigrant welfare grants for community agencies, English courses for children and adults, and the first steps toward a Telephone Interpreter Service.

By the 1970s, it was becoming clear that assimilation policy had failed to prevent structural exclusion for many NESB immigrants, which encouraged linguistic and cultural maintenance and the emergence of ethnic neighborhoods with their own associations and business. Yet, political assimilation had partly succeeded, since enough immigrants had become naturalized to constitute an important group of voters, especially in urban-industrial areas. This contradiction between failed socioeconomic and cultural assimilation and successful political assimilation was at the root of the shift to multiculturalism.

The new voters were concentrated in the traditional heartland of the Australian Labor Party (ALP). The party leaders set out to woo the "migrant vote," setting up Greek and Italian sections, paying attention to migrants' educational and welfare needs, advertising in the ethnic press, and selecting a few migrants as candidates.[110] The victory of the ALP in the 1972 election, after twenty-three years of conservative government, was partly attributable to this policy, and led to the official ending of assimilation policy and the introduction of multiculturalism. In return, this change produced a new philosophy for social policy with special emphasis on social and educational disadvantage of immigrants.[111] Apart from improving access to a range of services and benefits, the new approach included extensive consultation of ethnic communities. The ALP government also finally abolished the White Australia Policy. Henceforth, Australia would have a nondiscriminatory immigration policy designed to admit three groups: workers and entrepreneurs with skill needed by industry, fam-

107. Davidson, 1997, p. 169.
108. Lever-Tracy and Quinlan, 1988, pp. 53–166.
109. See, generally, Martin, 1978.
110. See Collins, 1997, pp. 135–37.
111. See, generally, Martin, 1978, pp. 50–78, 119–20.

ily members, and refugees. By the 1980s, Asia was to become the main source area for immigrants.

When the Liberal-Country Party Coalition returned to power in 1975, Prime Minister Fraser set out to win the support of ethnic community leaders by emphasizing the value of multiculturalism as a way of maintaining social cohesion in an ethnically diverse society. The bodies set up to promote multicultural ideas included the Australian Institute of Multicultural Affairs (AIMA) and the Special Broadcasting Service (SBS), which was to provide multicultural television and radio services. The Adult Migration Education Program was expanded, and a Multicultural Education Program was developed with the aim of developing consciousness of cultural diversity for members of all ethnic groups. Multiculturalism was redefined according to an "ethnic group model" in which Australian society was seen as consisting of a number of distinct ethnocultural communities held together by a set of "overarching values." Ethnicity was defined in primordial terms as something natural and fixed. This notion of ethnicity was used as a justification for delegation of welfare functions to ethnic organizations, which fitted the privatization program of the neoliberal government.[112]

The election of an ALP government in 1983 eventually led to a radical rethinking of multiculturalism as way of managing ethnic difference. At first, the Hawke government treated the notion of ethnicity with some skepticism and seemed inclined to return to the traditional ALP focus on class-based social welfare. In the 1986 budget, "the ALP Government abolished the [AIMA], and cut funding for English as a Second Language teaching and for the Multicultural Education Program."[113] Plans were also made to merge the SBS with the ABC.[114] But these cuts led to protests and demonstrations by migrant organizations. This ethnic mobilization threatened the ALP hold on marginal seats in Sydney and Melbourne. In a rapid reversal, many of the measures of 1986 were reversed in early 1987. "The new direction was signalled by the establishment of an Office of Multicultural Affairs ('OMA')" and the dropping of the proposed SBS-ABC merger.[115]

In social policy, the government moved away from services for specific ethnic groups. The slogan of "mainstreaming" was adopted as a principle for restructuring services, which implied that all government agencies should be aware of the needs of the various groups within the population and plan their

112. See Jakubowicz, 1989; see, also, Foster and Stockley, 1988, p. 33.
113. Castles, 1992, "Australian Multiculturalism," pp. 184, 188–89.
114. See Castles, 1992, "Australian Multiculturalism," p. 189.
115. Castles, 1992, "Australian Multiculturalism," p. 189.

services so that they are accessible to everybody. All Commonwealth government departments were required to produce annual "Access and Equity Statements" designed to show that their services were responsive to the needs of a diverse population. Most state governments adopted similar measures.

The most significant statement of the ALP is a new approach to multiculturalism contained in the National Agenda for a Multicultural Australia that identified "three dimensions of multicultural policy" cultural identity:

—1. The right of all Australians, within carefully defined limits, to express and share their individual cultural heritage, including their language and religion;

—2. Social justice: the right of all Australians to equality of treatment and opportunity, and the removal of barriers of race, ethnicity, culture, religion, language, gender, or place of birth; and

—3. Economic efficiency: the need to maintain, develop, and use effectively the skills and talents of all Australians, regardless of background.[116]

In the National Agenda, multiculturalism was portrayed as a system of rights linked to citizenship. These rights were limited by an overriding commitment to the nation; a duty to accept the Constitution and the rule of law; and the acceptance of principles such as tolerance and equality, English as the national language, and equality of the sexes. Multiculturalism was not defined as cultural pluralism or minority rights, but as part of the cultural, social, and economic rights of all citizens in a democratic state. The program contained in the document was based on the recognition that some groups were disadvantaged by educational and social factors, together with discrimination based on race, ethnicity, and gender. The National Agenda may be seen as a shift in the concept of multiculturalism away from an "ethnic group model" and toward a "citizenship model."[117] Multiculturalism thus emerged as a public policy model to manage Australia's increased ethnic diversity. In this respect, it is different from the way the term is used in the United States, where it is related to issues of history and culture, and often associated with programs of affirmative action based on race and ethnicity.

Encouraging immigrants to become citizens remained an integral part of multicultural policy, just as it had been in the assimilationist period. But now official discourses emphasized that it was not necessary to adopt Anglo-Australian values and cultural practices to be a citizen. This civic concept of belonging had a number of consequences. The first was that it was still regarded as necessary to encourage immigrants to become citizens, albeit for somewhat different

116. Australia, Office of Multicultural Affairs, 1989, p. vii.
117. See Castles, 1997, "Multiculturalism Citizenship," pp. 5, 14–15.

reasons. In most respects, immigrants could be full members of Australia's multicultural society not only without cultural assimilation, but also without naturalization, for there was little difference in the rights of citizens and lawful permanent residents.[118] To secure the high level of "commitment to Australia" regarded as necessary, citizenship campaigns or "Years of Citizenship" were periodically organized (for instance in 1989 and 1994). A second consequence was the need to define what citizenship actually meant. In the late 1980s and early 1990s, this need gave rise to policy debates on constitutional changes to define citizens' rights. These debates, however, led nowhere, because of con-servatism of both Australian politicians and the public, who were reluctant to "tinker with the Constitution."[119] A third consequence was discussion of the need to upgrade civics education for school students and the public at large—an area that never had much priority in Australia.[120] A major civics education pro-gram was decided upon in the last years of the ALP government but was drasti-cally cut back after the change in government in 1996.[121] Finally, a civic notion of citizenship implied the need to ensure equal chances of economic and social participation, which required measures from the government to combat dis-crimination and social disadvantage of minorities.

The period from 1987 to 1996 was marked by an institutionalization of multiculturalism. At the federal level, OMA had a wide-ranging brief that in-cluded monitoring bills and cabinet submissions, vetting departmental Access and Equity Statements, and publicly promoting multicultural policies. The De-partment of Immigration and Ethnic Affairs (DIEA) was responsible for a range of settlement services, including the Adult Migrant Education Program (mainly English courses); grants-in-aid to migrant welfare organizations; and the Tele-phone Interpreter Service, which provides interpreters for all languages throughout Australia. DIEA also funded a quasi-autonomous Bureau of Immi-gration, Multicultural and Population Research (BIMPR). The Department of Employment, Education and Training (DEET) ran a National Office of Over-seas Skills Recognition. Most state governments had a similar range of multi-cultural agencies.

Yet, major shifts away from multiculturalism occurred from the mid-1990s. The Liberal and National Party governments elected in most states put far less emphasis on multicultural policies. Agencies concerned with the needs of im-migrants and ethnic communities were drastically cut. In the March 1996 fed-

---

118. See *infra* Rights and Benefits for Citizens and Noncitizens.
119. Davidson, 1997, p. 115.
120. See Davidson, 1997, Chapter 4.
121. See, generally, Davidson, 1997, Chapter 4.

eral election, a Liberal-National Party Coalition was elected with a large majority. Before the election, the Coalition parties had promised to retain the social safety net but also to cut government expenditure and deregulate the labor market. The August 1996 budget contained cuts to many government services, including measures for the unemployed, health services, aged care, and tertiary education. During the 1996 election, racism played an important role, with several conservative candidates criticizing provision of special services for minorities. In one Queensland electorate, the Liberal Party candidate, Pauline Hanson, attacked services for Aboriginal people in such an extreme way that she was disendorsed as a candidate by her own party.[122] Despite this fact, she won the seat, with one of the biggest anti-Labor swings in the country. This vote was widely taken as a signal that antiminority discourses were now seen as acceptable by a large share of the population.

After the 1996 election, major cuts were quickly introduced in the immigration and multicultural area. The immigration intake was reduced, and there was increased emphasis on skilled immigration. Fees for visas and English courses were increased drastically.[123] At the same time, many occupational English courses were abolished. New immigrants' waiting period for eligibility for social security benefits like unemployment support was increased from six months to two years, which was expected to save $663 million. The BIMPR was closed. Perhaps the most important change in political terms was the abolition of OMA, which appeared to be a clear signal that the government did not see multicultural policy as an important area. A covert return to assimilationist principles seemed possible.

Loss of Citizenship

The laws governing the loss and resumption of Australian citizenship are also contained in the Australian Citizenship Act, 1948. There are five main ways in which Australian citizenship may be lost:

—First, by the *acquisition of another nationality or citizenship*.[124] This is dealt with in section 17 of the act, which states that a person shall cease to be an Australian citizen where they are eighteen years of age or more and undertake any act or thing whose dominant purpose and effect is to acquire the nationality or citizenship of a foreign country;

---

122. See Jones, 1996, p. 17.
123. See Australia, Department of Immigration and Multicultural Affairs, February 25, 1997.
124. See Australian Citizenship Act, 1948, §17(1)(a)-(b).

—Second, by the *renunciation* of Australian citizenship.[125] In this case, a person shall cease to be an Australian citizen where they are eighteen years of age or more and a national or citizen of a foreign country, or were born or normally resident in a foreign country and under that law are not entitled to acquire the citizenship of that country because they are an Australian citizen, and lodge with the minister a declaration renouncing their Australian citizenship;[126]

—Third, a person may lose their Australian citizenship where they are a citizen of a foreign country and *serve in the armed forces* of that country if it is at war with Australia;[127]

—Fourth, citizenship may be lost through *ministerial deprivation*.[128] This discretion normally relates to persons who make false or misleading statements when applying for citizenship or those who are convicted of an offense under an Australian or foreign law that is punishable by death, life imprisonment, or imprisonment for twelve months or more, before the grant of citizenship;

—Fifth, when the parent of a child less than eighteen years of age ceases to be an Australian citizen because they have acquired another citizenship, renounced their Australian citizenship, or served in the armed forces of an enemy country, and their child is recognized by the law of that respective country as a citizen of that country, then their child also ceases to be an Australian citizen from that time.[129] Where the minister exercises his or her discretion of deprivation of citizenship under section 21, the minister may also direct that all or any of the children of that person less than eighteen years of age also cease to be Australian citizens.

Laws regarding loss of citizenship, especially due to acquiring the citizenship of another country or dual citizenship, have been of particular concern to Australians of immigrant origins, and in many cases their Australian-born children. In part as a response to this pressure, in August 1995 Senator Nick Bolkus, who was then the labor minister for immigration, announced new policy guidelines to facilitate the resumption of Australian citizenship that had been lost on the acquisition of another citizenship.[130] In order to resume Australian citizenship, people must show that they (a) did not know they would lose their Australian citizenship or that they would have suffered significant hardship or

125. See Australian Citizenship Act, 1948, § 18(1)(a)-(b).

126. See Australian Citizenship Act, 1948, §§ 18(5A), 6(a)-(b) (describing the minister's duty to refuse a renunciation under certain conditions).

127. See Australian Citizenship Act, 1948, § 19.

128. See Australian Citizenship Act, 1948, § 21(1)(a)-(b).

129. See Australian Citizenship Act, 1948, § 23(1)-(2).

130. Bolkus, August 25, 1995 (stating "Each year, several hundred Australians lose their Australian citizenship because they choose to take out another citizenship").

detriment had they not acquired the other citizenship; (b) have lived in Australia for a total of at least two years during their lifetime and either indicate that they will continue to reside in Australia, or if now a resident overseas, that they will reside in Australia within three years; and (c) have maintained a close and continuing association with Australia.[131] The broader guidelines were a recognition that many Australian citizens continue to have links with their countries of origin for economic or cultural reasons and that dual citizenship (which in some ways this policy allows retrospectively) is beneficial. In announcing the policy, Senator Bolkus stated, "The new, broader guidelines allow for a wide range of circumstances to be considered as factors which would be acceptable examples of 'significant hardship and detriment' . . . [ranging] from loss of cultural heritage to restrictions on access to social security benefits or difficulties associated with frequent travel."[132]

Furthermore, people who have lost their Australian citizenship can apply to be granted Australian citizenship after twelve months from when they lost it, if they have been present in Australia as a permanent resident for twelve months out of the two years immediately before lodging their application for citizenship.[133]

Dual Citizenship

Dual citizenship has been an issue of increasing debate and discussion in Australia over the past decade. The Australian Citizenship Act, 1948, does not explicitly recognize dual citizenship, and section 17 of the act provides for the loss of Australian citizenship for those who take up the citizenship of another country.[134] A legal reason for this is that Australia is a signatory to the Hague Convention,[135] which is based on single citizenship. Despite this fact, it has been estimated that in 1986 there were 3 million dual citizens in Australia,[136] with the number now probably being closer to 5 million. The majority of these dual citizens fall within one of the following four categories:

—1. People not born in Australia who have applied for Australian citizenship, yet have retained their previous citizenship, if the citizenship laws of their respective country of origin allows them to do so;

131. See Bolkus, August 25, 1995
132. Bolkus, August 25, 1995
133. See Australia, Department of Immigration and Multicultural Affairs, March 11, 1996.
134. Australian Citizenship Act, 1948, § 17(1).
135. Convention on Certain Questions Relating to the Conflict of Nationality Laws, April 12, 1930, the Hague, 179 L.N.T.S. 91.
136. Davidson, 1997, p. 139.

—2. People who were born in Australia who by descent (*jus sanguinis*) laws are recognized as citizens by their parents' country of birth;

—3. People born overseas of Australian parents, who are therefore Australian citizens by descent, but who may also acquire the citizenship of their country of birth if that country allows citizenship by *jus soli* rules;

—4. Australian citizens who have applied for the citizenship of another country without informing the relevant authorities of their action.

It is only people in this last group who risk losing their Australian citizenship under section 17 of the act.[137] Australian citizenship law is therefore inconsistent with respect to its treatment of dual citizenship. This fact was recognized in the 1994 report of the Parliamentary Joint Standing Committee on Migration (JSCM), which argued that present laws were discriminatory[138] and recommended that section 17 of the Citizenship Act be repealed and that former Australian citizens who had lost their citizenship under section 17 have the right to apply for its resumption.[139] The JSCM Report was also significant in that it represented one of the first official views to explicitly support dual citizenship. Upon examining the citizenship laws of other countries, it found that dual citizenship was increasingly accepted, especially because of the needs of individuals and states in an increasingly interconnected world and the recognition that loyalty and commitment are borne of factors other than just holding a single passport. Elite opinion seems to be ahead of broad community support on this issue, however, and political parties are wary of alienating the electorate by explicitly supporting dual citizenship. As a result, the response of both the former Labor government and the current Coalition government to the JSCM recommendations has been lukewarm, preferring to leave them in the "too hard basket." The official government response to the JSCM Report stated that its recommendations raised "policy issues which require careful consideration be-

---

137. People must have deliberately sought and acquired the citizenship of another country in order to lose their Australian citizenship; if they acquire it automatically rather than by taking some action to acquire it they do not lose their Australian citizenship. See Australian Citizenship Act, 1948, §17(1)(a)-(b).

138. Section 17 of the Australian Citizenship Act, 1948, discriminates against Australian citizens by birth compared with those who become citizens by naturalization. While the former, in most cases, are not allowed to acquire another citizenship, the latter may, in some cases, retain their previous citizenship. A view has also been expressed that section 17 particularly discriminates against Australian-born women who marry overseas. Women tend to live longer than their husbands and are more likely to acquire their husband's citizenship. Their rights to return home, for instance, have in some cases been dependent on their husbands' acquired Australian citizenship. See Fitzsimons, January 27, 1997, p. 11.

139. See Joint Standing Committee on Migration, 1994.

fore any legislative amendments are introduced . . . the government has decided that they should be considered further."[140]

The current Coalition government has referred the issue of dual citizenship along with a review of the Australian Citizenship Act to an Australian Council on Citizenship, which it announced in its 1996 budget package.[141] Recent statements by the minister for immigration and multicultural affairs suggest that a greater acceptance of dual citizenship may be possible:

> Increasing [globalization] is forcing us as a nation to re-examine our notions of citizenship. Still fundamental are the notions of allegiance, loyalty and participation in a civic and legal sense. However, the issues have become more complex. Debate is now focusing on whether loyalty needs to be a singular concept and whether it is possible for individuals to owe their allegiance to different countries simultaneously.[142]

Given the silence of the Australian Constitution with respect to citizenship, it is ironic that most of the legal debates surrounding dual citizenship have revolved around the interpretation of section 44(i) of the Constitution, which provides for the disqualification of a person from being chosen or of sitting as a senator or House of Representatives member if they are "under any acknowledgment of allegiance, obedience, or adherence to a foreign power, or is a subject or a citizen or entitled to the rights or privileges of a subject or a citizen of a foreign power."[143]

In other words, intending candidates for parliamentary office cannot be eligible for, or hold, dual citizenship. Section 44 of the Constitution has caused several problems for candidates whose right to stand for Parliament was challenged under this provision, and who were generally found to be in breach of section 44 by the High Court. For instance, in 1992 the High Court found by a majority of five to two that two candidates in a House of Representatives

---

140. Commonwealth Government of Australia, 1995, p. 5.

141. See Australia, Department of Immigration and Multicultural Affairs, August 20, 1996.

142. Ruddock, January 20, 1997. Mr. Ruddock was a member of the JSCM and, within a month of coming to power in March 1996, went to Cabinet with a proposal that the law regarding dual citizenship was discriminatory and should be changed. His proposal was rejected, with Cabinet arguing that allowing dual citizenship would undermine government attempts to use national identity arguments in defense of other policies. See Middleton, March 14, 1997, p. 6.

143. Australian Constitution, 1900, ch. I, pt. 4, §44(i).

by-election were ineligible because of section 44(i) and therefore a recount could not be conducted.[144]

The two candidates found to be ineligible were John Charles Delacretaz and Bill Kardamitsis.[145] The former was born in Switzerland, migrated to Australia in 1951, and lived in Australia since that time. He became a naturalized Australian in 1960. The latter was born in Greece, migrated to Australia in 1969, and has lived in Australia since that time. Kardamitsis also became a naturalized Australian in 1975, at which time he renounced all other allegiance. Upon becoming an Australian citizen, he had surrendered his Greek passport, and his two subsequent visits to Greece were undertaken with his Australian passport.[146]

All the High Court judges agreed that the relevant test was whether a person had taken "all reasonable steps" to renounce the nationality of the other country. The majority found that although Delacretaz and Kardamitsis were both naturalized Australians, they had not taken "reasonable steps" to renounce their Swiss and Greek citizenship respectively. As one justice argued:

It is not sufficient . . . for a person holding dual citizenship to make a unilateral declaration renouncing foreign citizenship when some further step can reasonably be taken which will be effective under the relevant foreign law to release that person from the duty of allegiance or obedience. So long as that duty remains under the foreign law, its enforcement—perhaps extending to foreign military service—is a threatened impediment to the giving of unqualified allegiance to Australia. . . . [Delacretaz and Kardamitsis] each failed to take steps reasonably open under the relevant laws of his native country . . . to renounce his status as a citizen of that country and to obtain his release from the duties of allegiance and obedience imposed on citizens by the laws of that country . . . accordingly, neither . . . was capable of being chosen as a Member of the House of Representatives.[147]

144. See *Sykes v. Cleary* (1992) 109 A.L.R. 577, available in LEXIS, Aust. Library, Ausmax File (High Court of Australia sitting as the Court of Disputed Returns).

145. See *Sykes v. Cleary* (1992) 109 A.L.R. 577. The case had been brought by Mr. Sykes, a candidate in the by-election against Phillip Cleary, arguing that the latter's election to the seat was void under section 44(iv) of the Constitution, which prohibits candidates or members from holding an "office of profit under the Crown." Mr. Sykes's petition then also challenged the eligibility of three other candidates under section 44(i) of the Constitution.

146. See *Sykes v. Cleary* (1992) 109 A.L.R. 577.

147. See *Sykes v. Cleary* (1992) 109 A.L.R. 577.

Two justices dissented, arguing that both candidates had renounced their previous nationalities when they had sworn their oath of allegiance and renounced any other allegiance during their naturalization ceremonies.[148] They also argued that the test to determine whether "reasonable steps" had been taken to renounce previous citizenships should be with respect to Australian law rather than the law of the other country concerned.[149] The renunciation of other allegiances in the naturalization ceremony by Kardamitsis, for instance, meant that

> he had a right to have any question of his Greek citizenship or his right or entitlement to the rights and privileges of a Greek citizen determined on the basis that the citizenship was effectively renounced and that, only if he reasserted it in some way, would the question be answered by reference to Greek law.[150]

The requirement for renunciation of all other allegiances was removed from the Australian Citizenship Act in 1986, although it still required an oath of "true allegiance."[151] The question therefore becomes whether "true allegiance" is satisfied in cases where there is dual citizenship. The oath of allegiance was replaced in 1994 by a new Pledge of Commitment in which mention of previous allegiances is virtually absent. People becoming Australian citizens must now pledge:

> From this time forward, [under God],[152]
> I pledge my loyalty to Australia and its people,
> whose democratic beliefs I share,
> whose rights and liberties I respect,
> and whose laws I will uphold and obey.[153]

Nevertheless, a literal reading of section 44(i) would tend to indicate that all dual citizens are excluded whether or not the other citizenship is renounced and this is accepted by the other country at issue. The High Court's 1992 decision in *Sykes v. Cleary* suggests that section 44(i) only disqualifies people who have

---

148. See *Sykes v. Cleary* (1992) 109 A.L.R. 577.
149. See *Sykes v. Cleary* (1992) 109 A.L.R. 577.
150. *Sykes v. Cleary* (1992) 109 A.L.R. 577.
151. Australia, 1986, Australian Citizenship Amendment Act, No. 70, § 11.
152. The use of the words "under God" is optional.
153. Australia, Department of Immigration and Multicultural Affairs 1997, *How to Apply*.

not renounced or attempted to renounce their other citizenship. This issue also raises the question of why a concept of "primary citizenship" to Australia should not be sufficient, especially in cases where laws of other countries make renunciation difficult, if not impossible. In a "nation of immigrants" such as Australia, these laws may have the effect of excluding millions of citizens from taking an active role in their parliamentary democracy. As Thornton argues:

> *Sykes v. Cleary* illustrates the residual resistance to diversity in the constitution of citizenship, albeit that Australia is an immigrant society, which boasts of its racial heterogeneity and beneficent multicultural policies. It takes no more than a small scratch to reveal the latent xenophobia beneath the bland surface of universalism that legal formalism [endeavors] to occlude.[154]

Several reports have dealt with the issue of dual citizenship and section 44(i) of the Constitution since the late 1970s, most recommending that section 44(i) be deleted from the Constitution, and that disqualification provisions be placed solely in the relevant statutory acts of Parliament.[155] Most recommendations, however, still favored retaining a provision for people to take steps to renounce any other citizenship they might hold or be entitled to in order to avoid disqualification. The most recent report of section 44 was undertaken by the House of Representatives Standing Committee on Legal and Constitutional Affairs. The committee, chaired by Kevin Andrews M.P., tabled a report on aspects of section 44 of the Constitution on August 25, 1997.[156] The committee made ten recommendations, the main one being that section 44(i) (prohibiting dual citizens from parliamentary positions) be deleted and replaced with the requirement that candidates and members of the Federal Parliament should be Australian citizens, which would therefore enable an Australian citizen who may also hold another citizenship to stand for Parliament. The report also recommended that Parliament should be empowered to enact legislation to deal with disqualification of candidates or members relating to any foreign allegiances or conflicts. Although the provisions of section 44(i) have been rarely used, after the *Sykes v. Cleary* decision up to forty sitting members of Parliament were thought likely to be affected by the decision because they held or had the right to dual citizen-

154. Thornton, 1996, pp. 73–74.
155. See, for example, Joint Committee of Foreign Affairs and Defense, 1976; Senate Standing Committee on Constitutional and Legal Affairs, 1981.
156. See House of Representatives Standing Committee on Legal and Constitutional Affairs, December 18, 1998.

ship.[157] The debate over section 44(i) illustrates some of the challenges that the postwar migration poses for Australia's institutions of governance that were established in an era of impervious borders. As one commentator noted:

> Section 44(i) goes right to the heart of a representative democracy. . . . Examining the operation of [s]ection 44(i) is necessary for determining what requirements can reasonably be imposed on elected representatives in a multicultural Australia after a century of Federation.[158]

Finally, it is the case that dual citizenship may pose certain practical problems for states and indeed for its citizens who are dual citizens. These arise with respect to issues such as liability for military service, marriage, divorce and custody of children, visas and passports, and consular assistance when traveling. When dual citizens are in Australia, only their Australian citizenship is recognized, and they are required to use their Australian passport when entering or departing Australia.

It is unlikely that the present government will move to relax restrictions on dual citizenship, because it regards dual citizenship as contrary to its views on national identity and commitment to Australia. This view has received some support from academics who have also been opposed to Australia's immigration program and policy of multiculturalism.[159] In contrast are those who see the refusal to accept dual citizenship as one of the final barriers to making Australia's citizenship laws amongst the most liberal and democratic in the world.[160]

Rights and Benefits for Citizens and Noncitizens

It is difficult to differentiate clearly between the rights of citizens and noncitizens in Australia because the rights of citizens themselves are not always clearly and consistently defined. This problem arises because the Constitution does not specify the rights of British subjects and hence, later, of Australian citizens. Rights of citizens and noncitizens are laid down in legislation at both the

157. Australian citizens who are also British nationals would also be included, because recent decisions by the High Court would suggest that British nationals would be regarded as subjects of a "foreign power" in section 44(i). See House of Representatives Standing Committee on Legal and Constitutional Affairs, December 18, 1998.

158. See House of Representatives Standing Committee on Legal and Constitutional Affairs, December 18, 1998.

159. See, generally, Betts, 1995, p. 58.

160. See Davidson, 1997, p. 90.

federal and state levels. Such important matters as the right to vote, access to public service employment, and eligibility for jury service are not consistently regulated throughout Australia. In addition, many significant issues are laid down in common law through court decisions.[161] As Chesterman and Galligan argue, the "States have retained power over a range of key citizenship areas, such as the conduct of criminal and civil trials, education, the use of land, and the State electoral franchise."[162]

Despite these ambiguities, it appears that in most legal areas the differences between the rights of citizens and of lawful permanent residents are quite small. Once accepted for entry as permanent settlers, immigrants enjoy a range of substantive citizenship rights that may be denied in many other countries of immigration. These rights include the following (though in some cases with certain exceptions or conditions):

—The right to enter and leave Australia (subject to obtaining a reentry permit before departing);

—The right to mobility within Australia;

—The right to own land or other real estate;

—The right to take up paid employment or to establish a business (in some cases subject to gaining recognition of overseas qualifications or membership of professional associations);

—The right to family reunion (subject to various regulations, which also apply to citizens seeking to bring in dependents from overseas);

—The right to medical services, social benefits, and social services (in some cases subject to a two-year waiting period for new immigrants); and

—The right to education for children of immigrants.[163]

In addition, all noncitizens in Australia (including permanent temporary entrants and even illegal entrants) enjoy a range of civil and political rights guaranteed to everyone by law. Although these rights do not add up to a principle of legal equality for aliens,[164] it is quite possible for permanent residents to live a full life in Australia without ever feeling the need to become naturalized. Jean Barbalet therefore argues that the "quality of Australian citizenship is quite thin."[165] The major benefits for citizens compared with noncitizens are the right (and duty) to vote, access to Public Service employment, and protection from

161. See Rubenstein, 1995, p. 514.
162. Chesterman and Galligan, 1997, p. 7.
163. See Davidson, 1997; Rubenstein, 1995; Wells, 1996, p. 45.
164. See Wells, 1996, pp. 49–50.
165. Barbalet, 1996, pp. 55, 68.

deportation; meanwhile the additional obligations are to perform jury service and defend Australia from attack should need arise.

Noncitizen residents in Australia may therefore be considered to have highly developed rights of quasi-citizenship, or of what Tomas Hammar in the European context has called "denizenship."[166] One aspect of this is the very strong right to naturalization after two years, which makes permanent residents appear as citizens-in-waiting. This erosion of the differences between Australian citizens and noncitizen residents goes against the intentions of the government when mass immigration was started. Minister for Immigration Calwell introduced the 1948 act by stating in Parliament that

> creation of an Australian citizenship . . . in no way lessens the advantages and privileges which British subjects who may not be Australian citizens enjoy in Australia. British subjects, whether they are now in this country or enter it in future, will continue to be free from the disabilities and restrictions that apply to aliens. They will qualify for the franchise and have the right to become members of Parliament or to enter the public services.[167]

In fact, British immigrants entering Australia today no longer have any privileges compared with other noncitizens. British immigrants, however, enjoyed all the rights of Australian citizenship, including the right to vote, up to the 1984 amendments to the Australian Citizenship Act, 1948.[168] British citizens resident at that time did not lose their privileges, so that they continue to have virtually all Australian citizenship rights without having been naturalized.[169]

We will now look briefly at some of the major areas of difference in rights and obligations between citizens and noncitizens. The right to participate in representative government may be seen as one of the most fundamental aspects of citizenship. It includes the rights to vote, to stand for public office, and to freedom of speech. As already noted, the Constitution does not regulate the right to vote in Australia. Rather, it is set out in laws of the Commonwealth and the states. These create not only a right of citizens to vote, but also an obligation. Those who do not vote in federal and state elections are liable to be fined. Some citizens, however, are excluded from the right to vote: persons of un-

---

166. See, generally, Hammar, 1990.
167. Chesterman and Galligan, 1997, p. 4 (quoting Arthur Calwell).
168. Australia, 1984, Australian Citizenship Amendment Act, No. 129, § 33.
169. They do, however, need to get a reentry visa before leaving Australia if they wish to return.

sound mind and prisoners.[170] "Therefore, Parliament has the power to decide which citizens have the right to vote."[171] Resident noncitizens do not have the right to vote or to stand for public office in federal and state elections. Noncitizens, however, may have the right to vote in local government elections in the states of Victoria, South Australia, Western Australia, and Tasmania, where persons holding rateable land in the area can be enrolled as voters, irrespective of citizenship.[172]

The main anomaly with regard to voting rights is that pre-1984 British immigrants still had the right to vote at all levels without being naturalized. The exact size of this group is unknown, but estimates of the number of non-Australian British citizens on the electoral rolls vary from 200,000 to 1 million. This anomaly is due to section 93 of the Electoral Act, 1918 (Cth), which allows "persons (other than Australian citizens) who would, if the relevant citizenship law had continued in force, be British subjects within the meaning of that relevant citizenship law and whose names were, immediately before 26 January 1984" on the electoral roll.[173] This matter has long been an issue of contention, especially with ethnic communities, as they see it as a continued discrimination in favor of British noncitizens. In 1989, Irene Moss, who was then the race discrimination commissioner, advised Lionel Bowen, who was then the attorney-general, that section 93 of the Electoral Act was in breach of the Racial Discrimination Act, 1975. More significantly, Moss opined that if a successful challenge to this provision by a noncitizen who was not a British subject was brought, the result would be that all noncitizens would become eligible to vote.[174] This issue has recently resurfaced in the context of the elections held in 1997 for the Constitutional Convention to debate whether Australia should become a republic, and in the context of a likely future referendum to decide the issue. Some groups think that the vote of these non-Australian citizen British subjects may decide an important issue of Australian national identity in a close election. At the end of 1997, a consortium of people and organizations were preparing a challenge to section 93 in the High Court, on the basis that it contravenes section 10(1) of the Racial Discrimination Act, 1975 (Cth).[175] This section states:

170. See Australia, Department of Immigration and Multicultural Affairs, March 11, 1996; see, also, Australia, 1984, Referendum Act, No. 44, § 45.

171. Rubenstein, 1995, p. 509.

172. See Rubenstein, 1995, p. 510.

173. Australia, 1918, Electoral Act, § 93.

174. Moss, letter to Bowen, February 8, 1989.

175. The case is being brought by a Sydney plumber, Lorenzo Poletto, who is an Italian citizen living in Australia since 1960. He is being backed by Ausflag and the Public Interest Advocacy Center.

> If, by reason of, or of a provision of, a law of the Commonwealth or of a State or Territory, persons of a particular race, [color] or national or ethnic origin do not enjoy a right that is enjoyed by persons of another race, [color] or national or ethnic origin, or enjoy a right to a more limited extent than persons of another race, [color], or national or ethnic origin, then notwithstanding anything in that law, persons of the first-mentioned race, [color] or national or ethnic origin shall, by force of this section enjoy that right to the same extent as persons of that other race, [color] or national or ethnic origin.[176]

Many see the current arrangements as a clear breach of this section, as British subjects are the only resident noncitizens to have a right to vote. A successful challenge might have seen the disenfranchisement of this group or the widening of an important citizen right to all resident noncitizens. However, this action was not successful.

The right to free speech is more complex. In principle it is not protected by the Constitution (either for citizens or noncitizens). The Aliens Power of the Constitution, section 51 (xix), gives Parliament power to enact discriminatory laws concerning aliens.[177] There is no Australian equivalent to the Fourteenth Amendment to the U.S. Constitution, which provides equal protection to all aliens, even, in some circumstances, to those illegally present in the United States. Rather, equal protection in basic civil rights areas such as the right to due legal process is the result of both statutes and common-law decisions. Common law does appear to recognize the general principle of equality before the law.

In any case, it might seem that Australia's ratification of the ICCPR should give equal civil and political rights to resident noncitizens in all areas but the right to vote and stand for public office, and the right to employment in the public service. Yet, the recent High Court decision on the right to free communication on political matters (one aspect of freedom of speech) has failed to confirm the existence of that right for aliens in Australia.[178] The High Court justices have linked free speech to the right to participate in representative government, which is not available to aliens.[179] This interpretation of citizenship is narrow and old-fashioned; resident noncitizens are affected by decisions of government and might therefore be thought to have a right of political expression concerning these. This issue is too complex and ambiguous to go into further here.[180]

176. Australia, 1975, Racial Discrimination Act, § 10(1).

177. Australian Constitution, 1900, ch. I, pt. V, § 51(xix); see, also, Wells, 1996, p. 70.

178. See Wells, 1996, p. 59.

179. See Wells, 1996, p. 59.

180. For a detailed treatment, see Wells, 1996, pp. 67–69; see, also, Rubenstein, 1995, pp. 515–16.

The Public Service Act, 1922, does not permit noncitizens to take up permanent positions in the Commonwealth Public Service.[181] Noncitizens may be employed on a probationary basis, provided they undertake to apply for Australian citizenship. State rules are inconsistent, however: in Victoria, for instance, resident noncitizens can become permanent public servants.[182] This limitation of the right to work is significant, since the public service includes not only central administration, but also policing and the judiciary. In contrast, the importance of the exclusion is tempered by the ease and rapidity with which immigrants can become citizens.

The Constitution lays down the right to trial by jury for serious offenses against Commonwealth law. The composition of juries is determined by state laws, however, which disqualify or exempt certain categories of people from jury service. Again, inconsistency is the rule, but noncitizens are altogether excluded from jury service.[183] In a country of immigration with a substantial noncitizen population, this exclusion might be seen as inconsistent with the principle that accused persons should be judged by a jury of their peers.

The duty of defending the nation against external attack is often seen as one of the key defining aspects of the "community of citizens."[184] Here, too, Australia is somewhat idiosyncratic. The Defence Act, 1903 (Cth), does not exclude noncitizens from voluntarily joining the armed forces. Nor have they been excluded from conscription at times of war. Resident noncitizens were conscripted during the Second World War and the Vietnam War, and this practice was upheld by a High Court decision in 1945. All persons who have resided in Australia more than six months and who are aged eighteen to sixty are liable for service, unless exempted on grounds of physical or mental disability.[185] Immigrants from hostile countries (such as Germany and Italy) were not conscripted during the world wars, but many were interned for lengthy periods.[186] The practice of conscripting noncitizens is questionable on the grounds that they were forced to defend a nation-state in which they had no right of political representation. Indeed noncitizens in the armed forces had no clear right of reentry to Australia after overseas service.[187]

An obvious area of inequality between citizens and noncitizens concerns mobility rights: the rights to enter Australia in the first place, and to leave and

181. Australia, 1922, Public Service Act.
182. See Rubenstein, 1995, p. 514.
183. See Rubenstein, 1995, pp. 510–11.
184. See, generally, Schnapper, 1994.
185. See Australia, 1903, Defence Act, §§59, 61A(a).
186. See, generally, Bosworth and Ugolini, 1992.
187. See Rubenstein, 1995, pp. 520–22.

return to Australia. Citizens have the right to come and go as they please,[188] but neither Australian nor international laws give aliens a right to enter Australia. Admission is a matter of national sovereignty, and the Migration Act, 1958, requires all entrants to apply for a visa before arrival.[189] The only exception is for New Zealanders due to an agreement on free movement between the two countries. Most entrants are short-term visitors—over 4.2 million overseas visitors entered Australia in 1996–1997 for short-term purposes (mainly tourism), compared with 95,100 long-term temporary immigrants, who came mainly for purposes of work or study.[190] Such temporary entrants are subject to a range of visa conditions, generally restricting them to work or study in a specific place for a specific period.[191] Change of visa category from temporary to permanent is usually not permitted.

Permanent settlers enter Australia primarily through one of the two official programs for visaed permanent entry: the Migration Program, or the Humanitarian Program. Australia's immigration policy is nondiscriminatory, in that persons from any country can apply to come, whatever their ethnic origin, sex, color, or religion. Applicants must, however, meet adequate health standards, be of good character, and meet skill or other requirements for particular visa types. The Migration Program provides entry for "Family stream" and "Skill stream" immigrants under various visa categories, together with a small number of other persons under the "Special Eligibility stream." The Humanitarian Program has three components. Consistent with the UN definition, refugee immigrants include persons outside their own countries seeking protection from persecution. Special Humanitarian entrants seek relief from forms of discrimination amounting to a substantial violation of human rights, while the Special Assistance Category permits entry to other overseas persons in particularly vulnerable situations who have close family or community links with Australia. Total planned admissions for 1997–1998 are 80,000, of which 32,000 are in the Family stream, 34,800 in the Skill stream, 12,000 in the Humanitarian Program, and 1,200 other entrants with visas.[192]

Citizens cannot be deported from Australia, although they can under certain circumstances be extradited to face prosecution overseas. By contrast, perma-

188. Even to this right there are exceptions. See Rubenstein, 1995, p. 512 (citing the case of the left-wing journalist Wilfred Burchett who was denied a passport and refused reentry to Australia in 1970).
189. Australia, 1958, Migration Act, §42.
190. See Australian Bureau of Statistics, July 1997.
191. Australia, 1958, Migration Act, §41.
192. See, for example, Australia, Department of Immigration and Multicultural Affairs, 1997, *1997–98 Migration*; Australia, Department of Immigration and Multicultural Affairs, 1997, *Australia's Humanitarian*.

nent residents can be deported for various reasons. The Migration Act, 1958, discriminated between British subjects and aliens.[193] The former could only be deported upon conviction of serious offenses within five years of entry.[194] Aliens could be deported on a wide range of grounds, including advocating violent overthrow of the government or mental illness, however long they had been in Australia, and even if they had been naturalized.[195] This discrimination was removed in 1984. People who have been permanent residents for less than ten years can now be deported only if convicted for an offense and sent to prison for at least one year, and the situation is the same for British subjects as for others.[196]

Restrictions in mobility rights may lead to situations where noncitizens are denied equality before the law. This case has arisen with regard to asylum-seekers in recent years. "Boat people" who have arrived from Cambodia or China have in some cases been detained for lengthy periods (up to five years) without conviction for any offense. Such administrative detention would not be permitted for a citizen, but in 1992 the government introduced amendments to the Migration Act, 1958, to permit detention without a warrant and custody for an indefinite period for an alien awaiting deportation. The legality of this was confirmed by the High Court,[197] on the grounds that the purpose of the detention was not punitive.[198] This implies a restriction of aliens' common-law right to liberty and security of the person. Moreover, the Department of Immigration has taken steps to curtail the access of detained aliens to legal advice, which has led to a currently pending appeal to the United Nations Human Rights Committee by a Cambodian detainee at Port Hedland Detention Center in Western Australia, on the grounds that prolonged detention and lack of access to the courts and legal facilities contravene the ICCPR.[199]

Finally, it should be noted that the longstanding principle of equal treatment of resident noncitizens and citizens with regard to welfare rights is currently being questioned. In 1988, an official inquiry in immigration policy recommended that a range of benefits and services should only be available to citizens. The aim was to encourage naturalization and to increase "commitment to Australia" by differentiating more sharply between the rights of citizens and

193. Australia, 1958, Migration Act; see, also, Jordens, 1997, p. 195.

194. See Jordens, 1997, p. 195.

195. See Jordens, 1997, pp. 195–96.

196. See Godard, 1997, p. 484.

197. See *Lim v. Minister for Immigration, Local Government and Ethnic Affairs* (1992) 176 C.L.R. 1.

198. See, for example, Wells, 1996, pp. 60, 70–72; Rubenstein, 1995, pp. 513–14.

199. See Wells, 1996, p. 62.

noncitizens.[200] In January 1993, the ALP government decided to deny unemployment and sickness benefits to immigrants for the first six months after arrival. Fees were introduced for English-language courses for adult migrants, although some categories such as refugees were exempted. People sponsoring their relatives as immigrants had to give a two-year "assurance of support" (that is, promise to support their relatives if these were unemployed or in need). Since 1996, the Liberal-National Party government has made further changes. Fees for visas and compulsory English-language courses for new immigrants have been sharply increased. The waiting period for most welfare benefits has been increased to two years for new entrants.[201] In addition, the Office of Multicultural Affairs, which had had an important role in monitoring services for immigrants, was abolished.

Issues of Current Public Debate

Making Australian citizenship more meaningful has become the policy of all the major political parties. As part of the government's response to the JSCM Report on citizenship laws,[202] several initiatives were announced as part of a four-year plan culminating in a Year of Australian Citizenship in 1999 to mark the fiftieth anniversary of Australian citizenship.[203] These included national citizenship achievement awards; voluntary courses for migrants; citizenship promotion campaigns; and redrafting the Australian Citizenship Act, 1948, including rewriting the act in plain English, expanding the preamble to the act, and reviewing the application process for citizenship with an aim to make it simpler and more meaningful.[204]

Furthermore, in 1995, the Senate Legal and Constitutional Committee prepared a report on the benefits and feasibility of establishing a series of citizenship benchmarks in Australia.[205] The report argued that what was needed was (1) a clear definition of the basic rights and duties of individual citizens; (2) identification and establishment of standards in policy areas necessary for social participation and well-being; and (3) consideration of the most effective ways to implement rights and duties and policy standards pertaining to citizenship. It went on to argue for a "fully developed, integrated system of social

200. See Committee to Advise on Australia's Immigration Policies, 1988.
201. See Australia, Department of Immigration and Multicultural Affairs, August 13, 1997.
202. See Commonwealth Government of Australia, 1995.
203. See Bolkus, September 4, 1995.
204. See Bolkus, September 4, 1995.
205. See Australia, Senate Legal and Constitutional References Committee, 1995.

benchmarks and indicators . . . [as] an important tool for public policy in the longer term."[206] Yet, the notion of citizenship benchmarks, with its emphasis on broadly defined rights and a strong role for government in implementing them, has not found favor with the current government's policy for privatization and reducing the role of the state.

The victory of the Coalition government in March 1996 has seen the introduction of several changes designed to give citizens greater benefits and advantages over those enjoyed by noncitizens. The government's first budget saw it allocate $700,000 over three years to establish and operate an Australian Council on Citizenship.[207] The role of the council is to provide advice on reviewing the Australian Citizenship Act, particularly:

—The meaning and value of citizenship;

—Residency, language, cultural, age, and other legal and community requirements for citizenship;

—Drafting a new citizenship act and reviewing the current pledge;

—Dual and multicitizenship issues;

—The relationship of citizenship to immigration and settlement policies; and

—How best to celebrate the fiftieth anniversary of Australian citizenship in 1999.[208]

Some have interpreted these guidelines as an indication of the government's desire to make the gaining of citizenship harder and more exclusive by extending the residency requirements and introducing more rigorous English-language tests. Furthermore, the idea is one of making citizenship more "valuable" by making it a prerequisite for government benefits and a condition for sponsoring family members as immigrants.[209] Any relaxation of dual citizenship regulations is also considered unlikely. The government's agenda on citizenship has been described by the previous minister of immigration as

anti-migrant, anti-cultural diversity . . . it would take us back to the 1960s, and the years of the White Australia Policy, when migrants who

206. Australia, Senate Legal and Constitutional References Committee, 1995, p. 15.

207. The establishment of the council was announced by the minister on August 7, 1998. It is chaired by Sir Ninian Stephen. See Australia, Department of Immigration and Multicultural Affairs, 1998. See also Australia, Department of Immigration and Multicultural Affairs, August 20, 1996.

208. Australia, Department of Immigration and Multicultural Affairs, August 20, 1996; see, also, Ruddock, January 20, 1997.

209. See Bolkus, February 19, 1996.

were British subjects simply had to register as Citizens, while migrants from anywhere else had to wait up to [fifteen] years for citizenship.[210]

This statement fits in with current government thinking on immigrant rights and multiculturalism. As noted above, recent policy changes restrict the rights of new immigrants and break with the principle of equal treatment with regard to social rights. The most recent sign of this change is a proposal by Minister of Immigration and Multicultural Affairs Paul Ruddock to admit parents of immigrants only as temporary entrants, so that they will have no access to medical and social benefits.[211] Government policies on multiculturalism and racism are decidedly vague. Prime Minister Howard studiously avoids the theme of multiculturalism and has refused to dissociate himself from racist statements, especially from Queensland Independent Member of Parliament Hanson, on the grounds that she had the right to free speech.[212] The Coalition government has effectively abandoned the previous ALP government's measures to reshape the relationship between ethnic difference and citizenship. Some official statements indicate a desire to return to a more traditional focus on common heritage, presumably based mainly on British traditions. It is not clear how this change would include Australians of other origins.

The leader of the opposition Labor Party, Kim Beazley, has recently announced that he would reinstitute the previous Office of Multicultural Affairs and return it to the Department of Prime Minister and Cabinet under a new name of the Office of Multicultural Affairs and Citizenship.[213] The Labor Party policy, as it currently stands, is to link the policy of multiculturalism more closely to national identity and citizenship, seeing the latter as a vehicle to create unity in an ethnically diverse society.

The retreat from multiculturalism since the Coalition victory in 1996 seems anachronistic in a society in which two out of five people are immigrants or children of immigrants. Most recent opinion polls indicate support for the principles of a multicultural society.[214] Although it is hard to study perceptions of national identity, some recent research does indicate a shift away from an ethnic notion of belonging and toward a more civic notion. For instance, a study based on the 1995 National Social Science Survey divided respondents into two main categories: "Australian nativists," who emphasized the importance of being

210. See Bolkus, February 19, 1996.
211. See Bolkus, February 19, 1996.
212. Lynch and Reavell, 1997, p. 44.
213. See Beazley, March 28, 1998.
214. See, generally, Jones, 1996.

born in Australia, having lived most of one's life in Australia, and being a Christian; and people committed to "civic culture," who emphasized the importance of respect for Australian laws and institutions, and feeling Australian.[215] The study found that only about a quarter of respondents were strongly committed to nativist views, while more than half subscribed to civic ideals (many respondents subscribed to both principles to some degree).[216] Nativists tended to be older and more religious, and to have lower levels of education. Supporters of civic culture belonged to all demographic groups but were specially represented among younger and better-educated groups.[217]

These results bade well for the ideas of several well-known public intellectuals in Australia who have been emphasising the need to foster and create a national "civic identity."[218] People such as Donald Horne argue that the coming centenary of Federation in 2001 provides an opportunity to have an explicit statement or document of what it means to be an Australian citizen. He argues that in an ethnically diverse society such as Australia, social cohesion can be achieved by the state having "civic unity," by providing a statement of the "core values" of Australia for the next millennium that would be taught in wide-ranging civics education programs. He suggests that at least five "core values" could make up Australia's civic compact:

—Respect for the rule of law;

—Equal rights of Australians under the law;

—The principles of a tolerant liberal democracy;

—Commitment to custodianship of the land; and

—Commitment to strengthening Australia as a fair society.[219]

This compact, he suggests, would be used and affirmed at oath takings in "Citizen's Days," which would be for all Australians when they turned eighteen and not just for naturalizing immigrants.[220] There is an increasing recognition that Australia's sense of national identity can no longer be based on notions of race and ethnicity, but built on its political institutions, values, and habits. A policy of multiculturalism can achieve this, however, by encouraging immigrants to become Australian "by adoption," while not excluding those not born in Australia. Policy makers must therefore look more closely at the features that

---

215. See Jones, 1996.
216. See Jones, 1996.
217. See Jones, 1996; see, also, Betts and Rapson, 1997, p. 55.
218. See, for example, Horne, 1997; Kalantzis, May 1992–1993, p. 28.
219. Horne, 1997, pp. 263–64.
220. See Horne, 1997, pp. 262–63.

citizenship should have in a multicultural society, or in other words, what would *multicultural citizenship* entail?[221]

A key issue for citizenship in Australia remains the position of Indigenous Australians. Full formal citizenship for Indigenous Australians was achieved as recently as 1983, when their electoral participation was subjected to the same rules as other citizens.[222] As Mick Dodson has argued, however, Indigenous Australians still do not enjoy full citizenship, since they remain politically, economically, and culturally marginalized.[223] The High Court's 1992 decision in *Mabo v. Queensland*[224] appeared to represent a step forward for Indigenous Australians, since it recognized their claim to original ownership of the land. This recognition was provided by the Native Title Act, 1993, which allowed Indigenous Australians, who could demonstrate a continuous attachment to the land, to apply for recognition of ownership rights. This act, however, affected only a minority of Indigenous Australians because most had been driven from their ancestral land and widely dispersed during colonization. A compensation fund was to be provided for this majority of Indigenous Australians who could not make claims. The Land Fund and Indigenous Land Corporation (ATSIC Amendment) Act, 1995 (Cth), established this fund to be administered by the Indigenous Land Corporation.[225]

The High Court's 1996 decision in *Wik Peoples v. Queensland*[226] led to new political conflicts, however, by declaring that native title could coexist with farmers' rights on pastoral leases. Farmers' and miners' representatives interpreted this to mean a threatening increase in the scope of land rights, although this interpretation is disputed by Indigenous organizations. The Coalition government introduced a "10-Point Plan" to amend the 1993 Native Title Act.[227] But this plan was strongly rejected by Indigenous Australians, who claimed that it would deny them basic rights.[228] The prime minister agreed to amend his original proposals based on discussions with an independent senator, allowing the bill to be passed by both houses of Parliament (July 1998).[229] Although Indigenous groups agree that the amended plan is an improvement on the government's original proposals, it has nevertheless meant a diminution of their rights

---

221. See, generally, Castles, 1995, "Multicultural Citizenship."

222. See discussion *supra* Who Are Citizens of Australia?

223. See, generally, Dodson, 1997.

224. *Mabo v. Queensland* (no. 2) (1992) 175 C.L.R. 1.

225. Australia, 1995, Land Fund and Indigenous Land Corporation (ATSIC Amendment) Act.

226. *Wik Peoples v. Queensland* (1996) 121 A.L.R. 129.

227. Australia, 1993, Native Title Act.

228. See Aboriginal and Torres Strait Islander Commission (ATSIC), April 14, 1999 (discussing and critiquing the 10-Point Plan). ATSIC is the main representative body for Indigenous Australians.

229. See Aboriginal and Torres Strait Islander Commission (ATSIC), April 14, 1999.

with respect to the 1993 Native Title Act.[230] Although Indigenous Australians make up only about 2 percent of the Australian population, the symbolic significance of this issue is enormous. There has been increasing realization in recent years that Australian identity and citizenship needed to be reconstituted on an inclusive basis. This required recognition of past wrongs, reconciliation with Indigenous Australians, and measures to guarantee full membership for them. Current trends represent a major step back to the old exclusionary notion of a nation based on white British identity—a constellation that cannot succeed, since it ignores the major shifts in Australian society over the past half-century.

Finally, it important to realize that debates on citizenship as full membership of the community are becoming increasingly significant for those Australians who find themselves marginalized by economic globalization and industrial restructuring. The key values put forward in debates on Australian citizenship have always included social solidarity and equal opportunities. Since 1945, the keys to implementing these values have been equal access to education, full employment, and a social safety net. Current trends in Australian society include restriction of free education (especially at the tertiary level), a fairly constant level of structural unemployment of 8 to 11 percent, and tendencies toward reduction of government medical and social services. Many working class and rural Australians no longer feel that they fully belong to society because of such changes.[231] An inclusive model of citizenship needs to address these issues, too. So far, official unwillingness to do so has left the door open for populist racists, who blame the problems on minorities.

Conclusion

One of the authors of this paper has argued elsewhere[232] that policies for incorporation of immigrants in highly developed countries can be classified according to three ideal-typical models.

The first is *differential exclusion*, in which immigrants are incorporated into certain areas of society (above all the labor market) but denied access to others (such as political participation). This model applies particularly in former "guest worker" recruiting countries like Germany, Austria, and Switzerland. In such countries it is very hard for immigrants to become citizens, because mem-

---

230. Australia, 1993, Native Title Act; see, also, Aboriginal and Torres Strait Islander Commission, 1998, Native Title; Aboriginal and Torres Strait Islander Commission, 1998, Howard/Harradine; Aboriginal and Torres Strait Islander Commission (ATSIC), April 14, 1999.

231. See Castles, 1992, "Australian Multiculturalism," p. 197.

232. See Castles, 1995, "How Nation-States Respond," p. 293; see, also, Castles and Miller, 1998, pp. 293–308.

bership of the political community is based on nationality, that is, membership of the dominant ethnocultural group.

The second is *assimilation*, according to which immigrants are incorporated into society through a one-sided process of adaptation: immigrants are expected to give up their distinctive linguistic, cultural, or social characteristics and become indistinguishable from the majority population. In return for this acculturation, immigrants can become full members of a community ostensibly based on political (rather than cultural) criteria. France is the most obvious example, although assimilation policies have existed in most immigration countries at one time or another, and continue to do so in many.

And the third is *pluralism*, or the acceptance of immigrant populations as ethnic communities that remain distinguishable from the majority population with regard to language, culture, social behavior, and associations over several generations. Pluralism implies that immigrants should be granted equal rights in all spheres of society without being expected to give up their diversity, though usually with an expectation of conformity to certain key values. The United States is the obvious example, but pluralist policies of varying strength and characteristics may be found in Australia, Canada, New Zealand, Sweden, the United Kingdom, and the Netherlands.

Australia, like other European settler colonies that have become mass immigration countries, has evolved from an assimilationist to a pluralist model of incorporation. It could be argued that this is the only way to create an inclusive national community when large parts of the population no longer share the ethnic origins of the founding group. Yet, substantial variations can be found among pluralist countries, for instance with regard to the role of the state in managing ethnocultural difference: Australian multiculturalism has involved a far more active role of the state in social and cultural policy than is to be found in the United States, where the tendency has been to rely on equal legal rights and to leave social and cultural matters to private initiative.

As we have discussed, Australia has developed complex ways of defining citizenship and managing ethnocultural difference. The failure of the Constitution to define citizenship rights has left such matters to the laws of the Commonwealth and the states, as well as to common law, which has resulted in a high degree of inconsistency in many areas. The background to the silence of the Constitution is the fact that Australia did not become fully independent in 1901, and Australians remained British subjects. Moreover, the Constitutional vacuum with regard to citizenship rights was designed to legitimate racial discrimination against Indigenous Australians and non-European immigrants. It was not until the 1960s, in response to growing non-British immigration and the pressure from international public opinion, that Australia's racist definition of belonging was officially changed.

Since the 1970s, great efforts have been made to redefine the meaning of citizenship in a more inclusive way. Important legal measures include the Racial Discrimination Act, 1975;[233] measures to enfranchise Indigenous Australians and to recognize their land rights; and changes in citizenship law to encourage easy naturalization, permit dual citizenship, and remove the privileges of British settlers. Major policy changes include the introduction and development of multiculturalism, and a whole range of measures designed to improve the social position of Indigenous Australians (albeit often with limited success). Yet, Australian citizenship remains contradictory and incomplete in many respects, both as a legal framework and as social membership. Moreover, current trends appear retrogressive. Many of the reform impulses of the late 1980s and early 1990s have been abandoned—often tacitly rather than overtly. The situation is marked by oscillation between conservative models based on nostalgia for a bygone age of British hegemony and neoliberal models based on the perceived needs of Australian business as part of globalized capital. There is no clear direction for Australian citizenship at present, which can only heighten the insecurity of immigrants, Indigenous Australians, and other minorities.

References

Aboriginal and Torres Strait Islander Commission. (Cited April 14, 1999.) <http://www.atsic.gov.au>

Aboriginal and Torres Strait Islander Commission. 1998. *Analysis of the Howard/Harradine Agreement.* <http://www.atsic.gov.au/native/harradine.htm>

Aboriginal and Torres Strait Islander Commission. 1998. *Native Title Agreement: Limited Gain but Still Much Pain.* <http://www.atsic.gov.au/media/July98/native_agreement.htm>

Australia. 1995. Land Fund and Indigenous Land Corporation (ATSIC Amendment) Act.

Australia. 1993. Native Title Act.

Australia. 1986. Australian Citizenship Amendment Act.

Australia. 1984. Australian Citizenship Amendment Act.

Australia. 1984. Referendum Act, No. 44.

Australia. 1975. Racial Discrimination Act.

Australia. 1962. Commonwealth Electoral Act.

Australia. 1958. Migration Act.

Australia. 1948. Nationality and Citizenship Act (later called the Australian Citizenship Act, 1948).

233. Australia, 1975, Racial Discrimination Act.

Australia. 1922. Public Service Act.

Australia. 1920. Commonwealth Nationality Act.

Australia. 1918. Electoral Act.

Australia. 1903. Defence Act.

Australia. 1903. Naturalization Act.

Australia. 1902. Commonwealth Franchise Act.

Australian Constitution, 1900.

Australia. Department of Immigration and Multicultural Affairs. 1998. *Australian Citizenship, Fact Sheet No. 66.* (Last modified November 20.) <http://www.immi.gov.au/facts/66cits.htm>

Australia. Department of Immigration and Multicultural Affairs. 1997. *1997–98 Migration Program Planning Levels, Fact Sheet 20.* <http://www.immi.gov.au/facts/20proga.html>

Australia. Department of Immigration and Multicultural Affairs. 1997. *Australia's Humanitarian Program, Fact Sheet 40.* <http://www.immi. gov.au/facts/40human.html>

Australia. Department of Immigration and Multicultural Affairs. 1997. *How to Apply for Grant of Australian Citizenship: Information Form 1027I.* <http://www.immi.gov.au/allforms/pdf/1027i.pdf>

Australia. Department of Immigration and Multicultural Affairs. 1997. *Immigration Update: June Quarter.* (On file with authors.)

Australia. Department of Immigration and Multicultural Affairs. August 13, 1997. *Two-year Waiting Period for Social Security Payments.* <http://www.immi.gov.au/settlement/twoyear.htm>

Australia. Department of Immigration and Multicultural Affairs. February 25, 1997. *Increased Fees, Media Release.* <http://www.immi.gov.au/deptrel/d97001.htm>

Australia. Department of Immigration and Multicultural Affairs. August 20, 1996. *Immigration and Multicultural Affairs Budget '96 Fact Sheet.*

Australia. Department of Immigration and Multicultural Affairs. March 11, 1996. *Citizenship of Australia, Fact Sheet No. 12.*

Australia. Office of Multicultural Affairs. 1989. *National Agenda for a Multicultural Australia.*

Australia. Senate Legal and Constitutional References Committee. 1995. *Discussion Paper on a System of National Citizenship Indicators.*

Australian Bureau of Statistics. July 1997. *Overseas Arrivals and Departures, Australia.* (On file with authors).

Australian Bureau of Statistics. 1993. *Australia in Profile.* (On file with authors.)

Barbalet, Jean. 1996. "Developments in Citizenship Theory and Issues in Australian Citizenship." *Australian Journal of Social Issues,* no. 31.

Beazley, The Honorable Kim. Speech at the Federation of Ethnic Communities' Councils of Australia Annual Conference: Multiculturalism and Democracy, March 28, 1998.

Betts, Katherine. 1995. "Multiple Citizenships: Two Reports and Some Implications." *People and Place,* no. 3.

Betts, Katherine, and Virginia Rapson. 1997. "Pride and Commitment: Patriotism in Australia." *People and Place,* no. 5.

Bolkus, Senator Nick. (February 19, 1996.) *Howard and Citizenship: Back to the '60s.* Press Release 31/96.

Bolkus, Senator Nick. (September 4, 1995.) *The Ties That Bind: A Four-Year Plan for Australian Citizenship.* Press Release 83/95.

Bolkus, Senator Nick. (August 25, 1995). *New Guidelines on Resumption of Australian Citizenship.* Press Release B76/95. (On file with authors.)

Bosworth, Richard, and Romano Ugolini, eds. 1992. *War, Internment and Mass Migration: The Italo-Australian Experience 1940–1990.* Rome: Gruppo Editoriale Internazionale.

Castles, Stephen. 1997. "Multiculturalism Citizenship: A Response to the Dilemma of Globalisation and National Identity?" *Journal of Intercultural Studies,* no. 18.

Castles, Stephen. 1995. "How Nation-States Respond to Immigration and Ethnic Diversity." *New Community,* no. 21.

Castles, Stephen. 1995. "Multicultural Citizenship." Research Paper No. 16.

Castles, Stephen. 1992. "Australian Multiculturalism: Social Policy and Identity in a Changing Society." In *Nations of Immigrants: Australia, the United States, and International Migration,* eds. Garry Freeman and James Jupp. Oxford: Oxford University Press.

Castles, Stephen. 1992. "The Australian Model of Immigration and Multiculturalism: Is It Applicable to Europe?" *International Migration Review,* no. 26.

Castles, Stephen, et al. 1992. *Mistaken Identity—Multiculturalism and the Demise of Nationalism in Australia,* 3d ed. Sydney: Pluto Press.

Castles, Stephen, and Mark Miller. 1998. *The Age of Migration: International Population Movements in the Modern World,* 2d. ed. London: Macmillan, and New York: Guilford Books.

Chesterman, John, and Brian Galligan. 1997. "Historical Definition of Australian Citizenship." Paper presented at the Globalization and Citizenship Conference, Melbourne, Australia, May 7–9.

Collins, Jock. 1997. *Migrant Hands in a Distant Land: Australia's Post-War Immigration,* 2d ed. Sydney: Pluto Press.

Committee to Advise on Australia's Immigration Policies. 1988. *Immigration: A Commitment to Australia, The Report of the Committee to Advise on Australia's Immigration Policies.* (On file with authors.)

Commonwealth Government of Australia. 1995. *The Ties That Bind: Government Response to the Report by the Joint Standing Committee on Migration "Australians All-Enhancing Australian Citizenship."* (On file with authors.)

Convention on Certain Questions Relating to the Conflict of Nationality Laws. April 12, 1930. The Hague, 179 L.N.T.S. 91.

Davidson, Alastair. 1997. *From Subject to Citizen: Australian Citizenship in the Twentieth Century.* Cambridge: Cambridge University Press.

Dodson, Michael. 1997. "Citizenship in Australia: An Indigenous Perspective." *Alternative Law Journal,* no. 22.

Fitzsimons, Robin. (January 27, 1997.) "Law Not Equal for All Citizens." *Canberra Times,* p. 11.

Foster, Lois, and David Stockley. 1988. *Australian Multiculturalism: A Documentary History and Critique.* Clevedon and Philadelphia: Multilingual Matters.

Galligan, Brian, and John Chesterman. 1997. "Aborigines, Citizenship and the Austra-
    lian Constitution: Did the Constitution Exclude Aboriginal People From Citizen-
    ship?" *Public Law Review,* no. 8.
Godard, Jane. 1997. *The Immigration Kit: A Practical Guide to Australia's Immigration
    Law,* 5th ed. Sydney: Federation Press.
Great Britain. 1948. British Nationality Act.
Hammar, Tomas. 1990. *Democracy and the Nation State.* Aldershot: Avebury.
Horne, Donald. 1997. *The Avenue of the Fair Go.* Sydney: Harper Collins.
House of Representatives Standing Committee on Legal and Constitutional Affairs. As-
    pects of Section 44 of the Australian Constitution—Subsections 44(i) and (iv). (Last
    modified December 18, 1998.) <http://www.aph.gov.au/house/committee.laca/
    Inquiryinsec44.htm>
Human Rights and Equal Opportunities Commission. 1997. *Bringing Them Home: Re-
    port of the National Inquiry into the Separation of Aboriginal and Torres Straight Is-
    lander Children from Their Families.*
International Convention on the Elimination of All Forms of Racial Discrimination,
    opened for signature March 7, 1966, 660 U.N.T.S. 212.
Jakubowicz, Andrew. 1989. "The State and the Welfare of Immigrants in Australia."
    Ethnic and Racial Studies, no. 12.
Joint Committee of Foreign Affairs and Defense. 1976. *Dual Nationality.* Parliamentary
    Paper No. 255. (On file with authors.)
Joint Standing Committee on Migration. 1994. "Australians All-Enhancing Australian
    Citizenship." (On file with authors.)
Jones, Frank. 1996. "National Identity and Social Values." *People and Place,* no. 4.
Jordens, Ann-Mari. 1997. *Alien to Citizen: Settling Migrants in Australia, 1945–75.*
    Sydney: Allen and Unwin.
Jordens, Ann-Mari. 1995. *Redefining Australians: Immigration, Citizenship and Na-
    tional Identity.* Sydney: Hale and Iremonger.
Jordens, Ann-Mari. August 1991. "Promoting Australian Citizenship 1949-71."
    Working Paper No. 22, Australian National University: Administration, Compliance
    and Governability Program, RSSS.
Kalantzis, Mary. May 1992–1993. "Citizenship Education After the Monarchy: Five
    Questions for the Future." *Educational Australia,* no. 19/20.
Lever-Tracy, Constance, and Michael Quinlan. 1988. *A Divided Working Class.* Lon-
    don: Routledge.
Lynch, Tony, and Ronnie Reavell. 1997. "Through the Looking Glass: Hanson, Howard
    and the Politics of 'Political Correctness.'" In *Pauline Hanson: One Nation and Aus-
    tralian Politics,* ed. Bligh Grant. Armidale, NSW: University of New England Press.
Markus, Andrew. 1987. *Australian Race Relations.* Sydney: Allen and Unwin.
Marshall, T. H. 1964. *Citizenship and Social Class, in Class, Citizenship, and Social De-
    velopment: Essays by T. H. Marshall.* New York: Anchor Books.
Martin, Jean. 1978. *The Migrant Presence.* Sydney: Allen and Unwin.
McQueen, Humphrey. 1975. *A New Britannia.* Ringwood, Vic.: Penguin.
Middleton, Karen. (March 14, 1997.) "Minister Shelves Nationality Push." *Age,* p. 6.
Moss, Irene, Race Discrimination Commissioner. (February 8, 1989.) Letter to the Hon-
    orable Lionel Bowen, MHR. <http://www.ausflag.com.au/debate/vote/moss.html>
Peterson, Nicolas, and Will Sanders, eds. 1998. *Citizenship and Indigenous Australians:
    Changing Perceptions and Possibilities.* Melbourne: Cambridge University Press.

Reynolds, Harry. 1987. *Frontier*. Sydney: Allen and Unwin.

Rowley, Chris. 1970. *The Destruction of Aboriginal Society*. Canberra: Australian National University Press.

Rubenstein, Kim. 1995. "Citizenship in Australia: Unscrambling Its Meaning." *Melbourne University Law Review*, no. 20.

Ruddock, Phillip, M.P. January 20, 1997. *Citizenship: A Bond Shared by All Australians*. Press release.

Schnapper, Dominique. 1994. *La Communauté des Citoyens*. Paris: Gallimard.

Senate Standing Committee on Constitutional and Legal Affairs. 1981. *The Constitutional Qualifications of Members of Parliament*. Parliamentary Paper No. 131. (On file with authors.)

Stephen, Sir Ninian. 1993. "Issues in Citizenship." Lecture at the Alfred Deakin Lecture Trust.

Thornton, Margaret. 1996. "The Legocentric Citizen." *Alternative Law Journal*, no. 21.

Wells, Belinda. 1996. "Aliens: The Outsiders in the Constitution." *University of Queensland Law Journal*, no. 19.

Zappalà, Gianni. 1994. "The Decline of Economic Complementarity: Australia and the Sterling Area." *Australian Economic Historical Review*, no. 28.

Legal Cases

Kioa v. West (1985) 159 C.L.R. 550.

Lim v. Minister for Immigration, Local Government and Ethnic Affairs (1992) 176 C.L.R. 1.

Mabo v. Queensland (no. 2) (1992) 175 C.L.R. 1.

Sykes v. Cleary (1992) 109 A.L.R. 577, available in LEXIS, Aust. Library, Ausmax File (High Court of Australia sitting as the Court of Disputed Returns).

Wik Peoples v. Queensland (1996) 121 A.L.R. 129.

The Dilemmas of Canadian
Citizenship Law

DONALD GALLOWAY

THE SECTIONS of the Citizenship Act[1] stipulating how Canadian citizenship can be obtained and lost are deceptively simple. Their commendable clarity and precision ensure that they have presented few problems to tax the ingenuity of lawyers or jurists. Yet, while the rules themselves may be precise, they say little of the social meaning and political significance of the status. Beneath the straightforward formal rules, one finds a tangle of principles, values, and political perspectives.

In this paper, I attempt to unearth and examine some of these underlying values, and to offer an assessment of the membership criteria and principles of regeneration that have been adopted in Canadian law. I begin with a truncated account of Canadian citizenship laws. Next, I discuss the role that the concept of citizenship plays in liberal political and legal theory. Taking note of the complexities that arise when borders are permeable—which permits the entry and residence of nonmembers—the nub of my claim is that citizenship laws should be shaped and evaluated by their effect on those who are excluded from the status, as well as those who are included.

The author is currently a member of the Convention Refugee Determination Division of the Immigration and Refugee Board. The views expressed in this article are the author's alone and are not intended to represent the views of the board. The author would like to thank Alex Aleinikoff for his constructive comments on earlier drafts.

1. See Canada, 1985, Citizenship Act, R.S.C., ch. C-29.

I next examine the underlying values that have contributed to the evolution and development of Canadian citizenship law. I focus on early naturalization and immigration acts, and the debates that preceded the Canadian Citizenship Act,[2] which came into force in 1947. Bringing the discussion up to the present, I note a continuing tension between nationalistic and postnationalistic as well as collectivist and individualist conceptions of citizenship, and I highlight those parts of the substantive law where conflicting values and principles have given rise to interpretive dilemmas. The entrenchment of the Canadian Charter of Rights and Freedoms[3] (the "Charter") in 1982 and recent judicial decisions that focus on the rights of immigrants and their claims for equal treatment with citizens offer a particularly rich source for examination and analysis.

Throughout the paper, I advert to recent proposals for change found in Bill C-63, entitled An Act Respecting Canadian Citizenship, which was introduced in Parliament by the government in December 1998. In my conclusion, I argue that the proposals constitute a modest tilt toward a nationalistic conception of citizenship—one that emphasizes a physical nexus to Canadian territory, and the importance of a cohesive national community. The modesty of the proposed legislation is illustrated by the fact that it does not adopt earlier recommendations that would have gone considerably further, particularly in restricting dual citizenship.

Canadian Citizenship Law

Canadian citizenship law is multifunctional. It recognizes the status of citizenship, defines the qualifications required for obtaining it, stipulates the means through which the status can be lost or renounced, and, most significantly, attaches to the status a package of rights, privileges, and burdens generally not available to others, although each part of the package may have a wider distribution. Citizenship laws are also frequently accompanied by political programs that encourage those identified as citizens to behave in particular ways, such as publicly celebrating their status, and even to conceive of their legal status as an integral aspect of their identity.

Citizenship law does more than distinguish those who belong to a legal community and the terms of membership. It also has a diachronic dimension. Citizenship law is the mechanism whereby a society achieves regeneration,

---

2. See Canada, 1970, Canadian Citizenship Act, R.S.C., ch. C-19. The Canadian Citizenship Act was enacted in 1946 but came into force only on January 1, 1947. It is colloquially known as the "1947 Act." In the ensuing years, it was amended frequently and was eventually superseded by the Citizenship Act, which came into force on February 15, 1977.

3. See England, 1982, Canada Act, ch. 11, sched. B (the "Charter").

retaining its identity while its constituent members are born and die, arrive and depart. Citizenship law provides the strands that connect the future to the past, by identifying the characteristics of those who will be recognized as worthy of special attention from the law.

I start with the premise that the Citizenship Act is the primary source of citizenship law. This statement, however, is controversial. The 1982 entrenchment of the Canadian Charter of Rights and Freedoms as one of the components of the Canadian Constitution complicates the legality of the provisions of the Citizenship Act, because citizenship and permanent residence—while recognized as statuses in the Charter, with various rights being guaranteed to the holders of each—are not defined therein. Nor does the Charter identify qualifications for obtaining either status, which raises the question of whether there are implied constitutional standards that must be met by a citizenship act. Is it constitutionally permissible to exclude classes of individuals from the status or to include others? The entrenchment of the Charter raises the possibility that a moral conception of citizenship, binding on the legislature, should be regarded as being the fundamental source of citizenship rather than the positive law conception found in the Citizenship Act. The absence of any constitutional definition, however, entails that the issue is left open. Three options seem available. First, and least persuasive, one could argue that the framers of the Charter embedded therein the definition of citizenship that existed in 1982, that which is found in the current Citizenship Act, which came into force in 1977, and that a constitutional amendment would be required to alter this definition. This option is not very persuasive. Not only have Canadian courts expressed suspicion of the need to rely solely on the framers' intent, but also there is no good reason to assume that the framers intended a static definition of citizenship rather than a flexible one. The second option is that the term "citizen" should be regarded as having a flexible definition, with the legislature being the proper body to make decisions about its content. This option seems counterintuitive. If the legislature could redefine those who are the beneficiaries of Charter rights, one would think that, analogously, it could also redefine "Government," the body that is subject to Charter obligations, and thereby immunize itself from its application. The third option is that the term should be regarded as having a flexible definition with the judiciary as the proper body to determine its content. The suggestion, however, that a body that is not accountable to the people should have the authority to determine who is a citizen is equally problematic.[4]

---

4. Peter Hogg, a leading constitutional lawyer, opts for the second of these options but quite ambivalently and without offering reasons for doing so. See Hogg, 1998.

The Citizenship Act recognizes three principal ways by which one may gain the status.[5] First, a person who is born in Canada is automatically a Canadian citizen,[6] unless he or she is the child of a foreign diplomat.[7] This rule maintains and modernizes the English common law of *jus soli*. As summarized by Mervyn Jones,

> Under the common law a person became a British subject, as a rule, by being born within the allegiance of the Crown, and the usual source of this allegiance was birth within His Majesty's dominions. The common law, as modified or amended by statutes of the Parliament of the United Kingdom was regarded as applying in all parts of His Majesty's dominions. . . .[8]

Second, a strand of *jus sanguinis* is also recognized in the Citizenship Act, in that a person automatically becomes a citizen by being born to a Canadian citizen outside Canada.[9] A qualification is attached, however: if the parent had also gained citizenship through this provision, the child will lose the status unless, before the age of twenty-eight, he or she applies to retain the status, registers as a citizen, and either resides in Canada for at least a year before applying or establishes a substantial connection with Canada.[10] These rules do not apply to children adopted by a citizen outside Canada, who must be sponsored as immigrants if they are to gain status in Canada. Should the sponsorship be permitted, the child will be admitted to Canada as a permanent resident and may later seek naturalization.[11] Similarly, the rules do not apply to the children of permanent residents who are born outside Canada.

The third principal method of gaining citizenship is outlined in section 5(1) of the Citizenship Act, which sets out the qualifications for citizenship by naturalization. It provides that:

5. The Citizenship Act also allows for some exceptional ways of becoming a citizen; for example, the Governor in Council (that is, the Federal Cabinet) has unrestricted discretion to direct the minister to grant citizenship in cases of hardship or to reward exceptional services to Canada. See Canada, 1985, Citizenship Act, § 5(4).

6. See Canada, 1985, Citizenship Act, § 3(1)(a).

7. See Canada, 1985, Citizenship Act, § 3(2).

8. Jones, 1956. The English common law did recognize exceptions from an early date. Children born overseas to English subjects were recognized as subjects, and, conversely, the children of foreign representatives born in England were not.

9. See Canada, 1985, Citizenship Act, § 3(1)(b).

10. Canada, 1985, Citizenship Act, § 8. The detailed requirements of the process are outlined in Canada, 1993, Citizenship Regulations, SOR/93-246, § 6.

11. The law relating to adopted children is to be found in Canada, 1985, Immigration Act, R.S.C., ch. I-2; and Canada, 1978, Immigration Regulations, SOR/78-172.

The Minister shall grant citizenship to any person who
(a) makes application for citizenship;
(b) is eighteen years of age or over;
(c) has been lawfully admitted to Canada for permanent residence, has not ceased to be a permanent resident pursuant to section 24 of the Immigration Act, and has, within the four years immediately preceding the date of the application, accumulated at least three years of residence in Canada. . . ;
(d) has an adequate knowledge of one of the official languages of Canada;
(e) has an adequate knowledge of Canada and of the responsibilities and privileges of citizenship; and
(f) is not under a deportation order. . . .[12]

Section 3(1) of the Citizenship Act also stipulates that a person who meets these requirements is a citizen only when he or she takes the oath of citizenship, a requirement that can be waived only in the case of a minor or a person with a mental disability.[13] Moreover, section 24 of the Immigration Act, to which reference is made, provides that a person ceases to be a permanent resident when he leaves Canada or remains outside Canada with the intention of abandoning Canada as his place of permanent residence, and that a person who has been outside the country for six months in a one-year period shall be deemed to have abandoned Canada unless he proves that he did not have that intent.[14] The Citizenship Regulations flesh out these statutory requirements. They provide, for example, that knowledge of Canada and of the responsibilities and rights of citizens is to be tested by questions relating to such matters as the election process, social and cultural history, political history, or physical and political geography.[15]

The Citizenship Act and the Citizenship Regulations also provide for loss and renunciation of citizenship. Section 10 of the Citizenship Act provides that where the Governor in Council (that is, the Federal Cabinet) is satisfied that a person has obtained citizenship "by false representation, or fraud or by knowingly concealing circumstances," the person ceases to be a citizen.[16] Moreover, where a person has gained permanent resident status through such means, he or

---

12. Canada, 1985, Citizenship Act, § 5(1).
13. Canada, 1985, Citizenship Act, § 3(1).
14. See Canada, 1985, Immigration Act, R.S.C., § 24.
15. See Canada, 1993, Citizenship Regulations, SOR/93-246, § 15.
16. Canada, 1985, Citizenship Act, § 10.

she is deemed to have obtained citizenship also by such means. These provisions have been used by the federal government in recent years, with mixed results, against individuals who have concealed alleged war crimes when applying for permanent resident status. To find such individuals guilty of the offenses would require proof beyond a reasonable doubt. To strip them of their citizenship, and therefore qualify them for deportation, requires only proof on the balance of probabilities.

While the Citizenship Act identifies the formal criteria for gaining and losing citizenship, its silence on a number of issues is quite deafening. The issue, for example, of whether a person may retain multiple nationalities is dealt with only by implication. There is no provision in the Citizenship Act that prevents a person from taking out citizenship in another country. Nor is there any provision to compel a naturalized Canadian to renounce his or her previous citizenship.

Perhaps the most significant omission is the failure of the Citizenship Act to identify the responsibilities and rights that attach to the status. Consequently, it does not offer any hint on how the life of a citizen will differ from that of other persons who may participate in the political, cultural, and social life of Canada. Such matters are dealt with elsewhere, both in other federal statutes and in the Constitution. Section 3 of the Charter, for example, recognizes that every *citizen* has the right to vote in federal and provincial elections and to be qualified for membership in the relevant legislature.[17] Section 6(1) of the Charter recognizes that every citizen has the right to enter, remain in, and leave Canada.[18] And section 23(1) of the Charter vests in citizens who meet certain qualifications the right to have their children educated in one of the two official languages.[19] As I point out below, however, the equality provisions in the Charter have rendered the status of citizenship a suspect ground for positive discrimination, and accordingly citizens and permanent residents receive equal access to social benefits, such as medical care, and welfare. The rare case in which citizenship has been used as a criterion for preferential treatment has proved problematic and has attracted judicial attention.[20]

Moreover, as noted earlier, the rules of positive law do not provide much insight into the social meaning of citizenship. To address this issue, I turn first to political and legal theory and then to historical records.

17. See England, 1982, Canada Act, ch. 11, sched. B, § 3.
18. See England, 1982, Canada Act, ch. 11, sched. B, § 6(1).
19. See England, 1982, Canada Act, ch. 11, sched. B, § 23(1). Section 6(2) of the Charter recognizes the right of every citizen and permanent resident to move and to take up residence in any province and to pursue the gaining of a livelihood in any province.
20. See discussion below in section entitled "The Rights of Citizens and Noncitizens."

Authority, Membership, and Social Regeneration

The political and social landscapes of the modern world have been shaped by the existence of borders: imaginary lines drawn across our maps that define the territorial span of discrete societies, and that, as much as any attribute of physical geography, have contributed to the flourishing of their diverse cultures and distinctive identities. Within these boundaries, autonomous legal systems have developed, each identifying the enclosed territory as its domain and claiming sovereignty over it. But the law also makes an additional claim of much greater significance. As Joseph Raz has drawn to our attention,[21] one of the identifying characteristics of a legal system is that it makes a moral claim: it claims to have legitimate authority over a population on whose behalf, or in whose service, it acts.[22] The problem of defining the conditions that could justify the claim to legitimacy is the central question of political theory, and a variety of conflicting accounts dominate current debates. While some, for example, would argue that legitimacy can be gained only if the law represents the will of the people and furthers the interest of each and all, others, such as Raz, tie it to the ability of the legal authority to assist people to act on reasons that bind them.[23] Raz argues persuasively that the law's claim to authority is premised on a more basic claim: that by following the law rather than by following their own direction, those governed by it will more likely achieve what they already have a reason to achieve, such as a fulfilling life or meeting their moral obligations to others. In order to make this claim persuasively, the law must, of course, be able to show that it can provide the population with the preconditions for a more fulfilling life or can effectively coordinate social interactions.

While these debates may define the core of political theory, they rely for support upon the prior determination of an even more fundamental issue: no matter how a legal system attempts to ground its claim to legitimacy, it must first identify the set of individuals who are its subjects and distinguish them from strangers. "Who belongs?" is the most basic question for a government that asserts legitimacy. The concept of citizenship has become a central device by which the law distinguishes those subject to it and served by it from strangers. Thus, citizenship has come to play a vital role in the fundamental question of politics. It is here that it gains much of its social significance.

To avoid misunderstanding, it is vital to stress that this concept of citizenship does not imply that legal authorities have no obligations to strangers or that strangers are morally irrelevant. On the contrary, acting on behalf of a popula-

---

21. See generally Raz, 1986.

22. The service conception of authorities, as articulated by Raz, is the view that "their role and primary function is to serve the governed." Raz, 1986, p. 56.

23. See Raz, 1986, pp. 53–57.

tion, legal authorities are under the moral obligation to respect the human rights of strangers and to treat them justly and fairly. But, because the law does not assume a position of authority over strangers, because it does not aim to serve them, the substantive content of its obligations will differ from that of its obligations to those who are under its claimed authority. The latter obligations will normally be more onerous. The relationship between legal authorities and those subject to and served by them has further dimensions, mirroring the one just noted. First, a legal authority may determine that its ability to serve its subjects is contingent on a willingness of the subjects to participate voluntarily and enthusiastically in social and political life. Accordingly, the law may provide positive incentives to its subjects to do so. It will defend such measures by reference to the negative consequences of not providing them. But it may not limit itself to providing encouragement. While a state may make demands on strangers not to interfere with its attempts to create order and promote the interests of its subjects, on the subjects themselves it may impose stronger demands. In particular, it may demand some level of commitment to the collectivity that, in circumstances in which social disintegration is threatened, may even amount to self-sacrifice. In brief, the need to distinguish between subject and stranger pertains to the allocation of burdens as well as benefits and incentives.

Citizenship law does more than distinguish those who belong to a legal community and the terms of membership. It also serves as the mechanism whereby a society achieves regeneration. This added dimension reveals a second aspect to law's basic claim. Not only does law claim authority over a collection of people, but it also claims that the collectivity will be better served by acknowledging particular principles of regeneration.

Of course, both these claims may—and frequently do—meet resistance. The debates that rage in texts of political theory spill over into real life. For a variety of normative reasons, the law may choose to identify as its subjects a group of people who do not self-identify as a single cohesive group. Alternatively, it may identify as subjects a group of people who see themselves as part of a larger social group. Furthermore, even if there is a correlation between the law's conception of a group as its subjects and that group's conception of itself as a society, there may be different conceptions of the proper principles of regeneration.

While the law may base its claim to authority on a normative determination that a group should identify itself in a particular way and adopt particular principles of regeneration that will continue to shape that identity, it may face the challenge that group identity and regeneration are matters of brute fact or nonpolitical negotiation. Whereas moral claims are based on balancing competing reasons for action, determinations of identity may be conceived as being based on a more fundamental appreciation of cohesiveness. To meet these challenges, the law must show not only that it is has the ability to weigh correctly competing reasons for action, but also that it can defend the principles of community identity that it has adopted.

Membership, Participation, and Open Borders

In the previous section, I stressed the importance of distinguishing strangers and members, but I ignored two important dimensions of modernity—the permeability and flexibility of borders and the mobility of populations. If borders were immovable and impermeable, and the law were able and willing to exclude all strangers from its territorial jurisdiction, there would be little difficulty in drawing the distinction between strangers and subjects and in allocating the appropriate level of concern to each. These are, however, counterfactual hypotheses, never strictly true, but more applicable in earlier centuries where it was only settlement or conquest that brought about the relocation of borders and the consequent redefinition of the class of individuals subject to the law's authority. In these times, the expense and difficulty of arranging transportation or communication meant that it was only the merchant, the explorer, the scholar, the soldier, or those who had no other choice who would have the opportunity or resources to assume residence in another society. As a result, particular communities, as long as they could protect themselves from invasion or conquest, were able to maintain and develop their own peculiar ethos and sense of identity with relative ease.

In the changed circumstances of this century, the legal authorities of each state, with varying levels of success, have come to rely on administrative machinery to control the entry and exit of people, seeking thereby to limit the size of the community and maintain its integrity. At the same time, however, states have also come to realize that benefits may flow from exercising a lax level of control over the imaginary borderlines. Thus, we witness throngs of temporary workers, businesspeople, students, refugees, long-term residents, illegal immigrants, and tourists entering, exiting, and reentering through the available gateways. No longer is the emigrant a hapless exile or the holder of a one-way ticket. As these groups of foreigners take residence, no matter how permanent or temporary, the ethos and cultural coherence of a community can be transformed. Newcomers form ties and relationships with subjects, which give rise to obligations of association[24] that are more concrete, demanding, and pressing than one's abstract duties to humanity at large. They form relations with the

---

24. I borrow this phrase from Ronald Dworkin who attempts to found the legitimacy of the state on associative obligations. See Dworkin, 1986.

state. Moreover, they will likely retain familial and cultural ties with people in their country of origin—ties that will constrain or severely qualify the opportunities of immigration. Furthermore, they will form liaisons with individual immigrants who are in a similar position. It is no longer possible to even approximate a hard-and-fast line between subject and stranger. Between these two poles remain a number of different classifications. Justice will demand that the peculiarity of each be respected. It will require that full account be paid to the undertakings made to those who fit within these classifications, and to the demands that are made of them. Moreover, individuals who form such ties with a state may question the legal criteria established to identify those whom the law is intended to serve. They may make a claim that justice requires that they, too, be recognized as its subjects and its beneficiaries.

Thus, the presence of large numbers of foreigners within a community presents a challenge to the authority of the state. The crux of the difficulty is the state's ability to distinguish between, on the one hand, the population on whose behalf it acts and, on the other hand, those others whom it has permitted to participate in social life, to whom it owes obligations of justice but whose welfare is not its primary concern or *raison d'être*.[25] A defense of citizenship laws should be based on both instrumental and noninstrumental evaluations of collective and individual well-being, and on assessments of justice. Likewise, a critical assessment of citizenship laws should be founded on an assessment of the ways in which these various factors have been taken into consideration and balanced. This theoretical account of citizenship clashes with the rhetorical accounts of citizenship found in some of the most important Canadian political debates, which seem to focus entirely on the interests of Canadians and of the polity. It is to these that I now turn, after a brief methodological excursus.

Archeological Inquiries

It is worthwhile to examine the ways in which citizenship has figured rhetorically in political and legal debates of earlier decades for three reasons. First, it

25. To defend its claim to legitimacy in a mobile world, a legal authority would need to develop citizenship laws that reflect the interplay of four separate determinations: (1) the present and future interests of the collectivity—including whether the society will be more likely to flourish if membership is limited to those with certain characteristics or virtues; (2) whether the link between the community and a putative member (such as birth or residence in the territory) is of such a nature to give rise to claim in justice that the individual be recognized as a member; (3) the strength of the interests of persons already defined as members (regarding, for example, membership for their children or the impact of new additions); and (4) the strength of the interests of persons excluded from membership. Full explication and application of this analysis is beyond the scope of this paper.

is important to take account of a widely held and, in my opinion, sound conviction that political assessments of a social institution or process must be based not only on abstract universal principles, but also on the particular social context in which the institution or process is located. This view, associated with communitarian political theorists, is expressed aptly by Michael Walzer, who advocates that our moral and political vocabulary should be both "thick and thin."[26] To concretize normative abstractions, we must develop a detailed and vibrant account of the social order in which they have been and are to be applied. The contextual accounts that I offer here are highly selective and not intended to be complete. In Canada, there is a surfeit of interpretations of our past and present, of our links with previous generations, of the glue that holds us together as a nation, and of the tensions that threaten to split us apart—and hence a surfeit of possible contexts in which the legal status of citizenship may be located. I offer an historical account of the processes that led to adoption of citizenship as a legal status, emphasizing the rhetorical gambits that were used to justify its introduction into the legal lexicon. It is against this historical backdrop that I shall project both the relevant abstract ideals and the current laws, in order to expose both subtextual subtleties and enduring anachronisms and also to emphasize contextual factors that have influenced and continue to influence debates about membership and justice. My aim in developing these themes is to make the point that the never-ending multivocal Canadian conversation about sovereignty, national identity, federalism, and national unity continues to impinge heavily on any discussion of citizenship law. It would not be off the mark to claim that these are the factors that have dominated the development of the status of citizenship and the content of the positive laws that define it today.

A second reason to consult the historical record is to show how debates about citizenship in Canada have relied on a variety of themes pulled from inconsistent theoretical traditions. While most influential legislators, for example, have defended citizenship laws by espousing a Burkean form of conservativism that respects traditional institutions, others have tried to defend the same laws by adhering to more liberal values that seek neutral resolutions to political problems, based on a search for an overlapping consensus.

A third reason is to provide critical purchase on the communitarian principle to which I referred above. I will suggest that it is inappropriate to allow the interest of social cohesion, promoted by supporting social traditions and cultural practices, to blind us to the consequences for those who seek membership or for those who have been admitted to a community to live within it, but who have not become institutionally recognized members. Ultimately, I am anxious to

---

26. See, generally, Walzer, 1994.

express a concern that, in Canada, undue political attention has been paid to promoting Canadian sovereignty, to building a strong and unified nation, and to generating a rich and unique heritage in which members can take pride. This focus has contributed to the undervaluation of the interests of noncitizens, and also of some individual citizens.

The Emergence and Evolution of Canadian Citizenship

Before 1946, the Canadian Parliament had made no effort to exhaustively define the status of Canadian citizenship, although it had made various ad hoc forays into the field, most obviously by enacting statutes dealing with naturalization. By and large, it had adhered to the nationality criteria of the English common law.[27]

Although the matter was never tested, Jones states confidently that, before the enactment of the Statute of Westminster in 1931,[28] the Canadian Parliament did not have the constitutional jurisdiction to amend the law of nationality that accorded the status of British subject to those born within the Empire. He writes: "[N]otwithstanding the fact that many colonies acquired a substantial degree of self-government during the late nineteenth and early twentieth centuries, legislation with respect to British nationality was considered to be exclusively within the province of the 'Imperial' Parliament."[29] Jones also notes that, while the exclusive authority of the Imperial Parliament over matters of nationality was accepted, at no time was this seen to curtail "the power of the colonies to provide for naturalization of persons as 'local' British subjects, *i.e.*, as British subjects within the limits of the colony."[30] This power was exercised early by the Canadian Parliament, acting under the authority of section 91 of the Constitution Act, 1867[31] (the "Constitution Act, 1867"), which granted legislative competence over "Naturalization and Aliens."[32]

In 1914, an attempt was made to develop a cooperative scheme of naturalization throughout the British Empire.[33] Naturalization laws were more or less

27. See Jones, 1956, p. 87.
28. See England, 1931, Statute of Westminster, 22 & 23 Geo. 5, ch. 4. Among other things, the Statute of Westminster granted to the Canadian Parliament the power to amend or repeal any legislation of the Imperial Parliament except the British North America Acts. It also provided that Canadian statutes repugnant to Imperial statute would no longer be void.
29. Jones, 1956, p. 87.
30. Jones, 1956, p. 87.
31. Previously known as the British North America Act, 1867, 30 & 31 Vict., ch. 3 (England).
32. In 1868, it enacted a statute repealing all pre-Confederation legislation, and in 1881 it enacted a statute dealing with naturalization, England, 1881, Naturalization Act, 44 Vict., ch. 13, which mirrored the provisions of the recently enacted U.K. Act.
33. See Parry, 1957.

imperialized by the enactment of the British Nationality and Status of Aliens Act[34] (the "British Nationality Act"), which allowed for "imperial" rather than merely local naturalization, with the proviso that it have effect in other Dominions only if they, too, adopted a parallel measure. The Canadian Parliament acquiesced in this common plan by reenacting the British Nationality Act.[35]

While the aim of the British government may have been to establish an empire in all parts of which British subjects were free to settle, it did not succeed. At most, it could be said that "[a]t the height of imperial development the British subject was . . . free so far as his personal circumstances allowed, to enter and reside *in the United Kingdom*."[36] The lack of success can be attributed to the fact that various Dominions, including Canada, did not share the same aspirations and had already begun to assert their developing status as independent countries rather than colonies.

The clearest proof that during this period of Canada's history, authority over the political status of Canadians was seen as a vital toehold in the climb toward independence can be found in two contemporary statutes that legalized the statuses of "Canadian Citizen" and of "Canadian National": the Immigration Act of 1910[37] and the Canadian Nationals Act of 1921.[38] The latter contained a definition of "Canadian National" based explicitly on the definition of "citizen" found in the former. The Canadian Nationals Act served a single purpose—to deal with the demand by the International Court of Justice that countries only be able to nominate their own nationals for membership of that court. Without a concept of citizen, Canada would not gain representation. Thus, we have a clear instance of a case where the concept of citizenship is invoked not to express a relationship between individual and the state or amongst members of a political community, but to accord to Canada a benefit accorded to other autonomous and independent countries.

The Immigration Act placed significant restrictions on citizenship. Canada's immigration laws were enacted by Parliament under the authority of the Constitution Act, 1867, which provided for federal legislation on "Immigration and Agriculture." Soon after confederation, acting under this head of power, Parliament began to enact restrictive immigration laws, allowing it to control the composition of the Canadian population. Immigration legislation thus acted as a surrogate for effective citizenship legislation. In effect, the Canadian Parlia-

34. See England, 1914, British Nationality and Status of Aliens Act, 4 & 5 Geo. 5, ch. 17.
35. See England, 1914, Naturalization Act, 4 & 5 Geo. 5, ch. 44.
36. British Section of the International Commission of Jurists, 1980, *British Nationality: The Report of a Working Party*, p. 1 (emphasis added).
37. See England, 1910, Immigration Act, 9 & 10 Edw., ch. 27.
38. See England, 1921, Canadian Nationals Act, 11 & 12 Geo. 5, ch. 4.

ment attempted to bypass any technical hurdles preventing it from defining its membership by controlling access to the country. By restricting membership in this way, it was able to create an image of itself (both to itself and to others) as an autonomous country. The de facto power that it wielded undermined any legal niceties of colonial constitutionalism.[39] The Immigration Act is particularly notable because it was the first legal instrument to introduce to this scheme the status of Canadian citizenship. It provided that a person who was a member of one of the listed prohibited classes could enter or remain in the country only if he or she was also a citizen or a person with Canadian domicile.[40] It defined a citizen as: (1) a person born in Canada who had not become an alien, (2) a British subject domiciled in Canada, or (3) a person naturalized in Canada not having lost domicile or become an alien.[41] In this way, the definition of citizenship derived from a system of immigration restriction. In memorable language, Moffat Hancock noted, "It should be remembered . . . that this high-sounding but slippery dignity of Canadian citizenship is simply a term of art among immigration officials, very important at the border, but having no effect upon civil or political rights."[42]

The statutory structure was somewhat peculiar because the definition of "citizen" appears to overlap to a great extent with the category of persons with a Canadian domicile. The immigration purposes of the statute could have been achieved simply by establishing two categories—persons born in Canada and persons not born in Canada who were domiciled in Canada. If there was no need to define British subjects and domiciled naturalized persons as citizens, why was it done? Clive Parry has justifiably commented that one sees in the statute a parliamentary intent to assert its authority to identify individuals as citizens, but to do so in a way that did not threaten confrontation with colonial superiors.[43]

39. It is ironic that Canada's success in this regard has served as a model for the province of Quebec to pursue a similar strategy today. Having negotiated an agreement on immigration with Canada that allows it to select its own immigrants, while acknowledging that it lacks authority on matters of citizenship, Quebec aims both to shape its future population and to present itself as the ultimate authority on the identity of its population. It is unlikely, however, that Quebec's attempts to use immigration standards as a lever to separate itself from Canadian authority will be as successful as the earlier parallel attempts by Canada against its colonial superior. The most important difference between the two cases is that Quebec does not have the power to prevent individuals from other provinces to settle in Quebec; nor does it have the authority to prevent its immigrants, once selected, from moving to other provinces.

40. England, 1910, Immigration Act, 9 & 10 Edw., ch. 27, § 3.

41. England, 1910, Immigration Act, 9 & 10 Edw., ch. 27, § 2.

42. Hancock, 1937.

43. See Parry, 1957, p. 451. One can find other examples of such nonconfrontational assertiveness. Consider, for example, the fact that the early Canadian naturalization statutes also covered matters that fall clearly outside that heading, such as expatriation and the status of women

Further evidence of a legislative subtext relating to national sovereignty is provided by the fact that when joining the cooperative scheme of 1914, the Canadian legislature did not merely adopt the provisions found in the section of the British Naturalization Act. Rather, it reenacted the whole statute, including those parts that related to broader issues of national status rather than naturalization, narrowly conceived. Again, this suggests that from the Canadian point of view, it was important to at least appear to have authority over all matters relating to nationality and citizenship. The most plausible explanation for promoting this image is that the Canadian government considered it an effective measure to create momentum in its attempts to gain independence from the United Kingdom.

Whatever the case before the Statute of Westminster in 1931, in the years after that date, it became evident that enacting a citizenship law was regarded as a way of asserting Canada's newly gained sovereignty. It is revealing that in 1931, the secretary of state proposed a Canadian citizenship bill that bore close resemblance to the one introduced fifteen years later.[44] Although it was withdrawn before it received third reading, this event suggests that citizenship was regarded as a fundamental aspect of the newly granted independence.

In the debates in the House of Commons that preceded the enactment of the 1947 Canadian Citizenship Act, one can readily see that the passage of the bill was motivated in large part by concerns that Canada begin to divest itself of the remaining vestiges of its colonial status. One of the themes that dominated the debates is that to be a citizen means belonging to an independent country: to be a citizen was not to be a colonial. Thus, Secretary of State Paul Martin, in introducing the bill, noted, "It is a discreditable position in which we find ourselves as a nation among nations of the world [today] not to be able clearly to address one another with the full sanction of the law and for all purposes as citizens of our own country."[45]

The historical association between independence and citizenship can be identified as a major reason for the continuing perception that citizenship laws play a critical role in social ordering. Other important themes are also visible, however, and they have maintained a position of prominence. First is the theme of Canada's international status. One can detect in the 1946 debates an almost

---

who marry aliens. See, for example, England, 1881, Naturalization Act, 44 Vict., ch. 13. Such legislation suggests that in Canada the distinction between nationality and naturalization was not as clearly drawn as Jones has asserted or that it was deliberately being rendered murky. Such sections also suggest that it was not universally accepted that nationality was the concern solely of the Imperial legislature.

44. Canada, 1931, 188 Debates, House of Commons 2021.

45. Canada, 1946, 249 Debates, House of Commons 503.

invisible shift from concern about the need to mark Canada's independence to concern about the need to establish a strong position in the international community by achieving a cohesive and loyal population. In Paul Martin's words,

> For the national unity of Canada and for the future and greatness of this country it is felt to be of the utmost importance that all of us, new Canadians or old, have a consciousness of a common purpose and common interests as Canadians; that all of us be able to say with pride and say with meaning: "I am a Canadian citizen."[46]

Themes of independence and full membership in the international regime of states represent state interests in a formalized concept of citizenship. But the development of Canadian citizenship also had deep implications for individuals and their relation to their state. The shift from subject to citizen is a shift from constitutional monarchism to liberal republicanism, implicating both governance of the state and rights held against the state.

Subjecthood, from the view of the common law, described a political status based upon a bond of allegiance with the monarch. The relationship between subject and monarch, as noted in *Calvin's Case*, signified "the mutual bond and obligation between the King and his subjects, whereby subjects are called his liege subjects, because they are bound to obey and serve him; and he is called their liege lord, because he should maintain and defend them."[47] That the relationship should be determined primarily by place of birth was regarded as a natural implication of the sovereign's claim over the territory in question. Moreover, it is clearly articulated in *Calvin's Case* that the allegiance of the subject is personal. It is not "owed to the crown nor to the law nor to the kingdom, but to the person of the king."[48]

The transfer of legal sovereignty from the monarch to the king or queen in Parliament and the recognition of the political sovereignty of the people necessarily redefined the relationship of the person to the state—just as it set the stage for the struggles for universal suffrage in the first two decades of the twentieth century. The personal allegiance a subject owed to a sovereign was replaced by a set of common bonds with other citizens who together now constituted the sovereign.

46. Canada, 1946, 249 Debates, House of Commons 502.

47. *Calvin's Case,* 7 Co. Rep. 1, 5 (1608).

48. Dunham has noted that "the ruling in f[avor] of Calvin . . . may have checked, but it did not prevent, the eventual comprehension of the ideas, realm, law, and king, within the term, crown—perhaps the most consequential of all constitutional concepts." Dunham, 1951.

The second aspect of the relation between citizen and state in a liberal republic is the idea of citizenship connoting rights held against the state. This theme was emphasized by Paul Martin in the parliamentary debates of 1946. Insisting on the connection between citizenship and civil and political rights and liberties, he stated, "Under this bill we are seeking to establish clearly a basic and definite Canadian citizenship which will be the fundamental status upon which the rights and privileges of Canadians will depend."[49]

This comment, in some important respects, was inconsistent with the practices of citizenship at the time. First, the legislation focused on the criteria of determining citizenship; it neither specified any particular rights and privileges that attached to the status, nor did it alter the election laws that granted voting privileges to all British subjects. More significantly, at the same time that the government was predicating one's basic rights on one's citizenship, it was engaged in an extended legal battle to deport Japanese Canadians who would have satisfied the criteria for citizenship based on their Canadian birth. The shameful story has been well documented elsewhere.[50] In brief, the government asked Japanese Canadians during the war to sign repatriation forms, and those who signed were designated as deportable. Also deportable were the wife and children less than sixteen years of age of any person against whom an order for deportation had been made. These included many individuals born in Canada. As Frank Scott points out, the voluntariness of the original signatures was open to challenge.[51] The deportations continued after the war had ended, with the government fighting a challenge to the validity of the relevant order-in-council to the Judicial Committee of the Privy Council.[52] It eventually succumbed to political pressure and rescinded it. This example indicates the deep tensions imbedded within the conception of citizenship that dominated Martin's plans. The idea of citizenship could be mobilized to strengthen the body politic by alienating those who were identified as potential risks; yet this strategy conflicted with the idea of citizenship as designating a set of equal rights-holders.

Although Canada has transcended the need to assert its independence from the United Kingdom, the spirit of nationalism and of patriotism that underlay this historical process has endured and continues to influence debates about cit-

49. Canada, 1946, 249 Debates, House of Commons 503
50. See, for example, Adachi, 1976.
51. Scott notes, "It is like offering a condemned man a pistol so that he may choose swift suicide to a public hanging. Is his death voluntary? Perhaps no one was 'forced' to choose repatriation, but the whole Canadian policy, the extreme racial hatred in British Columbia, the refusal of other provinces to co-operate in resettlement . . . all this was the compulsion." Scott, 1977.
52. *Cooperative Comm. on Japanese Canadians v. Canada,* A.C. 87 (1947).

izenship law. To this day, Canada's status as an equal nation among nations, as a country with an important role to play in global politics, is frequently represented as being dependent upon it having a strong sense of self, and a unified population. Nevertheless, there has been widespread disagreement about the essential characteristics of the entity that requires protection and support. The model of Canada as a nation founded on two pillars—one English, one French—committed to developing a single unified cultural heritage on this footing, competes with a model of a three-pillared nation, founded by First Nations as well as by the English and French. It also competes with models that promote cultural dualism and with a liberal, multicultural model that aims to transcend and transform the assumptions that dominated the political debates of 1867 and the notion of founding nations.[53]

I now turn to examine three examples to show how these varying perspectives—which I will group under the labels of "nationalist" and "postnationalist" or "multicultural"—are in play in current policy debates about citizenship norms. The first concerns the acceptability of a person holding dual or multiple nationalities; the second, a disagreement over the meaning of the term "residency" in the naturalization rules; the third concerns allocating preferential treatment to citizens over permanent residents.

Dual Citizenship

In 1946, the legislature did not require its new citizens to renounce their previous citizenship. While it was thought to be important for Canadians to see themselves as holding a common status, it was not regarded as problematic that some Canadians also held a second nationality. The Canadian Citizenship Act, however, did provide that citizens could lose their status by voluntarily taking out citizenship of another country. Thirty years later, on the other hand, the Citizenship Act embraced a wholly permissive stance on the issue of multiple nationality. After 1977, Canadians naturalizing in another state did not lose their Canadian citizenship, nor were persons who naturalized in Canada required to renounce their prior citizenship. The reasons for the change are difficult to discern because the matter was not raised in the Parliamentary debates.

53. As these models compete to gain acceptance, so do different ideas of the rights and responsibilities of citizens. Thus, the language of citizenship is used by conservatives to defend the position that minority cultural groups should not be given special privileges or be immune from social burdens on grounds of their cultural difference, while liberals also try to find a place for limited cultural protection within their analysis. For a theoretical account of such a liberal view, see, for example, Kymlicka, 1995.

The issue of whether it is defensible to permit a person to hold more than one nationality has not disappeared but has reemerged in the 1990s. In 1994, the Parliamentary Standing Committee on Citizenship and Immigration issued a report that included three recommendations regarding dual nationality: that the government consider the possibility of stripping of their citizenship those Canadian citizens who voluntarily acquire a second citizenship; that those who hold dual citizenship by virtue of events beyond their control, while living in Canada, accord primacy to their Canadian citizenship; and that those becoming naturalized be required to declare that they will accord primacy to their Canadian citizenship over all other citizenships.[54] Specifically, the report states,

> The Committee finds persuasive the arguments of most of our witnesses who expressed concerns about the current practice of allowing dual citizenship. They questioned how it is possible to swear loyalty and allegiance to more than one country, and believe the practice diminishes the value of our citizenship. It may also aid and abet those who view Canadian citizenship primarily as a convenient commodity, useful to enhance their international trading ability, or as an "insurance policy", which they may wish to use in the future, while in the meantime residing elsewhere. Among the advantages of such a "policy" would be the guaranteed right to retire to Canada and have access to whatever benefits are then available to residents—health care in particular—without having contributed in taxes to the country.[55]

It may be naive to take the committee's recommendations at face value. They were published shortly before a referendum was to be held in Quebec to determine if it should remain a part of Canada, at a time when federalists were anxious to convince undecided voters that the consequences of an affirmative vote would be extreme. Nevertheless, the Parliamentary Committee does express a widely held view that loyalty to the nation should not be compromised, even when the nation is unthreatened. From this perspective, it is not sufficient that individuals should regard themselves as members of the same community; rather, solidarity demands undivided loyalty.

The committee's recommendations leave open a number of basic questions. First, it is difficult to identify any formal means by which Canadians are today

54. See Canada, 1994, Minutes of Proceedings and Evidence of the Standing Committee on Citizenship and Immigration, p. 16.

55. Canada, 1994, Minutes of Proceedings and Evidence of the Standing Committee on Citizenship and Immigration, p. 15.

required to show their loyalty (perhaps other than refraining from committing a criminal offense against national interest). There is no demand that Canadians vote, support the government or the Canadian Olympic team, sing the national anthem on formal occasions, or treat national symbols with respect. To that extent, the liberal virtue of individual nonconformism has gained widespread support. In such a context, requiring displays of loyalty from those with two nationalities appears oppressive. There is also the problem of determining how one shows preference for Canada when loyalties conflict. Would it be contrary to one's declaration of loyalty to send money to one's family overseas? To vote in a foreign election for a government whose goals conflict with the goals of the current Canadian government? In the face of such problems, it is not too surprising that the citizenship bill introduced by the government in 1998 makes no recommendations for altering Canadian dual nationality law. The Parliamentary Committee's recommendations, it would seem, have vanished—at least temporarily.

Physical Presence in Canada

The proposed legislation takes a different tack on another issue in citizenship law that has been in dispute—the residency requirement for naturalization. As noted above, the current law requires that applicants "accumulate at least three years of residence in Canada" within "four years immediately preceding the date of application."[56] The question that has arisen is whether an applicant must maintain actual physical presence in Canada for three years, or whether the standard can be met by showing that the applicant has centralized his ordinary mode of living in Canada. The issue is critical for those who have gained permanent resident status in Canada as entrepreneurs or investors whose business projects are transnational and who may wish to maintain their business associations in their country of origin. While they may have legitimate reasons for continued periods of absence, they also risk being regarded as opportunists who wish a Canadian passport as a form of insurance to protect against the economic ramifications of political turbulence in their country of origin.

Opinions of two federal trial court judges illustrate two different reactions to the "physical presence" question. Mr. Justice Muldoon has defended the "physical presence" interpretation on the ground that actual presence in Canada for three years is important for acculturation: "Canadianization . . . happens by 'rubbing elbows' with Canadians in shopping malls, corner stores, libraries, concert halls, auto repair shops, pubs . . . —in a word wherever one can meet

56. See discussion accompanying note 12 above.

and converse with Canadians—during the prescribed three years."[57] By way of contrast, Mr. Justice Cullen has written, "The strict interpretation of the term . . . ignores today's reality of the global village and the frequent necessity to work under contract with an employer outside Canada."[58]

The two views reveal an important difference in attitude toward assimilation as a prerequisite for naturalization. While Mr. Justice Muldoon's approach does not suggest that there is a single homogenized Canadian way of interacting, it does suggest that Canadian ways of interacting are different from those that happen abroad and that it is necessary for the applicant to learn these. Mr. Justice Cullen's approach, however, suggests that the three-year period is a probationary period during which an individual may make a contribution to Canadian society, without running afoul of Canadian law. From this perspective, the minimal requirements of knowledge of language, of Canada, and of the rights and responsibilities of citizenship are more formal than substantive, a token of the individual's good faith, as it were. While Mr. Justice Muldoon's interpretation seems to be shaped by the idea that the naturalization criteria are based on a determination of the state's best interest, Mr. Justice Cullen's interpretation is founded on the idea that citizenship is due when a positive contribution has been given. The validity of this latter interpretation is confirmed by the presence of other provisions in the act that allow for the minister to waive the knowledge requirements on compassionate grounds for any applicant,[59] but allow him or her to waive the residency requirement only in the case of a minor who also has had the age requirement waived.[60]

The recent report of the Immigration Legislative Review Advisory Group weighed in on this debate, recommending three years of physical presence in Canada and active participation in Canadian society demonstrated by the fulfillment of two out of three conditions: employment, study, and community service.[61] This position, however, has not gone unchallenged. Perhaps the clearest statement of the opposing position was made a number of years ago by Joseph Carens. In "Membership and Morality: Admission to Citizenship in Liberal Democratic States,"[62] Carens argues that those admitted into a country to live and work should be granted the right to naturalize "following a modest passage

57. Pourghasemi, 1993.
58. "Hasan v. Canada," 1993, pp. 39, 41.
59. See Canada, 1985, Citizenship Act, R.S.C., ch. C-29, § 5(3)(a).
60. See Canada, 1985, Citizenship Act, R.S.C., ch. C-29, § 5(3)(b).
61. Canada, 1997, Citizenship and Immigration, Immigration Legislative Review Advisory Group, 1997, Not Just Numbers, p. 40.
62. Carens, 1989, p. 31.

of time and some reasonable formalities."[63] He takes issue with what he calls "discretionary models of naturalization"—that is, schemes that demand that the resident show that they have in some way integrated into the society's cultural practices.[64] As Carens notes,

> To make claims to citizenship depend on cultural assimilation is a very dangerous path to tread. It suggests that social membership may be defined in terms of social conformity. All states in Europe and North America include some citizens who belong to minority groups that differ from the majority in significant ways. To link the moral claim to citizenship to cultural assimilation would be to suggest that these minority citizens are not true members of society, that their moral claim to the citizenship they possess rests on weaker foundations than the claim of citizens who share the majority culture.[65]

It seems that in recent years the government has adopted an interpretation more akin to that of Mr. Justice Muldoon. It has been seeking judicial review of all cases in which the applicant was granted citizenship despite having spent overseas more than 50 percent of the time required for Canadian residency.[66] Moreoever, the legislation proposed by the government in 1998 adopts a similar posture. It would require physical presence in Canada for three years, although it would increase the time to accumulate residence from four to five years. In its explanatory report, the government has explained the proposal in the following terms:

> Residence is an important and meaningful condition of citizenship in that it demonstrates an individuals attachment to Canada. It also provides an opportunity for the applicant to become familiar with Canadian society and to experience and discover its values, language, culture and physical environment.[67]

The example of physical presence in Canada as a requirement for citizenship, like the example of multiple nationality, reveals continuing tensions in the ways in which we conceive of the individual and the state. Over the years, Can-

---

63. Carens, 1989, p. 31.
64. Carens, 1989, pp. 34–36.
65. Carens, 1989, p. 40.
66. A total of sixty-one cases has been documented. See Oziewicz, August 4, 1998, p. A3.
67. Canada, 1998, Citizenship and Immigration, Citizenship of Canada Act, p. 5.

ada has revealed an ambivalence about how loyalty and individuality should be given expression. This ambivalence is connected closely to the issue of national identity. Citizenship debates have gained a quality of urgency, not only because of the seemingly ever-present threat of Quebec separating, but also because parties to the debates express concern about protecting the essential aspects of national identity from foreign influences, particularly those from the United States, which might jeopardize the country's individuality. In this context, it is unsurprising to find that the laws that define the criteria for gaining the status of citizenship and that identify those who may enjoy the privileges are defended on the ground that there is an overwhelming need to promote loyalty, to preserve the Canadian way of life, and to achieve unity.

The Rights of Citizens and Noncitizens

The impetus for recognition of the legal status of citizenship in Canada came not only from those who sought to present Canada as a unified and equal nation among nations, but also from those who, at least some of the time, sought to place a hybrid of liberal republicanism at the heart of the Canadian Constitution, and from those who sought to ensure a universal commitment to certain values across the country. The common sharing of common rights by citizens has both an internal and external dynamic. Internally, it argues for equal citizenship rights; externally, it suggests a basis for distinguishing citizens from noncitizens for certain purposes. This section addresses both these issues.

In the early decades of the twentieth century, it was clear that the possession of Canadian citizenship did not guarantee an equality of rights. Writing in 1937, Hancock noted:

> Although the Dominion possesses exclusive legislative authority over "naturalization and aliens," the provinces are quite competent to enact laws which discriminate against naturalized British subjects or bear harshly upon them. Such legislation is common in British Columbia where special restrictions and impositions are laid upon Orientals. The discriminations are based upon race, not nationality, so that naturalized Chinese or Japanese are affected equally with their alien brethren.[68]

Despite Hancock's confidence that racist laws do not impinge on the federal power over naturalization and aliens, there has always been a powerful undercurrent of dissent. In some cases, the court would identify a racist provincial

68. Hancock, 1937, p. 98.

law as an attempt to exercise power over "naturalization and aliens" even when the law applied both to aliens and subjects, on the basis that its real aim was to harm the interests of aliens and that it was using an overinclusive classification as a ruse.[69]

During the period when the Canadian Constitution did not explicitly guarantee political rights and freedoms, influential jurists in the Supreme Court of Canada relied on the concept of citizenship as a device to prevent provinces from enacting laws that burdened fundamental rights. Most prominent among these was Mr. Justice Ivan Rand, who asserted that being a citizen meant being able to exercise basic human rights and freedoms in all parts of the country.[70] In essence, his argument was that the federal legislature's authority over citizenship included authority over those rights that define the meaning of citizenship. At different moments, Mr. Justice Rand identified the right to free speech and the right of mobility as constituent elements of the status rather than incidental benefits. Consequently, any attempt to curtail these would be an attack on the status of citizenship and would therefore be beyond the powers of the provinces.[71] Thus, Mr. Justice Rand found in the concept of citizenship a device that promised to achieve two goals simultaneously—protecting fundamental human rights and maintaining a powerful central government.

The entrenchment of the Charter rendered obsolete the need to find indirect means to protect human rights. The nexus between individual rights and citizenship has proved to be problematic, however. As noted above, the Charter guarantees specific rights to citizens, such as the right to vote and to enter and leave Canada.[72] Yet, the Charter also includes a general equality clause, section 15(1), that applies to "every individual":

> Every individual is equal before and under the law and has the right to equal protection and equal benefit of the law without discrimination and, in particular, without discrimination based on race, national or ethnic origin, [color], religion, sex, age or mental or physical disability.[73]

The mere fact that citizens are guaranteed constitutional rights appears to conflict with the guarantee of equality to every individual. This conflict can be avoided if the sections that guarantee particular rights to citizens are read as re-

69. See, for example, *Union Colliery Co. v. Bryden*, A.C. 580 (1899).
70. See Price, 1958.
71. See, for example, *Switzman v. Elbling*, S.C.R. 285 (1957), and *Winner v. S.M.T.*, S.C.R. 887 (1951). See, also, Sharpe, 1993.
72. See England, 1982, Canada Act, 1982, ch. 11, sched. B, §§ 3, 6.
73. See England, 1982, Canada Act, 1982, ch. 11, sched. B, § 15(1).

quiring that at least citizens enjoy these rights, while leaving open the question whether the equality provisions require that others enjoy them, too. This option, however, has not been pursued.[74] I shall pass over it and turn to a second focus of conflict—the situation where a legislature attempts to reserve benefits for citizens. A clear understanding of the nature of the conflict can be gained only from an analysis of equality jurisprudence.

In Canada, the case law relating to the equality section is dominated by several related themes.[75] It is settled that the section does not simply require that government treat like cases alike, with unconstrained license to determine for itself the criteria of likeness. It is also settled that the section does not commit the government to a program of massive redistribution of resources. Instead, a middle ground between these two extremes is considered appropriate. The governing principle is that individuals must be treated with *equal concern and respect*; the obligation is to respect the inherent dignity of the individual, and to avoid treatment that can be regarded as an attack on the individual's moral personality.[76]

In unpacking the idea of equal concern and respect, the Canadian courts have emphasized the need to take a "contextualized" approach to the problem, looking beyond the formal text of the law to the way in which the law is experienced by individuals and groups. A law that on its face treats people similarly may impose more burdens on some than on others. The courts have also held that the imposition of extra burdens on one group of individuals is not necessarily contrary to the equality rights provision; a measure will be discriminatory only if it is an attack on the individual's moral status. This may be achieved in one of two ways. If the burden imposed is particularly egregious, any individual singled out to bear the burden may justifiably claim that he or she is not being accorded sufficient respect—that they are being sacrificed for the benefit of others.[77] Moreover, where an individual belongs to a social group that is socially or economically disadvantaged or politically powerless, any additional burden imposed by the law will be identified as discriminatory on the ground

---

74. See discussion of *Chiarelli v. Canada*, S.C.R. 732 (1992), below at note 104 and accompanying text.

75. I develop these themes elsewhere. See Galloway, 1993.

76. It is perhaps more apt to speak of a dominant principle rather than a governing principle since this issue is extremely contentious and has attracted many influential dissenting opinions. The leading cases are *Andrews v. Law Society of British Columbia*, S.C.R. 143 (1989); *Miron v. Trudel*, S.C.R. 418 (1995); *Egan v. Canada*, S.C.R. 513 (1995); and *Thibaudeau v. Canada*, S.C.R. 627 (1995).

77. This point may be extrapolated from the judgment of *Madam Justice Wilson in R. v. Turpin*, S.C.R. 1296 (1989). See Galloway, 1993.

that such a measure shows lack of concern for the situation of the individual concerned.

While there still exists a middle road between formal equality and demands for redistribution, this controversial conception of equality has been difficult to implement in practice. Particularly difficult has been the problem of dealing with a law neutral on its face, that will affect a disproportionate number of individuals from a disadvantaged group. Such laws have been sustained on the somewhat specious ground that they do not reinforce their disadvantaged status. Courts will not, in the guise of enforcing the equality provision, lightly intrude to dismantle structures of systemic discrimination.[78]

A potentially radical reading of the equality section is also undercut by interpretations of section 1 of the Charter, which stipulates that the guaranteed rights are subject "to such reasonable limits prescribed by law as can be demonstrably justified in a free and democratic society."[79] While this section allows governments to adopt legislation that burdens rights, courts have imposed heavy demands on a government attempting to do so, because the rights identified in the Charter are regarded as essential elements of human dignity or moral status. Specifically, not only must the government's objectives be pressing and substantial, but also the measures taken to achieve these objectives must be proportional to the objectives and must be tailored to have minimal impairment on individual rights.[80]

The leading case applying these norms to differential treatment of citizens and aliens is the Supreme Court of Canada judgment in *Andrews v. Law Society of British Columbia*,[81] which invalidated a provision of a British Columbia statute that made Canadian citizenship a prerequisite to admission to the legal profession within the province. The Court determined that the denial of such admission to a permanent resident amounted to discrimination on a ground analogous to those listed within section 15(1) and that such discrimination could not be justified under section 1.

Madam Justice Wilson, supported by two other justices, found that "relative to citizens, [permanent residents] are a group lacking in political power and as

---

78. See, for example, *Sauvé v. Canada,* F.C. 857 (T.D.) (1996). This case dealt with a section of a statute that disqualified citizens serving a sentence of two years or more in a correctional institution from voting in elections. It was argued that the measure had a greater impact on Aboriginals than it did on non-Aboriginals, since Aboriginals are overrepresented in prison populations. This argument was rejected on the ground that although more Aboriginals were affected by the measure, each was not affected more harshly than anyone else in the prison population.

79. England, 1982, Canada Act, 1982, ch. 11, sched. B, § 1.

80. See *R. v. Oakes,* S.C.R. 103 (1986).

81. See *Andrews v. Law Society of British Columbia,* S.C.R. 143 (1989).

such vulnerable to having their interests overlooked and their rights to equal concern and respect violated."[82] Citing John Stuart Mill, she stressed that "in the absence of its natural defenders, the interests of the excluded is [sic] always in danger of being overlooked."[83] She also adopted U.S. terminology by referring to permanent residents as a "discrete and insular minority."[84] The denial of access to the legal profession therefore amounted to an infringement of an equality right that discriminated on an inappropriate ground.

In a concurring opinion, Mr. Justice La Forest held that discrimination, to fall within the meaning of section 15(1), must be based on "irrelevant personal differences."[85] Specifically, he held that:

> There is no question that citizenship may, in some circumstances, be properly used as a defining characteristic for certain types of legitimate government objectives. I am sensitive to the fact that citizenship is a very special status that not only incorporates rights and duties but serves a highly important symbolic function as a badge identifying people as members of the Canadian polity. Nonetheless, it is, in general irrelevant to the legitimate work of government in all but a limited number of areas. By and large, the use in legislation of citizenship as a basis for distinguishing between persons . . . [harbors] the potential for undermining the essential or underlying values of a free and democratic society that are embodied in [section] 15. . . . It requires justification.[86]

Thus, after *Andrews*, it seems that measures that provide for differential treatment to citizens and permanent residents are *prima facie* constitutionally suspect. This conclusion is, from one perspective, a curious one. Unlike the minority religious or racial group, the class of permanent residents is a product of the law. That is, by creating a class of permanent residents, the law itself is responsible for the class's powerlessness. If adding to the burdens of a disadvantaged group is a form of discrimination, then it would seem that the creation of the class itself must also be discriminatory.

At this point, we begin to see how equality rights destabilize the hierarchy of recognized statuses of noncitizens, since the creation of statuses that do not wield the same amount of political power ought to demand strong justifications

82. *Andrews v. Law Society of British Columbia*, S.C.R. 152 (1989).

83. *Andrews v. Law Society of British Columbia*, S.C.R. 152 (1989).

84. *Andrews v. Law Society of British Columbia*, S.C.R. 152–53 n.4 (1989) (citing *United States v. Carolene Products Co.*, 304 U.S. 144 (1938)).

85. *Andrews v. Law Society of British Columbia*, S.C.R. 193 (1989).

86. *Andrews v. Law Society of British Columbia*, S.C.R. 196–97 (1989).

from the government. As regards permanent residents, three solutions to this paradox suggest themselves: (1) permanent residents should be naturalized immediately on gaining the status (thereby providing them with political participation rights); (2) permanent residents should be given the same access to political power as citizens, such as voting rights; or (3) we should admit the discriminatory structure of the system, and then turn to section 1 of the Charter to assess whether strong and pressing reasons exist for not taking one of the other two options. Perhaps unsurprisingly, it is this last option that has gained ascendancy.

When addressing the applicability of section 1 of the Charter, Madam Justice Wilson made some important remarks on the justifiability of discriminating in favor of citizens. First, she noted that it may be desirable to have as lawyers people who are familiar with Canadian institutions, but a citizenship requirement is "not carefully tailored to achieve that objective and may not even be rationally connected to it."[87] In response to the argument that citizenship evidences a real attachment to Canada, she quotes the opinion of Madam Justice McLachlin, then of the British Columbia Court of Appeals: "While no doubt most citizens, natural-born or otherwise, are committed to Canadian society, Canadian citizenship does not ensure that this is the case. Conversely, non-citizens may be deeply commited [sic] to our country."[88] In response to the argument that lawyers perform a government function, and this service can justify a citizenship requirement, she comments,

> To my mind, even if lawyers do perform a government function, I do not think the requirement that they be citizens provides any guarantee that they will [honorably] and conscientiously carry out their public duties. They will carry them out, I believe, because they are good lawyers and not because they are Canadian citizens.[89]

On this last point, Mr. Justice La Forest concluded that the practice of law is a private profession, but that a "requirement of citizenship would be acceptable if limited to Crown Attorneys or lawyers directly employed by government and, therefore, involved in policy-making or administration, so that it could be said that the lawyer was an architect or instrumentality of government policy. . . ."[90]

---

87. *Andrews v. Law Society of British Columbia*, S.C.R. 156 (1989).
88. *Andrews v. Law Society of British Columbia*, S.C.R. 156 (1989).
89. *Andrews v. Law Society of British Columbia*, S.C.R. 157 (1989).
90. *Andrews v. Law Society of British Columbia*, S.C.R. 203–04 (1989).

In summary, within the majority opinions in *Andrews*, one sees a high level of skepticism about attempts to show preferential treatment to citizens, at least when the issue is access to the legal profession. Madam Justice Wilson's skepticism seems to be the more severe. She avoids constructing a test to determine when section 1 would justify preferential treatment toward citizens, and she suggests that it would not even be justified in relation to governmental employment benefits. Citizenship is presented as a communal interest that will generally be insufficiently powerful to overwhelm equality rights. She does not, however, attempt to identify or analyze the values that underpin the status. Mr. Justice La Forest's skepticism seems to be more tempered: while admitting that discrimination in favor of citizens will violate equality rights, he at least acknowledges some situations where this might be justifiable. His references to government policy making suggest that he connects the status of citizenship with high levels of loyalty toward the state.

The issues raised in *Andrews* have not faded. They were raised again in the Trial Division of the Federal Court in *Lavoie* v. *Canada*,[91] in which was considered the constitutionality of a statutory provision that granted preference to citizens in open competitions for jobs in the public service. One of the plaintiffs had failed to take out Canadian citizenship, though qualified to do so, because by doing so she would automatically lose her Austrian citizenship. She stated that she did not wish to become a "foreigner in [her] own country."[92] She was also concerned about losing future employment opportunities in Austria.[93] Another plaintiff, from the Netherlands, "expressed concerns regarding the possible need to return to Holland to care for her aging parents."[94]

The case is an interesting one because both parties called political theorists as expert witnesses—Peter Schuck for the government and Joseph Carens for the plaintiffs. Mr. Justice Wetston held that the discriminating provision had two purposes: "to enhance the meaning, value and importance of citizenship and, secondly, to provide an incentive to naturalize."[95] In dealing with the first of these, Mr. Justice Wetston stated that "if the differences between citizenship and permanent resident status disappear or are rendered virtually meaningless, then citizenship could suffer the same result."[96] In dealing with the second, he

91. See *Lavoie v. Canada*, F.C. 623 (T.D.) (1995).
92. See *Lavoie v. Canada*, F.C. 629 (T.D.) (1995).
93. See *Lavoie v. Canada*, F.C. 629 (T.D.) (1995).
94. See *Lavoie v. Canada*, F.C. 632 (T.D.) (1995).
95. See *Lavoie v. Canada*, F.C. 657 (T.D.) (1995).
96. See *Lavoie v. Canada*, F.C. 658 (T.D.) (1995).

noted that in 1991, of 711,000 permanent residents who had met the residency qualification for citizenship, 611,000 had taken no steps to become citizens.[97]

When addressing the question of whether these objectives were sufficiently pressing, Mr. Justice Wetston sided with Schuck, who had testified that there are differences between citizens and noncitizens that are significant enough to give special meaning, value, and importance to citizenship. He furthermore noted that "Professor Schuck does theorize that the greater the difference between citizenship and non-citizenship the greater the value of citizenship; and the greater the value of citizenship, the greater the incentive to naturalize."[98] Mr. Justice Wetston also cited the fact that in Australia one of the explicit reasons expressed by the government for limiting public service jobs to citizens was "to enhance the significance of citizenship as a unifying factor in a multicultural society."[99]

The court thus rejected the opposing views of Joseph Carens, who had argued that "the fewer the differences between citizens and non-citizens, the greater the value in citizenship and the greater the incentive to naturalize."[100] The nub of Carens's position seems to be that a community that takes equality rights seriously is more worthy than one that does not, and that membership in such a community is a more valuable possession than membership in a discriminating community. By offering incentives to people to join, the community demeans itself. Arguably, a person who becomes a member in order to get a public service job is not someone who is embracing citizenship as an aspect of her or his identity. Such instrumental calculation reveals an absence of a sense of belonging. The person who identifies with a community when there are no short-term incentives is more likely to feel the bond of loyalty that cohesion requires.

Carens's argument raises grave doubts about one of the assumptions underlying Mr. Justice Wetston's opinion, namely that one can use citizenship law as an effective tool for forging social cohesion or unity. To achieve this purpose, qualifications for gaining citizenship must be carefully calibrated; they can neither be difficult nor easy to meet. If they are difficult to meet, then people will either choose not to become citizens, or they will be unable to meet the qualification. In either case, there will be a significant proportion of the population who will not be part of the citizenry, which is hardly consistent with achieving a cohesive society. If the qualifications are easy to meet, such as by birth in the

97. See *Lavoie v. Canada*, F.C. 659 (T.D.) (1995).
98. See *Lavoie v. Canada*, F.C. 659 (T.D.) (1995).
99. See *Lavoie v. Canada*, F.C. 661 (T.D.) (1995).
100. See *Lavoie v. Canada*, F.C. 660 (T.D.) (1995).

country, then many people will be admitted as citizens whose membership may not promote the good of the collectivity, or who see no need to balance their personal interests with those of the citizenry.

There is the further problem that the only device that the law can use to persuade individuals to become citizens is to offer incentives for doing so and to make the status more attractive than that of the noncitizen. Use of this device, however, will mean that many of those who become citizens will be doing so for reasons of personal gain, rather than as an expression of social solidarity. Conversely, if the law offers no incentive, many citizens will see no reason for relinquishing the status of permanent resident. Aleinikoff neatly summarizes these challenges: "We face a paradox. . . . Attempts to make citizenship matter more by increasing distinctions between citizens and aliens are likely to produce behavior that is seen as 'cheapening' citizenship; while erasing distinctions between citizens and aliens seems to reduce citizenship to a mere personal affiliation."[101]

Mr. Justice Wetston does not address these issues. With remarkably cursory analysis, he identifies the statutory requirements as proportional to the breach of the equality rights and sufficiently tailored to impair the equality rights of the plaintiffs as little as reasonably possible, and therefore defensible under section 15.[102] In doing so, he makes the briefest of references to *Andrews*, merely citing a comment by Mr. Justice La Forest that preferential treatment to citizens may be acceptable, but it requires justification.[103]

By virtually ignoring the discussion in the Supreme Court of Canada, Mr. Justice Wetston may be acknowledging that since the decision in *Andrews*, debates about the comparative importance of equality and citizenship have intensified throughout society. One can find evidence of changing attitudes even within the Supreme Court of Canada itself. Particularly noteworthy is the Supreme Court's decision in *Chiarelli v. Canada*,[104] which considered the constitutionality of the deportation of a long-term resident who had not become a citizen but who, nevertheless, had been a part of the Canadian community for an extended period.[105]

Chiarelli had entered Canada in 1975, at the age of fifteen. In 1984, he pled guilty to unlawfully uttering threats to cause injury and to possession of narcotics with the purpose of trafficking, both offenses for which sentences of more

---

101. Aleinikoff, 1998, p. 18.
102. See *Lavoie v. Canada*, F.C. 623, 677–78 (T.D.) (1995).
103. See *Lavoie v. Canada*, F.C. 662 (T.D.) (1995).
104. *Chiarelli v. Canada*, S.C.R. 711 (1992).
105. Currently, Canadian law has not accepted the claims of such individuals that they be considered de facto citizens. See "*Machado v. Canada*," 1996, p. 121.

than five years could be imposed. He received a sentence of six months' imprisonment, which rendered him deportable. A review committee impaneled under the Canadian Security Intelligence Service Act reported that there were reasonable grounds to believe that Chiarelli was involved in organized crime. Accordingly, the minister of Employment and Immigration issued a certificate determining that he was a security risk. Where this has been determined, the Immigration Act disallows the usual ground of appeal to the Immigration Appeal Division on "all the circumstances of the case" that would allow for compassionate consideration of the deportee's connection with Canada.[106]

Chiarelli challenged the process under section 7 of the Charter, which declares that "everyone has the right to life, liberty and security of the person and the right not to be deprived thereof except in accordance with the principles of fundamental justice."[107] The Court rejected the claim. Reasoning that "the principles of fundamental justice are to be found in the basic tenets of our legal system,"[108] it noted that the "most fundamental principle of immigration law is that non-citizens do not have an unqualified right to enter or remain in the country."[109] The Court furthermore found no violation of equality rights protected by section 15 of the Charter: under section 6(2) of the Charter only citizens are afforded the right to enter, remain in, and leave Canada; thus "there is . . . no discrimination contrary to [section] 15 in a deportation scheme that applies to permanent residents, but not to citizens."[110]

The Court's ruling is troubling on several grounds. First, it is based on the idea that issues of fundamental justice are to be resolved by consulting entrenched legal practice rather than considering transcendent abstract principle. While this view pays homage to contextualization, it contains the unfortunate suggestion that we should determine how to treat noncitizens in the future in accordance with practices that were developed during a time of nation building. The constitutional protection of individual rights begins to take on a hollow appearance if we are bound to perpetuate practices that developed in a previous era.

Second, it is not hard to make a persuasive argument that fundamental justice requires that an immigrant's personal situation and the depth of his or her connection with the community should be considered when determining individual rights. Social membership and participation are connected concepts: by adopting Canada as one's home and by participating in ways of life, the individ-

---

106. Canada, 1985, Immigration Act, R.S.C., §§ 70(1), 70(4).
107. England, 1982, Canada Act, ch. 11, sched. B, § 7
108. *Chiarelli v. Canada,* S.C.R. 732 (1992).
109. *Chiarelli v. Canada,* S.C.R. 733 (1992).
110. *Chiarelli v. Canada,* S.C.R. 736 (1992).

ual will have become immersed in the tangled networks of meaningful relations that define the cultural ethos. To disown such an individual is to deny his or her contributions.

Third, section 6(2) of the Charter can be read as guaranteeing rights to citizens but not exclusively. Instead of reading it as reserving the rights to enter and remain in Canada for citizens only, it can be read as leaving open whether others also have these rights. Finally, by upholding a distinction drawn on citizenship, *Chiarelli* implicitly tolerates a line between long-term residents who have chosen to naturalize and long-term residents who have not. Arguably, there are significant differences between these groups. As was noted above, for example, the former will have sworn an oath of loyalty and will have passed a citizenship test, which reveals an ability to communicate in one of the official languages and knowledge of Canadian culture. The critical question, however, is whether these factors are sufficiently powerful to justify such a disparity in treatment. While such differences may justify minor differences in treatment, it is questionable whether they can justify deportation of one group but not the other.

Chiarelli reveals a marked departure from the principles enunciated in *Andrews*. The deep commitment to equality expressed in the latter case does not demand that citizens and noncitizens may never be distinguished. It does not demand, for example, that we jettison all our immigration laws and regulations, but it does demand that we consider whether our laws treat all individuals with equal concern and respect. Yet, long-term residents who have not become naturalized but who have become part of the Canadian community may well appear to be similarly situated with citizens, and based on their long-term contributions to Canadian society, their removal may well be seen as a denial of equal concern and respect. From this perspective, the deportation provisions of the Immigration Act that permit the deportation of long-term residents[111] could be said to establish discriminatory treatment of long-term residents vis-à-vis citizens.

While I have focused on case law in these pages, it should be noted that law reformers have also picked up the theme of equality. The report of the Parliamentary Standing Committee on Citizenship and Immigration, *Canadian Citizenship: A Sense of Belonging,* relies on a conception of equality when mounting a critique of current citizenship laws. It identifies as discriminatory and contrary to constitutional principles of equality, for example, the rules that stipulate that children adopted by a citizen outside Canada must be sponsored as immigrants, while those born outside the country automatically gain the status. The committee recommended that children adopted overseas be granted automatic citizenship "subject to adequate rules to avoid adoptions of conve-

111. See Canada, 1985, Immigration Act, R.S.C., § 4.

nience . . . and appropriate medical, criminal and security checks."[112] Whether it is possible to devise such rules is questionable. Moreover, it is relatively easy to identify reasons for discrimination against adopted children. Justification for any differential treatment could, for example, be sought in the fact that there is a greater chance that the children of citizens will spend their childhood becoming acquainted with Canadian life and culture. A similar level of guarantee is unlikely with adopted children. In the light of broad interpretations of section 1 of the Charter, it is questionable whether this discrimination would be held to be unconstitutional. Nevertheless, in the recently introduced bill, Bill C-63, the government has adopted the suggestion that adopted children be granted automatic citizenship, but without being subject to any medical, criminal, or security checks.

Conclusion

I have attempted to show that throughout Canada's history, the concept of citizenship has not only been used as a means of identifying a community's membership and its principles of regeneration, but it also has played a variety of rhetorical roles. In essence, the concept of a "citizen" has been regarded as one-half of a dichotomy and, at different times, different dichotomies have shaped the ambit of political debates. Thus, the citizen has been juxtaposed with the king's subject; with the colonial; with the resident of a province; and more recently, with the permanent resident and others who are recognized by our immigration laws. As political and economic conditions have changed, the themes of political debate have also changed. The concept of citizenship has always played an important role, but it has been molded to fit each context.

I have attempted to illustrate the nature of current debates by focusing on three distinct issues—dual citizenship, residence, and equality. In my discussion of each, I have tried to reveal that two distinct philosophies are at odds: a nationalistic or collectivist vision that emphasizes the utility of citizenship law as a device to promote and stabilize social cohesion, and a more individualistic approach that emphasizes the need to respect individuals as equals. One can infer from the provisions of the recent Bill C-63 that national unity and identity continue to rank highly in importance. The redefinition of those who are entitled to the status of citizenship, particularly the emphasis placed on physical presence in Canada, suggests that social cohesion and assimilation are currently preferred concerns.

112. Parliamentary Standing Committee on Citizenship and Immigration, 1994, *Canadian Citizenship: A Sense of Belonging*, p. 19.

I have argued that the entrenchment of the Charter has been an important milestone. Its impact has been substantial in reducing the legal differentials between citizens and noncitizens, while also ensuring that the concept of citizenship continues to play a prominent role in debates about equality. Yet, it must also be conceded that the Charter has contributed to growing cynicism about the government's commitment to another idea at the heart of liberal democratic politics—that political sovereignty lies with the people. There have emerged undercurrents of dissatisfaction about the amount of political power transferred to the judiciary since 1982. Here two other aspects of citizenship—popular sovereignty and rights protection—seem in deep tension.

Furthermore, both these aspects of citizenship are brought under pressure by recent government eagerness to sign multinational economic agreements such as the North American Free Trade Agreement, or the now defunct Multilateral Agreement on Investment. The central concern is that the government will divest itself of power by adopting such agreements and thereby transfer its legal sovereignty to nongovernmental bodies that will be immune from political challenge. Not only is there significant doubt about the government's ability to enforce the parts of these agreements that aim to protect cultural integrity, but one can also detect a deeper concern that the reins of power are being transferred to bodies that are not responsible to the citizenry. It is thus commonplace to hear assertions that both national identity and the status of citizenship are being diluted.

References

Adachi, Ken. 1976. *The Enemy that Never Was*. Toronto: McClelland and Stewart.

Aleinikoff, T. Alexander. 1998. *Between Principles and Politics: The Direction of U.S. Citizenship Policy*. Washington, D.C.: Carnegie Endowment for International Peace.

British Section of the International Commission of Jurists. 1980. *British Nationality: The Report of a Working Party*. London: Justice.

Canada. 1998. Citizenship and Immigration, Citizenship of Canada Act. (On file with author.)

Canada. 1997. Citizenship and Immigration, Immigration Legislative Review Advisory Group. *Not Just Numbers*. (On file with author.)

Canada. 1994. Minutes of Proceedings and Evidence of the Standing Committee on Citizenship and Immigration. (On file with author.)

Canada. 1993. Citizenship Regulations, SOR/93-246.

Canada. 1985. Citizenship Act, R.S.C.

Canada. 1985. Immigration Act, R.S.C.

Canada. 1978. Immigration Regulations, SOR/78-172.

Canada. 1970. Canadian Citizenship Act, R.S.C.

Canada. 1946. 249 Debates, House of Commons 503.

Canada. 1931. 188 Debates, House of Commons 2021.

Carens, Joseph H. 1989. "Membership and Morality: Admission to Citizenship in Liberal Democratic States." In *Immigration and the Politics of Citizenship in Europe and North America*, ed. William Rogers Brubaker. Lanham, Md.: University Press of America.

Dunham, William H. Jr. 1951. "Doctrines of Allegiance in Late Medieval English Law." *New York University Law Review*, no. 26.

Dworkin, Ronald. 1986. *Law's Empire*. Cambridge: Harvard University Press.

England. 1982. Canada Act.

England. 1931. Statute of Westminster, 22 & 23 Geo. 5.

England. 1921. Canadian Nationals Act, 11 & 12 Geo. 5.

England. 1914. British Nationality and Status of Aliens Act, 4 & 5 Geo. 5.

England. 1914. Naturalization Act, 4 & 5 Geo. 5.

England. 1910. Immigration Act, 9 & 10 Edw.

England. 1881. Naturalization Act, 44 Vict.

England. 1867. British North America Act, 30 & 31 Vict.

Galloway, J. Donald C. 1993. "Three Models of (In)Equality." *McGill Law Journal*, no. 38.

Hancock, Moffat. 1937. "Naturalization in Canada." In *The Legal Status of Aliens in Pacific Countries*, ed. Norman MacKenzie. Oxford: Oxford University Press.

"*Hasan v. Canada*." 1993. *Immigration Law Review*, no. 22, 2d, p. 39.

Hogg, Peter W. 1998. *Constitutional Law of Canada*. 4th ed. Scarborough, Ontario: Carswell.

Jones, J. Mervyn. 1956. *British Nationality Law*. Oxford: Clarendon Press.

Kymlicka, Will. 1995. *Multicultural Citizenship*. New York: Oxford University Press.

"*Machado v. Canada*." 1996. *Immigration Law Review*, no. 33, 2d, p. 121.

Oziewicz, Estanislao. (August 4, 1998.) "Ottawa Fighting More Citizenship Decisions." *Globe and Mail*, p. A3.

Parliamentary Standing Committee on Citizenship and Immigration. 1994. *Canadian Citizenship: A Sense of Belonging*. (On file with author.)

Parry, Clive. 1957. *Nationality and Citizenship Laws of The Commonwealth and of The Republic of Ireland*. London: Stevens & Sons Ltd.

Pourghasemi, Re. 1993. *Immigration Law Review*, no. 19, 2d.

Price, Ronald R. 1958. "Mr. Justice Rand and the Privileges and Immunities of Canadian Citizens." *University of Toronto Faculty Law Review*, no. 16.

Raz, Joseph. 1986. *The Morality of Freedom*. Oxford: Oxford University Press.

Scott, Frank R. 1977. *Essays on the Constitution: Aspects of Canadian Law and Politics*. Toronto: University of Toronto Press.

Sharpe, Robert J. 1993. "Citizenship, the Constitution Act, 1867, and the Charter." In *Belonging: The Meaning and Future of Canadian Citizenship*, ed. William Kaplan. Montreal, Quebec: McGill-Queen's University Press.

Walzer, Michael. 1994. *Thick and Thin: Moral Argument at Home and Abroad*. Notre Dame: University of Notre Dame Press.

Legal Cases

Andrews v. Law Society of British Columbia, S.C.R. 143 (1989).

Calvin's Case, 7 Co. Rep. 1, 5 (1608).

Cooperative Comm. on Japanese Canadians v. Canada, A.C. 87 (1947).
Chiarelli v. Canada, S.C.R. 732 (1992).
Egan v. Canada, S.C.R. 513 (1995).
Lavoie v. Canada, F.C. 623 (T.D.) (1995).
Miron v. Trudel, S.C.R. 418 (1995).
R. v. Oakes, S.C.R. 103 (1986).
R. v. Turpin, S.C.R. 1296 (1989)
Sauvé v. Canada, F.C. 857 (T.D.) (1996).
Switzman v. Elbling, S.C.R. 285 (1957).
Thibaudeau v. Canada, S.C.R. 627 (1995).
Union Colliery Co. v. Bryden, A.C. 580 (1899).
United States v. Carolene Products Co., 304 U.S. 144 (1938).
Winner v. S.M.T., S.C.R. 887 (1951).

CHAPTER FOUR

Between Principles and Politics: U.S. Citizenship Policy

T. ALEXANDER ALEINIKOFF

WE CONCEIVE of the world as divided into states, with each state exercising sovereignty over a territory and a population. The population of a state consists primarily of its "citizens." In an increasingly mobile world, however, many persons—sometimes millions—are not citizens of the state in which they reside. Most have gained admission to the state lawfully, as settled immigrants, refugees, or temporary visitors or workers; many have entered illegally, although their continued residence may be tolerated to some degree.

In everyday life, little may separate citizens from aliens. But status has important political and affiliational implications. Citizenship is generally understood to connote "full membership" in a state. Citizens are (usually) those endowed with the political rights in the state. They are those on whose behalf the state is understood to act; and they are those seen as owing a degree of loyalty and commitment to the state that is not asked of noncitizen residents. Other benefits accompany citizenship, such as eligibility for a passport, the right to not be deported, and the ability to seek protection by their home government when traveling in a foreign country. In many states, moreover, social benefits and government employment are limited to citizens.

But the advantages of citizenship should not obscure the fact that immigrants in many states enjoy rights and opportunities largely on equal terms with citizens. They are permitted to work, to travel freely within the state, and to have access to the educational and legal systems of the state, and they may be eligible for social benefits. Their individual liberties are protected by emerging international human rights norms and, frequently, by domestic constitutions and legislation. These protections, as well as the day-to-day lives of settled immigrants, suggest an understanding of membership that goes beyond the status of citizenship.

In the United States, discussions about citizenship have increased markedly in recent years. Record numbers of immigrants are seeking naturalization. Questions have been raised about birthright citizenship for the children of undocumented aliens, naturalization standards, and dual citizenship. Moreover, in a dramatic shift in public policy, Congress in 1996 eliminated the eligibility of permanent resident aliens for most federal means-tested benefit programs.

This study examines current policy debates within the context of a broader description of the nature of U.S. citizenship and perspectives on membership. The first section focuses on the acquisition of U.S. citizenship. The central norm of U.S. citizenship law is that citizenship accrues to all those born in the territory of the United States. This norm of *jus soli* is not followed by most countries, and it is currently under challenge by those who would deny it to U.S.-born children of undocumented aliens. This paper recommends that this challenge be rejected.

Citizenship may also be granted by way of naturalization. The central requirements for naturalization have not altered much over the past two centuries. But the recent dramatic increase in the number of persons seeking citizenship has brought naturalization policies to the forefront of policy debate. Some observers have argued that standards regarding English proficiency and knowledge of U.S. history and civics must be raised; others have suggested a reconsideration of the requirement that an applicant renounce citizenship elsewhere when naturalizing.

The second section considers norms regarding loss of U.S. citizenship. Rulings by the Supreme Court make loss of U.S. citizenship virtually impossible without the consent of the citizen—other than on grounds that naturalization was wrongly obtained. A U.S. citizen taking citizenship in another country does not automatically lose U.S. citizenship.

The interplay of U.S. rules on acquisition and loss of citizenship, combined with similar rules in foreign states, has produced significant numbers of dual citizens in the United States. The third section examines the causes and policy implications of dual citizenship, taking particular note of the recent amendment to the Mexican Constitution that permits Mexican citizens to retain Mexican nationality despite acquisition of U.S. citizenship.

The fourth section examines differential treatment of citizens and aliens in terms of rights held against the government, rights to participate in government, and access to benefits and opportunities. As noted above, citizens are endowed with certain rights and privileges not extended to noncitizens. But the actual al-location of constitutional and statutory rights and obligations is complicated, and the relevant legal norms establish varying degrees of "membership" for cit-izens and aliens.

The first four sections provide the basis for the discussion in the fifth section of competing models of membership. Rejecting at the outset understandings of membership based solely on ethnic and racial criteria, or on mere presence in the United States, the study examines in detail three other models:

—1. *Citizenship as membership* adopts the view that citizenship is the pri-mary currency of membership and that immigrants are aliens, guests, nonmem-bers; under this perspective, limiting benefits and opportunities to citizens is appropriate.

—2. *Lawful settlement as membership* represents the best description of U.S. law and practice before the passage of the 1996 welfare legislation. While valuing citizenship as the most complete form of membership, this model also recognizes membership in the form of lawful residence in, participation in, and contribution to U.S. society.

—3. *Transnational membership* is based on the perspective that, increas-ingly, immigrants are and can be members of both their home countries and their countries of settlement.

The study concludes that citizenship is a concept of considerable impor-tance, worth valuing and preserving, but that our long constitutional and statu-tory traditions recognizing degrees of membership for resident aliens should not be cast aside in a desire to make citizenship "mean more." A robust citizen-ship, one that reinvigorates notions of allegiance and commitment, is not ulti-mately served by social policies that diminish the status and opportunities of immigrants. The study therefore suggests affirmation of the traditional "lawful settlement as membership" perspective.

A number of interrelated causes have put citizenship on policy agendas around the world. Developed states have witnessed high levels of immigration in recent decades. U.S. immigration, for example, has reached levels not seen since the early decades of this century. In the United States the foreign-born percentage of the total population is nearly 10 percent—double that of 1970. In Germany, noncitizens account for 8.5 percent of the population, and in France, for 6.3 per-cent. Many of these immigrants came as sojourners or temporary workers but have become settlers. In countries interested in integrating these large for-eign-born populations, naturalization has become a focal point of social policy.

Interest in citizenship has also been sparked by the perceived challenge to the sovereignty of nation-states from both above and below. From above, the activities of international, supranational, and nongovernmental organizations—and the reach and enforcement of international law—have constrained states in areas in which they formerly were largely unfettered. Subnational groups, too, have demanded—and sometimes received—rights of self-governance or other attributes of autonomy. Ethnic and religious groups within countries have challenged those traditions and symbols of nation-states that they believe contribute to their subordination.

In these circumstances, states are likely to search for overarching affiliations and identifications that can both hold together a polyethnic society and serve as a national rallying point for the assertion (or preservation) of state interests in an increasingly constraining supranational sphere. The concept of citizenship, appealing directly to the dedication of the citizen to the state, can be one such device.

Political developments in the world have also produced serious interest in citizenship and membership. The European Union's Maastricht Treaty declares the existence of "European citizenship";[1] the breakup of the Soviet Union has focused international attention on the citizenship rules adopted by the Baltic countries; and the Helsinki Agreement and the Dayton Accords have established novel political structures that challenge traditional notions of sovereignty and membership.

These demographic, social, and political developments raise a number of distinct issues regarding the relationship of people to a state. The first is a definitional question: Who are the citizens of a state? This question focuses attention on rules of birthright citizenship and naturalization. A second issue concerns the rights and obligations of citizenship, and centers on the difference that citizenship makes from the perspectives of both governments and individuals with or without this civic status. A third issue is normative: What is expected of citizens—in effect, what does it take to be a "good citizen"? A fourth issue is the degree to which questions of citizenship are linked to broader concerns of cultural pluralism and integration in a society.

Clearly, these issues are related. The rights granted citizens, for example, may make citizenship more or less attractive and therefore influence naturalization rates. Or, the society's expectations of "good citizenship" may be more or less friendly to maintaining other loyalties and therefore may affect immigrants' decisions to naturalize and the manner in which they integrate into U.S. society. In its examination of the relationship of citizenship and membership,

---

1. Treaty on European Union ("Treaty of Maastricht"), Title II, Part II, Article 8. Translated in Corbett, 1993, pp. 380, 389.

this study will give primary attention to the first two questions: Who is a citizen? What are the rights and obligations of citizenship?

Who are citizens of the United States?

Virtually all human beings acquire citizenship at birth, and the vast majority of people are citizens of the country in which they were born and currently reside. The near-universality of these facts—which seem so natural that we rarely think about them—is recent, correlating with the growth and development of the nation-state.[2] Birthright citizenship occurs in two ways: Under the principle of *jus soli*, a person is a citizen of the territory in which he or she is born; under the principle of *jus sanguinis*, citizenship is based on descent. Because most people are born to parents who are citizens of the country in which they reside, these two modes of citizenship acquisition usually overlap. But *jus soli* and *jus sanguinis* represent very different understandings of the nature of citizenship and have important implications for the integration of immigrants and their children.

This section examines how the principle of *jus soli* (literally, right of the soil) has been interpreted in U.S. law. It then considers how this principle has been and should be applied to the acquisition of citizenship by U.S.-born children whose parents are undocumented aliens. At the other end of the spectrum are the children born outside the territory of the United States to parents who are U.S. citizens. This section looks as well at how the United States has applied the principle of *jus sanguinis* (or right of blood) to these limited instances. Citizenship may also be acquired by naturalization, of course, and this section concludes by looking at the rules governing naturalization in the United States and at the larger policy issues informing the debate over these rules.

Jus soli, *American Style*

The United States has operated under the principles of both *jus soli* and *jus sanguinis* since its founding. Although neither the Constitution nor federal law defined birthright citizenship until after the Civil War, state and federal authorities recognized *jus soli* as part of the common law inherited from England.

---

2. Although the term "nation-state" is sometimes used in an ethnocultural sense, I will use the term more in its American sense, as interchangeable with "state," "country," and "polity."

Jus soli is sometimes criticized as an ill-fitting remnant of medieval times.[3] The classic statement of the principle dates back to a 1608 opinion by Sir Edward Coke in *Calvin's Case*. In U.S. law, *jus soli* was explicitly affirmed by the adoption in 1868 of the Fourteenth Amendment, which states that "all persons born or naturalized in the United States and subject to the jurisdiction thereof, are citizens of the United States and of the State wherein they reside." The amendment constituted an express overruling of Chief Justice Taney's opinion in the *Dred Scott* case (1857)[4] that *free blacks* born in the United States were not citizens. Taney's reasoning was that the term "citizens" meant "the people of the United States," and that the latter term was defined historically to include only those persons deemed to be part of "the people of the United States" at the time of the nation's founding. Examining the historical record, Taney concluded that persons of African descent born in the United States had not been included in "the people of the United States" at the time of the adoption of the Constitution, and thus free blacks born in the United States were not citizens at birth. Taney's analysis has been roundly rejected by scholars;[5] his conclusion was rejected by the nation with the ratification of the Fourteenth Amendment.

Because the principle of *jus soli* is so fundamental to the U.S. legal tradition, it has particular power in American culture. Its strength is evident in the 1898 decision of the Supreme Court in *United States v. Wong Kim Ark*.[6] At issue in the case was whether children born to Chinese immigrants in the United States were citizens. The government argued that the children of immigrants were not "subject to the jurisdiction" of the United States within the meaning of the Fourteenth Amendment. It further noted that federal law at the time prohibited Chinese immigrants from naturalizing in the United States. Nonetheless, the Court concluded that the children were citizens, upholding "the fundamental rule of citizenship by birth within the dominion of the United States."[7] *Wong*

---

3. See, for example, Schuck and Smith, 1985, p. 73.

4. *Scott v. Sandford,* 60 U.S. (19 How.) 393 (1857).

5. See Kettner, 1978, pp. 307–33.

6. *United States v. Wong Kim Ark,* 169 U.S. 649 (1898).

7. *United States v. Wong Kim Ark,* 169 U.S. 649, 688 (1898). As the Court noted in the case, such reasoning did not apply to children born to American Indians, "standing in a peculiar relation to the National Government, unknown to the common law." *United States v. Wong Kim Ark,* 169 U.S. 681 (1898). Indeed, the Court had held fourteen years earlier that an Indian born in the United States who left his tribe and integrated into white society did not acquire citizenship under the Fourteenth Amendment. *Elk v. Wilkins,* 112 U.S. 94 (1884). Eventually Congress adopted legislation conferring citizenship on all Indians born in the United States by the Immigration and Nationality Act (1952) section 301(b).

Kim Ark is an extraordinary decision, delivered in the same era as *Plessy v. Ferguson* (which sustained the constitutionality of Jim Crow laws) and a set of opinions limiting the application of the Constitution to recently acquired overseas territories.[8] Clearly the ghost of *Dred Scott* casts a long shadow.

The Debate over Citizenship for Children Born to Undocumented Aliens

While *jus soli* appears secure in the United States as a constitutional and political principle for children born to lawfully admitted permanent resident aliens, in recent years questions have been raised regarding the principle's application to children of undocumented aliens. Yale professors Peter Schuck and Rogers Smith argued in 1985 that no judicial precedent directly supported birthright citizenship for children of undocumented aliens and that political theory supported a contrary conclusion. Recognizing "the splendor of its constitutional pedigree," Schuck and Smith nonetheless suggest that "birthright citizenship is something of a bastard concept in American ideology":

> Birthright citizenship originated as a distinctively feudal status intimately
> linked to medieval notions of sovereignty, legal personality, and alle-
> giance. At a conceptual level, then, it was fundamentally opposed to the
> consensual assumptions that guided the political handiwork of 1776 and
> 1787. In a polity whose chief organizing principle was and is the liberal,
> individualistic idea of consent, mere birth within a nation's border seems
> to be an anomalous, inadequate measure of expression of an individual's
> consent to its rule and a decidedly crude indicator of the nation's consent
> to the individual's admission to political membership.[9]

The authors accept that the Fourteenth Amendment and the Supreme Court's decision in *Wong Kim Ark* establish birthright citizenship for children of citizens and permanent resident aliens. But they argue that the Fourteenth Amendment ought to be reinterpreted to incorporate a "consensualist" approach that would make birthright citizenship for children of illegal and temporary-visitor aliens "a matter of congressional choice rather than of constitutional prescription."[10]

A number of commentators have pointed out that Schuck and Smith's constitutional argument is difficult to square with the Fourteenth Amendment's ex-

---

8. See *Downes v. Bidwell*, 182 U.S. 244 (1901); *Balzac v. Porto Rico*, 258 U.S. 298 (1922).
9. Shuck and Smith, 1985, pp. 2–3.
10. Shuck and Smith, 1985, p. 5.

press affirmation of the common-law principle of *jus soli*.[11] Moreover, a consensualist approach seemed to underlie Justice Taney's opinion in *Dred Scott*, and nothing could be clearer than the nation's intent to overrule that decision by adopting the Amendment.[12] At a joint hearing of two subcommittees of the House Judiciary Committee in 1995, the Department of Justice rejected Schuck and Smith's constitutional reasoning, arguing that their theory "would require repudiation of the language of the Constitution itself, the clear statement of the framers' intent, and the universal understanding of 19th and 20th century courts."[13]

If the Supreme Court were to agree with the Department of Justice that the Constitution guarantees citizenship for the U.S.-born children of undocumented aliens, Congress would be without power to enact legislation to deny citizenship to such children. But such a ruling would not end the debate. Congress could, of course, propose a constitutional amendment denying such children citizenship and submit it to the states for ratification. Ensuing debates would need to consider the policy arguments raised by Schuck and Smith: that the rise of the welfare state, coupled with federal failure to effectively prevent undocumented migration, has made full application of the *jus soli* principle expensive. Assessing the cost burden is difficult at present. Congressman Elton Gallegly told the subcommittees at their joint hearings in 1995 that there are an estimated 250,000 citizen children of undocumented aliens in Los Angeles County alone, and that children of undocumented aliens (including both citizens and noncitizens) receive an estimated $500 million annually in welfare and health benefits.

These costs must be weighed against the benefits of *jus soli*. A weak justification is the argument that the current rule provides a clear-cut or "bright line" test, easy of application. In fact, most countries administer *jus sanguinis* regimes; indeed, the United States follows *jus sanguinis* for children born to U.S. citizens overseas. A more persuasive argument in favor of *jus soli* notes its strong assimilative advantages. David Martin, professor of law at the University of Virginia and former Immigration and Naturalization Service (INS) general counsel, has pointed out that, unlike European countries, the United States has no "second generation problem" because it has no second generation aliens: For children born here,

---

11. See Neuman, 1987; Martin, 1985; Carens, 1987.
12. See Neuman, 1987; and Carens, 1987.
13. "Children Born in the United States to Illegal Parents, 1995" (hereafter Hearings, 1995), p. 81. Statement of Walter Dellinger, Assistant Attorney General, Office of Legal Counsel.

a secure citizenship status forms a basic foundation for the shaping of identity and involvement in the polity. They are thereby encouraged to embrace life here as full participants, not as half-hearted, standoffish "guests." Equally important, other citizens are induced to treat them as coequal members of the polity, not as intruders who stay too long.[14]

Today, when some are raising concerns about the ability of a polyethnic society to maintain unity, abandoning birthright citizenship seems a step in the wrong direction.

Interestingly, Schuck and Smith conclude that, important as the cost analysis is, it should not ultimately drive the decision. Rather, "the question should be resolved in the light of broader ideals of constitutional meaning, social morality, and political community." Their view is that "it is simply morally perverse to reward law-breaking by conferring the valued status of citizenship."[15] A number of witnesses at the congressional hearing made similar claims. Representative Gallegly argued that current "law bestows citizenship on a kind of technicality, based more on logistics and timing than on roots, community, or legality. This is clearly inappropriate."[16] Furthermore, in a world constituted largely by *jus sanguinis* states, the denial of birthright citizenship to children of aliens cannot be persuasively characterized as a violation of fundamental human rights.

There are, however, moral arguments on the other side as well. U.S. Assistant Attorney General Walter Dellinger noted in his congressional testimony that

academics may conceive of nation-states in which citizenship would not necessarily extend to those who lack the approval or mutual consent of existing citizens. But the country in question is not some theoretical conception, but our own country with its real existence and its real history. It would be a grave mistake to alter the opening sentence of the Fourteenth Amendment without sober reflection on how it came to be part of our basic constitutional charter.[17]

Significantly, in testimony before Congress in 1995, Schuck himself urged Congress not to adopt legislation denying citizenship to children of undocu-

14. Martin, 1985, pp. 283–84.
15. Schuck and Smith, 1985, p. 113.
16. Hearings, 1995, p. 23. Statement of California Representative Elton Gallegly.
17. Hearings, 1995, p. 82. Statement of Walter Dellinger, Assistant Attorney General, Office of Legal Counsel, Department of Justice.

mented aliens. He argued that "feckless enforcement policies" virtually guarantee the existence of a large number of undocumented aliens in the United States and that, without a birthright citizenship rule, "these illegals, their children, and their children's children will continue to be outsiders, mired in an inferior and illegal status, and deprived of the capacities of self-protection and self advancement."[18] For Schuck, any change in citizenship rule would be irresponsible if not preceded by effective efforts to reduce illegal immigration.

In his testimony, Schuck briefly mentions French citizenship rules as an alternative *jus soli* system worth considering. Under the current French system, third-generation immigrants are attributed citizenship at birth, while second-generation immigrants (that is, the children of persons who immigrated to France) have the right to acquire French citizenship. In recent years, the exact provisions of the system have been in a state of flux. Before 1993, French rules governing the acquisition of citizenship by second-generation immigrants permitted the nearly automatic acquisition of citizenship "without formality" at the age of majority (eighteen), as long as the youth could provide proof of residence for the preceding five years and fulfill a few other conditions, including the absence of substantive criminal convictions. A 1993 reform of the French nationality code revised the system of *jus soli* to require that second-generation immigrants formally apply for citizenship between the ages of sixteen and twenty-one, in addition to showing proof of residence the preceding five years and fulfilling other conditions. Most recently, 1998 legislation returned the *jus soli* system to its pre-1993 form (with a few exceptions). It reinstituted the semiautomatic acquisition of citizenship ("without formality") for second-generation immigrants at majority, while retaining a procedure of declaration for youth sixteen to eighteen years of age.[19] Whatever the merits of France's *jus soli* system, it could not be adopted in the United States without a constitutional amendment.

In sum, *jus soli* is the foundation of U.S. citizenship policy, and, for historical reasons of enduring importance, the principle of *jus soli* appears virtually unassailable. *Jus soli* has significant implications for the integration of immigrants in U.S. society. A contrary citizenship rule in a country of high immigration tends to create "a hereditary caste of permanent aliens."[20] The assimilative characteristics of *jus soli* should not be abandoned in the search for better control of U.S. borders.

---

18. Hearings, 1995, pp. 96, 97. Statement of Peter Schuck.
19. For a fuller account of these legal developments, see Feldblum, forthcoming.
20. Hearings, 1995, p. 109. Statement of Gerald Neuman, Professor, Columbia Law School.

Jus sanguinis Rules

The United States follows *jus sanguinis* principles for children born to U.S. citizens outside its territory.[21] Perhaps no more than 50,000 children attain citizenship in this fashion annually—a number dwarfed by the number of persons who naturalize each year. The central policy issue in the transmission of citizenship to persons born outside the United States is whether adequate contact with U.S. traditions and culture is maintained as citizenship is passed from expatriate generation to expatriate generation.

Over the past century, Congress has consistently loosened the requirements for the transmission of citizenship *jure sanguinis*. In earlier days, U.S. law required that both the child and (at least one) parent reside in the United States for a specified duration for the child to retain U.S. citizenship. Since 1978, residency requirements for children have been dropped; however, a person who attains citizenship *jure sanguinis* cannot transmit citizenship to his or her children born outside the United States unless he or she has established residence in the United States before the birth of the child. Despite the relative ease with which citizenship may be transmitted overseas, little controversy has emerged about the *jus sanguinis* rules.[22] (The central policy concern they raise—their contribution to dual citizenship—will be discussed below.)

Citizenship by Naturalization

The Constitution grants Congress the power to establish a "uniform Rule of Naturalization," and the first naturalization statute was enacted in 1790.[23] Historically, U.S. naturalization laws have reflected U.S. views on race. The 1790 statute limited naturalization to "any alien, being a free white person." The law was amended in the wake of the Civil War to include persons of "African nativity, . . . and descent," a formulation that continued to exclude Asians and others. Chinese were not entitled to naturalize until 1943 (although children born to

---

21. The Supreme Court has held that such persons obtain citizenship by virtue of federal statutes, not the Fourteenth Amendment. *Rogers v. Bellei,* 401 U.S. 815, 828-31 (1971). Applicability of the Fourteenth Amendment to persons born in U.S. territories has never been fully determined, but Congress has provided by statute that persons born in Puerto Rico, Guam, and the Virgin Islands are citizens at birth.

22. There have been some significant legal controversies concerning the impact of earlier gender discrimination in the *jus sanguinis* rules. See, for example, *Wauchope v. U.S. Department of State,* 985 F.2d 1407 (9th Cir. 1993)—invalidating earlier statutory provision that allowed transmission of citizenship by U.S. fathers but not mothers. See also *Miller v. Albright,* 118 S. Ct. 1428 (1998).

23. For a history, see Ueda, 1994.

Chinese immigrants were citizens by way of the Fourteenth Amendment). A fully race-neutral naturalization law was not adopted until 1952.

For those not excluded by racial qualifications, the naturalization process was fairly liberal, and it remains so today. Immigrants must establish five years of permanent residence in the United States, demonstrate good moral character, prove knowledge of U.S. history and civics, and be able to "read, write, and speak words in ordinary usage in the English language."[24] (The English requirement is waivable for certain elderly persons who have resided in the United States for a considerable period, and the civics and English requirements may be waived for persons who "because of physical or developmental disability or mental impairment" are unable to comply with them.[25]) Various classes of aliens are deemed by statute not to possess "good moral character"—such as persons convicted of committing aggravated felonies and drug and gambling offenses, or habitual drunkards. Naturalizing citizens must take an oath that affirms allegiance to the U.S. Constitution and a commitment to contribute to the national defense. Significantly, the oath also requires renunciation of allegiance to any "foreign prince, potentate, state, or sovereignty."[26]

In the 1970s and 1980s, the number of persons filing U.S. naturalization applications averaged 150,000 to 250,000 annually. While U.S. immigrants have tended to naturalize at rates significantly higher than aliens in European countries, naturalization rates have varied considerably by national origin. Immigrants from Asian countries have had the highest naturalization rates; immigrants from Mexico and Canada traditionally have had far lower rates.[27]

Today there is a substantial pool of persons—perhaps as many as 6 or 7 million—who are eligible for naturalization but have chosen *not* to become citizens. The reasons usually ascribed to low naturalization rates are several. First, until recently, few benefits and opportunities were available to citizens for which permanent resident aliens were not also eligible. Second, because of *jus soli*, immigrants do not need to naturalize in order to provide for the U.S. citizenship of their U.S.–born children. Third, some immigrants find the language and history requirements daunting. Fourth, some immigrants are unwilling to take the oath because it requires renunciation of other allegiances; such a renun-

24. Immigration and Nationality Act (INA) section 312(a), 8 U.S. Code section 1423(a).

25. INA section 312(b), 8 U.S. Code section 1423(b). Immigration and Naturalization Service (INS) regulations implementing the waiver for physical or mental impairment still require the applicant to be able to take the oath of allegiance. *Federal Register* 62, p. 12915.

26. INA section 337, 8 U.S. Code section 1448.

27. In the 1990s, immigrants from Asian nations have had a nationalization rate of 57.6 percent; those from North America have a rate of 32.2 percent. (The rate is based on an INS analysis of a sample of immigrants admitted in 1977.) Immigration and Naturalization Service, *1994 Statistical Yearbook of the INS,* Table 58.

ciation either may be psychologically difficult or may cut off the immigrant's ability to travel, to own property, or to inherit in the country of origin.

The past five years have witnessed an unprecedented increase and level of naturalization applications:[28]

Fiscal Year	Applications
1995	959,963
1996	1,277,403
1997	1,571,797
1998	794,749
1999	720,468

This massive increase has occurred for a number of reasons. In the 1990s, the Immigration and Naturalization Service (INS) introduced a new resident alien card (green card) and required permanent resident aliens to replace their old ones, informing immigrants that naturalization would cost just a few dollars more than a new green card and suggesting they consider seeking citizenship. Many did. More significantly, the more than 3 million aliens whose status became legal under the 1986 Immigration Act began to become eligible for naturalization in the mid-1990s.

The anti-immigrant rhetoric of the past few years has also helped swell application numbers. Many immigrants see attaining citizenship as a way to protect themselves against unfriendly legislative and administrative policies.[29] Citizenship also protects their access to the social safety net. This latter consideration is of obvious significance in light of the 1996 welfare reform legislation, which terminated the eligibility of permanent resident aliens for most means-tested benefit programs. The resulting increase in filings outpaced INS resources to adjudicate naturalization applications. By summer 1995, the pending caseload was about 800,000 and waiting times in the largest offices exceeded two years. In August 1995, the INS announced CitizenshipUSA, a program intended to reduce the significant backlog of naturalization applications accumulating in INS field offices and return to historical processing times of approximately six months. The program targeted those cities with the largest

---

28. *1994 Statistical Yearbook of the INS,* Table 58; *1996 Statistical Yearbook of the INS,* Table 44; *End-of-Year FY 1998 Monthly Statistical Report, Naturalization Benefits;* and *September 1999 Monthly Statistical Report, End of FY 1999, Naturalization Benefits.*

29. In the 1920s, when anti-immigrant legislation and feelings were prevalent, naturalization rates rose sharply. In the years 1907–1910, an average of 54,679 petitions for naturalization were filed each year. In the 1920s, despite strict quota laws limiting the number of immigrants, an average of 188,427 petitions for naturalization were filed each year. *1994 Statistical Yearbook of the INS,* Table 45.

number of pending cases: Chicago, Los Angeles, Miami, New York, and San Francisco.[30] In FY1996, processing of naturalization applications more than doubled; 1.3 million cases were adjudicated, and of those, approximately 1.04 million were granted. The approval-denial rates were roughly consistent with earlier years.

CitizenshipUSA came under heavy fire from Congress, however. Investigative committees charged that it had been politically motivated—alleging that the administration sped up processing to naturalize citizens in time for them to vote in the 1996 elections—and that it had been incompetently administered. Substantial changes were undertaken in response, as the Department of Justice has contracted with outside firms to monitor a review of the 1996 naturalizations and to prepare a plan for a "reengineering" of the application and adjudication process. These developments produced a backlog of pending cases that topped 2 million by the end of 1998. Subsequent reforms have significantly reduced that number.

Concern about the integrity of INS procedures has been a recent focal point of public attention. But a broader and deeper set of naturalization issues are involved. In U.S. political culture, naturalization is more than an administrative adjudication; it is seen as a "rite of passage." It represents the solemn forswearing of other allegiances and the taking on of a new set of important commitments—to the U.S. Constitution and to the American people. Most Americans view that which is granted—U.S. citizenship—as one of the most sought-after and valuable statuses in the world. The expectation is that persons receiving such a benefit should demonstrate their awareness of the significance of what has been bestowed by giving something in return: undivided loyalty to the United States.

Naturalization thus has a symbolic importance that may well exceed its practical significance for many naturalized citizens and may belie the relative ease with which it may be obtained. The current debate about the naturalization process is grounded in a concern that this symbolic value has been "cheapened," both in its perceived mass-production and because of the reasons persons seek U.S. citizenship. Some claim that immigrants are naturalizing for *instrumental* reasons (such as maintenance of welfare benefits) rather than for *affective* reasons (such as love of country, patriotism).

It might be thought that the best route to "affective" naturalization is to make very few, if any, distinctions based on citizenship.[31] The reasoning would be

---

30. Together, these offices carried about 75 percent of the naturalization workload.
31. See "The Functionality of Citizenship," 1997.

that, if little of practical value turns on naturalization, then those seeking citizenship must be doing so for reasons of loyalty and commitment, not personal gain. But erasing all distinctions between citizens and aliens would seem to undermine the concept of citizenship as a status that defines a core group of members.

We face a paradox, then: attempts to make citizenship matter more by increasing distinctions between citizens and aliens are likely to produce behavior that is seen as "cheapening" citizenship; while erasing distinctions between citizens and aliens seems to reduce citizenship to a mere personal affiliation.

Attempting to fine-tune benefit eligibility in order to produce "proper" motivations for naturalization is not a wise strategy. Naturalization decisions have always constituted a mix of affective and instrumental reasons. The decision to naturalize in order to bring family members here, for example, may be seen as primarily instrumental, but it may also reflect the citizen's desire to live with his or her family in a country he or she holds dear. The solution is to ensure that those going through the naturalization process—for whatever reasons—meet appropriate standards and understand and accept the commitment they make in becoming U.S. citizens. The current naturalization oath does a fairly good job of this. To become a U.S. citizen, a person must swear:

(1) to support the Constitution of the United States; (2) to renounce and abjure absolutely and entirely all allegiance and fidelity to any foreign prince, potentate, state, or sovereignty of whom or which the applicant was before a subject or citizen; (3) to support and defend the Constitution and the laws of the United States against all enemies, foreign and domestic; (4) to bear true faith and allegiance to the same; and (5)(A) to bear arms on behalf of the United States when required by law, or (B) to perform noncombatant service in the Armed Forces of the United States when required by law, or (C) to perform work of national importance under civilian direction when required by the law.[32]

The language is, to be sure, somewhat archaic. But the sentiment is about right. The naturalizing citizen swears "allegiance" to the Constitution and pledges to "bear arms" or to undertake other service in defense of the nation. The oath is not a statement about identity or culture. It is about *loyalty* and, if circumstances demand, *sacrifice*—two crucial elements of patriotism. These

32. INA section 337(a), 8 U.S. Code section 1448(a).

characteristics are not a function of what benefits citizens do or do not receive in common with immigrants. Persons are likely to be loyal to, and to make sacrifices for, a nation that provides them with rights they value and that stands for values they deem right. The favored treatment they enjoy over other residents of the state is not likely to be a significant part of that judgment.

In sum, while benefits granted or denied immigrants may well affect decisions to naturalize, the crucial issue is not how to calibrate the incentives but rather how to foster the commitment the nation appropriately asks of naturalizing citizens. The current procedure is working: no evidence suggests that naturalizing citizens as a class are any less loyal to this country than native-born citizens. Concern over the knowledge and commitment of naturalizing citizens might best manifest itself in publicly funded programs of civics and English-language education (like those provided in the early decades of this century).[33]

Loss of Citizenship

Citizenship may be lost in three ways: expatriation, denaturalization, and denationalization.

Expatriation means the voluntary relinquishment of citizenship, usually by renunciation. In the early years of the Republic, it was an open question whether a citizen could unilaterally divest himself or herself of U.S. citizenship. Under English common law, a subject was a subject for life. (Indeed, one of the causes of the War of 1812 was the attempt by the English to impress into the Royal Navy English-born sailors who had become naturalized U S. citizens.)[34]

Congress resolved this issue in 1868 by enacting legislation declaring "the right of expatriation . . . a natural and inherent right of all people." The immediate motivation for the statute was British assertion of authority over naturalized U.S. citizens in Ireland participating in anti-British activities; but the statute was immediately understood to establish the right of U.S. citizens to shed their citizenship. That right has not been questioned since, although Congress has recently expressed displeasure at persons believed to have expatriated for tax reasons. The 1996 immigration legislation provides a new exclusion ground for

---

33. See U.S. Commission on Immigration Reform, *Becoming an American,* 1997, pp. 36–45.

34. In the early years, concern was also raised about malefactors who sought to expatriate themselves in order to avoid the reach of federal law. See, for example, *Talbot v. Janson,* 3 U.S. (3 Dall.) 133 (1795), involving U.S. citizens who purported to expatriate themselves in order to join in a conflict between two foreign nations without violating U.S. law requiring citizens to remain neutral.

persons determined by the attorney general to have renounced U.S. citizenship "for the purpose of avoiding taxation."[35]

Denaturalization means the revocation of wrongfully obtained naturalization. As discussed above, this process has received attention recently because of allegations that, under the CitizenshipUSA program of the INS, several thousand persons ineligible for naturalization because of their criminal records were nonetheless granted citizenship. In cases of clearly wrongful naturalization, the INS may use authority granted by Congress in 1994 to revoke naturalization administratively. Other cases must be presented to federal district courts, for which the Supreme Court has established fairly rigorous procedural protections. In frequently quoted language, the Court stated that

> in its consequences [denaturalization] is more serious than a taking of one's property, or the imposition of a fine or other penalty. For it is safe to assert that nowhere in the world today is the right of citizenship of greater worth to an individual than it is in this country. It would be difficult to exaggerate its value and importance. By many it is regarded as the highest hope of civilized men. Thus, citizenship could not be revoked without the clearest sort of justification and proof.[36]

Judicial protection of citizenship reaches its zenith in the third form of loss of nationality, *denationalization*—deprivation of citizenship because of conduct or legal status.[37] (Both native-born and naturalized citizens are subject to denationalization.) Congress has asserted the power to denationalize citizens since the early years of this century. The 1907 Expatriation Act, aimed at the problem of dual citizenship, in effect created denationalization grounds by establishing conditions under which U.S. citizens would be deemed to have expatriated themselves—including naturalization in a foreign state and, for naturalized aliens, extended residence in their native countries. The act also notoriously provided that American women who married foreigners would lose their U.S. citizenship (for the duration of the marriage).[38]

---

35. INA section 212(a)(10)(E), 8 U.S. Code section 1182(a)(10)(E), as added by the Illegal Immigration Reform and Immigrant Responsibility Act (1996) section 352. Expatriation is regulated to some degree: one must be outside the country (except in time of war). INA sections 349(a), 351(a), 8 U.S. Code section 1481(a), 1483(a).

36. *Schneiderman v. United States,* 320 U.S. 118, 122 (1943).

37. See generally Aleinikoff, 1986.

38. Upheld in *Mackenzie v. Hare,* 239 U.S. 299 (1915). The provision was repealed in 1922.

In 1940, the grounds for denationalization were expanded to include serving in the armed forces of a foreign country, voting in a foreign election, holding office in a foreign government, or being convicted for desertion in time of war or treason. Departure from the United States in time of war to avoid military service and conviction for subversive activities were later added as grounds for denationalization.

Some of these grounds for loss of citizenship were not conditioned on acquisition or retention of citizenship elsewhere. They therefore raised the specter of congressionally mandated statelessness. Over the past three decades, the Supreme Court, again stressing both the value of U.S. citizenship and also recognizing the potential dangers of statelessness, has rendered a number of decisions that severely limit congressional power to take away U.S. citizenship. In a dissenting opinion that became the basis of the Court's later restrictive approach, Chief Justice Earl Warren wrote:

> Citizenship *is* man's basic right for it is nothing less than the right to have rights. Remove this priceless possession and there remains a stateless person, disgraced and degraded in the eyes of his countrymen. He has no lawful claim to protection from any nation, and no nation may assert rights on his behalf. . . . This government was not established with power to decree this fate.[39]

In a subsequent case, the Court also noted its concern that broad congressional power to denationalize might be misused by current majorities to strip their opponents or other disfavored groups of citizenship.[40]

These concerns led the Court to declare that a citizen "has a constitutional right to remain a citizen . . . unless he voluntarily relinquishes that citizenship."[41] The Court's holdings mean that, in order to take away citizenship, the government must demonstrate that an expatriating act is accompanied by an intent to terminate U.S. citizenship. In short, the Court collapsed denationalization into expatriation. In 1988, Congress amended the Immigration and Nationality Act (INA) to reflect the Court's rule, and the statute now reads that a person shall lose U.S. nationality "by voluntarily performing [an expatriating act] with the intention of relinquishing United States nationality."[42] This language does not necessarily require that a person *express* an intention to give up

---

39. *Perez v. Brownell,* 356 U.S. 44, 64-65 (1958) (emphasis in original).

40. *Afroyim v. Rusk,* 387 U.S. 253, 267-68 (1967).

41. *Afroyim v. Rusk,* 387 U.S. 253, 267-68 (1967) (invalidating loss of citizenship for citizen who voted in Israeli election).

42. INA section 349(a), U.S. Code 1481(a).

U.S. citizenship when undertaking an expatriating act. Thus, some conduct—for example, attaining a high office in a foreign country—might be deemed, under certain circumstances, to evidence such an intention whether or not the person formally renounced U.S. citizenship. In practice, however, the State Department has virtually stopped declaring loss of citizenship unless a U.S. citizen has specifically declared an intention to give up citizenship.[43]

When contrasted with naturalization rules, the standards for denationalization create a peculiar asymmetry: An immigrant who naturalizes in the United States must renounce citizenship elsewhere; a U.S. citizen who naturalizes in another country cannot have his or her U.S. citizenship removed unless he or she expressly intends to lose it. The first rule seeks to prevent dual citizenship; the second rule virtually guarantees dual citizenship. The rules regarding denationalization might seem overprotective, but they are constitutionally based and, as such, may not be altered by statute or administrative regulation.

Dual Citizenship

International law and practice generally regard dual citizenship with disfavor. The preamble to the Hague Convention *Concerning Certain Questions Relating to the Conflict of Nationality Laws* (1930) represents the traditional view. It states that "it is in the interest of the international community to secure that all members should recognize that every person should have a nationality and should have one nationality only."[44] Dual citizenship raises concerns for states regarding diplomatic protection (particularly when a citizen resident in one country travels to another country in which he or she holds citizenship), military service, and voting rights. Beyond these more technical issues, there are deeper questions of divided loyalty. The German Federal Constitutional Court has stated:

43. Indeed, the Department of State indicated in 1995 that it would submit legislation that would have made explicit renunciation before an officer of the United States the only fashion in which citizenship could be lost. See, for example, Goldstein and Piazza, April 22, 1996.

44. The disfavor in which states traditionally hold dual nationality is also reflected in the Council of Europe's 1963 *Convention on Reduction of Cases of Multiple Nationality and Military Obligations in Cases of Multiple Nationality*. The council found that "cases of multiple nationality are liable to cause difficulties and . . . joint action to reduce as far as possible the number of cases of multiple nationality . . . corresponds to the aims of the Council of Europe." Ibid., p. 222. It should be noted that, in a 1997 Opinion, the Parliamentary Assembly of the Council of Europe acknowledged that the 1963 convention was ill-designed to handle the current situations facing European nations in the area of dual nationality.

It is accurate to say that dual or multiple nationality is regarded, both do-
mestically and internationally, as an evil that should be avoided or eliminated in the interest of states as well as in the interests of the affected
citizen. . . . States seek to achieve exclusivity of their respective nationalities in order to set clear boundaries for their sovereignty over persons;
they want to be secure in the duty of loyalty of their citizens—which extends if necessary as far as risking one's life—and do not want to see it
endangered by possible conflicts with a loyalty to a foreign state.[45]

The most serious loyalty issue arises in times of war. But today, in the post–cold
war setting, *political* loyalty is a more relevant concern. The fear is that a dual
citizen of countries A and B could participate in the political system of country
A with the interests of country B in mind, or could exploit dual citizenship status for inappropriate personal gain in carrying on business or collecting government benefits. In such cases, it might be questioned whether the citizen
possesses the identification with one state that many states seek to foster in their
citizens.

In a world nominally dedicated to the idea of assuring that every person is a
citizen of at least one but not more than one nation-state, dual citizenship is tolerated to a surprising degree. Without more effective cooperation among states,
the rising incidence of individuals with plural citizenship will probably continue. It remains an open question whether this trend should be welcomed as the
harbinger of a new internationally mobile world or feared as a potential threat to
the political, social, and cultural unity of modern polyethnic states.

To begin to answer that question, this section seeks to weigh the costs, benefits, and consequences of this trend as well as to consider the policy options
available to deal with it. The recent change in Mexican naturalization law offers
an illustrative case to explore the complexity of the conflicting motives, perceptions, and national interests that affect choices in naturalization rules and that
constrain the feasible policy alternatives of individual states.

In the United States, the incidence of dual citizenship is far more widespread
than is generally recognized. Plural citizenship may arise in four situations:

—1. *Birth in the United States to immigrant parents.* A citizen of country A
moves to the United States and has a child. The child is a dual citizen if country
A has *jus sanguinis* rules that recognize the child as a citizen of country A. (Example: a German citizen has a child in Chicago. Note that if a German citizen
marries a British citizen and they have a child in the United States, the child
may be born with three nationalities.)

45. Opinion of German Federal Constitutional Court, May 21, 1974, 254–55.

—2. Birth outside the United States to one parent who is a U.S. citizen and another who is a foreigner. A citizen of the United States marries a citizen of country A and has a child in country A. If the U.S. citizen has maintained the ties to the United States necessary for the transmission of citizenship *jure sanguinis*, the child is a citizen of both country A and the United States. (Example: A native-born U.S. citizen marries a British citizen and has a child in the United Kingdom.)

—3. Naturalization with a renunciation requirement, but renunciation not recognized by country of origin. A citizen of country A naturalizes in the United States. Even though the U.S. naturalization oath demands renunciation of other citizenships, country A does not deem naturalization elsewhere as expatriating the citizen. (Example: A Canadian citizen naturalizes in the United States. The U.S. oath requires renunciation, but Canada does not regard naturalization in the United States as expatriating unless the person specifically notifies Canadian authorities of an intent to renounce citizenship.)

—4. Naturalization, loss of citizenship, and resumption of citizenship. A citizen of country A naturalizes in the United States. Country A deems the person to have lost citizenship but provides for the resumption of citizenship. (Example: Under Australian law, a citizen who naturalizes in the United States loses Australian citizenship. The person can, however, subsequently apply to resume Australian citizenship—this is not a naturalization process—without losing U.S. citizenship unless he or she expresses the intent to do so.)[46]

The U.S. government does not record and has not estimated the number of U.S. dual citizens, but the total may be quite large. Any U.S.-born child of immigrants in the United States is likely at birth to be a citizen of both the United States and the parents' country of origin. Some of the largest "sending" countries to the United States—including Mexico, the Philippines, the Dominican Republic, Canada, and India—recognize children born to their nationals here as citizens of their countries. The Census Bureau's March 1996 *Current Population Survey* provides data that can supply a rough estimate of the number of children born dual nationals in the United States each year. The study reports that 540,000 U.S.-citizen children less than one year of age were living with at least one foreign-born parent who was not a naturalized U.S. citizen. It is reasonable to assume that most of these children are dual citizens, although the

---

46. In the late nineteenth century, the rule was generally that a wife took the citizenship of her husband. This rule is now almost universally rejected, the result being that individuals preserve their own nationality after marriage, although spouses are frequently given preferential treatment under the immigration quotas. See INA section 201(b), 8 U.S. Code section 1151. This twentieth-century development is a major contributing factor to increases in dual citizenship, since under *jus sanguinis* rules a child will obtain citizenship from each parent.

number is not a precise measure. It *under*counts, for example, the number of dual citizens by omitting (1) U.S.-born children whose foreign parents left the United States within a year and (2) children of foreign-born parents who have naturalized in the United States but who are still able to transmit the citizenship under their home countries' *jus sanguinis* rules. The number may also *over*count the number of dual nationals by including the children of foreign-born parents whose home countries do not permit the transmission of citizenship overseas if the foreign-born child obtains another citizenship at birth (China is the most significant example). Nonetheless, half a million is probably an acceptable order of magnitude for the number of children who obtain dual citizenship at birth each year in the United States. Because most countries do not require dual citizens to elect one citizenship over the other, the status may continue for life, and, indeed, can be passed to generations beyond.[47]

The rising incidence of dual citizenship is also due to the growing number of countries that have altered their laws to permit their citizens to retain nationality despite naturalization elsewhere. Canada adopted such a policy in 1977, as (more recently) have Argentina, Colombia, Costa Rica, the Dominican Republic, El Salvador, France, Ireland, Israel, Italy, Panama, Switzerland, and the United Kingdom.[48] Even in states that deem naturalization in the United States to constitute expatriation, authorities are likely to be unaware of the U.S. naturalization and therefore may continue to treat naturalized individuals as citizens.

Is Dual Citizenship a Problem?

Both theoretically and symbolically, dual citizenship may appear problematic. A regime of nation-states arguably functions more smoothly when persons are assigned citizenship in just one state. Unitary citizenship not only resolves various state administrative problems but also, it might be claimed, provides for an indivisible loyalty that states are likely to seek and value.

But the world is more complicated than this ideal allows, and a desire for tidiness is often in conflict with the practicalities of human life. Migration, mar-

---

47. Many countries require that, in order to pass on citizenship to future generations, a citizen born outside the state territory must reside for some number of years in the state. But this residency requirement does not prevent successive generations of dual citizens. A child born to an Australian in the United States, for example, is a dual national. If he or she returns to Australia at some point for two years and then moves back to the United States, then his or her children will be both Australian and U.S. citizens.

48. This list is not all inclusive. For a more complete list, see Goldstein and Piazza, April 22, 1996, pp. 545–47.

riage, and birth ensure that neither states nor their citizenries are hermetically sealed. Indeed, dual citizenship cannot be attributed simply to the (intentional or unintentional) actions of individuals. The existence of plural citizenships is a function of the unwillingness of the international community to establish international norms on the acquisition and maintenance of citizenship; international law leaves such matters to the discretion of states, and the resulting welter of rules is wholly a product of state choices.

Although a postnational world still seems far away, it is clear that the world is increasingly transnational. Modern communications and transportation have brought the world to the United States' door as never before, and many of those coming are less willing to leave their countries of origin behind. This reluctance characterizes business elites that seek to take advantage of commercial opportunities in more than one country as well as lower-skilled workers who seek to improve their condition abroad but to remain connected to home communities.[49] And, as already noted, "sending" countries show an increasing interest in maintaining ties with their diaspora populations.

From one perspective, these developments represent a healthy development, making commercial and social ties between nations deeper and stronger, opening up new markets, and fostering appreciation of cultural diversity.[50] Little evidence exists that widespread dual citizenship in the United States has been harmful to the national interest. While some dual citizens (and naturalized citizens) have committed espionage against the United States, so have persons of only one nationality—either native-born citizens or immigrants. Similarly, while concerns have been voiced that dual nationals may vote the interests of their countries of origin ahead of the interests of the United States, the same would be possible whether or not the person officially retains the citizenship of his or her home country.

From another perspective, there is cause for concern. The growing interest of countries of origin in dual citizenship for their nationals may make it a different phenomenon than it was in the past. Furthermore, with the sovereignty of the nation-state being challenged from both within and without, the idea of citizenship may take on increasing importance. Insistence on unitary citizenship could serve as a brake on transnational developments that undermine the loyalty and commitment needed for the healthy functioning of a polyethnic state.

These differing perspectives can be examined in two specific contexts: (1) recent changes in Mexican nationality law; and (2) debate regarding the retention of the renunciation requirement in the naturalization oath.

49. See Basch et al., 1994; Guarnizo, forthcoming 1998; and Graham, 1996.
50. For a discussion of postnationalism, see Basch et al., 1994.

Dual Nationality and Mexico

Under Mexican law, persons born in Mexico are Mexican nationals.[51] As in the United States, aliens naturalizing in Mexico must renounce other citizenships. Until recently, Mexicans obtaining citizenship in a foreign country were deemed to lose Mexican nationality, while Mexican *jus sanguinis* rules permitted the indefinite transmission of Mexican nationality to overseas generations (although persons born dual nationals had to elect Mexican nationality if they sought a passport or other identification document after the age of eighteen).

These latter rules underwent dramatic change based on an amendment to the Mexican Constitution published on March 20, 1997, and effective a year later (see table 4-1). First, Mexicans naturalizing elsewhere will be able to maintain Mexican nationality, a change that will affect the status of tens of thousands of Mexicans who naturalize in the United States each year.[52] Naturalized U.S. citizens of Mexican origin will also be permitted to apply for reacquisition of Mexican nationality. The amendment's use of the word "nationality" is intentional and is not coterminous with citizenship. Mexicans who retain nationality will be able to travel anywhere on a Mexican passport, to own coastal and border land forbidden to aliens, and to benefit from other rules regarding inheritance, business opportunities, and property ownership that treat Mexicans more favorably than non-Mexicans. Significantly, however, nationality does not, by itself, include a right to vote in Mexican elections; this would require a separate change in Mexican election law.

The second major change under the constitutional amendment alters *jus sanguinis* rules. Mexican nationality by descent would not be transmitted beyond the second generation; that is, U.S.-born children of Mexican nationals born or naturalized in Mexico would be Mexican nationals, but their children would not. This rule is stricter than that applied by the United States, Canada, or Australia, all of which permit transmission of citizenship beyond the second generation provided that some degree of contact occurs with the home country. Together, these two changes have an important impact on the citizenship of second- and third-generation Mexicans in the United States.

---

51. Under Mexican law, nationality and citizenship are distinct concepts. Nationality—a broader concept than citizenship—connotes belonging to the state; it entitles one to basic membership rights short of political rights. Citizenship is accompanied by full political rights.

52. Significant numbers of Mexicans have obtained U.S. citizenship by naturalization in recent years—some 39,300 (9.1 percent of total) in 1994; some 81,600 in 1995 (16.7 percent of total); and some 255,000 in 1996 (24.4 percent of total). *1995 Statistical Yearbook of the INS,* p. 145; *1996 Statistical Yearbook of the INS,* pp. 138, 146. The INS routinely revises its data calculations to make them as accurate as possible. The numbers cited here are the most recently published.

Table 4-1. *The 1990 Amendment to Mexico's Citizenship System*

Status of native-born Mexicans	First generation	Second generation	Third generation
Before amendment			
Naturalized in United States	U.S. citizenship only	U.S. citizenship only	U.S. citizenship only
Residing in United States	Mexican nationality only	1. Mexican nationality[a] 2. U.S. citizenship	1. Mexican nationality[b] 2. U.S. citizenship
After amendment			
Naturalized in United States	1. Mexican nationality 2. U.S. citizenship	1. Mexican nationality 2. U.S. citizenship	U.S. citizenship only
Residing in United States	Mexican nationality only	1. Mexican nationality 2. U.S. citizenship	U.S. citizenship only

a. To exercise the right to Mexican nationality, the person has to elect that status after attaining the age of majority. Election must be accompanied by renunciation of U.S. citizenship. That renunciation, however, would be effective under U.S. law only if the person intended to give up U.S. citizenship.

b. If elected by parent (see note a).

Under the old rules, naturalization produced one citizenship (U.S.) for Mexicans who naturalized and their children. Mexicans who chose to live in the United States without naturalizing transmitted Mexican nationality to their offspring, who were then dual nationals at birth. If the second generation elected at the age of majority to retain their Mexican nationality, they could transmit it to the third generation (and so on) despite their possession of U.S. citizenship. In short, the old rules produced the possibility of dual nationality for all subsequent generations, provided the first-generation parent did not naturalize. Under the new rules, children born to Mexican parents in the United States, whether or not the parents naturalize, will be dual nationals, but their children will not acquire Mexican nationality.

The retention (or reacquisition) of Mexican nationality by naturalized U.S. citizens may cause some Americans concern. The existence of dual nationality implicitly raises the issue of divided loyalty, and the Mexican amendment may be viewed as going further—as attempting to gain for Mexican nationals in the United States access to the U.S. welfare state and influence in the political system without the corresponding attachment to the United States that the naturalization laws are generally thought to secure. The amendment was written, at least in part, as a response to California's Proposition 187, which was widely perceived in Mexico as largely anti-Mexican. The Mexican Ministry of Foreign Relations has stated that the amendment

> corresponds to the Mexican government's interest in taking preventive measures to strengthen migrants' security and interests. . . . [It will] improv[e] the protection of their rights where they reside, support . . . fuller development of their potential in their host countries, and improv[e] their voice and their ability to exert greater influence on the decisions that the communities of which they are a part make.

This line of reasoning parallels that of other states that have recently permitted their nationals to maintain their citizenship when naturalizing in the United States. A 1994 amendment to the Dominican Constitution, clearly aimed at Dominicans in the United States, allows Dominicans to naturalize elsewhere without losing Dominican citizenship. As Pamela Graham has noted, a "prominent theme" in the debate over whether to amend Dominican law "involved the definition of U.S. naturalization as a practical step that did not signal any abandonment of the country of origin." She quotes a proponent of dual citizenship as follows:

> Our people here [in the United States] need to integrate themselves into the political process of this country. It is the only manner of obtaining solutions for problems and attention to the matters that harm us. Because of this, the Dominican must understand that he is not turning his back on his country through accepting U.S. citizenship; to the contrary he is involving himself in the rules of the game. That is absolutely legitimate. We contribute here with funds. . . . Why ignore the benefits of becoming citizens?[53]

In evaluating such statements, one must be attentive to what they do and do not say. First, the claim that naturalization will aid in the protection of the rights of U.S. residents is distinct from the promotion of Mexican (or Dominican) national interests in the U.S. political system. Thus, this motivation for the Mexican amendment does not necessarily implicate the major concern regarding dual nationality: that the dual national will pursue the interests of his or her

---

53. Graham, 1996, p. 166, quoting an excerpt in Viviana Hall, "La doble nacionalidad sigue preocopando al dominicano," *El Dominicano en el Exterior* 11 (June 1985).

country of origin over the interests of fellow Americans. Second, instead of seeing such statements as signs of questionable loyalty, one might view them as emblematic of precisely the kind of behavior that is generally praised in U.S. politics: active involvement in interest-group politics—particularly when it is pursued on behalf of disempowered individuals and groups.

Furthermore, the Mexican amendment was intended to serve goals beyond securing Mexican nationals a place in the U.S. political process. It was responsive also to the desires of Mexicans in the United States who want to maintain ease of travel to and from Mexico for both social and economic reasons. As the Foreign Ministry has stated, the amendment provides "an irrevocable guarantee that [Mexicans] can return to their country of origin at any time . . . with the same rights and obligations as all other Mexicans."

Concern about dual nationality occasioned by the amendment might also be tempered by recognition of the large number of dual nationals previously created by Mexican *jus sanguinis* rules. The March 1996 *Current Population Survey* reported that 260,000 U.S.-citizen children of one year of age or less were living with a Mexican national who had not been naturalized in the United States.[54] All these children presumably obtained dual citizenship at birth—like hundreds of thousands of U.S.-born children before them. Indeed, as mentioned above, the amendment to the Mexican Constitution might cause this number to *decrease* on an annual basis because the amendment limits transmission of citizenship *jure sanguinis* to one generation born outside Mexico.

Finally, there is nothing necessarily inconsistent in being an effective member of the U.S. polity and maintaining commercial or sentimental ties with one's country of origin. The Mexican amendment removes the concern that might keep Mexicans from naturalizing in the United States because of their fear that naturalization would deny their affective ties to Mexico. These deep and understandable human emotions do not necessarily get in the way of loyalty to the United States and successful integration into its social and political system.

The United States could take steps to counteract the effect of changes in other countries' citizenship laws. It could alter the naturalization process to require persons to demonstrate that they have relinquished citizenship elsewhere as of the date of naturalization. This requirement would, for example, make it necessary for Canadians seeking naturalization in the United States to expatriate themselves under Canadian law. Such an approach would be similar to German administrative regulations that require naturalization applicants to renounce citizenship under the laws of their countries of origin. The German

54. Bureau of the Census, March 1996, *Current Population Survey.*

regulations provide an exception for persons from countries that do not permit expatriation (or make it difficult to obtain);[55] but expatriation under Mexican law is possible and not hard to accomplish.

It might be argued that such U.S. action would accomplish what has been intended by the naturalization oath for almost 200 years: that naturalization result in the possession of just one citizenship. But pursuing such a tit-for-tat approach might not be without costs. First, it could be readily evaded by foreign states, which could permit citizens who "expatriate" to keep their passports—or could grant certificates indicating expatriation as people naturalize and simply return citizenship after U.S. naturalization is complete. Australia currently permits "resumption" of citizenship under certain circumstances—for example, when a person can demonstrate that he or she acquired another citizenship (thereby losing that of Australia) in order to avoid significant hardship or detriment.

Second, although a change in U.S. rules could be defended as simply returning the situation to the previous status quo, such a change must be viewed as part of a broader context of growing migration and interdependence. The United States can attempt to turn the clock back to an ideal (but nonexistent) past, or it can recognize a changing world and adapt to it. That world includes the production and maintenance of complicated personal identities—for example, that of a commercial trader operating in two countries under the North American Free Trade Agreement, or a long-term resident unskilled worker who, with the help of modern communications and better transportation, can make both the United States and his or her country of origin "home." Finally, a U.S. rule requiring relinquishment of previously held citizenship prior to naturalization would have the effect of denying citizenship to immigrants from countries that do not permit their citizens to expatriate, making such decisions subject to the control of the state rather than the individual.

There is a better solution than required expatriation that not only would be more open to the complexities of human attachments but also would help sort out some of the problems occasioned by dual citizenship. The United States could enter into bilateral agreements with other countries that provide for the allocation of rights and duties (such as voting, welfare benefits, military service) based on residence or some other criterion. The United States might, for example, conclude a treaty with the Dominican Republic whereby dual citizens

---

55. Exceptions exist, including (a) if the law of the country of nationality does not allow for expatriation; (b) if renunciation is conditioned on unreasonable requirements; (c) if the applicant is a refugee or stateless. "Naturalization Guidelines, section 5.3 (International Aspects)," in *Nationality and Statelessness.*

could vote only in the country in which they are residing, or whereby dual citizens could choose one and only one country in which to vote. This solution would not prevent naturalization for instrumental reasons, but it would help ameliorate some of the perceived problems.

Some might object that this proposal is ineffective because it does little to foster the kind of patriotic sentiment that is perhaps even more crucial today than in the past, given the increasing polyethnism of most developed nations. But it must be remembered that, in the U.S. case, we are primarily speaking about a one-generation concern; because of *jus soli*, the second generation acquires U.S. citizenship automatically and by all accounts is fully acculturated in the U.S. community. Furthermore, while the number of dual citizens born in this country each year is substantial, the United States has never required them to elect one citizenship over the other.

The Renunciation Element of the U.S. Oath

The naturalization oath requires that the applicant "renounce and abjure absolutely and entirely all allegiance and fidelity to any foreign prince, potentate, state, or sovereignty of whom or which the applicant was before a subject or citizen." If one's country of origin holds that naturalization in the United States is not expatriating, what does it mean to swear to this oath? Suppose the naturalized citizen chooses to travel on a passport issued by his or her country of origin, or chooses to travel home to vote. Has the oath been violated, even if the person's actions are entirely legal under the law of his or her country of origin?[56]

One remedy for these perceived difficulties would be to delete the renunciation requirement from the oath. The result, of course, would be an open embrace of dual citizenship for naturalized citizens. Peter Spiro has supported such a move:

> In a world of liberal states . . . the necessity of exclusive allegiances has largely dissipated; where peace prevails, there is no inconsistency in dual or even multiple attachments. . . .
>
> Maintaining additional national attachments becomes an expression of individual identity, both a reflection of and a contributor to community ties, and a mechanism for undertaking civic participation in that sphere;

56. And, what notice, if any, should the United States take of a naturalized citizen's attempt to reestablish Mexican nationality? (Under Supreme Court doctrine described above, presumably naturalized citizens could seek to reestablish nationality in their country of prior citizenship without loss of U.S. citizenship.)

and the facilitation of these virtues will . . . ultimately benefit society as well as the individual. . . .

Now secure in its unrivaled strength, the U.S. should move fully to embrace those to whom it has otherwise opened its doors.[57]

Deletion of the renunciation requirement would end the anomaly (mentioned earlier) whereby persons naturalizing in the United States must renounce other allegiances, while U.S. citizens naturalizing in other countries are under no such obligation. This would be consistent with the more welcoming attitude toward dual citizenship now developing in Europe and elsewhere,[58] and it would remove an existing disincentive to naturalization.

How strong are these arguments when weighed against the 200-year history of the renunciation requirement? The argument that a renunciation requirement unreasonably dissuades immigrants from naturalizing has been pressed primarily by commentators in Germany, where naturalization rates have historically been low.[59] Sustaining this claim in the United States is difficult, however, because the United States has always had a relatively high naturalization rate and is witnessing record levels today. Furthermore, because of *jus soli*, the impact of the renunciation requirement is in the case of United States limited to one generation, whereas in the case of Germany, which has no *jus soli* provisions, it affects the second generation and beyond.

Thus the argument for deleting the renunciation requirement is not compelling. Yet with increasing numbers of countries not considering naturalization in the United States as grounds for removing the citizenship of their nationals, the "renounce and abjure absolutely" language puts naturalizing citizens in a peculiar position, to say the least.

Lawrence Fuchs has suggested a route out of this conundrum that neither requires proof of relinquishment nor calls for simple deletion of the renunciation mandate. He proposes an oath that recognizes the *primacy* but not necessarily the *exclusivity* of allegiance to the United States. His oath would read:

57. Spiro, 1997, pp. 1416, 1484. Indeed, part of Spiro's argument for abandoning the renunciation requirement is that it is a disincentive to naturalization. See similar arguments concerning Germany in Brubaker, 1992, pp. 77–78. See also, Hammar, 1989.

58. In 1997, the Council of Europe drafted a proposal to amend the 1963 convention on the reduction of dual nationality that would allow children born with dual nationalities and individuals acquiring dual nationality by marriage to retain their original nationality. Council of Europe Parliamentary Assembly, 1997. In addition, the proposal would provide that states could not condition the acquisition or retention of nationality on the renunciation or loss of another nationality "where such renunciation or loss is not possible or cannot reasonably be required."

59. See Hammar, 1989. See also, Brubaker, 1992; and Neuman, 1992.

I, [name], take this solemn oath . . . freely and without mental reservation or purpose of evasion. My allegiance is to the United States of America above any other nation. I promise to support and honor the Constitution and laws of my new country and their principles of liberty and justice for all. I pledge to defend them by force of arms, noncombatant military service, or civilian work of national importance if necessary.[60]

Fuchs's proposal is consistent with a recommendation of a committee of the Canadian Parliament in a 1994 report on citizenship. The report expressed concern about dual citizenship and suggested a reconsideration of the 1977 citizenship law that permitted Canadians to retain Canadian citizenship when naturalizing in another country. It did not propose a renunciatory oath for immigrants seeking Canadian naturalization, recommending instead that naturalizing citizens "be required to declare as a condition of receiving their citizenship that they will accord primacy to their Canadian citizenship over all other citizenships."[61]

Such proposals preserve the important message of the oath that naturalization in the United States is about more than obtaining rights or benefiting from a welfare state. Attaining citizenship signifies belonging, commitment, loyalty, a willingness to sacrifice if called upon to do so. But it also recognizes that loyalty is not indivisible. As current U.S. practice shows—given the growth of dual citizenship attributable to the numbers of children born in the United States to alien parents—dual loyalties can exist without shaking the foundations of the Republic. While some see dual citizenship as membership bigamy, it is probably more appropriate to recognize it as the relationship that one has with one's family and one's in-laws. Such relationships at times produce conflict and need negotiation, but one can still be a functioning member of two families, loyal to both.

A "primacy, not exclusivity" oath would continue to serve the gatekeeping function provided by the current renunciation requirement. Immigrants who feel themselves unable to affirm the primacy of their allegiance to the United States would not be able to naturalize. At the same time, such an oath would assist immigrants who want to naturalize but are caught between an oath that requires renunciation and laws in their home country that permit dual nationality.

60. "Citizenship 1996," Hearings, October 22, 1996. Testimony of Lawrence Fuchs.

61. Canada, Parliament—House of Commons, Standing Committee on Citizenship and Immigration, 1994, *Canadian Citizenship*, pp. 15–16. In Austria, the citizenship oath established in 1948 did not require renunciation of former citizenships, but a provision was added in 1973 that provided for the explicit renunciation of prior citizenships.

Finally, it should be recognized that a growing acceptance of dual citizenship is not simply the unilateral product of "sending" countries' changes in law. Constituencies in "receiving" countries—particularly commercial ones—have recognized the benefits of dual citizenship for fostering binational ties. Thus, a 1994 submission by the Australian Department of Immigration and Ethnic Affairs considering changes in citizenship law noted support from the business community for dual citizenship because of the advantages of possessing a foreign passport (particularly within the European Union) in facilitating international travel.

Rights and Benefits: How Citizenship Makes a Difference

In a famous essay, T. H. Marshall notes that "citizenship is a status bestowed on those who are full members of a community." The possessors of that status "are equal with respect to the rights and duties with which the status is endowed."[62] The concept of "equal citizenship" has, since adoption of the Fourteenth Amendment, been a core constitutional principle.[63] What are the rights and duties equally endowed to citizens that define the status of citizenship—and that are, by pertaining to citizens as citizens, by inference denied to noncitizens? The following three sections examine this question in relation to individual rights held against the government, the right to participate in government, and the legality of differential treatment based on alienage.

Rights Held against the Government

The Constitution applies most of its protections to "persons," a term generally understood to be more capacious than "citizens." Accordingly, aliens—as well as citizens—are guaranteed due process in criminal and civil proceedings, benefit from the First Amendment's protection of freedom of speech and religion, are entitled to a lawyer at a criminal trial, may assert a right against self-incrimination, and may not be subjected to unreasonable searches and seizures. These rights apply *irrespective of immigration status*; they protect permanent resident aliens, nonimmigrant visitors, asylum-seekers, and undocumented aliens alike. The Constitution's focus on "persons" led constitu-

---

62. Marshall, 1992, p. 18.

63. See Karst, 1997. I have argued elsewhere that "equal citizenship"—not color blindness—is the true message of Justice Harlan's celebrated dissent in *Plessy v. Ferguson,* 163 U.S. 537 (1896). See Aleinikoff, 1992.

tional scholar Alexander Bickel, writing in 1975, to note that "remarkably enough . . . the concept of citizenship plays only the most minimal role in the American constitutional scheme."[64]

Rights to Participate in Government

The right to political participation is frequently identified as the core difference that citizenship makes. Aliens are not entitled to vote in state or federal elections.[65] Although it is not generally known, immigrants did vote in the United States throughout the nineteenth century—at a time when the majority of U.S. citizens could not vote, because of exclusions based on race and gender (1928 was the first presidential election in which no state permitted aliens to vote).[66] The close linkage drawn today between citizenship and voting rights is thus of fairly recent vintage. Furthermore, there are some indications that alien voting may be regaining acceptability at the local level. Several U.S. localities have recently made permanent resident aliens eligible to vote in local elections;[67] and the European Union's Maastricht Treaty grants citizens of member states the right to vote in local and EU elections when they reside in any member state.[68]

Although aliens have no constitutional right to participate in elections, they do enjoy First Amendment rights. They would therefore be protected against legislation that purported to bar their participation in political demonstrations or other nonvoting activities. Accordingly, current proposals to prohibit immigrants from making campaign contributions raise difficult constitutional questions.[69]

64. Bickel, 1975, p. 33.
65. The Colorado Supreme Court, in a decision the U.S. Supreme Court refused to review, found that it is clearly constitutional to deny aliens the right to vote. *Skafte v. Rorex,* 553 P.2d 830 (1976); appeal dismissed 430 U.S. 961 (1977). But see also, Rosberg, 1977, p. 1092.
66. See Rosberg, 1977; Raskin, 1993.
67. See, for example, Raskin, 1993 (discussing the 1992 decision of the people of Takoma Park, Maryland, to amend the city's charter and extend the franchise to noncitizens in local elections).
68. Maastricht Treaty, translated in Corbett, 1993. In the fall of 1990, however, the Federal Republic of Germany's Federal Constitutional Court invalidated statutes of two states granting certain resident aliens the right to vote in local elections. See Neuman, 1992, p. 260.
69. It is an interesting question whether prohibitions on campaign contributions are constitutional. See, for example, Brown, 1997, p. 503. See also, "'Foreign' Campaign Contributions and the First Amendment," 1997.

The Constitution draws but one distinction between native-born and natural-ized citizens:[70] Only a native-born citizen may be president of the United States. (This rule means, for instance, that Secretary of State Madeleine Albright, who otherwise would be the first woman to stand fourth in the line of presidential succession, is ineligible to serve as president.)

Differential Treatment Based on Alienage

In the nineteenth century, aliens faced a wide array of restrictions on land-ownership, inheritance, access to occupations, and governmental employment. The Supreme Court was willing to nullify state discrimination that it attributed to racial animus (chiefly against Chinese and Japanese immigrants) or that it found to interfere with federal regulation of immigration.[71] But most state rules drawing distinctions based on alienage were upheld well into this century. The significant shift came in the 1972 case *Graham v. Richardson*, which invalidated state laws denying immigrants welfare benefits made available to citizens. In a terse discussion, the Court held that aliens constitute a "discrete and insular" minority on whose behalf the judiciary would closely scrutinize discriminatory state laws. Laws not supported by a compelling state interest and not drawn in a precise manner would be held to run afoul of the Fourteenth Amendment's equal protection clause.[72] After *Graham v. Richardson*, the Court invalidated state laws that prohibited aliens from being civil engineers, lawyers, and state civil servants, or barred aliens from eligibility for state higher-education grants.[73]

The high-water mark of protection was reached in 1982, when the Court struck down a Texas statute authorizing local school districts to exclude undocumented alien children from public schools.[74] While it recognized that undocumented aliens were not a class entitled to special protection under the Fourteenth Amendment, the Court nonetheless invalidated the Texas policy. It found unpersuasive the state's justifications for the statute (including the claim

70. No other significant differences in federal statutes exist except for denaturalization, which, of course, only applies to naturalized citizens.

71. See, for example, *Yick Wo v. Hopkins*, 118 U.S. 356 (1886); *Takahasi v. Fish and Game Commission*, 334 U.S. 410 (1948); *Truax v. Raich*, 239 U.S. 33 (1915).

72. *Graham v. Richardson*, 403 U.S. 365 (1971). The phrase "discrete and insular minority" is a term of art for the Court, signaling groups for whom special judicial protection is appropriate. See *United States v. Carolene Products Co.*, 304 U.S. 144, 152 n.4 (1938).

73. *Examining Board of Engineers v. Otero*, 426 U.S. 572 (1976) (civil engineering); *In re Griffiths*, 413 U.S. 717 (1973) (admission to the bar); *Sugarman v. Dougall*, 413 U.S. 634 (1973) (state civil service); *Nyquist v. Mauclet*, 432 U.S. 1 (1977) (education grants).

74. *Plyler v. Doe*, 457 U.S. 202 (1982).

that the policy would deter illegal immigration), particularly when these were weighed against the harm imposed on the children—and ultimately on U.S. society:

> [The statute] imposes a lifetime hardship on a discrete class of children not accountable for their disabling status. The stigma of illiteracy will mark them for the rest of their lives. By denying these children a basic education, we deny them the ability to live within the structure of our civic institutions, and foreclose any realistic possibility that they will contribute in even the smallest way to the progress of our Nation.[75]

Not all state laws based on alienage are impermissible, however. The justices carved out an exception to *Graham v. Richardson*, recognizing that "some state functions are so bound up with the operation of a State as a governmental entity as to permit the exclusion from those functions of all persons who have not become part of the process of self-government."[76] The exception has been read, rather expansively, to uphold state statutes disqualifying aliens from being teachers, police officers, and probation officers.[77]

The Supreme Court has been far more tolerant of *federal* laws that discriminate against aliens. The Court has given Congress wide berth to enact immigration regulations, upholding statutes that would be unconstitutional if applied to citizens.[78] Indeed, exercise of the immigration power constitutes one of the chief ways in which aliens and citizens are treated differently: aliens are subject to Congress's deportation power; citizens are not—there is no congressional power to exile or banish U.S. citizens. Furthermore, citizens have significant advantages over immigrants in sponsoring immigrant relatives to the United States. And only citizens are eligible for U.S. passports and for protection by U.S. authorities outside the territory of the United States.

The Court's deference to congressional exercise of the immigration power is based on its belief that immigration regulations frequently involve foreign affairs matters, an area where judicial intervention is deemed inappropriate. In several startling opinions, the Supreme Court has declared that aliens at the bor-

---

75. *Plyler v. Doe,* 457 U.S. 223 (1982).

76. *Ambach v. Norwich,* 441 U.S. 68, 73 (1979); see also *Sugarman v. Dougall,* 413 U.S. 634 (1973).

77. *Ambach v. Norwich,* 441 U.S. 68, 73 (1979) (teachers); *Foley v. Connelie,* 435 U.S. 291 (1978) (police officers); *Cabell v. Chavez-Salido,* 454 U.S. 432 (1982) (probation officers).

78. *Fiallo v. Bell,* 430 U.S. 737 (1977), for example, upholding law making it harder for alien fathers to reunite with illegitimate children than alien mothers. Judicial deference is traceable to the Court's validation of the ignominious Chinese Exclusion laws. *Chae Chan Ping v. United States,* 130 U.S. 581 (1889). See Henkin, 1987, p. 853.

der of the United States seeking initial entry have no constitutional rights; "whatever the procedure authorized by Congress is," the Court wrote in a 1950 case, "it is due process as far as an alien denied entry is concerned."[79] These cases, remnants of the attitudes of an earlier day, continue to be cited with approval by the Court.[80]

The Court has applied this lax standard of review not only to immigration regulations regarding classes of entrants and grounds of exclusion and deportation, but also to federal regulations based on alienage. Thus, it has upheld federal laws that discriminate against aliens in the receipt of federal benefits and access to the federal civil service[81]—even though similar laws adopted by states would be held unconstitutional.

Despite its power to discriminate on the basis of alienage, however, Congress has not done so, until recently, to any significant degree. Indeed, settled immigrants live lives largely indistinguishable from those of most U.S. citizens. Although they cannot vote and may be ineligible for some government employment, they work, own property, have access to the courts, can be members of most professions, and exercise most constitutional rights on the same terms as native-born and naturalized citizens.

The 1996 welfare law sharply deviates from this general picture. The statute draws a hard line between immigrants and citizens, disqualifying future entrants from eligibility. (Initially the law terminated assistance to resident aliens already within the United States. In the budget agreement of 1997, disability payments under Supplemental Security Income [SSI] were reinstated for these immigrants; and in 1998 eligibility for food stamps was restored for some.) The legislation mandates states to deny some benefits and authorizes them to withhold others. These latter provisions pose the serious constitutional question of whether the federal government can authorize states to discriminate against aliens in a manner that would be unconstitutional if adopted by the state alone.

In the view of some, the welfare law simply provides a necessary extension of existing rules of responsibility for immigrants and their sponsors. Congressmen Lamar Smith (R-Tex.) and E. Clay Shaw Jr. (R-Fla.) have argued that, for many years, immigration law has barred the entry of aliens "likely to become a public charge," and has required some sponsors to execute affidavits of support promising to take care of the relatives they bring to the United States should they fall on hard times. Congressmen Smith and Shaw further note the high

---

79. *United States ex rel. Knauff v. Shaughnessy,* 338 U.S. 537, 544 (1950); *Shaughnessy v. United States ex rel. Mezei,* 345 U.S. 206 (1953).

80. *Fiallo v. Bell,* 430 U.S. 737 (1977); *Landon v. Plasencia,* 459 U.S. 2 (1982).

81. *Mathews v. Diaz,* 426 U.S. 67 (1976); *Hampton v. Mow Sun Wong,* 426 U.S. 88 (1976).

level of immigrant participation in welfare programs, particularly the SSI program (in 1996, legal immigrants constituted less than 6 percent of the population but received more than 50 percent of SSI benefits paid to the elderly).[82] In this view, the welfare law is closely linked to Congress's traditional exercise of the immigration power.

From another perspective the welfare law represents a paradigm shift in this nation's thinking about the difference that citizenship makes. Some defended the disqualification of immigrants in definitional terms: Congressman Frank Riggs (R-Calif.), for example, stated that "the message that we are sending here, and we are clearly stating to our fellow citizens, [is] that we really are going to put the rights and needs of American citizens first."[83] This bright line, on-off switch is a dramatic shift from post–World War II era public policy understandings, which were based on a recognition that settled immigrants participate in and contribute to their communities and the nation in ways similar to those of U.S. citizens and therefore are entitled to equal treatment. The Supreme Court adopted this latter position in the *Graham v. Richardson* case, where it noted its agreement with a lower court's reasoning that the

> justification of limiting expenses is particularly inappropriate and unreasonable when the discriminated class consists of aliens. Aliens like citizens pay taxes and may be called into the armed forces. . . . [They] may live within a state for many years, work in the state and contribute to the economic growth of the state.[84]

Models of Membership

So far this study has examined rules regarding citizenship and naturalization and the rights and opportunities that accompany the status of citizenship. These rules vary widely among nations of the world, and even among Western democracies. The welter of rules may appear incoherent—for example, why must aliens who naturalize in the United States renounce prior citizenship while U.S. citizens naturalizing elsewhere are allowed to keep their U.S. citizenship? Why does Australia have precisely the opposite rules? It is probable that the underlying structure of each nation's membership rules taps deep into its own political and cultural traditions and historical experience.[85] As the following discussion

82. Shaw and Smith (May 28, 1997), p. A19.
83. U.S. House of Representatives, Congressman Riggs speaking about H.R. 3406, *Congressional Record,* 104th Cong., 1st sess., 1995, vol. 141, p. 412.
84. *Congressional Record,* 104th Cong., 1st sess., 1995, vol. 141, p. 376.
85. See, for example, Brubaker, 1992, pp. x–xi.

will demonstrate, this structure rests as much on the rejection of certain traditional principles of membership as it does on the embrace of others.

Despite a legal history of citizenship replete with racial exclusions,[86] the
United States' architecture of membership is not based on the principle of
ethnocultural unity. There is no ethnic or racial group for which the United
States has been created or sustained, and an impregnable tradition of *jus soli*
coupled with immigration from all over the world guarantees a polyethnic nation. Although some recent literature, which has received widespread attention
in the media, has identified the United States as a "white nation" under threat
from immigration from nonwhite countries of origin, this view remains outside
the mainstream of U.S. politics. It has been repudiated by a several-hun-
dred-year history to the contrary and a deeply held political commitment to ethnic pluralism.

At the other end of the spectrum is the principle of membership based on
mere *physical presence* in the United States. Support for this principle appears
both in political and legal theories that extend the Constitution's protections to
all persons within U.S. territory and in international human rights law. The preceding discussion makes clear that, in the U.S. legal system, presence counts
for something—the Constitution does apply to all persons within the geographical boundaries of the United States. Indeed, the fact that U.S.-born children of
undocumented aliens are U.S. citizens lends some support to the claim that the
U.S. membership model turns primarily on presence.

But the principle of citizenship also counts for something in the U.S. system.
Its significance is clearest in the distribution of political rights. The exercise of
state authority over individuals might seem like grounds for endowing them
with political rights, but it has never been argued that the right to vote should be
extended to all persons within the territory of the United States. While some
scholars have declared the coming of a postnational world,[87] the U.S. model of
membership remains far from postnational.[88]

An appropriate U.S. model of membership cannot define full membership in
ethnocultural terms, and it must give weight to both presence and citizenship. In
this middle space are three models of membership: *lawful settlement as membership, citizenship as membership*, and *transnational membership*.

---

86. See Smith, 1997; and López, 1996.
87. See, for example, Appadurai, 1993.
88. And however persuasive one might find Yasemin Soysal's account of a "postnational"
membership in Europe, it does not seem an apt description of the U.S. system. See Soysal, 1994.

Lawful Settlement as Membership

Most immigrants reside in the United States in a manner that differs little from the everyday lives of citizens. Tomas Hammar has labeled this model of membership "denizenship," an English concept dating back centuries under which the monarch granted aliens the right to reside in the kingdom and to enjoy most of the privileges of citizenship. Hammar describes denizenship as follows:

> Some noncitizens . . . stand in a close relationship to the state, a relationship defined by an array of rights and duties . . . that links a citizen to his state. Some noncitizens, like citizens, have the right to enter the state's territory from abroad, to settle in the country, to take up work there, to receive social benefits, even, in some circumstances, to vote. Legal differences between citizens and these privileged noncitizens have tended to diminish.[89]

The crucial element here is lawful settlement, which in the United States is a creation of constitutional and statutory precedent. As noted above, the Supreme Court has extended constitutional rights to aliens and has struck down most state laws that discriminated on the basis of alienage. Federal statutory law entitles permanent resident aliens, refugees, asylees, and other classes of aliens to reside and work in the United States and to leave and reenter. Before the passage of the 1996 welfare law, permanent resident aliens were eligible for most federal benefits available to citizens.

The lawful settlement model takes notice that resident aliens function in U.S. society in a manner largely indistinguishable from citizens. They work, attend houses of worship, join social organizations, attend sporting events, and participate in their children's schools. Many are also the parents of U.S. citizens. Along with their residential ties, their contribution to the economic and social life of the nation—in terms of both participation and tax payments—entitles them to social benefits.

Lawful settlement does not, however, entail political rights. It understands immigrants to be members in one sense, but it also recognizes that citizenship remains the basic currency of self-government. Citizens may choose to give immigrants certain political rights, including the right to vote in local elections.

---

89. See Hammar, 1989, p. 83. Hammar is thinking particularly here of children of immigrants in *jus sanguinis* countries: "Some [denizens] may have been born in the country and never lived anywhere else; they may speak the language of the country with perfect fluency, and may perhaps speak no other language." Hammar, 1989, p. 84.

This is consistent with the model's recognition of the close ties that settled immigrants develop with their communities of residence.

It is important, however, to distinguish the lawful settlement model from a membership model based simply on presence. Status is crucial to the former, but not the latter. Immigrants granted membership rights have a status entitling them to work and to remain indefinitely in the United States. Thus, lawful settlement describes the situation of permanent resident aliens, refugees, and asylees, but not nonimmigrants (visitors, students, temporary workers) or aliens granted a temporary protected status. The 1986 legislation legalizing the status of long-term illegal immigrants is the exception that proves the rule: The legalization programs recognized both the contributions of long-term undocumented aliens and the fact that many were, for all intents and purposes, members of U.S. society. But the programs did not extend social benefits to this population; rather, the legislation legalized their status (permitting them to apply for permanent resident alien status a number of months later), and rights and benefits followed from that legalized status.

The lawful settlement as membership model rests on a distinction similar to one drawn by Rainer Bauböck between social membership in a society and political membership in a polity. These two realms of membership overlap but are not coextensive. Bauböck argues that social membership "is acquired gradually and mainly as a function of the length of residence."[90] By contrast, political membership is determined more by volitional choice. In his view, if liberal democratic polities do not confer the necessary menu of social rights to enable all resident aliens to participate fully in civic life, they risk undermining the social foundations of democratic governance by creating a permanent subclass of marginalized members.

A lawful settlement model might well support "statutes of limitations" on deportation grounds. After a certain number of years of lawful residence in the United States, an immigrant might be deemed to be so much a part of U.S. society that his or her deportation would constitute an unduly harsh penalty. Congress has never gone so far,[91] but it has provided long-term residents the opportunity for relief from deportation. In keeping with this model, permanent resident aliens have an easier time obtaining relief than other aliens.

The lawful settlement model is consistent with *jus soli* or *jus sanguinis*. Because little, other than political rights, would separate resident aliens and citizens, it could tolerate a *jus sanguinis* regime that produced several generations

---

90. Bauböck, 1994, p. 173; see also generally, pp. 172–77, 232–48.
91. It should be noted that some deportation grounds are limited to certain number of years after entry.

of aliens in the host country. The equal treatment of immigrants and citizens would not provide an incentive to naturalize; naturalization would be, however, available on fairly easy terms for those immigrants who wanted, for affective reasons, to attain citizenship. Dual citizenship might well be tolerated under a lawful settlement model, but the state would have no reason to foster it. Crucial to the model is the contribution of residents (citizen and immigrant) to the society. If immigrants are seen as almost full members, there is little reason to deny membership to those who choose to naturalize but also want to maintain a prior allegiance.

If the basis of the lawful settlement model is recognition of the social ties and economic contributions of long-term resident aliens, then the model would suggest skepticism toward the transmission of citizenship to generations born outside the country. Under an ethnocultural model, citizenship *jure sanguinis* outside the territory of the country is not a problem; blood, not geography, is the motivating factor. The lawful settlement model's focus on the social and economic participation of residents, in contrast, raises questions about whether overseas citizens are adequately attached not to the nation's political philosophy but to its daily life. This concern is heightened in the case of a mature welfare state in which overseas citizens can return home and claim access to state benefits simply on the basis of their citizenship. Developments in German nationality law display this concern: at the same time that Germany is considering easing naturalization requirements for long-term resident immigrants, it is reducing benefits to ethnic Germans born outside its borders who, in cold war days, were entitled to enter Germany and were eligible for significant public support. A recent Canadian parliamentary report also notes concern that some Canadian dual citizens view Canadian citizenship

> as an "insurance policy," which they may wish to use in the future, while in the meantime residing elsewhere. Among the advantages of such a "policy" would be the guaranteed right to retire in Canada and have access to whatever benefits are then available to residents—health care in particular—without having contributed in taxes to the country.[92]

Citizenship as Membership

In 1996—in a statement that underscores the predominant understanding of membership in lawful settlement terms—Saskia Sassen could write that "when

---

92. Canada, Parliament—House of Commons, Standing Committee on Citizenship and Immigration, 1994, *Canadian Citizenship*, p. 15.

it comes to social services (education, health insurance, welfare, unemployment benefits) citizenship status is of minor importance in the United States and Western Europe."[93] But the subsequent U.S. immigration and welfare legislation of the same year requires amendment of Sassen's declaration: citizenship status has come to mean a great deal in terms of eligibility for social benefits. So, too, does the significant tightening of provisions for relief from deportation indicate movement away from lawful settlement as an adequate rendering of membership. The United States seems to be shifting to a different model—one that is here labeled as citizenship as membership.

Citizenship as membership identifies citizens as the core members of the nation who constitute the body of people charged with exercising state power and on whose behalf the state acts. It is, as it were, government of the citizenry, by the citizenry, and for the citizenry. A model that starts with these premises views noncitizens as nonmembers. Supreme Court Justice Byron White captured this image in a case upholding a state requirement that parole officers be citizens of the United States:

> The exclusion of aliens from basic governmental processes is not a deficiency but a necessary consequence of a community's process of political self-definition. Self-government, whether direct or through representatives, begins by defining the scope of the community of the governed and thus of the governors as well; *aliens are by definition outside this community.*[94]

Justice Hugo Black, in an important denationalization case, put it this way: "Citizenship in this Nation is a part of a cooperative affair. Its citizenry is the country and the country is its citizenry."[95]

These statements appear to make citizenship as membership the natural consequence of the establishment of a political community. But to recognize that citizens belong to "a cooperative affair" is not necessarily to equate citizenship with membership. As described above, noncitizens in the United States possess a wide array of rights protected by the United States Constitution. These are not acts of grace and charity extended by a beneficent government of citizens. They are written into the fundamental document establishing this political community. One can thus talk of a constitutional community of which all persons present in the United States are members. This does not "disprove" a citizenship as

93. Sassen, 1996.
94. *Cabell v. Chavez-Salido,* 454 U.S. 432, 439-40 (1982), italics added.
95. *Afroyim v. Rusk,* 387 U.S. 253, 268 (1967).

membership model; but it does mean that such a model is not mandated simply by the concept of citizenship.

More important, the statements by the justices are a bit hyperbolic. Resident immigrants are not "outside the community of the governed"; they are subject to the laws and the authority of the United States. Nor is "the country" in any obvious way constituted only by citizens—unless one simply asserts that, by definition, the millions of aliens in the United States are not included in the term "the country." Both statements do, however, represent a deeply held view that U.S. citizenship is exceedingly valuable, that it stands for something, and that its value is not measured simply by the number of rights granted to citizens and denied to aliens. Citizens *are*, and feel themselves to be, part of a cooperative venture. The question is what should follow from that fact—not as a matter of definition, but as a matter of policy.

Citizenship as membership draws a sharp line between citizens and aliens, placing aliens not just within the next concentric circle but outside the circle of membership altogether. Aliens are guests, present at the sufferance of and under the conditions established by a government ruled by and for citizens. They are not entitled to social benefits,[96] they may be ineligible for state and federal employment, and they may be excluded from opportunities in the private sphere that citizens want to maintain for members only. Such logic underlies several recent legislative proposals, such as banning resident aliens from contributing money to political campaigns and adopting special rules for resident aliens seeking to purchase firearms.[97]

Supreme Court case law casts doubt on the complete realization of the model. The Court has held that states may not exclude aliens from most benefit programs and job opportunities (public and private). As noted above, however, such restrictions do not apply to the federal government; and Congress, in the 1996 welfare legislation, made the most of its authority—not only cutting off lawful permanent resident aliens from most means-tested federal programs but also purportedly authorizing states to do the same.

Citizenship as membership leans toward—though it does not compel—a regime of *jus sanguinis*. It would be sensible under this model for citizenship to pass by descent only from other citizens. *Jus soli*, in contrast, allows nonmem-

---

96. As Justice Stevens wrote in *Mathews v. Diaz*, "Neither the overnight visitor, the unfriendly agent of a hostile foreign power, the resident diplomat, nor the illegal entrant, can advance even a colorable constitutional claim to a share in the bounty that a conscientious sovereign makes available to its own citizens and Some of its guests." *Mathews v. Diaz*, 426 U.S. 67, 80 (1976).

97. It is interesting to see the National Rifle Association (NRA) take up the rights of aliens in opposing a legislative proposal that would have limited some legal alien's ability to purchase guns. See, for example, Rovella (March 17, 1997), p. A9.

bers (even illegal nonmembers) to create new members. The state might well be open to naturalization, perhaps even promoting it in a desire to grant rights to those living in its territory, while maintaining citizenship as the relevant category for rights possession.

The model views dual citizenship with disfavor. Given the core significance of citizenship, it might well be questioned how a person could develop an appropriate level of commitment and loyalty to two separate polities.

Transnational Membership

A third membership model understands the symbolic importance of citizenship but also takes into account the increasingly fluid world in which we live. The lawful settlement model focuses on the concrete experiences of settled immigrants; *transnationalism* goes one step further. It recognizes that persons may well fully function as members of two societies: that of the country of their (or their parents') birth and that of their current country of residence. Without denying the existence or relevance of borders and states, transnational membership recognizes the increasing possibility of individuals being members of two states, either as citizens of one and settled immigrants of another, or as citizens of both.

The transnational membership model has both descriptive and normative aspects. Modern communications and transportation not only support migratory flows but also make possible the retention or creation of relations with communities in countries of origin. Popular mythology aside, immigration to the United States has never been a one-way affair; perhaps as many as a third of those who came to the United States during the great wave of immigration in the early decades of this century returned to their countries of origin.[98] These migratory circuits are far easier to establish and maintain today than in the past (not only by way of jet planes and telephones but also by fax and electronic mail). Thus, a naturalized U.S. citizen born in India can own a chain of hotels in Pennsylvania and seek to expand to Bombay;[99] a Mexican with a green card can live in Tijuana and cross the border daily to work in San Diego; a Dominican American can be a political leader in Washington Heights and Santo

---

98. Portes and Rumbaut, 1996, p. 101. The majority of immigrants entering the United States in the 1920s considered themselves transitory sojourners whose ultimate goal was to return to their country of origin. "Although most were to settle eventually in America, this final outcome did not preclude their viewing the journey as temporary and instrumental."

99. Wysocki, (May 12, 1997), p. B1.

Domingo;[100] a Haitian migrant in the United States is considered a member of the "Tenth Department" of Haiti.[101]

The normative element of the transnational model is the claim that membership in more than one state is good for individuals as well as for the two societies. It affirms important aspects of human identity by not forcing a person to choose one set of relations over another; and it allows communities to benefit from the cosmopolitanism fostered by connections with other parts of the world.

The transnational membership model would adopt the lawful settlement perspective on access to social benefits. It would recognize that citizenship elsewhere would not necessarily undermine one's attachment to and participation in the United States. But it would go further than the lawful settlement model by valuing, rather than simply tolerating, close ties with the home country and dual citizenship. It would conclude that, on balance, the benefits of multiple memberships outweigh the costs (which are arguably significantly diminished in a world largely at peace). Viewing multiple allegiances as largely nonthreatening, transnationalism would also be open to the idea of dual citizens voting in both countries of citizenship.

Transnationalism is not postnationalism. It recognizes, as does a postnationalist perspective, that states are not impermeable geographic or social units. While the transnational perspective values citizenship and notions of loyalty and commitment, it recognizes that human beings can, and frequently do, maintain plural allegiances. While some may view the multiple allegiances affirmed by transnationalism as fundamentally inconsistent with the degree of commitment required by citizenship, supporters of the transnational model can reply that the vast majority of U.S. citizens achieve citizenship by birth in the United States and thereby acquire a firm grounding in U.S. culture and history that is likely to make their U.S. citizenship of primary significance.

Reaffirming the Lawful Settlement Model of Membership

In many countries, the nation preceded the state. In the United States it has been the other way around: the state created the nation, and the nation is identified not by ethnic or racial background but by the status of citizenship. U.S. citizens are the "We, the People" of the U.S. Constitution, and they are the "Americans" referred to by the rest of the world. Bounded political communities need a definition of membership, and democracies need a concept of the

100. See Graham, 1996; Guarnizo, forthcoming 1998.
101. Basch et al., 1994.

"demos," or the people. Citizenship can serve that function, defining the governors and those on whose behalf they govern. These theoretical premises undergird the significant intuitive appeal of the citizenship as membership model—an appeal heightened by the sense of fragmentation-at-large in the world today. The citizenship as membership model offers unifying concepts that can call forth loyalty and allegiance—not in the name of a particular ethnic group or religion, but in the name of a self-governing political community.

A concept of who governs, however, is not necessarily congruent with a concept of membership. Nor does the identification of governors necessarily identify those on whose behalf they govern. Although citizenship as membership has intuitive appeal, it is not the model of membership that has prevailed in the United States for some time. As noted above, the Constitution's protections extend significantly beyond citizens, and federal law has—until very recently—extended most benefits and opportunities to large numbers of resident immigrants. Immigration law has made naturalization available on fairly easy terms, and has provided avenues of relief from deportation for long-term resident aliens. These attributes of U.S. law and policy display a model of membership broader than citizenship; they seem most consistent with the lawful settlement model.

Why is this? Why has U.S. membership policy not made more turn on the concept of citizenship? First, the acquisition of citizenship traditionally has been understood as part of the broader process of immigration and acculturation. Naturalization is seen as a good thing—as a major step in fully joining the U.S. polity. A membership theory broader than citizenship gives recognition to this process of acculturation. It recognizes that resident immigrants are not merely nonmembers; rather, they are full-members-in-training. Citizenship is not commanded of immigrants, but it is expected of them.

Second, the United States conceives of itself as a "nation of immigrants." Except for the Native Americans, we all came from somewhere else. Thus we see in the current flow of immigrants our past and our nation's past. Immigrants are not merely guests. They are the history and the future of the United States.

Third, notions of membership are frequently linked with notions of contribution. People who work, pay taxes, and volunteer in organizations lay a claim to membership. In the past, the polity has responded to the implicit claim of lawful resident immigrants for rights and opportunities in recognition of their economic, social, and cultural contributions.

A decision to move beyond the lawful settlement understanding of membership to a citizenship as membership approach would not be indefensible. But it would be inadvisable. Quite simply, there are ways to make citizenship special—to affirm values of loyalty and allegiance—other than by disadvantaging

immigrants, particularly when such measures in fact increase demand for naturalization for the very reasons deemed troubling by supporters of citizenship as
membership.

Maintaining the lawful settlement approach also argues against a transnational understanding of membership. Transnationalism recognizes important
developments in modern migrations, but it is ultimately a one-generation
story.[102] The fact that all children born in the United States are automatically citizens begins a powerful acculturation process that usually overwhelms the influences from the home country. While many Americans (of whatever
generation) value the cultures of their ancestors' home states, little evidence has
appeared that transnationalism—in the sense of simultaneous memberships of
equal strength in two states—is strongly felt among second and later generations in the United States. Furthermore, a transnational model of membership,
which values and affirms multiple allegiances, is likely to foster a strong political backlash with uncertain consequences.

Conclusion

In a 1989 essay, Peter Schuck called attention to what he termed the "devaluation of American citizenship."[103] Schuck noted that citizenship was easy to obtain (under *jus soli* principles and easy-to-meet naturalization requirements)
and hard to lose (given Supreme Court doctrine on denationalization). Furthermore, the possession of the status did not make much of a difference in terms of
one's entitlement to state and federal benefits. Recent developments—including changes in foreign law producing a higher incidence of dual citizenship, a
perception that persons are seeking naturalization primarily for instrumental
reasons, and an alleged lowering of standards for naturalization—have renewed concerns about the "cheapening" of citizenship.[104] Rogers Brubaker has
identified similar concerns regarding the devaluation of citizenship in France.
His quotation of a French nationalist echoes views expressed by some in the
United States today:

> On the pretext of humanism . . . France has received and conferred its na-
> tionality on families whose sole bond of attachment to the national com-
> munity consists in pecuniary advantages. What is more, the persons

102. In states that continue to receive large numbers of immigrants over time, a "transnational"
account may be a necessary component of a full description of membership.

103. Schuck, 1989.

104. See Geyer, 1996.

concerned preserve their original allegiance and often take French nationality as one takes the Carte Orange [the subway and bus pass used by
Parisian commuters].[105]

These concerns are only heightened by academic musings that we are witnessing the decline of the nation-state and the dawning of a postnational era.

One can attempt to "revalue" citizenship by making it matter more—for example, by widening the differences between citizens and immigrants. The 1996
welfare legislation may be seen as such an intervention. But this strategy can be
self-defeating if it results in an increase in the number of applications for naturalization. As Schuck notes, "Whether this incentive is the kind of motivation
for naturalization that proponents of a more robust citizenship have in mind is a
question that is seldom asked."[106]

A better strategy would be to take the concept of citizenship seriously in an
affirmative sense, and to reinvigorate it by focusing on issues of loyalty, political participation, and civic involvement. Citizenship has a crucial role to play in
the functioning of a polyethnic society. It signals a commitment to a larger political enterprise above and beyond ethnic, racial, gender, or other associations.
Although citizenship may be an aspect of identity, it is not fundamentally about
identity or lineage. Rather, it is about belonging—to a land, to a history, to a
polity, and to a group of fellow citizens.

If it is believed that citizenship needs to be revalued, then attention should be
given to public policies and programs that reaffirm values of commitment and
loyalty. Examples might include an expanded voluntary national service program or mandatory national service, a national holiday for voting (or weekend
voting), renewed focus in public education on the fundamental documents of
the U.S. political system such as the Declaration of Independence, the Constitution, and the Gettysburg Address.

Concern that persons are naturalizing without an adequate knowledge of the
English language or U.S. history is rarely coupled with proposals that public
funds be spent on "citizenship education" for immigrants. Public and private
organizations sponsored such programs for new immigrants in the early decades of this century. With the return of high levels of immigration and a dramatic increase in applications for naturalization, education programs would
benefit both immigrants (who may appropriately be seen as "citizens in training") and U.S. society. Proposals for these sorts of programs occupy a promi-

105. Brubaker, 1992, p. 147 (quoting Jacques Toybon in *Le Monde*, November 5, 1986).
106. Schuck, 1997, p. 19.

nent place in the 1997 final report of the U.S. Commission on Immigration Reform.[107]

Some might argue that a lawful settlement model of membership contributes to a devaluation of citizenship by effacing most distinctions between citizens and immigrants. At a time when national communities appear particularly fragile, so the argument goes, undermining citizenship could threaten the unity, and ultimately the stability, needed for a well-functioning democracy. But this charge would be difficult to sustain if the lawful settlement model is an accurate picture of the membership rules that have prevailed in the United States for some time. Extending constitutional protections to immigrants or granting them social benefits has not materially undermined U.S. conceptions of the importance of citizenship or the stability of the U.S. political system. Indeed, if the major "threat" to citizenship today is thought to be the possibility that immigrants are seeking naturalization for instrumental reasons, it can be argued that anti-immigrant rhetoric and the recent denial of benefits to immigrants—both of which conflict with a lawful settlement model of membership—are the chief causes behind this rise in instrumental motives.

A conception of membership that includes resident immigrants does not dismiss citizenship as irrelevant or outdated. It assigns the concept to a different, but vitally important, sphere. Lawful settlement membership is based on notions of contribution and participation; citizenship is based on loyalty and commitment. The first resonates with values of fair treatment for similarly situated people; the second is attuned to a more symbolic set of relationships, one with a shared past and future. Lawful settlement is largely a social and legal status; citizenship provides a sense of belonging and is frequently an important aspect of personal identity.

The decline of the nation-state is regularly predicted. It is said that, in the "postnational" world to come, individuals will be protected by (perhaps internationally enforced) human rights norms, and human beings will cross borders with the same ease as goods and capital. Citizenship will become a concept as outdated as "subjecthood"—its use recalling a transitory era between feudalism and universalism (or at least regional supranationalism). So the prognosis goes.

---

107. "To help achieve full integration of newcomers, the Commission called upon federal, state, and local governments to provide renewed leadership and resources to a program of Americanization that requires: developing capacities to orient both newcomers and receiving communities; educating newcomers in English language skills and our core civic values; and revisiting the meaning and conferral of citizenship to ensure the integrity of the naturalization process." U.S. Commission on Immigration Reform, *Becoming an American,* 1997, pp. 29, 36–48.

This vision may well turn out to describe the world at some future date. But in the meantime, states will continue to control their borders, adopt rules for birthright citizenship and naturalization, and parcel out benefits and opportunities to a greater or lesser degree on the basis of citizenship. If there is an unfolding medium-term trend, it appears to be one that defines membership in terms of social contribution more than descent: sweat as well as blood. Thus, rights to participation in the welfare state will be more closely drawn to those who have contributed to the society from which they are now asking for assistance. There are hints of this trend in the recent amendment to the Mexican Constitution cutting off citizenship *jure sanguinis* after the first generation born overseas. It is also evident in recent changes in German policies that make it easier for long-term resident aliens to naturalize even as they afford fewer benefits to "ethnic Germans" born outside of Germany. The 1996 U.S. immigration legislation is the glaring counterexample, which ought to give U.S. policy makers serious grounds for reconsideration.

It is unlikely that the states of the world will soon agree on one set of citizenship rules—the *jus soli* of France and the *jus sanguinis* of Germany appear to be fairly firmly set in distinct political cultures. But the understandings of membership may well be converging, and will be seen in eased naturalization standards, welfare state participation for lawfully resident immigrants, and an increased tolerance for dual citizenship.

References

Aleinikoff, T. Alexander. 1992. "Symposium on Race Consciousness and Legal Scholarship: Re-Reading Justice Harlan's Dissent in Plessy v. Ferguson: Freedom, Antiracism, and Citizenship." *University of Illinois Law Review,* 1992, pp. 961–77.

Aleinikoff, T. Alexander. 1986. "Theories of Loss of Citizenship." *Michigan Law Review,* vol. 84, pp. 1471–503.

Appadurai, Arjun. 1993. "Patriotism and its Futures." *Public Culture,* vol. 5, no. 3, pp. 411–30.

Basch, Linda G., Nina Glick Schiller, and Christina Blanc Szanton. 1994. *Nations Unbound: Transnational Projects, Postcolonial Predicaments, and Deterritorialized Nation-States.* Amsterdam: Overseas Publishers Association, Gordon and Breach.

Bauböck, Rainer. 1994. *Transnational Citizenship: Membership and Rights in International Migration.* Brookfield, Vt.: Edward Elgar Publishing Ltd.

Bickel, Alexander. 1975. *The Morality of Consent.* New Haven: Yale University Press.

Brown, Bruce D. 1997. "Alien Donors: The Participation of Non-Citizens in the U.S. Campaign Finance System." *Yale Law and Policy Review,* vol. 15, pp. 503–51.

Brubaker, Rogers. 1992. *Citizenship and Nationhood in France and Germany.* Cambridge, Mass.: Harvard University Press.

Bureau of the Census. March 1996. *Current Population Survey.* Washington, D.C.: U.S. Department of Commerce.

Canada. Parliament. House of Commons, Standing Committee on Citizenship and Immigration. 1994. *Canadian Citizenship: A Sense of Belonging.* Ottawa: Queen's Printer for Canada.

Carens, Joseph H. 1987. "Who Belongs? Theoretical and Legal Questions about Birthright Citizenship in the United States." *University of Toronto Law Journal,* no. 37, pp. 413–43.

Corbett, Richard. 1993. *The Treaty of Maastricht.* Harlow, Essex: Longman Group.

Council of Europe. 1963. *Convention on Reduction of Cases of Multiple Nationality and Military Obligations in Cases of Multiple Nationality.* Dublin: Stationery Office.

Council of Europe Parliamentary Assembly. 1997. Opinion No. 200 on the draft. European Convention on Nationality, session 7.

Federal Register, vol. 62, no. 53 (March 19, 1997), p. 12915.

Feldblum, Miriam. Forthcoming. *Reconstructing Citizenship: The Politics of Nationality Reform and Immigration in Contemporary France.* Albany, N.Y.: State University of New York Press.

"'Foreign' Campaign Contributions and the First Amendment." 1997. *Harvard Law Review,* vol. 110, pp. 1886–903.

"The Functionality of Citizenship." 1997. *Harvard Law Review,* vol. 110, pp. 1814–31.

Geyer, Georgie Anne. 1996. *Americans No More: The Death of Citizenship.* New York: Atlantic Monthly Press.

Goldstein, Eugene, and Victoria Piazza. (April 22, 1996.) "Naturalization, Dual Citizenship and Retention of Foreign Citizenship: A Survey." *Interpreter Releases,* no. 73, pp. 517–21.

Graham, Pamela M. 1996. "Re-Imagining the Nation and Defining the District: The Simultaneous Political Incorporation of Dominican Transnational Migrants." Unpublished Doctoral dissertation. University of North Carolina, Chapel Hill.

Guarnizo, Luis Eduardo. Forthcoming, 1998. "The Rise of Transnational Social Formations: Mexican and Dominican State Responses to Transnational Migration." In *Political Power and Social Theory,* vol. 12, ed. Diane Davis. Stamford, Conn.: JAI Press.

Hammar, Tomas. 1989. "State, Nation, and Dual Citizenship." In *Immigration and the Politics of Citizenship in Europe and North America,* ed. William Rogers Brubaker. New York: University Press of America, pp. 81–95.

Henkin, Louis. 1987. "The Constitution and United States Sovereignty: A Century of Chinese Exclusion and its Progeny." *Harvard Law Review,* vol. 100, pp. 853–86.

Immigration and Nationality Act (INA), U.S. Code 1101 et seq. (1952), amended thereafter.

Immigration and Naturalization Service. 1994, 1995, and 1996. *Statistical Yearbook of the Immigration and Naturalization Service.* Washington, D.C.: U.S. Department of Justice.

Karst, Kenneth L. 1977. "Foreword: Equal Citizenship Under the Fourteenth Amendment." *Harvard Law Review,* vol. 91, pp. 6–68.

Kettner, James H. 1978. *The Development of American Citizenship, 1608–1870.* Chapel Hill, N.C.: University of North Carolina Press.

Lopez, Ian F. Haney. 1996. *White by Law: The Legal Construction of Race.* New York: New York University Press.

Marshall, T. H. 1992. "Citizenship and Social Class." In *Citizenship and Social Class,* ed. T. H. Marshall and T. Bottomore. London: Pluto Press, pp. 3–51. Originally published in T. H. Marshall, *Citizenship and Social Class and Other Essays* (Cambridge: Cambridge University Press, 1950).

Martin, David A. 1985. "Membership without Consent: Abstract or Organic?" *Yale Journal of International Law,* vol. 11, pp. 278–96.

Naturalization Guidelines, Section 5.3 (International Aspects) in *Nationality and Statelessness: A Collection of National Laws,* vol. 1, Humanitarian Series. Ferney-Voltaire, France: Independent Bureau for Humanitarian Issues (established in collaboration with the Office of the U.N. High Commissioner for Refugees), 1996, pp. 372–96.

Neuman, Gerald L. 1992. "'We Are the People': Alien Suffrage in German and American Perspective." *Michigan Journal of International Law,* vol. 13, pp. 259–335.

Neuman, Gerald L. 1987. "Back to Dred Scott." *San Diego Law Review,* vol. 24, pp. 485–500.

Opinion of German Federal Constitutional Court. May 21, 1974. *Bundesverfassungsgericht,* vol. 37.

Portes, Alejandro, and Ruben G. Rumbaut. 1996. *Immigrant America: A Portrait.* Berkeley, Calif.: University of California Press.

Raskin, Jamin B. 1993. "Legal Aliens, Local Citizens: The Historical, Constitutional and Theoretical Meanings of Alien Suffrage." *University of Pennsylvania Law Review,* vol. 141, pp. 1391–470.

Rosberg, Gerald M. 1977. "Aliens and Equal Protection: Why Not the Right to Vote?" *Michigan Law Review,* vol. 75, nos. 5 and 6, pp. 1092–136.

Rovella, David E. (March 17, 1997.) "NRA: Let Aliens Have Guns." *The National Law Journal.*

Sassen, Saskia. 1996. *Losing Control? Sovereignty in an Age of Globalization.* New York: Columbia University Press.

Schuck, Peter. 1997. "The Re-Evaluation of American Citizenship." *Georgetown Immigration Law Journal,* p. 1.

Schuck, Peter. 1989. "Membership in the Liberal Polity: The Devaluation of American Citizenship." *Georgetown Immigration Law Journal,* vol. 3, pp. 1–18.

Schuck, Peter, and Rogers M. Smith. 1985. *Citizenship without Consent: Illegal Aliens in the American Polity.* New Haven: Yale University Press.

Shaw, E. Clay Jr., and Lamar Smith. (May 28, 1997.) "Immigrants, Welfare and the GOP." *Washington Post,* p. A19.

Smith, Rogers M. 1997. *Civic Ideals: Conflicting Visions of Citizenship in U.S. History.* New Haven: Yale University Press.

Soysal, Yasemin Nuhoglu. 1994. *Limits of Citizenship: Migrants and Post-National Membership in Europe.* Chicago: University of Chicago Press.

Spiro, Peter J. 1997. "Dual Nationality and the Meaning of Citizenship." *Emory Law Journal,* vol. 46, pp. 1412–85.

Ueda, Reed. 1994. *Postwar Immigrant America: A Social History.* Boston: Bedford Books, St. Martin's Press.

U.S. Commission on Immigration Reform. 1997. *Becoming an American: Immigration and Immigrant Policy.* Washington, D.C.: U.S. Government Printing Office.

U.S. Congress. House of Representatives. "Children Born in the United States to Illegal Parents, 1995: Hearings Before the Subcommittees on Immigration and Claims and on the Constitution of the House Committee on the Judiciary." 104th Cong., 1st sess., December 13, 1995. Testimony of Walter Dellinger and Elton Gallegly.

U.S. Congress. House of Representatives. Congressman Frank Riggs speaking about H.R. 3406. 104th Cong., 1st sess., *Congressional Record* (1995), vol. 141, p. 412.

U.S. Congress. "Citizenship, 1996: Hearings before the Subcommittee on Immigration of the Committee on the Judiciary, Senate." 101st Cong., 2nd sess., October 22, 1996.

Wysocki, Bernard Jr. (May 12, 1997.) "Elite U.S. Immigrants Straddle Two Cultures." *Wall Street Journal,* p. B1.

Legal Cases

Afroyim v. Rusk, 387 U.S. 253 (1967).

Ambach v. Norwich, 441 U.S. 68, 73 (1979).

Balzac v. Porto Rico, 258 U.S. 298 (1922).

Cabell v. Chavez-Salido, 454 U.S. 432 (1982).

Chae Chan Ping v. United States, 130 U.S. 581 (1889).

Downes v. Bidwell, 182 U.S. 244 (1901).

Elk v. Wilkins, 112 U.S. 94 (1884).

Examining Board of Engineers v. Otero, 426 U.S. 572 (1976).

Fiallo v. Bell, 430 U.S. 737 (1977).

Foley v. Connelie, 435 U.S. 291 (1978).

Graham v. Richardson, 403 U.S. 365 (1971).

Hampton v. Mow Sun Wong, 426 U.S. 88 (1976).

In re Griffiths, 413 U.S. 717 (1973).

Landon v. Plasencia, 459 U.S. 2 (1982).

Mackenzie v. Hare, 239 U.S. 299 (1915).

Mathews v. Diaz, 426 U.S. 67 (1976).

Miller v. Albright, 118 S. Ct. 1428 (1998).

Nyquist v. Mauclet, 432 U.S. 1 (1977).

Perez v. Brownell, 356 U.S. 44, 64-65 (1958).

Plessy v. Ferguson, 163 U.S. 537 (1896).

Plyler v. Doe, 457 U.S. 202 (1982).

Rogers v. Bellei, 401 U.S. 815, 828-31 (1971).

Schneiderman v. United States, 320 U.S. 118, 122 (1943).

Scott v. Sandford, 60 U.S. (19 How.) 393 (1857).

Shaughnessy v. United States ex rel. Mezei, 345 U.S. 206 (1953).

Skafte v. Rorex, 553 P.2d 830 (1976); appeal dismissed, 430 U.S. 961 (1977).

Slaughter-House Cases, 83 U.S. (16 Wall.) 36 (1873).

Sugarman v. Dougall, 413 U.S. 634 (1973).

Takahasi v. Fish and Game Commission, 334 U.S. 410 (1948).

Talbot v. Janson, 3 U.S. (3 Dall.) 133 (1795).
Torres v. Puerto Rico, 422 U.S. 654 (1979).
Truax v. Raich, 239 U.S. 33 (1915).
United States ex rel. Knauff v. Shaughnessy, 338 U.S. 537 (1950).
United States v. Carolene Products Company, 304 U.S. 144, 152 n.4 (1938).
United States v. Wong Kim Ark, 169 U.S. 649 (1898).
Wauchope v. U.S. Department of State, 985 F.2d 1407 (9th Cir. 1993).
Yick Wo v. Hopkins, 118 U.S. 356 (1886).

PART TWO

Citizenship in the Aftermath of Major Political Transformations

CHAPTER FIVE

Introduction

KATHLEEN NEWLAND

THE POLITICAL transformation of a state almost invariably raises questions about the boundaries and content of citizenship. How inclusive or exclusive is the new or transformed state in defining who is entitled to full membership in the polity? Are all those who thought of themselves as citizens of the previous political entity accepted into the new one? What rights and duties give content to the formal status of citizenship, and how are they manifested in practice?

The three chapters in this section address these questions in relation to Russia, South Africa, and the three Baltic states of Latvia, Lithuania, and Estonia. Comparison of these three cases shows that, despite facing common dilemmas, each transformed state deals with citizenship issues in a unique context and in its own way. Citizenship policy is cast in the mold of historical experience and the current political agenda.

The Baltic states have used citizenship policy as a tool to separate themselves from their Soviet past and reinforce their national identity. Lithuania's relatively small ethnic Russian population posed no particular challenge to this project and, thus, was admitted to citizenship along with all other legal permanent residents at the time of independence. In Latvia and Estonia, however, the Russian minority was so large that it was seen as posing a mortal threat to the restoration of a distinctively Latvian or Estonian nation-state. In response to the perceived threat, citizenship was restricted to those who could trace their residency or descent to before the period of Soviet annexation. This, in effect, disenfranchised the great majority of ethnic Russians resident in the two states.

Lowell Barrington recounts and analyzes the subsequent struggle to reach accommodation on the issues of minority rights, democratic development, and political representation that arose from the first basic decision on admission to citizenship.

Left out of citizenship, what options remained to the ethnic Russian residents of Latvia and Estónia? They could either go through the deliberately slow and difficult process of naturalization, become Russian citizens and thereby give up the prospect of citizenship rights in their place of residence, or remain stateless. The Baltic governments have come under considerable pressure from international organizations to reduce statelessness by adopting more inclusive policies. This has been an important point of leverage, as the Baltics are eager to join European institutions. The two methods of distinguishing their European present from their Soviet past—excluding Russians from citizenship and meeting the human rights standards for membership in European institutions—thus have come into conflict. As Barrington shows, the latter seems to be winning.

Unlike the Baltic states, post-Soviet Russia did not emerge from its political transformation with an ethnoterritorial conception of statehood. The contentious issues of citizenship were not, therefore, issues of admission (or, rather, nonadmission) but of state succession. What state "inherited" the responsibility for the citizens of the former USSR? The leaders of the Russian Federation defined themselves into that role with a citizenship law that included not only all legal residents of Russian territory but also, in theory, all USSR citizens who within a defined period wished to claim Russian citizenship. Preferring the term "continuator" to "successor state," the Russians implied that the Russian Federation was the USSR writ small, to use George Ginsburgs's formulation.

For the 25 million or so Russian-speakers who resided in other parts of the Soviet Union, the breakup of the USSR brought agonizing choices: stay in successor states where they would be a distinct and unpopular minority or return to Russia and claim the proffered citizenship. Millions of Russians rushed back and found that the reality of being recognized as citizens was far more complex than the law made it sound. While the Soviet local-residency permit (*propiska*) had formally been abolished, local officials commonly refused to recognize the citizenship rights of those who did not possess one—and would issue them only to those who could prove their citizenship. The catch-22 was tolerated—even manipulated—by authorities who did not believe that Russia could cope with a headlong rush to return by Russians in Central Asia and Eastern Europe.

Some observers also suspected that Russian authorities were glad to retain a Russian population in the "near abroad" as a sort of fifth column that would give them some leverage over events in those countries. Certainly that appeared to be the view of many politicians in the other Soviet successor states. This suspicion has made the issue of dual citizenship extremely contentious and important in the former Soviet space. What Russian legislators portrayed as a mere insurance policy to calm the fears of Russian-speakers in a period of political transition, the other successor states saw as a license for Russian interference in their internal affairs. The impasse has left millions of people in a juridical limbo, uncertain of their status and prospects. Ginsburgs explains the intricacies of Russian citizenship law, which have both added to and attempted to resolve these uncertainties.

If Baltic citizenship issues have been defined around admission, and Russian issues have been defined around state succession, then the political transformation of South African citizenship centered on the imperatives of rectification. Apartheid-era citizenship policy had excluded more and more black South Africans through the creation of nominally independent "homelands" to which blacks were assigned. Post-apartheid legislation distinguished itself by its inclusivity, although, as in the other states considered in this section, practice has often differed from the theoretical norm of inclusion—for example, with respect to homelands residents.

The citizenship issues that remain salient in South Africa today have less to do with drawing the boundaries of citizenship than with defining its content. The key promise of the inclusive approach to membership in the South African polity is equality of rights and the ability to exercise them. Civil rights, such as access to the courts and equal treatment in the justice system, are thus more of a test of inclusion than admission to the franchise. The number of citizenship determinations that are outstanding is dwarfed by the number of South Africans who have had no form of identity papers and have still to register for the ID books that would allow them to claim some of the more tangible benefits of citizenship. Both symbolically and concretely, the challenge for South Africa is to educate all its citizens—not only those who might be eligible for naturalization—in the rights, obligations, and values of citizenship in the post-apartheid state.

All the states discussed in this section continue to struggle with the impact of their citizenship policies on the loyalty of their residents, often an issue with respect to those who hold dual or multiple citizenship. All must deal with the often glaring discrepancies between the citizenship laws on the books and the practices of administrative officials, particularly at the local level. And all have discovered, in some cases painfully, that an inclusive and consistent citizenship policy is one of the keys to acceptance in the company of liberal democratic nations.

CHAPTER SIX

Migration and Admittance to Citizenship in Russia

GEORGE GINSBURGS

RUSSIA IN THE post-Soviet era is experiencing major population movements. For the most part, these movements involve former Soviet citizens who are trying to establish their juridical and physical homeland within the framework of state succession practice. This sorting-out exercise will duly run its course. The people involved make up a distinct constituency whose members are afforded a special set of privileges and priorities under the principles that apply when a state ceases to exist and a successor state "inherits" responsibilities toward its citizens.[1]

The pool of migrants also contains a sizable—and growing—assortment of adults and their progeny whose status under Russian law and treatment at the hands of local authorities are shaped both by their current citizenship (or lack thereof) and by their ability and willingness to acquire Russian citizenship through the circumstances of their birth, naturalization, or other standard means of conscription or enlistment. This element comprises, among others, bona fide foreigners, asylum seekers, refugees, and illegal aliens. While their numbers may fluctuate from year to year, they can be counted upon to remain a fixture on the Russian scene. Their position will often be crucially affected by the available options for formal enrollment in the ranks of the host country's civic community. This chapter concentrates on this ordinary brand of outlanders and looks at how

---

1. For an assessment of Russia's performance record on the count of state succession in citizenship matters, see Ginsburgs, 1998.

they have fared in the *Sturm und Drang* mode of Russia's political culture during the period stretching from the entry into force of the new Constitution on December 25, 1993, to the present with regard to either negotiating voluntary conversion to Russian citizenship or incurring its award to a member of the family by legislative fiat (essentially on the principle of birthright).

The array of norms deployed to police Russia's citizenship operations is now codified in the statute on the citizenship of the Russian Soviet Federative Socialist Republic (RSFSR) of November 28, 1991 (in effect from February 6, 1992),[2] as amended on June 17, 1993, and February 6, 1995.[3] The 1993 Constitution of the Russian Federation adds some key pieces to the mosaic. Between them, these two sources virtually blanket the field and convey the tenor of the Yeltsin administration's policy on every significant aspect of its citizenship agenda.

Before we plunge into the thick of legal analysis, a glance at some statistical data will convey a sense of the magnitude of the problem Russia faces. Between February 6, 1992, and the close of 1996, 1.5 million persons acquired the citizenship of the Russian Federation by request or application. In the same period, about 40,000 persons renounced it—33,000 of them in the near abroad countries, the other fourteen successor states of the Soviet Union that many Russians refer to as the "near abroad." Ukraine and Belarus were responsible for 28,000 of that subtotal. Of those who received Russian citizenship, more than 800,000 lived in the near abroad and 100,000 in the far abroad. From that first group, more than half subsequently moved to Russia. The tendency to relocate in Russia differs from country to country: about 80 percent of new "converts" decide to emigrate from Azerbaijan, Kazakhstan, and the Central Asian republics; in the Baltic states and Moldova, virtually all of them choose to stay. The size of the annual increment also fluctuates, of course. In 1996 alone, for example, 490,000 individuals acquired Russian citizenship. Of the 360,000 who did so on the territory of Russia, most were arrivals who came from the members of the Commonwealth of Independent States (comprising all the newly independent Soviet republics except Estonia, Latvia, and Lithuania) and the Baltic states. The remaining 130,000 originated outside the confines of the Russian Federation—115,000 in the near abroad zone and 15,000 in the far abroad area (compared with 10,800 in the previous year).[4]

2. *Vedomosti,* 1992, no. 6, item 243.

3. *Vedomosti,* 1993, no. 29, item 1112; *SZ RF,* 1995, no. 5, item 496. The citizenship statute (Art. 31) also recognizes international treaties as a source of norms for regulating citizenship matters and stipulates that "if an international treaty of the Russian Federation prescribes rules different from those contained in the present Law, the rules of that treaty are applied."

4. Kutafin, 1997; Zubakov, 1997; *Rossiiskie vesti,* March 18, 1997.

For the period from 1992 until January 1, 1998, 5.1 million people reportedly migrated to Russia. Some 1.2 million of their number were registered as
forced resettlers and refugees[5] (or, to quote another source, 1.2 million forced
resettlers, plus 150,000 refugees whose status gave them some claim to government assistance).[6] On a micro scale, for instance, the figures compiled by the
State Committee for Statistics record that 286,475 souls moved to Russia in the
first half of 1996 from the Baltic and C.I.S. countries, with the majority hailing
from Ukraine, Kazakhstan, Uzbekistan, and Tajikistan. A total of 80 percent of
the immigrants consist of people of Russian stock.[7] The prognosis for the future
is that by the year 2001, the nation can expect an additional influx of 600,000
forced resettlers and refugees owing to fresh arrivals from the ex-republics of
the USSR, of which 500,000 are expected to originate from Central Asia and
Kazakhstan.[8] In the bigger picture, some computations forecast that a swarm of
more than 3 million individuals will have trekked to Russia by the year 2000 as
refugees and migrants from the C.I.S. countries, the Baltic region, and far
abroad.[9]

At this point, the far abroad component of the sample includes, according to
the director of the Federal Migration Service, 2,300 foreigners who had managed to acquire the formal status of refugees. In addition, 80,000 others of that
ilk are now classified as "legalized" refugees, namely, they are known to the authorities. Afghans constitute the largest element here—approximately a third of
the total.[10]

By official count, 300,000 foreign workers came to Russia by invitation in
1996, mostly from Ukraine, Turkey, and China. The vast majority of such guest
workers, however, went unreported.[11] Consider the following. Moscow's Bu-

5. Kamakin, 1998.
6. *Diplomaticheskii vestnik,* 1997, no. 9, p. 44.
7. *Rossiiskie vesti,* March 18, 1997.
8. *SZ RF,* 1997, no. 47, item 5406. "Concerning the Federal Migration Program for
1998–2000."
9. Churakova, January 13, 1998, VI.
10. Kamakin, 1998. By that calculation, the number of Afghan refugees in Russia would come
to about 26,600. A series of newspaper articles on the travails of the Afghan diaspora in Russia published in 1997–1998 wrote of 100,000 to150,000 Afghan exiles on the territory of Russia, of whom
50,000 to 60,000 were concentrated in Moscow and the Moscow region. Perhaps most of the Afghans located on Russian territory fit under the administrative heading of "illegal immigrants"
rather than "foreign refugees." Grankina, December 30, 1997; Bondarenko, 1998; Alekseev, 1998.
11. *Argumenty i fakty,* 1997, no. 29, p. 16. Back in the first weeks of 1995, a newspaper piece
already complained that Moscow and the Moscow region harbored a community of more than
60,000 to 70,000 illegal resettlers who were not Russian citizens, that is, refugees, transients, hired
workers, their children, "gastarbeiters," and members of the new propertied classes. A total of
6,000 foreigners and stateless persons from the far abroad were said to be living in the Moscow region. See Nikonorov, January 19, 1995.

reau for Coordinating Labor Resources, Migration and Employment of the Population planned to issue 50,000 permits for the hiring of foreign workers. Meanwhile, private sources claimed a further 250,000 Vietnamese, Romanians, Turks, Belorussians, Ukrainians, and Moldavians were locally employed on construction sites and in transportation services without a license.[12] In fact, even these estimates may be far too low: one sees published references to a pool of 0.5 million to 1 million illegal labor migrants in Russia and reads startling stories in the newspapers about "as many as a million foreign workers in and around Moscow."[13]

Finally, no one really knows how many illegal aliens have infiltrated Russia's home space. The chief government spokesman's guess is that there could be as many as 700,000,[14] whereas in the opinion of the International Organization of Migration between 500,000 and 1 million illegal migrants (particularly Afghans, Iranians, and Iraqi Kurds) are living in the Russian Federation.[15] Note that the phenomenon of Chinese trespassers is omitted from this census, and the assessments in their case range from several hundred thousand to 2 million and more.[16] What can be expected on this front for the next few years? According to one version, "matters are much more complicated as regards the problem of uncontrolled entry into the territory of Russia of citizens from countries with an undeveloped economy. Just officially, the size of this category of immigrants will amount annually to roughly 100,000 persons."[17]

General Principles

With this background, we can turn our attention to Russia's legal framework for setting procedures that let some among this crowd of outsiders normalize their life by incurring title to Russian citizenship.

Right to Citizenship

The 1991 statute opens with the grand pronouncement that in the Russian Federation every person has a right to citizenship, a formula lifted from the 1948 Universal Declaration of Human Rights and imported into the Russian constitutional repertory in April 1992 as an amendment to the 1977 charter that

12. Korovin, October 30, 1997.
13. Khorev, 1997; Bohlen, June 13, 1998, p. A3.
14. Kamakin, 1998.
15. *Central Asia Monitor,* 1998, no. 1, p. 24.
16. See, for example, Osenev, 1997.
17. Churakova, January 13, 1998, VI.

advertised that "every person has the right to acquire and terminate the citizenship of the Russian Federation in accordance with the laws of the Russian Federation."

The point has been made in Russian writing on this subject that, while the humanistic impulses behind this choice of language are understandable, all the talk about rights in this context gives people the mistaken impression that a quality of "automatism" is forthwith meant to govern the regime of acquisition and loss of Russian citizenship.[18] In that vein, for instance, an official commentator on the terms of the 1991 enactment interpreted the clause to mean that every person who satisfied the conditions set forth in the law on citizenship for a right to citizenship "cannot be refused the right to be a citizen of the Russian Federation."[19] That view prompted objections that the resulting "tilt" had the unintended effect of "downgrading the role of the other party—the Russian state" inasmuch as it seemed to offer the competent agencies no alternative but to grant citizenship whenever a petition was duly filed. Instead, we are told, what the lawmakers truly had in mind all along was to consider such an application as a bid to claim Russian citizenship that, in turn, was entitled to be treated and decided "with maximum good will," but without forgetting that the statute also listed several grounds for denying a request—which plainly attested to the fact that the apparatus was by no means bound to rubber-stamp the would-be conversion.[20]

Presumably, awareness of the need to clear the air on the subject caused the authors of the 1993 Constitution to eschew resorting to expressions like "right to citizenship" and "right to acquire and lose citizenship" in favor of a neutral call for citizenship to be acquired and lost in accordance with federal laws.

Rhetorical flourishes notwithstanding, anyone even slightly conversant with local administrative reality will know that the official guardians of the nation's portals have continued to maintain tight control over who may join the club. In discharging that function, they feel free to behave as a senior contracting party motivated by its own interests and not in the least as a mechanical recorder of the self-nominated candidate's personal wishes.

The second paragraph of Article 1 of the Law on the Citizenship of the RSFSR decrees that in the RSFSR no person can be deprived of his citizenship or the right to change his citizenship, which is a stronger version of the original injunction enshrined in the Universal Declaration of Human Rights and its various copies in latter-day Soviet legislation. The uncompromising tone of the cur-

18. Avakian, 1994, pp. 8–9.
19. Krylov, 1992, p. 9.
20. Avakian, 1994, p. 9.

rent bar against involuntary forfeiture of citizenship is attributed to a desire to avoid possible lapses into "subjectivism and, worse yet, arbitrariness" of the kind that plagued the Soviet period. Today, then, both this piece of legislation and the 1993 Constitution forbid resorting in any circumstances to such an extreme sanction as robbing an individual of his Motherland.[21] Consequently, we are assured, in only one case is the termination of Russian citizenship now contemplated otherwise than at the express initiative of the person concerned, namely, where the state has issued a decision to revoke admission to citizenship upon learning that the person in question had submitted false information and documents in order to pass the test.[22]

Note, too, that the 1991 statute speaks of the impermissibility of any person in the Russian Federation—not just a citizen of Russia—being stripped of his citizenship or denied the right to change it. As a practical matter, of course, a state is apt to be indifferent to how a foreign state treats one of its citizens or what a foreigner does to his citizenship, even if the party happens to reside on its territory at the time. So, not surprisingly, the authors of the 1993 Constitution opted to get rid of the verbal overkill by correcting the phrasing here to read that "a citizen of the Russian Federation cannot be deprived of his citizenship or the right to change it."[23]

Citizenship of the Russian Federation and of the Republics in the RSFSR

The citizenship of the Russian Federation (RF) vests in persons who have acquired RF citizenship in the manner prescribed by the 1991 statute. Under the terms of the treaty of March 31, 1992, between the central government of the

21. Avakian, 1994, p. 10. The Constitutional Court of the Russian Federation had occasion to rule in the Smirnov case that involuntary loss of Russian birthright citizenship was barred by law (May 16, 1996), *Rossiiskaia gazeta,* May 28, 1996; *SZ RF,* 1996, no. 21, item 2579.

22. Sukalo, 1996, p. 27. A draft of a federal law concerning changes and supplements to the citizenship statute is currently under consideration. *Inter alia,* the bill calls for additions to Article 24 of the statute designed to make it spell out "in greater detail the procedure for rescinding a decision to grant the citizenship of the Russian Federation with regard to a person who became a citizen on the basis of deliberately false data and invalid documents. This call is prompted by the experience of daily life." *Rossiiskie vesti,* March 18, 1997.

23. Proposed changes in the citizenship law would bring the language of the statute in line here with that of the Constitution to record that a citizen of the Russian Federation cannot be deprived of his citizenship or the right to change it. *Rossiiskie vesti,* March 18, 1997, and May 6, 1997. Note, too, that the 53rd session of the UN Commission on Human Rights adopted a resolution that condemned depriving persons of citizenship by reason of racial, national, ethnic, or religious attributes. "The resolution adopted at Russia's initiative" confirmed "the important right of every person to citizenship as an inalienable right of the human persona" and marked "the first time that at the level of the UN deprivation of citizenship on ethnic grounds was pronounced a violation of human rights." *Pravda,* April 16, 1997, and May 14, 1997.

RF and the component republics of the Federation (which defined the scope of their respective jurisdictional packages) and the 1993 Constitution, exclusive power to deal with matters of citizenship in the Russian Federation was assigned to the federal branch. The 1991 citizenship law defines the citizenship of the RSFSR as equal irrespective of its mode of acquisition, whereas the 1993 Constitution describes it as "uniform and equal" in every case. The sense is the same and invites the conclusion that (1) all citizens enjoy equal rights independently of whether they contract citizenship by birth or acquire it on some other grounds, and (2) the citizens of the Russian Federation cannot be divided into groups or classes that entail different sets of rights or duties. Or, to quote the 1993 Constitution, "every citizen of the Russian Federation possesses on its territory all the rights and freedoms and bears equal obligations as called for by the Constitution of the Russian Federation."

As usual, citizens alone are eligible to exercise political rights and are required to fulfill political duties. According to secondary sources, the "national regime" standard applies to all legally present foreigners and stateless persons, which reportedly means that they enjoy virtually all the rights and freedoms and owe obligations on an equal footing with local citizens—except for those that fall into the political basket. Special rules also operate for noncitizens when it comes to opening enterprises, bank accounts, engaging in various types of production activity, landing a job in the Russian Federation, and so on.[24]

The second clause of Article 2 of the 1991 statute enunciates the principle according to which citizens of the RSFSR who permanently reside on the territory of a republic that forms part of the RSFSR are simultaneously considered citizens of that republic. The "double citizenship" model maintains a Soviet tradition in this venue, *mutatis mutandis*, which was and still is called upon to give tangible expression to the sovereignty that is officially said to vest in designated component units of the Federation. In the case of the Russian Federation today, the exercise of this parallel right is reserved for the twenty-one republics that are listed in the Russian Constitution as subjects of the Russian Federation.

The present arrangement produces two crops of Russian citizens: those who permanently reside on the territory of the Russian Federation outside the confines of any "national" republic of the Federation possess the citizenship of Russia/Russian Federation; those who permanently reside on the territory of one of the "national" republics incorporated into the Russian Federation count as citizens of both the Federation and the home republic. The scheme is intended to underscore once again the unity of the Russian Federation, with the republics contributing to the theme by pursuing an agenda aimed at "solidifying

24. Avakian, 1994, p. 11.

the unison of federal citizenship and the citizenship of the republics."[25] Reference is made in this connection to the good example set here by the Constitution of the Republic of Sakha (Iakutiia) in broadcasting the twin message to the effect that "the Republic of Sakha (Iakutiia) possesses its own citizenship" and "a citizen of the Republic of Sakha (Iakutiia) is a citizen of the Russian Federation."

What the authors of the federal legislation truly had in mind was that the citizenship of the republics would, in practical terms, function as a passive appendage to federal citizenship. Thus, the sole requirement for a citizen of the Russian Federation to incur the citizenship of a republic is the incidental fact of his permanent residence on the territory of the respective republic, which, in turn, has prompted the telling pronouncement that "any attempt to impose any other supplementary conditions for acquisition by a citizen of the Federation of the citizenship of a republic besides permanent residence therein contravenes the law and violates the equal rights of citizens of the Russian Federation."[26]

This treatment of how the center and the republics are meant to interrelate in citizenship matters has occasioned deep resentment in some republics where the local authorities refuse to shut their eyes to the glaring incompatibility between the public portrayal of their fiefdoms as sovereign entities and the purely symbolic quality of the corresponding citizenship mandate. Remember that the 1993 Constitution charges the federal branch with exercising exclusive jurisdiction over the institution of citizenship in the Russian Federation. The tenor of the assignment connotes full authority to regulate federal citizenship as well as prescribe general rules governing citizenship that are incumbent on the subjects of the Federation. Although the republics are entitled to adopt their own normative acts on citizenship questions and do so, the duly sanctioned procedure for acquiring republic citizenship attests to how little control they were originally supposed to exert over this vital attribute of their "sovereign" personality.

The tensions generated by these contradictions between the dictates of the doctrinal canon and the proposed mode of their implementation are vividly captured in the following comments by a Russian expert on his country's citizenship practice. The decision to equate republic citizenship with permanent residence on its territory, he believes,

can draw objections from both the citizens and the republics. In the circumstances of a unified state space, many citizens are indifferent to

25. Krylov, 1992, pp. 10–11.
26. Krylov, 1992, pp. 10–11.

where they reside. After graduating from institutes, they live for decades in republics located far from the center, work there as geologists, engineers, etc. They have quarters for permanent residence in those republics, although they maintain title to living space in Moscow or other populated spots. That is why whether or not to consider them citizens of the republic depends on what this particular citizenship affords. Besides, just as important is the issue of what they might stand to lose in the place where they do not now permanently reside, but to which they intend to return in time. As for the republics, the above decision may prompt objections on their part because by reason of the wording of Art. 2 of the Law they do not admit into the citizenship of the republic, but instead sort of receive citizens "covertly" by approving the purchase of houses, granting residency permits, providing residential quarters, etc.[27]

Reviewing this corner of the Russian Federation's constitutional scene, a 1994 survey expressed satisfaction that the constitutions of all the republics, except Chechnia, matched the tone of the federal Constitution's prescriptions applicable to citizenship questions.[28] The Constitution of the Chechen Republic alone called for a "uniform citizenship" without reference to the citizenship of the Russian Federation, which would seem to indicate that what the charter meant was the citizenship of the Chechen Republic. As a Russian observer correctly pointed out at the time, the Chechen provision went far toward validating the assumption that "the intention here is to make use of the institution of citizenship as one of the means for seceding from Russia."[29]

Curiously enough, the aforementioned audit of the contents of the republics' constitutional closet failed to pay attention to the unorthodox position taken by Tatarstan's authorities on the subject of the republic's citizenship and how it was expected to fit into the matrix of a "unified" federal citizenship. While not as "divorce-minded" as their Chechen colleagues, the authors of the Tatarstan Constitution set the republic's citizenship on a par not only with that of the Russian Federation, but also with that of every other sovereign state, thus coming up with a model that managed to house both concerted citizenship and dual citizenship *stricto sensu*. One observer states, "Apart from the urge to acquire the trappings of state sovereignty, a clear tendency manifests itself in this instance to carve out a special status for the republic within the frame of the Russian Federation, marked

27. Avakian, 1994, pp. 13–14.
28. "Analiticheskii," 1994, pp. 19–20.
29. Vasilev, 1992, p. 60.

by greater independence than the others."[30] Among the motives cited to explain this distancing is a feeling shared by many in Tatarstan that "ethnic Tatars living in the United States or Turkey and wishing to acquire the citizenship of their home republic should not at all be compelled to acquire for that reason the citizenship of Russia. Under the existing legislation, this is mandatory."[31]

The constitutions of all the republics, with the exception of Ingushetiia and Kalmykiia, established that the grounds and mode of acquisition and termination of the republic's citizenship are elaborated in the republic's law on citizenship. The republic constitutions are also faulted, however, for not recording that the republic laws on citizenship must comport with the postulates of the relevant federal legislation. Recommendations were made to correct these defects by supplementing the federal citizenship statute with suitable instructions.

Next, notice was taken of the fact that the constitutions of the individual republics expressly contemplated their right to admit individuals into the citizenship of the republic. Given the differences in approach to the citizenship phenomenon as evidenced by the wording of the appropriate articles in the federal and republic charters, the possibility exists that foreigners and stateless persons could acquire the citizenship of a maverick republic in circumvention of standards required by federal law. The rights of the citizens of the Russian Federation may be infringed as a consequence. Consider, for example, how the Constitution of the Republic of Tyva does not shrink from declaring that

> the Republic of Tyva sets its own citizenship. The procedure of acquiring citizenship is determined with due account of the demographic situation in the Republic of Tyva and serves to maintain the stable prevalence of the native nationality, safeguard its ethnic and cultural heritage and patrimony. Individuals of Tyva origin living abroad have priority rights over other foreigners in obtaining the citizenship of the Republic of Tyva.[32]

30. Vasilev, 1992, p. 60.

31. Sharapov, October 16, 1992. About 1 million Tatars were estimated to be living in the far abroad.

32. When, for instance, reports were published that the legislative chamber of the State Assembly of Bashkiriia had approved at first reading the bill On the Citizenship of the Republic of Bashkortostan, its authors were quoted as claiming that the new law would not contravene Russian legislation. *Inter alia,* the draft text contemplated the concurrent operation of the citizenship of Bashkiriia and the citizenship of the Russian Federation. *Nezavisimaia gazeta,* February 16, 1996. Subsequently, however, the proposed version was severely criticized for condoning several major deviations from the corresponding federal writ, and calls were issued to eliminate these contradictions by tailoring the republic document to the federal prototype. Malikov, 1997, pp. 21–24. Note that at the time this piece was published, the Republic of Bashkortostan still did not have a citizenship statute.

Keep in mind, too, that even where the republic apparatus might decide—for the sake of appearance, if nothing else—to go along with the notion that permanent residency on the republic's soil begets local citizenship, the competent authorities at that level can still manipulate eligibility for citizenship by closely rationing access to the residency.[33]

Because of persistent tremors along the fault lines that run across the Federation's constitutional landscape, the citizenship arena remains the site of much doctrinal controversy. First, a new layer of complexity was introduced when Russia and Belarus concluded the Union Treaty of April 2, 1997.[34] The Charter of the Union appended thereto announced the debut of a Union citizenship with every citizen of the Russian Federation and every citizen of the Republic of Belarus simultaneously considered a citizen of the Union. Possession of Union citizenship by a citizen of the Russian Federation or by a citizen of the Republic of Belarus was not meant to detract from his rights and freedoms or exempt him or her from discharging duties entailed by citizenship in the respective partner state.

Union citizenship bestows on its holder, *inter alia*, a right to receive on the territory of third states, where representations of the member state of which he is a citizen do not operate, protection from the diplomatic representations or consular institutions of the other member state on an equal footing with the latter's citizens. Furthermore, a Union citizen permanently residing in the other member state has the right to elect and be elected to the organs of local self-administration on the latter's territory. Dropped from the final edition of the covenant was a companion clause featured in an earlier draft that indicated that the citizens of the member states could, at their request, be issued a separate document attesting to citizenship in the Union.[35] The omission lends credence to the charge of one Russian analyst, who dismissed Union citizenship as that of a "nonstate" with no legal purpose and recommended instead the conclusion of an agreement either on the mutual recognition of dual citizenship or equalizing the status of citizens of the Russian Federation and the Republic of Belarus in the two territories.

The irony behind the whole concept of citizenship in a Belarus-RF union lies in the fact that Belarus is one of the countries most intolerant of dual citizenship

---

33. A newspaper story by a high official on the staff of the Office of the Procurator-General of the Russian Federation tells of how a "real war erupted on the federal level for the repeal in several subjects of the Federation of bans against and restrictions on entry and settlement on their territory." See Churilov, November 23, 1996.

34. Text in *SZ RF*, 1997, no. 30, item 3596; *Diplomaticheskii vestnik*, 1997, no. 6, pp. 30–39; *Biulleten mezhdunarodnykh dogovorov*, 1997, no. 9, pp. 66–79.

35. See, for example, *Rossiiskaia federatsiia*, 1997, no. 8, pp. 6–9.

in the C.I.S. Its legislation contains a direct ban against it for citizens of Belarus. And inhabitants of the country who receive, *inter alia,* Russian citizenship thereby lose Belarus citizenship—with all the attendant consequences. Such a rigid position has brought about a situation where citizens of Russia living in Belarus exit from the citizenship of their primary Motherland. (A similar tendency can be observed only in Ukraine. Of the 33,000 who drew up final papers to leave Russian citizenship, 28,000 live in Belarus and Ukraine—but the latter has no immediate plans to enter into a tight Union with Russia.)[36] Nonetheless, reports published at the end of October 1998 indicated that the agenda of the November 2–3 session of the parliamentary assembly of the Union of Belarus and Russia in Iaroslavl featured, *inter alia,* the "problems of citizenship" and "electoral rights of citizens residing in Russia and Belarus." At the session, the deputies approved the draft text of the law "On the Citizenship of the Union," which envisaged "the right of citizens of the RF and Belarus not to be considered foreigners on the territory of the partner state."[37]

At the opposite end of the spectrum is Chechnia, which continues to wage its struggle to secede from Russia. Logically enough, that campaign has spilled over into the citizenship sector. In April 1998, stories were circulating in the mass media that the republic's government had just instructed the competent authorities not to issue any more passports of the federal type. How inhabitants of Chechnia were now expected to travel outside the republic was not explained. Local passport offices did not stock any sample forms of Chechen passports, of which only about 300 had been distributed thus far. The reason given for deciding to dispense with so-called Moscow passports was that their further deployment was bound to cause harm to the independence of the Chechen Republic.[38]

36. Sadkovskaia, May 14, 1997. Sadkovskaia returns to the subject in her newspaper article "Obshchee grazhdanstvo po ustavu i v zhizni," *Rossiiskie vesti,* November 27, 1997, where she discusses the need to elaborate legislation on joint citizenship to make the Union a true political amalgam, notes the difficulties of doing so (among the obstacles, Belarus's aforementioned antipathy to the notion of dual citizenship), and suggests that the first step toward that goal might involve synchronizing their respective citizenship laws. In the latter connection, her sense is that Russia's standards are higher than Belarus's—as witness the fact that Russia was one of the first states to ratify the European Convention on Citizenship—which would then require Belarus to raise the quality of its performance here to Russia's level.

37. *Nezavisimaia gazeta,* October 29, 1998, and Olegov, November 4, 1998.

38. *Nezavisimaia gazeta,* April 16, 1998. Around the same time, a story appeared in the Russian press about how the president of Chechnia had allegedly applied for a visa to travel to England and been informed by the British Embassy in Moscow that an entry visa would only be entered in his Russian-issued foreign passport, that he could be received in England solely as the head of one of the subjects of the Russian Federation and so the visit would have to be unofficial. The British consular staff would neither confirm nor deny the account. Charodeev, March 4, 1998.

Bitter controversy erupted in 1997 when the federal authorities unveiled their design for a new internal passport of the Russian Federation that no longer contained a space in which the bearer was required to enter his or her national identity. In liberal and pro–human rights circles, the proposed elimination of this notorious "fifth point," which had been a staple of Soviet practice, was greeted as a crucial step toward eliminating a prime source of past discrimination against local minorities and upgrading Russia's performance here to international standards.[39] Even among Russians, however, some denounced the reform as a misguided attempt to push an assimilationist line inspired, it was charged, by the desire to promote at any cost a vision of Russia's multiethnic population welded into a unified communal entity.[40] Joining the chorus of critics was a ragtag band of republic politicians and spokesmen for various Jewish groups with a stake in promoting the interests of their particular constituencies, whose membership effectively depended on the nationality index.

One of the first to raise his voice in protest was the president of Tatarstan. He went so far as to threaten to introduce special Tatarstan passports in the republic to protect his people's self-image. The Parliament of Tatarstan promptly followed suit by voting in favor of suspending the issuance of the new Russian passports.[41] The president of Ingushetiia likewise signaled his intention to fight to retain the nationality designation in the republic's repertory.[42] The scene then shifted to the lower house of the Russian Parliament, whose die-hard majority seized the opportunity to vent its antigovernment mood by passing a resolution that called for the restoration of the nationality slot in the planned passports.[43] In milder tones, the Council of the Federation soon after addressed a request to the government urging it to take into account the wishes of the ethnic minorities to keep the "fifth point" in the passport.[44] A compromise solution that was being discussed in the wake of these events contemplated the possibility of adding to the future passports for citizens of republics forming part of the Russian Feder-

39. Tishkov, October 22, 1997; Sachs, September 14, 1997, p. A21; Starovoitova, 1997, p. 5.
    The proponents of the revised format invoked in their legal arguments for discarding the "fifth point" the constitutional injunction (Art. 26) against requiring anyone to designate and indicate his nationality and the language of the European Convention on Citizenship that Russia planned to sign, which defined citizenship as the legal relations of an individual with the state without reference to ethnic origin. See *Rossiiskie vesti,* November 19, 1997.
    40. See, for example, Davydov, August 19, 1997; Khetagurov, December 19, 1997.
    41. Chugaev, October 24, 1997. See, too, Lebedev, November 11, 1997; Morozov, November 21–28, 1997; Shaimiev (president of the Republic of Tatarstan), 1997, p. 5.
    42. Sadkovskaia, October 24, 1997.
    43. Chugaev, October 24, 1997.
    44. Katanian, November 11, 1997.

ation extra pages to record the nationality of their owner or resorting to double entries by duplicating the principal data and the title of the document in the official language(s) of the respective republic, where applicable.[45] In fact, shortly thereafter it was reported that the inhabitants of the Komi Republic had cast their ballots for a bilingual passport—simultaneously in Russian and Komi. The leaders of the national movement considered the latest passports with entries only in Russian as "illegitimate."[46]

In Tatarstan, however, the nationalist fervor was not so easily appeased and, in February 1998, the republic State Council took up the bill On the Citizenship of the Republic of Tatarstan, which contained several provisions whose tenor could not be reconciled with the corresponding pronouncements of the federal Constitution or the federal citizenship statute. *Inter alia*, the draft text called for introducing a passport for citizens of Tatarstan and letting denizens of the republic renounce Russian citizenship while retaining the citizenship of Tatarstan. One article went so far as to proclaim that "hereditary descendants of the population of the Republic of Tatarstan acquire the citizenship of Tatarstan in a simplified manner." To Russian analysts, this proclamation sounded like an invitation to double or triple the population of the republic by enrolling citizens who have Tatar roots but live and will continue to live elsewhere.[47]

At any rate, cooler heads prevailed and the document was remanded to a commission for further study.[48] Meanwhile, the federal authorities also moved to defuse the issue by making changes in the law on certificates of registration, the effect of which was to entitle an individual, if he so desires, to have his nationality inscribed in his birth certificate upon reaching legal age. The amendment was obviously meant to respond to "the fact that many republics within

45. Chugaev, October 24, 1997; Tishkov, November 4, 1997. Interestingly enough, the largest exodus was predicted from Russian and Tatar identity once people were free to choose their own ethnic origin and would proceed to do so without regard to the categories listed in the catalogue of officially recognized nations that had effectively limited their options under the Soviet regime. Dozens of new nationalities were expected to resurface, now that these restrictions no longer applied, and cut into the size of the larger ethnic stocks in whose ranks these mini-groups had been forced to "take shelter" in the past. See, too, Postnova, June 2, 1998. In Dagestan, for instance, the passport/nationality issue seems to have generated little public interest, although the republic minister on Nationalities and Foreign Liaisons was quoted as saying that an insert would have to be designed for the new passports where the bearer's nationality would be indicated. Kisriev, December 16, 1997.

46. Borisevich, November 22, 1997.

47. Bronshtein, February 12, 1998; Mikhailin, February 21, 1998; Postnova, February 14, 1998.

48. *Izvestiia,* February 13, 1998; Gogolev, February 13, 1998; Shaimiev, February 14, 1998. See, too, York, April 13, 1998, p. A9.

Russia have insisted on this right and have wanted to state nationality in some legal documents."[49]

For the time being, at least, an uneasy truce reigns on this front. A number of Russian legal experts have expressed concern that citizenship matters, among other items on Russia's constitutional agenda, are being held hostage to each republic's political ability to extract concessions from the center, thus resulting in an array of ad hoc accommodations whose terms differ in concert with the prevailing power balance between the respective contracting parties. A uniform standard here would, in their opinion, serve the country's needs better, and, while most seem to prefer a strong federal system backed by a national brand of citizenship, some are prepared to concede that reality might require acceptance of a confederal version where the constituent republics would function as peer consorts of the federal regime by running their own citizenship shop.[50]

The public squabbling over how the central and republic authorities are supposed to interrelate under the tenets of Russia's constitutional culture has had the unfortunate consequence of injecting an element of uncertainty into the treatment of various technical procedures regulating the mode of admission into the country's citizenship. Going by the letter of the law currently on the books, for example, a foreigner who duly converts to the citizenship of the Russian Federation must, if he happens to be maintaining permanent residence in a subject republic, forthwith be assigned the latter's citizenship by virtue of that connection alone. In principle, then, no formal mechanism of admission to republic citizenship enters the picture.

Circumstantial evidence suggests, however, that an arrangement that once looked completely straightforward may since have lost that cachet and now fuels speculation about the way that system is really scheduled to function. Consider what is at stake when the author of a leading study on the citizenship law of the Russian Federation suddenly detours into a discussion of the need to spell out more precisely how, upon acquisition of the citizenship of the Russian Fed-

---

49. "In Russia," July 4, 1998. In the latest round of maneuvering, Tatarstan was reported to have drafted a letter addressed to Prime Minister Primakov with a request for his assistance to settle the festering problem of the new Russian passports. Not a single one of the 80,000 passports delivered to the republic had been issued to their intended owners so far and Tatarstan was seeking the inclusion of supplementary pages where entries would be made in the Tatar language, including data on the nationality of the *de cujus*. Soon after, the State Council of Tatarstan adopted at the second reading the bill On the Citizenship of the Republic of Tatarstan. The proposed statute records that Tatarstan has its own citizenship, that citizens of Tatarstan possess the citizenship of the RF, that termination of the citizenship of Tatarstan does not entail termination of RF citizenship. We are told that "the deputies adopted a softened formulation in regard to the document certifying the identity of a citizen of Tatarstan." *Izvestiia,* October 24, 1998, and October 31, 1998.

50. See, for example, Malikov, 1997, pp. 22, 24.

eration by a foreigner or stateless person, to answer the question of republic citizenship. According to him, several problems demand attention in this case:

> The Law requires that, when tackling questions of citizenship which affect the interests of a republic, the Commission on questions of citizenship attached to the office of the President of the Russian Federation take into account the views of competent organs of the republic (Art. 34). But from this it does not follow that pursuant to a decision of the federal organs adopted in conformity with said procedure the individual also receives the citizenship of the republic. The situation becomes even more complicated if the republic objected altogether to the granting of Russian citizenship.[51]

No hesitation is expressed, however, when talk turns to the duty of the Federation to stop every attempt by the republics to regulate citizenship traffic on the basis solely of national affiliation, indigenous population, and so forth. Oddly enough, that lesson is drawn from the experience of the former Soviet Union, where the practice of certain republics that sanctioned discrimination in such matters is cited as a "warning for Russia."[52]

Why dwell on this "crisis" in Russia's constitutional life? The reasons are twofold: First, the crisis illustrates the tenuousness of the central regime's control over this operation of citizenship regulations and raises valid doubts about the extent to which the norms of the federal statute can be relied upon when venturing into this arena. Second, any substantial erosion of the powers of the federal apparatus on citizenship matters is likely to work to the detriment of individuals concerned with their citizenship status, because republics are sure to pursue policies in this venue that will espouse standards less generous than those set at the federal level.

Dual Citizenship

The initial wording of Article 3(1) of the 1991 Law on RSFSR Citizenship decreed that "acquisition of the citizenship of the RSFSR by a foreign citizen can occur contingent on his renunciation of his former citizenship, except where otherwise provided by an international treaty of the RSFSR." Some Russian scholars saw this clause as proof that their country's law now sanctioned dual citizenship, that is, "the possibility of acquiring . . . the citizenship of the

51. Avakian, 1994, pp. 14–15.
52. Avakian, 1994, pp. 14–15.

Russian Federation while in possession of the citizenship of another state."[53] The innovation was generally well received for effecting a significant improvement compared with the old repertory that had bid to outlaw dual citizenship. Nevertheless, the reform must be rated as much more modest in scope than the above judgment suggests. In reality, the application of dual citizenship by the legislation of the Russian Federation was even then meant to be strictly limited—as witnessed by the requirement that a foreigner seeking to acquire Russian citizenship first shed his former citizenship, save where its retention is authorized by a treaty between the Russian Federation and the state of which the would-be inductee was already a citizen.

In 1993, however, the original edition of Article 3(1) was discarded in favor of a paragraph ordaining that "a person who is enrolled in the citizenship of the Russian Federation is not recognized as belonging to the citizenship of another state unless otherwise contemplated by an international treaty of the Russian Federation." From this statement it follows that henceforth "if someone claims Russian citizenship, he is no longer summoned to submit a document attesting to the absence on the claimant's part of any other citizenship."[54] Without that screen, then, the picture one gets is that any individual in possession of a foreign citizenship can at present obtain Russian citizenship through, say, normal naturalization procedures without having to indicate that letting him do so will instantly turn him into a de facto *bipatride*.

The scene is awash in paradox. Upon its debut, the 1991 model was praised by Russian analysts for validating the status of dual citizenship in Russian law, although even a cursory glance at the script shows that its design was actually animated by the desire to limit the incidence of dual citizenship. If complied with, it was bound to have precisely that effect. When the legislators shifted gears in 1993 and plainly reverted to the precedent that reigned during the Soviet era, they left no doubt that what they had in mind was simply to ignore any legal consequences that possession of dual citizenship might—and elsewhere

---

53. Lediakh, 1992, p. 29.
54. Andreev, January 15, 1994. Accordingly, Article 37(3) of the 1991 citizenship statute decreeing that persons acquiring the citizenship of the RSFSR and possessing the citizenship of another state must append to their declaration or solicitation a document confirming the termination of the former citizenship of the *de cujus*, except in certain designated cases, was now repealed. However, local authorities do not always bother to observe the new procedure. As late as 1997, for instance, a high official of the RF Ministry of Foreign Affairs was moved to note that in the Krasnodar and Stavropol Krays and the Rostov and Volgograd Oblasts, according to reports from "our embassies," there occur "frequent refusals to draw up the necessary papers for Russian citizenship in accordance with the Edict of the President of the Russian Federation (No. 2007 of 24 October 1994): in those places, they still demand certificates attesting to the absence of a foreign citizenship." Zubakov, 1997, p. 45.

generally does—entail, while simultaneously removing all barriers to its gene-
sis in the context of a bid to acquire Russian citizenship. In other words, an invitation was extended to each would-be convert to Russian citizenship to feel free
to add that membership card to his foreign citizenship packet and, in the same
breath, notice was posted that this foreign citizenship would enjoy no currency
wherever Russian law claimed the right to exercise sole jurisdiction.

The statute next addressed itself to the need to regulate the dual citizenship
phenomenon in the case of traffic running in the opposite direction, coming up
with the answer that "a citizen of the RSFSR may be permitted upon his request
to possess simultaneously the citizenship of another state with whom a corresponding treaty of the RSFSR exists." The logical inference is that the absence
of a duly approved request and suitable treaty license estops a Russian citizen
from obtaining or retaining the citizenship of another state—thus presumably
aiming to nip in the bud any attempt on his part to shop around for a second affiliation or count on availing himself of the services of one already owned.

Before the 1993 change of heart, this bid to keep Russian nationals from getting entangled in dual citizenship made sense, since in those days the Russian
regime operated with an agenda that also sought to prevent foreigners from
contracting Russian citizenship under circumstances that led them to incur dual
citizenship. After the switch to a laissez-faire outlook on dual citizenship as an
accompaniment to the acquisition of Russian citizenship by foreign nationals,
continuing to stick to the old policy of not letting Russian citizens enjoy the
same opportunity to add a foreign citizenship to their portfolio suggests a conscious decision to practice a double standard in this department. The new procedures were calculated to facilitate the acquisition and deployment of Russian
citizenship by citizens of other states in tandem with their own, while striving to
protect Russia's domestic monopoly from dilution by foreign brands of citizenship.

From all the above, the conclusion is inescapable that at this point Russian
legislation had not yet come to grips with the problem of dual citizenship. It
sanctioned the ad hoc inception of de facto dual citizenship by refusing to ask
the kind of questions that could prevent its occurrence, but it did not explicitly
enshrine the institution of dual citizenship in the local legal canon. The federal
Constitution, however, then took a significant step in the proper direction (Article 62) by prescribing that a citizen of the Russian Federation can have the citizenship of a foreign state (dual citizenship) in accordance with federal law or an
international treaty of the Russian Federation. Not only was dual citizenship
now referred to by name, but also federal law was cited along with international
treaties as a medium for validating a Russian citizen's right to claim title to dual
citizenship. Given that dual citizenship is always fraught with potential for

complications, the Constitution is praised for eschewing abstract endorsement of that condition and, instead, making its legitimacy contingent on compliance with whatever special terms might be attached to its operation in the Russian environment by applicable law or treaty.[55]

A slate of proposed amendments to the citizenship statute has been crawling through the lawmaking maze for a long time and at last seems poised to emerge. Among other things, the draft reportedly calls for Article 3 to be recast to spell out the principles governing acquisition of dual citizenship. The bill reportedly

> establishes that a person's belonging to a foreign citizenship poses no obstacle to his application for acquisition of the citizenship of the Russian Federation. Where a Russian simultaneously possesses the citizenship of a foreign state and is located on its territory, he enjoys the protection and sponsorship of the Russian Federation within the limits allowed by international law and the treaties of the Russian Federation and that country.[56]

Once the measure is passed, the mood of uncertainty that clings to the status of the dual citizenship phenomenon in Russia's legal repertory should be dispelled.

Ever since Russia switched to the pro–dual citizenship track, the Russian authorities have steadfastly maintained that its primary aim in doing so is to afford the members of the Russian diaspora a sense of security that they can always "go home" if need be. Therefore, they should not rush to repatriate, because their Motherland is not yet in shape to receive them properly. The official story is that the longer the influx can be postponed, the better Russia's chances are to recover its economic strength and marshal its domestic resources in order to stage a suitable welcome for its returning sons and daughters. Whether or not that tactic has had the desired effect has never been—and probably cannot be—empirically verified. Analysts do know that masses of people have moved to Russia from the other ex-republics of the former Soviet Union, but they cannot tell for sure whether their numbers would have been larger or smaller if they had not had ready access to both Russian citizenship and that of the respective successor state. Other factors intrude to affect the process, chiefly the level of the standard of living in the current host country compared with the conditions in Russia. Thus, possession of dual citizenship alone cannot really be viewed as the sole—or even the principal—element in catalyzing such decisions to reset-

---

55. Sadkovskaia, November 15, 1996.

56. *Rossiiskie vesti,* March 18, 1997. See, too *Rossiiskie vesti,* May 6, 1997, and Grigoreva, September 16, 1997.

tle. One is thus left to conjecture about whether Moscow's flirting with dual citizenship practice has increased the size of the exodus from the feeder countries, has reduced it, or has had no substantial impact on the volume of the traffic one way or the other.

Of course, the regime claims that its policy has largely succeeded in stemming the outflow and its recent move to recognize the dual citizenship mode *expressis verbis* in the revised version of the citizenship statute is presumably meant to be read as a vote of confidence in the quality of its performance here to date. Be that as it may, critics of the scheme paint a very different picture of what strikes them as an ostentatious display of liberal indulgence. In their considered opinion,

> possession of dual citizenship by the Russian-speaking residents of the newly independent states does not enhance the defense of their rights and freedoms. For those in whose name the institution was launched the procedure of acquiring Russian citizenship was facilitated by every means, but few benefits were reaped in the end. On the other hand, the generosity of the Russian piece of legislation is actively exploited by other citizens from the CIS countries. Here is just one example. Before the USSR fell apart, 600 thousand Russian-speaking individuals resided in Georgia. To this day, 170 thousand ethnic Russians and around 700 thousand Georgians have relocated to Russia. So, the question comes up: should there be retained in the law a provision of which it is very doubtful that our compatriots in the near abroad will be able to make full use, but which allows anyone to barge into our country who wishes to as long as he resides on the territory of the former USSR.[57]

Also worth noting in this connection is the technical distinction that Russian commentators insist on drawing between cases of dual citizenship *stricto sensu* and occasions where a person happens to hold two passports. Dual citizenship, as they see it, calls for the respective states to sign an agreement that specifies the relevant details and lets the eligible individual incur new relations with both contracting parties. At the same time, the latter determine in concert who extends what rights to the newly minted *bipatride* and who can demand the discharge of what duties.

In instances where an individual acts on his own initiative to add a foreign passport to the Russian document he already possesses, however, or vice versa, the competent Russian authorities are said to assume the posture of pretending

57. Sadkovskaia, May 14, 1997.

that they have no interest in the matter. Thus, having granted such a person the designated quota of rights, the administrative apparatus can then require that he fulfill all the obligations he owes the state, namely, payment of taxes, military service, compliance with the letter of Russian law, and so on. The result is a "legal situation where the problem does not exist as far as the state is concerned, it has no legal consequences. It is the private business of the dual citizen himself." To the question of whether, in the absence of a corresponding treaty, a "doubly connected" individual must satisfy his civic obligations in both of the countries with which he has opted to affiliate himself, the answer is that what he does to perform his duties or not "is his problem along with everything which this entails. The Russian state only fully recognizes the citizenship of those countries with whom we have concluded appropriate international treaties. In all other cases . . . we behave as though this is simply of no interest to us."[58]

Since Russia's current diplomatic inventory contains just two agreements of the type described above (with Turkmenistan, December 23, 1993, and Tajikistan, September 7, 1995), the bulk of its dual citizenship package must consist of the "two passport" brand, which, if the preceding statements can be trusted, means that the members of this constituency are largely left to their own devices, except for how Russia chooses to treat them in their capacity as Russian citizens. The focus on the Russian citizenship half of their identity to the total exclusion of the foreign "increment" accounts, among other factors, for the tenor of Article 3(3) of the citizenship statute, which records that "citizens of the RSFSR who also have another citizenship cannot for that reason be restricted in their rights, evade the performance of their obligations or be released from responsibilities stemming from the citizenship of the RSFSR." The 1993 Constitution, Article 62(2), sends virtually the same message, except to make adherence to the prescribed protocol contingent on the possibility that federal law or an international treaty of the Russian Federation might decree otherwise.

What incited the Russian regime to adopt such a rigid attitude toward its dual citizenship subjects is a mystery, especially in light of the fact that the decision to tinker with the legal script that made it easier to get dual citizenship with a Russian ingredient was entirely its own. Equally hard to explain is why the Russian authorities refuse to apply harsher or more lenient standards here depending on whether they are called upon to deal with those who went shopping for a second citizenship—and so have nobody to blame for their predicament but themselves—and those who were stuck with dual citizenship as a consequence of being trapped in a conflict of laws. Certainly, even a primitive sense of fairness about punishing culpability and rewarding innocence would counsel a

---

58. Sadkovskaia, November 15, 1996.

more nuanced approach, instead of which the "guilty" and the "victims" are lumped together and addressed in the same summary—and rough—manner.

Nor can one accept at face value the official claim of successful disengagement from the travails of de facto dual citizenship. Putting the onus on the individual caught in a dual citizenship squeeze works well enough in some situations, for example, where the *de cujus* is faced with the prospect of being drafted for military service or paying taxes in both countries of which he is formally a citizen. Other such collision cases are not so easily dropped in the lap of the "responsible" private party, with the contestant states calmly walking away from the scene of the accident. In the absence of a corresponding entente, the difficulties occasioned by disputes over citizenship attribution are quite apt to end up poisoning relations between the states themselves on a broad range of issues, especially whenever the agenda happens to feature pieces of business so loaded with potential to ignite public controversy as split loyalties, extraditability exemptions, and the like.

At any rate, a perfect example of the latter phenomenon recently cropped up on Russia's civil calendar in 1996. At stake were the circumstances surrounding the appointment in 1996 of B. A. Berezovskii to the post of deputy secretary of the Security Council of Russia, although at the time he apparently held the citizenship of both Russia and Israel.[59] The pros and cons of the proceedings in this case as well as the legality of such practice in general were thrashed out in the local press. The incident eventually prompted the State Duma to pass a resolution that directed the Ministry of Internal Affairs of the Russian Federation to check up on any evidence of possession of dual citizenship by citizens of the Russian Federation employed in government service, invited that similar verification be conducted with regard to the deputies of the State Duma, and suggested that the results of the investigation be reported to the State Duma by April 1, 1997.[60]

59. See, for example, Rumiantsev, November 15, 1996; Agafonov, November 22, 1996.

60. *Vedomosti RF,* 1997, no. 7, item 293; *SZ RF,* 1997, no. 9, item 1030. A legal consultantship service for the population offered by the journal *Iuridicheskii vestnik* subsequently discussed the issue of dual citizenship and service in the state apparatus in response to a letter from a reader without indicating what, if any, further action had so far been taken pursuant to the Duma resolution (February 1998, no. 3, p. 15).

A resolution of the government of the Russian Federation (No. 1003 of August 22, 1998) ratified the regulation on the procedure of allowing persons possessed of dual citizenship, stateless persons, as well as persons from among foreign citizens, emigrants, and re-emigrants, access to state secrets. *Inter alia,* persons with dual citizenship, obtained in accordance with the RSFSR law On the Citizenship of the RSFSR are given access to state secrets in the manner set for official persons and citizens of the Russian Federation. The designated persons are given access to information constituting state secrets classified as "secret" only after being checked by the organs of the federal security service. Text in *Rossiiskaia gazeta,* September 4, 1998.

Note, too, that starting in 1956 the USSR signed a string of bilateral conventions "to regulate the question of citizenship of persons with dual citizenship" in concert with Yugoslavia, Hungary, Romania, Albania, Czechoslovakia, Bulgaria, North Korea, Poland, Mongolia, and East Germany. Except for the treaties with East Germany and Hungary, which after the collapse of communism in East-Central Europe and the Soviet Union were formally declared as no longer in effect, the rest of these pacts has each been included in the respective succession package and so continues to operate—at least on paper. In reality, however, the available evidence suggests that the provisions of these agreements are generally ignored—on both sides of the corresponding border. A recently published account bemoaned the fact that various people in Poland were openly purchasing foreign passports and then claiming every imaginable immunity on the pretext that they are citizens of other countries. Despite the valid agreement between Poland and Russia, the Poles were doing nothing to police the phenomenon even vis-à-vis Russia and apparently neither were their Russian counterparts. This inaction caused the commentator to ask whether perhaps it was not about time that the Russian law-enforcement organs began to worry more about these problems.[61]

Retention of RSFSR Citizenship by Persons Living Outside the RSFSR

According to Article 4 of the citizenship statute, the sojourn of a citizen of the RSFSR outside the confines of the RSFSR does not terminate his citizenship. Presumably, the law's authors wanted to make sure that the bare fact of a Russian citizen going abroad—no matter what the duration of his stay there—would in no way impair his juridical ties with the Motherland, since they conceived of citizenship as a stable legal bond between the individual and the state that was intended to operate "independently of space."[62] Hence, its validity beyond the perimeter of the state's territorial jurisdiction was to remain unaffected even in the case of a decision by the person in question to settle overseas.

Without any designated cutoff date, this provision would seem to indicate that an expatriate's title to Russian citizenship is meant to be inherited from generation to generation if the proper combination of conditions stays in place for the effects of the *jus sanguinis* principle to persist. Under this set of circumstances, chances are good that such emigrants will acquire the citizenship of their host country somewhere down the line and then be doomed to carry the

---

61. Shapovalov, February 13, 1998.
62. Krylov, 1992, p. 12.

germs of dual citizenship *ad infinitum*—unless, of course, they ultimately take steps to snap the chain by winning formal release from their Russian affiliation.

Protection and Sponsorship of RSFSR Citizens Located Outside the RSFSR

Per Article 5 of the citizenship statute, RSFSR citizens outside the confines of the RSFSR enjoy the protection and sponsorship of the RSFSR. The state organs of the RSFSR, diplomatic representations and consular institutions of the RSFSR, and their official personnel are obliged to help ensure that RSFSR citizens are guaranteed the opportunity to exercise in full the rights established by the legislation of their host state, the international treaties of the RSFSR, and international customs. They must also defend the rights of the RSFSR citizens abroad and their legally protected interests and, if need be, instigate measures to redeem the rights of RSFSR citizens that have been violated.

The aspect of this formula that is relevant to the theme of the present study concerns, once again, the status of dual citizens and the limits of possible intervention by the Russian regime on their behalf because they still qualify as Russian citizens—although, of course, the other state whose citizenship they hold is equally justified in considering them its own. What one must remember here is that the whole pitch of Russia's citizenship canon on the subject of dual citizenship has from the start emphasized Russia's claim to such *bipatrides* and refusal to take into account the legal consequences accruing from concurrent possession by an individual of the citizenship of another state or the latter's title to the person in question by virtue of that parallel connection. Hence, very little room is left for compromise on these occasions when Moscow has made it perfectly clear that it is not willing to distinguish between passive and active brands of citizenship, or to take a backseat in instances where the logic of pragmatism might recommend accepting the empirical evidence of Russia's citizenship's lapse into a secondary, or dormant, role.

Obviously, this scenario creates ample opportunity to meddle in the affairs of other states by citing the duty owed one's citizens even when they count as citizens of and reside on the territory of the opposite party—and particularly so in Russia's case because the priority assigned to Russia's jurisdiction over the members of this constituency is not hedged in with any reservations whatever for the sake of accommodating the other state's stake in the same individual. A breakthrough on this front seemed to be forthcoming in 1999 judging by reports that the proposed revisions in the 1991 citizenship act now wending their way through the legislative pipeline contemplate, *inter alia*, that if a Russian simultaneously possesses the citizenship of another state and is located on its territory, he enjoys the protection and sponsorship of the Russian Federation within the limits sanctioned by international law and in accordance with the international treaties of the Russian Federation and that country.[63] The new version would mark a major improvement over the tone of the previous score, provided that practice duly observes the applicable *dicta* of international law at the implementation stage.

RSFSR Citizenship and Marriage

Russia's citizenship legislation follows Soviet precedent by pronouncing that the conclusion or dissolution of marriage of a citizen of the RSFSR with a person not belonging to the citizenship of the RSFSR entails no change in citizenship and that change of citizenship by one spouse does not entail change of citizenship of the other spouse. The principles embodied in this policy are said to be motivated by the desire to enhance the stability of the individual's legal bond with the state and immunize it from the effects of the vagaries of private life. Local spokesmen likewise praise the entry for comporting with the letter and spirit of the 1957 Convention on the Citizenship of the Married Woman whose primary intent is to shield married women from exposure to involuntary acquisition or loss of citizenship contingent on their marital status or changes in the citizenship affiliation of their spouse. The convention contains an added safeguard that calls for enabling a foreign wife to acquire the citizenship of her husband through a special simplified mode of naturalization, with the reservation that this procedure may be circumscribed in the interests of state security or public order. In light of the Russian citizenship statute's underlying concern here to abide by the standards of the convention, the law makes an arrangement that, in fact, goes one step further than its model for expedited treatment to facilitate the conversion of either a foreign husband or a foreign wife to the citizenship of his or her Russian spouse by medium of simple registration. Ultimately, then, marriage can entail consequences for the citizenship status of the partners, except that Russian analysts are quite right in noting that these changes do not occur *sua sponte* and at least require the interested party to go to the trouble of filling out registration forms.[64]

---

63. *Rossiiskie vesti,* March 18, 1997.

64. There is also, of course, the matter of "fictitious" marriages. As noted by Stepanov, 1998, p. 9: "This is always an 'instrument' of illegal migration. According to information furnished by state organs, it is used mostly by persons hailing from the republics of Transcaucasia and Ukraine, who thereby seek to transfer to Russian nationality. The state has a duty to protect itself from 'illegal aliens.' Chez nous, however, nobody pays any attention to them." He points out that failure to take appropriate measures means that national "resources earmarked for social purposes are squandered on a multitude of legal and illegal migrants."

A separate clause expands the coverage by specifying that dissolution of a marriage entails no change in the citizenship of children born of the marriage or adopted children. In this case, too, the ostensible goal is to maintain the stability of citizenship relations and guarantee the interests of children, except that an extra dose of care is now provided for the sake of this constituency by sanctioning restoration of Russian citizenship by medium of registration for persons whose Russian citizenship lapsed as a consequence of change in the citizenship of their parents. Those eligible for such summary reinstatement are allotted five years from the time they reach eighteen to file the proper papers.

Reduction of Statelessness

Under this rubric, the citizenship law records that the RSFSR encourages acquisition of the citizenship of the RSFSR by stateless persons and does not impede acquisition by them of another citizenship. The significance of the problem of statelessness lies primarily in the need to ensure the true equality of all persons, inasmuch as in many countries stateless persons are often discriminated against, as well as to defend their rights and freedoms in case conflicts arise. Reference is made in this connection to the 1961 convention on reducing statelessness devoted to the task of reducing the pool of individuals thus cast adrift. Russia's commitment to this proposition is attributable to a growing malaise in official circles over the appearance on its territory of a substantial number of persons who are refugees from the countries of their permanent abode and have de facto lost their citizenship. To deal with this phenomenon, local legal experts argue in favor of elaborating legislation to define the procedure of acquisition of the citizenship of the RSFSR by individuals suffering from this infirmity.[65] For instance, G. Stepanov cites the case of "refuseniks" who, for the most part, hail from Iraq and Syria:

During the period when the USSR existed and good relations prevailed with these states, their youth received higher education here. Many, after graduating from the institutions of higher learning, continued their graduate studies, entered into matrimony with Russian citizens and, as foreigners, received residence permits and continue to live here up till now.

But, over the last 10-15 years, the situation in those states changed and the majority of Iraqis and Syrians simply fear to approach their embassies for prolonging the duration of their passports. Their foreign passports

65. Krylov, 1992, p. 15.

have expired, they do not want to become stateless persons and claim
Russian citizenship.

The question arises: whom are we dealing with? At first blush, everything looks simple—these are persons without citizenship. But, recognizing this must be preceded by certain legal procedures and receipt of a
corresponding document.[66]

The same philosophy, incidentally, is shared by other members of the Commonwealth as witnessed by the tenor of the "recommended legislative act" con-
taining a set of "concerted principles for regulating citizenship" that was
adopted by the Commonwealth's Inter-Parliamentary Assembly at its session
of December 29, 1992.[67] The designated purpose of the proposed guidelines
was to upgrade the level of protection of human rights within the Commonwealth, curb the occurrence of statelessness, facilitate contacts among people,
and establish and maintain friendly and good-neighbor relations with all states
that are prepared to consider them as a basis for their domestic legislation on
citizenship. On the subject of statelessness, that document echoes the theme of
offering encouragement to stateless persons to acquire citizenship (though
without repeating the second portion of the Russian equation that promises not
to impede acquisition by them of another citizenship), and it espouses the norm
that children born on the territory of one of the member states of the C.I.S. must
not become stateless persons.

Russian citizenship heeds that latter injunction by riding to the rescue where
children face the prospect of incurring statelessness, even though, as already
mentioned, it is strangely remiss in not extending a commensurate helping hand
to adults sentenced to that fate—beyond recognizing the possibility of cutting
in half the residency requirement for admission to RF citizenship in processing
applications from individuals who qualify as refugees under the terms of the
law or the international treaties of the Russian Federation or waiving all preconditions where a person has received asylum on the territory of the Russian Federation. Add to the spartan fare a one-time rescue mission mounted for the
benefit of stateless persons who on the date of entry into force of the citizenship
act permanently resided on the territory of the RSFSR or other republics directly forming part of the late USSR as of September 1, 1991: the members of

66. Stepanov, 1998. The general lack of sympathy for the plight of adult *apatrides* on the Russian scene is reflected in Stepanov's accompanying comments to the effect that the "refuseniks"
usually get upset that Russian law-enforcement agencies find no grounds for granting them Russian
citizenship and really have no right to do so. Instead, he says, "they should thank the Russian Federation for the fact that they are located on its territory and are not expelled."

67. Mitskevich, 1996, pp. 75–77.

this flock were given one year from the date of entry of the citizenship statute into force to record their wish to acquire the citizenship of the RSFSR just by going through the process of registration. By contrast, special dispensations do operate *sine die* for children faced with the threat of statelessness. For instance, where the parents of a child have different citizenships, one of them being a citizen of the Russian Federation at the time of the child's birth and the other a citizen of another country, the question of the citizenship of the child regardless of place of birth is decided by written agreement of the parents. In the absence of a corresponding agreement, the child acquires the citizenship of the Russian Federation if it is born on the territory of the Russian Federation or would otherwise end up stateless.

Next, a child located on the territory of the Russian Federation both of whose parents are unknown is considered a citizen of the Russian Federation, except that its citizenship may change if the identity of at least one of the parents, guardian, or trustee subsequently comes to light. Then, a child born on the territory of the Russian Federation of parents who are citizens of other states is assigned the citizenship of the Russian Federation if those states do not grant him their citizenship. Finally, a child born on the territory of the Russian Federation to stateless persons counts as a citizen of the Russian Federation.

Comparable measures are deployed to prevent children from being precipitated into statelessness in various other circumstances. To cite one such example that fits the thematic focus of this study: if a child who is not a citizen of the Russian Federation is adopted by spouses one of whom is a Russian citizen and the other has a different citizenship, he or she becomes a citizen of the Russian Federation by agreement of the adopting parents. Without such an agreement, the child becomes a citizen of the Russian Federation if he or she sojourns on the territory of the Russian Federation or would otherwise remain or become a stateless person.

The bottom line is a fairly comprehensive safety net designed to forestall a child slipping into the limbo of a stateless existence. Russian law seems to feel free to intervene unilaterally in these circumstances on behalf of a child headed for statelessness either as a result of accidentally falling through gaps in the legal fabric or by default of the parents in not taking appropriate action to spare their progeny that hardship. The Russian government does not appear to be bothered by the idea of pinning Russian citizenship on a child caught in that kind of trap through the *ex parte* exercise of its legal powers. Where adults stuck in such a predicament are concerned, "forcible" conversion even of stateless individuals sounds wrong and is not practiced by the local authorities who prefer instead to persuade the affected individual to take the right steps toward obtaining the citizenship of Russia or perhaps some other state. Of course, as noted above, no fast lane has as yet been installed for servicing this need in the Russian environment—an oversight that marks a serious discrepancy between word and deed.

Modes of Admittance to Russian Citizenship

Having described the legal framework, we can now turn to the proceedures by which persons may acquire citizenship of the Russian Federation.

At Birth

The basic rule here postulates that a child born to parents who possess the citizenship of the RSFSR is considered a citizen of the RSFSR no matter where the birth takes place. Although Russia also applies the principle of *jus soli* in certain circumstances and recognizes other grounds for assigning its citizenship to children at birth, the *jus sanguinis* test is given priority on the premise that the central role in deciding the issue is played by the common citizenship of the child's parents. If only one of the parents of the child at the time of its birth possesses the citizenship of the RSFSR and the other parent is a stateless person, the child counts as a citizen of the RSFSR regardless of place of birth. Here, too, the scale is tipped in favor of Russian citizenship in order, reportedly, better to serve "the interests of the child"[68] and help "reduce the number of stateless persons."[69]

In cases where the parents have different citizenships, one of them at the time of the child's birth possessing Russian citizenship and the other holding a foreign citizenship, the question of the citizenship of the child is determined by written agreement of the parents. "If the agreement was not duly filed in final form and a dispute erupts, the child acquires Russian citizenship since the law always sides with the parent who possesses the citizenship of the Russian Federation."[70] Without a corresponding agreement, the child acquires the citizenship of the RSFSR if it is born on the territory of the RSFSR or would otherwise end up stateless. Ancillary regulations (as amended in 1993) detail that where parents with different citizenships (one of them being a Russian citizen) choose the newborn's citizenship, they must submit before the child turns one a copy of the birth certificate and the written agreement that confirms their choice of citizenship to the organs of internal affairs or the consular office at their place of residence. In this context, the authorities rely on the parents' preference. Only

68. Avakian, 1994, pp. 29–30.
69. Krylov, 1992, p. 21.
70. Krylov, 1992, p. 21.

where that fails to work do they look for relief to the norm of *jus soli*, if that element is present, or the norm of *jus sanguinis* if it is not and the child is otherwise bound to incur statelessness. The regime's willingness to shift gears repeatedly to achieve a positive outcome evinces a creditable streak of pragmatic flexibility that deserves commendation for, among other things, sparing the individuals concerned a brush with statelessness.

The law envisages further cases where neither the will of the parents nor *jus sanguinis* is a viable factor in various contingencies surrounding a child's birth and so designates the principle of *jus soli* to fill the void. Thus, a child located on the territory of the RSFSR both of whose parents are unknown is considered a citizen of the RSFSR, with the proviso that the attribution of Russian citizenship may be reversed once the identity of at least one of the parents, guardian, or trustee has been established. First, the foundling is registered in the organs of registry of acts of civil status on the presumption that his parents are Russian citizens.[71] The recognition of parental rights is possible only by applying to the organs of guardianship and trusteeship armed with an appropriate court order. Next, a child born on the territory of the RSFSR to stateless individuals forthwith receives Russian citizenship, a procedure that calls for a finding to that effect by the organs of the Ministry of Internal Affairs or Administration of Internal Affairs that is attached to the personal file of one of the parents, and a corresponding inscription is entered or stamped into the child's birth certificate.

Finally, a child born on the territory of the RSFSR is considered a citizen of the RSFSR if its parents are citizens of other republics that formed part of the USSR as of September 1, 1991, or foreign states and if these republics or states withhold their citizenship from the child. The reference to the other ex-republics of the Soviet Union (subsequently deleted from the text in favor of a general statement concerning foreign states) allegedly reflected the RSFSR's view of itself as successor to the USSR. That reasoning does not extend, of course, to the foreign states mentioned in the same breath. Thus, this provision is another sample of Russia's generosity toward children threatened with statelessness that entails staking them to Russian citizenship in order to save them from that undesirable experience. Still, as one local spokesman notes, the picture is unclear about whether *jus soli* kicks in "automatically or at the request of the parents."[72]

---

71. Krylov, 1992, p. 21. Oddly enough, Avakian, 1994, p. 31, takes the opposite view and claims that "what is most likely the case here is that the child has been abandoned and its skin color indicates that the parents or one of them has a foreign provenance." The argument in favor of the state's intervention on the foundling's behalf would then be predicated on the fact of abandonment by a foreign parent or parents from which no relief can reasonably be expected.

72. Avakian, 1994, p. 31.

By Naturalization

A person who is not a citizen of the Russian Federation, has dispositive capacity, and is eighteen years of age or older can apply for admission into the citizenship of the Russian Federation regardless of origin; social status; racial or national appurtenance; gender; education; language; and rapport with religion, political, and other convictions. The normal condition for admission into the citizenship of the Russian Federation is permanent residence on the territory of the Russian Federation: for a foreign citizen or stateless person, a total of five years or three years uninterrupted immediately prior to filing the application; for refugees recognized as such by law or treaty of the Russian Federation, the designated terms are cut in half. The stint of residence on the territory of the Russian Federation is considered to be continuous if the person in question went abroad for study or medical treatment for no more than three months. The only unusual item in the package pertains to the permanent residency requirement for naturalization purposes whose appearance in the 1991 citizenship statute marks its debut in Russia's legislative canon. Even so, local sources refer to the prescribed length of local residency as "not high."[73]

The law also catalogues a number of circumstances that can facilitate admission into Russian citizenship by entitling the applicant to a reduction of the respective waiting period, including the possibility of waiving the test altogether. The following grounds are cited as warranting preferential processing of a naturalization request: (1) past possession of the citizenship of the former USSR; (2) adoption of a child who is a citizen of the RSFSR; (3) a record of high accomplishments in the fields of science, technology, or culture, as well as possession of a profession or skill that is of interest to the RSFSR; (4) a record of meritorious service to the peoples pooled in the RSFSR, toward the renaissance of the RSFSR, and the attainment of universal human ideals and values; and (5) grant of asylum on the territory of the RSFSR.

Some of the items on this list call for a closer look. The special dispensation for people adopting Russian children is said to be prompted by the same concern that is often encountered in other countries as well for the care of one's young, which, *inter alia*, means letting them be adopted by foreigners only in exceptional cases. Encouraging such foreigners to convert to the child's Russian citizenship on short notice is thus intended to enable them to get around that roadblock while living up to one's sense of responsibility toward the minor by arranging to keep him in the fold notwithstanding the "transfer." Next, objections have been voiced to the idea of giving easy access to local citizenship

73. Krylov, 1992, p. 25.

in order to attract a certain brand of "quality immigrant." The United States, for instance, is criticized for practicing an immigration policy that fuels a brain drain in other countries, and Russia itself is portrayed as a victim of this phenomenon. Now, Russia has opted to emulate the U.S. example, and the decision to do so has not met with universal approval on the home scene.[74]

Finally, award of territorial asylum in Russia as a prelude to quick admission into Russian citizenship remains a dead letter in today's political reality. On the one hand, the 1993 Constitution takes the trouble to advertise that "the Russian Federation grants political asylum to foreign citizens and stateless persons in accordance with the universally recognized norms of international law." On the other hand, if the chairman of the commission on questions of citizenship attached to the office of the president of the Russian Federation can be believed, as of mid-1996 that panel had received only two requests for asylum: one involved a citizen of North Korea whose application was approved and who subsequently moved to South Korea; no action was taken on the second petition, which had been submitted by the former president of Azerbaijan, A. Mutalibov.[75] Many more requests for territorial asylum are filed, of course, but they are routinely rejected at lower levels of the administrative apparatus and never reach the upper rungs of the hierarchy for review on the merits. In a lone departure from such stonewalling tactics, subordinate agencies did give visas to a handful of applications from thirteen (or sixteen by another count) journalists who by 1994 had fled to Russia from Tajikistan (out of a batch of approximately one hundred fellow exiles), but solely "by way of exception."[76] Even Russian spokesmen now concede that "although the granting of asylum is envisaged by the Russian Constitution, to get it is virtually impossible."[77] Since asylum thus remains out of reach as a practical proposition, all talk of its role in expediting the extension of Russian citizenship to asylum seekers is moot at this stage of the game.

Even more stringent controls may be in the offing for policing the procurement of sanctuary on Russian soil. Calls have recently been heard for establishing a special permanent bureau of the Commonwealth to coordinate the struggle against and deal effectively with the scourge of drug addiction. Among the views broached in this connection is a recommendation that "the grant of

74. Avakian, 1994, pp. 35–36.
75. See interview by Shcherbachenko, June 14, 1996, and by Shcherbina, July 11, 1996. According to a leading human rights activist in Moscow, "No person who has turned to the Russian authorities for political asylum has been granted it since the moment Russia joined the UN Convention on the status of refugees" in 1992. Lyubarsky, May 1996, p. 21.
76. Urigashvili, September 22, 1994, and Grankina, June 7, 1996.
77. Grankina, June 7, 1996.

political asylum be barred . . . for persons accused and wanted by law-enforcement organs for illegally trafficking in drugs. . . ."[78]

Although the citizenship statute says nothing about using treaties to institute
a simplified mode of naturalization for the nationals of the respective signatory
parties, concerted arrangements along those lines have, in fact, been made on
two occasions that have introduced a quasi-instant regime for converting from
one designated citizenship to the other. The agreement between Russia and
Kazakhstan contemplating a "fast lane" procedure for acquisition of citizenship
by citizens of the Russian Federation arriving for permanent sojourn in the Republic of Kazakhstan and citizens of the Republic of Kazakhstan arriving for
permanent sojourn in the Russian Federation was concluded on January 20,
1995. A twin version, *mutatis mutandis*, was contracted between the Russian
Federation and the Kyrgyzstan Republic on March 28, 1996. It is safe to predict
that no comparable ententes with non-Commonwealth partners are forthcoming since the tenor of these operations is tailored to the specific conditions prevailing in the post-Soviet geopolitical space, chiefly the continued search for
relief from the trauma of state succession still afflicting so many subjects of the
former USSR.

Admission into citizenship is a two-way street where an individual expresses a desire to acquire the citizenship of the Russian Federation and the latter responds to that request. Hence, the state cannot be indifferent to the
credentials of a candidate. It sets conditions under which an application to obtain Russian citizenship will be refused, namely, where the applicant (a) calls
for use of force to change the constitutional order of the RSFSR; (b) is a member of a party or organization whose activities are incompatible with the constitutional principles of the RSFSR; or (c) has been convicted and is serving
sentence to loss of freedom for acts for which he can be charged under the laws
of the RSFSR.

Interestingly enough, the pitch of point (b) has been severely criticized on
the grounds that

> this strange, to say the least, wording is obviously murky which allows
> one to ascribe to it any interpretation whatever, depending on who the pe-
> titioner happens to be and the mood of the Russian functionary handling
> the case. Furthermore, the aforecited wording plainly contradicts para. 1
> of the same Art. 19 which indicates that a person can petition for admis-
> sion into the citizenship of the Russian Federation without regard, *inter
> alia*, to his "political or other convictions."[79]

78. See, for example, Gasanov, November 13, 1997.
79. Avakian, 1994, p. 36.

These negative comments must have struck a sore nerve, judging from reports that this section of the statute is scheduled to be rephrased and in its new guise will single out "parties and social organizations employing terrorist methods in their activities."[80]

Clause (c) also gives pause. Read literally, the pronouncement would seem to refer to instances where a person seeking Russian citizenship is at the time he files the corresponding application convicted and serving sentence entailing physical detention. Certainly, much more must be at stake here. First, such persons can apparently submit relevant explanations in their defense, the substance of which must be addressed by the proper authorities, although, of course, there is no guarantee that the claim will be upheld. Second, the competent agencies are expected to conduct their own investigations into an applicant's history for possible brushes with the law that might make him undesirable as a recruit for the national constituency. Thus, the Ministry of Internal Affairs checks the applicant to see whether or not he is wanted or has been charged. After that, the data are forwarded to the Federal Security Service, which verifies them through its own channels, and only then are the documents relayed to the commission on questions of citizenship attached to the office of the president of the Russian Federation. The materials are next examined by the commission, including those findings that prompted the preceding instances to recommend that the petition be rejected. On occasion, the commission's conclusions differ from those of the departments that assist it in running this operation. After discussion at a session of the current crop of naturalization applications, the commission submits to the president a proposal concerning each of them, which, practically speaking, represents a draft version of the decree awaiting signature by the head of state.[81]

The Russian authorities have good reason for carefully screening individuals wishing to acquire Russian citizenship. Remember that the citizenship law postulates that a citizen of the RSFSR cannot be surrendered to another state otherwise than on the basis of the law or a treaty of the RSFSR. By contrast, the 1993 Constitution takes a harder line on that score and dictates that a citizen of the Russian Federation cannot be banished outside the confines of the Russian Federation or surrendered to another state. The bar against involuntary exile had already been raised to constitutional level on April 21, 1992, and was meant to preclude any repetition of the sorry experience during the 1970s when persons critical of the regime, that is, dissidents, were summarily expelled and, more often than not, coincidentally stripped of Russian citizenship. As for transnational rendition, the 1993 Constitution eschews any mention of circum-

---

80. *Rossiiskie vesti,* March 18, 1997.
81. *Rossiiskie vesti,* March 18, 1997.

stances that might warrant the extradition of a Russian citizen to a foreign state and ends up flatly forbidding such transfer. The language of Article 3(1) of the citizenship act is slated to be rewritten to conform with the tenor of the constitutional model's absolute injunction against the rendition of Russian citizens abroad.[82]

Thorough scrutiny of a would-be citizen's past makes extra sense where the state is likely to get stuck with a criminal and subsequently incur considerable expenditure of time and money in a bid either to cancel his naturalization as having been fraudulently obtained or to prosecute him locally where the imputed act qualifies as a criminal offence under Russian law as well. The issue is a live one. The chairman of the federal commission on questions of citizenship, for example, has had occasion to cite in a press interview instances where a person who had committed a crime back home tries to acquire Russian citizenship in the knowledge that Russia does not surrender its citizens to other countries to face criminal charges. At any rate, he quickly dismissed "such a method of self-defence" as "naive."[83]

In a second episode, the Office of the Procurator-General of Russia reached a decision on May 16, 1996, to surrender to the Uzbek authorities the president of the financial-industrial consortium Rusti-Rosti registered in Moscow and former general director of the stock company Uzgosnefteprodukty, A. Khusainov. The suspect was arrested on December 22, 1995, by order of the General Procuracy of the Russian Federation at the behest of the Uzbek authorities who accused him of abuse of official powers. Already after his arrest, Khusainov managed to obtain Russian citizenship through the Russian Embassy in Tashkent. The presidential commission on questions of citizenship concluded that Khusainov received Russian citizenship in violation of established procedures, but left the final decision on the matter to the Ministry of Foreign Affairs. The procedure for surrendering Khusainov to the Uzbek au-

---

82. *Nezavisimaia gazeta,* September 16, 1997. See also *Rossiiskie vesti,* March 18, 1997, and May 6, 1997. Two cases confirm the rule against the rendition of Russian citizens to foreign states: *in re Lozhkin,* 1995, pp. 14–15, and *in re Podshebiakin,* 1995, pp. 5–6, although in the latter case the Criminal Bench of the RF Supreme Court still mouthed the obsolete formula that a citizen of the Russian Federation cannot be surrendered to a foreign state except on the basis of a law or international treaty. In any event, both cases were remanded to local courts of first instance for trial. Lozhkin's offence (committed in Kazakhstan) was squarely covered by a corresponding provision of the Russian Criminal Code, but in Podshebiakin's case the lower court was instructed to determine whether an equivalent existed in the Russian Criminal Code for the offence imputed to him under the Criminal Code of Uzbekistan.

83. Interview by Shcherbachenko, June 14, 1996.

thorities contemplates revoking his Russian citizenship; Uzbek authorities contest the legality of Khusainov's acquisition of Russian citizenship.[84]

Proposals for still tighter policing in such matters are awaiting legislative endorsement. When passed, the changes would add to the slate of grounds for
blackballing a petition for naturalization the following: forcible eviction of the
individual from the Russian Federation in the course of the three years preceding submission of the application, the solicitor's record as a repeat offender,
and so on.[85] Also being discussed at the Commonwealth level in connection
with joint projects to combat the drug problem are plans for vesting a special
permanent organ of the C.I.S. to coordinate the campaign against and mount an
effective response to the spread of drug addiction with the power to block the
procurement of citizenship and right of sojourn in any member state of the
Commonwealth to all persons accused of and being sought by law-enforcement
agencies for illegally trafficking in drugs.[86]

The real irony here, however, is that the test whose deployment has sin-
gle-handedly managed to turn the country's entire naturalization process into a
game of Russian roulette—I am speaking of the notorious practice of *propiska*
or residency permit—has no legislative mandate to play this role and no recognized relation to this function. Yet, the administrative agencies responsible for
"assigning" living quarters to Russia's inhabitants have for years wielded that
power in a totally discretionary fashion to approve or deny a person's choice of
abode. Although repeatedly struck down by the Constitutional Court for contra-
vening the charter's guarantees of the individual's freedom to pick his place of
domicile and recently recast as residency registration to emphasize that it is intended as a mere bookkeeping device for recording the address indicated by the
de cujus as his dwelling spot with no right of refusal to do so, *propiska*-registra-
tion continues to thrive in the Russian environment and remains the bureaucracy's most potent weapon for controlling as it pleases access to the country's
citizenship rolls.

The arbitrary exercise of this authority can best be judged from the tenor of
widely circulated accounts reporting how employees of the institutions performing these duties have blandly informed persons entangled in their web that
"without *propiska*, you cannot get citizenship, and, without citizenship, you
cannot get *propiska*." The prospects for breaking this vicious circle in the foreseeable future are bleak and the consequence is that the naturalization system so

84. *Nezavisimaia gazeta,* May 18, 1996.
85. *Rossiiskie vesti,* March 18, 1997.
86. Gasanov, November 13, 1997.

neatly outlined in the legislative canon is, in fact, in shambles and will stay that way until the nation's bureaucratic juggernaut is brought to heel—should that ever happen.[87] In the plus column, the legislative script's message on this subject sounds civil enough and, if the so-called subnormative distortions were erased, its pronouncements could afford the pool of potential customers a quality of service that would, on balance, comport with the general standards governing these matters.

A quick look at what sort of people have so far succeeded in obtaining Russian citizenship through naturalization will help round out the picture. Overwhelmingly, the newcomers are drawn from the ranks of those who have past nationality-citizenship ties with pre-Soviet Russia or the USSR. Until now, bona fide foreigners were conspicuously absent from the scene, to a point where a recent presidential decree ratifying the admission of 234 adults into the citizenship of the Russian Federation drew special attention in Moscow's press for the unusual detail that sprinkled among the latest recruits were a few genuine foreigners: three individuals born in Afghanistan, two born in Korea, two born in China, and one born in Vietnam.[88] The event may portend an era of greater liberality ahead in extending Russian citizenship to alien immigrants who aspire to gain full legal enrollment in the host community—albeit with no assurance at all that the influx will at any time soon be allowed to swell to tidal proportions.

Meantime, the question must be asked about how firm is an acquired deed to Russian citizenship. The answer is that the citizenship law does allow for the revocation of Russian citizenship, but only in instances where the *de cujus* received it on the basis of deliberately falsified information and counterfeit documents. The fact of committing such perjury is established in court proceedings and the rescission of the naturalization decision does not exempt the offender from facing legal charges. On a somewhat more positive note, the law does not extend the sanction of repeal of the naturalization decision to the spouse and children of the culprit who acquired the citizenship of the Russian Federation together with him or her if it is not proved that they knew that the citizenship of the Russian Federation was being obtained by illegal means. Important, too, is the companion proviso that stipulates that reversal of the

87. Thus, a recently published article on the subject of procuratorial supervision over the implementation of legislation on citizenship discusses in considerable detail the applicable procedures and sets out what the procuratorial apparatus ought to be doing to perform this assignment, but sheds no light whatever on anything that it has, in fact, done in this province. See, Churilov and Vinokurov, 1998, pp. 12–18. From other sources, one gets the distinct impression that the procuratorial branch has been singularly remiss in exercising its jurisdiction in this venue.

88. *Rossiiskaia gazeta,* March 7, 1998; *SZ RF,* 1998, no. 10, item 1189.

naturalization decision on the grounds indicated is possible during a five-year period from the date of admission.

Incidentally, legitimate doubts have been expressed about how effective this brand of punishment is likely to be given that where the innocent spouse retains his or her Russian citizenship, the guilty party can after a while petition for what amounts to preferential admission into Russian citizenship through registration channels that are open to persons whose spouse is a citizen of the RSFSR.[89]

By Derivative Naturalization

An important element of any naturalization package is the treatment that lies in store for minors upon change in the citizenship affiliation of one parent or both parents. The cornerstone rule in Russian law under this rubric is that the citizenship of children under fourteen years of age follows the citizenship of the parents. The citizenship of children between the ages of fourteen and eighteen changes contingent on their consent, which must be couched in written form and certified by a notary. The citizenship of children does not change upon change in the citizenship of parents deprived of parental rights nor does change in the citizenship of the children require the consent of parents who have been deprived of parental rights. These norms are admittedly harsh, but their deployment is justified by the need to protect the children: parents deprived of parental rights in effect lose their children and the capacity to influence their fate.[90]

If both parents acquire or a sole parent acquires the citizenship of the RSFSR, the citizenship of the children changes accordingly. For children under the age of fourteen, the relabeling is automatic; those between the ages of fourteen and eighteen must record their consent thereto in a written document validated by a notary. If one of the two parents who do not have Russian citizenship acquires it, the child is granted the citizenship of the RSFSR upon request of the parent who acquired Russian citizenship, which must be accompanied by the other parent's endorsement of the "vote"—again, couched in written form and duly authenticated by a notary.

The bill to amend the citizenship statute that is currently under consideration includes a proposal to simplify the procedure of admission into and release from the citizenship of the Russian Federation in the case of children under eighteen if there is a corresponding joint statement by the parents where one of them is a Russian citizen and the other a foreign national.[91]

89. Avakian, 1994, p. 44.
90. Mikhaleva, 1992, p. 32.
91. *Rossiiskie vesti*, March 18, 1997.

Adoption raises similar problems. Thus, a child who is not a citizen of the RSFSR, if adopted by a citizen of the RSFSR or a couple who are citizens of the RSFSR, instantly becomes a citizen of the RSFSR. If such a child is adopted by a couple, one spouse being a citizen of the RSFSR and the other a stateless person, the child is also forthwith assigned the citizenship of the RSFSR. Finally, if a child who is not a citizen of the RSFSR is adopted by a couple, one spouse being a citizen of the RSFSR and the other holding a different citizenship, the child becomes a citizen of the RSFSR by agreement between the parents. Without such agreement, the child becomes a citizen of the RSFSR if it resides on the territory of the RSFSR or if otherwise it would remain or become a stateless person.

Appeal from Decisions on Citizenship of the RSFSR

Decisions by a competent organ denying registration of acquisition or termination of the citizenship of the RSFSR or possession of the citizenship of the RSFSR can be appealed to a court within one month for review on the merits of the ruling. Refusal to accept statements and petitions on questions of citizenship, violation of the deadlines set for examining statements and petitions, as well as other actions by official personnel of the competent organs that violate the regime for treating cases of citizenship and the regime for executing decisions on questions of citizenship of the Russian Federation may be appealed in the prescribed manner to the respective superior official or a court. Persons permanently residing outside the confines of the Russian Federation file appeals against such actions by the diplomatic representations or consular institutions of the Russian Federation to the Moscow city court. On such occasions, the aggrieved individual is not challenging a decision taken on the merits of his claim but is appealing procedural irregularities committed by the corresponding officials. Note, though, that the decisions by the president of the Russian Federation regarding petitions on questions of citizenship are final and cannot be contested in court.

The question of which court can hear this category of cases is not addressed in the statute. A secondary source has emphasized that it would be desirable to clarify that issue and direct the traffic to the district or city court of general jurisdiction, or the court of a subject of the Russian Federation, or, lastly, the Supreme Court of the Russian Federation. The point made here is that the

common logic of procedural regulation is that where the law says "appeal to a court", what is being talked about is the district (city) court at the place where the organ or official person is located. However, this logic is frequently subject to exceptions in the legislation itself. And, in order to be completely certain, it would be best to designate the level of court to which disputes over citizenship shall be submitted.[92]

In any event, so far I have not run across any reported case of a decision by a regular court relating to citizenship matters.

Since the applicable provisions of Russia's citizenship law and the mode of their implementation have been analyzed and criticized piecemeal in the course of the preceding narrative, elaborate conclusions would serve no further purpose except to rehash what has already been said. Instead, let me offer once again an observation that has repeatedly been made throughout the study: As written, Soviet citizenship law sounds fine in terms of the signals it sends to individuals seeking to obtain Russian citizenship papers. The trouble comes in the implementation, where wholesale administrative mangling of the law's pronouncements has created an environment in which many of these liberal promises remain a dead letter. The treatment accorded to a person who wants to convert to Russian citizenship bears scarcely any resemblance to the message posted on the legislative billboard. Often, today's performance is so bad as to recall the abuses perpetrated in the Soviet era. Forecasting that Russia will or will not manage to get rid of this curse—and, if yes, when—depends on whether the person offering the judgment is an optimist or a pessimist. Where Russia's political and legal mores are concerned, I am afraid that I belong in the pessimist camp.

References

Agafonov, S. (November 22, 1996.) "O grazhdanstve Borisa Berezovskogo. V poslednii raz." *Izvestiia.*

Alekseev, S. 1998. "Kto pomozhet bezhentsam? Tysiachi afgantsev prevrashchaiutsia v bomzhei." *Nezavisimaia gazeta—Regiony,* no. 1.

"Analiticheskii obzor konstitutsii respublik, vkhodiashchikh v sostav Rossiiskoi Federatsii." 1994. *Rossiiskaia federatsiia,* no. 21, pp. 18–27.

Andreev, I. (January 15, 1994.) "Vyezd za granitsu: utochnenie v pravilakh." *Izvestiia.*

Argumenty i fakty. 1997, no. 29, p. 16.

Avakian, S.A. 1994. *Grazhdanstvo Rossiiskoi Federatsii.* Moscow: Rossiiskii iuridicheskii izdatelskii dom.

Biulleten mezhdunarodnykh dogovorov. 1997, no. 9, pp. 66–79.

Bohlen, C. (June 13, 1998.) "Moscow Jobs Beckon, but Let the Migrant Beware." *New York Times,* p. A3.

92. Avakian, 1994, p. 55.

Bondarenko, M. 1998. "Chem zaniatsia afgantsu na Donu." *Nezavisimaia gazeta—Regiony,* no. 1, p. 11

Borisevich, T. (November 22, 1997.) "Pasporta budut na dvukh iazykakh." *Rossiiskie vesti.*

Bronshtein, B. (February 12, 1998.) "Parlament Tatarstana vnov stavit vopros o grazhdanstve." *Izvestiia.*

Central Asia Monitor. 1998, no. 1, p. 24.

Charodeev, G. (March 4, 1998.) "Prezidenta Chechni pustiat v London kak grazhdanina Rossii." *Izvestiia.*

Chugaev, S. (October 24, 1997.) "Budet vam 'piatyi punkt'." *Izvestiia.*

Churakova, E. (January 13, 1998.) "K novomu tysiachiletiiu Rossiiu popolniat tri milliona immigrantov." *Finansovye izvestiia,* VI.

Churilov, A., and Iu. Vinokurov. 1998. "Prokurorskii nadzor za ispolneniem zakonodatelstva o grazhdanstve." *Zakonnost,* no. 7, pp. 12–18.

Churilov, A. (November 23, 1996.) "600 tysiach narushenii zakonov vyiavili za poslednie 2.5 goda prokurory vo vsekh sferakh deiatelnosti gosudarstva i obshchestva." *Rossiiskie vesti.*

Davydov, G. (August 19, 1997.) "I snova—rodina slonov. . . ." *Nezavisimaia gazeta.*

Diplomaticheskii vestnik. 1997, no. 9, p. 44.

Diplomaticheskii vestnik. 1997, no. 6, pp. 30–39

Gasanov, E. (November 13, 1997.) "Skhvatka s narkomafiei." *Nezavisimaia gazeta.*

Ginsburgs, George. 1998. *From Soviet to Russian International Law, Studies in Continuity and Change.* M. Nijhoff: The Hague/Boston/London.

Gogolev, A. (February 13, 1998.) "Shaimiyev Holds Deputies Back from a Clash with Moscow." *Kommersant-Daily,* condensed text in *Current Digest of the Post-Soviet Press,* 1998, no. 6, pp. 13–14.

Grankina, V. (December 30, 1997.) "V Moskve zhivet bolee 60 tysiach afganskikh bezhentsev." *Nezavisimaia gazeta.*

Grankina, V. (June 7, 1996.) "Sudba bezhentsev v Rossii." *Nezavisimaia gazeta.*

Grigoreva, E. (September 16, 1997.) "Vstrechi v Kremle." *Nezavisimaia gazeta.*

"In Russia a Citizen May Have a Nationality Only if He Wishes to." (July 4, 1998.) *Novye izvestiia,* in *Current Digest of the Post-Soviet Press,* 1998, no. 27, p. 14.

Izvestiia, October 24, 1998, and October 31, 1998.

Izvestiia, February 13, 1998.

Kamakin, A. 1998. "Interview with Tatiana Regent, Director of the Federal Migration Service of Russia." *Nezavisimaia gazeta—Regiony,* no. 8, p. 10.

Katanian, K. (November 11, 1997.) "Otkaz ot piatogo punkta." *Nezavisimaia gazeta.*

Kisriev, E. (December 16, 1997.) "Natsionalnyi pasport ili natsionalnost v pasporte?" *Nezavisimaia gazeta.*

Khetagurov, G.A. (December 19, 1997.) "Vnov po povodu piatogo punkta." *Nezavisimaia gazeta.*

Khorev, B. 1997. "Rossiia: 'Velikoe pereselenie narodov'." *Dialog,* no. 5, p. 27.

Korovin, D. (October 30, 1997.) "Moskovskie gastarbaitery budut zhit po zakonu." *Izvestiia.*

Krylov, B.S. 1992. In *Zakon o grazhdanstve Rossiiskoi Federatsii (nauchno-prakticheskii kommentarii).* Moscow: Izdanie Verkhovnogo Soveta RF.

Kutafin, O. E. 1997. In *Diplomaticheskii vestnik,* no. 2, p. 41.

Lebedev, P. (November 11, 1997.) "Opiat budem pisat: mat—russkaia, otets—iurist?" *Rossiiskaia gazeta.*

Lediakh, I. 1992. "Kommentarii Zakona 'O grazhdanstve RSFSR'." *Sovetskaia iustitsiia,* no. 6, p. 29.

Lozhkin. 1995. *Biulleten Verkhovnogo Suda Rossiiskoi Federatsii,* no. 5, pp. 14–15.

Lyubarsky, K. (May 1996.) "Inhospitable Russia." *New Times,* p. 21.

Malikov, M.K. 1997. "Grazhdanstvo Rossiiskoi Federatsii i grazhdanstvo ee sub'ektov." *Gosudarstvo i pravo,* no. 8, pp. 21–24.

Mikhailin, D. (February 21, 1998.) "Odin pasport dva gosudarstva?" *Rossiiskaia gazeta.*

Mikhaleva, N.A. 1992. In *Zakon o grazhdanstve Rossiiskoi Federatsii (nauchno-prakticheskii kommentarii).* Moscow: Izdanie Verkhovnogo Soveta RF.

Mitskevich, A.V. 1996. *Kommentarii zakonodatelstva gosudarstv—uchastnikov SNG o grazhdanstve.* Moscow: Izdatelstvo "Iuridicheskaia literatura."

Morozov, N. (November 21–28, 1997.) "Bars protiv orla." *Pravda.*

Nezavisimaia gazeta, October 29, 1998.

Nezavisimaia gazeta, April 16, 1998.

Nezavisimaia gazeta, September 16, 1997.

Nezavisimaia gazeta, May 18, 1996.

Nezavisimaia gazeta, February 16, 1996.

Nikonorov, N. (January 19, 1995.) "70 tysiach tainykh emigrantov." *Rossiiskaia gazeta.*

Olegov, F. (November 4, 1998.) "Deputaty 'dvoiki' aktiviziruiut sotrudnichestvo." *Nezavisimaia gazeta.*

Osenev, V. 1997. "Zhong Guo (China)." *Russian Politics and Law,* no. 6, p. 87.

Podshebiakin. 1995. *Biulleten Verkhovnogo Suda Rossiiskoi Federatsii,* no. 6, pp. 5–6.

Postnova, V. (June 2, 1998.) "Tak Bulgary ili vse zhe tatary?" *Nezavisimaia gazeta.*

Postnova, V. (February 14, 1998.) "Gossovet Tatarii obsuzhdaet proekt zakona o grazhdanstve." *Nezavisimaia gazeta.*

Pravda, April 16, 1997, and May 14, 1997.

Rossiiskaia federatsiia. 1997, no. 8, pp. 6–9.

Rossiiskaia gazeta, September 4, 1998.

Rossiiskaia gazeta, March 7, 1998.

Rossiiskaia gazeta, May 28, 1996.

Rossiiskie vesti, November 19, 1997.

Rossiiskie vesti, May 6, 1997.

Rossiiskie vesti, March 18, 1997.

Rumiantsev, O. (November 15, 1996.) "Iavnyi pravovoi probel." *Nezavisimaia gazeta.*

Sachs, S. (September 14, 1997.) "Russia's New Passport Hailed by Rights Activist." *Philadelphia Inquirer,* p. A21.

Sadkovskaia, T. (November 27, 1997.) "Obshchee grazhdanstvo po ustavu i v zhizni." *Rossiiskie vesti.*

Sadkovskaia, T. (October 24, 1997.) "'Piatipunktovyi' konflikt." *Rossiiskie vesti.*

Sadkovskaia, T. (May 14, 1997.) "Chetyre pasporta mogut okazatsia v karmane rossiianina." *Rossiiskie vesti.*

Sadkovskaia, T. (November 15, 1996.) "Dvoinoe grazhdanstvo—ne 'dvoinoe dno.'" *Rossiiskie vesti.*

Shaimiev, M. (February 14, 1998.) "Podlinnyi federalizm vsegda na storone regionov." *Rossiiskaia gazeta.*

Shaimiev, M. 1997. *Argumenty i fakty,* no. 45, p. 5.

Shapovalov, A. (February 13, 1998.) "Kupite pasport—pro zapas." *Rossiiskaia gazeta.*

Sharapov, A. (October 16, 1992.)"Grazhdanstvo ne dar, a iskonnoe pravo." *Rossiiskaia gazeta.*

Shcherbachenko, M. (June 14, 1996.) "Pozvolte prinadlezhat Otechestvu." *Rossiiskaia gazeta.*

Shcherbina, N. (July 11, 1996.) "Nikto ne razrushit most grazhdanstva." *Rossiiskie vesti.*

Starovoitova, G. 1997. *Argumenty i fakty,* no. 45, p. 5.

Stepanov, R. 1998. "Rossiia—zemlia obetovannaia." Iuridicheskii vestnik, no. 22, p. 9.

Sukalo, A. E. 1996. In *Kommentarii k Konstitutsii Rossiiskoi Federatsii.* 2nd ed. Moscow: Izdatelstvo BEK.

SZ RF. 1998, no. 10, item 1189.

SZ RF. 1997, no. 47, item 5406.

SZ RF. 1997, no. 30, item 3596.

SZ RF. 1997, no. 9, item 1030.

SZ RF. 1996, no. 21, item 2579.

SZ RF. 1995, no. 5, item 496.

Tishkov, V. (November 4, 1997.) "Natsionalnosti i pasport." *Izvestiia.*

Tishkov, V. (October 22, 1997.) "Proshchanie s piatym punktom." *Nezavisimaia gazeta.*

Urigashvili, B. (September 22, 1994.) "Ne zhdali. U rossiiskikh vlastei net ne tolko sredstv pomogat politicheskim bezhentsam, no net, kazhetsia, i zhelaniia." *Izvestiia.*

Vasilev, V. 1992. "Grazhdanstvo posle raspada SSSR." *Narodnyi deputat,* no. 18, p. 60.

Vedomosti RF. 1997, no. 7, item 293.

Vedomosti. 1993, no. 29, item 1112.

Vedomosti. 1992, no. 6, item 243.

York, G. (April 13, 1998.) "Tatarstan Forges Model of Independence." *Globe and Mail* (Toronto), p. A9.

Zubakov, Iu.A. 1997. In *Diplomaticheskii vestnik,* no. 2, pp. 44, 45.

CHAPTER SEVEN

Post-Apartheid Citizenship in South Africa

JONATHAN KLAAREN

CITIZENSHIP IN SOUTH AFRICA is an unfolding story that cannot be easily separated from other issues, as South Africans struggle to remake their political, social, and economic order in the post-apartheid era. This paper will aim at only a small part of that story. It focuses on enactment of the first post-apartheid legislation concerning citizenship, the South African Citizenship Act 88 of 1995. My central theme is that although the 1995 act was the first major piece of citizenship legislation since 1949, it did not make far-reaching substantive changes to the preexisting South African rules of citizenship—except in the significant aspect that it made citizenship rules uniform throughout the Republic.

Of course, the passage of the 1995 citizenship act is not the only recent significant event regarding citizenship in South Africa. Important administrative measures were taken with respect to voting in the liberation election of 1994 and with respect to unifying the various administrative departments concerned with immigration and citizenship. So, too, citizenship issues arose in the drafting of the final Constitution.[1] Citizenship has been influenced by the post-apart-

---

The author would like to thank Alex Aleinikoff, Raylene Keightley, and Doug Klusmeyer for helpful comments.

1. Constitution of the Republic of South Africa Act 108 of 1996 (1996 Constitution) section 3 on citizenship provides: "(1) There is a common South African citizenship. (2) All citizens are (a) equally entitled to the rights, privileges and benefits of citizenship; and (b) equally subject to the duties and responsibilities of citizenship. (3) National legislation must provide for the acquisition, loss and restoration of citizenship."

heid cabinet-approved grants of amnesty to three categories of persons present in the Republic in violation of immigration laws (mine workers, South African Development Community citizens, and Mozambicans). It has also been shaped by the Department of Home Affairs' inaction in revamping the primary piece of immigration legislation, the Aliens Control Act 96 of 1991. Even the Truth and Reconciliation Commission process has raised citizenship issues.[2]

Analysis of the passage of the 1995 act—the constitutionality of which I have explored elsewhere[3]—leads to exploration of the principles underlying citizenship in the new South Africa. Before getting to that story, I will briefly canvass the history of formal citizenship in South Africa during apartheid, the basic structure of citizenship and permanent residence law, and current patterns of immigration to South Africa. After a brief look at the rights of aliens in the new South Africa, I will conclude with a discussion of the essential continuity of the new citizenship regime with its predecessors and possible reasons for this continuity.

A Brief History of South African Citizenship from 1949 to 1995

This section conducts a brief survey of South African citizenship law from 1949 to the passage of the 1995 act, focusing on the formal legislation rather than the historical context.[4] This period spans from the passage of the primary piece of citizenship legislation governing during apartheid, the South African Citizenship Act 44 of 1949, until its repeal by the 1995 South African Citizenship Act. The period can itself be split into three phases with the division between the first and the second marked by the Bantu Homelands Citizenship Act 26 of 1970[5] and the division between the second and the third marked by the Restoration of South African Citizenship Act 73 of 1986. This last act was preceded by former state president P.W. Botha's 1985 statement, "The Govern-

---

2. Klaaren, 1998, "Truth and Reconciliation."

3. The constitutionality of some of the major provisions of the South African Citizenship Act of 1995 is discussed briefly in Klaaren, 1998, "Immigration."

4. This section adopts the perspective of South African constitutional law. The term "national" is used to refer to the international law aspect of nationality-citizenship, and "citizen" to refer to the domestic-constitutional law aspect. For a history of formal citizenship law developments in South Africa before 1949, see Schmidt, 1993, pars. 343–47. The historical literature on documented immigration to South Africa and the administration of the system of pass controls is surprisingly thin. Peberdy, 1997, p. 2; Hindson, 1987, p. 1. The same appears to be the case for formal citizenship administration.

5. This act was later renamed the Black States Citizenship Act and even later, in 1980, the National States Citizenship Act.

ment does not regard the loss of South African citizenship to be the inevitable result of a national state becoming independent."[6]

In South Africa for the twenty years or so before 1949, there were no South African citizens, only British subjects and Union nationals. In 1926, the South African Parliament defined the status of a British subject for the purposes of South African law.[7] In 1927, another piece of legislation was put into place that created a distinct South African nationality, the status of a Union national.[8] Aliens were defined as persons who were not British subjects in terms of the 1926 act.[9] While not all British subjects had status as Union nationals, all Union nationals were considered by South African legislation as British subjects, and the overlap was nearly complete.

These conditions changed with the South African Citizenship Act of 1949. The 1949 act instituted the status of South African citizenship, essentially substituting that status for that of Union nationality.[10] A British subject would henceforth be either a South African citizen or a citizen of another Commonwealth country or the Republic of Ireland.[11] Even after the 1949 act was passed, however, certain preferences for Commonwealth subjects remained. As initially passed, the South African Citizenship Act of 1949 contained a provision allowing citizens of other Commonwealth countries to register and thereby obtain South African citizenship.[12] For instance, a Canadian citizen could become a South African citizen by registration by fulfilling some residence and other conditions. This registration provision was abolished a year after South Africa declared its status as a republic in 1961.[13]

6. Budlender, 1985, "Common Citizenship?" Some might start this phase earlier. See Dugard, 1980.

7. British Nationality in the Union and Naturalization and Status of Aliens Act of 1926.

8. Union Nationality and Flags Act of 1927. This 1927 act replaced the earlier effort to determine British nationality on the basis of a common code with other Commonwealth states as attempted in the British Nationality in the Union and Naturalization and Status of Aliens Act of 1926.

9. Union Nationality and Flags Act of 1927, section 9.

10. See, for example, South African Citizenship Act of 1949, section 38, providing that, as a matter of interpretation, references in other legislation to Union nationality should be taken as references to South African citizenship.

11. The act differed significantly from earlier legislation defining Union nationals by providing that a married woman did not derive her citizenship status from that of her husband. South African Citizenship Act of 1949, sections 12–14.

12. South African Citizenship Act of 1949, section 8. See Schmidt, 1993, par. 351.

13. Commonwealth Relations Act of 1962, section 19. The declaration of republic status did affect citizens of Botswana, Lesotho, and Swaziland. From 1963, they were no longer treated as Union nationals and, with certain exceptions, were treated under South Africa's alien legislation. See Peberdy, 1997, p. 7.

The establishment of the status of South African citizenship was also the first phase of apartheid citizenship. Citizenship was a necessary but not sufficient qualification for the franchise. Race was an additional qualification for the franchise but not for citizenship. While the status of citizenship was common, not all citizens were equal.[14]

The second phase of apartheid citizenship legislation began in 1970 with the Bantu Homelands Citizenship Act.[15] Applying only to blacks, this act ensured that every black South African was granted an additional status of citizenship on the basis of connection to one of the designated homelands through language, culture, or race. Initially, this status was additional to and not diminishing of the common (if empty) South African citizenship.[16] For instance, people who were granted Transkeian citizenship retained their status as South African citizens and as South African nationals.

When the homeland to which a person was linked was granted independence by means of South African legislation, however, that person lost both South African citizenship and nationality. As Professor Dugard describes the situation, "Prior to independence all persons linguistically or culturally connected with the homeland were already citizens of the territory but nationals of South Africa. On independence such persons became both citizens and nationals of the homeland and ceased to be South African nationals."[17] For instance, the Transkei was granted independence on October 26, 1976, pursuant to the Status of Transkei Act. By this South African legislation, Transkeian citizens ceased to be South African citizens from that time.[18] Thus from the

14. That blacks did not enjoy full rights of civil and political participation such as the franchise in the Republic led many to condemn this citizenship status as empty. "In South Africa, Blacks are not really citizens since they do not exercise full civil and political rights in the central political process." Dugard, 1980, p. 22.

15. The concept of an additional status of citizenship on the basis of race had been introduced to South African law seven years earlier in the Transkei Constitution Act of 1963. Section 7 of this act made "every Xhosa-speaking Bantu person in the Republic" who did not belong to another homeland (such as Ciskei) a citizen of Transkei.

16. Section 2(4) of the Bantu Homelands Citizenship Act read in part: "A citizen of a territorial authority area [for example, a homeland] shall not be regarded as an alien in the Republic and shall, by virtue of his citizenship of a territory forming part of the Republic, remain for all purposes a citizen of the Republic and shall be accorded full protection according to international law by the Republic." Of course, blacks were placed one conceptual step away from the common South African citizenship by enjoying that common citizenship only "by virtue of" their homeland citizenship.

17. Dugard, 1980, p. 25. Professor Dugard did not term blacks as South African citizens before independence on account of his view that true citizenship must mean full civil and political rights.

18. Status of Transkei Act of 1976, section 6. As Dugard, 1980, p. 25, wrote, "The independence-conferring statutes carefully refrain from depriving persons of South African nationality on grounds of race. Instead, they prescribe language and culture as the criteria for denationalization. There can, however, be no doubt that in practice they are intended to apply to Blacks only as this accords with declared government policy. Certainly there is no known instance in which a white, col-

viewpoint of South African law, these people had lost their South African citizenship.[19]

The most extreme formulation of the homelands citizenship policy was probably made by C.P. Mulder, the minister of Bantu Administration and Development, in 1978. He stated:

> If our policy is taken to its full logical conclusion as far as the black people are concerned, there will be not one black man with South African citizenship. . . . Every black man in South Africa will eventually be accommodated in some independent new state in this honourable way and there will no longer be a moral obligation on this Parliament to accommodate these people politically.[20]

At the same time that South Africa was forcibly divesting many of its black citizens of their status, it was forcing that status on a completely different group of potential citizens, white males of an age to perform military service. From 1978, with certain conditions, persons permanently resident in the Republic for five years automatically became citizens by naturalization.[21] The purpose was to render noncitizen male residents eligible for military service.[22] The South African Defence Force was increasingly used during the 1970s and 1980s to support the apartheid state, and its troops were deployed in both regional and domestic military action.[23]

The third phase of formal citizenship under apartheid is characterized by legal confusion but also by a growing if halting formal acceptance of the notion of a common South African citizenship.[24] Its start can be marked by the passage of the

---

ored, or Asian person connected with the Transkei, Bophuthatswana, or Venda has been deprived of his nationality since the conferment of independence on these states."

19. From 1978 (and for Bophuthatswana from its independence in 1977), provision was made for a citizen of an independent homeland to recover South African citizenship by becoming a citizen of a nonindependent homeland. See Dugard, 1980, pp. 25–26; van Wyk, 1978, p. 148.

20. House of Assembly Debates (Hansard), col. 579, February 7, 1978 (as quoted in Dugard, 1980, p. 16). As Dugard points out, it was this type of overreaching that doomed the homelands strategy to political failure: "If Transkeian nationality had not been compulsorily extended to all persons connected with Transkei, however remotely, it might have been possible to view Transkeian independence as a simple achievement of statehood. But once South Africa set the denationalization of all persons ethnically or culturally linked with Transkei as the price for independence, the goal of recognition became impossible."

21. See Schmidt, 1993, par. 352. See also van Wyk, 1978.

22. South Africa, "Memorandum on the Objects of the South African Citizenship Bill, 1995" (B23–95), par. 3.2.

23. The legal relationship between citizenship and military service was a complex one. For one part of it, see *Kelleher v. Minister of Defence,* 1982 (3) SA 278 (SECL).

24. This confusion was built in and planned for in the citizenship regime. For instance, section 6 of the each of the four status acts (Status of the Transkei Act of 1976, Status of Bophuthatswana Act of 1977, Status of Venda Act of 1979, and Status of Ciskei Act of 1981) provided for a board to

Restoration of South African Citizenship Act of 1986. The significant pieces of legislative action during this phase were the Restoration and Extension of South African Citizenship Act of 1993 and the 1993 interim Constitution.

South African human rights lawyers greeted with suspicion the government's initial moves toward a common citizenship.[25] They noted that the denationalization process had affected different groups of people in different ways and were quick to point out the gaps in the stated policy (detailed below). They questioned the content of the offered citizenship, querying whether the right to live and work in South Africa, the right to reside in urban areas, and the right of access to courts were included. They were also concerned that the government was offering merely common nationality rather than common citizenship; in short, a passport without the vote was not acceptable.

Such fears were well founded. The Restoration of South African Citizenship Act passed in 1986 was no more than a "half a loaf" type of statute. Recall that prior legislation had denationalized persons with citizenship in one of the independent homelands—Transkei, Bophuthatswana, Venda, and Ciskei (TBVC citizens). The 1986 statute restored citizenship only to those TBVC citizens who were permanently resident in South Africa. Thus, the bulk of the approximately 9 million people denationalized—those permanently resident in the territory of the independent homelands—remained without South African citizenship.[26] Moreover, even those people eligible for restoration of citizenship needed to go through a complicated administrative application procedure to enjoy the benefits of the act. By 1992, it was estimated that less than half of the 1.8 million people who in the government's estimate could benefit from the 1986 act would, in fact, do so.[27] In the end, the 1986 act was really no more than a "ninth of a loaf" and a small step toward a common South African citizenship.[28]

---

be established between the Republic and each of the four homelands to finally determine the citizenship of people whose status was unclear. See Schmidt, 1993, par. 357. See also Dugard, 1980, p. 21, who noted, "There is much confusion in South Africa today over the policies of the South African Government with respect to citizenship."

25. Budlender, 1985, "Common Citizenship?" pp. 210–17. For an account of the basis for such wariness laid during the legal struggle against the pass laws, see Abel, 1995, pp. 24–65.

26. See Dugard, 1992, p. 16.

27. Dugard, 1992, pp. 16–17; see also Budlender, 1989, p. 51.

28. The administrative manifestation of these developments in citizenship policy was the abandonment of the influx control system in 1986: Abolition of Influx Control Act of 1986. The influx control system applied to Africans. At the same time as the abolition of influx control, a limited set of controls on the movement of Indians within two provinces of the Republic, the Orange Free State and Natal, was repealed. Dugard, 1992, p. 17. State regulation over the movement of people into the cities was not itself abandoned, however. The government replaced the racially based influx control system with an ostensibly nonracial policy of "orderly urbanization." As noted below, the 1986 act has also been criticized in that when read together with *Tshwete v. Minister of Home Affairs*, 1988

Parallel to this tentative legislative restoration of citizenship, there was much confusion evident in the courts over the exact effects of denationalization.[29] Some of the confusion centered on a provision in the Status of Transkei Act and the other status acts and legislative and administrative action that appeared to mitigate the effects of denationalization by providing that citizens of the independent homelands resident in the Republic would not forfeit existing rights, privileges, or benefits on account of the status act.[30] In interpreting these internally contradictory provisions, the Appellate Division (the AD, then the highest court in South Africa) failed to challenge the denationalization policy in any significant way. For instance, in *Tshwete v. Minister of Home Affairs,* the AD held that "the only way in which the citizens of Transkei, Bophuthatswana, Venda, and Ciskei ('TBVC citizens') can claim a right of permanent residence in South Africa, is by relying on s 12 of the Aliens Act, which provides that aliens domiciled in South Africa do not need a permanent residence permit."[31] Read with a later provision in the 1986 restoration act, this statement, in fact, had the effect of denying permanent residence in South Africa to TBVC citizens resident there.[32] While the logic of the court's decision was murky (and roundly criticized), the judicial support for executive-determined citizenship policy was clear. Legislative developments in formal citizenship policy in the homelands added to the confusion. Each of the four independent homelands had constitutional provisions and a statutory framework governing citizenship that constituted a formal part of the South African citizenship regime during this period.[33] Citizenship policy was thus further made uncertain by formally separate citizenship regimes.

This legislative and judicial confusion had to be addressed by legislative developments surrounding the transition to the post-apartheid Government of National Unity. The Restoration and Extension of South African Citizenship Act 196 of 1993 was part of a package of legislation agreed upon by the negotiating

(4) SA 586 (A), it confirmed the loss of the right of permanent residence to those TBVC citizens resident in South Africa.

29. Budlender, 1985, "Incorporation and Exclusion," pp. 3–9.

30. For instance, section 6(3) of the Status of Ciskei Act of 1981 provided: "No citizen of the Ciskei resident in the Republic at the commencement of this Act shall, except as regards citizenship, forfeit any existing rights, privileges or benefits by reason only of the other provisions of the Act."

31. Budlender, 1989, p. 50. See *Tshwete v. Minister of Home Affairs,* 1988 (4) SA 586 (A).

32. Budlender, 1989, pp. 53–54.

33. See sections 57 and 58, Republic of Transkei Constitution Act of 1976 (Transkei); section 80, Republic of Bophuthatswana Constitution Act of 1977 (Bophuthatswana); sections 59 and 60, Republic of Venda Constitution Act of 1979 (Venda); section 67, Republic of Ciskei Constitution Act of 1981; Citizenship of Transkei Act of 1976; Bophuthatswana Citizenship Act of 1978; Citizenship of Venda Act of 1980; and Ciskeian Citizenship Act of 1984.

parties in the drafting of the interim Constitution. The act automatically restored South African citizenship to those people who had lost their citizenship by force of the status acts' grants of independence to the former homelands. It further automatically granted South African citizenship to those who would have been South African citizens by birth or descent had the status acts not been passed, for example the children of parents who had only TBVC citizenship when those children were born. It also adopted the principle that all other people who were TBVC citizens (such as those who were naturalized by the homelands) would have to apply for South African citizenship by naturalization.[34] Finally, the citizenship provisions of the status acts were made nonapplicable to South African citizens and those to whom citizenship had been restored or extended.

The priority accorded to the legislative provision of citizenship at this time was driven by the need to provide an administrative structure for the participation of TBVC citizens in the April 27, 1994, elections. The Restoration and Extension of South African Citizenship Act thus took effect from January 1, 1994, four months before the April 27 elections. Two months later, the constitutional protection of the franchise took effect.[35] The repeal of the status acts and the reincorporation of the independent homelands would wait until the election date itself to be effected in terms of a schedule to the interim Constitution. Thus, the constitutional entrenchment of a common citizenship can be dated from April 27, 1994.[36]

Despite the creation of a common South African citizenship, the separate citizenship regimes of the former independent homelands continued to operate in each of the formerly independent homelands. While the interim Constitution did repeal the Bantu Homelands Citizenship Act, it left untouched legislation such as the Citizenship of Transkei Act of 1976 (Transkei). This act and others like it were enacted by the homelands legislatures themselves. It took the 1995 South African Citizenship Act to formally repeal these pieces of homelands citizenship legislation and provide for a single statutory instrument governing citizenship across the Republic.[37] The passage of this act is examined in detail below.

34. This principle was revisited during the passage of the 1995 act as discussed below.

35. Section 6 of the interim Constitution took effect from March 9, 1994. In this sense, one can state that a common constitutional right to vote preceded a common South African citizenship.

36. Section 5(1) of the interim Constitution provided: "There shall be a South African citizenship."

37. Even after the passage of the 1995 act, there remain strong legal traces of the homelands citizenship legislation. For instance, in *Bangindawo and Others v. Head of the Nyanda Regional Authority and Another* 1998 (3) SA 262 (Tk), the court was willing to attach some meaning to the concept of "Transkei citizenship," despite the provision for a common citizenship in the Constitution, for the limited purpose of determining the jurisdiction of the regional authority courts. Where

Current Migration Patterns

South Africa is currently witnessing substantial migration across its bor-ders.[38] Noncitizens are entering the country, especially from Mozambique and other states of the Southern African Development Community (SADC). Deter-mining the precise number of immigrants is difficult, but it is clear that post-apartheid South Africa has seen "a massive escalation in legal and undocu-mented migration of workseekers to South Africa from the region."[39] Migra-tion, in the sense of movement of people unregulated by the state, is a major feature of the contemporary South African polity.[40]

The best estimates of the population of noncitizens in the country range from 500,000 to 1.5 million in a total population of 37.9 million.[41] This figure repre-sents a sizable portion of the population; but it is far less than figures thrown around in popular and policy discourse, which have gone as high as 12 million people.[42]

Reflecting both the reality and the perception of this increase, a muscular re-sponse has been forthcoming. In 1996, a record number of repatriations were conducted: more than 150,000 people were transported out of the country, more than 80 percent of whom went to Mozambique. Deportation figures have shown a dramatic escalation over the past five years.[43] Perhaps most worrying has been a rising trend of xenophobia.[44] One of the most dramatic incidents oc-curred in September 1998 when three Senegalese citizens were killed by a crowd of unemployed people on a Johannesburg-bound commuter train as the crowd was returning from a protest march in Pretoria.

---

the accused in a criminal case or all the parties in a civil case are "citizens of the Transkei," these courts exercise concurrent jurisdiction with magistrates' courts.

38. One part of this migration has been a refugee flow where South Africa participates in a continent-wide trend. See Maluwa, 1995. For a brief historical survey of immigration and migra-tion patterns to South Africa, see South Africa, "Draft Green Paper on International Migration," par. 2.2. For a more complete picture of current patterns, see Peberdy, 1997, and Crush, 1997.

39. Crush, 1997, p. 30.

40. Jacobson, 1996, p. 9.

41. See Human Rights Watch, 1998, pp. 19–22. The population figure is based on the prelimi-nary results of the first post-apartheid census conducted by the government's Central Statistical Services. These results are available at http://www.css.gov.za/CensRes/prelimin.htm.

42. Crush, 1997, p. 18. See also South Africa, "Draft Green Paper on International Migration," 1997, par. 3.1.3 (noting figure of 5.1 million). The "Draft Green Paper" is a comprehensive assess-ment of South African migration policy.

43. Crush, 1997, p. 20.

44. According to Human Rights Watch, 1998, p. 4, "In general, South Africa's public culture has become increasingly xenophobic, and politicians often make unsubstantiated and inflammatory statements that the 'deluge' of migrants is responsible for the current crime wave, rising unemploy-ment, or even the spread of diseases."

Legal Provisions for Permanent Residence and Citizenship

This section aims to state briefly the current legal regime for citizenship and permanent residence in South Africa.[45] South African citizenship is granted in three primary ways: by birth, by descent, and by naturalization.[46] Under existing statutes, citizenship by birth is limited to a child of a South African citizen or to a child whose parents are both permanent residents.[47] As implemented by the Department of Home Affairs, however, this rule is relaxed to a significant degree: if only one of the parents is a permanent resident, then the citizenship by birth may be claimed by the child of that parent.[48] Children born in South Africa to temporary residents and to the population of undocumented persons do not acquire citizenship at birth.

Citizenship by descent is granted to children born outside the Republic who have at least one parent with South African citizenship, where notice of the birth is given to South African authorities. There is no cutoff to this transmission; thus, citizens born outside of South Africa may apparently transmit citizenship to their children born outside South Africa.

The citizenship system, therefore, is a mix of *jus soli* and *jus sanguinis* principles. Although most South Africans become citizens under *jus soli* rules, large numbers of persons born in South Africa do not acquire citizenship at birth. Nonetheless, as is indicated in the legislative debates considered below, it seems clear that there is comparatively greater weight placed on the *jus soli* principle in South Africa than in many other countries.[49]

The bar against citizenship for a large class of people born in South Africa makes the conditions for obtaining naturalization of particular importance.[50] For people born in South Africa to parents without permanent residence, the

---

45. The material in this section borrows from Klaaren, 1998, "Immigration."

46. South African Citizenship Act of 1995 (SACA), sections 2–4.

47. SACA, 1995, section 2(2). There are exceptions for children adopted by South African citizens and (as lobbied for by the Black Sash, an organization of primarily white women long concerned with human rights issues in South Africa) for stateless children registered in terms of the Births and Deaths Registration Act of 1992. SACA, 1995, section 2(4). See Keightley, 1998.

48. Telephone interview on March 2, 1998, by author with Mrs. Joubert, citizenship supervisor, Department of Home Affairs. Under the accepted doctrine of legitimate expectations, it appears unlikely that the Department of Home Affairs could change this practice without parliamentary approval. See *Administrator, Transvaal v. Traub* 1989 (4) SA 731 (A) (a legitimate expectation may be based on long-standing practice or an express promise).

49. See Aleinikoff, 1998, p. 7. The principle of *jus soli* was explicitly depended upon by the minister of Home Affairs in order to justify the granting of South African citizenship to children born in the Republic who have no rightful claim for the citizenship or nationality of any country. South Africa, *Debates of the Senate,* col. 2607 (Thursday, September 7, 1995).

50. It is unclear what percentage of children born within South Africa to noncitizens have at least one permanent resident parent and are thus capable of claiming citizenship.

only opportunity to become a citizen is through naturalization. In order to be naturalized, a person must be over twenty-one, must be admitted for permanent residence, must have been continuously resident for one year before applying for naturalization, must have been ordinarily resident for at least four of the eight years preceding the application,[51] must be of good character, must intend to continue to reside in the Republic, must be able to communicate in one of the official languages, and must have knowledge of the responsibilities and privileges of South African citizenship.[52] Minors admitted to permanent residence may be granted citizenship without satisfying these conditions upon application by a parent.[53] In the case of permanent resident aliens married to South African citizens, the only requirement for citizenship is residence with the citizen spouse in South Africa for two years.[54] Citizenship by naturalization thus depends upon prior admission for permanent residence.

Permanent residence is governed by the Aliens Control Act.[55] From December 1, 1996,[56] a permit for permanent residence (newly termed an immigration

51. In an apparent change from the previous citizenship legislation, periods of temporary residence do not count toward fulfilling the requirement of residence or ordinary residence. SACA, 1995, section 5(3)(b). Periods of stay that were in contravention of any law continue not to count. The legislation also prohibits periods of time during which an alien has "conditionally" sojourned from counting. It is not clear how this section should be interpreted. At first glance, it would appear to include the employment conditions that may be imposed without any statutory limit and are often attached to permanent residence permits for three years. See, for example, Aliens Control Act of 1991 (ACA), section 25(3). Since ACA section 25(3) apparently mandates a minimum employment condition of twelve months, the minimum naturalization period may be effectively lengthened by a year. If an employment condition is imposed but not time-limited, then a permanent resident would be barred indefinitely from naturalization. Giving effect to these distinctions among varying employment conditions would probably violate the equality clause. The reasons for placing such conditions may bear no relation to an applicant's fitness for naturalization. A court should thus interpret SACA, 1995, section 5(3)(b) in order to avoid such a constitutional violation.

52. SACA, 1995, section 5(1).

53. SACA, 1995, section 5(4). There is no requirement that the parents themselves be naturalizing.

54. SACA, 1995, section 5(5).

55. Until 1986, South African immigration legislation was explicitly racial, requiring that applicants for permanent residence be "readily assimilable by the white inhabitants." Especially from 1960, the government recruited white skilled workers, offering them permanent residence, but in recruiting black workers continued to prohibit their time of employment from counting toward naturalization. The effect of these policies was that permanent residence status was reserved for whites and not for blacks. Indeed, although the racial clause to the assimilation requirement was removed in 1986, the requirement itself remained until 1996. Moreover, it was administered by the all-white Immigrants Selection Board, a body whose membership and procedures remained secret. See, for example, Edmonds, March 29, 1996. Because the law of naturalization (as well as other legislation) depends on permanent residence status, a strong if indirect constitutional equality claim thus exists. See Peberdy and Crush, 1998.

56. The Aliens Control Amendment Act of 1995 came into operation on July 1, 1996, with the exception of sections 11 and 12, which substitute the sections of the ACA dealing with the Immi-

permit) is available to an applicant who is of good character, who will be a desirable inhabitant of the Republic, who is not likely to harm the welfare of the Republic, and who does not and is not likely to pursue an occupation in which there are already sufficient numbers of people available in the Republic.[57] Other provisions allow for (but do not mandate) immediate permanent residence without conditions for destitute, aged, or infirm family members and for spouses or dependent children of permanent residents and citizens.[58] Normally, applicants for permanent residence apply from outside South Africa. There are exceptions for persons in possession of a temporary residence work permit; persons who are destitute, aged, or infirm and a member of the family of a permanent resident or citizen who is able and willing to support that person; and persons who are married to, or dependent children of, permanent residents or citizens.[59]

Of course, the discussion of legal doctrine must be seen in the South African context. Three aspects of this context make the above brief exposition of the citizenship laws on the books particularly vulnerable to reality checks. The first is the degree to which the legal regime of the South African Citizenship Act of 1995 has only recently been extended to the people previously governed by the formerly independent homelands. As noted above, those citizenship regimes differed from those of the Republic, presenting more than the usual selection of nonenvisaged situations for the act to cover. The scope for administrative discretion and for implementing rules differing from the terms of the formal legislation is therefore broadened. The second is the significant level of informal action taken outside the formal rules by administrative officials in the area of citizenship. In both this respect and the next, the Department of Home Affairs is known to be struggling with significant problems of corruption. The third aspect is the degree to which status as a citizen may be less significant in practical terms, such as gaining access to banking facilities, than possession of a formal identification status—evidenced in South Africa

---

grants Selection Board and permanent residence permits. These sections came into operation on December 1, 1996.

57. ACA, section 25(4)(a). The application of this criterion of national employment availability to an applicant's occupation is to be made by a regional committee in respect of people intending to reside in that region.

58. ACA, sections 25(4)(b) and 25(5). Of course, these sections would have to be interpreted to include citizens within the meaning of the term "a person permanently and lawfully resident in the Republic." Section 25(6) requires that a regional committee be satisfied that a marriage was not contracted for the purposes of evading any provision of the ACA. The administrative practice of Home Affairs in relation to this section is to require a job offer in order for spouses to be given permanent residence. Personal communication to the author from Sheena Duncan of the Black Sash, November 2, 1996.

59. ACA, section 25(9).

by a government-issued ID document. The number of ID documents issued by administrative authorities dwarfs the number of formal citizenship determinations on an annual basis. For instance in 1994 (an election year), 4.6 million ID documents were issued and in 1995, 2.8 million. In contrast, citizenship actions are measured in the thousands not millions.[60] By the end of 1995, 27.6 million people were on record.[61] Given that the total population is around 37.9 million, there is a large backlog of formal registration.[62]

The Passage of the 1995 South African Citizenship Act

This section examines aspects of the legislative history of the 1995 citizenship act. The act made five main changes to South African citizenship law.[63] The first was the repeal and national application of the citizenship law. Second, the policy of tolerance with respect to dual citizenship was resurfaced but reaffirmed. Third, there were a series of adjustments to naturalization policy. Fourth, the declaration of allegiance was amended. Fifth, citizenship by birth for stateless children was introduced.

Consideration of the act in the Senate was lengthy, nearly six months, although the consideration in the National Assembly was quick.[64] During parliamentary debate, significant modifications were made to the proposed legislation in all these areas, except the dual nationality provisions.[65] The only opposition to the legislation came from the relatively small (and relatively white) Democratic Party, which dissented.[66]

60. For instance, the number of citizenship grants by descent was 5,235 in 1995 and the number of naturalizations, 6,153.

61. See South Africa, Department of Home Affairs, *Annual Report,* 1995.

62. See the preliminary results of the first post-apartheid census conducted by Central Statistical Services. These results are available at http://www.css.gov.za/CensRes/prelimn.htm.

63. Questions of the act's provisions relating to resumption of citizenship status are not treated here.

64. South Africa, *Debates of the Senate,* col. 2606 (Thursday, September 7, 1995). Senator C. R. Redcliffe of the National Party hopefully saw in this period an emerging norm: "We should resist any attempt at bulldozing legislation through portfolio committees and therefore through Parliament." South Africa, *Debates of the Senate,* col. 2610 (Thursday, September 7, 1995).

65. This paper does not consider the extent to which these parliamentary passages may influence the interpretation of the statutes. In a preconstitutional era, Geoff Budlender has argued with respect to the citizenship policy area that legal interpretation should take into account parliamentary speeches. See Budlender, 1989. While there are strong hints of change, preconstitutional South African law did not allow reference to parliamentary speeches as an aid to statutory interpretation. See *S v. Makwanyane,* 1995 (3) SA 391 (CC), pars. 12–15.

66. The Democratic Party (which counts Helen Suzman as one of its members) had 3 of 90 representatives in the Senate and 7 of 400 representatives in the National Assembly.

One Common Citizenship

The primary impetus for the South African Citizenship Act of 1995 was the need to repeal the various homelands legal regimes governing citizenship and to create a unified national citizenship regime.[67] This purpose was mentioned by the minister of Home Affairs, Dr. Buthelezi of the Inkatha Freedom Party (IFP), in his introduction and reflected in the speeches of some of the party representatives.[68] In terms of the transitional provision of the interim Constitution, the citizenship laws of the Republic as well as of the four "independent" homelands (Transkei, Bophuthatswana, Venda, and Ciskei) remained valid.[69] Upon unification of the Republic, the need for amending legislation administered by and structuring the Department of Home Affairs was a priority matter. A number of bills, including what became the 1995 citizenship act, were passed in a single session.[70] Repealing the homelands citizenship acts, the 1995 citizenship act extended to the entire country legislative provisions for a single citizenship regime.

Creation of a single citizenship regime was a huge step toward eradicating the results of apartheid citizenship policies and aligning citizenship in terms of South Africa's new Constitution.[71] Indeed, Parliament went further in this regard than Home Affairs' proposed legislation, amending the 1993 restoration law that had required naturalized citizens in the homelands to naturalize in order to get South African citizenship.[72] In Parliament, the proposed continuation of the 1993 act was seen to be discriminating unconstitutionally against the category of TBVC citizens. The 1995 law as enacted makes automatic the acquisi-

67. The act repealed in whole or in part twenty-five pieces of legislation.

68. South Africa, *Debates of the National Assembly,* cols. 4315, 4320 (Thursday, September 14, 1995). In terms of the constitutional provisions for a Government of National Unity, minority parties such as the IFP had several ministries, including the Ministry of Home Affairs.

69. Section 229 of the interim Constitution.

70. Beyond the 1995 citizenship act, three other important pieces of rationalizing legislation within the province of the Department of Home Affairs were also passed in 1995: the Aliens Control Amendment Act of 1995, the Identification Amendment Act of 1995, and the Home Affairs Laws Rationalisation Act of 1995.

71. It was claimed that this 1995 legislation was needed to fulfill the requirement in the interim Constitution that there be national legislation regulating citizenship. Constitution of the Republic of South Africa, Act 200 of 1993 (interim Constitution), section 5(2). The prior existing legislation, however, probably already satisfied that requirement. In any case, the 1995 act certainly satisfies the similar requirement in section 3(3) of the 1996 Constitution (which took effect in most part on February 4, 1997).

72. As originally conceived by the Department of Home Affairs, people with citizenship status granted by the independent homelands were not to be automatically granted South African citizenship. In the bill as submitted to Parliament, people who were not South African citizens but had become citizens of the TBVC states had to apply for South African citizenship by naturalization. This provision followed what had previously been the case in the Restoration and Extension of South African Citizenship Act of 1993.

tion of South African citizenship by those persons who acquired homelands citizenship by naturalization. The minister of Home Affairs noted this change from his original proposal in the following terms: "A word of caution needs, however, to be expressed. All naturalised South African citizens who have obtained a certificate of naturalisation by means of fraud, false representations, or concealment of a material fact, can in terms of measure proposed in the Bill, be deprived of their South African citizenship."[73]

Anti-apartheid policy was also reflected in the deletion of the provision granting automatic citizenship to whites residing for five years in South Africa, a section intended to increase the pool of persons liable for military service. Other constitutionalizing features included rejection of a department-proposed rule that naturalized citizens living abroad for more than seven years would lose their citizenship (subject to a system of ministerial exemptions), adoption of citizenship for stateless children born in the Republic, and the inclusion of a section explicitly affirming judicial review of ministerial decisions in terms of the 1995 act.[74]

Dual Citizenship Policy

Traditionally, dual nationality has been tolerated in South Africa. Dual nationality resulted when permanent resident aliens had South African children, when citizens of different countries married, or often when persons naturalized, because South African citizenship law contained no renunciation requirement. Indeed, the principle of dual nationality is deeply rooted in the historical emergence of the status of South African citizenship in the period from the 1920s to the 1940s. This tolerance has not been complete, however. In terms of the pre-1995 legislation, South African citizens naturalizing elsewhere were liable to losing their South African citizenship by ministerial order. In terms of the 1995 act, this loss of citizenship rule became automatic, subject to application to the minister of Home Affairs for exemption from deprivation prior to the acquisition of the other citizenship.[75] Most of the persons who benefited from dual

73. South Africa, *Debates of the Senate,* col. 2609 (Thursday, September 7, 1995).
74. SACA, 1995, sections 2(4) (stateless children) and 25 (judicial review).
75. SACA, 1995, section 6. Citizens by birth or descent who have already lost their citizenship may apply directly to the minister for its resumption with the intent of permanently residing in South Africa. Citizens by naturalization in a similar situation may apply for resumption only after succeeding in an application for a permanent residence permit. SACA, 1995, section 13(3). The harsher treatment meted out to noncitizens who were formerly citizens by naturalization as opposed to citizens by birth or descent in SACA, 1995, section 11(3) and section 13(3) could be argued to be an apparent violation of the rights of citizens because it subjects one class of citizens to a stricter potential sanction.

nationality were whites. Until 1986, only such persons were eligible for permanent residence, which is a major cause of dual nationality through having children or as a precondition to naturalization. Since the 1990s, members of the liberation movement who, in exile, attained citizenship and attachments elsewhere have also joined the visible ranks of dual citizens. As reflected in the parliamentary debates, this latter feature may explain the continued tolerance of dual nationality.

Most of the debate over dual citizenship took place within the context of deprivation of citizenship. Under pre-1995 law, some provisions for loss of citizenship applied to dual citizens as well as to other South African citizens. South African citizenship would be lost upon acquiring another citizenship or becoming a prohibited immigrant.[76] Citizens by naturalization or registration (a procedure for acquisition of citizenship largely used for British subjects) would cease to be citizens upon seven years of residence outside the country. Such citizens could also be deprived of their status upon proof of fraudulent naturalization or registration. With procedural safeguards, the minister also had the power to order deprivation of citizenship upon a variety of grounds, including conviction for treason (for all citizens) or conviction for a crime carrying with it a sentence of a year's imprisonment (for citizens by naturalization or registration within five years of the grant of their citizenship). Furthermore, the acquisition of another citizenship if done by voluntary act was grounds for deprivation of South African citizenship.

Dual nationals would also lose citizenship upon serving in the armed forces of their other country while it was at war with South Africa. Dual nationals (only) could voluntarily lose their South African citizenship by making a declaration of renunciation. Law further provided that the minister had the power to deprive a dual citizen of South African citizenship if he or she made use of the citizenship of the other country.[77] Most dramatically, the minister had the power to deprive dual nationals of South African citizenship "if he is satisfied that it is in the public interest that such citizen shall cease to be a South African citizen."[78]

The 1995 act changed the provisions specifically regarding dual nationals in two respects. First, deprivation of citizenship on grounds of being sentenced to imprisonment for a year for a crime in any country, provided that the offence would be similarly punished in South Africa, is now applicable only to dual na-

---

76. See, generally, South African Citizenship Act of 1949, sections 15–22.
77. South Africa, *Debates of the National Assembly,* col. 4316 (Thursday, September 14, 1995).
78. South African Citizenship Act of 1949, section 19 bis(b).

tionals (rather than to all citizens by naturalization) and may be triggered by imprisonment at any time rather than only within five years of the date of naturalization. This first change passed without comment. The second change was more significant. Treating the grounds for depriving dual nationals of citizenship because of use of the other citizenship, the 1995 act innovated by referring to two specific situations—voting in one's other country of nationality or using a passport issued by that country—which indicated use of a second nationality.[79] The resultant fear was that the government was becoming less disposed toward dual citizenship. In his speech introducing the South African Citizenship Act of 1995, the minister of Home Affairs referred to this expression of fear by holders of dual citizenship. Dr. Buthelezi responded as follows:

Although the Government is appreciative of the fact that there are strong arguments for and against the principle of dual citizenship, it has no intention to legislate against dual citizenship. I am certain that the majority of South African citizens who also hold the citizenship of another country are as loyal and respectful to the Republic and its Constitution as our own

79. SACA, 1995, section 9(1) provides: "The Minister may by order deprive a South African citizen of his or her South African citizenship if he or she also has the citizenship or nationality of another country, and has at any time made use of the franchise or the passport facilities of that country or performed such other voluntary act which, to the satisfaction of the Minister, indicates that such citizen has made use of the citizenship or nationality of that other country." This statutory provision must be seen together with prior and subsequent administrative practice, particularly in relation to passport use. The number of people actually deprived of citizenship is very low. In 1995, 533 persons voluntarily renounced their citizenship. Three naturalized citizens were deprived of their citizenship by order of the minister, and ten such citizens lost their citizenship by virtue of prolonged residence outside South Africa. No dual citizens were deprived of citizenship in terms of section 9. It is not clear if the three persons deprived of citizenship were subject to the order by the minister on the grounds of fraud in naturalization, or, if they were dual citizens, for crimes resulting in a sentence of not less than twelve months, or upon the minister's satisfaction of what is in the public interest. The grounds of fraud in naturalization appear most likely. South Africa, Department of Home Affairs, *Annual Report*, 1995, p. 12.

Before 1995, the minister of Home Affairs had a practice of writing letters of consent for use of foreign passports. After the 1995 act, the previously existing administrative procedure for granting exemptions for passport use was continued. See South Africa, Department of Home Affairs, Passport Control Instruction (PCI) No. 93 of 1995 requiring use of a South African passport by citizens departing from South Africa. The previous understanding that the writ of Home Affairs extended only to departure from and arrival to the Republic—based on an argument against extraterritorial application—was contested by the department, however. In 1997, the administrative procedure by which dual citizens could be granted written permission to use the passports of their other countries was added at this level of primary legislation but was stated to apply globally. PCI No. 93 of 1995 suggested that the requirement of the use of the South African passport (and by extension the prohibition on the use of the foreign passport) extends only to departure from South Africa. The 1997 act is explicit, however, that the exemption from prohibition extends only to the entrance and leaving of the other country of which the dual citizen holds a passport.

citizens who hold no other citizenship. The Bill consequently contains no proposals that deviate from the present legal tolerance of dual citizenship. At present the Minister has the power to deprive someone with dual citizenship of his or her South African citizenship if he or she makes use of the citizenship of the other country. The Bill contains a similar proposal, but it deviates from the present provisions in the sense that the use of the other country's franchise or passport facilities is being introduced as a particular example of making use of another country's citizenship. At present, dual citizenship is allowed to enable people to make use of the other country's passport facilities in meritorious cases, if those concerned apply in writing beforehand, and we will continue with this practice—on stricter terms, however—once this Bill becomes law.[80]

The speech, while probably written by the departmental legal adviser (and nearly word for word the same as the one delivered in the Senate), is vintage Dr. Buthelezi—managing to speak on both sides of a difficult issue.

The debate over the dual citizenship issue was scattered to the point of confusion. Indeed, Senator Mnisi of the liberal Democratic Party (DP) took the position that the legislation did not address the question of dual citizenship because it did not clearly distinguish between citizenship and nationality.[81] The contributions also reflected considerable dissension on the point within the parties themselves. Mr. Sikakane of the African National Congress (ANC) alluded to "debate and disagreement" within his party's study group on migration. His endorsement of the concept was based on the notion that "it would serve no good purpose at this point in time to argue for the abandonment of dual citizenship. In fact, it will be destructive to our needs."[82] He then explored the underlying issue of loyalty, stating, "Now, the question arose: should we shoot down the Bill just because of the provision concerning dual citizenship? How does one measure loyalty? Where does loyalty begin and end? Our memories should not fail us, but we should remember what our own people have done. . . ."[83] This understanding of loyalty contrasted sharply with the understanding of the representative of the Afrikaner-based Freedom Front (FF) in the National Assembly:

---

80. South Africa, *Debates of the National Assembly*, col. 4316 (Thursday, September 14, 1995).

81. South Africa, *Debates of the Senate*, col. 2614 (Thursday, September 7, 1995).

82. South Africa, *Debates of the National Assembly*, col. 4319 (Thursday, September 14, 1995).

83. South Africa, *Debates of the National Assembly*, col. 4319 (Thursday, September 14, 1995).

We welcome the provision . . . which places strict restrictions on the exercising of dual citizenship. A person who in any way makes use of a second citizenship, places his South African citizenship in jeopardy, and the Minister is authorised to deprive him of it. We welcome this because we believe that a person cannot serve two masters. He cannot have two loyalties towards two different countries.[84]

The leader of the Senate Committee ended the debate in that House with a statement of the rationale for tolerating dual citizenship. According to Dr. Cwele, the ANC's view was that

the legislation as it stands tolerates dual citizenship, but it has some restrictions so as to prevent abuse. It is our view that dual citizenship must only be tolerated to the extent that it does not undermine the loyalty of an individual to this country, to the Constitution or to the sovereignty of our nation.[85]

Dr. Cwele went on to note the practical realities, focusing on English-speaking whites[86] and exiles.[87] At the time of the referendum among whites on continuing the direction of reform, English-speaking whites who were permanent residents of South Africa were even encouraged to become citizens and were "promised that they would always retain their original country's citizenship."[88] Moreover, the ANC's representative went on to note that blacks in exile had the same experiences: "Some of the people involved in the liberation movement, because of their suffering of being away from their country, acquired the citizenship of

---

84. South Africa, *Debates of the National Assembly,* col. 4322 (Thursday, September 14, 1995) (Mr. W. A. Botha).

85. South Africa, *Debates of the Senate,* col. 2619 (Thursday, September 7, 1995).

86. The reality of a number of whites with dual citizenship figured significantly in the debate. Indeed, Dr. Buthelezi defended dual citizenship at the end of the National Assembly debate in the following terms: "Many people may not realise that it could completely destabilise our country if it was revoked suddenly, especially if I take into cognisance the fact that almost a million English-speaking South Africans in this country have that dual citizenship. In this stage of transition through which we are going as a country, I can imagine that if we were to revoke the dual citizenship, a lot of people would run away from our country. That would not be in the interests of our country." *Debates of the National Assembly,* cols. 4324–25 (Thursday, September 14, 1995).

87. The representative for the Inkatha Freedom Party in the Senate felt that the provisions for applying for permission to use the citizenship of another country meant that "members of Parliament can rest at ease. If they need to use a foreign passport to get to a country for which they have no time to apply for a visa, all they do is apply for permission to the department, to the Minister or to somebody delegated to give them that approval." *Debates of the Senate,* col. 2618 (Thursday, September 7, 1995) (Senator R. Rabinowitz).

88. South Africa, *Debates of the Senate,* col. 2620 (Thursday, September 7, 1995).

sympathetic adopted countries. Some of them even used the franchise in these countries. These are the practical realities."[89] Dr. Cwele said "more important" these people had properties in one or both of the counties. If one did away with dual citizenship, what would happen to these properties?

In addition to this general defense of the toleration of dual citizenship, Dr. Cwele addressed the specifics of the cases of passport use and the franchise. Deprivation of citizenship on the grounds of use of franchise was justified because "it is a restrictive mechanism preventing people from undermining the sovereignty of our country, and because we find that some individuals may vote in all the countries, thereby influencing the world political order in different nations and in that manner undermining the sovereignty of the state."[90] Deprivation of citizenship on the grounds of abuse of passport facilities was justified because "if a person has multiple nationality, then in cases of conflict the question arises as to who will actually protect that individual. What will happen when the countries of one's dual nationality have conflict?"[91]

Ms. Smuts of the Democratic Party would have allowed deprivation of dual citizenship on grounds of fraud or fighting against South Africa but not otherwise. With regard to the introduction of deprivation on grounds of use of a passport, she charged that the Department of Home Affairs was being turned into "a kind of department of un-South African activities, especially when we, ie South Africa, have allowed permanent residents the franchise here."[92] Her approach was a rights-based one and she made the most of it, claiming that it was only her party that cared about fundamental rights. Her pleas, however, proved unsuccessful, as the legislation was enacted with the broader grounds for loss of South African citizenship.

It is worth noting that the citizenship policies of neighboring countries (arguably extremely relevant to the policy debate) figured in the discussion hardly at all.[93] The laws of the Customs Union states, Botswana, Lesotho, and Swaziland, as well as Mozambique and Zimbabwe, in particular would bear examination.[94] Most of southern Africa has been reported to have a prohibition on dual citizenship.[95]

---

89. South Africa, *Debates of the Senate,* col. 2620 (Thursday, September 7, 1995).

90. South Africa, *Debates of the Senate,* col. 2620 (Thursday, September 7, 1995).

91. South Africa, *Debates of the Senate,* cols. 2620–21 (Thursday, September 7, 1995).

92. South Africa, *Debates of the National Assembly,* col. 4322 (Thursday, September 14, 1995).

93. According to Senator Mnisi, "We should also have looked into the legislation of the Southern African states which will be affected by this piece of legislation." See South Africa, *Debates of the Senate,* col. 2614 (Thursday, September 7, 1995).

94. See Centre for Sociopolitical Analysis, 1996 (covering the United States, the United Kingdom, Canada, Namibia, Swaziland, Zimbabwe, and Kenya; not investigating dual citizenship).

95. See Cheater and Gaidzanwa, 1996, p. 197.

Combined with the topic of the next section, naturalization, South Africa exhibits its own peculiar statutory asymmetry, one different from that of the United States. In the United States, "an immigrant who naturalizes in the United States must renounce citizenship elsewhere; a U.S. citizen who naturalizes in another country cannot have his or her U.S. citizenship removed unless he or she expressly intends to lose it."[96] In South Africa, the naturalizing citizen has no need to renounce his citizenship elsewhere, but once naturalized is in potential danger of losing South African citizenship if he or she uses the foreign citizenship in any way.

Naturalization

The 1995 act effected four major changes in the naturalization policy of the previous regime. First, the act took away automatic acquisition of citizenship upon five years' residence. As mentioned above, this acquisition had previously been provided for by section 11A of the act of 1949, a section introduced in 1978. The deletion of this apartheid provision was an uncontroversial issue.[97]

Second, the act repealed the prior law that persons who had gained TBVC citizenship by naturalization could attain South African citizenship only by way of naturalization. This change was consistent with the major purpose of the legislation to provide a single citizenship law for South Africa. The minister of Home Affairs had initially supported the status quo ante, but accepted the change with a word of caution that naturalized citizens who obtained that status by fraud could be deprived of their citizenship.[98]

The third change to the naturalization regime was a significant reduction of the minister's discretion in terms of the grant of naturalization. As introduced, the legislation continued to provide for the minister's discretion, in special cases, to waive two of the four years required for naturalization and to waive the language requirement in the case of former citizens. The Senate Committee deleted both clauses. According to Senator Lamani of the ANC:

Furthermore, I am pleased to say that sections 6 and 7 have been repealed [by our committee], because they contained a lot of problems. The Minis-

---

96. See Aleinikoff, 1998, p. 22.

97. According to Mrs. I. Mars, "We are also very pleased to find that section 2 of the existing South African Citizenship Act has been omitted, as we will hopefully never again have the need for compulsory military service." South Africa, *Debates of the National Assembly,* col. 4320 (Thursday, September 14, 1995).

98. South Africa, *Debates of the Senate,* cols. 2608–09 (Thursday, September 7, 1995).

ter was given discretionary powers in granting a certificate of naturalisation. In section 7, for example, the Minister was even given powers to
waive some of the requirements for an applicant, if such applicant satisfied the Minister that he or she had previously been in South Africa. How
can one allow a Minister to waive these requirements? Does that not lead
to corruption? I am pleased that we got rid of that section.[99]

In response, the minister cited the administrative justice clause of the Constitution and noted the constitutional entrenchment of judicial review.[100] But
these references did not satisfy the opponents of ministerial discretion. Senator
Lamani, for example, commented, "We do not expect people who do not even
know that they have a right of appeal, to go to the Constitution and read the
paragraph that gives them such a right."[101] It was further suggested that the existing right to appeal directly to the minister be supplemented by an independent appeal structure within the department. The Inkatha Freedom Party (led by
Dr. Buthelezi, the minister of Home Affairs) thought such an innovation unnec-
essary; but the Democratic Party (which was the sole party to dissent from the
legislation) stated as one of its reasons for not supporting the legislation the fact
that it did not include "independent administrative review procedures and structures . . . to give real content" to the constitutional right to administrative justice.[102] The appeals structure was not adopted.

The lack of provision for the minister's discretion proved short-lived, however, as the 1997 act authorized the minister to grant a certificate of naturalization in exceptional circumstances where the residential periods had not been
fulfilled.[103] Indeed, the entire period of residence may apparently be waived. A
modest check on discretion remains: the minister must table in Parliament in
the first fourteen days of each year the names of people granted naturalization
together with reasons.

Finally, the 1995 act took away provision for the denationalization of naturalized citizens by virtue of extended residence outside the country. This
change was made by the Senate Committee. The version as introduced by the
Department of Home Affairs had proposed that naturalized citizens living

99. South Africa, *Debates of the Senate,* col. 2612 (Thursday, September 7, 1995).
100. South Africa, *Debates of the Senate,* col. 2609 (Thursday, September 7, 1995).
101. South Africa, *Debates of the Senate,* col. 2613 (Thursday, September 7, 1995). Senator
Lamani was discussing a similar provision.
102. South Africa, *Debates of the Senate,* col. 2617 (Thursday, September 7, 1995) (Senator R.
Rabinowitz); South Africa, *Debates of the National Assembly,* col. 4323 (Thursday, September 14,
1995) (Ms. Smuts).
103. Section 4 of the South African Citizenship Amendment Act 1997.

abroad for not less than seven years would lose their citizenship.[104] This issue, too, sparked little debate. The reason for the change was apparently the argument that naturalized citizens should not be treated differently from other citizens.[105]

Citizenship Oaths and Education

The purest symbolic expression of citizenship in the laws of a country perhaps comes with oaths or declarations of allegiance. The South African Citizenship Act of 1949 provided a short oath of allegiance. It stated simply: "I, A. B., do hereby declare on oath that I will be faithful to the Republic of South Africa, observe its laws, promote all that which will advance it and oppose all that may harm it. So Help Me God."[106] Naturalizing citizens over the age of fourteen were required to make this oath.[107]

As introduced, the 1995 act proposed a much more extensive declaration of allegiance "to fit the occasion and to bring the duties, rights and privileges of a South African citizen into better perspective."[108] This declaration was in the following form:

> I, _____ (A. B.), do hereby solemnly declare that I will be faithful to the Republic of South Africa, and I hereby undertake to carry out my duties as a South African citizen to the best of my abilities.
>
> I especially commit myself to:
> —obeying the laws of my country;
> —exercising the franchise to ensure that my country's affairs rest in good hands;
> —defending my country;
> —paying such taxes as may be levied;

---

104. South Africa, Parliament, "Memorandum on the Objects of the South African Citizenship Bill, 1995" (B23–95), par. 4.1(v).

105. As Senator R. Rabinowitz said, "There was general agreement that, provided that the criteria for granting citizenship were not unnecessarily lenient and flexible, once individuals had citizenship there should be no distinction between them and other South Africans." South Africa, *Debates of the Senate,* col. 2616 (Thursday, September 7, 1995).

106. South African Citizenship Act of 1949, First Schedule (repealed).

107. Persons objecting on religious grounds to the taking of an oath were permitted to make a corresponding solemn affirmation. South African Citizenship Act of 1949, section 10(11) (repealed).

108. South Africa, Parliament, "Memorandum on the Objects of the South African Citizenship Bill, 1995" (B23–95), par. 9.

—assisting in the preservation of the natural beauty of my country and to conserving its soil;

—developing my physical, intellectual and social capacities so that I shall be an asset to my country and its people;

—being tolerant towards my fellow citizens and to fostering good relations.

I also declare that I am fully aware of my rights and privileges as a citizen of South Africa, and I commit myself to exercising those rights and privileges in such a manner that it will promote the common weal in my country, and oppose all that may harm my country and my fellow citizens.

The Senate Committee formulated a simpler oath, to be sworn by naturalizing citizens over the age of eighteen: "I _____(A. B.), do hereby solemnly declare that I will be loyal to the Republic of South Africa, promote all that will advance it and oppose all that may harm it, uphold and respect its Constitution and commit myself to the furtherance of the ideals and principles contained therein."

This revised oath's reference to the "ideals and principles" of the Constitution provides a contrast with the more positivist, rule-of-law tone of the first proposed oath. Significantly, neither the 1949 oath nor the oaths considered in 1995 require the renunciation of prior citizenships, which clearly leaves open the possibility of dual nationality for naturalizing citizens—at least so long as maintaining the other citizenship is not inconsistent with the "loyalty" due South Africa under the oath.

Under past and existing practice, citizenship is not conferred in a special ceremony.[109] Some speakers in the parliamentary debates suggested that such a ceremony would be an appropriate way to express the significance of acquiring South African citizenship. One representative stated that "if we follow the American example and celebrate the acquisition of South African citizenship, we will actually be enhancing it and making people proud of being South African citizens."[110] The Freedom Front welcomed "the declaration of allegiance which every new citizen must make and [trusted] that this will always be and re-

109. At present, the entire naturalization process may be conducted through the post. Upon approval of an application for a certificate of naturalization, a blank Declaration of Allegiance is posted to the applicant with a letter requesting the applicant to sign the declaration (in the presence of two witnesses) and to return the signed declaration to the Department of Home Affairs. Upon receipt of the declaration, a certificate of citizenship is issued and forwarded to the applicant.

110. South Africa, *Debates of the National Assembly*, col. 4320 (Thursday, September 14, 1995) (Mrs. I. Mars).

main a dignified and solemn occasion."[111] This suggestion was specifically welcomed by Dr. Buthelezi, who stated that the department was looking into the possibility of a citizenship ceremony.[112]

Parliament also plugged for the value of citizenship by considering closely the Department of Home Affairs' proposed provision regarding instructing naturalizing citizens in the responsibilities and privileges of South African citizenship. The Senate Select Committee on Health, Welfare and Population Development and Home Affairs, the parliamentary committee dealing with the proposed legislation, extended the legislative sanction for citizenship education from people naturalizing to citizens as well.[113] The impetus for this change derived from a belief in the importance of rights-based citizenship education. As Mrs. I. Mars put it: "The subject of dissemination of information to our previously deprived community is a very, very important one. We must let our citizens know what their rights are, and what their obligations to the State as citizens are."[114] The chairperson of the Senate Committee supported this provision by noting that

> because the majority of us were not previously regarded as full citizens we were sometimes given bad or empty citizenship. It may also be important to empower the Minister further to inform all persons or categories of persons. We are talking about Blacks who may not know of the privileges or the responsibilities of being a South African citizen.[115]

For the Freedom Front, this push to citizenship education for all South Africans was the "most important change now being made."[116]

111. South Africa, *Debates of the Senate,* col. 2612 (Thursday, September 7, 1995) (Senator J. R. De Ville).

112. South Africa, *Debates of the Senate,* col. 2621 (Thursday, September 7, 1995).

113. The committee added subsection (a) to SACA, 1995, section 21, which now provides: "Instruction in responsibilities and privileges of South African citizenship. The Minister may in respect of— (a) South African citizens, make such arrangements as he or she deems fit; or (b) applicants for certificates of naturalisation, establish such facilities as may appear necessary or desirable—to enable such citizens or applicants to receive instruction in the responsibilities and privileges of South African citizenship."

114. South Africa, *Debates of the National Assembly,* col. 4320 (Thursday, September 14, 1995).

115. South Africa, *Debates of the Senate,* col. 2619 (Thursday, September 7, 1995) (Dr. S. C. Cwele).

116. South Africa, *Debates of the Senate,* col. 2612 (Thursday, September 7, 1995) (Senator J. R. De Ville).

Stateless Children

A significant change from the previous citizenship regime was the provision of South African citizenship to the stateless children. Although it had not been in the legislation as introduced, the minister justified this provision with explicit reference to the principle of *jus soli*:

> In many countries of the world, the *ius soli* principle in terms of which a birth in a particular country automatically leads to the nationality or citizenship of that country is applied. I am satisfied that the proposals contained in clause 2 are sound and that they provide much more legal certainty and equitability than the present provisions regarding citizenship by birth.[117]

While it was not a topic of debate, the recognition of the principle of citizenship by birth appeared to be supported by other representatives as well.[118]

The Rights of Citizens and Aliens

What significant difference is made by the status of citizenship in South Africa? The Bill of Rights of the 1996 Constitution provides that almost all rights benefit all persons within South Africa, whether they are citizens or aliens. Save for the rights to trade, occupation, and profession, citizenship, some parts of movement and residence, and political rights, the 1996 Constitution guarantees its rights to "everyone" rather than "every citizen." For instance, section 29(1)(a) states: "Everyone has the right to a basic education, including adult basic education." Of course such rights may be limited, but the starting point of the Bill of Rights at least is one where aliens enjoy nearly the same constitutional rights as citizens.

Dealing with the specific distinction between permanent residents and citizens, the Constitutional Court has also affirmed a near equality of rights to employment. The Constitutional Court applied the equality provisions of the interim Constitution to non–South African citizens and struck down a Depart-

117. South Africa, *Debates of the Senate,* cols. 2607–08 (Thursday, September 7, 1995).
118. South Africa, *Debates of the Senate,* col. 2612 (Thursday, September 7, 1995) (Senator N. E. Lamani) and cols. 2616–17 (Senator R. Rabinowitz) (noting that such numbers were extremely limited).

ment of Education regulation prohibiting foreign citizens from being permanently employed as teachers in state schools.[119]

Nonetheless, many acts of Parliament restrict the rights of aliens by comparison with citizens. Many of these laws restrict aliens from holding office in various statutory bodies.[120] Other statutes restrict aliens from important welfare rights such as old-age pensions and social assistance grants.[121] Other restrictions occur at the level of regulation. For instance, the Gauteng Department of Education requires that "illegal aliens" who are parents of children applying for admission to public school must show evidence that they have applied to the Department of Home Affairs to legalize their stay in the country.[122] Finally, in 1998, the electoral act that had governed the April 27, 1994, election was replaced with a new act providing for voter registration of South African citizens only and not of permanent residents (as had previously been the case).[123]

Conclusion

One might have thought that South Africa's radical transformation—from apartheid state to human rights state—would have produced a radical transformation in its citizenship law. But this was not the case. The basic principles of South African citizenship were reaffirmed in the first post-apartheid citizenship law. There were some minor changes in *jus soli* rules and naturalization rules and some tinkering with—but essential continuation of—the policy of toleration of dual nationality. Outside of the citizenship laws, the rights of aliens are undergoing some legislative and executive erosion but have nonetheless demonstrated judicial support. The chief thrust of the recent citizenship laws has been the unification of the country through the repeal of homelands laws and the extension of citizenship to all those who lost citizenship or would have been citizens without apartheid laws as well as to those naturalized in the homelands. As with deleting the provision for automatic citizenship after five years of residence, the focus is on ridding South Africa of the vestiges of apartheid.

Following the establishment of a newly nonracial democracy, one might have thought that a strong sense of citizenship would be seen as necessary in or-

119. *Larbi-Odam and Others v. The Member of the Executive Council for Education (North-West Province) and Another*, 1998 (1) SA 745 (CC). See Klaaren, 1998, "Non-Citizens."

120. See, for example, Medical Schemes Act of 1967, section 6(1)(c).

121. Aged Persons Act of 1967, section 12(1)(b)(i); Social Assistance Act of 1992, section 3(c).

122. Gauteng Province, 1998, p. 4.

123. Electoral Act of 1998, section 8(2) (replacing Electoral Act of 1993).

der to bring together those previously divided. Such a strong sense of citizenship might well have rejected dual loyalties, tightened up the access requirements, and even more strongly distinguished between citizens and aliens. While there are undoubted pressures in those directions of closure, one cannot conclude that such is the case based on an examination of the 1995 citizenship act. Like its predecessors, the new South African citizenship is one that remains fairly open.

One can speculate about three themes of South African history that might help account for the continuity of this fairly open membership regime. First, but paradoxically given its racism, South Africa has never been a place of firm and set boundaries. In the mines and the factories, the formal designation of citizenship mattered less than did the enforcement patterns of the pass laws. Noncitizens are not *non*members; they are *less-than-full* members. The post-apartheid amnesties approved by President Mandela's cabinet to three categories of people present in South Africa without lawful status (mine workers, SADC citizens, and Mozambican refugees) accord with this theme of permeable legal distinctions as do the fairly easy naturalization policies of the South African citizenship regime.

Second, there is an important narrative that South Africans are united in their diversity. Radical cultural divisions among citizens make some of the divisions between citizens and noncitizens pale in significance. Given racism and the arbitrariness of the Southern African borders, linkages between citizens and noncitizens have in cases been greater than those between citizens.[124] This case was particularly true during the period of formal homelands citizenship when large parts of those populations resided outside their putative homelands. It remains the case with the populations of Botswana, Lesotho, and Swaziland as well as perhaps with other neighboring countries.

Third, there is something significant about a national coming-of-democratic-age in an era where the dominant institution is no longer a parliament responsive to an electorate but a court interpreting a justiciable bill of rights. The important conceptual framework built during the struggle against apartheid citizenship may not have been the franchise itself but rather the *right* to vote as part of a package of human rights. Such a focus on individual rights may lead to a more open membership regime.

The 1995 South African Citizenship Act has the flavor of a conclusive chapter in South Africa's development of citizenship, unifying the post-apartheid

124. For an application of W. Kymlicka's *Multicultural Citizenship: A Liberal Theory of Minority Rights* (1995) argument to South Africa, see Sacks, 1997. For a brief discussion of women's citizenship, see Meintjes, 1997; see also Cheater and Gaidzanwa, 1996.

nation at the level of individuals' legal status. While more citizenship chapters will be written, the story's focus may now be shifting to the rights of aliens.

References

Abel, Richard. 1995. *Politics By Other Means: Law in the Struggle Against Apartheid, 1980–1994.* New York: Routledge.

Abolition of Influx Control Act 68 of 1986.

Aged Persons Act 81 of 1967.

Aleinikoff, Alex. 1998. "Citizenship and Membership: A Policy Perspective." Unpublished paper presented to the Carnegie Comparative Citizenship Project.

Aliens Control Act 96 of 1991.

Aliens Control Amendment Act 76 of 1995.

Bantu Homelands Citizenship Act 26 of 1970 (renamed the Black States Citizenship Act and later renamed the National States Citizenship Act).

Births and Deaths Registration Act 51 of 1992.

Bophuthatswana Citizenship Act 19 of 1978 (Bophuthatswana).

British Nationality in the Union and Naturalization and Status of Aliens Act 18 of 1926.

Budlender, Geoff. 1989. "On Citizenship and Residence Rights: Taking Words Seriously." *South African Journal on Human Rights,* vol. 5, pp. 37–59.

Budlender, Geoff. 1985. "A Common Citizenship?" *South African Journal on Human Rights,* vol. 1, pp. 210–17.

Budlender, Geoff. 1985. "Incorporation and Exclusion: Recent Developments in Labour Law and Influx Control." *South African Journal on Human Rights,* vol. 1, pp. 3–9.

Centre for Sociopolitical Analysis, Human Sciences Research Council. 1996. "A Comparative Study of Immigration Legislation in Selected Countries with Specific Reference to the South African Aliens Control Act, 1991, (as amended)." Unpublished study compiled at the request of the South African Department of Home Affairs.

Cheater, A. P., and R. B. Gaidzanwa. 1996. "Citizenship in Neo-Patrilinear States: Gender and Mobility in Southern Africa." *Journal of Southern African Studies,* vol. 22, pp. 189–200.

Ciskeian Citizenship Act 38 of 1984 (Ciskei).

Citizenship of Transkei Act 26 of 1976 (Transkei).

Citizenship of Venda Act 8 of 1980 (Venda).

Commonwealth Relations Act 69 of 1962.

Constitution of the Republic of South Africa, 1996, Act 108 of 1996.

Constitution of the Republic of South Africa, 1993, Act 200 of 1993.

Crush, Jonathan, ed. 1998. *Beyond Control: Immigration and Human Rights in a Democratic South Africa.* Cape Town: Southern African Migration Project.

Crush, Jonathan. 1997. "Covert Operations: Clandestine Migration, Temporary Work and Immigration Policy in South Africa." In *Migration Policy Series,* no. 1. Cape Town: Southern African Migration Project.

Dugard, John. 1992. "The Law of Apartheid." In *The Last Years of Apartheid: Civil Liberties in South Africa,* eds. John Dugard, Nicholas Haysom, and Gilbert Marcus. Ford Foundation, pp. 3–31.

Dugard, John. 1980. "South Africa's 'Independent' Homelands: An Exercise in Dena-tionalization." *Denver Journal of International Law and Policy,* vol. 10, pp. 11–36.

Dugard, John. 1978. *Human Rights and the South African Legal Order.* Princeton, N.J.: Princeton University Press.

Duncan, Sheena. (November 2, 1996.) Personal communication with author, Johannes-burg.

Duncan, Sheena. (September 1, 1995.) "We Need Debate About Citizenship." *Mail and Guardian.*

Edmonds, Marion. (March 29, 1996.) "Home Affairs Frustrates Would-Be Immi-grants." *Mail and Guardian.*

Electoral Act 73 of 1998.

Electoral Act 202 of 1993.

Gauteng Province. Department of Education. "Admission Policy" for ordinary public schools for 1999." Circular Grade 133/1998, December 10, 1998, pp. 1–4.

Hindson, Doug. 1987. *Pass Controls and the Urban African Proletariat.* Johannesburg: Ravan Press.

Home Affairs Laws Rationalisation Act 44 of 1995.

Human Rights Watch. 1998. *"Prohibited Persons": Abuse of Undocumented Migrants, Asylum Seekers, and Refugees in South Africa.* Human Rights Watch.

Identification Amendment Act 47 of 1995.

Jacobson, David. 1996. *Rights Across Borders: Immigration and the Decline of Citizen-ship.* Baltimore: Johns Hopkins University Press.

Joubert, Mrs. Telephone interview by author, Pretoria, March 2, 1998.

Keightley, Raylene. 1998. "The Child's Right to a Nationality and the Acquisition of Citizenship in South African Law." *South African Journal on Human Rights,* vol. 14, pp. 411–29.

Klaaren, Jonathan. 1998. "Contested Citizenship in South Africa." Unpublished paper.

Klaaren, Jonathan. 1998. "Immigration and the South African Constitution." In *Beyond Control: Immigration and Human Rights in a Democratic South Africa,* ed. Jonathan Crush. Cape Town: Southern African Migration Project, pp. 55–78.

Klaaren, Jonathan. 1998. "Non-Citizens and Constitutional Equality." *South African Journal on Human Rights,* vol. 14, pp. 286–97.

Klaaren, Jonathan. 1998. "The Truth and Reconciliation Commission, the South African Judiciary, and Constitutionalism." *African Studies,* vol. 57, no. 2, pp. 197–208.

Kymlicka, Will. 1995. *Multicultural Citizenship: A Liberal Theory of Minority Rights.* Oxford: Clarendon Press.

Maluwa, Tiya. 1995. "The Refugee Problem and the Quest for Peace and Security in Southern Africa." *International Journal of Refugee Law,* vol. 7.

Medical Schemes Act 72 of 1967.

Meintjes, Sheila. 1997. "Gender, Citizenship and Democracy in Post-Apartheid South Africa." In *Gender Research Project Bulletin,* Spring 1997. Johannesburg: Centre for Applied Legal Studies.

Peberdy, Sally. 1997. "Obscuring History? Contemporary Patterns of Regional Migra-tion to South Africa." Forthcoming in *South Africa in Southern Africa: Reconfig-uring the Region,* ed. David Simon. London: James Currey.

Peberdy, Sally, and Jonathan Crush. 1998. "Rooted in Racism: The Origins of the Aliens Control Act." In *Beyond Control: Immigration and Human Rights in a Democratic South Africa.* Cape Town: Southern African Migration Project, pp. 18–36.

Republic of Bophuthatswana Constitution Act 18 of 1977 (Bophuthatswana).

Republic of Ciskei Constitution Act 20 of 1981 (Ciskei).

Republic of Transkei Constitution Act 15 of 1976 (Transkei).

Republic of Venda Constitution Act 9 of 1979 (Venda).

Restoration and Extension of South African Citizenship Act 196 of 1993.

Restoration of South African Citizenship Act 73 of 1986.

Sacks, Vera. 1997. "Multiculturism, Constitutionalism, and the South African Constitution." *Public Law,* pp. 672–91.

Schmidt, C. W. H. 1993. "Citizenship and Nationality." Revised by F. Venter. In *The Law of South Africa (First Reissue),* vol. 2, ed. W. A. Joubert. Durban: Butterworths, pp. 343–57.

Smith, Rogers. 1997. *Civic Ideals: Conflicting Visions of Citizenship in U.S. History.* New Haven: Yale University Press.

Social Assistance Act 59 of 1992.

South Africa. Department of Home Affairs. (May 30, 1997.) "Draft Green Paper on International Migration." General Notice 849 of 1997. *Government Gazette,* vol. 383, no. 18033.

South Africa. Department of Home Affairs. 1995. *Annual Report.* RP 69/1996.

South Africa. Department of Home Affairs. (November 14, 1995.) "Dual Citizenship: Permission To Make Use of a Foreign Passport." Passport Control Instruction No. 93 of 1995. Unpublished.

South Africa. National Assembly. *Debates of the National Assembly* (Hansard). 1995. Second Session, First Parliament.

South Africa. Parliament. 1995. "Memorandum on the Objects of the South African Citizenship Bill, 1995." B23–95.

South Africa. Senate. 1995. *Debates of the Senate* (Hansard). Second Session, First Parliament.

South African Citizenship Act 88 of 1995.

South African Citizenship Act 44 of 1949.

South African Citizenship Amendment Act 69 of 1997.

Status of Bophuthatswana Act 89 of 1977.

Status of Ciskei Act 110 of 1981.

Status of Transkei Act 100 of 1976.

Status of Venda Act 107 of 1979.

Transkei Constitution Act 48 of 1963.

Union Nationality and Flags Act 40 of 1927.

van Wyk, David. 1978. "The Ebb and Flow of South African Citizenship Law." *1978 South African Yearbook on International Law,* vol. 4, pp. 148–52.

Legal Cases

Administrator, Transvaal v. Traub, 1989 (4) SA 731 (A).

Afroyim v. Rusk, 387 U.S. 253 (1967).

Bangindawo and Others v. Head of the Nyanda Regional Authority and Another, 1998 (3) SA 262 (Tk).

Kelleher v. Minister of Defence, 1982 (3) SA 278 (SECL).

Kellerman v. Minister of the Interior, 1945 TPD 179.

Larbi-Odam and Others v. The Member of the Executive Council for Education (North-West Province) and Another, 1998 (1) SA 745 (CC).

S v. Makwanyane, 1995 (3) SA 391 (CC).

Tshwete v. Minister of Home Affairs, 1988 (4) SA 586 (A).

CHAPTER EIGHT

Understanding Citizenship Policy in the Baltic States

LOWELL W. BARRINGTON

WHETHER CITIZENSHIP should be limited or whether all permanent residents should be granted citizenship has been an important question in the post-Communist, newly independent Baltic states. The amendments to the Latvian citizenship law passed in June 1998, the opposition's successful bid to force a national referendum on the issue, the attention paid to the referendum outside Latvia, and the vote of the population in favor of upholding the inclusive amendments have once again demonstrated that the issue of citizenship remains at the center of ethnic, regional, and international relations in the Baltic states. This fact should not be surprising. As much as any decision made by the government of a newly independent state, citizenship inclusiveness influences the lives of a state's residents and, potentially, stability in the region. This article lays out and attempts to explain the citizenship choices made by the governments of three post-Communist states where the citizenship debate has been especially lively: Estonia, Latvia, and Lithuania.

Citizenship policy development has not received the attention of other developments in the post-Communist world, such as economic turmoil in Russia or NATO expansion. Yet citizenship affects voting, occupation, and residence, and it increases tensions between those who receive it and those who do not. The exclusion from citizenship of minority groups in one state can affect the actions of other states because of the heterogeneous populations of central Europe and Eurasia. Groups such as the Organization for Security and Cooperation in Europe (OSCE) and the European Union (EU) continue to monitor events surrounding citizenship precisely because of their potential to bring violence, actions outside the normal political arena, increased tensions between states, and further territorial division.[1]

The goal of this article is to go beyond a description of the policies and explain the factors driving the inclusiveness of the policies. While an overview of the inclusiveness of the policies is provided, the central question is: *what factors led the governments of the Baltic states to develop a more inclusive or more exclusive citizenship policy?* To help answer this question, the development of the citizenship policies in Estonia, Latvia, and Lithuania is explored by breaking the broader question down into four specific puzzles generated by these cases: (1) Why was the citizenship policy of Lithuania more inclusive than the policies of Estonia and Latvia? (2) Why was the citizenship policy in Estonia more inclusive than the citizenship policy in Latvia? (3) Why were the citizenship policies of both Estonia and Latvia more inclusive than they might have been? (4) Why is the citizenship policy in Latvia more inclusive today than it was only five years ago? Examining these questions will produce a better understanding of the citizenship policies in these cases, as well as an idea about the forces—internal and external—that can affect citizenship policy decisions in other states.

Citizenship and Its Importance

First, it is necessary to discuss in some detail how citizenship is treated in this article. Citizenship is crucial to understanding "the state" and politics within it. All states set citizenship guidelines, which differentiate among the population living within a state. Citizenship sets the boundaries for "full membership" in the political community.[2] The percentage of residents that is granted citizenship affects perceptions of the state by those inside and outside its borders.

Despite its importance—or perhaps because of it—there is little agreement on the meaning of citizenship. Richard Norman states that political theorists often discuss citizenship as a bundle of political, civil, and social rights.[3] Raymond Plant attempts to justify an idea of citizenship that includes social (welfare) rights as well as political rights.[4] Some see citizenship as defined by passive rights, while others think that the citizen "experiences citizenship as

---

1. Before 1995, OSCE was known as the Conference on Security and Cooperation in Europe (CSCE). Thus, in this article either "OSCE" or "CSCE" will be used, depending on the year at issue.
2. Walzer, 1983.
3. Norman, 1992.
4. Plant, 1992.

practice (active participation in the determination, protection, and promotion of the common good)."[5] This practice of citizenship is related to another idea about being a citizen: duty. Citizenship has even been defined as the performance of these duties, as a "good citizen."

This idea of bringing rights and duties directly into the definition has generated much of the complexity and confusion in the political theory literature on citizenship. It leads to a blurring of citizenship with memberships that carry *some* of the same rights. William Safran states that citizenship carries with it certain rights, but because noncitizens also have certain rights, the distinction between citizen and noncitizen can be less than clear-cut if one bases the definition on rights alone.[6] Distinctions based on rights have even been made between citizenship and "full citizenship."[7] In addition, rights for people most would agree to call citizens can vary from country to country and time to time. Therefore, selecting a fixed set of rights and duties to use as the basis of a definition is problematic at best, impossible at worst.

By coming up with a definition of citizenship that does not depend on certain rights, we are not restricted from discussing rights. But we should be able to separate the rights of citizenship from the formal membership guidelines. As Norman states, "We need to know what it is about citizenship that gives rise to these kinds of rights."[8] What "it is" is that citizenship is a special kind of membership. It is official membership in the state. The idea that the individual is connected to the state on an equal basis with other citizens "gives rise" to the rights and duties many have associated with citizenship. Thus, citizenship is defined as follows: *it is the highest form of official membership in the state granted to the general public, its boundaries are set by a government representing the state, and it implies a certain equality among members.* Citizenship *policy* is the set of official rules and de facto procedures that affect this official membership. Thus, this article concerns who is, and who can be, in the body of citizens.

Citizenship and Political Rights

Separating the definition of citizenship from the rights and duties connected to it does not imply that they are unimportant. In fact, it is the difference in duties and rights between citizens and noncitizens in a given state that makes citi-

5. Peled, 1992.
6. Safran, 1997.
7. Bendix, 1964.
8. Norman, 1992, p. 36.

zenship such a potent issue. While the goal of this article is to provide an understanding of *admission into citizenship*, it is necessary to discuss the consequences of this membership as well in order to understand why inclusion matters.

Residents in newly independent states know that noncitizens are unlikely to receive all the rights granted to citizens. Often in democracies only citizens may fully participate politically. Noncitizens are denied the opportunity to run for office, form parties, or even vote. In Estonia, an important right, the right to vote in national elections, had a major impact on the 1992 presidential and parliamentary elections. September 20, 1992, marked Estonia's first national elections since the restoration of independence. The impact of disfranchisement before these "founding elections" was severe.[9] How can noncitizens feel loyalty to a new state when one of its first actions is to deny the vote to those who had it before independence?[10] The lack of political rights for noncitizens alienated even those non-Estonians who participated in the Estonian independence movement.[11] Beyond the psychological effect, the makeup of the electorate had a direct political effect. Despite the large Russian population in Estonia and twenty-three Russian representatives in the old Supreme Soviet, *no* Russian representatives were elected to the new Riigikogu (National Assembly), reducing the likelihood that the Parliament would represent the interests of Russian-speakers.[12] Noncitizens in Estonia were also prohibited from holding national or local political office and joining political parties.[13] In subsequent local elections, the former ethnic Russian leader of the Narva City Council was barred from running for office.[14] Thus, while noncitizens were allowed to vote in local elections, their choices were limited.

Other basic rights in Estonia differ between citizens and noncitizens. While "all persons legally present in Estonia shall have the right to freedom of movement and choice of abode," and everyone "shall have the right to leave Estonia," only citizens are protected from deportation and extradition.[15] Citizens

---

9. Stepan, 1994. For an overview of the negative reaction from Europe to the elections, see "Council of Europe," 1992.

10. All residents of the Estonian SSR had voting rights as late as the March 1990 republic-level elections.

11. Stepan, 1994, p. 138.

12. "Russian Envoy," January 27, 1993, p. 64.

13. Bungs et al., December 18, 1992, p. 39. Interestingly, noncitizens are allowed to form "non-profit associations and leagues." See Estonian Constitution, (last modified September 15, 1998), Article 48.

14. For more information on the local elections, see "Local Government," October 14–17, 1993.

15. Estonian Constitution, (last modified September 15, 1998), Articles 36–38.

also cannot be prevented from settling in Estonia (a right also granted to all ethnic Estonians regardless of citizenship), although the Estonian Constitution
leaves open the possibility that noncitizen residents who leave could be denied
the opportunity to resettle in the country.[16]

In Latvia, political opportunities for noncitizens are even more restricted
than in Estonia. Noncitizens cannot vote, even in local elections. Those without
citizenship have been prohibited from holding state office, from serving as
judges or barristers, and from taking part in diplomatic and consular service.[17]
While citizens are protected from extradition, noncitizens do not share such
protection. In addition, only a citizen has the right to "freely choose his/her residence in any part of Latvia's territory" and to "freely leave Latvia and to freely
return to Latvia."[18] Finally, although "all people have the right to form public
organizations and participate in their activities," only citizens can establish political parties.[19]

In Lithuania, noncitizens also face a significant restriction of rights. As in
Latvia, they cannot vote in local or national elections, or hold political office or
serve as police officers.[20] Like both other states, they are not protected from extradition in the way that citizens are.[21] Unlike Lithuanian citizens, noncitizens
are also not guaranteed in the Lithuanian Constitution the right to choose their
place of residence freely, the right to return to Lithuania, and the right to form
"societies, political parties, and associations."[22] The law On Public Organizations specifically prohibits noncitizens from forming or joining public organizations.[23]

When those denied citizenship tend to coincide with ethnic identity, the excluded ethnic group's ability to protect itself through the political system is se-

16. Estonian Constitution, (last modified September 15, 1998), Article 36.

17. These differences are laid out in On the Rights and Responsibilities of Citizens and People,
1991, Latvia; On Judicial Power, 1992, Latvia; On the Bar, 1993, Latvia; and On the Republic of
Latvia Diplomatic and Consular Service, 1993, Latvia. These laws are cited in Tsilevich and
Ruchkovsky, 1994.

18. On the issues of extradition, location of residence, and right of return, see Latvia, 1991, The
Rights and Obligations of a Citizen and a Person, Articles 6, 10.

19. On the issues of political party and public organization formation, see Latvia, 1991, The
Rights and Obligations of a Citizen and a Person, Article 31.

20. See Lithuania, 1991, On the Legal Status of Foreigners in the Republic of Lithuania, Article 9; Lithuania, 1994, On Elections to Local Government Councils, Article 2; Lithuania, 1990,
Law on Police, Article 5.

21. See Lithuanian Constitution, (last modified September 15, 1998), Article 32.

22. See Lithuanian Constitution, (last modified September 15, 1998), Articles 32, 35.

23. See Lithuania, 1995, On Public Organisations, Articles 4, 8. The 1996 law On Associations
declares that association members can be noncitizens, but it also states that the associations can
limit membership of noncitizens in their statutes. See Lithuania, 1996, On Associations, Article 4.1.

verely limited. In democratic theory, the "intensity" of minorities is often discussed as a way that minorities can be protected in systems based on majority rule.[24] It is argued that a minority will have more at stake on a given issue that affects it, while the majority will be less committed. In this situation, the intense minority can break apart the less intense majority.[25] This argument rests on two large assumptions. First, it is assumed that the majority will be passive.[26] In a climate of ethnonationalism where the survival of the nation is perceived to be at stake, however, the majority will not be passive. Second, it is assumed that the members of the minority have access to the political system.[27] With political rights attached to citizenship, membership in the citizenry is essential for making claims on the political system.

Citizenship and Social Rights and Benefits

Citizenship also brings a greater assurance of social rights. George Ginsburgs states that "full-fledged citizenship affords the most reliable surety of enjoyment of the ensemble of social rights practiced in a particular community. . . ."[28] This "surety" comes from the political rights that citizens enjoy, allowing them to pressure the system for protection. It also comes from a belief that, given their special membership status, citizens deserve special protection from the state that noncitizens do not deserve.

In Latvia, noncitizens have been prohibited from owning land and other natural resources, from purchasing housing from the state, and in some cases from purchasing privatized cooperative apartments.[29] In addition, noncitizens have received fewer privatization vouchers and a smaller pension.[30] Noncitizens in Latvia continue to complain that their housing and social benefits have been re-

24. See, for example, Dahl, 1956 (discussion of the power of minorities in the U.S. political system).

25. See Dahl, 1956, pp. 90–123.

26. See Dahl, 1956, p. 133.

27. See Dahl, 1956, p. 137. "A central guiding thread of American constitutional development has been the evolution of a political system in which all the active and legitimate groups in the population can make themselves heard at some crucial stage in the process of decision."

28. Ginsburgs, 1990, pp. 3, 14.

29. See On the Rights and Responsibilities of Citizens and People, 1991, Latvia; On State and Municipal Assistance in Solving the Problem of Housing, 1993, Latvia; and On Privatization of Cooperative Apartments, 1991, Latvia; in Tsilevich and Ruchkovsky, 1994. According to Tsilevich and Ruchkovsky, 1994, Article 7 of On Privatization of Cooperative Apartments states that those residing in Latvia for more than sixteen years are entitled to buy privatized apartments regardless of citizenship, yet some municipalities have restricted this right only to citizens.

30. See On Privatization Certificates, 1992, Latvia; and On Interim Rules of State-Paid Social Security Benefits, 1993, Latvia; in Tsilevich and Ruchkovsky, 1994.

duced because of their "second class status."[31] In Estonia, everyone has the right, according to the Estonian Constitution, to health care.[32] But it leaves open the possibility that other laws could restrict certain benefits. Only citizens, for example, are absolutely guaranteed by the Constitution "state assistance in the cases of old age, inability to work, loss of provider and need" and the right "to freely choose his or her field of activity, profession and place of work."[33] In Lithuania, the Constitution grants only to citizens the guarantee of free higher education for those who show "suitable academic progress."[34] In addition, only citizens may own land, and only citizens are guaranteed by the Constitution "old age and disability pension."[35] Yet other laws state that noncitizen permanent residents also enjoy such rights.[36] This is not the case with land ownership, which is restricted only to citizens.[37] Noncitizens also cannot be founding members of cooperatives, although they can be members.[38]

While people in the West tend to focus on the political rights granted to citizens, these social rights and benefits may be even more important. Given the chaotic environment in the former Communist world, the lack of access to housing, work, or welfare benefits is an even greater worry than it would be in the less chaotic West. In the period immediately after independence, this worry was fueled by rumors about impending action against noncitizens in Estonia and Latvia. Reports in the Russian press in 1993, for example, discussed the possible expulsion of some Russians from their apartments in Estonia.[39] These concerns continue today. Gennady Kotov, cochairman of the Latvian Human Rights Committee, claims that there are sixty-nine differences in political, social, and economic rights between citizens and noncitizens, making Latvia "an apartheid state."[40]

Thus, much of the emotion that comes from debates over citizenship is due to the importance of the social rights of citizens and the uncertainty of such rights for noncitizens. This uncertainty over what the final difference between rights of citizens and noncitizens will look like makes the issue of citizenship

31. See "Western Press," April 9, 1998.
32. Estonian Constitution (last modified September 15, 1998), Article 28.
33. Estonian Constitution (last modified September 15, 1998), Articles 28–29.
34. See Lithuanian Constitution (last modified September 15, 1998), Article 41(3).
35. See Lithuanian Constitution (last modified September 15, 1998), Articles 47(1), 52.
36. See Lithuania, 1991, On the Legal Status of Foreigners in the Republic of Lithuania, Article 18 (stating that permanent residents have the same "rights to social security as citizens"). Article 22 states that such residents also share citizen rights to education.
37. See Lithuania, 1994, Law on Land, Article 3.
38. See Lithuania, 1993, Cooperative Law, Articles 3, 4.
39. See "Otnosheniya," June 24, 1993, p. 1.
40. See Stephens, September 21, 1998, p. A1.

more contentious than if these rights were completely clear from the start. Particularly in the newly independent states of the former Soviet Union, therefore, it has been very unsettling not to receive citizenship.

Citizenship Policies and Citizenship Laws

So far, citizenship has been discussed both in terms of the specific citizenship law and with a more vague reference to citizenship "policy." The latter is the focus of this article, although the former is obviously included in the policy. Why focus on citizenship policy rather than on citizenship law? Limiting the examination to official laws can miss important dimensions of the comprehensive citizenship policy. In the area of citizenship, differences between policy and official law could include the refusal to pass qualified applicants during the testing stage of naturalization as well as related issues such as the treatment of those denied citizenship, or access to language training for those seeking naturalization. A 1995 U.S. Department of State report, for example, criticizes the behavior of the Latvian Citizenship and Immigration Department for arbitrary behavior regarding noncitizen residency status.[41]

Exclusion from citizenship clearly matters, but what is an exclusive citizenship policy? What is an inclusive one? In fact, it is somewhat misleading to imply that citizenship laws can be thought of in such dichotomous terms. All citizenship laws exclude by their nature. By defining citizens, a government is defining noncitizens. Where naturalization is allowed, citizenship laws contain guidelines for naturalization (how foreigners become citizens) that make it impossible for simply *anyone* to enter a country and claim citizenship. In addition, a provision called "automatic replenishment determines whether or not one can be born into citizenship."[42]

While all citizenship laws set boundaries, the requirements for crossing these citizenship boundaries differ from country to country. Therefore, it *is* possible to describe one country's citizenship policy as more—or even much more—exclusive than another's. A law that requires ten years of residency for naturalization, for example, is more exclusive than one that requires only five. In the case of "replenishment," laws that do not guarantee citizenship to those born in the country are more exclusive than those that do.

In addition to setting policy on naturalization and replenishment, governments of newly independent states face a decision that rulers of existing states do not. They must decide who makes up the initial base of citizens to which birth and nat-

---

41. See Zwadiuk, March 6, 1996.
42. Brubaker, "Citizenship Struggles," 1992, pp. 269, 277.

uralization add. A law that creates a base from 60 percent of the permanent residents is more exclusive than one that allows all existing permanent residents to become citizens. Because of the unique situation of creating a base of citizens and the number of people affected, the guidelines for initial, "automatic" citizenship are by far the most important part of the citizenship policy in newly independent states. Here, provisions for automatic citizenship are weighted most heavily in discussing the inclusiveness of a citizenship policy.[43]

Citizenship Policies in the Baltic States

Most of the states that emerged from the collapse of the Soviet Union chose the "zero option" for citizenship, by which all permanent residents were granted citizenship without naturalization. In Lithuania, separate designations were made for those who could trace their own or their parents' citizenship back to the period before incorporation into the Soviet Union (1940) and those who came during the Soviet period.[44] Yet this latter group was not excluded from citizenship but, rather, was required simply to apply for citizenship without a formal naturalization process.[45] In Estonia and Latvia, however, those who came during the Soviet period—mostly Russian-speaking and, of these, mostly ethnic Russians—were excluded from simple registration. They were required to naturalize, in the case of Estonia, and barred completely from citizenship in the case of Latvia until a citizenship law was finally passed in 1994.[46] Even then, strict limits were placed on naturalization.[47] In June 1998 the Latvian government enacted a reform to make citizenship automatic for children born on their territory after independence. Similarly, the Estonian parliament in December 1998 passed an amendment making children under the age of 15 who were born in postindependence Estonia and do not have citizenship of another country eligible for citizenship through application rather than through the full naturalization process.

---

43. One could envision ideal types of inclusive and exclusive citizenship policies in newly independent states. In the inclusive policy, all permanent residents would receive citizenship without naturalization. Later arrivals would have minimum naturalization requirements (for example, one year of residency plus an oath of loyalty). Children born in the country would be citizens regardless of the status of their parents. In the ideal exclusive policy, automatic citizenship would be severely restricted and favor a certain group over others. Naturalization would not be allowed. Children born in the country would not necessarily be citizens. While none of the three states examined in this chapter perfectly fit either of these ideal types, the imaginary types provide a useful benchmark for comparing the citizenship policies.

44. See Girard, 1998.

45. See Girard, 1998.

46. See Barrington, 1995, pp. 731, 735–39.

47. See the discussion *infra* on the development of the Latvian citizenship law.

Space does not permit me to provide all the details of the citizenship policies of the Baltic states. The summary of the inclusiveness of the policies follows.

Citizenship Policy in Lithuania

Of the three states, Lithuania developed the most inclusive citizenship policy by far, in terms of both its official provisions, particularly in the crucial area of automatic citizenship, and its effect on the population of the state. Nearly all permanent residents were able to become citizens without residency and language requirements. As a result of the Lithuanian policy, roughly 95 percent of the adult population of Lithuania in 1994 had acquired Lithuanian citizenship.

The Supreme Soviet of the Lithuanian Republic passed a law on citizenship that went into effect on November 3, 1989. Since Lithuania was still part of the Soviet Union, the citizenship guidelines were technically for the Lithuanian Soviet Socialist Republic (LiSSR). The Lithuanian law began by stating that all persons who had been citizens before June 15, 1940, and all their descendants living in Lithuania were automatically citizens.[48]

In addition, however, the law contained two provisions that broadened the base of initial citizens. First, all permanent residents born in Lithuania or those who could show that one of their parents or grandparents was born there were also granted automatic citizenship, provided they did not have citizenship from another country.[49] Second, those residing on the territory who did not meet the other criteria could still become automatic citizens by signing, within two years, a loyalty declaration stating that they would support the Lithuanian Constitution and the laws of the LiSSR as well as "respect its state sovereignty and territorial integrity."[50] Thus, the Lithuanian law was based strongly on the principle of *jus soli* (law of the soil). Naturalization was possible by showing a knowledge of the Lithuanian language, being a permanent resident for the previous ten years, possessing a permanent source of income, promising to obey and showing a knowledge of the Lithuanian Constitution, and signing a loyalty statement similar to that of automatic citizens but also stating a respect for Lithuania's state "language, culture, customs, and traditions."[51]

48. See Lithuania, 1989, O grazhdanstve Litovskoi SSR, Article 1.
49. See Lithuania, 1989, O grazhdanstve Litovskoi SSR, Article 1.
50. See Girnius, 1991, p. 21; Brubaker, "Citizenship Struggles," 1992, p. 281; and Lithuania, 1989, O grazhdanstve Litovskoi SSR, Article 1.
51. Brubaker, "Citizenship Struggles," 1992, p. 280; Lithuania, 1989, O grazhdanstve Litovskoi SSR, Article 17.

While the naturalization demands were not easy, the requirements for automatic citizenship were quite inclusive. Nearly everyone was eligible for citizenship under these guidelines. Out of a population of more than 3.3 million, only about 350,000 permanent residents did not receive citizenship before the two-year period expired; the failure to acquire citizenship by these people, however, appears to be due more to choice or ignorance than to any kind of legal or de facto exclusion.[52]

With the end of the two-year period and with independence a reality, a new citizenship law was put in place. On December 5, 1991, the 1989 citizenship law was replaced by a new law passed by the Sajudis-controlled Parliament.[53] This law generally eliminated the possibility of automatic citizenship for current permanent residents. As *The Economist* described it, Lithuania had "at first magnanimously granted citizenship to all permanent residents who asked for it—but the offer expired in November 1991."[54] This view is not completely accurate. Those who were citizens of Lithuania before 1940—as well as their children and grandchildren—were still granted citizenship without naturalization, as long as they had not taken citizenship of another state.[55] For the purposes of this part of the law, "another state" did not include the Soviet Union; rather, this provision was targeted at those who left Lithuania, went abroad, and took citizenship of their new state of residence.[56] In addition to those who had been pre-1940 citizens, those who were permanent residents of Lithuania from January 9, 1919, to June 15, 1940, and their children and grandchildren, would receive citizenship without naturalization if they were currently permanent residents and had not taken citizenship of another state.[57]

Elements of *jus sanguinis* (law of blood descent) could be found in the new law. For those who had taken citizenship of another state, Article 18 of the 1991 law stated that Lithuanian citizenship could be restored to "persons of Lithuanian descent who were citizens of the Lithuanian Republic and who left Lithuania in the period between 15 June 1940 and 11 March 1990 and now live in other states."[58] A law passed on December 10, 1991 (five days after the new citizenship law) included amended wording to this article. The new wording in-

52. But see Ginsburgs, 1993, pp. 233, 238 (claiming that administrative problems may have kept this number from being even lower).

53. See Lithuania, 1991, Zakon o grazhdanstve Litovskoi Respubliki, Ekho Litvi.

54. "Citizenship; One of Us," July 31, 1993, p. 45.

55. See Lithuania, 1991, Zakon o grazhdanstve Litovskoi Respubliki, Ekho Litvi, Article 1.

56. This follows logically from the idea of post-Soviet Lithuania as a "restored" state, and the establishment of Soviet citizenship for Lithuanian residents as an invalid act of an illegal regime.

57. See Lithuania, 1991, Zakon o grazhdanstve Litovskoi Respubliki, Ekho Litvi, Article 1.

58. See Lithuania, 1991, Zakon o grazhdanstve Litovskoi Respubliki, Ekho Litvi, Article 18.

cluded the phrase "as well as their children who, being born in another state, have not acquired citizenship of that state."[59] This change made it easier for children of émigrés abroad to become Lithuanian citizens. In addition, those of Lithuanian descent who were not citizens could implement their right to citizenship by renouncing "citizenship of another state, and moving to Lithuania for permanent residence, as well as taking the oath to the Republic of Lithuania."[60] This ethnic-based right to citizenship had not existed in the 1989 law.[61]

The 1991 citizenship law also stipulated that dual citizenship was not allowed. The exception would be in the case of an international treaty on the topic. As outlined in Article 36 of the law, international treaties take precedence over the 1991 law.[62] While the citizenship law did not make specific reference to the Soviet Union, a resolution passed five days later made it clear that obtaining Lithuanian citizenship meant that citizenship of the Soviet Union was considered invalid for that person by the Lithuanian government.[63]

Naturalization requirements in the 1991 law were similar to those in the law passed in 1989. As outlined in Article 12 of the law, naturalization required passing a written and spoken test in Lithuanian, permanent residence in Lithuania for ten years, employment or a constant legal source of income from within Lithuania, knowledge of the Lithuanian Constitution, and renunciation of prior citizenship.[64] New citizens also had to take an oath similar to the one in the 1989 law. One difference in the naturalization articles in the two laws was a line inserted at the end of Article 12 in the 1991 law. After the naturalization requirements, the article concluded, "Persons meeting the conditions specified in this Article shall be granted citizenship of the Republic of Lithuania *taking into consideration the interests of the Republic of Lithuania.*"[65] This statement seemed to open the door for the refusal of naturalization even for those who met the requirements, although there have been no significant concerns expressed about such denial of naturalization for qualified applicants taking place in practice. The citizenship oath again included a pledge to protect the "territorial integrity of the state" and to "respect the state language, culture and customs of Lithuania." Differences from the 1989 law's oath included the requirement to

---

59. Lithuania, 1991, O deistvii dokumentov o grazhdanstve Litovskoi Respubliki i vnecenii dopolnenia v zakon o grazhdanstve, Ekho Litvi.

60. Lithuania, 1991, Law on Citizenship, Articles 17, 18.

61. See Lithuania, 1989, O grazhdanstve Litovskoi SSR, Article 22.

62. See Lithuania, 1991, Zakon o grazhdanstve Litovskoi Respubliki, Ekho Litvi, Article 36.

63. See Lithuania, 1991, On the Procedure for Implementing the Republic of Lithuania Law on Citizenship, Resolution of the Lithuanian Supreme Council.

64. See Lithuania, 1991, Zakon o grazhdanstve Litovskoi Respubliki, Ekho Litvi, Article 12.

65. See Lithuania, 1991, Zakon o grazhdanstve Litovskoi Respubliki, Ekho Litvi, Article 12 (emphasis added).

pledges in the 1991 law's oath to be "loyal to the Republic of Lithuania," to "defend the independence of Lithuania," and to "strengthen the democratic Lithuanian state."[66]

Over the next five years, the 1991 law was heavily amended. In November 1992, the Lithuanian Supreme Council simplified the procedures for granting citizenship to children and grandchildren of ethnic Lithuanians living outside of Lithuania.[67] A second set of amendments to the 1991 law was passed in July 1993. The revisions included new guidelines for demonstrating past Lithuanian citizenship.[68] In December 1993, another amendment affecting the émigré community was passed. The amendment overturned provisions in the 1991 citizenship law by waiving both the requirement to have not taken citizenship of another state, outlined in Article 1, to receive automatic citizenship and the need to renounce citizenship of that state to receive *restored* citizenship.[69] This change paved the way for émigrés who met the qualifications to hold citizenship of Lithuania and of their country of residence.[70]

In October 1995, several additional amendments were added to the law. One of these equated adopted children with natural children under the rules for children acquiring (or losing) citizenship based on the citizenship status of their parents.[71] Another modified the rules for naturalization to allow those sixty-five or older and those with certain disabilities, such as blindness and deafness, to naturalize without taking a language test or exam on provisions of the Constitution.[72] This modification was important for older residents who had not understood the need to *apply* for automatic citizenship during the period from 1989 to 1991. Yet another change at this time involved children of émigré citizens. It allowed these children to claim citizenship, even if they had taken citizenship of

66. For English-language versions of the oaths, see Lithuania, 1989, Law on Citizenship, Article 17; and Lithuania, 1991, Law on Citizenship, Article 15.

67. See "Supreme Soviet," November 20, 1992, p. 59. The amendments passed in November 1992 also included the provision that children, one of whose parents is a Lithuanian citizen and the other of whom is stateless, can become Lithuanian citizens by application of the citizen-parent. See Lithuania, 1996, Law on Citizenship, Article 25.

68. See Lithuania, 1996, Law on Citizenship, Article 28.

69. Lithuania, 1991, Law on Citizenship, Article 18 (concerning the restoration of Lithuanian citizenship, requiring the applicant to give up citizenship of his state of residence to have his Lithuanian citizenship restored). In addition, according to paragraph 3 of Article 18—even after the new wording added on December 10, 1991—the émigrés' children *who had acquired citizenship of another state* were not eligible for automatic restoration. See Article 18(3).

70. The qualifications, however, were important. Those of Lithuanian ethnic background fared best. Those without such background but who had been citizens could get their citizenship back without naturalization only if they had not given up their Lithuanian citizenship.

71. See Lithuania, 1996, Law on Citizenship, Article 24.

72. See Lithuania, 1996, Law on Citizenship, Article 12.

another state, provided that they had not renounced Lithuanian citizenship.[73] The October 1995 changes also included a clearer definition for Lithuanian ethnic identity. A person could claim Lithuanian origin if at least one of his parents or grandparents was ethnically Lithuanian, and if he considered himself Lithuanian as a result. The final change in the law during this period went into effect in February 1996. It extended the right to claim Lithuanian citizenship for an indefinite period to children of pre-1940 citizens living in other states who had not repatriated.[74]

Citizenship in Latvia

The Latvian citizenship policy was far less inclusive than the Lithuanian one, and the least inclusive of the three Baltic policies. Latvia did not even adopt an official law after independence, but simply restored the citizenship of those who had it before the Soviet period and their descendants.[75] Except for this resolution restoring citizenship to pre-1940 citizens, the Latvian government did all it could to put off adopting an official law. First, Supreme Council Chairman Anatolijs Gorbunovs proposed a referendum to solve the issue.[76] Then, Latvian officials argued that the official citizenship law, passed either by Parliament or by referendum, could come only after the reestablishment of the Saeima (Parliament) as a replacement for the existing Supreme Council. Under this argument, naturalization could not be allowed in practice, as the naturalization rules in the 1991 resolution had been established by the Supreme Council, a body of the Soviet occupation period. Latvian Foreign Minister Georgs Andrejevs, in a letter to CSCE High Commissioner on National Minorities Max van der Stoel, argued, "[T]he current Latvia Supreme Council is a transitional parliament and has no legal mandate under the restored 1922 Latvia Constitution to change the body of Latvia citizenship through naturalization or other means."[77] Why naturalization provisions from this body should be deemed illegitimate as distinct from restoration of pre–World War II citizenship or even the declaration

73. See Lithuania, 1996, Law on Citizenship, Article 1. Interestingly, this right was not extended to grandchildren, who could still claim automatic citizenship only if they had not acquired citizenship of another state.

74. See Lithuania, 1996, Law on Citizenship, Article 17.

75. See Latvia, 1991, On the Renewal of Republic of Latvia Citizens' Rights and Fundamental Principles of Naturalization, Resolution of the Republic of Latvia Supreme Council. The Supreme Council also passed amendments to this resolution on November 27, 1991, that restored citizenship to émigrés even if they maintain the citizenship of their country of residence. This resolution thus allowed dual citizenship for émigrés, while prohibiting it for most citizens. See Staprans, 1991, p. 2.

76. See "Gorbunovs," March 23, 1992.

77. Andrejevs, letter to van der Stoel, April 18, 1993.

of independence was never discussed.[78] Regardless of the explanation for the delay, the lack of a citizenship law before the Saeima elections, combined with the lack of voting rights for noncitizens, ensured that most non-Latvians would not be able to vote for the Saeima in June 1993. The eventual citizenship law that the Saeima would produce was, as a result, more exclusive than if these people had been able to elect representatives to the new assembly. Thus, while Latvia lacked an official citizenship law, it had a citizenship policy.

Few in the Russian community could become citizens until the official law was passed. Since most Latvian politicians did not object to the Russians' lack of citizenship, there was little incentive for the Latvians to establish official citizenship guidelines, until Europe made it clear that to receive Council of Europe membership Latvia must change its "lawless policy" and adopt a citizenship law.[79] Up to the time of the new law, 700,000 to 800,000 residents of Latvia were shut out of the citizenship process with no chance at automatic citizenship and doubts about whether they would ever be allowed to naturalize. Thus, while the lack of an official law on citizenship was not a purely *jus sanguinis* policy,[80] the effect was similar to that of a law that banned most of the non-Latvians from becoming citizens.

The citizenship law that was finally passed went through many versions, with much of the controversy surrounding the issue of naturalization quotas (which would limit the number of naturalized citizens each year regardless of the number of qualified applicants). Residency requirements were also argued over, although the length of time required was less important than the issue of from what date the residency period would be counted, since so many of the residents had been in Latvia more than a decade. Five parties in the Saeima pro-

78. When I asked this question of Inese Birznece, a member of Latvia's Way and one of the drafters of the Saeima ruling coalition's draft citizenship law versions, she responded that the naturalization provisions in the 1991 Supreme Council resolution were not binding on the Saeima, but something like restoring citizenship was acceptable for the Supreme Council to do because technically the restored citizens were citizens the entire time of the Soviet period; the Soviet government had just failed to recognize this. Birznece, interview, May 10, 1994. It is clear, however, that this argument was applied to citizenship because of the highly controversial nature of nearly all proposals on the issue and because the lack of a law with binding naturalization features had the same effect as a highly exclusive law. According to Latvian American political scientist Neils Muiznieks, the lack of a formal citizenship law was part of a strategy by nationalists who originally argued that expanding citizenship would take place after pre-WWII citizenship was restored. These politicians knew, however, that expanding citizenship would be too controversial to happen any time soon after the October 1991 resolution.

79. For a more detailed discussion of the effect of Council of Europe pressure, see "Lack of Citizenship Law," February 1, 1994, p. 69; Girnius, August 26, 1994, pp. 29–33; and the discussion of European action *infra*.

80. A portion of those who could trace citizenship back to the interwar period were not ethnic Latvians.

duced draft proposals of the law for the first reading; three of these were given to standing committees on September 23, 1993, for review.[81] The two versions not sent to the committees were the two most inclusive proposals.

The draft law that emerged from the bargaining and amendment included quotas and strict naturalization requirements. The 0.1 percent quota provision remained in the final version of the draft law and became part of the basis for the presidential rejection of the bill and his demand for a reconsideration.[82] The president also demanded, at the request of Western officials, clearer deadlines for the review of naturalization applications.[83] Parliament could have simply passed the law again and the president, according to the Latvian Constitution, would have been forced to sign it. Instead, the president got his wishes. The revised (and final) version contained a schedule for naturalization, the so-called window policy.[84] There were no fixed quotas limiting the number of applications that could be accepted among those who qualified according to the application schedule. The president signed the bill into law.

The absence of quotas did not mean, however, that naturalization would be easy. According to the guidelines of the law,[85] applicants for naturalization must be registered;[86] must have lived in Latvia for five years counted from no earlier than May 4, 1990, unless they came after July 1, 1992, in which case the five years begins with the issuance of a permanent residence permit; must have a "command of the Latvian language";[87] must have a legal source of income; must take a loyalty oath to Latvia; and must know the national anthem and his-

81. See Birznece, interview, May 10, 1994.

82. This provision meant that as a result of the naturalization process, the body of citizens could only be expanded by 0.1 percent per year. In the version of the law passed at the first reading, the quota was to be determined annually, "taking into consideration the demographic and economic situation in the country, in order to ensure the development of Latvia as a single nation-state." Latvia, 1993, Citizenship Law.

83. See Boulton, July 23, 1994, p. 2.

84. According to Article 14 of this final version, the application review was to be based on the age and place of birth of the applicant. Starting in 1996, applications from those born in Latvia who are sixteen to twenty years old will be considered; in 1997, those born in Latvia who are up to twenty-five years old may apply; in 1998, those born in Latvia who are up to thirty years old may apply; in 1999, those who are forty or younger and born in Latvia will be considered; in 2000, all those born in Latvia may apply; in 2001, those born outside Latvia but who came to Latvia as minors may apply; in 2002, those who were born outside Latvia but entered the country up to the age of thirty may apply; and in 2003, all others may apply. This last group of applicants, however, will have preference given to those who have lived in Latvia the longest. See Latvia, 1994, Law on Citizenship, Article 14.

85. See Latvia, 1994, Law on Citizenship, Article 12.

86. This detail became an issue when many Russians claimed that they were unfairly denied registration, making them ineligible for naturalization.

87. Latvia, 1994, Law on Citizenship, Articles 19–21 (describing procedures for testing for command of the Latvian language).

tory of Latvia as well as the basic principles of the Latvian Constitution and the constitutional law Rights and Obligations of a Citizen and a Person.

Because of the controversial nature of the citizenship law, there was a general understanding by Latvian politicians that the issue needed to be taken off the table for a while. In other words, despite the international community's desire for greater inclusiveness, the prospects for significant changes in the law in the period immediately after its adoption were remote. While amendments to the law were passed in March 1995, these were minor changes having little effect on the vast majority of the noncitizens.[88] This reluctance to make alterations in the law began to change in 1997 and, in particular, during 1998. In February 1998, the Parliament voted on, but rejected, an amendment to grant citizenship to postindependence children of noncitizens.[89] But in March 1998, police dispersed, with batons drawn, a demonstration by Russian-speaking pensioners.[90] Russia immediately linked this incident to the citizenship issue and portrayed it as an example of human rights violations in Latvia, something it has claimed repeatedly since the restoration of Latvian independence.[91] In early April 1998, an antipersonnel mine exploded outside the Russian Embassy in Riga.[92] This event followed a march by several Latvian SS veterans, in which a number of senior Latvian army officers participated.[93] In response to these various events, Russia threatened economic retaliation against Latvia, including the reduction of the export of Russian crude oil from the Latvian port of Ventspils.[94] These incidents further weakened Latvia's case for EU membership, after the EU passed it over for the next wave of expansion of the organization.[95]

In late April 1998, the Latvian government began to move forward with changes to the citizenship policy supported by European officials and the Latvian president.[96] The road to passage was not easy, however, as Fatherland and Freedom–LNNK, a party in the ruling coalition, initially announced its opposi-

88. For a text of the changes, see Naturalization Board of the Republic of Latvia, 1997, On Naturalization in Latvia, pp. 62–63 (section describing the "Amendments to the Law on Citizenship").

89. See "Latvian Lawmakers," February 13, 1998.

90. See Goble, March 9, 1998.

91. It should be noted that the human rights violation charge has been rejected by nearly all international observers. A U.S. State Department report in 1997 supported the position that Latvia is not a country with significant human rights abuses. Its main criticism was the occasionally excessive use of force against prisoners by the police and Latvian Interior Ministry. See U.S. Department of State, Bureau of Democracy, Human Rights, and Labor, *Latvia Report on Human Rights Practices for 1997* (January 30, 1998).

92. See "Latvia Reels," April 7, 1998.

93. See "Latvia Reels," April 7, 1998.

94. See "Latvia Urges Russia," April 21, 1998.

95. See "Latvia Reels," April 7, 1998.

96. The government announced its decision on April 21.

tion to any changes to the law. A working group, established by the government parties, hit several snags over the issue of the naturalization "window" policy.[97] Finally, the amendments were agreed to, and they were passed by the Parliament on June 22, 1998. The amendments eliminated the naturalization schedule (the window policy) and allowed children born to noncitizens in Latvia since the restoration of independence to claim automatic citizenship.[98]

The nationalists in Parliament immediately moved to force a national vote on the issue. A week after the vote in Parliament, thirty-six deputies, including all nineteen of the Fatherland and Freedom–LNNK Party, forced the president to delay implementation of the law.[99] A petition drive was organized, and well more than the required number of signatures was obtained, leading to a vote on October 3, 1998. The results of the referendum, in which the amendments were supported by just over 53 percent of those voting,[100] may still not close the door on the citizenship issue. Further inclusive changes are not out of the question, especially if naturalization numbers remain as low as they have been.

Once the Latvian government finally moved toward a citizenship law in 1994 that would allow at least limited naturalization, it also discussed the need for a new body to oversee the naturalization process. This discussion was due in great part to concerns about the Citizenship and Immigration Department, a body accused by many in Latvia and Europe of doing what it could to discourage non-Latvians from integrating into Latvian politics and society. As a result, the Latvian Naturalization Board was created by a decree of the Cabinet of Ministers on October 18, 1994.[101] The Naturalization Board was given the task of educating the population about naturalization, reviewing applications for citizenship, and administering the naturalization tests. It has also overseen and employed research on the attitudes of noncitizens and their potential for naturalization.

The Naturalization Board has tried to make the process of naturalization as accommodating as possible by, among other things, producing books and pamphlets on the testing process that include sample questions. As a result, more than 90 percent of those who have taken the naturalization tests have passed

97. See "Latvian Working Group," April 15, 1998.

98. See Johnson, 1998.

99. See Johnson, 1998.

100. See "Latvian Vote," October 6, 1998, p. 3.

101. In a not-too-subtle comment on the Citizenship and Immigration Department, a publication of the Naturalization Board stated that training of Naturalization Board officials was a priority, because "in the state there were no employees who would be competent in dealing with citizenship and naturalization." See Naturalization Board of the Republic of Latvia, 1997, On Naturalization in Latvia, p. 13.

them.[102] Significantly fewer people than had been anticipated, however, have applied for naturalization. Of the more than 33,000 sixteen- to twenty-year-olds eligible for naturalization, only 560 applied.[103] Of the 140,000 residents who were eligible to apply by 1998, only approximately 10,000 had applied, and only 7,477 had become citizens by March 31, 1998.[104] In addition, fewer than 50 percent of the applicants were ethnic Russians, while nearly one-quarter of them were Lithuanians and Estonians.[105] The bulk of those applicants who were not Lithuanian or Estonian were married to citizens, making naturalization slightly easier for them.[106] While these numbers helped justify the need for the inclusive amendments passed in the summer of 1998, they have also created problems for the Naturalization Board. Its budget has come under attack, and it has been forced to turn to funding from Europe for some of its projects.[107]

Citizenship in Estonia

The citizenship policy of Estonia fell between Lithuania and Latvia in terms of inclusiveness. Yet Estonia's law was much more exclusive than Lithuania's, because automatic citizenship was not extended to the majority of ethnic Russians in the country, and special privileges were given to descendants of ethnic Estonians. The policy was more inclusive than Latvia's "lawless policy" of 1991 to 1994, and also more inclusive than the Latvian policy based on the law of 1994. Unlike Latvia, Estonia did not restrict those eligible for naturalization. Otherwise, the naturalization requirements were similar.

Like their counterparts in Lithuania, Estonian politicians considered a republic citizenship law during the Soviet period. Unlike Lithuania, Estonia did not pass such a law until after the restoration of independence. Less than a month after the failed Soviet coup solidified Baltic independence, the Estonian

102. See Karklins, 1997.

103. See Karklins, 1997. The reasons for the lack of interest in Latvian citizenship include the negative atmosphere surrounding the perceived treatment of non-Latvians, the limited knowledge of Latvian, ability to travel to countries such as Russia and Ukraine without paying for a visa, and the desire to avoid service in the military.

104. See Latvia, 1998, Republic of Latvia Naturalization Board, Information about Acceptance and Review of Naturalization Applications, by June 30, 1998.

105. See Latvia, 1998, Republic of Latvia Naturalization Board, *Naturalization Process in Latvia: 1995, 1996, 1997, 1998, Main Indices* (by June 30, 1998).

106. See, generally, Latvia, 1998, Republic of Latvia Naturalization Board, *Information about Acceptance and Review of Naturalization Applications* (by June 30, 1998); and Latvia, 1998, Republic of Latvia Naturalization Board, *Naturalization Process in Latvia: 1995, 1996, 1997, 1998, Main Indices* (by June 30, 1998).

107. The book *On Naturalization in Latvia,* for example, was published with the financial support of the Swedish Helsinki Committee for Human Rights.

special commission on citizenship submitted a draft law to the Supreme Council. Like the law that had emerged in Lithuania, this first draft law was quite inclusive regarding the initial base of citizens.

According to this proposal, the initial population of citizens would come from two groups. Those who were citizens before June 16, 1940, and their descendants would be granted automatic citizenship; those who were permanent residents on the date that the "transition period to full independence" began could apply for citizenship and have two of the naturalization requirements waived, competence in the Estonian language and ten years of residency.[108] Naturalization would be possible for others by fulfilling the requirements above as well as taking an oath of loyalty.[109] The draft law would have eliminated the automatic citizenship of spouses but would have allowed mothers to pass on citizenship as well as fathers.[110] While the naturalization requirements of the draft law were difficult, the possible waivers in the areas of language and residency requirements meant that the draft of the law was quite inclusive, a "variation on the 'zero option.'"[111] Most of the non-Estonian population would have had an opportunity to become citizens with little difficulty.

With its inclusive provisions, this version of the citizenship law was very controversial. It was amended on the floor of the Supreme Council to such an extent that the special committee on citizenship removed it from consideration. Only a week after submitting the first proposal, the citizenship committee announced that a new draft law would be submitted. This second version called for automatic citizenship only for pre-1940 citizens and their descendants. All others had to be naturalized, and the waivers in the first draft for the language test and ten-year residency requirement were eliminated.[112]

Exclusive guidelines for citizenship became law on February 26, 1992, after the adoption of the Supreme Council resolution On the Application of the Law on Citizenship.[113] This resolution differed from both of the two previous drafts. It essentially reinstated the 1938 citizenship law, creating the base of postindependence citizens from those who were citizens before the Soviet period and their descendants.[114] Dual citizenship with Russia was denied. Naturalization residency requirements in the final version, however, were more

108. See Kionka, 1991.
109. See Kionka, 1991.
110. The interwar law had allowed only fathers to pass citizenship to descendants.
111. See Kionka, 1991, p. 24.
112. See Kionka, 1991, p. 25.
113. See Estonia, 1992, "On the Application of the Law on Citizenship," Resolution of the Estonian Supreme Council.
114. See Estonia, 1993, Law on Citizenship; and Estonia, 1992, "On the Application of the Law on Citizenship," Resolution of the Estonian Supreme Council.

inclusive than the second draft law. Those ineligible for automatic citizenship could apply for citizenship after two years of permanent residency.[115] Qualified applicants would be granted citizenship one year after application.[116] The catch for applicants was that the two years of residency would be counted only after March 30, 1990.[117] Thus, someone not given automatic citizenship could, at the earliest, become a citizen on March 30, 1993. Until that date, even those who had lived their entire lives in Estonia but could not trace their roots to interwar Estonia remained noncitizens.

The language requirements for naturalization were unclear in the law, and it appeared initially that there would be room for discretion of local government officials. Language guidelines were clarified by a law that went into effect on February 25, 1993.[118] Nonetheless, learning Estonian was not easy, given the vast differences between Russian and Estonian and the lack of Estonian schooling for would-be applicants.[119]

The law did contain two provisions that granted automatic citizenship to a broader base. First, Article 7 of the law stated that those of Estonian ethnic descent could be naturalized without meeting the language and residency requirements.[120] While this provision made it easier for some people to become citizens, it could be seen as not especially inclusive, since it gave preferential treatment based on ethnic identity. Second, the so-called special merits clause in Article 7 of the law allowed simplified procedures for residents who "provide particularly valuable service to the national defense of the Republic of Estonia or who are widely known for their talents, knowledge or work."[121]

Despite concern over the special merits provision, it remained, and it was used by the Estonian government to stack the deck in local elections. Ethnic Russian politicians that Estonian leaders believed to be most supportive of Tallinn were given citizenship for special merits and, thus, allowed to run in local elections; those who had opposed Tallinn in the past were denied such citizenship.[122] While the total number of people affected by this part of the policy was small, the use of the clause was significant given the importance of local political elites in organizing Russian opposition to policies in Tallinn.

115. See Brubaker, "Citizenship Struggles," 1992, p. 282.
116. See "Russkiye Pribaltiki," January 3, 1992, p. 3.
117. See Brubaker, "Citizenship Struggles," 1992, p. 282.
118. See Estonia, 1993, On Estonian Language Requirements for Applicants for Citizenship.
119. The schooling problem remains an issue today. See discussion *infra* on language training.
120. See Estonia, 1938, Law on Citizenship, Article 7(1).
121. See Estonia, 1993, Law on Citizenship, Article 7(2).
122. See, generally, Laitin, 1993.

The citizenship law was amended in 1993, nudging the policy in a more inclusive direction. First, several amendments were adopted in February 1993. The most important for the inclusiveness of the law was the provision that anyone who registered for citizenship before the elections of the Congress of Estonia after independence would have the residence and language requirements for naturalization waived.[123] This position had been supported by the Congress of Estonia, since these people had demonstrated their loyalty to an independent Estonian nation-state by applying for citizenship well before independence was guaranteed. Another amendment, passed in March 1993, reinstated one of the original draft law provisions: the passage of citizenship through the maternal side as well as the paternal side for those with roots to pre-1940 citizens.[124] While these provisions did not add significantly to those who could receive automatic citizenship, they were steps toward inclusiveness.

Yet, the law was exclusive enough that around three-quarters of the non-Estonians were unable to receive automatic citizenship,[125] and no Russians were elected to the new Parliament when elections were held. A *Helsinki Watch* report claimed the citizenship law was discriminatory because "it allows in principle a certain group of people to become citizens, but qualifies their citizenship entitlements by putting them on 'second-class' footing with 'real' Estonian citizens with respect to the most important political and economic events in the near future."[126] The tone set by the law, as well as by a June 1992 national referendum in which broadening the electorate was rejected, and the resulting perceptions of exclusion by noncitizens were probably more important than the provisions themselves.[127]

Those noncitizens who learned the basic Estonian required of citizens and who wanted to naturalize were eligible to apply in 1992. As mentioned above, differences between Estonian and Russian, and the lack of mass schooling for those wanting to learn Estonian, made this difficult. In addition, the general temper of the citizenship debate made mass application for naturalization unlikely. By late July 1993, nearly 12,500 people were new citizens of Estonia, adding to the base already established.[128] Of these people, nearly two-thirds had

---

123. See Estonia, 1993, Law on Amendments to the Republic of Estonia Supreme Council Resolution "On the Application of the Law on Citizenship." The Congress of Estonia was a representative body elected by citizens of interwar Estonia and their descendants that acted as an alternative to the Estonian Supreme Soviet from the late 1980s until the election of the Riigikogu.

124. See Estonia, 1993, Law on Amendments to the Law on Citizenship.

125. See Kelam, June 30, 1993.

126. "New Citizenship Laws," April 15, 1992, p. 3.

127. See "'Draconian' Law," March 6, 1992, p. 71.

128. See Estonia, Ministry of Foreign Affairs of the Republic of Estonia, Estonian Citizenship Statistics as of July 26, 1993 (no date, on file with author).

become citizens because of their ethnic Estonian background; more than one-quarter became citizens because of their registration before the Congress of Estonia elections.[129] *Fewer than 700* gained citizenship through naturalization, roughly the same number that received it for "special merits."[130] Figures in March 1994 showed a slight improvement in naturalization, perhaps because of the changes in the language guidelines. Still, of the roughly 29,000 new citizens, fewer than one-eighth had been naturalized by meeting the language and residency requirements in the citizenship law; yet almost 13,000 had become citizens because of their ethnic identity.[131]

On January 19, 1995, the Riigikogu passed a new version of the citizenship law. With the president's signature, the law went into effect on April 1, 1995. This law brought together provisions from a collection of laws including the existing citizenship law and the Estonian Constitution. Among other things, the new law changed the residency requirement from two years to five years.[132] This new period of residency, however, applied only to those who entered Estonia after the law was put in place; it did not affect the permanent residents already in Estonia.[133] The law also clearly spelled out the provisions of the citizenship policy and the Constitution that applicants need to know to become naturalized. Important for the role of the citizenship policy in affecting identity, dual citizenship was still not allowed, except for *ethnic Estonians* who are already citizens of another country.[134]

Shortly before the new law passed the Parliament, the Estonian government also announced that it was ending the practice of granting citizenship "on general grounds."[135] Interior Minister Kaido Kama told reporters that "the moratorium did not concern ethnic Estonians and the republic's permanent residents who registered prior to the country's independence."[136] The government justified the change by stating that members of the Citizenship and Migration Department had allegedly sold passports illegally.[137] The Citizenship and Migration Department blamed applicants, stating that many had forged documents.[138] Some Russians in Estonia, however, argued that the purpose of the

129. See Estonia, Ministry of Foreign Affairs of the Republic of Estonia, Estonian Citizenship Statistics as of July 26, 1993 (no date, on file with author).

130. See Estonia, Ministry of Foreign Affairs of the Republic of Estonia, "Estonian Citizenship Statistics as of July 26, 1993" (no date, on file with author).

131. See "Over 16,000," March 23, 1994, p. 67.

132. See "Estonia Passes," January 20, 1995.

133. See "New Estonian Citizenship," February 2, 1995.

134. See "Estonia Passes," January 20, 1995.

135. See "Estonia Suspends," January 5, 1995.

136. See "Estonia Suspends," January 5, 1995.

137. "Estonia Suspends," January 5, 1995.

138. See "Many Have Passport Wrongfully," January 20–26, 1995, p. 3.

change was to limit the number of non-ethnic Estonians qualified to vote in the March 1995 national elections.

The Estonian citizenship law has been left alone for the most part since 1995. As in Latvia, however, discussion in 1997 and 1998 emerged about the need to amend the law. Since Estonia did not have the "window" naturalization policy adopted in Latvia, the focus was on granting citizenship to children born to noncitizens after the restoration of independence. This amendment has the support of Europe and of many scholars who study the issue of statelessness and international law.[139] It was first submitted to Parliament in December 1997, and enacted a year hence.

Slowing naturalization figures created the need for the new amendment. While the rate passage of the naturalizations tests has been quite high (more than 90 percent for the test on the Constitution and citizenship law and more than 80 percent for the language test), the number of applicants has declined over the past several years. After nearly 23,000 people were naturalized in 1996, just over 8,000 became citizens through naturalization in 1997.[140] In early 1998, still fewer than 100,000 people had been naturalized since the 1992 citizenship law had been adopted.[141] Another concern the government has had to consider when contemplating inclusive changes is the large number of Estonian residents who have taken Russian citizenship. According to official Estonian government statistics, more than 120,000 such people have become citizens of other countries, and the vast majority of these have taken on Russian Federation citizenship.[142] This situation raises the stakes in the Estonian-Russian relationship, and it gives Russia a more solid position under international law to express concern about the fate of Russians in Estonia.

While not part of the citizenship law, the issue of language training can certainly be considered a part of the citizenship policy. Since knowledge of the Estonian language is a requirement for naturalization, access to language training affects the prospects for the integration of noncitizens. On this point, Estonia has been criticized by Russians in the country and by European officials. One of the concerns has been the cost of such language instruction. The programs that did exist were not free, creating problems in particular for pensioners.[143] There

139. See, for example, Girard, 1998.
140. See "Estonian Government Seeks," January 5, 1998.
141. See "Citizenship Statistics: An Update as of March, 1998," March 19, 1998.
142. See "Citizenship Statistics: An Update as of July, 1997," July 8, 1997.
143. In my discussions with several noncitizen pensioners in Tallinn, the issue of costs was a central theme. Not only did these retirees have to pay for the language training, but they also had to

have also been concerns about the quality and even the availability of language training in the country. While several million dollars had been spent by the Estonian government from 1993 to 1997 on the teaching of Estonian to non-Estonians, even Estonian government officials question how good the language training was.[144] Finally, Estonian is a very difficult language, and one with few similarities to Russian.

In late 1998, the Estonian government launched a program, funded and coordinated by the European Union and the United Nations Development Program, to improve the language abilities of the noncitizens, in the hopes of increasing the number of naturalized citizens and improving noncitizen social integration.[145] State language courses were to be organized, and the program was to pay for half of the expenses of study for noncitizens who pass the state language examination. It may take a while, however, for the program to have an effect. In October 1998, the government announced that half of the fifty positions for official language teachers in Estonia were vacant.[146]

The Crucial Factors Influencing Inclusiveness

In this article, four variables that had the greatest effect on the development of the citizenship policies in the Baltic states are emphasized. There are, of course, other factors as well, but none of the others are as necessary to understanding the variation in inclusiveness as these four. Three of the four crucial variables are *understandings* about the nation and the state. The other central factor is the role of international organizations, especially the Organization for Security and Cooperation in Europe (OSCE), the Council of Europe, and (particularly recently) the European Union, in pushing citizenship policy inclusiveness. These four variables will be used to solve the four puzzles laid out in the introduction: (1) Why was the citizenship policy of Lithuania more inclusive than the policies of Estonia and Latvia? (2) Why was the citizenship policy in Estonia more inclusive than the citizenship policy in Latvia? (3) Why were the citizenship policies of both Estonia and Latvia more inclusive than they might have been? (4) Why is the citizenship policy in Latvia more inclusive today than it was only five years ago?

---

pay to apply for naturalization. Most felt that, given their age and income, it was not worth it to try to learn the language and naturalize.

144. See "Linguistic Environment," September 20–26, 1998 (comments by Andra Veindemann, Minister without Portfolio in Charge of Inter-Ethnic Relations).

145. See "EU and UNDP," October 11–17, 1998.

146. See "New Official Language Teachers," September 20–26, 1998.

Understandings, Perceptions, and Policy Making

Much of the next section deals with understandings and perceptions. The reader may already be thinking, "Understood and perceived by *whom*?" Since citizenship policy is a policy, it is necessary to look at the perceptions of the members of the political elite making the decisions. One cannot completely exclude the masses (since presumably the elites are taking mass attitudes into account, and referendums may be used to solve controversial issues—something that happened in Estonia and, most recently, in Latvia). In general, however, members of the legislature and the executive are making the final decisions. The political elite is not a unitary actor; there will be competing ideas about the nation and the state within the group of people vying for political power in a newly independent state. It may have mattered, for example, that Lithuania's citizenship law was put in place before Sajudis swept to power in republic-level elections. Yet, there was a surprising degree of consensus about the ideas related to the nation and the state, even among politicians at different ends of the political spectrum. A solid case can be made that elites in the newly independent states are generally starting with an ethnic definition of the nation. Whether this will change over time is another question, but, in the short run, the Soviet legacy will continue to have a significant impact. The word for nation (*natsiya* in Russian) is understood by Russians (and to my knowledge other nationalities in the former Soviet Union as well) to mean a large, *ethnically* defined nation. Likewise, "Estonian" means "ethnic Estonian" to Estonians and Russians.

Understandings about the Nature of the Nation and the State

The first two variables crucial to citizenship policy inclusiveness in the Baltic states are two understandings about the nation and the state: *whether the nation is ethnically or politically defined and whether the new state is seen as a nation-state or a multinational state*. While these can be thought of as two separate variables, the understandings of the nation and the state must be examined together, since only a specific combination of answers can make citizenship exclusion possible (see below). Citizenship defines members of a state. Yet, since the eighteenth century, the ideas of state and nation have become intertwined. Thus, it is likely that defining official membership in the state would be affected not only by ideas about the state but also by ideas about the nation.

UNDERSTANDINGS ABOUT THE NATION. Rogers Brubaker argues that conceptions of national identity affect the formation of inclusive or exclusive citizenship policies.[147] In his work on Germany and France, Brubaker contends

147. See, generally, Brubaker, *Citizenship and Nationhood,* 1992.

that "differing definitions of citizenship have been shaped by and sustained by distinctive and deeply rooted understandings of nationhood."[148] He argues that the more exclusive nature of the German law is mainly due to a definition of the German nation based on descent. In France, however, a political definition of nationhood (based on territory as well as allegiance to the French state) led to a more inclusive law. Thus, the key is *whether the nation is defined ethnically or political-territorially.*

This explanation for these two cases is instructive. It is, however, inadequate to explain the citizenship outcomes in the Baltic states because of the general lack of variation in this explanatory variable. In Lithuania, like Latvia and Estonia, the nation is defined in ethnic terms, which would imply, following Brubaker's logic, that all three of the Baltic states should have exclusive citizenship policies. Instead, the Lithuanian policy was more inclusive than the others' policies, particularly in the most crucial element, automatic citizenship.

In Latvia and Estonia, there is little doubt among the elite that the nation is based on ethnic identity. Showing this tendency, the secretary general and press secretary of the Fatherland Party in Estonia, which was ruling at the time, stated in 1993 that the Estonian policies were not discriminatory, asking how 1 million people could discriminate against 150 million.[149] Further evidence of the ethnically defined nation comes from Peet Kask, who served on the special citizenship committee that drafted the versions of the citizenship law. He stated, "An ethnic Swede living in Finland is called a 'Swedish-speaking Finn.' It would be normal if we could use the term 'Russian-speaking Estonians' but we are still far from that."[150] *All* the politicians and academics with whom I spoke in Latvia divided the population into "Latvians" and "non-Latvians," with non-Latvians being those who were not *ethnically* Latvian.

In Lithuania, the relatively inclusive citizenship policy was not due to a civic idea of the nation. Generally, as with their neighbors to the north, Lithuanians define their nation in ethnic terms. As Erika Umbrasaite, a reporter for *Europos Lietuvis*, said, "There is no real desire to develop 'Lithuanian' into a civic concept. Poles are not seen as Lithuanian even if they have citizenship. They are Poles with Lithuanian citizenship."[151]

UNDERSTANDINGS ABOUT THE STATE.   Alfred Stepan points out the second perception related to the idea of the type of nation and state that could affect treatment of ethnic minorities: *whether or not the newly independent state is*

148. See, generally, Brubaker, *Citizenship and Nationhood,* 1992, pp. x–xi.
149. See Rull and Aleksius, interview, July 7, 1993.
150. Kask, letter to Barrington, August 11, 1993.
151. Umbrasaite, interview, May 4, 1994.

seen as a nation-state or as a multinational state.[152] He claims that the identification of Estonia as a nation-state led directly to a policy of excluding those who were not ethnically Estonian from obtaining automatic citizenship. Indeed, the sentiment of the state as a nation-state and therefore that the Russian population should not be privileged as it was in the past has been an important factor in Estonia. Some government officials in Estonia also hoped that making the Russians feel that they did not belong would force many of them to leave. As Ole Kvarno, CSCE mission leader in Narva, Estonia, put it, "It is becoming more and more clear that the basis of the problem is not actually integration or assimilation, but that a lot of Estonian politicians simply want the Russians out."[153]

Many statements point to the understanding of Estonia as a nation-state. The post-Soviet Estonian Constitution opens with, "Unwavering in their faith and with an unswerving will to safeguard and develop a state which is based on the inextinguishable right of the Estonian people[154] to national self-determination . . . which shall guarantee the preservation of the Estonian nation and its culture throughout the ages. . . ."[155] As a member of the Estonian Institute for Human Rights described, "Certainly Estonia as a country is the only homeland for Estonians, we do not have any other country where we should feel [at] home."[156] Sociologist Aksel Kirch added that Estonians see Estonia as a nation-state, while Russians there see it as a multinational state.[157] In the clearest support of the *effect* of this understanding, Kask stated that the final version of the citizenship law "did reflect the attitude 'Estonia for Estonians,'" although the rhetoric has sometimes been different.[158]

In Latvia, the understanding of the state as the nation-state for ethnic Latvians is strongly held by members of the Latvian political elite. The policy implications range from ideas that the Russians need to develop a sense of loyalty to the Latvian state to the idea that they should "return" to Russia. As Viestur Karnups, creator of the LNNK Party version of the draft citizenship law, stated,

> The question really is what to do with the colonists. No one outside Latvia, especially in the West, wants to admit that there are 700,000 colonists

152. See Stepan, 1994.
153. Kvarno, interview, July 11, 1993.
154. Note that the statement is not "people of Estonia." This shows a different emphasis in Estonia from that seen in, for example, Ukraine.
155. See Estonian Constitution (last modified September 15, 1998), Preamble.
156. Estonian Institute for Human Rights, letter to Barrington (no date, on file with author).
157. See Kirch, interview, May 30, 1996.
158. Kask, letter to Barrington, August 11, 1993.

in Latvia. . . . Our recipe for this is to encourage voluntary repatriation to the country where they came from or their ethnic homeland. We will do everything we can to encourage this.[159]

Bringing together the ideas of Latvia as a nation-state, exclusive citizenship provisions, and their intended consequences, Karnups added that the population of Latvia should be at least 75 percent ethnic Latvians because "Latvia is an ethnic nation-state. That's why it's called 'Latvia' and not 'Russia.' . . . There's no other Latvian nation-state. This is the only one we've got."[160]

In Lithuania, the idea of the state as a nation-state exists but was not a central issue for those shaping citizenship policy. Rather, a much greater emphasis was placed on interethnic harmony. In 1994, Severinas Vaitiekus, vice-director of the government's Department of Nationalities, stated, "In our blood we have no such idea of 'Lithuania for Lithuanians.' Our history taught people to live together in a multicultural society."[161] Irenijus Cerkasovas, who was head of the Special Commission on the Questions of Citizenship at the time, added, "Lithuania . . . comprises not only Lithuanians, but Polish, Russian and Jewish people live there, and there are certain laws which protect their rights as national minorities."[162] This idea is also indicated by the way Lithuanians, in writing on the history of Lithuania, seem to stress the multinational character of the territory to a greater extent than similar works by Estonians or Latvians.[163] Even the national anthem stresses Lithuania as a homeland but does not mention for whom. The last line reads, "May the love of Lithuania brightly burn in our hearts. For the sake of this land, let unity blossom."[164]

One should not assume from these statements that Lithuania was seen as a multinational state in the way that a state such as Ukraine was by much of its political elite. One can certainly say that Lithuania was seen by most of the political elite as a nation-state. This tendency to lean toward the nation-state idea has combined with an ethnic idea of the nation to produce some of the provisions of the policy allowing easier acquisition of citizenship for ethnic Lithuanians. What makes Lithuania different from its Baltic neighbors in this regard, however, is a willingness not to emphasize the idea of the state as, above all, the homeland of ethnic Lithuanians.

159. Karnups, interview, May 11, 1994.
160. Karnups, interview, May 11, 1994.
161. Vaitiekus, interview, May 4, 1994.
162. Cerkasovas, interview, April 29, 1994.
163. See, for example, Center of National Researchers of Lithuania, 1992; and Media and Public Relations Department of the Seimas, Lithuania, 1994.
164. Media and Public Relations Department of the Seimas, Lithuania, 1994, p. 3.

*   *   *

The understandings of the nation and state must be considered together. While they can be thought of as separate variables, it is the intersection of the two that is important for policies such as citizenship. In order to lead to exclusive citizenship policies, the understanding of the nation as an ethnic one and the understanding of the state as a nation-state must both be present. If either the state is seen as a multinational state or the nation is defined in political-territorial terms, inclusive policies would result. Thus, if the state is considered a multinational state, an ethnic definition of the nation would not lead to an exclusive policy: the recognition of the multinational character of the state by the majority national group would lead those of a minority ethnic nation within the state to acquire "official membership." Likewise, if a new state is seen as a nation-state but has a political-territorial definition of nationhood, the resulting citizenship policy would be inclusive. Because the nation is defined by political membership, permanent residents in the state at the time of independence, regardless of ethnic identity, would receive citizenship easily.

Thus, although state and nation are different things, the *combination* of a state seen as the national homeland and an ethnic definition of the nation is a necessary step for exclusive citizenship requirements. Both Stepan and Brubaker are correct in pointing out the importance of these perceptions about the nation and the state. Each author alone, however, does not tell a complete story. By not making clear that his argument applies only to ethnically defined nations, for example, Stepan's point about the nation-state and exclusion is less persuasive than it might have been. In combination, the ethnic nation understanding and nation-state understanding lead to the perception of the state as an *ethnic-nation-state*. As such, official membership in the state is likely to be difficult for ethnic minorities to obtain.

Perceptions of "Threat" to the Nation

While the particular intersection of the views about the nation and the state made exclusion in the Baltic states possible, perceptions of the threat posed by including members of the ethnic minority as citizens in Estonia and Latvia both triggered exclusion and affected the degree of exclusion that was seen. Thus, the next crucial factor is a perception related to the ethnic minority: whether or not the minority poses a threat to the cultural survival of the dominant nation. In Brubaker's article on the Soviet successor states, he examines the idea of a perceived *threat to the survival of the nation* as an explanatory variable.[165] The per-

---

165. See Brubaker, *Citizenship and Nationhood,* 1992, pp. 274, 285.

ception that the cultural survival of the nation is threatened makes it easier to justify protecting the nation in any way possible, including limiting the rights of the minority that is perceived to be a threat. Immigration into the republics of Latvia and Estonia during the Soviet period significantly reduced the percentage of the native population of the republic, feeding such perceptions.

Given the size of the minorities and the relatively constant level of ethnic Lithuanians as a percentage of the population, there was little discussion in Lithuania of threats to "survival."[166] The lack of a sense of threat was the major factor that pushed the Lithuanian policy in a more inclusive direction than the Estonian and Latvian ones. As Rimantas Markauskas, a member of Parliament and of the Committee on Human and Citizens' Rights and Nationality Affairs in 1996, stated, Lithuanians never had the kind of "fear" that was present in Estonia and Latvia.[167] Another member of this committee, as well as a member of the President's Special Commission on Citizenship, Valdas Petrauskas, stated that Lithuania had the "best demographic situation" of the three Baltic states, reducing the sense of threat posed by the ethnic Russians.[168] In 1994, Vilius Kavaliauskas, press secretary for the Lithuanian Seimas (Parliament), argued, "The situation is different than in Estonia and Latvia policies. There is no threat to the majority from the minority here. When you are not threatened as a nation, you can afford to be democratic."[169]

In Estonia, there was a much greater sense of urgency by the political elite to protect the cultural integrity of the nation. These feelings, and the consequences for citizenship, are shown by statements from the Congress of Estonia, an alternative Parliament in Estonia mentioned earlier. One resolution of the Congress stated:

Subsequent to its annexation of the Republic of Estonia, the Soviet Union organized extensive immigration by its citizens into Estonia. As a result of this, non-citizens form over one-third of the population of Estonia, *which is now threatening the preservation of the native population of Estonia* and the security and unity of the entire Estonian nation. . . . Before

166. While the percentage of the titular populations in Estonia and Latvia dropped significantly during the Soviet period, the percentage of the population of the Lithuanian SSR that was ethnically Lithuanian remained near 80 percent from 1945 to 1991.

167. See Markauskas, interview, June 11, 1996. He also stated, in response to my question about the timing of initial citizenship law, that even if the law had first been adopted under the Sajudis government, it would have been very inclusive because of the lack of a perception of threat.

168. See Petrauskas, interview, June 12, 1996. Like Markauskas, Petrauskas thought that even if the 1991 law had been the first citizenship law (since 1939) in Lithuania, it would have been very inclusive.

169. Kavaliauskas, interview, May 2, 1994.

the elections to the Riigikogu, the body of citizens can only be extended by persons *who are of Estonian ethnic origin* or who applied for Republic of Estonia citizenship before the elections to the Congress of Estonia.[170]

An official statement of the Estonian government in 1997 made the link between the citizenship law and the ideas of the nation, state, and cultural survival even more clearly:

Estonia is the only home for the Estonian people and therefore, Estonia's people, language, and culture must be preserved and developed here. Our citizenship law is based on that premise. The spirit of national cultural traditions and their preservation is the basis for our laws regarding foreign residents, our language, and the education of our younger generation.[171]

Here, the differences between Lithuania and Estonia cannot be overemphasized. As Brubaker states, "The national movement in Lithuania sought to restore the Lithuanian state, not to save the Lithuanian nation."[172] In Estonia, however, nationalists felt independence was more than regaining sovereignty; it was a matter of cultural survival.[173]

Nowhere in the former Soviet Union was the idea of a threat to the survival of the ethnic nation more a part of political conversation than in Latvia. The major reason for the feeling of threat was the change in population percentages in the Latvian Republic during the Soviet period. The percentage of ethnic Latvians in Latvia dropped from 77 percent in 1939 to a low of 52 percent in the late 1980s.[174] Since that time, the percentage of Latvians has increased, as Russian immigration to Latvia has virtually stopped and Russian emigration from the state has increased.[175] At the time the citizenship law was passed, the percentage had climbed to more than 54 percent, according to estimates of the State Statistics Committee, and ethnic Latvians made up 56.5 percent of Latvia's popula-

170. Congress of Estonia, 1992, "Congress of Estonia Position on the Immigrants from the Former USSR Residing in the Republic of Estonia" (emphasis added).

171. Veering, January 16, 1999.

172. Brubaker, *Citizenship and Nationhood,* 1992, p. 285.

173. Brubaker, *Citizenship and Nationhood,* 1992, p. 285.

174. See Smith, 1996.

175. In 1991, for example, immigration of Russians from the rest of the USSR into Latvia was less than 10,000, while out-migration of Russians from Latvia to the USSR was more than 20,000. See Kirch et al., 1993, Table 10. According to the Population Information Site of Latvia, from 1991 to 1995, 30,842 immigrants entered Latvia and 145,810 emigrants left the country. See "Population Information Site of Latvia," March 3, 1999.

tion in 1998.[176] This change is a noticeable increase from the low point a decade earlier.

Yet, despite the out-migration and increasing percentage of "natives," the belief in "national extinction" played an important role in the citizenship debate. As Gvido Zemrido, the chief justice of the Latvian Supreme Court, put it in a speech at the University of Michigan in 1993, "It is clear that Latvians want to regain their national identity and that they are trying to preserve that identity against what they consider foreign intruders."[177] Elmars Vebers adds:

The Latvians are worried about the survival of the nation, a nation which has been systematically emaciated throughout this century. The public consciousness of the Latvians is very sensitive, reacting to everything that could possibly harm the demographic interests of the nation. The feeling of ethnic vulnerability affects the whole political climate, and political parties and other organizations of a political nature are becoming more radical on the demographic question.[178]

While views about the threat to the nation were significant for the development of the initial postindependence laws in both Estonia and Latvia, concerns about threats to the cultural survival of the nation have waned in the past few years. Independence has been restored, and the political system has been under the control of the majority groups for more than seven years. Education policies, language laws, and other state programs to protect the culture have been put in place. The native populations have slowly but steadily increased as a percentage of the population.

The change in thinking about such a threat is reflected in the Estonian government's Basic Goals for 1997 and 1998, which presents seventeen objectives.[179] While the Basic Goals document discusses the connection between the citizenship law and protecting the national culture, the order of the goals is telling. Of the seventeen, the goal to "provide conditions for preservation and development of the Estonian language, culture, and nation" is fourteenth on the list. This item is only one position ahead of "assist non-Estonians with integration into Estonian society" (number 15), and well down the list from "do everything in our power to be in the first wave of nations admitted into the European Union (EU)" (number 2), and "improve political and economic relations with

176. See Central Intelligence Agency, March 3, 1999.
177. Zemrido, February 4, 1993.
178. Vebers, 1993.
179. See Veering, January 16, 1999.

Russia" (number 4).[180] Clearly, only a few years earlier, protecting Estonian culture would have been much higher on the list. The shift in thought about the prospects for national cultural survival, along with the pressure from international organizations discussed below, is a key reason why the citizenship policy amendments were passed in Latvia—and upheld by the referendum—and why similar changes will likely be made in Estonia as well.

Answering Questions 1 and 2

In answering the question of why the citizenship policy of Lithuania was more inclusive than those of Estonia and Latvia, the understandings related to the nation and the state are crucial. In Lithuania, there was an understanding of an ethnic nation and of the state as a nation-state. But, this conception was not emphasized as it was in Estonia and Latvia, and—more important—there was little sense of threat to the nation from the inclusion of ethnic minorities as citizens. In Latvia and Estonia, however, the understandings of an ethnic nation and nation-state were reinforced by feelings of threat to the cultural survival of the nation.

As for the difference between Estonia and Latvia, the perception of threat is again important. While talk of threats to "national survival" appeared in both states, this talk was central to the citizenship discussions in Latvia in a way that was unmatched in Estonia. This focus is likely due to the difference in the percentage of the majority ethnic groups in the populations of both states. As mentioned above, while Latvians were quickly approaching less than 50 percent of the population of Latvia by the late 1980s, Estonians still composed well over 60 percent of the population of Estonia. This fact meant that it was at least possible to consider naturalization provisions in Estonia, while in Latvia they were put off as long as possible. What ended the possibility of continued delay in Latvia in 1994 is the subject of the next section.

Answering Questions 3 and 4: The Role of International Organizations

As central as the "understanding and perception" variables are to explaining variation in inclusiveness, the role of international organizations was what kept the policies in Latvia and Estonia from being as exclusive as the understanding and perception variables would predict. The role of international organizations interested in interethnic peace, in particular the Council of Europe, CSCE (now OSCE), and the EU, is often overlooked by those trying to explain the absence

180. See Veering, January 16, 1999.

of ethnic conflict in the Baltic states. Yet it is increasingly apparent that understanding events and policies related to ethnic relations within a state requires one to look to external factors, such as international organizations, as well. The development of citizenship policy in the Baltic region is no exception.

International organizations from human rights groups such as Helsinki Watch to the European Union have monitored citizenship legislation in the post-Communist states. Not all groups have had an equal impact on the eventual policies, however. Examination of the development of the citizenship policies in the Baltic states indicates that there are two considerations when analyzing the impact of international organizations: the expressed interest of the international organizations in the given state's citizenship policies and the willingness of the government of that state to listen to these organizations.

If the international community is not interested in the formation of citizenship policies, it will obviously not have an effect. If interested, it must have something to offer the state's leaders. One thing European organizations can offer is acceptance of the newly independent as a part of Europe. If the government of a newly independent state has a strong desire for its state to "join Europe" (be accepted into European organizations, increase trade with European states, or even simply be considered a "European" state), it is much more likely that the government will consider European criticism of its citizenship policy. Of course, if European organizations can offer financial aid or military protection, the incentive to listen is even stronger. In both Estonia and Latvia, the presence and activity of such international organizations guided the policies back in a more inclusive direction, both during the drafting of the laws and during the amending of the laws in the years after their implementation.

INTERNATIONAL ORGANIZATIONS IN ESTONIA. At least three inclusive changes in the Estonian citizenship policy, as well as the pending amendment on children born since independence, were greatly influenced by the actions of the European representatives who saw problems with the existing citizenship law. First, the provisions for naturalization were originally very open to interpretation, especially regarding the language test. A CSCE report in September 1992 stated, "Commission staffers got the impression that procedures for obtaining citizenship, if not entirely clear in statute, may be even less clearly applied in practice."[181] Better-defined guidelines for the language test and assurances that local officials would not arbitrarily deny citizenship to qualified applicants were needed, according to the CSCE representatives. Second, an-

---

181. Commission on Security and Cooperation in Europe, 1992.

other CSCE report called for easier naturalization for elderly and disabled applicants.[182]

Just two months after the publication of the CSCE report *Russians in Estonia,* the prime minister of Estonia announced that no arbitrariness on language tests would be permissible.[183] This announcement was followed by the law On Estonian Language Requirements for Applicants for Citizenship, which set clearer language requirements.[184] This law also authorized the government to set policy on simplified provisions for the elderly. A government order two months later did just that, waiving fees for elderly and invalid applicants as well as easing the test requirements. In 1993, Ole Kvarno, CSCE mission leader in Narva, said that these changes appeared as a result of the specific demands of CSCE.[185]

Third, the March 1993 amendment on maternal descent was added "to bring Estonia's citizenship law in line with the constitution and European standards and to facilitate Estonia's admission to the Council of Europe."[186] The change "was made under pressure from the Council of Europe, which Estonia hopes to join. . . ."[187]

Finally, the change in the citizenship law being discussed in late 1998 to give automatic citizenship to all children born in the country since 1991 has been of great interest to OSCE, the EU, and NATO.[188] While Estonia has not acted as quickly on the amendment as Latvia did, Europe has made a strong case for its eventual adoption. When the president made the amendment his top priority for the session of Parliament that began in the fall of 1998, "strong recommendations" from Europe likely played a central role.[189]

INTERNATIONAL ORGANIZATIONS IN LATVIA. Europe was slow to put pressure on the Latvians to develop an official citizenship law immediately after independence. As Russia and Russians in Latvia increased their complaints, pressure from Europe increased. This pressure eventually forced Latvia to

182. See Conference on Security and Cooperation in Europe, 1992.
183. See "Prime Minister Forbids," November 5, 1992, p. 71.
184. See Estonia, 1993, On Estonian Language Requirements for Applicants for Citizenship.
185. See Kvarno, interview, July 11, 1993.
186. "Estonia Amends," March 24, 1993.
187. "Constitution Watch: Estonia," 1993.
188. In the case of OSCE, see Organization for Security and Cooperation in Europe, 1998. The interest of NATO is indicated by Estonian President Lennart Meri's mention of the proposed changes to the citizenship law in a speech before the North Atlantic Council on November 4, 1998. See Meri, 1998.
189. See "Opposition Rejects," September 18, 1998; and "Law Must Change," September 16, 1998.

adopt an official citizenship law. European organizations were very active in monitoring the development of the official of law, compelling the ruling coalition to remove the vague reference to quotas and the reference to Latvia as a "single-nation state" from the draft passed at the law's first reading.[190]

When the president returned the draft of the citizenship law that was finally passed by the Saeima for further consideration, he did so because of strong pressure from Europe for changes in the law, again especially over the quota issue. His statement to the Saeima urged legislators to "take into account the recommendations of the Conference on Security and Cooperation in Europe and the Council of Europe."[191] Prime Minister Valdis Birkkavs added, "We shall not allow this law to bar our way to Europe, the only place where Latvia can survive."[192]

The CSCE recommendations had come mainly from CSCE High Commissioner on National Minorities Max van der Stoel. Pointing out that most noncitizens would like to become Latvian citizens, van der Stoel criticized, in a letter to the Latvian foreign minister, the possibility of the prevention of any naturalization given the combination of the Saeima having the power to set the annual quota and that the quotas were to "ensure the development of Latvia as a single-nation state."[193] He warned, "If the overwhelming majority of non-Latvians in your country is denied the right to become citizens, and consequently the right to be involved in key decisions concerning their own interests, the character of the democratic system in Latvia might even be put into question."[194] He also made specific recommendations about a way to replace the quota system by allowing naturalization in stages based on the length of time that one had lived in Latvia.[195]

In addition to CSCE, suggestions from the Council of Europe played an important role in the formation, and especially the final version, of the Latvian citizenship law. In early 1992, Latvian officials had expressed optimism over their likely induction into the Council of Europe.[196] Soon, however, it became clear

---

190. See van der Stoel, letter to Andrejevs, December 10, 1993. The letter makes numerous suggestions that were later adopted, and it contains strong criticism of the "single-nation state" phrase.

191. "Saeima to Review," July 1, 1994, p. 60.

192. "President, Government to Review," June 28, 1994, p. 71.

193. See van der Stoel, letter to Andrejevs, December 10, 1993.

194. See van der Stoel, letter to Andrejevs, December 10, 1993.

195. See van der Stoel, letter to Andrejevs, December 10, 1993.

196. Some of this optimism was likely due to the comments of Council of Europe Secretary-General Catherine Lalumiére, during a February 18, 1992, trip to Riga. Radio Riga reported that Lalumiére had said that Latvia had "made much progress toward democratization, implementation of human rights, and economic reforms." See "Lalumiére in Latvia," February 19, 1992.

that the unresolved citizenship issue would keep Latvia out of the organiza-tion.[197] The Council of Europe had made clear that an acceptable citizenship law was a condition of Latvian membership.[198] As a result of the more tangible ben-efit of pleasing the Council of Europe, the Latvian government was even more willing to incorporate Council of Europe recommendations than suggestions from CSCE. The ruling coalition sent the first reading version to the Council of Europe for suggestions, and experts from the Council of Europe made trips to Riga to discuss their specific objections to the draft law.

After the first reading, a Council of Europe report argued against certain provisions in the Latvian law and made specific recommendations.[199] As with CSCE criticism, the strongest objections were raised over the natural-ization provisions. Referring often to "European standards," the Council of Europe report criticized the vagueness of the provisions; the fact that most of the noncitizens would not know when they would even be eligible for nat-uralization; and, like van der Stoel, the idea that naturalization should take into account Latvia's struggle to be a "single-nation state."[200] The report pointed out that in Eastern Europe "'nation' is more commonly understood as the ethnic group which forms the dominant group within the state."[201] Thus, the Council of Europe members stated that the single-nation state idea "augurs badly for non-Latvian ethnic elements and their continued presence within the state" and that the Latvian law implies that the state "belongs" to ethnic Latvians.[202] They suggested removing the reference to a single-nation state and setting up a naturalization system based on the age of the applicant rather than leaving the decision about quotas to the Latvian Saeima.[203] In ad-dition, they supported a reduction of the residency requirement from ten years to five years and stated that language tests must be uniform and consis-tently applied.[204]

The changes from the first to second reading versions were nearly word for word the European suggestions. But during second-reading amending, the 0.1 percent quota idea was again added under pressure from nationalists in the

197. See Barne, July 9–15, 1993, p. 5.

198. This point was made to me by several Latvian government officials during interviews in 1994 in Riga, Latvia.

199. Specific recommendations can be found in Council of Europe, January 24, 1994.

200. See Council of Europe, January 24, 1994, p. 4.

201. See Council of Europe, January 24, 1994, p. 5.

202. See Council of Europe, January 24, 1994, p. 5.

203. See Council of Europe, January 24, 1994, p. 6.

204. See Council of Europe, January 24, 1994, p. 7 (residency requirement), p. 8 (language tests).

Saeima who threatened a referendum if they did not get their way.[205] Thus, the 0.1 percent quota became part of the third reading version. Representatives of the Council of Europe and the CSCE mission in Latvia then turned to the president. As with the changes from the first to second drafts, European suggestions were the driving force behind the president sending the law back to the Parliament for further consideration and the changes in the law that followed. The European suggestions were reincorporated into the final version of the law.[206]

Latvia was rewarded for implementing the changes suggested by Europe, as an August 1994 Council of Europe mission to Riga recommended Latvia's acceptance into the Council of Europe. Fredrich Vogel, mission member, stated that the newly refined citizenship law complied with Council of Europe standards.[207] Visiting Riga in January 1995, Council of Europe Parliamentary Assembly President Miguel Angel Martinez stated that Latvia would become a member of the Council of Europe in February. He pointed to Latvia's willingness to compromise on the citizenship law as the key factor in its acceptance.[208]

But Europe continued to push Latvia for a more inclusive policy, even after the 1994 law was passed, especially after the events of the spring of 1998. For the first time, the European Union moved to the forefront of European involvement. Since Latvia was not a member of the EU—but strongly sought such membership—the organization arguably had more influence over the process in 1998 than either OSCE or the Council of Europe. Several European officials stated that the events of March and April had hurt Latvia's EU membership prospects, and that the EU remained highly interested in a resolution to the disagreements over the status of noncitizens in the country.[209] The EU also urged Latvia to pursue dialogue with Russia to reduce tensions. After these statements

205. Such a referendum is allowed under Latvian law if supporters get 10 percent of the registered voters to support it, something most politicians felt would be a formality. The ease with which signatures were collected to force the 1998 referendum indicates that they were probably correct.

206. Perhaps the best evidence of the impact of European suggestions comes from the Latvian Naturalization Board's publication, On Naturalization in Latvia. The sections "Co-Operation with the International and Organizations and Foreign State and Social Institutions" and "The Latvian Citizenship Law and its Incorporation of International Recommendations" describe the role of numerous Western groups in the citizenship process. The sections especially highlight the efforts of OSCE and the Council of Europe and the way in which their recommendations were brought into the law. See Naturalization Board of the Republic of Latvia, 1997, pp. 18–19, 64–67.

207. See "Visiting Experts," August 9, 1994, p. 59.

208. See Birzulis, January 20–26, 1995, p. 4.

209. See, for example, "Dini," April 8, 1998 (statements of the Italian foreign minister). Among other things, Foreign Minister Dini stated, "Events like those of recent days distance Latvia further from the process of preliminary membership," and "I would stress that a necessary condition admission into the European Union is the presence of . . . established democratic institutions and especially full respect of the rights of ethnic minorities."

and behind-the-scenes pressure, by the end of April the Latvian government's ruling coalition had announced its intention to move ahead on the European-supported amendments. The European reaction to these comments was positive.[210]

Once the amendments to the citizenship law were passed in June, the West attempted to indicate its support for the amendments in the face of the October referendum, while hoping not to appear as if it was trying to strong-arm Latvian voters. The European Commission quickly stated its support for the amendments; Latvian Radio carried statements by the Italian undersecretary of state, who emphasized that supporting the amendments would be a step toward EU membership; the Swedish foreign minister warned of "international consequences" if the amendments were overturned; the U.S. ambassador to NATO linked the amendments to NATO membership for Latvia; and even the outgoing U.S. ambassador to Latvia indicated that failure to uphold the amendments would lead to a questioning of Latvia's desire to integrate into the remaining European organizations in which it is not a member.[211] Max van der Stoel visited Latvia in August, pushing the link between European integration and the amendments.

The line between suggesting and pressuring is sometimes a fine one, and this was certainly the case with Western comments during the months leading up to the vote. The Latvian president, a strong supporter of the amendments, at one point even warned van der Stoel to temper his comments, and he criticized the OSCE for its at times "over-exaggerated advisory methods" as well as expressing concerns more generally over "pressure from the international community."[212] Nonetheless, the referendum passed. The results were praised by European officials as a "step towards Latvia's integration into Europe."[213]

210. OSCE said the proposed changes had its "full backing." High Commissioner Max van der Stoel stated, "I feel confident that the legislative changes which the government is going to propose will be in full conformity with the recommendations I have been making." See "Latvia Urges," April 21, 1998.

211. See "Italy Urges," September 16, 1998; "US Envoy Reiterates," September 11, 1998; "US Envoy to NATO," September 3, 1998; "OSCE Commissioner," August 26, 1998.

212. The president's statements were discussed in a LETA news agency report. See "Latvian President Warns," August 24, 1998. Similar negative comments about European pressure were heard during debate in the Parliament on the amendments.

213. See "Latvian Vote," October 6, 1998, p. 3 (comment from Austria's foreign minister, writing on behalf of the EU). Ironically, an Estonian Foreign Ministry press release also welcomed the vote, even though Estonia had yet to pass a similar amendment on children born since the restoration of independence.

Conclusion

Citizenship is one of the most important policy decisions for newly independent states—it is an essential step in state building. In all three Baltic states, there are significant differences in political rights, and social and economic rights and benefits, between citizens and noncitizens. In Estonia, noncitizens can vote in local elections, provided they are permanent residents. In Latvia and Lithuania, however, there is no such local election voting right, and in none of the Baltic states can noncitizens vote in national elections or hold public office. Social and economic rights and benefits are restricted to similar degrees across all three states. In some cases, laws state that permanent residents enjoy equal benefits to citizens. But even on these issues, the constitutions leave open the possibility of future restrictions.

Despite the importance of citizenship in shaping rights and benefits, we know surprisingly little about the reasons for variation in citizenship policies across states. The main argument of the most impressive work to date on the causes of citizenship variation, for example, cannot be used to account the difference among the policies of the three Baltic states.[214] As this article describes, there is no simple answer to the puzzle of citizenship inclusiveness. The answer to the central question of citizenship inclusiveness involves understandings, perceptions, and external actors.

Breaking down the question of citizenship inclusion in the Baltic states into four answerable puzzles helps. When approached in this way, it becomes clear that understandings and perceptions about the nation, the state, and threats to national survival made exclusion likely in Estonia and Latvia but much less likely in Lithuania. In addition, international organizations worked with the governments as laws were drafted and pushed already-existing laws in a more inclusive direction. They kept the policies in Estonia and Latvia from being as exclusive as they were headed to being in the early stages. And they "encouraged" Latvia to adopt an official law with naturalization requirements but without quotas, which led to a more inclusive policy than the "lawless" one between 1991 and 1994.

The difference between the citizenship policy of Lithuania and its neighbors to the north highlights the need to treat these countries individually. They are more than a single entity called "the Baltic states." They are often lumped together because they share many similarities,[215] and indeed this common history

214. See, generally, Brubaker, *Citizenship and Nationhood,* 1992.

215. All three republics were brought into the Soviet Union in 1940 as a result of the Molotov-Ribbentrop pact, the native populations of all three had strong national identities before the Soviet period, and each had been an independent state during the interwar period. They took

is important for dismissing certain explanations about the development of citizenship policies in the region. While Velo Pettai, for example, discusses the importance of the interwar period as a reference point for laws and even constitutions, the idea of the Baltic states as "restored states" does not explain the exclusiveness of the citizenship policies in Latvia and Estonia.[216] If this condition were the cause of exclusive policies, the Lithuanian policy should have been as exclusive as the others—which it was not—and there should have been no significant differences in exclusion between Estonia and Latvia—which there were. Although the common events and characteristics cannot explain the policy differences, this article has outlined factors that can help one to understand the disparity between the inclusive, automatic citizenship policies in Lithuania and the more exclusive approaches taken by Estonia and Latvia.

While citizenship policy is shaped by issues of identity, the choices made by elites in this policy area are precisely that: choices. The incorporation of the Baltic states in the Soviet Union gave elites in post-Soviet Estonia and Latvia a way to justify exclusion, but this exclusion did not necessarily have to occur. Both the Lithuanian policy and the changes in the Estonian and Latvian policies over time demonstrate this fact. Citizenship policy is not only a domestic issue. The choices of elites can be affected by international pressure, especially from international organizations of which the state in question is a member or, even more, seeks to join. As a result, citizenship policy in the Baltic states—as well as other parts of the world—is likely to continue to evolve as new elites come to power, new international organizations become drawn into the issue, and new choices are made.

References

Andrejevs, Georgs, Latvian Minister of Foreign Affairs, letter to Max van der Stoel, CSCE High Commissioner on National Minorities. April 18, 1993. (Copy provided by the CSCE mission in Riga, Latvia.)

Barne, Jonathon. (July 9–15, 1993.) "Riga Opts for Caution on CE Membership." *Baltic Independent,* p. 5.

Barrington, Lowell. 1995. "The Domestic and International Consequences of Citizenship in the Soviet Successor States." *Europe-Asia Studies,* no. 47.

---

turns leading the drive for independence from the Soviet Union (although Latvia often lagged behind the other two because of the presence of the large Russian minority), and all three refused to join the Commonwealth of Independent States. Finally, the national movements in all three states considered the post-Soviet period a time of restoration rather than creation of independence. See, generally, Brubaker, "Citizenship Struggles," 1992.

216. See Pettai, 1993.

Bendix, Richard. 1964. *Nation-Building and Citizenship.* Berkeley: University of California Press.

Birznece, Inese, Member, Latvia's Way. Interview by Lowell Barrington. Riga, Latvia. May 10, 1994.

Birzulis, Philip. (January 20–26, 1995.) "Latvia as Good as In, Russia on Hold for CE Membership." *Baltic Independent,* p. 4.

Boulton, Leyla. (July 23, 1994.) "Latvia Relents over Curbs on Citizenship." *Financial Times* (London), p. 2.

Brubaker, Rogers. 1992. *Citizenship and Nationhood in France and Germany.* Cambridge, Mass.: Harvard University Press.

Brubaker, W. Rogers. 1992. "Citizenship Struggles in Soviet Successor States." *International Migration Review,* no. 26.

Bungs, Dzintra, et al. (December 18, 1992.) "Citizenship Legislation in the Baltic States." *RFE/RL Research Report,* p. 39.

Center of National Researchers of Lithuania. 1992. *National Minorities in Lithuania.* Produced for the Ministry of Foreign Affairs and the Department of Nationalities of Lithuania.

Central Intelligence Agency. *The World Factbook, 1998: Latvia.* (Cited March 3, 1999.) <http://www.odci.gov/cia/publications/factbook/lg.html>

Cerkasovas, Irenijus. Head of the Special Commission on the Questions of Citizenship (Lithuania). Interview by Lowell Barrington. Vilnius, Lithuania. April 29, 1994.

"Citizenship; One of Us, or One of Them?" (July 31, 1993.) *Economist.*

"Citizenship Statistics: An Update as of March, 1998." (March 19, 1998.) *Estonia Today.* <http://www.vm.ee/eng/estoday/1998/03cits.html>

"Citizenship Statistics: An Update as of July, 1997." (July 8, 1997.) *Estonia Today.* <http://www.vm.ee/eng/estoday/1997/06cits.html>

Commission on Security and Cooperation in Europe. 1992. "Russians in Estonia: Problems and Prospects."

Conference on Security and Cooperation in Europe. 1992. "Report of the CSCE ODIHR Mission on the Study of Estonian Legislation."

Congress of Estonia. 1992. "Congress of Estonia Position on the Immigrants from the Former USSR Residing in the Republic of Estonia."

"Constitution Watch: Estonia." 1993. *Eastern European Constitutional Review,* no. 2.

Council of Europe. "Comments on the Draft Citizenship Law of the Republic of Latvia." January 24, 1994.

"Council of Europe Reviews Estonian Elections." (September 28, 1992–October 4, 1992.) *Estonian Review.* <http://www.vm.ee/eng/review/1992/92er2804.09e.html>

Dahl, Robert A. 1956. *A Preface to Democratic Theory.* Chicago: University of Chicago Press.

"Dini Says Russian Row Hurts Latvia EU Case." (April 8, 1998.) *Russia Today.* <http://www.russiatoday.com/rtoday/news/98040807.html>

"'Draconian' Law Encroaches Minorities." (March 6, 1992.) *F.B.I.S. Daily Report: Central Eurasia,* p. 71.

Estonia. 1993. Estonian Law on Citizenship. *InfoPress* publication of the Estonian Ministry of Foreign Affairs.

Estonia. 1993. Law on Amendments to the Law on Citizenship. (Unofficial translation provided the Estonian Ministry of Foreign Affairs.)

Estonia. 1993. Law on Amendments to the Republic of Estonia Supreme Council Reso-
    lution "On the Application of the Law on Citizenship." (Unofficial translation pro-
    vided by the Estonian Ministry of Foreign Affairs.)
Estonia. 1993. "On Estonian Language Requirements for Applicants for Citizenship."
    (Unofficial translation provided by the Estonian Ministry of Foreign Affairs.)
Estonia. 1992. "On the Application of the Law on Citizenship." Resolution of the Esto-
    nian Supreme Council. (Translation provided by the Estonian Ministry of Foreign
    Affairs.)
Estonia. Estonian Constitution. Trans. M. Scheinin. (Last modified September 15,
    1998.) <http://www.uni-wuerzburg.de/law/en00000_.html>
Estonia. Ministry of Foreign Affairs of the Republic of Estonia, "Estonian Citizenship
    Statistics as of July 26, 1993." (No date, on file with author.)
"Estonia Amends Citizenship Law." (March 24, 1993.) RFE/RL Daily Report.
    <http://www.friends-partners.org/friends/news/omri/1993/03/930324.html>
"Estonia Passes New Citizenship Law." (January 20, 1995.) OMRI Daily Digest.
    <http://solar.rtd.utk.edu/friends/news/omri/1995/01/950120II.html>
"Estonia Suspends Granting Citizenship." (January 5, 1995.) OMRI Daily Digest.
    <http://solar.rtd.utk.edu/friends/news/omri/1995/01/950105.html>
"Estonian Government Seeks to Integrate Russian Speakers." (January 5, 1998.)
    RFE/RL NewsLine. <http://www.rferl.org/newsline/1998/01/050198.html>
Estonian Institute for Human Rights. Letter to Lowell Barrington, Department of Politi-
    cal Science, University of Michigan. (No date, on file with author.)
"Estonian Parliament Passes Amendments to Citizenship Law." (December 9, 1998.)
    RFE/RL NewsLine. <http://www.rferl.org/newsline/1998/12/091298.html>
"EU and UNDP Launch Major Language Training Program in Estonia." (October
    11–17, 1998.) Estonian Review. <http://www.vm.ee/eng/review/1998/98101117.
    htm>
Ginsburgs, George. 1993. "From the 1990 Law on Citizenship of the USSR to the Citi-
    zenship Laws of the Successor Republics" (Part II). Review of Central and Eastern
    European Law, no. 3.
Ginsburgs, George. 1990. "The Citizenship of the Baltic States." Journal of Baltic
    Studies, no. 21.
Girard, Francoise. 1998. "The Latvian and Estonian Laws on Citizenship and the Prob-
    lem of Statelessness in International Law." Paper presented at the annual meeting of
    the Association for the Study of Nationalities, New York, April 18.
Girnius, Saulius. (August 26, 1994.) "Relations Between the Baltic States and Russia."
    RFE/RL Research Report, pp. 29–33.
Girnius, Saulius. (September 19, 1991.) "The Lithuanian Citizenship Law." RFE/RL Re-
    search Report, p. 21.
Goble, Paul. (March 9, 1998.) "Latvia: Analysis from Washington—Russia Plays the
    Ethnic Card." RFE/RL Features. <http://search.rferl.org./nca/features/1998/03/
    F.RU.980309133140.html>
"Gorbunovs on Citizenship Referendum." (March 23, 1992.) RFE/RL Daily Report.
    <http://solar.rtd.utk.edu/friends/news/omri/1992/03/920323.html>
"Italy Urges Citizenship Amendment Approval in Latvia." (September 16, 1998.) BBC
    Monitoring Former Soviet Union—Political. <http:/proquest.umi.com>

Johnson, Steven. "People Get the Last Word on Citizenship Reform." (July 2–8, 1998.) *Baltic Times.* <http://www.lvnet.lv/baltictimes/news.html>

Karklins, Rasma. 1997. "Ethnopolitics and Language Strategies in Latvia." Paper presented at the annual convention of the American Political Science Association, Washington, D.C., August 28–31.

Karnups, Viestur, LNNK Party. Interview by Lowell Barrington. Riga, Latvia. May 11, 1994.

Kask, Peet, Adviser, Centrist Faction, State Assembly of Estonia, letter to Lowell Barrington, Department of Political Science, University of Michigan. August 11, 1993.

Kavaliauskas, Vilius, Press Secretary for the Lithuanian Seimas (parliament). Interview by Lowell Barrington. Vilnius, Lithuania. May 2, 1994.

Kelam, Tunne, Head of the Estonian Delegation. 1993. Statement at the Council of Europe Parliamentary Assembly, June 30. (Provided by the Estonian Ministry of Foreign Affairs.)

Kionka, Riina. 1991. "Who Should Become a Citizen of Estonia?" *RFE/RL Report on the USSR,* no. 27.

Kirch, Aksel, Sociologist. Interview by Lowell Barrington. May 30, 1996. Tallinn, Estonia.

Kirch, Aksel, et al. 1993. "Russians in the Baltic States: To Be or Not to Be?" *Journal of Baltic Studies,* no. 24.

Kvarno, Ole, CSCE Mission Leader in Narva. Interview by Lowell Barrington. Narva, Estonia. July 11, 1993.

"Lack of Citizenship Law Mars CE Membership Hope." (February 1, 1994.) *F.B.I.S. Daily Report: Central Eurasia,* p. 69.

Laitin, David D. 1993. "The Russian Speaking Nationality in Estonia: Two Quasi-Constitutional Elections." *Eastern European Constitutional Review,* no. 2, p. 23.

"Lalumiére in Latvia." (February 19, 1992.) *RFE/RL Daily Report.* <http://solar.rtd.utk.edu/friends/news/omri/1992/02/920219.html>

Latvia. 1998. Republic of Latvia Naturalization Board. *Information about Acceptance and Review of Naturalization Applications.* (By June 30, 1998.)

Latvia. 1998. Republic of Latvia Naturalization Board. *Naturalization Process in Latvia: 1995, 1996, 1997, 1998, Main Indices.* (By June 30, 1998.)

Latvia. 1994. Law on Citizenship. (Unofficial translation provided by the Latvian Foreign Ministry, on file with author.)

Latvia. 1993. Citizenship Law. Trans. Inese Birznece. (Draft law version passed on November 25, 1993, on file with author.)

Latvia. 1991. On the Renewal of Republic of Latvia Citizens' Rights and Fundamental Principles of Naturalization. Resolution of the Republic of Latvia Supreme Council. (Official translation.)

Latvia. 1991. The Rights and Obligations of a Citizen and a Person. Trans. M. Scheinin. <http://www.uni-wuerzburg.de/law/lg03000_.html>

"Latvia Reels Amid Bombs, SS Row with Russia." (April 7, 1998.) *Russia Today.* <http://www.russiatoday.com/rtoday/news/98040702.html>

"Latvia Urges Russia Talks, Gets OSCE Support." (April 21, 1998.) *Russia Today.* <http://www.russiatoday.com/rtoday/news/07.html>

"Latvian Lawmakers Reject Amendment to Citizenship Law." (February 13, 1998.) *RFE/RL   NewsLine.*   <http://www.rferl.org/newsline/1998/02/3-CEE/cee%2D130298.html>

"Latvian President Warns against OSCE Interference in Citizenship Affairs." (August 24, 1998.) *BBC Monitoring Former Soviet Union—Political.* <http:/proquest.umi.com>

"Latvian Working Group Divided over 'Naturalization Windows.'" (April 15, 1998.) *RFE/RL NewsLine.* <http://search.rferl.org./newsline/1998/04/150498.html>

"Latvian Vote Wins Praise." (October 6, 1998.) *Financial Times* (London), p. 3.

"Law Must Change to Grant Citizenship to Children Born in Estonia—Meri." (September 16, 1998.) *BBC Summary of World Broadcasts,* available in LEXIS, Academic Universe, SU/D3333/E.

"Linguistic Environment Needs to be Changed." (September 20–26, 1998.) *Estonian Review.* <http://www.vm.ee/eng/review/1998/98092703.html>

Lithuania. 1996. Law on Citizenship. (Amended version, official translation, provided to the author by the press department of the Seimas of Lithuania.)

Lithuania. 1996. On Associations. (English version.) <http://www.litlex.lt/Litlex/Eng/Frames/Laws/Documents/361.HTM>

Lithuania. 1995. On Public Organisations. (English version.) <http://www.litlex.lt/Litlex/Eng/Frames/Laws/Documents/352.HTM>

Lithuania. 1994. Law on Land. (English version.) <http://www.litlex.lt/Litlex/Eng/Frames/Laws/Documents/174.HTM>

Lithuania. 1994. On Elections to Local Government Councils. (English version.) <http://www.litlex.lt/Litlex/Eng/Frames/Laws/Documents/168.HTM>

Lithuania. 1993. Cooperative Law. (English version.) <http://www.litlex.lt/Litlex/Eng/Frames/Laws/Documents/204.HTM>

Lithuania. 1991. Law on Citizenship. (English version.) <http://www.litlex.lt/Litlex/Eng/Frames/Laws/Documents/55.HTM>

Lithuania. 1991. On the Legal Status of Foreigners in the Republic of Lithuania. (English   version.)   <http://www.litlex.lt/Litlex/Eng/Frames/Laws/Documents/FOREIGN.HTM>

Lithuania. 1991. On the Procedure for Implementing the Republic of Lithuania Law on Citizenship. Resolution of the Lithuanian Supreme Council. (Unofficial translation, on file with author.)

Lithuania. 1990. Law on Police. (English version.) <http://www.litlex.lt/Litlex/Eng/Frames/Laws/Documents/105.HTM>

Lithuania. 1989. Law on Citizenship. (English version.) <http://www.litlex.lt/Litlex/Eng/Frames/Laws/Documents/216.HTM>

Lithuania. 1989. O grazhdanstve Litovskoi SSR. (Russian-language version provided by the Lithuanian Seimas archive department.)

Lithuania. Lithuanian Constitution. Trans. M. Scheinin. (Last modified September 15, 1998.) <http://www.uni-wuerzburg.de/law/lh00000_.html>

Lithuania. (December 28, 1991.) O deistvii dokumentov o grazhdanstve Litovskoi Respubliki i vnecenii dopolnenia v zakon o grazhdanstve, Ekho Litvi. (On file with author.).

Lithuania. (December 28, 1991.) Zakon o grazhdanstve Litovskoi Respubliki, Ekho Litvi. (On file with author.)

"Local Government Elections Held." (October 14–17, 1993.) *Estonian Review.* <http://www.vm.ee/eng/review/1993/93101417.html>

"Many Have Passport Wrongfully." (January 20–26, 1995.) *Baltic Independent*, p. 3.

Markauskas, Rimantas, Member of Parliament and of the Committee on Human and Citizens' Rights and Nationality Affairs (Lithuania). Interview by Lowell Barrington. Vilnius, Lithuania. June 11, 1996.

Meri, Lennart. (Npvember 4, 1998.) "Address of the President of the Republic of Estonia, Mr. Lennart Meri, before NATO." <http://www.nato.int/docu/speech/1998/s981104a.htm>

Naturalization Board of the Republic of Latvia. 1997. On Naturalization in Latvia.

"New Citizenship Laws in the Republics of the Former USSR." (April 15, 1992.) *Helsinki Watch*, p. 3.

"New Estonian Citizenship Law Signed." (February 2, 1995.) *OMRI Daily Digest.* <http://solar.rtd.utk.edu/friends/news/omri/1995/02/950202II.html>

"New Official Language Teachers Take up Posts." (September 20–26, 1998.) *Estonian Review.* <http://www.vm.ee/eng/review/1998/98092703.htm>

Norman, Richard. 1992. "Citizenship, Politics and Autonomy." In *Liberalism, Citizenship and Autonomy*, eds. David Milligan and William Watts Miller. Aldershot, England: Avebury.

"Opposition Rejects President's Citizenship Appeal." (September 18, 1998.) *BBC Summary of World Broadcasts*, available in LEXIS, Academic Universe, SU/D3335/E.

Organization for Security and Cooperation in Europe OSCE. 1998. Report from the High Commissioner on National Minorities. *OSCE Newsletter*, June. <http://www.osce.org/e/docs/newsletr/nl-98-06/nl0698e.htm>

"OSCE Commissioner, Latvian President Discuss Referendum on Citizenship Law." (August 26, 1998.) *BBC Monitoring Former Soviet Union—Political.* <http://proquest.umi.com>

"Otnosheniya prinimayut konfrontatsionii kharakter." (June 24, 1993.) *Nezavisimaya gazeta*, p. 1.

"Over 16,000 Said to Receive Citizenship." (March 23, 1994.) *F.B.I.S. Daily Report: Central Eurasia*, p. 67.

Peled, Yoav. 1992. "Ethnic Democracy and the Legal Construction of Citizenship: Arab Citizens of the Jewish State." *American Political Science Review*, no. 86.

Petrauskas, Valdas, Member of the Committee on Human and Citizens' Rights and Nationality Affairs and the President's Special Commission on Citizenship (Lithuania). Interview by Lowell Barrington. Vilnius, Lithuania. June 12, 1996.

Pettai, Velo. 1993. "Contemporary International Influences on Post-Soviet Nationalism: The Cases of Estonia and Latvia." Paper presented at the annual meetings of the American Association for the Advancement of Slavic Studies, Honolulu, Hawaii, November.

Plant, Raymond. 1992. "Citizenship and Rights." In *Liberalism, Citizenship and Autonomy*, eds. David Milligan and William Watts Miller. Aldershot, England: Avebury.

"Population Information Site of Latvia." *International Migration.* (Cited March 3, 1999.) <http://www.lanet.lv/popin/statistics/migracij.html>

"President, Government to Review Citizenship Law." (June 28, 1994.) *F.B.I.S. Daily Report: Central Eurasia*, p. 71.

"Prime Minister Forbids the Discussion of Ousting 'Russian-Speakers.'" (November 5, 1992.) *F.B.I.S. Daily Report: Central Eurasia,* p. 71.

Rull, Ivo, Secretary General of the Fatherland and Freedom Party, and Malle Aleksius, Press Secretary of the Fatherland and Freedom Party. Interview by Lowell Barrington. Tallinn, Estonia. July 7, 1993.

"Russian Envoy Says Elections Not Democratic." (January 27, 1993.) *F.B.I.S. Daily Report: Central Eurasia,* p. 64.

"Russkiye Pribaltiki." (January 3, 1992.) *Nezavisimaya gazeta,* p. 3.

"Saeima to Review Ulmanis Demand on Citizenship Law." (July 1, 1994.) *F.B.I.S. Daily Report: Central Eurasia,* p. 60.

Safran, William. 1997. "Citizenship and Nationality in Democratic Systems: Approaches to Defining and Acquiring Membership in the Political Community." *International Political Science Review,* no. 18.

Smith, Graham. 1996. "The Resurgence of Nationalism." In *The Baltic States,* ed. Graham Smith, p. 126. New York: St. Martin's Press.

Staprans, Alda. (December 6–12, 1991.) "Latvian Emigrés Granted Citizenship Rights." *Baltic Observer,* p. 2.

Stepan, Alfred. 1994. "When Democracy and the Nation-State Are Competing Logics: Reflections on Estonia." *European Journal of Sociology,* no. 35.

Stephens, Ken. (September 21, 1998.) "Divided Freedoms: Latvia's Russians Struggle for Citizenship Following Nation's Independence." *Dallas Morning News,* p. A1.

"Supreme Soviet Ends Last Session, Creates Army, Amends Citizenship Law." (November 20, 1992.) *F.B.I.S. Daily Report: Central Eurasia,* p. 59.

Tsilevich, Boris, and Alexander Ruchkovsky. 1994. "Difference in Status and Rights between Citizens and Permanent Residents (Non-Citizens) of Latvia." Trans. Alex Grigorievs. Unpublished manuscript. (On file with author.)

Umbrasaite, Erika, Reporter for *Europos Lietuvis.* Interview by Lowell Barrington. Vilnius, Lithuania. May 4, 1994.

U.S. Department of State, Bureau of Democracy, Human Rights, and Labor. (January 30, 1998.) *Latvia Report on Human Rights Practices for 1997.* <http://dosfan. lib.uic.edu>

"US Envoy Reiterates Support for Latvia Despite Citizenship Law Referendum." (September 11, 1998.) *BBC Monitoring Former Soviet Union—Political.* <http:// proquest.umi.com>

"US Envoy to NATO Urges Latvia to Press Ahead with Citizenship Reform." (September 3, 1998.) *BBC Monitoring Former Soviet Union—Political.* <http:// proquest.umi.com>

Vaitiekus, Severinas, Vice-Director of the Lithuania's Department of Nationalities. Interview by Lowell Barrington. Vilnius, Lithuania. May 4, 1994.

van der Stoel, Max, CSCE High Commissioner on National Minorities, letter to Georgs Andrejevs, Latvian Foreign Minister. December 10, 1993. (On file with author.)

Vebers, Elmars. 1993. "Demography and Ethnic Politics in Independent Latvia: Some Basic Facts." *Nationalities Papers,* no. 21.

Veering, Uno. *The Government's Basic Goals for 1997 and 1998.* (Cited January 16, 1999.) <http://www.rk.ee/valitsus/valproto.html>

"Visiting Experts to Endorse CE Membership." (August 9, 1994.) *F.B.I.S. Daily Report: Central Eurasia,* p. 59.

Walzer, Michael. 1983. *Spheres of Justice: A Defense of Pluralism and Equality.* Oxford: Blackwell.

"Western Press Review: Latvia Stares into Russian Economic Gun Barrel." (April 9, 1998.)   *RFE/RL   Features.*   <http://search.rferl.org/nca/features/1998/04/F. RU.980410130821.html>

Zemrido, Gvido, Chief Justice of the Supreme Court of the Republic of Latvia. 1993. "Human Rights in the Baltic Republics." Speech delivered at the University of Michigan, February 4. (On file with author.)

Zwadiuk, Oleh. (March 6, 1996.) "U.S. Says Latvia Generally Respects Human Rights." *RFE/RL   Features.*   <http://www.rferl.org/nca/hr/1996/03/F.HR.96031215432618. html>

PART THREE

Dual and Supranational Citizenship: Limits to Transnationalism

CHAPTER NINE

Introduction

RAINER BAUBÖCK

THE CASE STUDIES explored in the two following chapters deal with very different phenomena. The Mexican study documents a major policy shift in a traditional "sending country" toward a toleration, or even encouragement, of dual nationality among its emigrants. The European Union study examines a slowly emerging supranational form of citizenship among a regional confederation of states. What the Mexican citizenship reform and citizenship of the European Union still have in common is that they illustrate how the traditional conception of citizenship as a singular membership in a sovereign national polity is gradually eroding under the impact of geographical mobility and regional integration. Yet, at the same time, both cases also show how legislators and policy makers attempt to curb this transnational dynamic by linking access to citizenship in problematic ways to national membership. The Mexican reform does this by distinguishing between Mexicans by birth who may become dual nationals and Mexicans by naturalization who are not allowed to hold another citizenship. The European Union does this by leaving it to its individual member states to define the requirements for naturalization and thereby also for admission to the common citizenship of the Union.

The amendment of the Mexican Constitution of March 20, 1997, and the law on nationality that came into effect one year later allows Mexicans by birth to retain their original nationality when they naturalize abroad. Those who had lost their Mexican nationality when they became U.S. citizens may regain it within five years. The large number of potential beneficiaries of this reform has aroused considerable concern among conservatives in the United States. They warn that Mexican Americans possessing dual nationality might use their franchise to promote Mexican rather than U.S. interests. The irony is that the reform really brings Mexican citizenship policies closer to the U.S. model.

First, it establishes the same combination of straightforward *jus soli* for those born in the national territory and *jus sanguinis* transmission of citizenship outside the country (whereas the previous law had followed the French model of granting those born to foreigners in Mexico only an option to citizenship at the age of majority). This combination attributes citizenship both to the offspring of immigrants in the country and of emigrants abroad and makes thus for the most inclusive allocation of citizenship in states that are simultaneously sending and receiving countries. (One should not forget that Mexico is also one of the most important destinations of migration from Central and South America.) It is this combination that inevitably generates dual citizenship at birth.

Second, whereas the previous law had allowed for an unlimited passing on of Mexican citizenship abroad, Mexico has now also adopted the U.S. policy of limiting an automatic acquisition of citizenship *jure sanguinis* to the first generation born abroad. The reform will thus create an option for dual citizenship among immigrants while removing automatic inclusion for their grandchildren. As dual ties will be certainly strongest among first-generation emigrants and their children, this change is reasonable if citizenship ought to reflect effective links to a country.

Third, since a 1967 Supreme Court decision, the United States no longer considers citizens who naturalize abroad as having expatriated themselves, and Mexico has simply adopted a similar rule. If the U.S. laws contribute thus to the proliferation of dual citizenship both at birth and at naturalization, it seems hardly fair to accuse another country of doing the same.

One might object that there is no symmetry here, because there are many more Mexicans living north of the Rio Grande than there are U.S. citizens in Mexico. Between these two states, however, fears of the other's power to encroach on national interests and sovereignty have certainly been greater on the Mexican side. One could say that Mexican policies have been driven by a dual historical trauma of losing territory and population to its wealthy northern neighbor. The new citizenship legislation can be interpreted as a shift in emphasis from the first to the second trauma. In Mexico, foreign owners of land have to renounce claims to diplomatic protection by their country of citizenship and must, in fact, apply for a status of Mexican quasi-nationality. There are further specific restrictions for owning land in coastal and border areas. These had also affected Mexican immigrants who had naturalized in the United States. The toleration of dual nationality removes this obstacle.

Mexico seems now more concerned about losing its emigrant population, whose remittances and investments represent a considerable economic asset, than about a potential sellout of the territory to Mexican Americans based abroad. Similar reasons have motivated policy reforms toward facilitating dual citizenship in Turkey, which is the major sending state of migration to Western Europe. Yet the Mexican government still appears to share concerns about the political impact of dual citizenship that are entirely symmetrical with those of U.S. conservatives. If the latter fear that Mexican issues might come to dominate U.S. elections in areas like Southern California, the former dread the prospect of a large vote for the opposition by emigrants politically socialized in the United States. Both concerns have, for the time being, prevented the introduction of absentee ballots for Mexican nationals.

The Mexican reform makes a terminological distinction between citizenship and nationality. Only when residing in Mexico do nationals enjoy the full rights of citizens. In international law the concept of "nationality" generally refers to the external effect of citizenship that affiliates a person to a sovereign state and restricts thereby another state's powers to submit him or her exclusively to its own laws. The Mexican usage concerns instead the relations of citizens living outside the territory to the Mexican state. It should therefore be thought of as an external citizenship, that is, a specific bundle of rights and obligations assigned to citizens when they reside abroad. This is not merely a terminological question. The Mexican reform seems to rest on the idea that a person can be a dual national but not a dual citizen. It appears to me that, in fact, it establishes dual citizenship with a differentiation of rights according to residence. While voting rights cannot be enjoyed when living abroad, the rights to own land and to return to Mexico are retained even for those who take up another citizenship abroad. When they move back to Mexico, they become again full citizens but lose their claims to diplomatic protection by the United States.

This halfway model of dual citizenship makes the citizenship of the other country to a large extent dormant. Rather than driving a wedge between citizenship and nationality by turning them into distinct legal categories, one should discuss one by one the list of rights and obligations entailed in full citizenship and see which among them can be meaningfully assigned to, and exercised by, those living abroad and holding a second citizenship. Such an approach could provide pragmatic answers to the generally exaggerated concerns about conflicting loyalties and duties or unjustified privileges of these groups. As far as voting rights are concerned, the basic requirement for exercising it should be some present involvement in the political community and some likelihood that the voters will themselves bear the future consequences of their political choices. If seems to me that with their high rates of cross-border mobility and strong transnational family networks, first-generation Mexican Americans perfectly qualify for a dual franchise.

There is another aspect in which the Mexican law uses a traditional understanding of "nationality" in order to make a distinction among different kinds of citizens. Only Mexicans by birth are fully protected against being deprived of their nationality. Naturalized Mexicans lose it by acquiring the citizenship of another country or may also be denaturalized after residing continuously abroad for five years. Once again, this distinction is not entirely alien to U.S. law, which bars naturalized immigrants from the highest political office. Yet, their weaker protection against a loss of citizenship in Mexican law is certainly a more serious matter.

First, this differentiation does not survive a simple test of generalization. (One should consider a Golden Rule for citizenship policies: Do not make provisions in your nationality law to which you would object if they were adopted by other states and affected your own citizens.) If the United States adopted the same rule, it would deny Mexican immigrants naturalization unless they renounce their Mexican citizenship. This move would thwart the whole Mexican reform by also depriving Mexican nationals by birth of its benefits.

Second, by considering naturalized immigrants, in a way, as merely probationary citizens, the Mexican laws give priority to a national community into which one is born over a political community that one may choose. It does not seem unreasonable to ask those who naturalize for an explicit declaration of their loyalty that is never demanded from those who acquire their citizenship at birth, which is what all democratic states do. Distrusting those who already have shown their consent by becoming citizens, however, undermines a democratic conception of citizenship as a consensual membership in a polity.

The European Union is not a federal state, but it is more than an alliance of states for limited purposes of market integration or common defense. This ambiguous character is revealed in its construction of a citizenship of the Union, formally introduced by the Maastricht Treaty. If citizenship is understood as membership in a democratic polity, then this move would imply that the European Union has reached a stage of integration at which it has become a polity. A closer examination, however, reveals that both the substance of rights and obligations implied in such membership as well as the social preconditions for conceiving of the Union as a political community are still extremely thin. Citizenship of the Union is, on the one hand, merely a compilation of an incoherent set of rights that reflect the present stage of economic and political integration, and, on the other hand, a symbolic exercise that announces a larger project still to be achieved in the future. Should we conclude that introducing this kind of quasi-citizenship was premature or merely an ideological move in order to sell the burdens of economic integration to a reluctant electorate? Even if the latter may have been the political motive, the question of whether the project of the Union needs a structure of citizenship remains.

In my view, the strongest need for a European citizenship emerges from the much-discussed democratic deficit. Democracy is a form of government in which all those who are affected by collectively binding decisions are equally represented in the decision making. The citizens of member states are today subjected to both the political powers of their national governments and those of the institutions of the Union. The legislative powers of the European Council and Commission and the judicial powers of the European Court of Justice have grown to such an extent that their actions can no longer be legitimated within an intergovernmental framework. Creating a citizenship of the Union spelled out that to live up to the democratic commitments of all its member states, the Union itself ought to be seen as a polity in the making with its own structure of inclusive individual membership. Affirming this project provides us with a yardstick for measuring the formidable obstacles for progress and the serious deficiencies of the present conception of citizenship.

The major obstacle is the lack of a common European civil society. Citizenship requires not only a common political authority, but also a network of associations embedded in a shared public sphere. Civil society in Europe is still compartmentalized into national societies. What is needed so that "ordinary citizens" can experience their membership in the emerging European polity as important? First, a European public sphere, including mass media and political parties that are no longer primarily attached to national publics and electorates. Second, spontaneous forms of voluntary association that cross national boundaries. Today's European NGOs are hardly genuine expressions of transnational self-organization of citizens but rather are pressure groups trailing the shifts of political power toward Brussels. Third, much higher rates of geographical mobility between member states. Only outside their country of national citizenship can individuals fully experience the relevance of their rights as citizens of the Union. Obviously, all three developments can only be politically facilitated or encouraged but cannot be directly brought about by legislation. As long as they persist, Union citizenship will remain a legal construction in limbo.

Even if one ought, therefore, to reject a voluntaristic approach, there are still serious deficiencies in the present provisions on citizenship that cannot be explained by these social limitations. The first striking thing about Union citizenship in the Maastricht Treaty is that the only rights listed there are those of free movement, diplomatic protection, petition, and political participation in municipal and European Parliament elections. And although the treaty stipulates that "citizens of the Union shall be subject to the duties imposed thereby," one searches in vain for a list of such legal duties. The Amsterdam Treaty has added an important provision against discrimination, which is, however, seriously hampered by requirements of unanimity for implementation. Certainly, fundamental civic and social rights are protected through the European Convention of Human Rights, the Social Charter, and other documents, but it seems significant that the framers of the Union have not felt the need to summarize and systematize them in a bill of rights that would document the full content and scope of Union citizenship. Jürgen Habermas has suggested that political integration in Europe will require developing a constitutional patriotism rather than a national sense of unity based on common culture and history. There is so far, however, no definition of citizenship that could provide a focus for such loyalty.

The second deficiency lies in the mode of access to citizenship and is linked to what we may call the European inclusion deficit. Citizenship of the Union is derived from being a citizen of a member state, and the nationality laws of the member states are vastly different in their rules for naturalization and for the acquisition of citizenship at birth. The common status of Union citizenship can thereby be reached in fifteen different ways, which may be characteristic for the early stages of federal integration in which the constituent units still act as gatekeepers for immigration and admission to political membership. Yet, a pressing European problem is the political integration of millions of disenfranchised immigrants who are third-country nationals. In some European states, naturalization requirements are extremely difficult to meet, *jus sanguinis* turns those born in the country into foreigners, and resident aliens are subjected to discriminatory laws. Union citizenship could become a vehicle for integration, but its present architecture highlights the exclusionary features.

There are three paths toward a more inclusive conception: one could give third-country nationals direct access to Union citizenship without requiring their previous naturalization in a member state; one could introduce a uniform legal status for permanent residents from third countries that would give them many of the rights but not the formal status of Union citizens; or one could harmonize the nationality laws of the member states so that access to both national and Union citizenship becomes easier and the same everywhere. None of these solutions currently has much chance of being adopted, but it seems to me that a combination of the second and third would be highly desirable, whereas the first one would merely result in a further devaluation of Union citizenship in the eyes of the native population and would consolidate exclusionary citizenship policies at national levels.

Union citizenship is today a supranational construction rather than a postnational or transnational one. It creates a thin layer of additional rights placed on top of the thicker national citizenships and accessible only to those who are recognized as members by one of the states of the Union. Mending its deficiencies would not require disconnecting it from national citizenship but enhancing its set of rights and addressing the inclusion deficit. Policy makers should finally acknowledge that the integration of immigrants has become just as much a European agenda as the control of immigration.[1] Once this task is taken seriously, the linkage between national and Union citizenship may stimulate a transmission of transnational dynamics from the European level down to the member states as well as a harmonization of their nationality laws from below.

---

1. The European Council meeting in Tampere, Finland, on October 15 and 16, 1999, took a first step by proposing that third-country nationals should enjoy rights comparable to those of European Union citizens.

CHAPTER TEN

Nationality in Mexico

MANUEL BECERRA RAMÍREZ

REGULATION OF THE population is a fundamental power of the sovereign state. The state determines who composes its population, which includes defining the legal status of its nationals and citizens.

The case of Mexico can be considered unique in some ways because of its extensive border with the United States. Mexican population flows between the two countries are substantial. The economy of Mexico is poor, with a chronic incapacity to provide employment to millions of people, mostly peasants, who find that they must emigrate in search of work. Naturally, they migrate northward where the U.S. economy is the strongest in the world. This migration to the United States is a frequent irritant to the bilateral relationship between the countries.

The Mexican government has dedicated itself to protecting the rights of its nationals in the United States, who are alleged to suffer from discrimination in employment opportunities, from the cutoff of benefits, and from the lack of political rights. During the recent welfare and migration reforms in the United States, it was alleged that Mexicans are subject to discrimination by virtue of their national origin.[1] In addition, the important contribution of these Mexicans to the economy of the United States usually goes unrecognized.

This chapter was translated by Mary Ann Larkin.

1. It is believed that Mexicans maintain their customs without adapting fully to the U.S. culture, which is interpreted as a threat to U.S. society.

In recent years, the Mexican government reached the conclusion that a considerable number of Mexican emigrants to the United States were not naturalizing in the United States in order to preserve their Mexican nationality. As a result, they have de facto accepted the legal, employment, administrative, and political disadvantages under which they live. As a response to this dilemma, the Mexican government launched a project to reform the Mexican legal system from the national Constitution down to provisions of specific laws to offer some relief. Reforms included passage of the Nationality Law in 1997, which permits dual nationality. Thus, dual nationality has shifted from being treated as a legal aberration to being fashioned as a solution for the legal system.

This article examines nationality and dual nationality in the international legal and scholarly context and provides a detailed account of nationality in Mexico. This review will trace nationality through Mexican constitutional history, including the most recent amendments on the subject passed by the National Congress in 1997. Finally, it will present in detail the subsequent incorporation of key passages on dual nationality into law and regulation.

Nationality from a Legal and Political Perspective

The concept of nationality has a variety of meanings as viewed from the different perspectives of sociology and law. In sociology, nationality refers to the sense of belonging felt by a group of persons who share one culture, including language, traditions, history, and social values.[2] By contrast, in the legal field, nationality refers to the relationship or link between individuals and the state that translates into certain reciprocal rights and responsibilities. A person may hold a nationality understood as a sociological matter that differs from their nationality as recognized by law; for example, person may be Jewish of Argentine, Russian, or even Mexican nationality and hold legal nationality from the United States, Germany, Canada, or another country.

Currently, Mexican nationality is undergoing profound revision from both perspectives. Officially, nationality has been rooted in its Indian past—*lo mestizo*. This concept of nationality stems from the ideology of the Mexican Revolution, which "reassessed the concept of the *mestizo* and came to see it as a quintessential national asset and, in doing so, redefined the essential elements of the nation."[3] In order to explicate the term "national" in Mexico, one must

---

2. Cabaleiro, for example, notes that the nation is "a group of individuals united by a common language, customs, culture, territory, common historic tradition. Together with these visible characteristics, some authors have imposed a subjective characteristic: the belief on the part of the group members in a common destiny." Cabaleiro, 1962, pp. 4–5.

3. Lomnitz, 1993, p. 188.

turn to the *mestizo* metaphor, which Lomnitz has argued resulted in the ascendancy of a complex set of authoritarian formulas of governance. By contrast, Lomnitz's own ideal centers the definition of nationality in the elevation of individual rights over the rights of the nation.[4] This all-encompassing icon of the *mestizo*, however, obscures the fact that Mexico has comprised, and continues to comprise, different groups of people with different cultural backgrounds (language, beliefs, customs, and so on), a society that anthropologists might describe as cosmopolitanism. The indigenous rebellion in Chiapas and the current discussion of indigenous rights demonstrate the fallacy and the limitations of the *mestizo* icon.

Nationality and citizenship are distinct concepts under Mexican law. Nationality binds an individual to the Mexican state; citizenship, one aspect of nationality, signifies the eligibility of nationals to participate in governance through the right to vote and hold office. Mexican nationality is usually established at birth or through naturalization. Citizenship is acquired automatically at the age of eighteen. The law also mandates that an individual must have led an "upright" life (*"tener un modo honesto de vivir"*), but this requirement is rarely enforced. A citizen may hold office after becoming twenty-one years old.

The Authority of the State to Regulate Nationality

By most standard definitions, the essential elements of the state are its population, its sovereignty, and its territory. Each element is inextricably linked: the population is subject to the laws and legal norms defined by the state by virtue of its sovereign power, subject to its territorial limits. In principle, the state has the power to establish norms that regulate the population, including norms that permit or deny entry of foreigners to its territory. The state's power in this area is undeniable, but has some limits. The first of these limits refers to those that the state accepts through entering into international treaties, especially human rights accords that form the basis for modern international human rights law.

The second set of limits on the state refers to treatment of individuals after they enter national territory. The assumption here is that the state has been organized to serve the general welfare of individual human beings, making it impermissible for the state to act in any way against its people—even those who do not hold the same nationality. Furthermore, international legal doctrine recognizes the existence of certain principles that regulate the attribution of nationality. According to the literature on the subject,[5] these principles have been born

4. Lomnitz, 1993, p. 194.
5. See Mancilla y Mejia, 1998, p. 30; Trigueros Gaisman, "La doble nacionalidad," 1996, p. 586.

of international practice. Some of these principles may not be legally binding, but they are nonetheless important as a source of emerging international norms and jurisprudential principles. Among these principles are the following:

—International law recognizes the right of each state to determine how nationality is acquired and lost;

—No state may determine conditions for the acquisition or forfeiture of a foreign nationality;

—The determination process for the conferring of nationality is limited by international law;

—International legal restrictions are the result of international covenants entered into by states, international custom, and the general principles of law, as universally recognized in Article 38 of the Statutes of the International Court of Justice;

—A declaration of nationality issued by one state within the limits of its competence under international law has legal implications for other states;

—If nationality is acquired through a transgression of international law, other states and international bodies are not bound to recognize this status. The conferral of nationality in this way will be effective for domestic purposes, based on the legal system in the state that granted nationality, only so long as it is not challenged by another state and, by its request, then revoked;

—Nationality is conferred on an individual from his or her day of birth;

—Single nationality is recognized;

—One has the right to change nationality;

—Dual nationality is a condition to be avoided;

—Nationality is not conferred automatically;

—One has the right to renounce one's nationality;

—The possibility of forfeiting one's nationality occurs only upon acquisition of another nationality;

—The threat of forfeiture of nationality may not be used as punishment.

In general terms, the state has the sovereign right to regulate its population. But, as shown, this right is neither absolute nor unlimited; it is limited by international law, including human rights law.

Regulation of Nationality in Mexico

Traditionally, Mexico's legislation has reflected its nationalist fervor. As with many other countries, Mexico's history plays an important role in the development of nationality law. The language of much of the Constitution is characterized by strong protectionism, which is understandable in the light of losses of territory over time, among other experiences.

The Constitution of 1857

Nationality law in Mexico has its roots in the Constitution of 1857. That document set out the general outline for matters related to foreigners, nationality, and citizenship that were retained in the 1917 Constitution. Reviewing particular articles, the earlier Constitution established the following:

—Article 30 based nationality on a combination of *jus sanguinis* and *jus soli*.[6] Moreover, the early text underscored the state's economic interest by including among those who could be considered Mexican, foreigners who acquire real estate;

—With regard to employment, Mexicans are entitled to preference in all cases over foreigners, in equal circumstances;

—Foreigners have rights, or enjoy individual guarantees, granted by the Constitution (Article 33);

—Citizenship, which is granted to all Mexicans of good moral standing at eighteen years of age, confers political rights (Article 35);

—Citizenship is forfeited by "naturalization in a foreign country" (Article 37). There was no mention of the loss of nationality, only the loss of citizenship. That is, an individual continues to be Mexican but holds no political rights.

The Constitution of 1917

The preceding provisions were carried forward by the Constitution of 1917. Currently, the following articles are among those that pertain to foreigners in the country:

—Article 1 refers to rights of individuals;

—Article 11 guarantees freedom of movement;

—Article 30 establishes that nationality may be acquired by birth or naturalization;

—Article 32 establishes the principles by which nationals are accorded preference in employment and public office, as well as those principles that reserve, for national security reasons, certain employment to native-born Mexicans;

—Article 33 refers to the rights and obligations of foreigners;

—Article 34 refers to citizens;

—Article 35 refers to the privileges of citizenship;

6. The Constitution of 1857, Article 30, establishes that Mexicans are
I. All those born of Mexican parents within or outside the territory of the Republic.
II. Those foreigners who naturalize in accordance with the laws of the Federation.
III. Those foreigners who acquire real estate or have Mexican children, as long as they manifest no intention of retaining their nationality.

—Article 36 sets out the obligations of citizens;

—Article 37 refers to the forfeiture of nationality and of citizenship;

—Article 38 regulates the cases in which the rights and privileges of citizenship may be suspended;

—Article 73, paragraph XVI, establishes the exclusive powers of the National Congress to issue laws governing nationality, legal status of foreigners, citizenship, and naturalization; thus, the individual states of the Federal Union are forbidden to deal with this federal issue, leaving it to the exclusive domain of the federal government.

I will now describe some of these provisions in greater detail.

RIGHTS OF INDIVIDUALS.   The current Constitution begins with the assertion that all persons enjoy the guarantee of their rights as individuals under the Constitution by merely stepping on Mexican soil (Article 1). The term "individual" is broadly defined to include both nationals and foreigners. This interpretation was confirmed by a passage relating to foreign slaves who "upon entry to national territory shall attain, by this sole act, their liberty and protection under law." Later, this blanket coverage was tempered by the possibility that the Constitution itself may restrict or suspend such "individual guarantees" (Article 1) and that only the Constitution may do so. In this way, the Mexican Constitution establishes certain limits on foreigners as detailed below.

FREEDOM OF MOVEMENT.   In principle, there are limits on the guarantee of freedom of movement (Article 11) that the 1917 Constitution recognizes for all individuals.[7] The Constitution authorizes legislation relating to emigration, immigration, and public health that places limits on foreigners[8] and, specifically, "undesirable aliens living in the country."[9] The concept of the undesirable alien, which comes from the Constitution of 1857, is overly broad. If by "undesirable," one means "dangerous," the criteria for determining this status remains unspecified. According to Montero Solana, "A foreigner's freedom to enter, exit, transit, and remain in Mexico is subject to legal restrictions."[10]

PROPERTY.   The passages of the 1917 Constitution that contain broad restrictions on foreign ownership of property have their roots in the nineteenth

7. Article 11 provides: "All men have the right to enter and leave the Republic, travel within its territory and move residence, without the need for a security pass, passport, safe conduct or other similar requirements."

8. Article 73, paragraph XVI.

9. Article 33.

10. Montero Solana, 1992, p. 37.

century. With half the nation's territory already lost, the fear that the "overflow-ing prosperity in North America" would spur further U.S. annexation led the Liberals (the political group victorious in the earlier Mexican civil war of the 1800s) to propose legislation to restrict the colonization of Mexico by anyone from the United States.[11] Thus, Article 27 of the 1917 Constitution provides for the following:

> I. Only Mexicans by birth or by naturalization and Mexican companies have the right to acquire ownership of land, water and waterfront prop-erty, or to obtain concessions for the operation of mines or waterways. The State will grant the same rights to those foreigners who appear before the Foreign Relations Secretariat as nationals with respect to such prop-erty and with the understanding that they will not invoke, for this reason, protection of their governments in matters relating to it, under penalty, in the event of breach of contract, of forfeiting for the good of the Nation the property that had been acquired by virtue of the same. Under no circum-stances will foreigners acquire direct ownership over land and waterways within one hundred kilometers of the border and fifty kilometers of the shoreline.
>
> The State, in accordance with domestic public interest and the princi-ples of reciprocity, will, at the discretion of the Foreign Relations Secre-tariat, grant authorization to foreign governments so that they may acquire in the permanent place of residence of the Federal Powers, the private real estate property necessary to service directly their embassies or missions.

Foreigners are prohibited from direct ownership of land, water, and waterfront property, unless they submit to the Calvo Clause before the Foreign Relations Secretariat, by which they agree to forfeit any diplomatic protection for the property by any other state. Absolute restrictions also exist regarding the border and coastal zones. The Restricted Zone now has exceptions, with the possibility of banking trusts open to foreigners and, more recently, with reforms concern-ing the nonrenunciation of other nationalities, which means that those who have dual nationality, including Mexican nationality, of course, will have access to the Restricted Zone.

---

11. Vallarta, 1986, p. 20. Ignacio Vallarta, an illustrious jurist at the time of the Constitution of 1917, wrote a now famous opinion regarding the legality under domestic and international law of Mexican restrictions on foreign ownership of property.

MEXICAN NATIONALITY.   Since the original text of the Constitution, Article 30 has included the recognition of two paths for acquiring Mexican nationality, one by birth and one by naturalization. Article 30 has come under several modifications over the years, in 1934,[12] 1969,[13] 1974,[14] and the latest in 1997, which will be described below.

Citizenship at birth. In general, Mexican nationality policy has been a combination of rules of *jus soli* and *jus sanguinis.*

—Jus soli. In 1934, the Constitution was amended to confer nationality upon all those born in the territory of the Republic, independent of the nationality of the parents.[15] Thus, by the mere act of having been born in Mexican territory, independent of the nationality of the parents, Mexican nationality is granted.[16] This provision has great current significance for the country, owing to the migration flows from countries such as Guatemala, El Salvador, and Honduras during the internal conflicts there in the 1980s. Even though Central America has now achieved peace, a large group of refugees from this region have decided to remain permanently in Mexico. Many now have Mexican-born children, who are legally Mexican and thereby entitled to all the rights the Mexican Constitution grants to its nationals.

Mexican legislative policy maintained some equilibrium insofar as it took into consideration the intentions of the Mexican-born children of foreign parents. Upon reaching the age of eighteen, the child of a foreigner may petition the secretary of Foreign Relations to opt for Mexican nationality, if and when proof of residence is demonstrated for the previous six years. Note that this rule, in effect, results in dual nationality until the age of eighteen for children born to non-Mexican citizens in Mexico.

—Jus sanguinis. The pre-1997 text referred to Mexicans by birth as those "children of Mexican parents, born within or outside the Republic." It did not require parents to have been born in Mexican territory. The 1997 amendments are described below.

Naturalization. Article 30(B) recognizes as Mexican nationals "foreigners who obtain a naturalization card from the Foreign Secretariat." This provision leaves open the possibility that future legislation may stipulate procedures for acquiring Mexican nationality by way of naturalization.

---

12. *Diario Oficial de la Federación,* del 18 de enero de 1934.

13. *Diario Oficial de la Federación,* del 26 de diciembre de 1969.

14. *Diario Oficial de la Federación,* del 31 de diciembre de 1974.

15. Article 30 of the Constitution provides: "Mexican nationality is acquired by birth or by naturalization: (a) Mexicans by birth: I. Those individuals born in the territory of the Republic, irrespective of the nationality of their parents."

16. Mexican territory is defined in Articles 27 and 42 of the Constitution.

FOREIGNERS.   The current text of Article 33 had its origins in Article 33 of
the Constitution of 1857. The government (it was not specified which part of
the government) had the power to "expel undesirable aliens," as an exception to
individual guarantees. The term "undesirable" was not further defined. Article
33 reads as follows:

> Foreigners are those who do not meet the criteria established in Article
> 30. They have the right to the guarantees granted under Chapter 1, Para-
> graph One, of the present Constitution, but *the Chief Executive will have
> the exclusive authority to order immediate expulsion from national terri-
> tory without need for prior trial of any foreigner whose stay is considered
> undesirable.*
> Under no circumstances may foreigners interfere in the political af-
> fairs of the country. [emphasis added]

Thus, the language remains broad and vague.

The drafters of the 1917 Constitution recommended more specific designation of the grounds for expulsion.[17] But the proposal was ultimately not accepted. It nonetheless appears reasonable. Although, as Professor Gutiérrez
Baylón has maintained, the state is recognized as having "undisputed territorial
jurisdiction in determining the stay of foreigners in its territory," in exercising
this authority, the state risks violating human rights, expanding the already ample powers of the executive (as has happened), or even creating a dangerous
precedent for Mexico.[18]

At a time when the protection of human rights has reached nearly universal
acceptance, an undisputed principle of law is that all individuals have the right
to a trial that conforms to standard formal procedures and guarantees a proper
defense. Every individual also has the right to present evidence at trial. Yet Article 33 does not provide for such rights. Indeed, it appears to negate the guarantee of a prior trial contemplated in Article 14—although it does not cancel the
guarantees against illegal search and seizure incorporated in Article 16 of the
Constitution. No known precedents exist, however, that contest it.

Article 33 also prohibits foreigners from "interfer[ing] in the political affairs
of the country." This statement raises the question of whether interference in
economic affairs may not be of equal concern today. Perhaps it is time to recon-

---

17. *Diario de Debates*, 1985, pp. 1127–28.
18. See, for example, the following thesis on the dangerous precedent for the country:
Gutiérrez Baylón, 1996, pp. 9–13.

sider the idea, proposed by the 1917 Constitutional Commission, that the Constitution designate specified causes for expulsion of foreigners.

HIGH OFFICE AT THE FEDERAL LEVEL. The Constitution requires that to become a federal deputy in the Chamber of Deputies or a senator in the Senate, one must be a Mexican citizen (Articles 55-I and 58). By contrast, until recently, to be eligible to be president, one must "be a Mexican citizen by birth enjoying full rights, be the child of a Mexican father or mother, and have resided in the country for at least 20 years."[19] This provision was modified in 1994 to permit a candidate with a foreign father or mother to be eligible for the presidency. The change, which will enter into force on December 31, 1999, will be in effect in the presidential election in the year 2000.

In order to become a justice on the Supreme Court, the highest court in the nation, one must "be a Mexican citizen by birth." Note the curious wording. As we know that a Mexican citizen is one who has reached the age of eighteen (Article 34-I), it is therefore impossible to be a Mexican citizen at birth.

Constitutional Reforms of March 20, 1997

The newest and most important aspect of the reforms begins from a premise that acknowledges the "permanence of nationality" or the "nonrenunciation of nationality." Both, in the opinion of Trigueros Gaisman, "occur frequently in Anglo-Saxon legal systems by the persistence of the notion of personal and perpetual alliance with the sovereign."[20] The much-expected constitutional reforms relating to nationality took effect in 1998.[21]

Citizenship at Birth

Article 30(A)(I), pertaining to *jus soli,* was not modified in 1997 and remains in the Constitution. Paragraph II, however, underwent a significant change. It now provides for nationality for "those individuals born abroad, children of Mexican parents who were born in national territory, of a Mexican father born in national territory or of a Mexican mother born in national territory." Before the reform, the text simply mentioned "those born abroad of Mexican parents, of a Mexican father or of a Mexican mother." Thus, *jus sanguinis* is now limited by the added requirement that one of the parents must have been

19. According to the reforms of 1994 (*Diario Oficial de la Federación,* I-VII, 1994).
20. Trigueros Gaisman, "Nacionalidad única," 1996, p. 96.
21. *Diario Oficial de la Federación,* del 20 de marzo de 1997.

born in national territory. That is, Mexican nationality for those born abroad is now limited to the first generation.

The 1997 reforms added a third paragraph to Article 30(A) that stipulates Mexican nationality for "those individuals born abroad to parents who are naturalized Mexicans, to a naturalized Mexican father or to a naturalized Mexican mother." Again, the principle of *jus sanguinis* is not applied beyond the first generation. That is, the children of a Mexican national who was born abroad to naturalized parents do not obtain Mexican nationality at birth, as they do not meet the requirement that at least one of their parents was born in Mexican territory.

The following hypothetical cases illustrate how Mexican nationality is conferred, according to the reforms:

—Individual born abroad to Mexican parents born in national territory. The person in this case will directly acquire Mexican nationality by virtue of having Mexican parents, but the individual may have a second nationality if the state in which he or she is born applies the principle of *jus soli* as a criterion in conferring nationality.

—Individual born abroad to a Mexican father born in national territory and a mother born in another country. Here, the child is Mexican; however, the scenario may produce double or triple nationality. If, for example, the mother has a different nationality from that which the child receives by place of birth, the potential exists for the child to acquire various nationalities: that of the father, which would be Mexican; that of the county of birth; and that of the mother, if the country of origin follows *jus sanguinis*.

—Individual born abroad to a Mexican mother born in national territory and father born in another country. As in the previous scenario, the child is Mexican and may hold two or three nationalities, depending on the law of those countries.

—An individual born abroad to naturalized Mexican parents. This individual will be a Mexican national at birth, but his or her children born outside of Mexico will not be Mexican nationals.

—Furthermore, paragraph IV of the constitutional reform, which earlier corresponded to paragraph III, establishes Mexican nationality for "those individuals born aboard Mexican ships or aircraft, be they of war or commercial craft." By extension, Mexican ships and aircraft are considered Mexican territory, and in the application of *jus soli*, nationality is conferred upon those born aboard these craft. It is not clear if paragraph II, which the requires the parents to have been born in national territory, applies to this paragraph. Likewise, the fact that Articles 27 and 42 of the Constitution do not include ships and aircraft under the rubric of "territory" leaves open the possibility that those Mexicans to which paragraph IV refers will not be considered as having been born in national territory on the terms laid out in paragraph II. This scenario, however, may not arise often, because women in their latter months of pregnancy typically do not travel by boat or plane. If the foreigners who give birth to a child aboard ship or aircraft were entitled as well to the nationality of the country of origin, of course, this hypothetical case could cause dual nationality.

—Children of foreigners who are born in territory occupied by Mexican embassies, such as asylum seekers in Mexican diplomatic missions abroad. Here, it would be logical that the children born under these circumstances would also have Mexican nationality, however, the eventuality is not mentioned at the end of Article 27, nor in Article 42.

Naturalization

The reforms also amended Article 30(B), paragraph II of which now recognizes Mexican nationality for "the woman or man who enters into marriage with a Mexican man or woman and has or establishes residence within national territory and complies with the remaining requirements on the matter as stipulated by law." The phrase "and complies with . . . " was added to the text. The two objectives in adding this phrase were to prevent the conferral of Mexican nationality by marriage alone and to avoid fraud, that is, to avoid marriage between foreigners and nationals for the mere purpose of obtaining Mexican nationality.

Forfeiture of Nationality and of Citizenship

One of the fundamental changes in the constitutional reforms referred to the forfeiture of nationality. Although there were several reasons for loss of nationality included in Article 37(A) of the prereform text, the reforms centered on the restriction contained in Article 37(A)(I) of the prereform text, which provided for loss of nationality "by voluntary acquisition of a foreign nationality." By contrast, the revised text reads: "No Mexican by birth shall be deprived of his or her nationality." (The amendment does lay out in revised Article 37(B) how *naturalized* Mexicans may lose nationality, which will be discussed below.)

The amendment for the nonforfeiture of nationality was accompanied by a provisional article that allows for its retroactive application: "This right may be exercised during a period of five years from the effective date [March 20, 1998] of this provision." This statement means that, for example, Mexicans who were deemed to have forfeited Mexican nationality by naturalizing in the United

States before March 20, 1998, will have until March 2003 to reclaim Mexican nationality.

The loss of citizenship was also addressed in the constitutional reforms in revised Article 37(C). Only the following item of six causes for loss of citizenship was amended, as follows: "I. By accepting or using titles of nobility of foreign governments." Edited out of the old text was the ending phrase "by accepting or using titles of nobility *that imply submission to a foreign government*" (emphasis added). The current provision is stricter than the previous version by clearly punishing with the loss of citizenship any acceptance or use of titles of nobility of foreign governments. Other causes for loss of citizenship may be addressed by future legislation.

The Issue of Dual Nationality

Traditionally, state doctrine and practice have considered dual nationality in negative terms. The general disfavor expressed toward this practice was illustrated by the Principle on Nationality adopted by the Institute for International Law in 1985, which reads, "no one may hold two nationalities simultaneously."[22]

Several developments in recent years have changed the tradition of Mexican nationalism. In the 1995–2000 National Development Plan, the executive branch declared a priority for constitutional and legal reforms that would permit Mexicans to retain their nationality independent of their state of residence or citizenship. Subsequently, on April 4, 1995, members of various political parties in the National Congress introduced a bill that set in motion a process that culminated in constitutional reform in 1997. A Special Pluri-partisan Commission was created to study and propose constitutional and corresponding legal reforms "to address the problem of dual nationality, as well as the citizenship of those Mexicans who reside abroad, and to update legislation on the matter."[23]

In justifying their proposal, the legislators cited the following considerations:

—A large number of Mexicans emigrate, for reasons related to the economy and economic opportunity, without losing touch with their roots, their Mexican identity, and their link to the country of origin;

22. Arellano García, 1992, p. 10. As we have seen, the constitutional reforms allow for the recognition of dual nationality. Although dual nationality was technically possible under the previous Constitution, it was treated as temporary in nature while an individual matured to the age of eighteen years. At that stage, he or she would choose a single nationality.
23. Taken from Arellano García, 1996, pp. 21–22.

—Many of these Mexicans, in order to maintain their nationality do not take the legal steps that would permit them greater expression of their social, civil, and political rights in their place of residence, even when living abroad for extended periods;

—Other Mexicans who do seek citizenship abroad even though they consider themselves Mexican encounter various barriers when carrying out their economic or family pursuits in their country of origin despite not having formally lost their nationality;

—Mexican children of Mexican parents born abroad carry dual nationality until they come of age and then must choose citizenship in one country;

—In comparing the legislation of various countries, many cases are recorded in which the possibility of dual nationality occurs without affecting basic principles of dignity and national sovereignty;

—Representatives of the different political parties of Mexico have advocated legislative reforms to ensure that Mexican nationals do not lose their nationality.[24]

This bill caused an interesting debate in Mexico with arguments both in favor and against dual nationality. Some of the major arguments in favor of dual nationality included the following:[25]

—Mexicans in the United States need protection because of an increase in xenophobia directed mainly at Mexicans;

—Despite its tainted image, dual nationality has gained worldwide acceptance over the past three decades in more than forty nations;[26]

—Dual nationality has been accepted in U.S. jurisprudence;

—Since the 1970s, Chicano groups in the United States have requested dual nationality with Mexico as a way to help themselves advance in U.S. society, while enjoying rights in Mexico, including their right to own border-front property on the Mexican side; it is estimated that some 1.2 to 2.5 million Mexicans are eligible for U.S. citizenship.

Arguments against dual nationality included the following:[27]

—U.S. law regarding naturalization requires that each person on whom citizenship is conferred must swear under oath before the court to, among other things, "absolutely, and entirely, renounce and abjure all allegiance and fidelity to any foreign prince, potentate, state or sovereign of whom or which [they]

24. Taken from Arellano García, 1996, pp. 21–22.
25. See García Moreno, 1995, pp. 193–98.
26. For example, Argentina, Costa Rica, Chile, the Dominican Republic, Ecuador, El Salvador, Guatemala, Nicaragua, Panama, Paraguay, Peru, Uruguay, France, Germany, Great Britain, Italy, Spain, and Switzerland
27. See Arellano García, 1996, p. 22.

have heretofore been a subject or citizen" and to "support and defend the Constitution, and laws, of the United States. . . ." The penalty for violation of the oath is to be charged with lying under oath or breech of solemn oath, which theoretically leaves no room for dual nationality;

—Mexicans who migrate lose their roots, their sense of Mexican identity, and their ties to the country of origin, transferring their loyalty to their new nationality;

—A large number of Mexicans in the United States either cannot qualify for or do not want U.S. citizenship;

—While Mexicans who take on other nationalities do encounter certain barriers upon return to Mexico, it is because of their foreign status, and legislation existing at the time eased this impact. Although the prereform Mexican Constitution (Article 37, A-I) declared that Mexican nationality was forfeited "by voluntary acquisition of a foreign nationality," the laws regulating its application clarified what was meant by voluntary acquisition. Article 22 of the Nationality Law of 1993 directed: "Voluntary acquisition of nationality will not be deemed to have taken place for purpose of law by virtue of simple residence or when nationality is a necessary condition for obtaining work or to maintain employment already acquired." In addition, Article 28 of the same stipulated the easy procedures for recovery of nationality once forfeited; Comparison of Mexican legislation with other countries' legislation is irrelevant;

—Naturalized U.S. citizens have no recourse under law nor the Constitution with respect to ownership of land in the border area restricted to foreigners.

Even before the 1997 reforms, however, Mexican law produced dual nationality, or at least tolerance of the phenomenon.[28] Nonetheless, the emphasis placed on the protection of Mexicans in the United States sent a strongly critical message to the United States. This criticism then became a foreign policy issue and yet one more item for discussion in the supremely complicated bilateral relationship.

A popular proposal with those who were in favor of adopting a dual nationality law was to regulate the rights of dual nationals by means of limiting their citizenship rights. This proposal was eventually adopted in the 1997 law. Dual nationality is allowed but only with limited rights. Although the Constitution gives dual nationals the right to vote, Mexicans living outside the coun-

---

28. Professor Laura Trigueros Gaisman reasons, "The renunciation of foreign nationality is made before the Mexican authorities, therefore, it becomes subject to the recognition of the foreign state; nevertheless, in U.S. naturalization proceedings, there is no stipulation that one must await the acceptance of such renunciation in order to confer nationality, which frequently results in dual nationality." See Trigueros Gaisman, "La doble nacionalidad," p. 591.

try are not entitled to participate in Mexican elections.[29] It is currently being debated whether voting outside of Mexico should be permitted, but pending legislative proposals would exclude dual nationals from voting abroad. In short, the goal of the constitutional change was to permit dual nationality, not dual citizenship.

The recognition of dual nationality as a permanent status is made clear by amendments to Article 32 of the Constitution, which authorizes legislation to regulate the legal problems that arise with dual nationality. Article 32 provides:

> The law will regulate the exercise of rights granted by Mexican legislation to those Mexicans who hold another nationality and will establish norms for the purpose of avoiding conflicts that arise because of dual nationality.
>
> Those government offices and functions for which, by the provisions of the present Constitution, the holder is required to be Mexican by birth, are reserved for those who meet this criterion and do not acquire another nationality. This restriction also will apply where stipulated in other laws legislated by the National Congress.
>
> In peacetime, no foreigner will serve in the Army, nor with the police or security forces. To join the Army in peacetime and the Navy or the Air Force at any time or to carry out any office or commission in these services, one must be Mexican by birth.
>
> It is imperative that the same requirement hold for captains, pilots, machinists, mechanics, and in general, for all personnel who serve on any ship or aircraft operating under the Mexican flag or merchant insignia. It will also be a necessary condition to fill the position of captain and all airport command and staff operations.
>
> Mexicans will be given preference over foreigners in equal circumstances for all types of concessions and for all government employment, public office, and commissions for which it is not imperative that one be a citizen.

Therefore, Article 32 provides the foundation for secondary legislation in various respects. While recognizing the possibility that an individual may hold

---

29. Some 7 million Mexican nationals are estimated to reside permanently in the United States, about one-third of whom are undocumented. See *Bi-National Study on Migration: Migration Between Mexico and the United States*, p. 7. According to the 1990 U.S. census, the main destinations of Mexican migrants are California, 45 percent; Texas, 29 percent; Illinois, 5 percent; Arizona, 5 percent; New Mexico, 2 percent; Colorado, 2 percent; Florida, 1 percent; Michigan, 1 percent; and New York, 1 percent (*Reforma*, 1998, p. 2A).

more than one nationality, the Constitution foresees the establishment of "norms to avoid conflicts that arise because of dual nationality." Significantly, under Article 32, dual nationals will be considered non-nationals and, hence, subject to the article's restrictions on military service and employment.

Article 27(I) of the Constitution restricts foreigners from acquiring direct ownership over lands and waterways within 100 kilometers from the border and 50 kilometers from the coast.[30] Unlike the restrictions of Article 32, these restrictions will not apply to dual nationals after the constitutional reforms. That is, a U.S.-Mexican may purchase land in the zone traditionally restricted to Mexican ownership. The reason for the change appears simple: foreign investment (that technically would not be foreign) can flow into these areas.

But surely this explanation gives rise to many questions: How is the reform consistent with the historical explanations for the ban on foreign ownership? Does the country run the risk of undercutting nationalism? Is national sovereignty jeopardized once again by such a provision? If there is substance to the concerns of some foreign experts that the United States has an insatiable appetite for territory and that Japan has a need to claim some territory to help propel its entry into other markets (such as the United States), then it is not so farfetched that territory would be acquired to suit foreign purposes and in such a way as to cause Mexico's loss of control over the territory. The recommended course would be to eliminate these new notions about ownership so that the original intent of the constitutional drafters in placing such restrictions may be respected.

The New Nationality Law

On March 20, 1998, the new Nationality Law went into effect. The law implements Articles 30, 32, and 37(A) and (B) of the amended Constitution of 1917.[31] The Nationality Law recognizes three types of Mexican nationality: Mexican nationality acquired by birth or by naturalization, and dual nationality.

Mexican Nationality by Birth

The Nationality Law does not define who are Mexicans by birth, as this was treated under Article 30 of the Constitution. The law refers only to certain "bonds" or obligations that devolve upon Mexicans by birth when they take on another nationality. Thus, for example, they should present themselves as na-

---

30. Mexican Constitution, Article 27 (1997).
31. Published in the *Diario Oficial de la Federación*, del 23 de enero de 1998.

tionals upon entry and exit from national territory (Nationality Law, Article 12).

In addition, Article 13 states that nationals by birth will conduct themselves as nationals with respect to the following:

> I. Legal action taken within national territory and in the areas of Mexican government jurisdiction in accordance with international law; and
>
> II. Legal action taken outside national jurisdiction, among them:
>
> a) Participation at any level in providing capital to any Mexican person of good moral standing or entity constituted or organized in conformance with Mexican law, or in the exercise of control over such persons or entities;
>
> b) Extension of credit to any person or entity referenced above;
>
> c) Holding of title to real estate located in national territory or other rights whose exercise are restricted to national territory.

The focus of this provision is to avoid a situation of diplomatic protection and to some extent is a result of the famous Calvo Clause found in the Mexican Constitution's Article 27. Relative to the actions mentioned, the Nationality Law provides for sanctions in the event of noncompliance. If anyone in this condition should invoke the protection of a foreign government, the provision directs, "the individual will forfeit for the good of the Nation any property or any rights for which he or she has invoked such protection."[32]

Despite the foresight on the part of Mexican legislators in these cases, one must remember that international law has clear rules for diplomatic protection where dual nationality applies. It is a principle of international law that a state may not legitimately attempt to extend diplomatic protection on behalf of a national against a state that also considers the same individual one of its own.

The Nationality Law also refers to the case of abandoned children and establishes the presumption that "unless proved otherwise, a foundling discovered in national territory is presumed to have been born in-country and to be the child of a Mexican father and mother."[33]

The law defines a Mexican of good moral standing in the way traditionally described in Mexican legislation: "Mexican nationals of good moral standing are those who comply with Mexican law and maintain their legal residence in national territory."[34]

32. Article 14 of the Nationality Law.
33. Article 7 of the Nationality Law.
34. Article 8 of the Nationality Law.

Mexicans by Birth Who Hold More than One Nationality

We may assume that Mexicans by birth who hold more than one nationality constitute a distinct category by the fact that the Nationality Law provides for certain restrictions on them. In principle, they may not invoke diplomatic protection under the terms described above.

Furthermore, dual nationals are not eligible for certain employment from which foreigners are barred. The Nationality Law stipulates that a public office or position may be reserved to persons who are citizens at birth and have no other nationality ("restricted employment") if such a restriction is "expressly stated in the applicable provision."[35] Dual nationals may, however, remove the bar by obtaining a Certificate of Mexican Nationality. The requirements for a certificate include renunciation of any other nationality to which he or she may be entitled (and to all foreign protection outside Mexican law and authority) and a declaration of allegiance, obedience, and submission to the law and authorities of Mexico.[36] Similarly, the authorities should demand proof of nationality before granting such employment.[37] In the event that an individual acquires another nationality in the course of discharging his or her duties in the restricted employment, the individual is expected to immediately cease his or her duties.

The Nonforfeiture of Nationality

A core objective of the constitutional reforms was to ensure the nonforfeiture of Mexican nationality for Mexicans by birth, a purpose now secured by Article 37(A).[38] These reforms, then, recognize dual nationality as a legitimate status. The decision of the Mexican government to accept dual nationality is significant and has been effected virtually without controversy.

Despite its importance, the article in the Nationality Law that refers to the recognition of the nonforfeiture of nationality appears merely as one of a number of provisional articles listed at the end of the law:

Fourth. In order to benefit from the provisions of Article 37, Part A, of the Political Constitution of the United States of Mexico, the interested party should:

---

35. Article 15 of the Nationality Law.
36. Article 17 of the Nationality Law.
37. Article 16 of the Nationality Law.
38. Article 37(A) states: "No Mexican by birth will be deprived of his or her nationality."

I. Present a written request to the Secretariat, Embassies or Consulates of Mexico, within five years beginning March 20, 1998;

II. Provide proof of Mexican nationality, as determined by this Law; and

III. Provide proof of identity to the authorities.

The Foreign Relations Secretariat estimates that between 2 and 3 million people who acquired other nationalities may recover their rights as Mexican nationals. Although dual nationality is not directed against any one country in particular, in political terms it is seen as directed primarily at the United States. The economic, political, and cultural factors related to Mexican migration to the United States surely weighed heavily in the Mexican government's decision to move to a policy of multiple nationalities.[39] Still pending is the issue of granting political rights to these Mexicans so that they may participate in Mexican elections, which will be subject to future debate.

In accordance with international law, it is the state's sovereign and irrefutable right to determine its nationals. Thus, Mexico's decision may not be contested. International law, however, also indicates that when a measure may affect a third country, that country should be consulted. In this case, however, Mexico, may not be obliged to act if a lack of reciprocity is demonstrated. In practice, for example, the United States does not take Mexico sufficiently into consideration when it legislates matters related to migration that affect the interests of Mexican migrant workers.

The boldness of the Mexican government's move on dual nationality must be acknowledged. At the same time, constructing the legal infrastructure that will make dual nationality operational and establishing boundaries against the use of dual nationality for the introduction of purely foreign interests constitute an enormous task. Where we must seek congruence, however, is in Mexico's dual position as an exporter of manpower to the United States and as a receiver of migrants in the south of the country.

Given the expectation that the nonforfeiture of nationality may give rise to conflicts, the Nationality Law stipulates specific rules for division of goods in

---

39. The director general for the Program for Mexican Communities Abroad, of the Secretariat of Foreign Relations, Rodolfo Figueroa, noted that the Hispanic community in the United States encompasses 27 million people, of whom 18 million are of Mexican origin; of those, approximately 10.5 million were born in Mexico, he reported. Of the remaining, 5 million are legal residents of the United States and 500,000 of those are naturalized in the United States. "This leaves 2.5 million undocumented, more or less." Estimates are that approximately 65 percent of the migrants return to Mexico within the first ten years, he pointed out. Figueroa noted that based on remittances and transfers registered by the Bank of Mexico, migrants send approximately U.S.$4 billion to Mexico annually. The average remittance is U.S.$225. (*Reforma*, 1998, p. 2A.)

the case of dual nationals (Article 13). These rules recognize the principle of primacy of the law of the court of jurisdiction (*ley del foro*). The opinion of Mexican foreign policy expert José Luis Siqueiros on this issue may prove useful to clarify the latter point. Siqueiros postulated that an intermediate or complementary point exists between the two traditional systems of determining nationality (*jus sanguinis, jus soli*). That midpoint, termed *jus domicili,* takes into consideration an individual's intention to remain (*animus manendi*) and has the added benefit of clarifying that an individual is subject to the law of the land in which he or she resides.[40]

Proof of Nationality

The documents necessary to prove nationality are defined in the Nationality Law and consist of the following:
—Birth certificate issued in conformance with the applicable provisions of law;
—Mexican Nationality Certificate, which will be issued by special petition, exclusively for the purposes of Articles 16 and 17 of the Nationality Law;
—Naturalization card;
—Passport; and
—Citizen identity card.

In the absence of the documents mentioned above, nationality will be proved by whatever means, in conformance with the law, convince the authorities that the requirements for attribution of Mexican nationality have been met.[41]

Mexican Nationality Certificate (CNM)

The Mexican Nationality Certificate has become an important document and, as explained above, a requirement for dual nationals who wish to obtain restricted employment. The Nationality Law defines the purpose of the Nationality Certificate, its regulation, and how it may be annulled.[42]

In order to obtain a Nationality Certificate, the applicant petitions the Foreign Relations Secretariat and must fulfill the requirements described above. With respect to annulment of the Nationality Certificate, the Nationality Law provides for the possibility that the Foreign Relations Secretariat may,

40. See Gómez-Robledo Verduzco, 1994, p. 325.
41. Article 3 of the Nationality Law.
42. Mexican Nationality Certificate: legal instrument that attests that an individual is of Mexican nationality by birth and holds no other nationality (Article 2(II) of the Nationality Law).

subject to an interview with the applicant, declare the certification null and void when it has been issued in violation of this law and procedures or when the applicant has not complied with the stipulations of the Law and procedures.

The annulment will specify the expiration date of the certificate. In all cases, third parties acting in good faith will be protected with respect to any legal action taken during the effective life of the certificate.[43]

From the text, one can see that the revocation of nationality is an administrative order of relative character: it is made valid only by the Foreign Relations Secretariat, its application is limited to the parties involved, and "third parties acting in good faith will be protected with respect to any legal action taken during the effective life of the certificate." The law does not mention a prescribed time limit but, rather, makes reference to supplementary laws. In this regard, the law provides that "for everything not foreseen in this Law, the provisions of the Civil Code for the Federal District in Ordinary Matters (*Materia Común*), for the entire Republic in Federal Matters, and provisions of the Federal Law on Administrative Procedure will be considered supplementary."[44]

The Mexican Nationality Certificate also may be revoked upon the presumption of loss of Mexican nationality.[45] Finally, the "interview with the applicant," consistent with Article 14 of the Constitution, is an important guarantee maintained under the Nationality Law.

Mexican Nationality by Naturalization

To acquire Mexican nationality by naturalization, the Nationality Law stipulated the requirements to be fulfilled by the applicant, as follows:

—Present request to the Secretariat indicating intention to acquire Mexican nationality;

—File renunciations and affirmations previously noted when processing the Mexican Nationality Certificate. The Secretariat will not require these affidavits to be filed until it has made a determination to grant nationality to the applicant. The naturalization card will be issued once the affidavits have been verified;

—Prove that one can speak Spanish, knows the history of the country, and is integrated into national culture; and

43. Article 18 of the Nationality Law.
44. Article 11 of the Nationality Law.
45. Article 32 of the Nationality Law.

—Provide proof of residence in national territory for the term established under Article 20 of this Law.[46]

With respect to residency, the law provides for four different cases of naturalization, as follows:[47]

Five years of residence is required under the following circumstance:

The foreigner who intends to naturalize as a Mexican must provide documentation that he or she has resided in national territory at least during the five years immediately preceding the date of application.

Two years residence is required immediately preceding the date of application when the applicant:

—is a direct descendant of a Mexican by birth;

—has Mexican children by birth;

—is from a country in Latin American or Iberian Peninsula; or

—at the discretion of the Secretariat, has provided service or achieved outstanding work of a cultural, social, scientific, technical, artistic, sport or business nature that benefits the Nation.

A foreign man or woman who marries a Mexican man or woman must present proof that they maintained a residence and lived together as husband and wife in that residence in national territory. It is not necessary for the residence to be in national territory if the Mexican couple travel abroad under orders or commission of the Mexican Government.

In the case of marriage between foreigners, the acquisition of Mexican nationality on the part of one of the parties after the marriage will enable the other party to obtain nationality, as long as he or she fulfills the requirements set out in this section.

The previous law resulted in disputes because of the lack of clarity about when nationality is acquired, whether automatically upon marriage or at the time the Mexican Nationality Certificate is issued. The latest reforms make it clear that nationality is acquired upon issuance of the Nationality Certificate.[48] The law also makes clear that those who acquire Mexican nationality in this

46. Article 19 of the Nationality Law.
47. Article 20 of the Nationality Law.
48. See Hernández Trillo, 1992, pp. 15–16.

way will preserve it even after the dissolution of the marriage, except in cases of annulment of the marriage attributed to the naturalized party.[49]

The Nationality Law provides for additional scenarios. First, *one year's residence*, immediately prior to the application, is required in the case of adoption, as well as of minors to the second generation, subject to Mexican parental authority. In the event that parents have not sought the naturalization of adopted children or minors, they themselves may do so within one year of their coming of age.

In cases in which parents have not sought naturalization for their children, residency must be uninterrupted.[50] In general, it should be noted that "temporary absences from the country will not interrupt residency, except when absence occurs within two years of presentation of the request and when it exceeds six months in total."[51]

Second, *no residence requirement* need be met to confer nationality in special circumstances. These circumstances refer to the discretionary and exceptional powers of the executive—as when in the judgment of the executive, the foreigner "has provided services or has achieved outstanding work of a cultural, social, scientific, technical, artistic, sport or business nature that benefits the Nation." In such cases, the residency requirement is waived.[52]

Naturalization Card

The Nationality Law provides the following rules with respect to the Naturalization Card, which is defined as the "legal instrument by which to prove that Mexican nationality has been conferred on a foreigner."[53] The Naturalization Card becomes effective on the day of issuance.

In general terms, the Nationality Law refers to suspension for cause and to revocation of the Naturalization Card. The procedure for obtaining the Naturalization Card is suspended when a formal arrest warrant is issued for the applicant or when he or she is taken into custody in Mexico, or its equivalents abroad.[54]

The Nationality Law stipulates that the Naturalization Card will not be issued under the following conditions:

49. Article 22 of the Nationality Law.
50. Article 20 of the Nationality Law.
51. Article 21 of the Nationality Law.
52. Article 20(I)(D) of the Nationality Law.
53. Article 2(II) of the Nationality Law.
54. Article 24 of the Nationality Law.

—Applicant is in non-compliance with the requirements of the Nationality Law;

—Applicant is completing a prison term for a serious crime in Mexico or abroad; and

—When, in the judgment of the Foreign Relations Secretariat, it is inconvenient to issue the Naturalization Card, in which case it must provide a reason for its decision.[55]

With respect to the revocation of the card,

> the Foreign Relations Secretariat will take action in the event that the card was issued fraudulently or without fulfilling the stipulated requirements. In all cases, third parties acting in good faith will be protected with respect to any legal action taken during the effective life of the certificate.[56]

The Forfeiture of Mexican Nationality by Naturalization

In reference to the forfeiture of Mexican nationality *acquired by naturalization*, the Nationality Law defers to the causes listed in Article 37(B), as amended.[57] Thus, subject to an interview with the applicant, a naturalized Mexican may lose nationality for the following reasons:

> I. By voluntary acquisition of a foreign nationality, by presenting oneself as a foreigner in a public transaction, by use of a foreign passport, by accepting or using titles of nobility that imply submission to a foreign State.[58]
>
> II. By residing five continuous years abroad.

The constitutional reform guarantees nationality only to Mexicans by birth. With this change, only Mexicans by birth, not by naturalization, have the possibility of dual nationality. To be clear, Mexicans by naturalization are prohibited from holding dual nationality. Upon taking Mexican nationality, naturalized Mexicans must renounce any other nationality they hold and, furthermore,

---

55. Article 25 of the Nationality Law.
56. Article 26 of the Nationality Law.
57. Article 27 of the Nationality Law.
58. With regard to determining when another nationality has been acquired, the circumstances are most important, according to the Nationality Law. Except when proven otherwise, it is presumed that a Mexican has taken on a foreign nationality when he or she has taken some legal action to obtain or preserve it or if he or she presents himself or herself as a foreigner to any authority or in any public document (Article 6 of the Nationality Law).

should they acquire another nationality at any point after taking Mexican nationality, they lose Mexican nationality. The same condition holds should they present themselves with a foreign passport or if they were to use a title of nobility that implied submission to a foreign state.

By residing for five continuous years outside the country, a naturalized Mexican risks being left without any nationality. In some instances, excused absence from the country may be the result of family, work, or other affairs but may not include acquiring another nationality. While one may become estranged from the country by prolonged absences, it does not necessarily mean that a naturalized Mexican has expressed his or her intent to establish links to another state. The following hypothetical example may be far from unique. A British citizen marries a Mexican student in Spain. The couple establish residence in Mexico and Mexican nationality is conferred upon the wife. The husband then accepts an important position in Spain that keeps them away more than five years. The result is that the wife of British origin and Mexican nationality by naturalization loses Mexican nationality with no intention of doing so.

Who takes action to demand the forfeiture of nationality by naturalization? In these cases, the federal government and other authorities are obliged to inform the Foreign Relations Secretariat when they discover that an individual falls into one of the categories mentioned above, which are listed in Article 37(B) of the Constitution. The Nationality Law stipulates that such notice must be given to the Secretariat within forty working days of the date on which an individual is suspected of violating the terms.[59]

Furthermore, the forfeiture of nationality by naturalization affects exclusively the individual on whom the charge falls.[60] In all cases of forfeiture of Mexican nationality by naturalization, the Foreign Relations Secretariat is obliged to seek the opinion of the Interior Secretariat before taking action.[61] Finally, when notice of the supposed violation of Mexican nationality is given, the process to revoke the Mexican Nationality Certificate commences. In the event of violation of the Nationality Laws, fines determined on a sliding scale may be imposed by the Foreign Relations Secretariat,[62] with discretionary authority.[63]

---

59. Article 28 of the Nationality Law.
60. Article 29 of the Nationality Law.
61. Article 31 of the Nationality Law.
62. The highest fine category ranges from 500 to 2,000 times the minimum salary "for those who marry with the sole intention of obtaining Mexican nationality" (Article 33-III of the Nationality Law).
63. Article 37 of the Nationality Law. In deciding to impose fines, the Secretariat must take into consideration the seriousness of the violation, damages, and injury caused, as well as the personal background and socioeconomic situation of the violator.

Adoption and Nationality

Adoption does not confer nor forfeit nationality for the child nor adopted parent. We must remember, however, that adopted children are in a privileged situation with respect to time, as they require only one year of residency in the country to acquire nationality, without prejudice as to the provision of Article 20, Section III, of the Nationality Law.[64]

Modifications to Other Provisions for the Purpose of Nonforfeiture of Nationality

With the constitutional reforms and the possibility for Mexicans to hold more than one nationality, additional reforms were carried out on a series of laws that restrict dual nationals from occupying various positions, the "restricted employment" laws.[65] Although some fifty-five regulations were identified,[66] only thirty-one laws were actually modified. The focus of the reforms was to carve out certain services, occupations, and employment prohibited to dual nationals and, of course, to foreigners.[67]

The creation of restrictions on dual nationals relates to the Mexican government's national security concerns with respect to protecting the armed forces, upholding justice, preserving political and labor rights, and so on. Given the logic for limiting dual nationals' access to restricted employment, the actual list of restricted jobs is short. To give one example, the Federal Law for Protection of the Consumer is omitted, in which Article 51 requires that the federal prose-

---

64. Article 30 of the Nationality Law.

65. *Diario Oficial de la Federación,* del 23 de enero de 1995.

66. García Moreno, 1995, p. 198.

67. In accordance with this package of reforms, the following laws were modified: Mexican Foreign Service Law, Regulation of the Mexican Army and Air Force (*Ley Orgánica*), Regulation of the Mexican Navy, Code of Military Justice, Military Service Law, Regulation of the Federal Judiciary, Regulation of the Federal Fiscal Tribunal, Law for the Treatment of Juvenile Defenders in the Federal District on Common Matters (*Materia Común*) and for the entire Republic on Federal Matters, Regulation of the Procuraduría General (Justice Department) of the Republic, Regulation of the Federal District Attorney's Office, Federal Code on Electoral Institutions and Procedures, Navigation Law, Civil Aviation Law, Federal Labor Law, Social Security Law, Law on the Institute for Social Security and Services for State Workers, Law on the Institute for Social Security of the Mexican Armed Forces, Federal Law on Non-governmental Entities, Regulation of Constitutional Article 27 Pertaining to Nuclear Matters, Law on the National Commission for Human Rights, Federal Brokerage Law, Regulation of the National Institution of Anthropology and History, Foreign Investment Law, General Law that Establishes the Bases for Coordination of the National Security System, Energy Regulatory Commission Law, Retirement Savings Systems Law, Constitution of Agrarian Tribunals, Bank of Mexico Law, Federal Law on Economic Competition, Federal Law on Public Service Workers—Regulation of Part 15 of Constitutional Article 123, and Law on the National Banking and Investment Commission.

cutor be a Mexican by birth. Thus, a dual national could theoretically assume this post.

These reforms do not address the problem of extradition. It remains unclear how the principle of nonextradition of nationals should apply to a suspect who holds more than one nationality. This extradition problem may be resolved by the principle of effective nationality.[68]

Conclusions

First, at this time, the concept of nationality in Mexico is being revisited. Various issues such as the reappraisal of the nationality of indigenous peoples and the decision to permit dual nationality have played a very important role in this reassessment.

Second, with respect to nationality, Mexico has maintained a policy of basic protection of its nationals. The result has left Mexico in a contradictory situation. On the one hand, Mexico protects and promotes the rights of its nationals in the international arena. On the other hand, it neglects the protection of those from countries to the south, who travel to Mexico in the hope of finding work in the United States just like Mexicans.[69]

Third, some observers express fear that the spread of dual nationality will undermine national culture, but Mexican national culture is strong. Because of this strength, Mexico should be more open to the outside world, working from the standpoint of equals. Mexican nationalism, as it has been traditionally handled, has a provincial character that is not appropriate in these days of economic opening and globalization.

Fourth, another concern is that Mexico cannot protect its Mexican nationals when they obtain U.S. nationality. International common law prohibits a first country from carrying out protection activities against a second country of which an individual is also a national. Thus, a certain sector of the Mexican-born population in the United States will remain outside the reach of the current reforms.

Fifth, one of the most interesting political implications of dual nationality with respect to the U.S.-Mexico relationship is the attraction Mexicans feel toward their roots in Mexico and their rejection of a policy based on "the melting pot." This phenomenon provides Mexico an important element for negotiation. Mexico needs to be prepared and clear about what it wants in its dealings with

---

68. Spain has taken this stance in its dual nationality policy. See Rodríguez Mateos, 1990, p. 477.

69. Aguayo Quezada, 1992, p. 39.

the United States. Mexico should, for example, work toward enhancing real respect and protection for the rights of Mexicans in the United States and toward commencing negotiation on an agreement regarding migrant workers.

Sixth, in general, dual nationality can be a controversial subject. But it should be noted that Mexico for the first time has taken the initiative in this matter and that making dual nationality operational may require negotiation with its northern neighbor.

References

Aguayo Quezada, Sergio. 1992. "Política Migratoria y Seguridad Nacional" (Migration policy and national security). In *Memoria del Simposio, Extranjeros y Derechos Humanos Según su Calidad y Característica Migratoria* (Report of the symposium on foreigners and human rights, depending on their category and migration characteristics). México: Comisión Nacional de Derechos Humanos.

Arellano García, Carlos. 1996. "Migración y doble nacionalidad, algunas implicaciones" (Migration and dual nationality: some implications). *Estudios Parlamentarios del Congreso,* año 2, número 3, primera época (mayo-junio).

Arellano García, Carlos. 1992. "La doble nacionalidad: situación en México y perspectivas" (Dual nationality: situation and perspectives in Mexico). Unpublished, Instituto de Investigaciones Jurídicas-UNAM, México, Agosto.

Bi-National Study on Migration: Migration Between Mexico and the United States. Washington, D.C., and Mexico City: U.S. Commission on Immigration Reform and Secretaría de Relaciones Exteriores.

Cabaleiro, Ezequiel. 1962. *La doble nacionalidad* (Dual nationality). Madrid: Instituto Editorial Reus.

Diario de Debates. 1985. Tomo II. México: Instituto Mexicano de Estudios Históricos de la Revolución Mexicana.

Diario Oficial de la Federación, del 23 de enero de 1998.

Diario Oficial de la Federación, del 20 de marzo de 1997.

Diario Oficial de la Federación, del 23 de enero de 1995.

Diario Oficial de la Federación, I–VII, 1994.

Diario Oficial de la Federación, del 31 de diciembre de 1974.

Diario Oficial de la Federación, del 26 de diciembre de 1969.

Diario Oficial de la Federación, del 18 de enero de 1934.

García Moreno, Victor Carlos. 1995. "La propuesta de reforma legislativa sobre doble nacionalidad" (The legislative reform proposal on dual nationality). *Revista de Derecho Privado,* año 6, número 18 (septiembre-diciembre).

Gómez-Robledo Verduzco, Alonso. 1994. "Derecho Internacional y Nueva Ley de Nacionalidad Mexicana" (International law and the new law of mexican nationality). *Boletin Mexicano de Derecho Copmarado,* UNAM, Mexico City, nueva serie, ano XXVII, no. 80 (Mayo-Agosto), p. 321.

Gutiérrez Baylón, Juan de Dios. 1996. "El artículo 33 constitucional y los elementos de generación de un estoppel en contra del gobierno norteaméricano" (Article 33 of the constitution and the creation of an etoppel against the U.S. government). *Lex*, año II, no. 8 (febrero).

Hernández Trillo, Luis. 1992. "Efectos jurídicos de la naturalización de los extranjeros casados con mexicanos" (Legal implications in the naturalization of foreigners married to Mexicans). In *Memoria del Simposio, Extranjeros y Derechos Humanos Según su Calidad y Característica Migratoria* (Report of the symposium on foreigners and human rights, depending on their category and migration characteristics). México: Comisión Nacional de Derechos Humanos.

Lomnitz, Claudio. 1993. "Hasta una antropología de la nacionalidad mexicana" (Toward an anthropology of Mexican nationality). *Revista Mexicana de Sociología*, número 2.

Mancilla y Mejia, María Elena. 1998. "Algunos aspectos de la nacionalidad" (Some aspects of nationality). *Lex, Difusión y Análisis*, 3a época, año IV, número 32 (Febrero).

Montero Solana, Gerardo. 1992. "La Facultad discrecional en material migratoria" (Discretionary power in migration matters). In *Memoria del Simposio, Extranjeros y Derechos Humanos Según su Calidad y Característica Migratoria* (Report of the symposium on foreigners and human rights, depending on their category and migration characteristics). México: Comisión Nacional de Derechos Humanos.

Reforma. (30 de marzo de 1998), p. 2A.

Rodríguez Mateos, Pilar. 1990. *Revista Española de Derecho International*, no. 2 (julio-dic).

Trigueros Gaisman, Laura. 1996. "Nacionalidad única y doble nacionalidad" (Single nationality and double nationality). *Alegatos*, Mexico City, numero 32 (Enero-Abril), p. 89.

Trigueros Gaisman, Laura. 1996. "La doble nacionalidad en el derecho mexicano" (Dual nationality in Mexican law). *Jurídica*, Anuario de Derecho de la Universidad Iberoamericana, número 26.

Vallarta, Ignacio L. 1986. *La propiedad inmueble por extranjeros* (Real estate ownership by foreigners). México: Secretaría de Relaciones Exteriores.

CHAPTER ELEVEN

Citizenship in the
European Union

MARCO MARTINIELLO

THE PAST DECADE has witnessed a return of the citizen and of citizenship both in academic and in political discourse.[1] The number of research projects, books, journals, conferences, and articles dealing with citizenship issues has also increased dramatically. The words *citizenship* and *citizen* are used in a growing number of different areas and social contexts. Whereas these words were traditionally linked exclusively to human beings, now discussions about citizenship extend to plants, animals, and corporations. In many ways, the concept of citizenship has become a political slogan.

But despite a renewed, extensive academic interest in citizenship issues, a comprehensive theory of citizenship broadly accepted by the academic community is still absent. Some scholars stress the formal dimension of citizenship, namely the juridical link between the individual and state. Others reduce it to a set of rights enjoyed by the individual by virtue of her or his belonging to a national community. Others find it more useful to study the participatory dimensions of citizenship in order to explore new forms of political mobilization and social movements in contemporary societies. Exchanges between these scholars, who often seem to be interested in quite different phenomena and processes, are afflicted with chronic misunderstandings. Dialogue between academics and policy makers or politicians is often even more problematic.

---

1. This report is largely based on my previous published and unpublished work on EU citizenship, which I have revised, updated, and corrected as necessary.

At least three features characterize current debates on citizenship issues. First, these discussions often become entangled with other diverse academic and political topics, such as the debates on international migration, the management and the impact of cultural diversity, and the place of the nation-state in the post–cold war era. Second, although liberal approaches to all these issues seem to predominate among academic scholars, the general public has proved sympathetic to illiberal views on ethnicity, nationalism, citizenship, and multiculturalism. These views increasingly find a channel of expression in extreme right-wing and conservative politics, such as the Vlaams Blok in Belgium and the Front National in France.[2] The gap between academic liberalism and a growing illiberalism among the general public is an important context for understanding the scope and meaning of citizenship in general, European Union (EU) citizenship in particular. Third, the confusion that has infused debates over citizenship is often rooted in the difficulty of distinguishing between normative concerns one the one hand and explanatory concerns on the other hand. Moreover, considerations fundamentally intended to answer the question "what ought to be?" are presented as mere analyses of the situation and vice versa.

These same difficulties plague the more specific debates on EU citizenship, in which both theoretical and political disputes abound. The issue of EU citizenship is closely linked to the issues of migration, cultural diversity, and the future of the nation-state in the old continent. The European Union is home to a wide variety of ethnocultural and national affiliations and identities. This diversity is not going to disappear under the pressure of globalization. Rather, Europeans have entered a process that will only magnify European diversity. The enlargement of the EU has and will increase the sheer range of national identities available within a common framework. Moreover, in several member states, such as Spain, France, Belgium, Italy, the United Kingdom, and so on, subnational mobilization promotes ethnoregional identities and group claims to recognition as national minorities. Along with these two sources is the reality of migration. Europe will continue to be a continent of immigration. Migrants come from all over the world following new patterns of migration. Some of them settle and adapt culturally while simultaneously enriching the local culture and the variety of ethnocultural identities. The European Union is highly diversified both in terms of ethnonational identities and in broader cultural terms. The myth of monoculture that is often invoked to justify exclusionary policies does not fit the sociological reality of any society. The European Union

2. See, for example, "Racism and Xenophobia," 1997.

will continue to be de facto a multicultural society, a culturally diversified society in which many collective identities coexist.

Despite the huge misunderstandings within the academic world over issues linked to EU citizenship and multiculturalism, many scholars seem to share a common starting point. They all acknowledge that in the current world, ideas of ethnocultural homogeneity, "natural" or created, do not mirror the actual sociological composition of the population, which is diverse. The traditional sequence *ethnies*–nations–citizenry–nation-state has seriously been challenged by international migration, European integration, and globalization. Therefore, crucial questions arise: How does the European Union deal with its de facto multicultural, multireligious, multiethnic, growing character while simultaneously reasserting its democratic exigencies and dealing with growing social and economic inequality and exclusion? In other words, how does it raise the question of a multicultural citizenship of the European Union?

The concept of EU citizenship has certainly entered into a process of change and development, but to predict how and in which direction it is going to evolve is fraught with uncertainties.[3] Could it develop by analogy with the U.S. federal citizenship?[4] Could it replicate the multidimensional Commonwealth citizenship? What are the prospects for a new imperial model of citizenship in Europe?[5] Should EU citizenship be entirely new? Can we imagine a multicultural model of citizenship for the European Union?[6] These questions are and will be very difficult to answer, and it is essential to underline that any thought about EU citizenship still remains largely prospective.

The aim of the present report is primarily to explicate the meaning and scope of the existing EU citizenship. It contains seven sections. The first section presents a definition of citizenship. The second section defines citizenship of the European Union and presents its development. The third section presents a critical view of EU citizenship in its current form. The two following sections deal with the implementation of EU citizenship and the use EU citizens make of EU citizenship rights. The sixth section examines the impact of the introduction of EU citizenship on the structure of citizenship in the European Union. The seventh and conclusive section deals with the further development of EU citizenship by distinguishing a top-down approach and a bottom-up approach. It also presents some general considerations on the project of a multicultural citizenship of the European Union.

3. Turner, 1990; Meehan, 1993.
4. Closa, 1992.
5. Leca, 1992.
6. Castles and Miller, 1993.

Defining Citizenship

As pointed out above, no general agreement has been reached on the definition of citizenship, let alone on its meaning and scope. Conceptions of citizenship vary according to the academic discipline but also according to the school of thought within the various academic disciplines. Furthermore, language is often an obstacle to mutual understanding. The English word *citizenship*, for example, can be translated in French as *citoyenneté* but also as *nationalité*. The distinction between *nationalité* and *citoyenneté* covers approximately the distinction between formal citizenship and substantive citizenship. The former refers to a formal link between an individual and a state, to the individual belonging to a nation-state, which is juridically sanctioned by the possession of an identity card or passport of that state. The latter refers to the bundle of civil, political, social, and also cultural rights enjoyed by an individual, traditionally by virtue of her or his belonging to the national community. It also refers to the participation of the individual in the management of the public affairs of a given national and political community. These realities are clearly linked, but they need to be distinguished just as clearly.

In order to clarify the terms for this study, it is useful to adopt a starting definition of citizenship. Three main features characterize modern citizenship.[7] First, citizenship is a juridical status granting civil, political, and social rights and duties to the individual members of a political entity, traditionally a state. Second, citizenship refers to a set of specific social roles (voter, activist, and so on) performed by citizens and through which they express choices with regard to the management of public affairs and, hence, participate in government. Citizenship thus implies some sort of access to the political system. Citizens have the ability to use their status in order to defend their interests in the political arena. Third, citizenship also refers to a set of moral qualities thought to be crucial for the existence of the good citizen. These qualities are often referred to as the expression of civic virtue. The recognition of the existence and primacy of a public interest transcending private ones is a crucial aspect of civic virtue.

Citizenship historically developed within the framework of state building. In an ideal world, the political and cultural boundaries of a people would neatly correspond with divisions drawn between independent political units, and all the members of a nation would share the same status as citizens. In the contemporary world, international migration, the issue of national and cultural minorities, and the emergence of supranational constructions like the European Union have revealed that political boundaries and cultural boundaries very rarely co-

7. Leca, 1991.

incide. Questions then arise: Is the traditional conception of citizenship still adaptable to recent social and political developments worldwide? How should EU citizenship be understood as a form of membership? What does it mean to be a citizen of the European Union since it is not a state? To answer these questions, the content and history of EU citizenship must first be explored.

Defining Citizenship of the European Union

Historically, the European integration process was the exclusive province of small bureaucratic and political elites who were in charge both of the European decision-making process and of the dissemination of knowledge about European integration. The citizens of the member states did not evince a deep interest in the integration process, and they were rarely consulted by the European elites.

The first serious attempt to involve the citizens of the member states in the European integration process and to flesh out the idea of a Citizens' Europe dates back to the summit of the heads of states or governments in 1974.[8] This attempt occurred soon after the report on European identity of 1973 and in parallel with the Tindemans report on the European Union. But it was only at the end of the 1980s and in the early 1990s that the issue of citizenship of the European Union (hereafter, EU citizenship) became salient, especially when work toward the Maastricht Treaty was initiated in 1991.

In 1992, the year before the official completion of the European internal market, various themes related to the European integration process, and especially the Treaty on the European Union, were given widespread public attention. The important newspapers and journals in most member states periodically provided space for critical discussion of integration issues by leading intellectual figures. This discussion stimulated a public debate on the construction of Europe. Maurice Duverger and Edgard Morin, for example, wrote often on different aspects of this topic in the prestigious French daily *Le Monde*. The pace and course of the European integration process became a major topic of public discourse in several member states.[9] This press and public interest started to decline after the French referendum on the Maastricht Treaty. The year 1993 was characterized by a worrying public silence on Europe's future, which expressed a growing *europessimism*. Again, experts within the European institutions tended to claim a monopoly of the knowledge about the European

---

8. As in the literature and in official documents, in this article I use two expressions that, in my view, cover the same meaning: "Citizen's Europe" and "Citizens' Europe."

9. Wolton, 1993.

integration process by using a kind of juridical and economical technocratic jargon that was opaque to the majority of the citizens of the member states. In the view of the internal European experts, nobody outside the European institutions was better suited than they to understand the process of European integration and to lead it.

Despite many difficulties, the Treaty on the European Union was ratified and entered into force on November 1, 1993. According to several observers, the Maastricht Treaty buried the old technocratic, economic, and elitist Europe and opened the way for a new political Europe in which the citizens would play a central part. In other words, the Treaty on the European Union was supposed to mark a complete change of nature of the integration process.[10] The issue of whether the treaty signified this magnitude of change is complex and contested, and cannot be discussed here. But in terms of EU citizenship, it is indisputable that the Maastricht Treaty, for the first time in the history of European integration, gave some juridical basis to that notion.

The Maastricht Treaty

The Maastricht Treaty set out certain basic elements of European Union citizenship, but one confined exclusively to the nationals of one of the member states of the European Union.[11] Under this treaty, Union citizenship consists of the following set of rights: the rights of freedom of movement and residence on the territory of the member states,[12] the right to vote and to be elected in the local elections and in the elections of the European Parliament in the member state of residence,[13] the right to diplomatic protection in a third country,[14] and the right to petition the European Parliament as well as the possibility to appeal to a European ombudsman.[15] The question of EU citizenship of the Union is also dealt with elsewhere in the treaty,[16] but in a more indirect way.

It should be underlined that the concept "citizenship of the European Union" and the expression "Citizens' Europe" do not cover the same realities. The former deals predominantly with civil and political rights, leaving aside social and economic rights. The latter included the free movement of persons as well as

10. Wolton, 1993; Cloos, Reinesch, Vignes, and Weyland, 1993.
11. Title II, Part 2, Articles 8, 8A, 8B, 8C, 8D, 8E.
12. Article 8A.
13. Article 8B.
14. Article 8C.
15. Article 8D.
16. Title II, Part 3, Articles 138A, D, E, and Article 157; Title VI, Article K1; Final Act of the Maastricht Conference, Declaration no. 2.

"special" political rights for the European citizens. But it also adopted a broad conception of the well-being of the individual by stressing the importance of culture, communication, public health, and the protection of privacy.[17]

In legal terms, EU citizenship undoubtedly constitutes only a minimal advance that could perhaps be developed in the future.[18] Article 8E of the Maastricht Treaty mentions the possibility of extension of EU citizenship but it says nothing more on this point, leaving the future open. The extension of EU citizenship is certainly not seen as a legal obligation but as a mere possibility.

The Amsterdam Treaty

Before and during the Intergovernmental Conference (IGC) that started in 1996 and led to the adoption of the Amsterdam Treaty in June 1997, several voices called for a revision and an extension of EU citizenship. The opportunity for the revision of the Maastricht Treaty opened the door to go further in terms of EU citizenship. As to the introduction of new citizenship rights, many proposals were made either by experts or by institutions like the European Parliament and the Migrants Forum. The European Parliament proposed that the Union should sign the Council of Europe Convention on Human Rights and Fundamental Freedoms. It also advocated the inclusion in a new version of the treaty of a clear reference to equality of treatment for all individuals independent of their race, gender, age, or religion.

The European Parliament also recommended grouping all citizenship rights in one single chapter of the treaty. In its view, the political aspects of citizenship should be deepened by stimulating the formation of European political parties. It called for stronger provisions to protect the equality for women and the rights of minorities.[19] Independent experts, on their part, proposed several new rights to be included in the treaty, such as a European right to association. Other proposals supported the extension of the EU citizenship to non-nationals of member states based on the criterion of residence. The Economic and Social Committee and the Migrants Forum advocated such an evolution. The Italian Socialist member of the European Parliament, Renzo Imbeni, advocated a similar step in his report on citizenship of the European Union. In his view, the IGC should have modified Article 8 in order to in-

---

17. Cloos, Reinesch, Vignes, and Weyland, 1993, p. 163.
18. Mira, 1991, p. 169.
19. European Parliament, 1995, PE 190.441/1; European Parliament, 1996, *Agence Europe*, no. 1982.

clude, under specific conditions, residents who are not nationals of one of the member states.[20] In her report on the status of third-country citizens in the European Union, the French ecologist and former member of the European Parliament Djida Tazdait advocated the granting of voting rights at the local level to third-country citizens on the basis of a period of five years of legal residence in the European Union.[21] Considering the fact that both the Economic and Social Committee and the Migrants Forum were not powerful enough to impose their views and that both the Imbeni report and the Tazdait report were rejected at the January 1994 plenary session of the European Parliament[22] for, among other reasons, "going too far," it was clear that no radical changes could be expected in terms of EU citizenship.

In a way, the last hopes for treaty revision vanished in December 1995 when the *groupe de réflexion* formed to prepare the IGC for the release of its report. It became clear that the IGC would, at most, clarify the foundations of EU citizenship rather than expand the rights associated with it. The governing idea behind the treaty was to stipulate more precisely the rights and duties of both EU citizens and third-state citizens residing in the EU as well as to enhance nondiscrimination and fundamental rights. For the pessimists, the risk that nothing would be done at all and that EU citizenship would not even be on the agenda of the IGC was real. Eventually, the worst fears were not realized and the theme of citizenship was finally included in the list of issues to be discussed during the IGC.

The end result reached in Amsterdam followed the line presented as early as December 1995. Three changes are worth mentioning, although none of them is radical in terms of either deepening or extending EU citizenship. These changes include amendments to Article 8, the adoption of an antidiscrimination clause in the Amsterdam Treaty, and the adoption of articles intended to better protect human rights and fundamental liberties.

A sentence stating that EU citizenship supplements national citizenship and does not replace it is added to Article 8.1. Clearly, this addition reinforces the approach of the Treaty of Maastricht, according to which EU citizenship is derived from national citizenship of one of the member states. Consequently, this change closes the door for now to the conferral of EU citizenship to third-country nationals residing on the territory of the EU. It reemphasizes the legal dis-

20. *Agence Europe*, no. 6150, January 17 and 18, 1994, p. 4.
21. *Agence Europe*, no. 6141, January 5, 1994, p. 11.
22. *Agence Europe*, no. 6152, January 20, 1994, pp. 4–5; *Agence Europe*, no. 6153, January 21, 1994, p. 11; Migration News Sheet, no. 131/94-02, pp. 8–9.

tinction between EU citizens and non-EU citizens, which can only impair the status of the latter. In this sense, the change can be interpreted as a setback because it emphasizes the link between EU citizenship and national citizenship, between citizenship and nationality—whereas EU citizenship has often been presented as an attempt to break this link. Possession of national citizenship of one of the member states remains the foremost condition for acquisition of EU citizenship.

Furthermore, a third paragraph is added to Article 8D. It states that EU citizens can write to any EU institution in the European language of their choice and get a reply in that same language. This provision is undoubtedly a step toward more transparency and nondiscrimination, but its scope remains quite limited. For the remainder, Article 8 of the Maastricht Treaty is left untouched in the new Amsterdam Treaty, which has caused a huge disappointment among antidiscrimination and pro-immigrant activists throughout Europe who had not abandoned their hopes earlier.

A more positive aspect is the introduction of an antidiscrimination clause in the Treaty of Amsterdam that could potentially strengthen EU citizenship. Article 6A of the treaty states that the council can adopt adequate measures to combat discrimination based on gender, race, ethnic origin, religion, age, sexual preference, and handicap. This new article constitutes progress because for the first time the principle of nondiscrimination is given a legal ground on which political and legal action can be based for both EU and non-EU citizens. It could, however, have gone further to include nationality in the list of discriminatory criteria. At present, discrimination based on nationality remains covered by the old Article 6. In practice, the implementation of Article 6A will depend on the emergence of considerable political will at the EU level. Any decision to implement a new measure to combat discrimination as defined in Article 6A requires unanimity among member states. This requirement will be difficult to meet.

Finally, fundamental human rights are slightly reinforced through the introduction of paragraph 1 in Article F of the Treaty on the European Union. It states that the European Union is grounded on the principles of democracy, freedom, and the respect of human rights and fundamental liberties. In other words, all member states are committed to respect these principles. In case of nonrespect by one of the member states, it may temporarily lose its voting right.

Clearly, despite some progress, the opportunity for the IGC to develop EU citizenship was largely missed. The Amsterdam Treaty confirms to a large extent the philosophy of the Maastricht Treaty as far as EU citizenship is concerned.

A Critical View of EU Citizenship

As discussed above, drawing a clear-cut distinction between analytical and normative accounts of citizenship in general is often very difficult. This observation is certainly relevant in the specific case of EU citizenship. Increasingly, an orthodox approach to EU citizenship has developed that reflects more a normative standpoint than a detached, analytical one. According to this standard approach, the introduction of EU citizenship marks a dramatic change in the process of European integration that would transcend the EU's economic underpinnings to transform it into a substantive political body in which citizenship would become a major priority. This approach also assumed that EU citizenship opens the way to a new form of postnational membership in which citizenship rights and nationality would be dissociated. Furthermore, this approach believed that the participation of the citizens would be crucial in the new phase of the European integration process. By this view, the construction of the European Union would cease to be a top-down process. It would become a bottom-up process based on active citizenship. Let us examine these three assumptions in a critical manner in order to get a more precise understanding of the meaning and scope of EU citizenship.

A Major Concern in the European Integration Process?

Since its inception, work toward a more united Europe has mainly been an economic project, as shown by the creation of the European Economic Community in Rome in 1958. The cultural, political, and social aspects of European integration have for a long time been neglected. The permanent primacy of the economic and monetary dimensions over all other dimensions in the process of European integration was again highlighted during the Maastricht Summit of 1991. At that time, the most significant results were reached in the field of the economic and monetary Union, and not in the field of a political Union. Despite the fact that the Maastricht Treaty deals with a move from the European Economic Community toward a broader European Union, the priority is, as in the past, to complete as soon as possible the internal market and to assure the conditions of its efficiency. The other dimensions, that is, the cultural, social, and political aspects, are still mainly conceived as supporting measures intended to facilitate the realization of the central economic and monetary goals.

The title of a report on social Europe published in 1988 by the interservice group of the European Commission offers a good example of the permanent subordination of noneconomic dimensions to economic ones in the process of

European integration: *The Social Dimension of the Internal Market*.[23] Further-more, the question of an EU citizenship was only briefly mentioned at the Edin-burgh Summit of December 1992 through a discussion on Article 8A concerning the free movement of people. This focus on the economic aspects has for a long time been the only dimension of EU citizenship that regularly re-ceived attention in broader debates over immigration controls and policy. The prevalence of economic and monetary dimensions over social, cultural, and po-litical aspects of European integration reflects both in the Intergovernmental Conference of 1996–1997 and in the Amsterdam Treaty to which it led in June 1997.

Therefore, EU citizenship for itself, which is part of the political Union, does not seem to be a major concern of the institution builders of a more integrated Europe. The political Union as well as an EU citizenship are required only to the extent that they are considered necessary for a more efficient completion and functioning of the internal market and Euro monetary area. Member states are too jealous of their own autonomy to cede their sovereignty in other areas.

From this perspective, the present minimal political Union and EU citizen-ship seem to be merely means to achieve economic and monetary goals and nothing more. They are not central objectives in their own right, and, hence, they still are minor concerns to the institutional constructors of Europe. The fact that Jacques Santer used the expression "citizenship" seventeen times in his first speech as number one of the European Commission does not necessarily mean that the issue of EU citizenship has gained central importance in the pro-cess of European integration.

Supranationalism or Postnationalism?

Any discussion about EU citizenship implies a debate about the nature of the European political society as well as a debate on the meaning of European iden-tity. In the present stage, the European Union is "neither a federative Empire, nor a nation-state elevated to the rank of a continental power. The European Union is an economic entity that could perhaps become political."[24] Many clas-sical elements of the state are present in the recent Maastricht and Amsterdam Treaties (for example, a territory, a currency, a foreign policy, a citizenship). Nevertheless, the European Union still has no juridical personality as a state in

23. Commission of the European Communities, 1988.
24. This is a free translation to English of the following quotation: "ni Empire fédérateur, ni Etat-Nation élevé en pouvoir continental: l'Union européenne est une entité économique qui, éventuellement, pourra devenir politique," Lafont, 1991, p. 27.

its own right.[25] The type of European political society that is envisioned will determine both the content and the shape of the EU citizenship. No unanimously shared conception exists of a future political European Union. The historical opposition between the Federalists and the Confederalists has not completely disappeared. The influence of the Federalists, however, who were led until the Maastricht Summit by Jacques Delors, has increasingly eroded. The Confederalists, and all those who fear that the European project will entail the dissolution of the nation-states, seem to have gained power during the 1990s throughout the European Union.

In this context, the agreement achieved in Maastricht and confirmed in Amsterdam with respect to EU citizenship must be viewed as the smallest common denominator between the two main historical conceptions of a political Europe. It is a compromise that does not irreversibly commit the member states in one way or the other and that leaves the gate open to both options. In other words, EU citizenship as introduced in the Maastricht Treaty and confirmed in the Amsterdam Treaty allows the Federalists to pursue their objective provided that they do not openly refer to the word *federation*. At the same time, it leaves Confederalists a strong basis to defend their position that nation-states within the Union retain the exclusive power to decide what should or should not belong to their individual purview. Among these matters is national citizenship. Only a decisive solution of this conflict in favor of the Federalists could bring new substantial developments in terms of a stronger and more complete EU citizenship. But the prospects of such a victory seem unlikely for the foreseeable future.

Therefore, in the present state of affairs, EU citizenship, as designed in Maastricht, is nothing more than a *functional* semicitizenship as opposed to a *substantive* citizenship. It merely formalizes under the official heading of EU citizenship a set of preexisting rights with a few novelties. (One such novelty is that some member states had to introduce the right to vote and to be elected in the country of residence for European citizens both at the local and at the European elections.)[26]

The conferral of these political rights is sometimes presented as a critical step toward the overcoming of the nation-state in dissociating the possession of a nationality and the possession and exercise of citizenship.[27] Here my analysis and Soysal's account of postnational membership converge.[28] In her view, the

---

25. Cloos, Reinesch, Vignes, and Weyland, 1993, p. 116.
26. Callovi, 1993.
27. Meehan, 1993; Tassin, 1991.
28. Soysal, 1994.

settlement of migrants in Western Europe forced European states to move beyond their traditional understanding of citizenship linked to national belonging. A new postnational membership has progressively developed based on human rights in which most citizenship rights that were historically reserved for nationals are now available also to legally residing foreigners. Soysal argues that citizenship rights and national identity have been increasingly decoupled in European immigration countries and how temporary guest workers have been progressively incorporated into their host countries.

In my view, both analyses are partly correct but also too optimistic. The concept of EU citizenship introduced in Maastricht is still largely derived from the national concept of citizenship.[29] The Amsterdam Treaty makes the point even more clearly than the Maastricht Treaty. Neither treaty creates any new juridical and political constructs. The main condition to be recognized as a citizen of the European Union is to be a citizen of one of its member states, that is, to have the nationality of one of the member states. This conception of European citizenship was earlier expressed in the Spanish proposal of September 1990. According to President Felipe Gonzales, citizenship of the European Union should "develop without weakening in any manner the national citizenship to which it should be a complement and not a substitute."[30] By and large, this approach to EU citizenship still seems valid about a decade later.

Therefore, EU citizenship as introduced in Maastricht and confirmed in Amsterdam can at present be viewed as a renewal of the nationalist logic in the Gellnerian sense.[31] Theoretically, it tries to stimulate a European political identity that is largely linked to a prior belonging of the individual to one of the fifteen nations corresponding to the member states of the European Union. In its present shape, EU citizenship is thus a sort of complementary supracitizenship that confirms the existence of the fifteen cultural and political identities corresponding to the fifteen member states of the European Union.

This renewal of nationalism under the form of a European supranationalism accounts for the exclusion of third-country nationals legally residing in Europe from the benefits of EU citizenship. This exclusion would have no legal justification if a sharp and complete dissociation of nationality and citizenship had been introduced. This important point merits further development. As stated above, many observers consider the establishment of EU citizenship a significant advancement toward postnationalism in the sense that the objective crite-

29. O'Keefe, 1992.
30. This is a free translation of the following quotation: "prendre corps sans entamer en rien la citoyenneté nationale dont elle serait un complément et non un substitut," "Opinion of the Commission on the Political Union of October 21, 1990," *Agence Europe*, no. 1659, October 31, 1990, p. 5.
31. Ferry, 1990.

rion of residence would replace the criterion of nationality to determine who should be granted the rights commonly associated with citizenship. Now, if this perspective had been effectively adopted, it would be incoherent and discriminatory to limit the access to EU citizenship to the nationals of one of its member states.

That it was not adopted is the core of the problem. By using an undifferentiated concept of citizenship,[32] or by selecting the dimension of citizenship that suits their argument, many analysts have neglected the fact that, as far as political rights are concerned—after all, one of the main novelties introduced by the Maastricht Treaty in the field of citizenship—EU citizenship does not break the association citizenship-nationality at all but renews it in a slightly different way. Some member states of the European Union have not waited for the Maastricht Treaty to move further on the way toward a larger dissociation between nationality and citizenship in the field of politics. States such as the Netherlands and Sweden, for example, granted local voting rights to foreigners more than ten years ago. To them, this dimension of EU citizenship is, in a way, a setback. As far as socioeconomic and civil citizenship are concerned, non-EU citizens were granted rights as individuals and as workers, regardless of their nationality, before the introduction of EU citizenship.[33]

In a sense, the Soysalian perspective is partially correct. But the Maastricht Treaty and the Amsterdam Treaty do nothing to advance the trend Soysal sees toward the dissociation between nationality and citizenship in most of the member states of the European Union. In short, the fundamental criterion for the granting of EU citizenship remains the possession of a nationality, that is, the belonging to a nation as sanctioned by nationality laws. This nationality may correspond to the state of residence, but a national of one member state may also reside in the territory of another. In acquiring a transnational European citizenship, the criterion of residence is still largely subordinated to the criterion of nationality. This subordination is unlikely to change in the near term. The passage to supranationalism and postnationalism may well not occur in the foreseeable future, even though some developments point in that direction. One such development is the decision taken by the European Parliament in January 1993 to grant the right to petition to non-EU citizens. This small step goes further than existing EU citizenship policy toward a dissociation between nationality and citizenship.[34]

---

32. The work of T. H. Marshall is crucial for the sociological study of modern citizenship, especially the distinction he made between three types of rights associated with citizenship, namely civil rights, political rights, and socioeconomic rights (Marshall and Bottomore, 1992).

33. North, 1992.

34. *Agence Europe,* no. 5905, January 25 and 26, 1993, p. 6.

The Result of a Top-Down Approach

In his article "Outline of a Theory of Citizenship," Turner extends the classical work of T. H. Marshall by introducing a useful distinction between a passive citizenship, developed "from above" by the state through the granting of rights, and an active citizenship developed "from below" by the citizens through their protest participation in various social movements.[35] EU citizenship has thus far been primarily constructed from above. The introduction of an EU citizenship through the conferral of a set of "special" rights to the citizens of the member states is to be understood as a compromise between the European institutions and the member states and not as the result of some kind of mobilization of the grassroots citizens of Europe.[36] During the preparation of the European Council of Dublin, the ministers of Foreign Affairs raised the question of

> how to integrate and to extend the notion of a communitarian citizenship to which specific rights (human rights, social and political rights, total freedom of movement and residence) are attached and which is granted to the citizens of the Member States *by virtue of the belonging of these States to the Union.*[37]

Clearly, the role played by the will and mobilization of the citizens of the European states in the process that led to the adoption of an EU citizenship in Maastricht was decidedly minor. Some of them have campaigned to bring forth a new political movement that would advance the development of the citizenship of the European Union.[38] But associations like ECAS (Euro-Citizen Action Service) or VOICE (Voluntary Organisations in a Citizen's Europe), which began to be active during the campaign for the French referendum on the Maastricht Treaty, remain far from forming a significant social and political movement of European citizens. In September 1993, for example, ECAS organized an important week-long seminar of the European citizen around the notions of equality and the struggle against discrimination. Since then, ECAS has never stopped being active in its attempts to promote a European Union that would be more open to the citizens and, hence, more democratic. But this type of initiative remains confined to a small circle of "enlightened" European citi-

35. Turner, 1990.
36. Bryant, 1991.
37. Emphasis added. This is a free translation of a quotation included in the document adopted by the ministers of the Foreign Affairs of the EEC at their meeting in Luxembourg on June 11, 1990 (*Agence Europe,* no. 1628, 1990). The aim of the meeting was to prepare the European Council of Dublin that took place June 25 and 26, 1990.
38. de Schutter, 1992.

zens who organize more like a lobby than like a transnational, grassroots citizens movement. Even in Brussels, where the ECAS has its seat, very few citizens know about it. Furthermore, the action of unions and political parties at the European level remains problematic. Workers' solidarity across European national borders, for example, is not easy to organize. As Jürgen Habermas observed, if EU citizenship is conceived as a potential basis for transnational collective action and as the consciousness of an obligation toward a shared European welfare, then it does not exist at present.[39]

If EU citizenship is more the result of a movement from above, of a top-down approach, than of a movement from below, why did both the European institutions and the governments of the member states introduce it in the Maastricht Treaty and confirm it in Amsterdam? At this stage, an analysis of the power relations between the various European institutions and the national governments would be useful, but it goes beyond the purpose of this report. Any such analysis would need to look closely at the impact of both intra-institutional and inter-institutional conflicts on the decision-making processes at the European level. In this regard, the institutions and the governments engaged in the European integration process should not be treated as homogeneous and undifferentiated bodies working exclusively in the framework of a positive cooperation.

Five reasons are commonly put forward to explain the introduction of EU citizenship of the European Union from above despite the relative low concern of the populations of the member states. The first reason is somewhat technical. The mobility of highly qualified workers and executives among the various European branches of the international companies is certainly one condition for the efficiency of the internal market. Therefore, it seems important to make this mobility and the residence abroad as comfortable as possible for those who are directly concerned. From this perspective, EU citizenship can be viewed as a means of granting an acceptable legal protection to those mobile, European, highly qualified workers and executives. The granting of political rights at the local and European levels could be considered an extension of the free movement of European workers.[40] This first reason may initially not seem compelling since EU citizenship does not offer any substantial advances with respect to socioeconomic and civil rights. But a closer examination of the provisions contained in EU citizenship reveals that, in fact, only moving European citizens benefit from it. This statement certainly makes this first reason more convincing.

39. Habermas, 1991.
40. Heymann-Doat, 1993.

The second reason issues from the general recognition of the "democratic deficit"[41] that affects the process of European integration. Effectively, the members of the European Council of the heads of states or governments, the national governments that take part in the negotiations in the framework of the Council of Ministers of the European Union, the European Commission members are not directly elected by the peoples of the various member states. The European Parliament is the only European institution elected by universal suffrage, but its powers remain limited. In this context, the introduction of EU citizenship has been analyzed as an attempt by the commission to solve the democratic deficit problem and to "assure a real participation of the citizens to the community work simultaneously and proportionately with the development of policies in the fields that affect them directly."[42]

If solving the democratic deficit problem were to be the main aim of EU citizenship, then the efficiency of this tool should be seriously questioned. The only voting and eligibility rights granted to the citizens of the Union under the Maastricht Treaty refer to local and general European elections. These rights could, therefore, be seen to confer only a second-class order of citizenship.[43] As far as the participation of European citizens in local elections of their country of residence is concerned, it is difficult to understand how it could increase the democratic participation at the European Union level. Concerning participation in the European elections, it should be stated that, despite the fact that the process of codecision has certainly increased the powers of the European Parliament, at least theoretically, it remains the least powerful of European Union institutions. Therefore, it is difficult to explain to what extent the right to elect a relatively powerless institution is likely to increase the citizens' participation in the European integration process and to reduce the democratic deficit it suffers. Furthermore, trying to reduce the democratic deficit through undemocratic, opaque decision-making processes such as the Maastricht and Amsterdam negotiations may seem paradoxical and not convincing in the citizens' view.

The third reason presupposes that the European Union's future is to become a singular nation or a quasi nation-state, sharing a common European culture and an ideology of cultural resistance against encroachments from poorer, non-Western regions to the south.[44] This vision of the future assumes the final victory of the Federalists over the Confederalists. From this perspective, EU

---

41. The French expression is "déficit démocratique."
42. This is a free translation of the following quotation: "pour assurer une véritable participation des citoyens à l'oeuvre communautaire au fur et à mesure que se développent des politiques dans des domaines qui les touchent directement," "Opinion of the Commission on the Political Union of October 21, 1990," *Agence Europe,* no. 1659, October 31, 1990, p. 5.
43. Moxon-Browne, 1992.
44. Balibar, 1989.

citizenship can be considered as the first step in the transfer of the national sociopolitical principle to the European Union level. The fact, however, that this victory is far from being achieved leaves viability of this vision questionable. Still, proponents of this view may be right that the introduction of EU citizenship will contribute to attempts to build a European culture and to promote a European identity.

In searching for ways to promote a common European cultural identity, two major options can be distinguished: the traditionalist option and the modernist option.[45] In the traditionalist and fundamentalist option, the "European culture" is seen as a given, an admitted fact on the basis of which a European "community of destiny" should be developed. The idea of the intangible existence of a natural European culture based on the common Judeo-Christian and humanist experience grounding a "European spirit" has been recurrent for a long time. In his project for a perpetual peace written at the turn of the seventeenth century, the Abbé de Saint-Pierre states that contrary to Asia or Africa, Europe is "a real society with its religion, its manners, its customs and its laws, and whose peoples can not deviate from it without directly causing troubles."[46] In 1924 Paul Valéry wrote that "every race and every land that has been successively romanized, christianized and submitted, as far as the spirit is concerned, to the discipline of the Greeks, is absolutely European."[47] In Valéry's mind, the Homo Europeus can thus be defined by a European spirit built through the ages by the Roman, Greek, and Christian heritage. At present, several advocates of Europe attempt to mobilize this heritage in order to ground the European culture and consequently the European "community of destiny" of tomorrow. For Pierre-Yves Monette, for example, the essential core of the European civilization, that is,

the European specificity, is explained by all that we have in common: our cultural Judeo-Christian basis, our marked taste for liberty, justice and democracy . . . our conception of the role of the woman which conflicts completely with other civilizations, our spirit of openness and tolerance which is not the integralism cultivated by some other peoples. . . .[48]

45. Ferry, 1990.
46. This is a free translation of the following quotation: "une société réelle qui a sa religion, ses moeurs, ses coutumes et ses lois, dont aucun des peuples qui la composent ne peut s'écarter sans causer aussitôt des troubles" (Coll, 1963, p. 107).
47. This is a free translation of the following quotation: "toute race et toute terre qui a été successivement romanisée, christianisée et soumise, quant à l'esprit, à la discipline des Grecs, est absolument européenne" (Coll, 1963, p. 99).
48. This is a free translation of the following quotation: "la spécificité européenne s'explique par tout ce qui nous est commun: nos fondements culturels judéo-chrétiens, notre goût prononcé pour la liberté, la justice et la démocratie . . . notre conception du rôle de la femme qui est en opposi-

In the modernist and constructivist option, a major political objective is to create a common European cultural space. From this perspective, the cultural construction of Europe should follow the same pattern as the economic construction. Policy initiatives in various fields such as plurilinguism, education and universities, multimedia, publishing, and so on have been launched to promote a common European identity.[49] Long neglected, considerable attention has been focused on education and universities in Europe since the implementation of the Maastricht Treaty.[50] Exchange programs for students, researchers, and academics such as Erasmus, Socrates, Human Capital, and Mobility, for example, have had growing success even though their implementation faces numerous problems (financial, administrative, and so on). Increasingly, European universities are harmonizing their curriculums, a process that will have an impact on a European academic culture and, perhaps, in the long term, on popular conceptions of European identity.

As witnessed by an Opinion of the Economic and Social Committee on a Citizen's Europe published in September 1992,[51] these two options for promoting a shared European cultural identity are not mutually exclusive. Article 128 of the Maastricht Treaty leaves both options open, with a formidable consequence in terms of exclusion from the "Europeanity" of those citizens living in Europe who are coming from non-Christian civilizations, for example, the immigrant origin populations coming from countries in which Islam is the main religion. Nevertheless, it seems at the moment a bit impetuous to defend the hypothesis that the European Union has entered into a proper "nationalization" process. As a matter of fact, such a movement is impeded by the strong resistance of the European national identities and states formed in the past.

Let us now turn to the fourth reason that could explain the introduction of an EU citizenship. The achievement of both the great internal market and the economic and monetary Union imply additional deprivations for the European population, whose standard of living has been significantly decreasing since the

---

tion complète avec celle de nombreuses autres civilisations, notre esprit d'ouverture et de tolérance qui n'est pas l'intégrisme cultivé par certains peuples. . . ." (Monette, 1991, p. 285).

49. Domenach, 1990.

50. The treaty established a juridical basis for cooperation in the field of education through Article 126 and Article 127.

51. "The key to a Citizen's Europe is its unity and diversity of culture, its pluralism of thought and tradition, its Christian heritage and appreciation of other faiths as well as humanistic and secular values and principles, and its fundamental attachement to liberty, peace, social justice, tolerance, human rights and the Rule of Law. The 'soul' of Europe is in fact imbued with humanistic principles (notably the right to human dignity), such principles constituting the bedrock and driving force of democracy. . . ." Economic and Social Committee, "Opinion on Citizen's Europe," CES(92) 1037, September 23, 1992, p. 2.

first oil crisis in 1973. The now famous "convergence criteria," which eleven out of fifteen member states have accepted to establish the new European currency system, the Euro, required severe austerity policies that further lowered the standard of living of the population. Before Maastricht, it was no secret that a certain degree of people's consent to this additional austerity would be necessary if the economic integration was to progress in Europe. In this respect, the heads of states or governments of the European Union declared at their Birmingham meeting of October 1992, "As a community of democracies, we can progress only with the support of our citizens."[52] According to some political actors, the stimulation of a European identity was one means to obtain the people's support and the people's consent in the face of additional deprivations.[53]

In this context, the introduction of EU citizenship may be viewed more as an attempt to create "a feeling of belonging to the European construction"[54] than as the expression of a political will to provide the European citizens with a real and direct means of participation in this construction and some real political power. This hypothesis is supported by the evolution of the debates and decisions that have led from the Citizens' Europe to EU citizenship. The first European Community decisions in this area stressed the importance of creating European symbols that were not seen as mere and futile gadgets but as central elements of identification to the European Community. This desire to promote shared loyalties explains the appearance of a European Union flag, passport,[55] and anthem. The same period saw the creation of a tool to control the evolution of European public opinion at the same time as it was trying to give birth to it, that is the *Eurobarometer.*[56]

The fifth reason, which is also the most logical one, is well summarized by the following quotation:

If one sticks to the creation of a political Union, whatever scope one wishes to give to the concept, it is at first advisable to solve the preliminary question of its domain of jurisdiction, both at the geographical level

52. This is a free translation of the following quotation: "En tant que communauté de démocraties, nous ne pouvons progresser qu'avec le soutien de nos citoyens," "Déclaration of Birmingham," *Agence Europe,* special edition, no. 5839, October 18, 1992, p. 3.
53. Bryant, 1991.
54. This is a free translation of the following quotation: "un sentiment d'appartenance à la construction européenne," "Opinion of the Commission on the Political Union of October 21, 1990," *Agence Europe,* no. 1659, October 31, 1990, p. 5.
55. The European Community passport is not a single passport but merely a document of uniform design issued and delivered only by the member states to their citizens (Closa, 1992).
56. For more details on the Citizens' Europe, it is useful to refer to the communication of the Commission to the Council "A Citizens' Europe," COM (88) 331 final, June 24, 1988.

and at the level of persons. Even from a purely logical point of view, it is not possible to conceive of a political Union without an accurate previous delimitation and without defining the persons belonging to the Union.[57]

From this perspective, the aim of EU citizenship should be to bring about this delimitation, but this aim raises again the question of determining membership criteria for citizens of the political Union. Here we need to refer back to the third reason, that is, to the construction of a European culture and the confinement of EU citizenship to those individuals who are supposed to belong to this culture.

In the end, it seems that the introduction of EU citizenship from above can be explained reasonably well by a combination of the first, third, fourth, and fifth explanations presented above. To the extent that EU citizenship is conferred on the basis of the individual's belonging to one of the European Union nations and on the basis of belonging to a shared European culture in construction, the result excludes from full membership numerous immigrants from different regions of the world who have already settled in Europe. It could also exclude those potential migrants who arrive in Europe as asylum seekers or as part of the family reunification process. The idea that one should be an EU citizen and "culturally" European to reap the benefits from Europe's relative economic well-being seems to be gaining growing public support. This support could lead to the assertion of an ethnoracial conception of the European society that could be used to justify the exclusionary practices suffered by the nonmembers of that European society. Any such justification would contradict the fact that all European societies are de facto multiethnic, multicultural, and multiracial. Indeed, the various minorities living in the member states whose presence is a consequence of colonialism, labor migrations processes, and other patterns of human mobility remain a living challenge to the mythical view of an ethnically, racially, and culturally homogeneous Europe.

The Implementation of EU Citizenship

The implementation of the various provisions contained in Article 8 can be analyzed both at the European level and at the national level. A quick and effective implementation depends on the interplay between the European institu-

57. This is a free translation of the following quotation: "Si l'on s'en tient à la création d'une Union politique, quelle que soit la portée que l'on souhaite donner à ce concept, il convient tout d'abord de résoudre la question préalable de son domaine de juridiction, tant sur le plan géographique que sur le plan des personnes. Même d'un point de vue purement logique, il n'est pas possible de concevoir une Union politique sans une délimitation préalable précise et sans que soient définies les personnes appartenant à l'Union" (Mira, 1991, pp. 168–69).

tions on the one hand, and the governments and the administration services of the member states on the other hand. In the present case, as in other matters, numerous technical and political problems have emerged that have impeded the process of EU citizenship implementation, which was not completed yet when the Intergovernmental Conference started in March 1996. In other words, the revision of Article 8 officially started before its full implementation.

Consider, for example, the case of the freedom of movement and settlement for European citizens within the European Union.[58] The Treaty on the European Union (TEU) does not provide for a general and total recognition of these rights. They are subject to a number of conditions and limitations according to European law. This issue is also connected with the more general issues of external migration toward the European Union and the establishment of a European space without borders. Furthermore, the abolition of internal borders is still impeded by the Anglo-Spanish dispute over Gibraltar, which renders impossible the adoption of the directive on the crossing of external borders of the Union. As a result, full implementation of the promised rights of freedom of movement for all European citizens has still not been achieved. For the time being, controls at the internal borders of the Union are still often operated, and freedom of circulation remains limited and conditional even for European citizens, let alone for third-country nationals.

As to the right of settlement, the European Commission has been very active in trying to improve the situation. The recognition of professional qualifications across Europe is here an important issue that has been handled through the adoption of various directives. Nevertheless, as in the case of the right to free movement, the right of settlement remains limited. One can wonder whether a European social security regime must first be established as a preliminary condition before this right can be fully implemented, but this question need not be addressed here. Whether or not such a regime is a necessary condition, little progress toward it has been achieved.

The implementation of Article 8B concerning the right to vote and to be elected in the elections of the European Parliament and in the municipal elections in the member state of residence is now completed at the European level. The voting and eligibility rights at the elections of the European Parliament are actually the first part of EU citizenship to have been implemented through a directive issued by the council in December 1993.[59] The directive is based on five

---

58. Article 8A of the Treaty on the European Union.
59. Council Directive 93/109/EC of December 6, 1993, laying down detailed arrangements for the exercise of the right to vote and stand as a candidate in elections to the European Parliament of citizens of the Union residing in a member state of which they are not nationals.

main policy options. First, it provides for minimum rules and avoids any hints toward a harmonization of member states' electoral systems. Second, it reasserts the principle of nondiscrimination between nationals and other European citizens. Third, European citizens remain free to choose where they want to vote or to stand as candidates. Fourth, European citizens are obliged to choose. They can not participate twice in the elections. Fifth, the same rules of disqualification are mutually recognized by the member states.[60]

Furthermore, because of pressure from Luxembourg, which has been supported by other member states such as Belgium, an important derogation was introduced in the directive that limits somewhat this new political right.[61] According to Article 14 of the directive, a member state in which the proportion of non-national European citizens of voting age exceeds 20 percent of the total electorate can restrict the right to vote to those who have resided in that member state for a minimum period (not more than five years). It can also restrict the right to stand as a candidate to those EU citizens who have been residing in that same member state for a minimum period (up to ten years). In Luxembourg, where more than a quarter of the population is made of non-national European citizens, most of whom are from Portugal, this derogation was meant to avoid any opposition between Luxemburgers and European citizens. Still, this example shows the willingness of the defenders of the nation-state to preserve some sort of political sovereignty and the ambiguities of the construction process of a political Europe. European citizens living in a member state other than their own are considered to be equal to EU citizens living in their own member state, but they are a bit less equal than them. The deadline to adopt regulations, laws, and administrative procedures to comply with this directive was February 1, 1994, just a few weeks before the European elections. This deadline was met, and since then European citizens can, at least in theory, exercise their new political right.

As to the right to vote and to be elected in the municipal elections in the member state of residence, a directive laying down and detailing arrangements for the exercise of these rights was issued only in December 1994.[62] It is very similar to the directive concerning the right to vote and to be elected in the European elections. In principle, the directive should have implemented the right of non-national European citizens to participate in the local administration and government of their place of residence on the basis of the principle of equality

60. Oliver, 1996.
61. Actually, the directive provides for a second derogation, the scope of which is more limited since it concerns exclusively Britain and Ireland.
62. Directive 94/80/EC, O.J. L368, 31.12.1994.

with national citizens. This generous principle, however, has been undermined in the final directive because of legal and political problems that emerged in some member states. The French Constitution, for example, provides that only French nationals can hold the office of mayor. In France, the mayor can also exercise governmental functions and participate in political elections. Since no political majority emerged to change this provision in France, the council decided to take this limitation to EU citizenship into account. The final directive, then, states that member states can reserve the office of mayor or its equivalent to nationals. Furthermore, member states may also stipulate that European citizens elected as members of a representative council shall not take part in the designation of delegates who can vote in a parliamentary assembly or in the election of the members of that assembly.

In December 1994, Belgium put pressure to include "a 20 percent derogation" as Luxembourg did in the case of European elections. According to Article 12 of the directive, a member state in which the proportion of non-national European citizens of voting age exceeds 20 percent of the total electorate can restrict the right to vote to those who have resided in that member state for a minimum period (no longer than the term for which the municipality council is elected). It can also restrict the right to stand as a candidate to those who have resided in that same member state for a minimum period (no longer than twice the term for which the municipality council is elected). The deadline to implement this directive was January 1, 1996. It was not met by the fifteen member states. Some of them were more than eighteen months late in transposing the directive into national law. Belgium, for instance, was so unwilling to do so that the commission had to appeal to the European Court of Justice against Belgium on this matter.

The delay in the process of implementation of Article 8B is not simply due to the usual technical problems. It can well reveal the political dilemma faced by some member states when dealing with the very sensitive issue of political citizenship. One the one hand, they agreed that no democratic political European Union would be possible without giving some political rights to non-national European citizens. On the other hand, most political rights were until recently reserved for nationals, which was considered normal. Therefore, the extension of some political rights to non-nationals raises the issue of political citizenship beyond nationality and raises questions about the future of the nation-state and its articulation with the European Union. Since the answer to that question is not clear, some member states seem to hesitate between the promotion of political integration for all EU citizens and nationalistic setbacks.

Furthermore, the issue of the implementation of Article 8B is also to be connected with internal political issues of some member states. Why, for example, is Belgium so slow on that matter? For the same reason that it demanded a derogation of the right to vote at the municipal level. The issue of the extension of these political rights to non-national European citizens has to be understood as a dimension of the perennial opposition between the Flemings and the Francophones in the Belgian State in which the Brussels area is of central importance. The Brussels periphery belongs politically to Flanders but hosts important Francophone minorities and many European civil servants. The latter are supposed to be more sympathetic with the Francophones than with the Flemings. Therefore, it is often feared in some Flemish political circles that the granting of local voting rights to Europeans will empower Francophone parties in the Flemish periphery of Brussels. Their resistance is directed less against an EU citizenship *in abstracto* than against what they see as a risk for their political and linguistic dominance in parts of their territory. Belgium, under the pressure of the Flemish majority in the federal government and Parliament, required a derogation to Article 8B and impeded the process leading to its implementation in order to avoid the issue of the participation of European citizens in the local elections of October 1994. Clearly, this case shows that issues of EU citizenship and attendant political rights often have more to do with national politics than with European politics.

As to the right to diplomatic and consular protection contained in Article 8C, which is not of central importance for most European citizens, the principle is generally accepted. The areas of protection remain unclear, however. Furthermore, the procedure to be followed in order to exercise this new right is not described clearly anywhere in the Maastricht Treaty. The right to petition the European Parliament and the right to appeal to a European ombudsman are now implemented. It nevertheless took more than a year after the European elections of 1994 to appoint the ombudsman in July 1995.

Before turning to the issue of the practice of EU citizenship, it must simply be repeated that its implementation has been a long and difficult process. There are certainly technical and legal reasons involved, but there are also political reasons connected to internal politics of some member states.

How Do Citizens Use EU Citizenship Rights in Practice?

As noted above, much attention has been given to the emergence of EU citizenship seen as a top-down process. Many studies on the attitudes of European citizens toward the process of European integration have also been conducted. One of the aims of *Eurobarometer* surveys is to monitor regularly the evolution of the attitudes of the European public opinion. But much less has been said about the practice of European citizenship. The concept of European citizenship practice has been widely explored by Antje Wiener.[63] In her view, it designates quite broadly the process of policy making and political participation that contribute to shaping the terms of EU citizenship. What I call the practice of EU citizenship is more restricted and refers to the uses of the "new" set of rights contained in EU citizenship by European citizens: To what extent have EU citizens used their new rights? To what extent have they practiced their "new" citizenship? From this perspective, EU citizenship is looked at as a bottom-up process.

Most observers acknowledge that the practice of EU citizenship has not been impressive so far. Among the many reasons that could explain why EU citizens have not used their new citizenship rights as extensively as some may have hoped, three are worth mentioning. First, there has been a problem of information. Many EU citizens still do not know precisely what EU citizenship involves and what the link between this new concept and national citizenship exactly is. After the introduction of the Maastricht Treaty, the European Commission received letters from citizens of some member states expressing their anxiety and at times their refusal to accept the new EU citizenship. Some of them declared that they already had a national citizenship with which they were happy and that they did not want to have it replaced by EU citizenship. This example illustrates perfectly the confusion that surrounded the introduction of EU citizenship within the population and the general ignorance of its content.

Second, for technical and political reasons related to its national implementation, some elements of EU citizenship have not been available yet, such as voting rights in local elections. This situation increased the confusion within the population: on the hand, EU citizens were in theory granted a new political right, on the other hand, they were told that they might have to wait as many as six years to exercise it. In Belgium, for example, prospective voters have been required to wait until the 2000 local elections to exercise their new political right. Third, most of the rights included in EU citizenship make sense only for citizens of the member states who live in a member state different from their own. In other words, only the small minority of mobile EU citizens can take advantage of most EU citizenship rights and exercise EU citizenship in their daily life. In that sense, EU citizenship may be seen as a de facto indirect discrimination against EU citizens who live in their own country! The latter are protected by guarantees concerned with freedom of movement, the right to petition the European Parliament, and the right to apply to a European ombudsman, but

63. Wiener, 1998.

only mobile EU citizens can enjoy the totality of the rights included in EU citizenship.

In order to assess how EU citizens have exercised their EU citizenship rights, let us look at a selection of them: the freedom of movement and residence within the territory of the European Union, and the voting and eligibility rights at the elections of the European Parliament.

On paper, EU citizens have the right to move and to reside freely within the territory of the member states under certain conditions.[64] Freedom of movement and of residence is a crucial element of any democratic citizenship. In practice, many EU citizens have used their right to move freely but few have used their right to reside in a member state other than their own. The European Union counts 370 millions inhabitants. Only 5.5 million of them live in a member state other than their own, that is, 1.5 percent, and this percentage has not seemed to increase.[65] EU citizens do travel within the European Union for their holidays, but they did not need the introduction of EU citizenship to do so. EU citizenship has implied a major change that facilitates intra-European tourist traveling: the reduction of border controls. But another element explains the growing tourist mobility within Europe more fundamentally: the development of fast and cheap transportation reduces the distance between some European capital cities. Brussels and Paris, for example, are only one hour and twenty-five minutes away from each other with the new high speed train *Thalys,* and the fare can be as low as $60 for a return tourist ticket. This evolution encourages short-term excursions within Europe but not necessarily the resolve to live in another European Union state.

Whereas capital flows readily from one member state to another, EU workers and citizens are not very mobile and do not move to another European Union country very easily. Generally, they do not favor moving within their own country either. Clearly, Europeans are far less mobile than U.S. citizens. In other words, Europeans show little interest in exercising this new right granted to them through EU citizenship provisions. Why this lack of interest? Several reasons can be given. Historically, mass intra-European workers migrations did take place in the twentieth century and especially from 1945 to the mid-1970s from the poorer rural areas of southern Europe to the industrialized cities in the north. These mass migrations were considered to be temporary even though they led to permanent settlement. The governments of the receiving and send-

---

64. Article 8A of the TEU.
65. *Memo d'Eurostat,* no. 0498, April 16, 1998; "Résumé du rapport du groupe de haut niveau sur la libre circulation des personnes présidé par Mme Simone Veil," *Agence Europe,* no. 2030, April 9, 1997.

ing countries organized these migration movements through bilateral agreements. These movements, then, were not spontaneous and, in a way, were stigmatized as the only way for poor Europeans to survive. The attachment to the native soil and environment seems historically much higher in Europe than it is in the United States.

Language is clearly another obstacle to mobility in Europe. For a European, moving to another European country often means adapting to a new and totally different linguistic environment. This difficulty reduces mobility. The fact that social benefits and social protection remain largely linked to the member state of which one is a national is another disincentive to move. Europeans often fear that moving to another European country will have negative consequences for their retirement benefits, their social rights and protection, their health care protection, and so on. To a certain extent, these fears are warranted and will continue to be until a common European social policy in these fields is designed and implemented. For all these reasons, moving within the European Union is much more problematic than moving within the United States, and the end result is therefore not surprising: mobility is much lower in Europe than it is in the United States.

Incentives are needed in order to encourage human mobility within the European Union. European institutions are aware of this necessity. The European Commission has published a practical guide informing EU citizens about their social security rights when they move within the Union.[66] But information is not enough. More Europeans will start moving when they are convinced that doing so will accumulate gains for them and their families in terms of salaries, quality of life, prestige, career, access to the labor market, and so on.

As to the participation of EU citizens living in a member state other than their own in the elections of the European Parliament of 1994, the results reveal a low turnout throughout the Union. Official figures indicate that the percentage of EU citizens who registered to vote in their country of residence did not exceed 44.11 percent of the potential EU voters, in the case of Ireland, for example.[67] The rate of registration was less than or equal to 5 percent in Belgium, Greece, France, Italy, Portugal, and the United Kingdom. It was between 6 percent and 10 percent in Germany, Luxembourg, and Austria. It was about 12 per-

66. Commission Européenne, "Vos droits de sécurité sociale quand vous vous déplacez dans l'Union Européenne, Guide Pratique," Luxembourg, Office des Publications officielles des Communautés Européennes, 1995.

67. "Rapport de la Commission Européenne au Parlement Européen et au Conseil sur l'application de la Directive 93/109/CE relative au Droit de vote et d'éligibilité aux élections au parlement européen pour les citoyens de l'Union résidant dans un autre état membre dont ils ne sont pas ressortissants," COM(97) 731 final, 07.01.1998.

cent for Spain and about 24 percent in the Nordic countries (Denmark, Sweden, Finland). Only one EU candidate was elected in a member state other than his or her own. Clearly, EU citizens have not demonstrated a deep interest in voting or competing for a seat in their country of residence, which in theory is a crucial aspect of EU citizenship as designed in Maastricht and confirmed in Amsterdam.

Various reasons can be adduced to explain low voter participation in European-wide elections. Declining electoral turnout is part of a broader trend that has occurred at the national level throughout Europe during the past few years. But other factors are also important to consider. The European Parliament is the least powerful European institution, and a significant number of EU citizens have probably wondered why they should make the effort to vote for members of a largely toothless body. In addition, serious problems of information persist. Many EU citizens have not known exactly what their new right meant. Could they vote in their country of residence for candidates in their home country? Or could they vote for candidates of their country of residence? Or could they perhaps vote for both? The need to register to vote and the somewhat complex registration procedures in some member states have also contributed to reducing the rate of participation. In some countries it could take at least half a day to register, and only the most motivated EU citizens have been inclined to do so.

Some observers have viewed low turnout as proof of the weakness of a European political identity among the European citizenry. This hypothesis should not be dismissed casually. But weak participation could also be interpreted as an expression of political resistance by EU citizens against the current evolution of the European integration process that has not corresponded to their wishes and needs. Not voting may reflect simple apathy but it can also be a political act. Not voting may in many cases represent a vote against the European Union in its present form, but it does not necessarily indicate that no shared European political identity exists or is possible.

According to a recent *Eurobarometer* survey, 70 percent of EU citizens declared that they are willing to participate in the 1999 elections of the European Parliament.[68] This level of participation may be an achievable goal. In order to succeed, though, information needs to be improved and registration procedures simplified. Beyond this plausible short-term goal, a general public debate on the meaning of EU political identity is necessary if the final aim is to build a more democratic European Union composed of equal and active citizens.

---

68. *Eurobarometer,* report no. 48, March 1998.

The Effect of EU Citizenship on Citizenship Structure in the European Union

Extending the work of Brubaker and Hammar, I have formulated elsewhere the hypothesis of the emergence of a triangular citizenship structure in the European Union.[69] In my view, the introduction of EU citizenship did confirm and sanction juridically this "triangularization" of citizenship in the European Union while modifying it slightly. Three main levels of citizenship, that is, three types of citizens, can be distinguished in the European Union depending on the particular mix of civil rights, socioeconomic rights, and political rights they enjoy.

Only the citizens of a member state living within the border of their nationality state possess the entire basket of civil, socioeconomic, and political rights, that is, full citizenship. But sharing full citizenship does not necessarily mean equality of status. A growing number of them are effectively excluded from the processes of redistribution of economic, social, and political resources.

At the next lower level are the citizens of a European Union member state who are residing in a member state other than their own. They enjoy only limited political rights (mainly the right to vote and to be elected at the local and European level). In other respects, their civil rights are not complete. Article 8A of the Maastricht Treaty, for example, does not guarantee the total freedom of settlement in another European Union country. In order to avoid movements of unemployed workers from member states with low social protection to member states that offer a high level of protection, European citizens must satisfy two conditions if they want to settle in another member state. These conditions are financial independence and no dependence on social security. Furthermore, the employment opportunities for European citizens in their country of residence of which they are not a national remains severely limited. Although this category of European citizens is largely protected by European Union law, the full equality between nationals and other European Union citizens has not yet been achieved. This problem is exacerbated by the fact that the social legislations of the member states are far from being fully harmonized. The idea of a coordinated European Union social policy has always faced strong opposition, and not only from the government of the United Kingdom.

The third category of citizens is actually divided into two subcategories. One may be understood as "denizens," that is, citizens of a third state (nonmember) who are legally settled in the European Union. Denizens have, to a certain extent, become integrated into the civil and socioeconomic life of European soci-

---

69. Brubaker, 1989; Hammar, 1990; Martiniello, 1992.

ety. As human beings and as workers, they enjoy fundamental civil and socioeconomic rights. But they generally have no significant political rights in the European Union.[70] For the past few years, the Forum of the Migrants of the European Communities has been working in this area. In theory, the forum should offer a means of expression for the third-country migrants at the European level as well as a platform for dialogue between them and the commission. The forum, however, has no decision-making power and is clearly located at the margins of the European polity.

The second subcategory, the "margizens," enjoy extremely limited civil, socioeconomic, and political rights. In many cases, they have almost no rights at all because they live illegally in a member state. I have grouped denizens and margizens together in the same category because they suffer analogous mechanisms of exclusion from the cultural and political "Europeanity." Between the denizens and the margizens, one could also mention a growing category of legal temporary residents or workers. Members of this category may have high-status positions while many more are severely marginalized.

This hypothesis concerning the emergence and consolidation of a triangular citizenship structure in the European Union requires qualification. The practical implementation of the rights associated with citizenship sometimes makes the distinctions among nationals, denizens, and margizens less clear-cut in daily life than in my proposed model. We must consider the growing socioeconomic exclusion processes affecting both nationals and foreigners in Europe, especially in urban settings, to understand the concrete realities shaping this triadic citizenship structure. Although, for example, the nationals in principle enjoy all the socioeconomic rights, including the right to work, a growing number of them are condemned in almost all member states to long-term unemployment, poverty, and exclusion. The living conditions of these nationals then tend to resemble that of some margizens.

This resemblance is especially, but not at all exclusively, the case for a significant proportion of black nationals in several European countries.[71] The possession of the nationality of a European state does not impede racial discrimination. No strict and binding guidelines intended to fight racism at the European level exist. No common policy in this area has emerged, and each member state has its own particular approach.[72] At the end of the 1997 European

70. In the framework of the negotiations between the EEC and some EFTA states in the perspective of an enlargement of the EEC and their accession to it, the status of the citizens of those EFTA states is likely to evolve rapidly.

71. Many member states of the European Union have a minority of dark-skinned citizens who are a legacy of their past colonial experiences. It is certainly the case of Britain, France, the Netherlands, and Germany, but also of Belgium and Italy.

72. Commission of the European Communities, 1992; Niessen, 1992.

Year against Racism, Padraig Flynn, the Irish commissioner in charge of social affairs, committed himself to introduce new antidiscrimination legislation before the end of the term of the European Commission in June 1999.[73] The European Commission indeed adopted a Communication in March 1998 that contains an Action Plan on the fight against racism. More recently, in November 1999, the new European Commission, led by Romano Prodi, approved a package of four proposals to combat discrimination on the basis of powers conferred by the Amsterdam Treaty. But at this stage these four remain merely proposals, which need unanimous approval from all the Member States to produce any effect.

Toward a Multicultural Citizenship of the European Union?

In order to envisage the further developments of EU citizenship, it is useful to differentiate between EU citizenship seen as a top-down construction (EU citizenship from above) and EU citizenship seen as a bottom-up process (EU citizenship from below). It is also instructive here to distinguish between short-term and long-term developments.

The development of EU citizenship from above in the short term raises the issue of its implementation as designed in Maastricht and confirmed in Amsterdam. A revision of the Amsterdam Treaty has already been planned in the short term, although no precise date has been set. A new institutional negotiation could commence when the number of member states of the European Union has reached twenty. It could also begin after the integration of a sixteenth member state.[74] In any case, given the fact that negotiations regarding enlargement are moving forward, the revision of the Amsterdam Treaty can be expected in the next five years. Will EU citizenship be included in the list of issues to be discussed during this revision? No one can predict with absolute accuracy.

In looking forward to future prospects, three main ways to develop EU citizenship can be theoretically distinguished. First, Article 8 could be technically improved and thus be subject to minor cosmetic changes. Second, new rights could be added for EU citizens either in Article 8 or elsewhere in the TEU. Third, EU citizenship could be extended to third-country nationals who have been residing legally within the European Union for a period to be fixed (five years, ten years). Obviously, these three developments could also take place simultaneously.

---

73. *Agence Europe,* no. 7128, December 24, 1997, p. 3.
74. Dehousse, 1997.

With respect to the first route, the introduction of cosmetic changes intended to improve technically the functioning of Article 8 is the easiest way to address from above concerns over EU citizenship, but it is not necessarily the most fruitful one. We can expect such changes as the most probable development in the short term, but they will not substantially advance the development of EU citizenship. As to the second way, many proposals have already been made regarding the introduction of new citizenship rights. These proposals have come both from independent experts and from institutions like the European Parliament, such as during the IGC that prepared the Amsterdam Summit of June 1997. More new proposals may emerge in the coming month and years. Which of these proposals could be adopted in the near future remains an open question. The third way—the extension of EU citizenship to third-country nationals who have legally been residing within the European Union for a period of years—does not seem to be politically feasible in the short term. Nevertheless, proposals have been made for this extension by basing citizenship eligibility on the criterion of residence rather than on nationality. Nothing precludes this extension juridically, but reaching a common agreement seems unlikely in the short and medium term. Therefore, no profound and significant developments of EU citizenship from above can be expected in the near future. The main barrier is the absence of political agreement on the future shape of a political European Union in the long term.

What are now the long-term prospects for EU citizenship, in particular, and the political Union, in general? Effectively, their respective evolution will be closely linked. The nature, the shape, and the content of the future EU citizenship will depend on the type of European society that will actually be constructed and vice versa. Will the EU vacillate between the present hybrid Confederalism and some kind of a vague European Federalism? Will the implementation of a European citizenship remain largely based on the national model to which some elements of a federal citizenship are added? What will be the impact of the dilemma of enlargement versus deepening of the Union on the future shape of a European polity and citizenship? When will the issue of a long-term project of a democratic European polity be publicly discussed? To address such questions would require a discussion about a real European social policy, a real European equal-opportunity policy, and a real European antiracism policy. No consensus exists among the member states on the adequacy of the European level to tackle such issues traditionally dealt with at the national level. Will there be some space for a postnational and postethnic political Europe and thus for a postnational and postethnic EU citizenship?[75]

75. Hollinger, 1995.

In Glotz's view,[76] Maastricht was more likely to be the end rather than the beginning of a political European Union. According to him, the European Community will continue to be a sort of loose confederation of nation-states that will cooperate in a free trade zone.[77] If we try to extend Glotz's analysis, it may well be that EU citizenship as introduced in Maastricht and confirmed in Amsterdam was an end, the greatest common denominator between the respective wills of the European institutions and of the member states that can be found. Forced to abandon parts of their sovereignty in other areas, the member states will strive to keep control of what is left of their sovereignty, namely the independent determination and delimitation of who can be considered as their nationals. Chabot's analysis follows the same lines when he asserts that an involvement of the member states in the construction of Europe is often followed by a withdrawal that makes all further progress impossible for a certain time.[78] Smith advances the hypothesis that a sort of pan-European nationalism could develop, grounded on the mobilization of a European cultural heritage, provided that it will not compete with the national identities and cultures. The political European Community could thus constitute a new kind of collective identity embracing the present nations without, however, abolishing them.[79]

At present, no development seems to herald the beginning of a postnational era cherished almost ten years ago by Ferry, Habermas, Lafont, Oriol, and many others. In Ferry's view, a postnational European society could be based on the principles of constitutional patriotism and cultural sovereignty.[80] Lafont does not use the same expression, but he aims at the same type of society in his argument for a "mixed" and transparent Europe as well as for a "deterritorialized" human being.[81] The same is true with Oriol when he states that "the Europe of the citizens can only be the Europe of all the resident citizens."[82]

For the time being, issues related to multiculturalism and issues related to citizenship are almost completely disconnected at the European level, and this disjuncture is reflected in the concept of EU citizenship that says nothing about the promotion of diversity in Europe. It also says very little about the social di-

---

76. Glotz, 1992.
77. It could easily be argued that the European Community is already far more than that, but the monetary clash of summer 1993 shows that setbacks are not to be excluded.
78. Chabot, 1987.
79. Smith, 1991.
80. Ferry, 1990; Ferry, 1991.
81. It is almost impossible indeed to translate Lafont's terms. The original expressions are "une Europe métisse et désopacifiée et un homme déterritorialisé" (Lafont, 1991).
82. This is a free translation of the following quotation: "l'Europe des citoyens ne peut être que l'Europe des citoyens résidents" (Oriol, 1992, p. 217).

mension of citizenship. Clearly, the idea of a multicultural citizenship for the European Union does not rank very high on the political agenda in Europe.

The fact that various and conflicting national narratives of citizenship and multiculturalism exist within the European Union impedes the emergence of that type of debate at the European level. In France, the republican rhetoric of national integration and citizenship underlines the divisive effects of a public recognition of cultural diversity. Multiculturalism is often presented as a new tribalism, as a balkanization of France, and, in the end, as a risk for citizenship. In Britain, things are different. The British have conflicting views on multiculturalism but the issue is at least openly discussed. The accommodation of diversity in the public sphere is less problematic. In Germany, a "multikulti" trend coexists with a quite exclusive conception of citizenship. Each country, for historic and political reasons, has its own way to address these issues and wants to keep its sovereignty in these matters. This concern with national sovereignty explains why debates over supranational European structures seldom receive much attention.[83]

Furthermore, in many member states of the European Union, debates on issues related to multiculturalism overlap with the debate on the position on ethnic immigrant minorities. Multiculturalism is not seen as a broad project for society at large. This narrow perspective discourages the development of a multicultural EU citizenship.

The necessity to accommodate ethnocultural and national identities in the European Union in a dynamic way seems clear. Any attempt to promote a homogeneous Europe will fail because Europe means diversity. Accommodation will require promoting a postethnic Europe based on the recognition of multiple and fluid identities and respect for the equality of opportunity for every inhabitant. This notion of accommodation differs from Kymlicka's model,[84] which runs the risk of essentialization and rigidification of ethnicities and which leaves aside the issue of economic and social inequality. Promoting cultural rights without promoting a fair share of economic and social resources between individuals would certainly not be a good solution for a democratic European Union. Inhabitants of the European Union, like any other individuals, display a complex and multidimensional identity that is the result of various affiliations and identificational processes: Muslims in Europe can affiliate with the European idea, second-generation immigrants, too, without necessarily renouncing other dimensions of their identity. This reality is often either underestimated or

83. Martiniello, 1997; Vertovec, 1998.
84. Kymlicka, 1995.

overestimated in the current debate. It should be taken into account more carefully.

The presence in the European Union of a variety of ethnocultural and national identities is not per se an obstacle for an EU citizenship and an EU political identity that rests on a commitment to a shared project of society. It can, nevertheless, become an obstacle should social and economic inequality continue to grow. If the holders of alleged illegitimate identities are also the excluded and the poor, and if the holders of alleged legitimate identities are also the included and the rich, then Europe as a focus of identification and commitment does not seem to make sense.

In my view, only a successful mobilization of the denizens and margizens together with the full citizens, that is, a significant pressure from below, for a new multicultural EU citizenship could bring about a decisive breach in the nationalist logic and open the way toward postnationalism and postethnicity in Europe. But what are the prospects of construction of EU citizenship from below? Generally, collective action is developing at the European level.[85] But transnational and European grassroots citizens' mobilization and collective action remains highly problematic and underdeveloped.[86] As Edgard Morin put it some years ago, the challenge of a democratic Europe at this stage would be to develop European political parties, European trade unions, and European associations committed to the construction of the Union.[87] Can such a process of development of an EU citizenship from below be stimulated from above? Probably to a certain extent. But in any case, without an active EU citizenship, the idea of a multicultural Eurodemocracy will remain an inaccessible dream, and EU citizenship could be blocked in its present embryonic stage for some time.

References

Balibar, Etienne. 1989. "Racism as Universalism." *New Political Science*, no. 16–17 (Fall), pp. 9–22.

Brubaker, William Rodgers, ed. 1989. *Immigration and the Politics of Citizenship in Europe and North America.* New York: University Press of America.

Bryant, Christopher. 1991. "Europe and the European Community 1992." *Sociology*, no. 25 (2), pp. 189–207.

Callovi, Giuseppe. 1993. "La nouvelle architecture de la Communauté européenne face à la migration." In *Migrations et minorités ethniques dans l'espace européen*, eds. Marco Martiniello and Marc Poncelet. Bruxelles: De Boeck Université, pp. 91–104.

85. Greenwood and Aspinwall, 1998.
86. Tarrow, 1997.
87. *Le Monde,* February 2, 1994, p. 2.

Castles, Stephen, and Mark J. Miller. 1993. *The Age of Migration: International Population Movements in the Modern World.* London: MacMillan.

Chabot, Jean-Claude. 1987. "La nation et l'unité européenne." *Communications,* no. 45, pp. 213–21.

Cloos, Jim, Gaston Reinesch, Daniel Vignes, and Joseph Weyland. 1993. *Le Traité de Maastricht: Genèse, Analyse, Commentaires.* Bruxelles: Bruylant.

Closa, Carlos. 1992. "The Concept of Citizenship in the Treaty on the European Union." *Common Market Law Review,* vol. 29, pp. 1137–69.

Coll. 1963. *Ecrits sur l'Europe.* Paris: Seghers, écrits.

Commission of the European Communities. 1992. *Legal Instruments to Combat Racism and Xenophobia.* Bruxelles-Luxembourg: CEE publications.

Commission of the European Communities. 1988. "The Social Dimension of the Internal Market." *Social Europe,* special issue. Bruxelles-Luxembourg: CEE Publications.

Dehousse, Franklin. 1997. "Le Traité d'Amsterdam, reflet de la nouvelle Europe." *Cahiers de Droit Européen,* no. 3–4, pp. 265–73.

de Schutter, Olivier. 1992. "La nouvelle citoyenneté européenne." *Cahiers Marxistes,* no. 186, pp. 103–20.

Domenach, Jean-Marie. 1990. *Europe: le défi culturel.* Paris: La Découverte, Essais.

European Parliament. 1996. "Resolution of the European Parliament on the Intergovernmental Conference." *Agence Europe* (Europe documents), no. 1982, April 13.

European Parliament. 1995. "Resolution of the European Parliament on the Functioning of the European Union," PE 190.441/1.

Ferry, Jean-Marc. 1991. "Pertinence du postnational." *Esprit,* no. 176, pp. 80–93.

Ferry, Jean-Marc. 1990. "Qu'est-ce qu'une identité postnationale?" *Esprit,* no. 9, pp. 80–91.

Garcia, Soledad, ed. 1993. *European Identity and the Search for Legitimacy.* London: Pinter and RIIA.

Glotz, Peter. 1992. "Democracy and Nation in the New Europe." Paper presented at the seminar "La théorie politique en Europe après les bouleversements de 1989," Bruxelles, Université Libre de Bruxelles.

Greenwood, Justin and Mark Aspinwall, eds. 1998. *Collective Action in the European Union.* London: Routledge.

Habermas, Jörgen. 1991. "Citizenship and National Identity. Some Reflections on the Future of Europe." Paper presented at the conference "Identités et différences dans l'Europe démocratique. Approches théoriques et pratiques institutionnelles," Bruxelles, Cellule de Prospective de la Commission des Communautés Européennes et Centre de Philosophie du Droit de l'Université Catholique de Louvain, May 23–25.

Hammar, Thomas. 1990. *Democracy and the Nation State.* Research in Ethnic Relations Series. Aldershot: Avebury.

Heymann-Doat, Arlette. 1993. "Les institutions européennes et la citoyenneté." In *Les étrangers dans la cité: expériences Européennes,* ed. O. Le Cour Grandmaison, et Catherine Withol de Wenden. Paris: La Découverte/Ligue des droits de l'homme, pp. 176–91.

Hollinger, David. 1995. *Postethnic America: Beyond Multiculturalism.* New York: Basic Books.

Lafont, Robert. 1991. *Nous, peuple européen.* Paris: Kim.

Leca, Jean. 1992. "Nationalité et citoyenneté dans l'Europe des immigrations." In *Logiques d'Etats et immigrations*, ed. Jacqueline Costa-Lascoux and Patrick Weil. Paris: Kim, pp. 13–57.

Leca, Jean. 1991. "La citoyenneté en question." In *Face au racisme 2: analyses, hypothèses, perspectives*, ed. P.-A. Taguieff (sous la direction de). Paris: La découverte, pp. 311–36.

Marshall, Thomas H., and Tom Bottomore. 1992. *Citizenship and Social Class*. London: Pluto.

Martiniello, Marco. 1998. "Réflexions sur la postethnicité et l'Europe." In *Constructions et Mobilisations Identitaires*, eds. Gabriel Gosselin and Jean-Pierre Lavaud. Lille: USTL-CLERSE.

Martiniello, Marco. 1997. "The Development of European Union Citizenship. A critical Evalutation." In *European Citizenship and Social Exclusion*, eds. Maurice Roche and Rik van Berkel. Aldershot: Ashgate, pp. 35–47.

Martiniello, Marco. 1997. "Les ressortissants communautaires et la pratique de la Citoyenneté de l'Union." In *De l'étranger au citoyen*, ed. Paul Magnette. Bruxelles: De Boeck Université, pp. 125–34.

Martiniello, Marco. 1997. *Sortir des ghettos culturels*. Paris: Presses de Sc. Po.

Martiniello, Marco. 1996. "La citoyenneté multiculturelle de l'Union Européenne. Une utpoie postnationale." In *Repenser l'Europe*, eds. Mario Telo and Paul Magnette. Bruxelles: éditions de l'Université Libre de Bruxelles, pp. 127–38.

Martiniello, Marco. 1992. *Leadership et pouvoir dans les communautés d'origine immigrée*. Paris: CIEMI, L'Harmattan.

Meehan, Elisabeth. 1993. *Citizenship and the European Community*. London: Sage Publications.

Mira, Pierre S. 1991. "La citoyenneté européenne." *Revue du Marché Commun*, no. 168–170.

Monette, Pierre-Yves. 1991. *Les Etats-Unis d'Europe*. Beauvechain-Bruxelles: Nauwelaerts-Bruylant.

Moxon-Browne, Eileen. 1992. "The concept of European Community citizenship and the development of political union." Paper presented at the ECPR Joint Sessions of Workshop, Limerick.

Newman, Michael. 1996. *Democracy, Sovereignty and the European Union*. London: Hirst and Company.

Niessen, Jan. 1992. "International instruments to combat racial discrimination in Europe." Briefing Paper no. 8. Brussels: Churches Committee for Migrants in Europe.

North, David. 1987. "Non Citizens' Access to Social Services in Six Nations." Unpublished report prepared for the German Marshall Fund.

O'Keefe, David. 1992. "European Citizenship." Paper presented at the conference "1993. Le marché unique et l'Europe des personnes." Liège, Université de Liège, Institut d'Etudes Juridiques Européennes, June 26.

Oliver, Peter. 1996. "Electoral Rights under Article 8B of the Treaty of Rome." *Common Market Law Review*, no. 33, pp. 473–98.

Oriol, Michel. 1992. *Les immigrés devant les urnes*. Paris: CIEMI, L'Harmattan.

"Racism and Xenophobia in Europe." 1997. *Eurobarometer Opinion Poll,* no. 47.1. Draft final report presented at the closing Conference of the European Year Against

Racism, European Commission, Employment and Social Affairs, Luxembourg, December 18 and 19.

Smith, Anthony D. 1991. *National Identity*. London: Penguin.

Sörensen, Jens M. 1996. *The Exclusive European Citizenship: The Case for Refugees and Immigrants in the European Union*. Aldershot: Avebury.

Soysal, Yasemin. 1994. *The Limits of Citizenship: Migrants and Postnational Membership in Europe*. Chicago: University of Chicago Press.

Tarrow, Sidney. 1997. "L'Européanisation des mouvements?" Paper presented at the University of Liège, Faculty of Law-Political Science, Liège.

Tassin, Etienne. 1991. "L'Europe, une communauté politique?" *Esprit*, no. 176, pp. 63–79.

Tarzi, Shah M. 1991. "The Nation-State, Victim Groups and Refugees." *Ethnic and Racial Studies*, no. 14 (4), pp. 441–52.

Turner, Brian J. 1990. "Outline of a Theory of Citizenship." *Sociology*, no. 24 (2), pp. 189–217.

Vertovec, Steven. 1998. "Multi-Multiculturalisms." In *Multicultural Policies and the State: A Comparison of Two European Societies*, ed. Marco Martiniello. Utrecht: ERCOMER, pp. 25–38.

Wiener, Antje. 1998. *"European" Citizenship Practice: Building Institutions of a Non-State*. Boulder: Westview Press.

Withol de Wenden, Catherine. 1997. *La citoyenneté européenne*. Paris: Presses de Sc. Po.

Wolton, Dominique. 1993. *La dernière utopie: naissance de l'Europe démocratique*. Paris: Flammarion.

PART FOUR

Ethnic Republics?
Citizenship in Israel and Japan

CHAPTER TWELVE

Introduction

ARISTIDE R. ZOLBERG

SOME CASES ARE more unusual than others, and there is no gainsaying the idiosyncrasy of Israeli citizenship. As is well known, its foundation stone is the Law of Return, which extends to every Jew in the world at large the right to immigrate, settle, and establish citizenship. Albeit grounded in the traditions of European nationalism, at least at the level of theory, the Law of Return in effect reverses the usual relationship and accords to immigrant Jews a superior status over the native-born. "Every Jew," indeed, but how does a person qualify? Jews of the Diaspora who live in liberal democracies generally insist that Judaism is a religion and, hence, a private and voluntary matter that falls outside the state's purview—for example, in the United States, "Jewish" is not available as an ethnicity within the white race in the census. Yet "Jew" for purposes of the Law of Return is evidently *not* established principally on religious grounds: although one can qualify on the basis of *conversion* to Judaism, neither religious practice, nor a belief in the deity specified in Judaic traditions, nor even a belief in a deity *tout court* is generally required. Rather, in keeping with the structure of Zionist ideology, formed in the mold of late-nineteenth-century European nationalism, qualification is commonly on the basis of membership in the tribe, established on the basis of ancestry. Although one Jewish parent suffices, the Jewishness of that parent is itself determined on the basis of ancestry—or at least putative ancestry, since in most cases, by virtue of the vagaries of regional history, records are not available—and so on until one enters the Andersonian realm of "imagined communities," of putative origins in the desert tribe that began its transformation into a settled territorial nation upward of five millennia ago. And if there is some doubt over lineage, the matter is to be settled on the basis of Jewish religious law. So, Israeli citizenship does rest on a religious foundation, after all. Or does it?

And these peculiarities, ambiguities, and contradictions, are only the beginning. The Israeli case is a misfit in relation to all the typological exercises set forth by social scientists as a prelude to theorizing on the subject of citizenship. In relation, for example, to the contrast drawn by Rogers Brubaker between the universalistic French model of citizenship and the ethnic German model, Israel clearly belongs in the German camp. The Israeli concept of citizenship is clearly republican, however, in the strong sense of that term, in that it entails not only rights but also obligations, centering on military service. Whereas this is easily understood in the light of the historical contingencies that have surrounded the state's existence since its inception, at a more theoretical level this republicanism is traceable to the French revolutionary tradition of the "nation in arms." In contrast with the "blood nation," a republican nation is constituted on the basis of active reciprocity: citizens are obligated to serve the republic, but in return the republic has stronger obligations toward its citizens than is the case for merely liberal states. Indeed, Hertzl's engagement in Zionism was precipitated by the French Republic's failure to meet its obligations toward a citizen who served, Captain Dreyfus. But Israel's republicanism is, in turn, jumbled up with outright communalism in the realm of family law, whereby marriage rules are determined on the basis of community affiliation. Derived from Ottoman tradition, this sort of pluralism belongs structurally in the realm of empire rather than of republic. Although pluralism in itself does not necessarily entail inequality—it is possible to be "separate and equal"—in Israel the communities in question are clearly *not* equal, but provide the foundations for what Ayelet Shachar terms "degrees of citizenship," a structural element that echoes the U.S. situation prior to the civil rights revolution, as well as South Africa in the epoch of apartheid.

Although Shachar's major objective is to provide a critical assessment of the Israeli situation, a task of which she acquits herself with the utmost intellectual integrity and admirable moral sensitivity, her paper also provides the makings of stimulating comparisons. As she astutely demonstrates, the uniqueness of Israeli citizenship arises from the disparate character of its constitutive elements, assembled on the basis of imperatives that are themselves highly disparate, ranging from the foundational principles of Zionism—themselves of mixed origin—to the realistic constraints of managing a heterogeneous population, whose differences are laden with ominous significance by way of their relationship to the tense international environment, and the hegemony of orthodox Jewish authorities in a state whose Jewish population is on the whole less religious than their American cousins. To this has been added, most recently, the experience of foreign guest workers, which links Israel with the United States during the era of the *bracero* program, Western Europe during the Bretton-Woods boom years, and, more recently, the Arab oil states of the Gulf. Somewhat paradoxically, the disparate character of the resulting Israeli configuration reveals aspects of these several elements that are not visible in their native habitat, and thereby enhances our understanding of their significance.

Japan and Israel surely stand out as the "odd couple" of the comparative citizenship project, each of them being an outlier in which one element of citizenship policy has been extrapolated into a dominant feature. In short, Japan comes closer than any other economically advanced constitutional democracy to retaining a fundamentalist version of *jus sanguinis*, and the "blood" involved is the immediate and concrete one of family or lineage, rather than merely the usual "imagined" national community.

In her balanced account, Chikako Kashiwazaki properly emphasizes the protracted problems encountered by former colonials and their descendents, but also provides a detailed review of the important improvements that finally were enacted in recent decades. Although matters are not all they might be, there is fortunately some light at the end of that tunnel.

Her conclusion, however, highlights the distance that separates Japan from the other countries considered in the project: unlike most European nonimmigration states, including now even Germany, Japan has still not adopted the perspective "of conceptualizing resident aliens as future citizens of Japan." Arguably, of course, this does not constitute a problem from a humanitarian or rights perspective, so long as a country is willing to forgo the economic advantages of immigration, and so long as it is willing to meet the obligations incurred as a member of the international community with regard to refugees. Indeed, for most of the post–World War II period, Japan in fact did adopt internal and external economic strategies that enabled it to ignore the temptation of guest workers. But more recently, Japan relented and hence acquired a significant foreign resident population whose status remains unacceptably marginal. Citizenship issues arising in the refugee sphere are less significant, but only because Japan has maintained an extremely restrictive stance with regard to asylum.

CHAPTER THIRTEEN

Citizenship and Membership in the Israeli Polity

AYELET SHACHAR

CITIZENSHIP MEANS drawing borders: between peoples, between states, between insiders and outsiders. Citizens assume their positions because of their legal status, their shared history, or their sense of identity. For a variety of historical reasons, the constituency of such a group may be distinctly heterogeneous. In Israel, a land of immigrants, roughly 80 percent of the citizenry is Jewish and 20 percent is Palestinian Arab.[1] A significant number of the Jewish Israeli citizens are foreign-born. In 1996, for example, after the large influx of Jews born in the former Soviet Union, approximately 38 percent of the Jewish population in Israel (1.75 million) had been born outside the country.[2] In other words, *one in every three Israelis* was an immigrant.

An earlier version of this paper was presented at the Third International Metropolis Conference, Zirchron Yaacov, Israel, November 30-December 3, 1998. I am grateful for the responses I received to previous drafts of this paper, particularly those from Ari Zolberg, Joe Carens, Christian Joppke, Doug Klusmeyer, Kathleen Newland, Demetri Papademetriou, Don Galloway, Miriam Feldblum, David Martin, Dan Friedman, Caroline Sand, and Lisa Brill. I would also like to thank the members of the Legal Department at the Association for Civil Rights in Israel (ACRI), especially Dan Yakir, Orna Kohn, and Anat Shekolnikov, for their insights regarding the issues raised in this article. Special thanks to Alex Aleinikoff for his comprehensive assistance and detailed comments.

1. As of May 1998, the Israel Central Bureau of Statistics announced that the current population of Israel was estimated at 5.94 million. Of the total population in 1998, approximately 4.76 million were Jews and 1.18 million were non-Jews. See *Israel at 50,* September 22, 1998.

2. See *Statistical Abstract of Israel,* 1997, p. 49.

By way of comparison, according to the United States Census Bureau, "in 1997 nearly one in ten residents of the United States (25.8 million) was for-eign-born,"[3] and that is in the context of one of the largest immigration waves in U.S. history.

In the words of Rogers Brubaker, "citizenship is a powerful instrument of social closure."[4] In Israel, immigration also serves as an important strategy in the project of nation building and a means to affect the demographic balance between Jews and non-Jews occupying the land.[5] Like any other modern state, Israel formally defines its citizenry, identifying a set of persons as its members, or "the people" in whose name the state is understood to act.[6] Any citizenship law and immigration policy must determine who is entitled to full membership in a given political community, and, therefore, who profits by the rights and who must fulfill the subsequent obligations. The unique nature of Israeli immi-gration policy rests in its perception of expanded state membership to any per-son who is entitled to the "right of return" that is codified in the 1950 Law of Return.

"Every Jew," proclaims section 1 of the Law of Return, "has the right to come to this country as an *oleh* [immigrant]."[7] This open invitation to immi-grate and settle in Israel (or "right of return") "is considered one of the most fundamental rights in Israeli law."[8] It is often described as reflecting the *raison d'être* and ideological underpinning of the State of Israel with the state's aim of the reuniting of the scattered Jewish people (the "exiles") in their ancient home-land.[9] The Law of Return views every Jew and his or her family members as *in potenia* citizens of the State of Israel, thus establishing a formal, legal link be-tween the State of Israel and the community of world Jewry, and expressing a fundamental Zionist value upon which the state itself is founded: that Israel

3. U.S. Census Bureau, April 9, 1998.

4. Brubaker, 1992, p. x.

5. See Goldscheider, 1990, pp. 131, 138. See, generally, Soffer, 1994, p. 289 (explaining the function of demography in the shaping of Israel).

6. Membership in the Israeli polity is formally defined in two major legal acts: The Law of Re-turn and the Citizenship Act. See, generally, Israel, 1950, The Law of Return, 4 L.S.I. 114; and Is-rael, 1952, Citizenship Law, 6 L.S.I. 50, (1951–52). (The Hebrew title of this law is *hok ha-ezrahot,* literally, "Citizenship Law." Note that the official government translation uses the term "National-ity Law" rather than "Citizenship Law.")

7. Israel, 1950, The Law of Return, 4 L.S.I. 114, § 1. For the purposes of the Law of Return, *Jew* "means a person who was born of a Jewish mother or has become converted to Judaism and who is not a member of another religion." Israel, 1970, The Law of Return (Amendment No. 2), 24 L.S.I. 28, § 4B. For further analysis of the question "who is a Jew," see discussion *infra* Citizenship by Return.

8. See Klein, 1997, p. 53.

9. "The Declaration of Independence," May 14, 1948, p. 1.

should provide a home to any Jew who so desires.[10] Yet, the obligation to immigrate, settle, and establish citizenship in Israel is not automatically imposed
upon a person simply because of his or her Jewishness. Rather, any person
who is considered a "Jew," according to the legal definition encoded in section 4B of the Law of Return, has an open invitation from the State of Israel to
establish his or her life in that country as a citizen. This invitation to settle in
Israel (or right of return) is also conferred upon family members of that person, up to a third generation, regardless of their own religious affiliation.[11]
Moreover, non-Jewish family members have an inalienable right to return
even if the person through whom the right is claimed has deceased or has
never settled in Israel.[12]

The centerpiece of Israeli immigration policy, the Law of Return, is effectively grounded in the romantic nationalist ideology of Zionism from the late
nineteenth century. This law reflects a perception of membership in the state
that is not territorially bound or defined,[13] but rather is based on a *preexisting* affiliation with the Jewish people, in its perception of that people as a "nation."[14]

10. Upon presenting the proposed Law of Return to the *Knesset* (Israeli Parliament) in 1950,
David Ben Gurion, Israel's first prime minister, observed that the right of return "existed before the
state did, and it is that which built the state." Lorch, 1993, p. 613.

11. Section 4A(a) of the Law of Return states that the right to return to Israel is also granted to
"a child and a grandchild of a Jew, the spouse of a Jew, the spouse of a child of a Jew and the spouse
of a grandchild of a Jew, except for a person who has been a Jew and has voluntarily changed his religion." Israel, 1970, The Law of Return (Amendment No. 2), 24 L.S.I. 28, § 4A(a). In the initial
wave of immigration to Israel in the late 1980s, about 15 percent of the immigrants from the former
Soviet Union entered the country as non-Jews entitled to the right of return based on their family affinity to a Jewish person. Since 1993, more stringent procedures of verification of the entitled person's "Jewishness" have been enforced, while at the same time, the numbers of non-Jews
"returning" to Israel has steadily grown.

12. See Israel, 1970, The Law of Return (Amendment No. 2), 24 L.S.I. 28, § 4A(b).

13. In the Israeli example, the criteria for membership by return are derived from a religious
definition of "who is a Jew," which the state then adapts. See Israel, 1970, The Law of Return
(Amendment No. 2), 24 L.S.I. 28, § 4B. Ironically, the criteria for acquiring membership, as laid out
by the Israeli Law of Return (a form of expanded *jus sanguinis*), has family resemblance to the German ethnocultural perception of membership, as expressed by section 116 of the German Basic
Law (*Grundgesetz*). See Klein, 1997, pp. 53–55.

14. I put the term "nation" in quotation marks because it reflects the Zionist view of the Jewish
people, developed in the late nineteenth century and the early twentieth century, that conceptual-
ized the "Jewish problem" not as a religious or social problem, but rather as a national problem.
Jews were, as Theodor Herzel put it, a "nation without a land," and like other nations, deserved a
homeland. "Let sovereignty be granted us over a portion of the globe large enough to satisfy the
rightful requirements of a nation," he wrote in 1896 in *Der Judenstaat* (the Jewish state). Herzl,
1943. This national perception of the Jewish people is modernist and secularized. It has never been
the only way to think about membership in the Jewish people, nor has it been accepted by all
branches of Judaism.

As it was written in 1950, in the aftermath of World War II and the Holocaust, the primary aim of the Law of Return was to help Jews and their family members "who continued to live in repressive societies or in places where the freedom to maintain their Jewish identity was restricted."[15] Today, while the Law of Return still formally maintains this original purpose, Jews in most countries are free to preserve their religious identity and have full membership rights in their respective political communities. Given the current political climate, the Law of Return, designed to be an inclusive law aimed at Jews, now also appears to be an exclusive law effectively excluding all those who do not have a pre-existing affiliation with the Jewish faith.[16] Unlike "returning" Jews, who are entitled to automatic citizenship in Israel, all other immigrants who wish to establish citizenship in Israel need to go through a relatively rigid naturalization process.[17] When evaluated from a comparative perspective, the prerequisites for naturalization in Israeli citizenship law are not more restrictive than immigration procedures in other developed countries in terms of residency or language proficiency requirements.[18] Yet, unlike most other countries, while Israel regulates the flow of immigrants to its territory, it also permits an unrestricted entitlement to membership for a particular group of persons: anyone entitled to the right of return.

The act of Jewish immigration to Israel has a special ideological position within Zionism and that is reflected by the word "*aliyah*,"[19] which has particular and strong connotations of self-fulfillment and ascent in the Hebrew language, and is a term that is not adequately translated by the standard English term "im-

15. Peretz and Doron, 1997, p. 62.
16. With the above-mentioned exception of non-Jewish family members who are entitled to the right of return. Israel, 1970, The Law of Return (Amendment No. 2), 24 L.S.I. 28, § 4A.
17. Israel, 1952, Citizenship Law, 6 L.S.I. 50, (1951–52), § 5. See also discussion *infra* Citizenship by Naturalization.
18. As in the United States and Canada, for example, Israeli citizenship law provides that a person seeking to gain citizenship by naturalization must fulfill a set of qualifications specified in law. In all three countries, an applicant for naturalization must have been lawfully admitted to the country. A minimal period of three years of physical residence is also required in all three polities (three years out of the five years immediately preceding the date of application in Israel and the United States, and three years out of the four in Canada). Knowledge of the official language is another standard requirement; however, unlike the United States and Canada, Israel does not impose a mandatory language proficiency test. See Israel, 1952, Citizenship Law, 6 L.S.I. 50, (1951–52), § 5; Israel, 1998, Immigration and Nationality Act, §§ 316, 312(a)(1), 8 U.S.C §§ 1427, 1423; Canada, 1999, Citizenship Act, R.S.C., ch. C-29, § 5. For a more detailed account of the prerequisites for naturalization as they are set out in section 5 of the Israeli Citizenship Law, 1952, see discussion *infra* Citizenship by Naturalization.
19. Literally, "ascent." *Aliyah* is the term used for the action of people immigrating under the Law of Return. See Israel, 1950, The Law of Return, 4 L.S.I. 114, § 1.

migration."[20] In order to establish Israeli citizenship by way of return, an eligible person need only express a desire to immigrate to the country and physically settle in Israel, or "make *aliyah*." The State of Israel actively attempts to solicit the immigration (*aliyah*) of Jews to Israel. Immigrants who are claiming the right of return are entitled to a host of benefits, such as language training programs underwritten by the state, tax breaks, employment training courses, and housing subsidies.[21] Furthermore, new immigrants by return are automatically entitled to *full membership*, that is, citizenship, as soon as they settle in Israel.[22] No waiting period is imposed on newcomers before they are granted formal inclusion in the body politic.[23] In other words, there is nothing equivalent to a naturalization process in the case of "returning" Jews because, as with other family-related perceptions of ethnocultural membership, Israeli citizenship law views persons eligible for return as *already* belonging to the constitutive community; that is, they are considered to have a status equal to Israeli-born citizens.[24]

Israel is unique in its active recruitment of Jewish immigrants and overwhelmingly accommodating policy of granting them immediate full participatory citizenship by way of return. The main problem with this immigration policy is that it does not apply to all potential immigrants. Only Jews and non-Jewish relatives of Jews (as specified in the law) may benefit from the Law of Return. Most importantly, other persons such as Arab Palestinians[25] do not have the benefits and privileges bestowed on the *olim*. For the purposes of this discussion, I refer to three different statuses Palestinians occupy in relation to the Israeli citizenship regime: (1) as citizens of the state; (2) as subjects of the

20. Thus, a Jewish immigrant who "returns" to Israel is termed, in Hebrew, an *oleh* (plural: *olim*), that is, "one who ascends." See Israel, 1950, The Law of Return, 4 L.S.I. 114, § 1.

21. See Ministry of Immigrant Absorption, 1996, pp. 42–51, 56–65, 71–72, 85–89.

22. See Israel, 1952, Citizenship Law, 6 L.S.I. 50, (1951–52), §§ 1, 2(a).

23. See Israel, 1952, Citizenship Law, 6 L.S.I. 50, (1951–52), § 2(b). "Israel nationality by return is acquired . . . by a person having come to Israel as an *oleh* after the establishment of the State—with effect from the day of his *aliyah*." Israel, 1952, Citizenship Law, 6 L.S.I. 50, (1951–52), § 2(b).

24. This perception is apparent, for example, in the Passports Law, 1952, which permits the issue of an Israeli passport to a new immigrant regardless of the time he or she has actually resided in the country after making *aliyah*. See Israel, 1952, Passports Law, 6 L.S.I. 76, (1951–52). An attempt to change this law and impose a one-year residence requirement before the issuing of an Israeli passport to a new immigrant was defeated because it was argued that it would have created an unwanted legal distinction between the new immigrant and the settled citizen. See Rubinstein, 1976, pp. 159, 177. On different variants of the ethnocultural citizenship model, see, for example, Brubaker, 1992 (on Germany); Peled, 1992, p. 432 (on Israel).

25. My usage of the term "Palestinians" refers to persons who were entitled to Palestinian residency or citizenship under the British Mandate, before the establishment of the State of Israel in 1948.

occupied territories in the West Bank and Gaza, and since 1993, as permanent residents under the jurisdiction of the Palestinian Authority (PA); and (3) as refugees in neighboring Arab states[26]—"all states which have, with the exception of Jordan, refused citizenship to Palestinians residing within their borders."[27]

While *aliyah* is the prime means for immigration to Israel, citizenship status can also be created in three other important ways: by residence in the country, by birth to an Israeli parent, or by naturalization. *One in every five Israelis* is a Palestinian Arab citizen[28] and must have acquired citizenship status by way of residence, birth, or naturalization.[29] I propose to analyze these three ways of establishing Israeli citizenship in greater detail below.

My discussion proceeds in four sections. The first section analyzes the different ways of establishing Israeli citizenship, paying special attention to the right of return. Like many other countries, Israel adopted a combination of *jus sanguinis* and *jus soli* principles, placing greater emphasis on the *jus sanguinis* principle.[30] As a destination country for immigrants, Israel is exceptionally lenient in permitting its new "returning" citizens to maintain their previous formal affiliations (that is, citizenship status) to the countries from which they emigrated.[31] Hence, Jewish Israeli citizens can maintain a dual citizenship sta-

26. Given the scope of this article, my discussion below of the legal implications of the Law of Return and the Citizenship Law upon non-Jews will focus on Palestinian citizens of Israel (the first category mentioned above), as opposed to the legal implications for Palestinian noncitizens who wish to enter the country (the second and third categories).

27. Weiner, 1997, pp. 1, 31.

28. As of 1998, the total population of Israel numbered approximately 5.94 million. Of the total population in 1998, approximately 4.76 million were Jews and 1.48 million were non-Jews. See *Israel at 50*, September 22, 1998.

29. While formally entitled to full and equal citizenship rights, Palestinian Arab citizens, in general, have not achieved full social, economic, or cultural equality in Israel. To provide just one illustration of this problem, the Israeli State's official symbols are clearly associated with the Jewish majority: the Israeli flag reflects Jewish symbols (it is inspired by the Jewish prayer shawl, the *tallit*, and includes the Shield of David), and the national anthem, *Hatikva* ("the Hope"), expresses, in Hebrew, the yearning of the Jewish people to be "a free people in our own land." None of these official symbols of the state make Israel a comfortable home for all its citizens, regardless of their religious or national affiliation. See, generally, Kretzmer, 1989; Peled and Shafir, 1996, pp. 391, 402–404.

30. The right to membership by descent, however, is not limited to the state's citizens. Rather, it may be "activated" by any person who belongs to the Jewish people and wishes to settle in Israel. See discussion *infra* Citizenship Acquisition by Return.

31. This, again, reflects the centrality of the Zionist concept of "gathering in of the exiles" in the legal construction of Israeli citizens. A person who made *aliyah* to Israel automatically acquires Israeli citizenship unless a declaration of refusal is filed within three months of arrival to the country. See Israel, 1952, Citizenship Law, 6 L.S.I. 50, (1951–52), § 2. There is no requirement that the new Israeli citizen renounce his or her previous citizenship status. See Israel, 1952, Citizenship Law, 6 L.S.I. 50, (1951–52), § 14. Many countries (including the United States) require a voluntary performance of an expatriatory act for a citizen to lose his or her citizenship status; under these legal

tus, either because they immigrated to Israel or because their parents immigrated to Israel and they acquired foreign citizenship by way of descent.[32]

The second section examines the rights and obligations of citizenship, illustrating how Israeli citizenship law emphasizes a republican perception of membership, as expressed in the emphasis on the *obligations* a citizen has toward the collective. According to this view, citizenship is not merely a bundle of rights (or a "passive" entitlement to membership in the body politic), rather it is an *active* practice epitomized in one's military service and ultimate willingness to sacrifice one's life for the nation. In analyzing the emphasis on military service as the virtue of full membership in the Israeli polity, I illustrate how selective recruitment policies tacitly preserve structural inequalities among citizens, particularly between Jews and Palestinian Arabs (members of the latter group are usually not called upon for the service).[33] Military service also serves to preserve more nuanced, and less obvious, structural inequalities, such as sustaining a power differential between men and women (although all Jewish women are, like men, obliged to do their compulsory national service). I label such state practices and legal rules that sustain power disparities among formally equal citizens' "degrees of citizenship."[34] Covert yet systemic differentiation among formally equal citizens based on criteria such as religion, ethnicity, race, national origin, or sex is anything but unique to the Israeli State. But because these cleavages are so visible in the Israeli context, they call attention to, and are illustrative of, a host of problems that may be "dormant" in other, less divided societies and citizenship regimes, such as the United States.[35]

---

circumstances, the automatic conferral of citizenship status by the State of Israel upon an *oleh* would not cause loss of citizenship in the native home country. See *Afroyim v. Rusk,* 387 U.S. 253 (1967).

32. The only exception to this rule is if an Israeli citizen has left the country illegally and resides or acquires citizenship in a country that is at a formal state of war with Israel. A list of these countries is mentioned in the Prevention of Infiltration (Offenses and Jurisdiction) Law, 1954. See Israel, 1954, Prevention of Infiltration (Offenses and Jurisdiction) Law, 8 L.S.I. 133 (1953–54). In such a case, the individual may lose his or her Israeli citizenship. This rule has a grave effect on Israel's Arab citizens, who may be denationalized if they permanently reside in a neighboring country that is at a formal state of war with Israel.

33. See Kretzmer, 1989, p. 98.

34. My analysis here builds on different critiques of the gap between the claim to universality of citizenship and its practical imposition of disproportionate burdens upon certain groups of citizens, such as minority-group members or women. See, generally, Young, 1989, p. 250; Kymlicka, 1995; Peled, 1992 (claiming that Israel's citizenship is best described as "ethno-republican").

35. Note, however, that there is also formidable historical evidence to race-based and gender-based restrictions on immigration and on full entitlement to citizenship in the United States. See, generally, Smith, 1997.

The third section further discusses the republican underpinnings of Israeli citizenship law that are also reflected in the legal requirements for relinquishing citizenship. In Israel, unlike the United States, expatriation is not viewed as an inherent right of a citizen. Rather, the Citizenship Law precludes a voluntary severance of national ties to Israel unless the consent of the government is obtained.[36] Hence, while Israeli citizenship is easily conferred upon every person entitled to the right of return, it is equally hard to surrender if one belongs to the dominant Jewish majority. This duty-bound understanding of citizenship, and its conception as a lifelong bond between the individual and the state, has remained surprisingly stable despite the dramatic changes that Israel has undergone in the past decade.

The fourth section will briefly explore new trends in Israeli immigration policy since the late 1980s, in light of changes related to the gradual emergence of a neoliberal order in Israel, the arrival of almost 1 million new immigrants from the former Soviet Union, the 1993 Oslo agreement signed between Israel and the Palestine Liberation Organization (PLO), and the growing numbers of foreign workers admitted to the country as nonimmigrant "temporary workers." This article, then, aims to provide a clear picture of how Israeli citizenship law is legally conceived and practiced; its relationship with the republican ethos of membership in the Israeli polity; and its role in creating different types of statuses, or "degrees of citizenship," among formally equal citizens of the Israeli state.

Finally, I reflect on how rapid socioeconomic, political, and demographic changes in Israel since the late 1980s have brought to the forefront of Israeli immigration policy fundamental questions associated with the tension embedded between the rollback of the welfare state and the increasing movement of persons, goods, and capital across frontiers (or "globalization"), on the one hand, and the republican, duty-bound, religious-based perceptions of membership with its more state-centrist understanding of identity, still encoded in Israeli citizenship law, on the other.

Establishing Citizenship Status in Israel

Israeli immigration and citizenship law is composed of two major legislative acts: the Law of Return (enacted in 1950, amended in 1970) and the Citizenship Law (enacted in 1952, amended in 1980).[37] Israeli citizenship can be established

36. Israel, 1952, Citizenship Law, 6 L.S.I. 50, (1951–52), § 10.
37. Israel, 1950, The Law of Return, 4 L.S.I. 114; Israel, 1970, The Law of Return (Amendment No. 2), 24 L.S.I. 28. Israel, 1952, Citizenship Law, 6 L.S.I. 50, (1951–52); Israel, 1980, Citizenship Law (Amendment No. 4), 34 L.S.I. 254, (1979–80).

only in accordance with the provisions of the Citizenship Law and the Law of Return. While the Law of Return establishes the right of every Jew to immigrate to Israel (the right of return), the Citizenship Law provides three other ways in which to acquire Israeli citizenship: residence, birth, and naturalization.[38] I examine each of these categories in turn.

Citizenship by Return

The cornerstone of Israeli citizenship law is the right of every Jew (and certain specified family members) to establish automatic citizenship in Israel (the right of return). The right of return is encoded in section 1 of the Law of Return and is grounded in the Zionist perception of the State of Israel as a safe haven for the Jewish people of the Diaspora,[39] who historically endured centuries of persecution and were considered less-than-full-members in almost every country in which they lived.[40] It encompasses an open door policy toward Jewish immigrants and is viewed as one of the country's founding principles. The Law of Return, then, is a statutory expression of the Zionist perception of independent statehood.[41]

The combined provisions of the Law of Return and the Citizenship Law send an open invitation to every Jew in the world to immigrate, settle, and establish citizenship in Israel.[42] This right to return is nonselective: the state is unable to restrict the number of Jewish immigrants who arrive in Israel under the Law of Return and is bound to provide automatic citizenship to every person who makes *aliyah* to Israel.[43] The idea behind this *carte blanche* granting of citizen-

38. See Israel, 1952, Citizenship Law, 6 L.S.I. 50, (1951–52), § 1. In exceptional cases, Israeli citizenship can also be "granted" by the state, at the discretion of the minister of the interior. See Israel, 1952, Citizenship Law, 6 L.S.I. 50, (1951–52), § 9.

39. As Robin Cohen observes, the word "diaspora" is derived from the Greek verb *speiro* (to sow) and the preposition *dia* (over). When applied to humans, the ancient Greeks thought of *diaspora* as migration and colonization. For the Jews, as well as other communities that have been dispersed from an original "center" to several foreign regions, the experience of diaspora often "signifies a collective trauma, a banishment, where one dreamed of home but lived in exile." Cohen, 1997, p. ix.

40. Sharkansky, 1997, pp. 71–72. See, generally, Cohen, 1997, pp. 3–20.

41. In Rubinstein's words, as "a deliberate reply to centuries of Jewish dispersion and suffering." Rubinstein, 1976, p. 160, n. 4.

42. Section 2(a) of the Citizenship Law is complementary to the right of return established in the Law of Return. It provides that "every *oleh* under the Law of Return shall become an Israel national." Israel, 1952, Citizenship Law, 6 L.S.I. 50, (1951–52), § 2(a).

43. The only qualifications to the right of return are found in section 2(b) of the Law of Return. The minister of the interior may refuse to grant *oleh* (immigrant) status to an individual who either "engaged in an activity against the Jewish people"; is likely to "endanger the public health or the security of the state"; or has a criminal background and is likely to endanger the public welfare. Israel,

ship reflects the Zionist view of Israel as the national home to the Jewish people. As David Kretzmer observes, the right of return (of foreign-born Jews to
Israel) encoded in the Law of Return "is one of the only cases in Israeli legislation in which an overt distinction is made between the rights of Jews and
non-Jews. . . . This aspect of the Law of Return [*aliyah*] is generally regarded as
a fundamental principle of the State of Israel, possibly even its very *raison
d'être* as a Jewish state."[44] As well as its practical success, in terms of
"chang[ing] the place of residence of the world's Jews from the Diaspora to
Zion," *aliyah* expresses the ideological underpinning of the Israeli state with its
aim of gathering in the exiles.[45]

From this perspective, the State of Israel is a "trustee" of the right to return,
which itself predates the inception of the state and is vested in a preexisting affiliation, that is, one's membership in the Jewish people.[46] It is this preexisting
membership in "a people" that is crucial for entitlement to citizenship in Israel
by right of return, to the extent that section 4 of the Law of Return states that every Jew—even one who was born in Israel—is in the same position as one who
immigrated under this law.[47] This reversal of priorities in the Israeli conception
of membership in the polity, under which a person who was born in the territory
to an Israeli parent is deemed to have the same legal status as a person who im-

---

1950, The Law of Return, 4 L.S.I. 114, § 2(b). Note, however, that there is no instance known in
which the minister of the interior has used the power to restrict immigration because of a situation in
which the security of the state was endangered, or because of an act against the Jewish people.
Some individuals, however, were denied this status because of health, insanity, the cumulative conditions of a criminal past, and the likelihood of endangering the public welfare. See, for example,
H.C. 125/80, *Angel v. Minister of the Interior,* 34(4) P.D. 329; H.C. 442/71, *Lansky v. Minister of
the Interior,* 26(2) P.D. 337.
     44. Kretzmer, 1989, p. 36. See Peretz and Doron, 1997, pp. 46–62, for a concise discussion of
the patterns of Jewish immigration to Israel since 1948. Various scholars have explored the impact
of Jewish immigration and Zionist nationality upon the citizenship status of Israel's non-Jewish
population. See, for example, Kretzmer, 1989; Kook, 1996, p. 199; Peled, 1992.
     45. Arian, 1998, p. 19. In 1882, there were 24,000 Jews in Palestine, or 0.31 percent of the
world's Jewish population at the time. By 1996, Israel's 4.6 million Jews constituted almost 36 percent of the world's Jews. Note, however, that this dramatic increase in the percentage of Jews living
in Israel out of the total Jewish population in the world is the result of both mass immigration to Israel and the tragic decrease in the world's Jewish population during World War II. By way of illustration, in 1914 the total Jewish population was approximately 14 million; in 1925, approximately
15 million; in 1939, at the eve of World War II, approximately 16 million. In 1945, the total Jewish
population in the world decreased to approximately 11 million. Today, the total world's Jewish
population is estimated at approximately 13 million, of which about one-third live in Israel. See
Statistical Abstract of Israel, 1997, p. 52.
     46. See Israel, 1970, The Law of Return (Amendment No. 2), 24 L.S.I. 28, § 4B. Section 4B
adopts a semi-*Halachic* definition of the term "Jew."
     47. See Israel, 1950, The Law of Return, 4 L.S.I. 114, § 4.

migrated to the country, reflects the legislatures deliberate attempt "not to make any distinction whatsoever between an *oleh* and a Jew born in Israel."[48]

This approach to immigration is clearly unorthodox in that it reverses the common hierarchy of statuses between a native citizen and a new immigrant. The standard case of immigration requires that the newcomer gradually becomes more like a member of the host society in the country of his or her choice, a process that is epitomized by the acquiring of the rights and status of citizenship. In Israel, a reverse logic is applied. There, "in the eyes of the law, it is not the new immigrant who is considered as though he were a native-born Israeli; [rather] the Jew born in Israel . . . [is] deemed to be [an] immigrant."[49] In the early days of the Zionist movement, emphasis was placed on gaining control of the immigration policy from the British Mandate. Crucial control over the definition of immigration policy came with sovereignty in May 1948. Section 13(a) of the Law and Administration Ordinance of 1948, the first legislative act passed by the Provisional Council of the State after independence, retroactively revoked British legislative restrictions on Jewish immigration to the country.[50]

Since the establishment of Israel as an independent state in 1948, the number of people making *aliyah* has varied from year to year. In total, however, about 2.7 million Jews immigrated to Israel between 1948 and 1998.[51] This is an extraordinarily high volume of immigration for a country whose total population in 1998 was approximately 5.94 million people.[52] There are no pertinent statistics in the Israeli Census about the color or racial origin of the population. The *Statistical Abstract of Israel,* however, published by the government's Central Bureau of Statistics, does report citizens' religion. Of the total population in 1998, approximately 80.5 percent were Jews, and 19.5 percent were non-Jews.[53]

---

48. Rubinstein, 1976, p. 161.

49. Gouldman, 1970, p. 21. The 1980 amendment of the Citizenship Law, however, has for the first time recognized a more conventional *jus sanguinis* principle. Section 4(a) of the amended Citizenship Law holds that "the following shall, from the date of their birth, be Israel nationals by birth: (1) a person born in Israel while his father or mother was an Israel national; (2) a person born outside Israel while his father or mother was an Israel national—a) by return; b) by residence in Israel; c) by naturalization; d) under paragraph (1)." Israel, 1980, Citizenship Law (Amendment No. 4), 34 L.S.I. 254, (1979–80), § 4(a). For further discussion of the 1980 Amendment of the Citizenship Law, see *infra* notes 111–116 and accompanying text.

50. Israel, 1948, Law and Administration Ordinance, 1 L.S.I. 7, § 13(a).

51. See *Israel at 50,* September 22, 1998.

52. See *Israel at 50,* September 22, 1998.

53. See *Israel at 50,* September 22, 1998. Arab Palestinian citizens of Israel are divided into three main groups: Muslim, Christian, and Druze. In 1996, approximately 78 percent of the Arab Palestinian population in Israel was Muslim, 14 percent was Christian, and 8 percent was Druze. See *Israel at 50,* September 22, 1998.

Arab Palestinians constituted almost 20 percent of the Israeli citizenry at the inception of the state in 1948. By the mid 1950s, however, "large waves of Jewish Immigration . . . changed the population composition in favor of Jews so that . . . [Palestinian] Arabs comprised only [eleven] percent of Israel's population."[54] The first massive wave of Jewish immigrants arrived in Israel from 1948 through 1951. In these formative years of nation building, almost 688,000 *olim*, an average of 172,000 immigrants per year, arrived in Israel, doubling the Jewish population of the state in these years.[55] This wave of immigrants was composed largely of refugees from the Nazi concentration camps, Jews who were refused entry to Israel under the British Mandate rules and were deported as "illegal immigrants" before the establishment of Israel, and Jews from Arab countries.[56] Between 1952 and 1989, about 1.2 million immigrants acquired Israeli citizenship by return. Of them, about 750,000 were Arab-speaking Jews who arrived in Israel during the 1960s and early 1970s from Iraq, Yemen, Syria, Lebanon, Egypt, Morocco, Tunisia, Algeria, and Libya.[57]

By the mid 1980s, *aliyah* "ha[d] decreased and the number of Jewish emigrants ha[d] increased."[58] By 1986, for example, approximately 18 percent of Israeli citizens were Arab Palestinian, and 24 percent of Arab population was between the ages of zero and four.[59] As Lewin-Epstein and Semyonov observe, the proportional increase of the Israeli Arab population "represents an average annual growth of 4.1 percent, a rate very close to the average rate in the Jewish population which stands at 4.3 percent."[60] Yet "almost half of the Jewish population growth (45.7 percent) is due to immigration whereas 1.6 percent of the Arab population growth is accounted for by immigration."[61] The Jewish population, then, is structurally dependent on *aliyah* to keep its numerical dominance in the state.[62]

In 1989, when it became possible for large numbers of Jews and their family members to leave the former Soviet Union, Israeli governmental and nongovernmental agencies actively solicited them to come to Israel to settle. It appears that a combination of "pull" and "push" factors led significant numbers of people from the former Soviet Union to seek a new home country in Israel

54. Lewin-Epstein and Semyonov, 1993, p. 16.
55. See Peretz and Doron, 1997, p. 47.
56. See Peretz and Doron, 1997, pp. 47–48.
57. See Peretz and Doron, 1997, p. 49.
58. Soffer, 1994, p. 296.
59. See Soffer, 1994, p. 297.
60. Lewin-Epstein and Semyonov, 1993, p. 16.
61. Lewin-Epstein and Semyonov, 1993, p. 16.
62. See Soffer, 1994, p. 297.

(see table 13-1).[63] The State of Israel granted these newcomers (by return) full citizenship and a host of social and economic benefits intended to ease their *kelitah* (or "absorption") in Israel.[64] Moreover, these *olim* were automatically entitled to an Israeli passport, and, with it, established a formal option to pursue a new life.[65]

In the past decade, automatic citizenship by return has been granted to approximately 722,400 immigrants from the former Soviet Union.[66] This massive wave of immigration again raised the complex question of "who is a Jew," and therefore who is accorded the right of return as set forth in the Law of Return and the Citizenship Law.[67] The question of "who is a Jew" for the purpose of entitlement to the right of return has plagued the State of Israel since its inception, mainly because it exposes a deep gulf between the two main paradigms for defining Jews: religious and secular. Of the different religious (*Halakhic*) definitions of Jewishness, the most important one politically in Israel has been the Orthodox definition, namely, birth to a Jewish mother or an Orthodox conver-

---

63. See, generally, Portes and Böröcz, 1989, p. 606 (discussing international "pull-push" migration theories). Note, however, that unlike the standard understanding of "push" and "pull" factors (which are primarily economically based) in the case of Jewish immigration to Israel, these factors also have an ideological dimension, reflected, for example, in the growing "pull" factor Israel had after the Six Day War, which brought a large number of immigrants from economically well-off countries (Europe and the United States), or a growing sense of anti-Semitism, as a "push" factor. See, generally, Sharkansky, 1997, pp. 71–84.

64. These benefits, known as the *sal-kelita* ("return packet"), included, for example, language training fully paid for by the state, universal health coverage, housing subsidies, employment training courses, and entitlement to financial support. The form and extent of financial assistance varied with the immigrant's country of origin, family size, age, and economic circumstances. It could take the form of a grant, stipend, loan, or standing loan (a loan that becomes a grant after a specified period of settlement in Israel). All immigrants who arrived from the former Soviet Union, however, were entitled to direct monetary aid upon their settlement in Israel. See Ministry of Immigrant Absorption, 1996, pp. 30–35, 42–55, 71–72, 85–89, 119–23.

65. For some of the *olim* who joined the massive exile from the former Soviet Union, "Israel was a transition station; for most, it became a permanent home." Peretz and Doron, 1997, p. 50.

66. See Ministry of Immigrant Absorption, June 1998, p. 2.

67. The Law of Return grants automatic citizenship to non-Jewish immigrants by return, if, for example, their spouse has a Jewish grandfather or grandmother. See Israel, 1970, The Law of Return (Amendment No. 2), 24 L.S.I. 28, § 4A; Israel, 1952, Citizenship Law, 6 L.S.I. 50, (1951–52), § 2(a). Before their *aliyah,* some of the Russian immigrants had only minimal affiliation with Judaism or with the State of Israel, and their entitlement to return was put into question. In 1984, another significant group of immigrants arrived in Israel, numbering approximately 7,000; these were Ethiopian Jews being brought to Israel in a rescue effort known as "Operation Moses." In 1991, another 15,000 *olim* from Ethiopia arrived from Addis Ababa in a dramatic airlift known as "Operation Solomon." The "authenticity" of these new returning immigrants' Judaism was also put into question. In their case, however, the challenge was by the Orthodox Rabbinical establishment, referring to the Ethiopian Jewish community as a whole, not to specific individuals' entitlement to the right of return as determined by the state's bureaucratic agencies. See Sharkansky, 1997, p. 82.

Table 13-1. *Immigration to Israel by Region of Origin, 1989–1997*

Region	Total immigrants	Percent of total immigrants
Total	847,900	100.0
Asia	10,000	1.2
Africa	40,100	4.7
Europe	761,600	89.8
(former Soviet Union)	(722,400)	(82.25)
North America and Oceania	20,400	2.4
Latin America	14,900	1.8
Other	900	0.1

Source: Ministry of Immigration Absorption, *Immigration and Absorption 1989*–1997, Annual Report (Jerusalem: 1998), p. 2.

sion to Judaism. The secular Zionist understanding of Jewishness, on the other hand, is expressed through Israeli nationality and self-identification of an individual with the state, and has little to do with the obligations or beliefs of traditional Jewish faith.[68] These two paradigms have been in direct conflict, pitting religious positions against the secular Zionist understanding of Jewishness. This conflict has manifested itself in the legal arena, time and again, and has been the subject of several landmark Supreme Court decisions in the 1960s and 1970s, of which I will discuss the most prominent decision: the *Shalit* case of 1968.[69]

In the 1960s and the 1970s the question of "who is a Jew" was aired in the debate about whether a person's Jewish identity and nationality should be defined by "external," religious (*Halakhic*) rules, or by "internal" decisions, such as self-identification and choices expressed through the person's actions, for example, by establishing a home in Israel and becoming rooted in its history and culture. In *Shalit*, the Court held in favor of the latter definition by a narrow five to four majority.[70] The Court ruled that for purposes of the population regis-

68. See, generally, Arian, 1998, pp. 6–11.

69. H.C. 58/68, *Shalit v. Minister of Interior,* 23(2) P.D. 477.

70. In *Shalit*, the Court had to decide whether the minister of the interior could register children born to an Israeli Jewish father and a non-Jewish mother as "Jewish," for purposes of the population registry, when under the *Halakhic* definition of membership they were not considered Jewish. The specific issue was whether children of an Israeli-Jewish father and an Israeli non-Jewish mother could be registered as Jews for the administrative purpose of the population registry, which invoked

try (and by analogy, for the purposes of the Law of Return), the government, through its administrative bodies, such as the Ministry of the Interior, had no authority to determine a person's national or religious affiliation. Rather, the only relevant criterion was a person's *bona fide* statement of such an affiliation.[71] The Israeli legislature thought differently, however. In an unusual move in Israeli politics, the Knesset overruled the Supreme Court by amending section 4B of the Law of Return to read as follows: "for the purposes of this Law, 'Jew' means a person who was born of a Jewish mother or has become converted to Judaism and who is not a member of another religion."[72]

To balance out this narrow, semi-*Halakhic* definition of Jewishness, the Knesset added another section to the Law of Return, which greatly expanded the right of return by granting this right to any family member of an entitled person (that is, a "Jew" by the above definition), up to a third generation and regardless of the family members' religious affiliation. Section 4A of the 1970 amendment vests in "a child and a grandchild of a Jew, the spouse of a Jew," the spouse of a child and a grandchild of a Jew all the rights of an *oleh* to Israel.[73] Here, again, we see the unusual conception of Israeli immigration law that goes to great lengths to determine who is an "insider" to the collective. Once a person is considered eligible for the right of return, however, then all the gates are open and a conscious effort is made to erase formal legal distinctions between the newcomer immigrant and the settled citizen.[74]

In its construction of the legal category of membership by return, of "who is a Jew" for the purposes of the Law of Return and the Citizenship Law, the 1970 amendment resolved the tension surrounding the question of who is by *family genealogy* or *marriage* entitled to Israeli citizenship. It established a middle ground between a religious definition of Jewishness (section 4B), and a secular Zionist understanding of Israeli national identity (section 4A), which generally welcomes non-Jewish family members who are willing to come to the country and establish their life as participants in its republic.[75] In other words, living in

---

the more general question of how to interpret the criteria for membership in the Jewish people in the context of the Law of Return. See H.C. 58/68, *Shalit v. Minister of Interior*, 23(2) P.D. 477.

71. In other words, the presumption is that a citizen's statement is truthful. The only way to rebut the person's statement is through a declaratory judgment of a district court to the effect that the information given to the registration officer was false. See H.C. 58/68, *Shalit v. Minister of Interior*, 23(2) P.D. 477, p. 489.

72. Israel, 1970, The Law of Return (Amendment No. 2), 24 L.S.I. 28, § 4B.

73. Israel, 1970, The Law of Return (Amendment No. 2), 24 L.S.I. 28, § 4A.

74. It is estimated that since the mid-1990s significant numbers of immigrants from the Soviet Union were not seen as "Jews" by the Orthodox *Halakhic* definition. In 1997, for example, only 56.4 percent of the immigrants by return were "Jews" by the Orthodox *Halakhic* definition. See Somech, June 12, 1998.

75. See, generally, Lahav, 1997.

Israel, taking part in its culture, and expressing willingness to serve or have their children serve in the military, is, according to the secular Zionist understanding of citizenship, as much a proof of those persons' affiliation with the state as any religious criteria for membership of the Jewish people.

The 1970 amendment of the Law of Return, however, remained silent on another issue—conversion—that proved to be a major controversy in the late 1980s and early 1990s. The Law of Return states in section 4B that any person who has converted to Judaism is entitled to Israeli citizenship by return, but the law does not specify the rules under which the conversion must take place, and thus has set the stage for current controversy over "who is a Jew."[76] In the 1980s and the 1990s, then, the debate shifted to an inquiry about the rites of passage that a person with no previous affiliation with Judaism or the State of Israel has to go through in order to be recognized religiously as a "Jew," and based on that definition, the individual may establish entitlement to citizenship by way of return. Specifically, the point at issue was whether *any* denomination of Jewish rabbi or religious institution could officiate a conversion to Judaism, or whether this authority was solely vested in the representatives of Orthodox Jewry.[77]

This debate brought to the surface the bitter division between the institutional power of Orthodox Jewry in Israel and the overwhelming opinion of (the mainly non-Orthodox) world Jewry. Many conversions to Judaism take place outside Israel and under the guidance and authority of non-Orthodox rabbis. In 1989, the Supreme Court held in *Sephardi Torah Guardians, Shas Movement v. Director of Population Registry* that for purposes of immigration, any person who converted to Judaism outside Israel, whether under an Orthodox, Conservative, or Reform religious institution, is automatically entitled to all the rights of an *oleh*, as stated in the Law of Return and the Citizenship Law.[78] In 1995, in *Pesarro (Goldstein) v. Minister of Interior*, the Supreme Court was again drawn into the muddy waters of identity politics.[79] This time, the question brought before the Court was whether a non-Jewish person who underwent a non-Orthodox conversion in Israel was entitled to automatic citizenship based on the right to return. The ostensibly insignificant fact of the location of the conversion is highly politically charged due to the Orthodox institutional monopoly over Jewish religious services in Israel (such as solemnizing of marriage and di-

---

76. See Israel, 1970, The Law of Return (Amendment No. 2), 24 L.S.I. 28, § 4B.

77. See Arian, 1998, p. 316.

78. H.C. 264/87, *Sephardi Torah Guardians, Shas Movement v. Director of Population Registry,* 43(2) P.D. 723.

79. H.C. 1031/93, *Pessaro (Goldstein) v. Minister of Interior,* 49(4) P.D. 661 (hereinafter *Goldstein*).

vorce), and the growing power of religious parties in the Knesset.[80] Had the Court ruled in favor of the petitioners in the *Goldstein* case, its actions would have been portrayed as "deregulating" the religious services arena, a step that could have caused a backlash by the legislature, as was indeed the case in the aforementioned 1968 *Shalit* case. In 1995, however, the justices were more cautious. The Court ruled that while in principle a non-Orthodox conversion may take place in Israel and have validity for the purposes of the Law of Return, they did not rule on the merits of the case brought before them. Even this carefully crafted judicial decision was viewed as inflammatory by religious parties in the Knesset who in return initiated a proposed new amendment to the Law of Return that would specify that only Orthodox conversion to Judaism could be valid for the purposes of the Law of Return and the Citizenship Law. This legislative proposal has been a source of great discontent to U.S. Jewry in particular, whose leaders view such an amendment to the Law of Return as potentially undercutting the bond between Israel and the rest of the Jewish world, which, for the most part, is not Orthodox. By claiming the illegitimacy of the main religious institutions of world Jewry in the very law that defines the centrality of the Diaspora to the sovereign Jewish state, the Orthodox parties could seriously erode relations between the Israel and world Jewry.[81] This legislative proposal has not materialized in law, but it has neither been fully removed from the political agenda.[82]

Citizenship by Residence

As explained above, all Jews born in Israel, or who immigrated to Israel, acquire automatic citizenship through the Law of Return. Non-Jews cannot generally acquire Israeli citizenship by way of return (unless they are family members of a person entitled to the right of return); rather, they must establish citizenship by way of residence, birth, or naturalization. These different methods of establishing citizenship were set in place in 1952, the formative years of nation building in Israel.[83] At that time, the citizenship law had to establish the requirements for citizenship by way of residence, a definition that had significant political implication in light of the following facts: until 1947, "Arabs constituted two-thirds of Palestine as a whole and made up nearly one-half of their

80. See Arian, 1998, pp. 127–33.
81. See Arian, 1998, p. 316.
82. See Sharkansky, 1997, p. 161.
83. See Israel, 1952, Citizenship Law, 6 L.S.I. 50, (1951–52), § 3.

residents in the area designated the Jewish state by the partition plan."[84] For complex reasons, the 1947 UN partition plan never went into effect.[85] Instead, British officials were to govern Palestine until May 15, 1948, the last day of the League of Nations Mandate over Palestine.[86] Between November 30, 1947, and May 15, 1948, the tensions between the Jewish and Arab communities escalated into violent incidents. Amid these events, on May 14, 1948, Israel was established as an independent state by the Declaration of Independence by Jewish leaders of the *Yishuv*. The following day, on May 15, with the official termination of British Mandate, the armies of Egypt, Syria, Lebanon, and Iraq joined forces in the battle to prevent the establishment of the a Jewish state. The 1948 war (which Israelis call the "War of Independence," and Palestinians call *al-Nakaba*, or "the Disaster")[87] officially ended in 1949 with a set of armistice agreements that solidified Israel's frontiers with its Arab neighbors until 1967.[88]

This war, like any other war in history, had many tragic consequences. Yet because both Israelis and Palestinians hold territorial and national claims over the same land, "there can be no agreement on what actually happened in 1948."[89] In terms of our discussion of citizenship, it is important to note that there is a continuing debate over how and why hundreds of thousands of Palestinians left their homes and lands after the establishment of the State of Israel in May 1948.[90] Many of those who left Israel later became refugees in neighboring Arab countries and are collectively referred to as the "1948 refugees."[91] Some international estimates suggest that "the number of 1948 refugees was approximately 604,000, about half of the Palestinian population living in Israel at the

---

84. Peretz and Doron, 1997, p. 55. The UN partition resolution recommended that Palestine be divided into a Jewish state, an Arab state, and an international enclave around Jerusalem. UN General Assembly Resolution 181 (Partition Plan), November 29, 1947.

85. The Jewish community in Palestine (the *Yishuv*) generally viewed the UN partition resolution as a significant step toward the fulfillment of the Zionist dream of "establishing in Palestine a national home for the Jewish people." This phrasing of the Zionist aspiration was incorporated in the Balfour Declaration given by Great Britain on November 2, 1917. This Declaration took the form of a public letter signed by Lord Alfred Balfour, the British foreign minister, which stated that "His Majesty's Government view with favor the establishment in Palestine of a national home for the Jewish people . . . it being clearly understood that nothing shall be done which may prejudice the civil and religious rights of existing non-Jewish communities in Palestine, or the rights and political status enjoyed by Jews in any other country." Hurewitz, 1979, p. 106.

86. See Peretz and Doron, 1997, p. 42.

87. See Kimmerling and Migdal, 1993, p. xv.

88. See Peretz and Doron, 1997, p. 42.

89. Shlaim, 1995, p. 287.

90. See Weiner, 1997, p. 7.

91. See, generally, Weiner, 1997, pp. 5–10.

time."[92] Yet the exact number of refugees has never been established. Several Israeli scholars place the figures between 600,000 and 750,000,[93] while certain Arab sources suggest that the numbers are even higher, ranging from 750,000 to 1,000,000.[94] A related dispute refers to the causes of this mass displacement. Roughly speaking, "most pro-Palestinian narratives claim that the Palestinian evacuation resulted from a carefully designed Israeli campaign to drive the Arabs out of Palestine," whereas the traditional view expressed by Israeli policy makers "is that most Palestinians left their homes during the 1948 war either because of a general sense of fear and confusion, or because they were prompted to evacuate by Arab leaders."[95] The question of voluntary or involuntary exodus is significant not only in terms of "getting the history right"; but also, it may also have major political implication: any comprehensive peace agreement between Israel, the Palestinians, and its neighboring Arab states must eventually address the 1948 refugees' claim for repatriation or establish a scheme of financial compensation (as a possible alternative to resettlement).[96]

In the eyes of the 1952 Israeli Citizenship Law, however, any Palestinian who discontinued his or her residency in Israel after the establishment of the state lost his or her entitlement to automatic Israeli citizenship by right of residence.[97] In other words, the official policy adopted by the Israeli government in

92. Weiner, 1997, p. 7.

93. See, for example, Lewin-Epstein and Semyonov, 1993, p. 16; Lustick, 1980, p. 28 (estimating the number of 1948 refugees to be 750,000); Soffer, 1994, p. 292 (estimating the number of 1948 refugees to be more than 700,000). See, generally, Morris, 1987.

94. See Kimmerling and Migdal, 1993, p. 147. The ArabNet, for example, a comprehensive online resource on the Arab world published by a Saudi research and marketing group, deals with this controversial issue in the following way: "as a result of the war, 780,000 Palestinians became refugees. About half that number left in fear and panic while those remaining were compelled to make room for Jewish immigrants from both European and Arab countries." *Palestine History*, January 19, 1999.

95. Weiner, 1997, pp. 15, 21–22. In recent years, a number of Israeli "revisionist" or "new historians" have challenged the traditional Israeli interpretation, arguing that while there was probably no Israeli plan to drive the Arab population from their homes and lands, certain local incidents of expulsion carried by individual commanders effectively spurred the Palestinian departure. See, generally, Morris, 1990.

96. See, generally, Weiner, 1997 (comprehensively analyzing the 1948 refugee problem and the Palestinians' "right to return").

97. Israel, 1952, Citizenship Law, 6 L.S.I. 50, (1951–52), § 3; Peled and Shafir, 1996, pp. 402–404. In many cases, persons who left the country or failed to register as inhabitants also lost their entitlement to property in Israeli territory. The Absentees' Property Law, 1950, regulated matters related to the administration of property "abandoned" by the Arab Palestinians refugees during the 1948 war. Interestingly, the definition of "absentee" in this law is similar to that of the requirements for entitlement to citizenship by way of residence encoded in the Citizenship Law of 1952. Both these laws were formulated to exclude as many Arabs as possible from the classification of citizenship, that is, those persons entitled to full civil, political, and social rights. See Hofnung, 1996, p. 105.

the 1950s was to prevent the 1948 refugees from establishing Israeli citizenship status.[98] The main idea behind the newly established state's citizenship policy toward Palestinians was, as one scholar aptly summarized it,

> that nationality by residence should be conferred only upon those non-Jews who remained in Israel after the establishment of the State or who subsequently entered Israel lawfully, e.g., under a family re-unification scheme. Those who crossed to the enemy lines during the War of Independence only to infiltrate back again later were not to be rewarded with the grant of Israel nationality.[99]

In the early years of statehood, the borders of the new Israeli State were far from sealed. Individuals managed "to cross from one side to the other without going through the official entry posts."[100] Indeed, "many [Palestinian] Arabs who had fled their homes, or had been expelled, to neighboring countries during the war managed to cross the border back into Israel."[101] Regardless of the causes that had led them to depart from their homes and lands during the war, these persons were understandably anxious to formalize their status as residents and to register in the Population Registry, in order to establish their Israeli citizenship.[102] Yet many Palestinian Arabs found it difficult to prove that they had met the stringent conditions laid down in section 3 of the 1952 Citizenship Law, and, as a result, were denied Israeli citizenship status.[103]

The provisions for acquiring Israeli citizenship by way of residence, set forth in section 3 of the Citizenship Law, consisted of three cumulative conditions: (1) residency; (2) presence in Israel *after* the establishment of the state in 1948; and (3) registration in the 1951 Population Registry.[104] Section 3 was clearly designed to grant automatic citizenship status to Arab residents who had stayed in Israel during the 1948 war, while denying this status to Arab residents who had left Israel during the war.[105] During the 1950s, the Supreme Court

---

98. This position was expressed, for example, by Israel's first foreign minister, Moshe Sharett, in a 1949 debate in the Knesset: "Allowing the refugees to return without a peace settlement with the neighboring countries would be suicide for the State of Israel; it would be like stabbing ourselves in the chest, no other state in our situation would even consider such a step." D.K. (1949) 721, Statement of Foreign Minister Moshe Sharett.

99. Gouldman, 1970, pp. 70–71.

100. Kretzmer, 1989, p. 37.

101. Kretzmer, 1989, p. 37.

102. See Kretzmer, 1989, p. 37.

103. See Hofnung, 1996, pp. 77–82.

104. See Israel, 1952, Citizenship Law, 6 L.S.I. 50, (1951–52), § 3.

105. See Kretzmer, 1989, pp. 37–38; Rubinstein, 1976, p. 171.

rarely overruled administrative decisions that denied Arabs' requests to be registered as residents or as citizens, even if these persons had been illegally deported from Israel and had later managed to return to their homes.[106] This policy left a class of persons who lived in Israel but were stateless, since they had lost their previous Palestinian citizenship (which was terminated with the end of the British Mandate) but were unable to prove the cumulative conditions set in the Citizenship Law in order to acquire Israeli citizenship by residence.[107] These persons de facto resided in Israel but had no *de jure* residence or citizenship status.

This problem was partly resolved with the 1960 *Mussa* case,[108] in which the Supreme Court changed its previous narrow reading of the Citizenship Law and held that because citizenship is one of the most precious entitlements an individual has, it cannot be denied because of procedural faults.[109] This change in policy meant that people who had left Israel with permission for a period during the war or shortly thereafter were entitled to Israeli citizenship, even if their residence was "interrupted" by the war. "Any other reading of the Citizenship Law," held the Court, "would deny Israeli citizenship to thousands of non-Jewish residents . . . a result which the Knesset would never have intended."[110] The 1980 amendment of the Citizenship Law finally resolved the problem of statelessness of Israeli Arab residents who were previously residents of the territory but could not prove their entitlement to citizenship by residence under the strict provisions of the original 1952 Citizenship Law. The 1980 amendment retroactively recognized these Israeli residents as citizens of the state since its inception in 1948.[111] More important, the amendment also granted automatic

---

106. See, for example, H.C. 64/54, *Bader v. Minister of Police,* 8 P.D. 970.

107. See, for example, H.C. 125/51, *Hassin v. Minister of Interior,* 5 P.D. 1386; H.C. 157/51, *Abad v. Minister of Interior,* 5 P.D. 1680. For a more detailed discussion of the attempts by former Arab residents to obtain Israeli citizenship, see, generally, Hofnung, 1996, pp. 76–86. The Citizenship Law did not resolve the status of thousands of Arab residents who returned to Israel illegally by crossing the border back into the state without the government's permission after the end of the 1948 war. Such denial of status had grave implications in terms of these persons' ability to claim ownership over "abandoned" homes, lands, and property that were left behind in Israeli territory. For further discussion of this troubling period in Israel's history, see Hofnung, 1996, pp. 101–12 (discussing the Absentees' Property Law of 1950).

108. H.C. 328/60, *Mussa v. Minister of Interior,* 16 P.D. 1793, aff'd F.H. 3/63, *Minister of Interior v. Mussa,* 17 P.D. 2467.

109. Technically, this decision meant that section 3 of the Citizenship Law need not be interpreted as requiring uninterrupted residence.

110. H.C. 328/60, *Mussa v. Minister of Interior,* 16 P.D. 1793, p. 1868.

111. See Israel, 1980, Citizenship Law (Amendment No. 4), 34 L.S.I. 254, (1979–80), § 3A(5)(b).

citizenship to the children of these residents by virtue of a *jus sanguinis* principle.

Note, however, that none of the above-mentioned changes in the Citizenship Law affected the legal status of the Palestinian Arab population in the West Bank and Gaza Strip, nor that of Palestinian refugees residing in neighboring Arab countries.[112] Between the Six Day War of 1967 and the signing of the 1993 Declaration of Principles (the Oslo peace accord) between Israel and the PLO, the Palestinian Arab population in the West Bank and Gaza Strip was subject to Israeli military occupation. Palestinians living in these territories enjoyed only heavily circumscribed rights, since they were considered neither citizens nor residents of Israel.[113] Thus, although noncitizen Palestinian Arabs were in many respects effectively part of the Israeli society and its economy, they were not legally incorporated into the state.[114] Their status was even less favorable than that of "denizens" in Europe and North America, since as occupied persons they were not permitted to establish a secure permanent residence status in Israel.[115] Instead, Palestinians in the West Bank and Gaza were granted "permanent residence" status in the occupied territories, by a registrar operated by the Israeli Civil Administration, under the Israeli minister of defense. As a result of the Oslo peace accord, the Palestinian Authority (PA) now has the general power to determine "permanent residence" status of persons under its territorial, functional, and personal jurisdiction over most of the West Bank and Gaza Strip.[116]

112. Israel, 1980, Citizenship Law (Amendment No. 4), 34 L.S.I. 254, (1979–80), § 4. Some of these refugees assumed citizenship status in Jordan or in other non-Arab countries where they resided, but many still claim their right of return to Israel. Politically, the problem of citizenship for refugees is likely to be resolved as part of a comprehensive peace settlement between Israel, the Palestinians, and the neighboring Arab countries. Several negotiation proposals refer to monetary compensation to the 1948 Palestinian refugees, assistance to help resettle the refugees in neighboring countries rather than a materialization of a Palestinian right of return to Israel or a future Palestinian entity. See, generally, Weiner, 1997.

113. After the Six Day War, Israel established a military occupation in the West Bank and Gaza in 1967, but it has never annexed these territories. East Jerusalem, however, was incorporated to Israel in 1967 and formally annexed to Israel in 1980. See *Basic Law,* January 3, 1999. For a concise overview of the complex legal and political problems of Jerusalem, see, generally, Sharkansky, 1997, pp. 115–47.

114. See, generally, Rubinstein, 1994, p. 237.

115. I use the old English word "denizens" as employed by Tomas Hammar to refer to a category of "privileged noncitizens." They are, in his definition, "foreign citizens who have a secure permanent residence status [in the host country], and who are connected to the state by an extensive array of rights and duties." Hammar, 1989, pp. 81, 84.

116. In effect, the accord provided that (1) all persons who were illegally residing in the West Bank and Gaza for a period of at least three years, before January 1996, were permitted to apply for Palestinian permanent residence status; (2) the PA acquired authority to register as "Palestinian permanent residents" in the territories, all children who were sixteen years of age or younger if one of

Citizenship by Birth

Returning to the discussion of the different ways of acquiring Israeli citizenship, it is important to note that any person born in Israel whose father or mother is an Israeli citizen is automatically granted Israeli citizenship at birth. There is no requirement that the child's parent be married or that both parents have Israeli citizenship. Similarly, the manner in which the parent acquired Israeli citizenship is irrelevant.[117] Hence, children of Jews and Arab citizens have a similar entitlement to birthright citizenship.[118] The 1980 amendment to the Citizenship Law resolves the anomaly present in the 1950 Law of Return, that children born in Israel to at least one Israeli Jewish parent are regarded as if they themselves were immigrants, or citizens by way of return (rather than by way of birth to an Israeli parent). In other words, the Citizenship Law now gives precedent to the principle of citizenship by birthright over the legal fiction of granting citizenship to children born in Israel based on the right to return.[119] This change is significant because it "normalizes" the pattern of acquiring Israeli citizenship (toward a standard *jus sanguinis* principle), and because it provides a universal definition of birthright entitlement to Israeli citizenship that is devoid of any religious-based distinctions.

Children born outside Israel to an Israeli parent are also granted automatic citizenship at birth. In fact, until the 1980 amendment to the Citizenship Law, Israeli citizenship was transmitted as a birthright by descent in perpetuity, regardless of the place of birth or of the parents' place of residence.[120] A person who attained citizenship *jure sanguinis* outside Israel

their parents had permanent residence status; and (3) the PA acquired authority to determine the legal status of nonresident spouses of Palestinian permanent residents (subject to Israeli approval of such an application). See Association for Civil Rights in Israel, 1996. See also Declaration of Principles, September 13, 1993; *Gaza-Jericho Agreement,* January 21, 1999.

117. See Israel, 1980, Citizenship Law (Amendment No. 4), 34 L.S.I. 254, (1979–80), § 4(a)(1).

118. The Law of Return states that all Jews born in Israel are regarded as if they were immigrants, hence Jewish children born in Israel are entitled to citizenship both by way of return and by way of birth. It would seem, then, as one commentator put it, that the "real 'citizenship beneficiaries' of section 4(a)(1) [of the Citizenship Law] regarding citizenship by birth are Arabs born to parents one of whom is an Israeli citizen." Kretzmer, 1989, p. 39.

119. See Israel, 1980, Citizenship Law (Amendment No. 4), 34 L.S.I. 254, (1979–80), § 4(a)(1).

120. Section 4 of the Citizenship Law, in its old version, provided that: "A person born while his father or mother is an Israel national shall be an Israel national from birth." Israel, 1952, Citizenship Law, 6 L.S.I. 50, (1951–52), § 4. The amended section 4 now provides that "(a) The following shall, from the date of their birth, be Israel nationals by birth: (1) a person born in Israel while his father or mother was an Israel national; (2) a person born outside Israel while his father or mother was an Israel national—(a) by return; (b) by residence in Israel; (c) by naturalization; (d) under paragraph 1." Israel, 1980, Citizenship Law (Amendment No. 4), 34 L.S.I. 254, (1979–80), § 4(a)(1).

could, in turn, transmit Israeli citizenship to his or her children even if that person never stepped foot in Israel and had no effective links to the state.[121] This imposition of Israeli citizenship in perpetuity imposed the duties of citizenship upon such children born outside the country. They were subject, for example, to recruitment to the military at the age of eighteen and were considered deserters if they did not fulfill this mandatory citizenship obligation. Moreover, because Israeli citizenship is only lost in extreme circumstances (as I discuss later in this chapter), the Citizenship Law forced membership upon individuals solely because one of their progenitors was once an Israeli citizen.[122] The 1980 amendment to the Citizenship Law changed this legal situation, and currently acquisition of citizenship *jure sanguinis* outside the state is limited to one generation only.[123] The only determining factor for acquiring citizenship in this fashion is that at the time the child is born outside Israel, one of the parents must be an Israeli citizen. If a child is born outside Israel after the death of the parent who was an Israeli citizen, the child is still granted automatic citizenship at birth.[124]

Citizenship by Naturalization

In contrast to the acquisition of Israeli citizenship by way of return, residence, or birth, which is *automatic*, naturalization is subject to the discretion of the minister of the interior. In order to qualify for citizenship by way of naturalization, the applicant must fulfill six prerequisites listed in section 5 of the Citizenship Law. That is, the applicant must (1) be in Israel; (2) have been in Israel three out of the five years preceding the day of submission of the application; (3) have been entitled to permanent residency; (4) have settled or expressed intent to settle in the Israel; (5) have basic knowledge of the Hebrew language (however, no mandatory language proficiency test is imposed); and (6) have renounced his or her prior citizenship or has proved willingness to terminate it upon becoming an Israeli citizen.[125] Upon approval of the application for naturalization by the minister of the interior, the naturalized person is entitled to Israeli citizenship after taking the following simple oath: "I declare that I will be a

121. See Rubinstein, 1976, p. 172.

122. See Israel, 1952, Citizenship Law, 6 L.S.I. 50, (1951–52), § 4.

123. See Israel, 1980, Citizenship Law (Amendment No. 4), 34 L.S.I. 254, (1979–80), § 4(a)(1).

124. See Israel, 1980, Citizenship Law (Amendment No. 4), 34 L.S.I. 254, (1979–80), § 4(b).

125. See Israel, 1952, Citizenship Law, 6 L.S.I. 50, (1951–52), § 5. Moreover, section 6(c) of the Citizenship Law exempts all people who were Palestinian citizens under the British Mandate (that is, before the establishment of the State of Israel in May 1948) from the language proficiency requirement. See Israel, 1952, Citizenship Law, 6 L.S.I. 50, (1951–52), § 6(c).

loyal [citizen] of the State of Israel."[126] These prerequisites for naturalization are in many respects no harsher than those of many other countries in the world;[127] however, they are extremely restrictive in comparison with the automatic grant- ing of citizenship by way of return to Jews and their non-Jewish family mem- bers who wish to make *aliyah* to Israel. While *olim*, for example, do not have to renounce their citizenship to other countries upon becoming Israelis, natural- ized immigrants are required to renounce or express willingness to renounce their prior citizenship.[128] This distinction is another reflection of the entrenched "ethnocultural" conception of Israeli citizenship and immigration policy. It likely assumes that a "feeling of solidarity and loyalty to the political commu- nity can be presumed only of those persons who by way of common interests or shared historical experience" are already part of the nation,[129] whereas those who are not by religion, ancestry, or family affinity related to the Jewish people, must assert their loyalty to the Israeli State by severing their citizenship ties to a former political community.[130] To provide further illustration to this problem, the next section considers the effect of Israeli citizenship law and immigration policy upon third parties, such as non-Jewish alien spouses of Israeli citizens (who until 1996 were treated differently if they were married to a Jewish Israeli citizen or a non-Jewish Israeli citizen).

Gender, Marriage, and Citizenship

Until recently, Jewish citizens received preferential treatment over non-Jew- ish citizens in matters where citizenship and marriage converged. Specifically, the minister of the interior implemented two different legal procedures for the acquisition of Israeli citizenship by an alien spouse, depending on the religion of the Israeli spouse.[131] In principle, if an alien spouse married a Jewish Israeli citizen, the alien spouse was *automatically* entitled to Israeli citizenship upon marriage. This automatic granting of citizenship was based on a long-estab- lished interpretation of section 4A of the Law of Return that states that the "rights of a Jew under this Law and the rights of an [*oleh*] under the [Citizen- ship] Law . . . are also vested in a child and a grandchild of a Jew [and] the spouse of a Jew."[132] It was taken for granted that the legislature intended to in-

---

126. See Israel, 1952, Citizenship Law, 6 L.S.I. 50, (1951–52), § 5(c).
127. See *supra* note 18 and accompanying text.
128. See Israel, 1952, Citizenship Law, 6 L.S.I. 50, (1951–52), § 5(a)(6).
129. Hailbronner, 1989, p. 75 (discussing the German right of return).
130. See Israel, 1952, Citizenship Law, 6 L.S.I. 50, (1951–52), §§ 5(a)(6), 5(c).
131. See Gouldman, 1970, p. 84; Klein, 1997, p. 61.
132. Israel, 1970, The Law of Return (Amendment No. 2), 24 L.S.I. 28, § 4A(a).

clude the "alien" spouse of an Israeli Jewish citizen within those family members who are entitled to citizenship by way of return, thus permitting the alien spouse of a Jewish Israeli citizen to bypass the prerequisites of naturalization (as set forth in the aforementioned section 5 of the Citizenship Law).[133] An alien spouse who married a non-Jewish Israeli citizen, however, could not use the Law of Return "bypass." Instead, the alien spouse had to go through the more complex procedure of seeking Israeli citizenship by way of naturalization.[134] In principle, an alien spouse of an Israeli citizen could obtain citizenship by way of naturalization, even if he or she had not met the prerequisites of naturalization. This is a privilege, however, not a right.[135] The minister of the interior has discretion over whether to grant such an exemption and what the scope of such an exemption might be, specifically, which of the prerequisites specified in section 5 may be waived in any particular naturalization case because of marriage.[136]

Since September 1996, the minister of the interior has adopted a new "hard line" against any person seeking citizenship by way of marriage to an Israeli citizen, even when the Israeli spouse is Jewish.[137] The minister of the interior now requires that alien spouses married to Israeli citizens, whether Jewish or non-Jewish, "leave the country for six weeks to confirm the 'sincerity' of the marriage."[138] Thereafter, the alien spouse can reenter the country on a temporary visa,[139] apply for permanent resident status from within Israel, and only then begin the citizenship process.[140]

---

133. See *supra* notes 128–31 and accompanying text.

134. See Israel, 1952, Citizenship Law, 6 L.S.I. 50, (1951–52), § 5. See also discussion *supra* Citizenship by Naturalization.

135. See Israel, 1952, Citizenship Law, 6 L.S.I. 50, (1951–52), § 7.

136. See Israel, 1952, Citizenship Law, 6 L.S.I. 50, (1951–52), § 7. Note, however, that if the marriage took place outside Israel, and the Israeli citizen was not Jewish, then in order for the alien spouse to legally enter Israel, the spouse has to initially enter Israel on a tourist visa. As tourists, these spouses are not covered by the state's otherwise universal health coverage, nor are they entitled to social security benefits (permanent residents, however, are entitled to these benefits). See Adalah (the Legal Center for Arab Minority Rights in Israel), March 1998, p. 40. The question of social entitlements is of special concern in Israel because many of the alien spouses who applied for naturalization were Palestinians from the West Bank and Gaza Strip or from one of Israel's neighboring Arab countries. Given the economic disparities among Israel, the West Bank and Gaza Strip, and neighboring Arab countries, establishing permanent residency or citizenship in Israel has great significance in terms of ensuring, on average, a higher standard of living both for the couple and their children. See Economist Intelligence Unit, 1993–1994 (describing the economic disparities).

137. See Reinfeld, November 24, 1998.

138. Reinfeld, November 24, 1998.

139. See Adalah, March 1998, p. 39.

140. See Reinfeld, November 24, 1998. See also H.C. 3497/97, *Kamella v. Minister of Interior*, decision given on December 4, 1997 (unpublished), cited in Adalah, March 1998, p. 40.

This new immigration policy has a "race to the bottom" rationale. Instead of making it easier for the alien spouse of a non-Jewish citizen to establish Israeli citizenship, it "equalizes" the hardships by imposing greater difficulties upon alien spouses of Jewish Israeli citizens. Apparently, this policy was changed by the minister of the interior as a means of preventing "fictitious marriages" for the purposes of acquiring Israeli citizenship.[141] It reflects the growing anxiety about the status of nonmembers in Israel, particularly foreign workers who began entering the country in substantial numbers in the late 1980s.[142] In this respect, the motives behind the tightening regulation of immigration policy toward alien spouses in Israel were not too different from those that led to the passing of stricter immigration requirements in other countries, such as the Immigration Marriage Fraud Amendments of 1986 adopted by the United States Congress.[143] Yet, unlike the United States, this new policy was not publicly debated in Israel, nor was it approved by the Knesset, although it represents a departure from the long-standing interpretation of the Law of Return as granting automatic citizenship status to alien spouses of Jewish Israeli citizens.[144]

In practice, for many alien spouses (whether they are married to Jewish or non-Jewish Israelis) the real issue pivots around establishing permanent residency, a status that grants most of the social and economic benefits that are attached to Israeli citizenship.[145] Yet establishing permanent residency may prove to be more difficult for some alien spouses than others. In particular, the minister of the interior seems to place serious bureaucratic obstacles before *male* alien spouses who wish to establish permanent residency based on their marriage to Israeli wives. This case has long been a problem in the context of "family reunification" requests put forth by Palestinian Arab Israeli women.[146] These administrative hardships create a de facto barrier from fulfilling the right of every Israeli citizen to establish his or her family in Israel and to grant immigration status to his or her spouse. The problem is most acute in the case of Arab Israeli women who marry Palestinian husbands from the West Bank or Gaza.[147]

141. See Reinfeld, November 24, 1998. See also "Petitioner's Brief," H.C. 3648/97, *Stemka v. Minister of Interior.*

142. See discussion *infra* New Trends in Israeli Immigration Law.

143. See, generally, Immigration and Marriage Fraud Amendments of 1986, Pub. L. No. 99-639, 11 Stat. 3537 (codified as amended in scattered sections of 8 U.S.C.).

144. The legality of this change in immigration policy is currently under review by the Supreme Court. See H.C. 3648/97, *Stemka v. Minister of Interior* (decision pending).

145. See Adalah, March 1998, pp. 39–40.

146. See Association for Civil Rights in Israel, 1996 (discussing the Association for Civil Rights in Israel's representation of Palestinian Arab women seeking permanent resident status for their spouses).

147. See Association for Civil Rights in Israel, 1996.

To be more specific, it seems that the minister of the interior is operating under archaic gender presumptions that echo the infamous common-law principle
of female coverture in marriage. That doctrine holds that "by marriage, the husband and the wife are one person in law; that is, the very being or legal existence
of the wife is suspended during the marriage, or at least is incorporated and consolidated into that of the husband."[148] Historically, this principle of family unity
(or "dependent citizenship") had a deleterious effect on the legal status of
women who married aliens,[149] leading, for example, in certain periods in United
States history, to automatic expatriation of "those [American] women who
dared marry a foreigner."[150] Men, however, were not subject to the same sanction if they married an alien wife.[151] This gender-based distinction was common
in most countries' citizenship and nationality laws until World War I and is still
practiced in several countries today.[152] Israeli law, however, never subscribed to
this concept of dependent citizenship.[153] Instead, it firmly adopted the principle
of "independent citizenship," whereby an Israeli woman's nationality and citizenship are not lost "upon marriage to an alien even if, under the husband's national law, marriage has the effect of bestowing the husband's nationality upon
her."[154] In short, nothing in the provisions of the Citizenship Law permits discrimination in bestowing citizenship upon an alien spouse based on the gender
of the Israeli citizen.[155] Yet, from the scattered evidence available about the
practice of the minister of the interior in the case of requests for permanent residency or naturalization based on marriage to non-Jewish Israeli wives, there
seems to be a pattern of imposing greater administrative hardships upon male
Arab husbands who wish to establish status in Israel based on the principle of
family unity than would be the case if a non-Israeli wife sought to join her
non-Jewish citizen husband in Israel.[156]

---

148. Ehrlich, 1959, p. 83.
149. See, generally, Committee on Feminism and International law, International law Association, May 1998.
150. Sapiro, 1984, pp. 1, 10.
151. See Sapiro, 1984, pp. 1, 10.
152. See, generally, Stratton, 1992, p. 195.
153. See Gouldman, 1970, p. 83.
154. Gouldman, 1970, p. 83.
155. In fact, the Citizenship Law clearly asserts the independence of each spouse in matters of
nationality (that is, Israeli citizenship is not automatically bestowed upon the alien spouse, whether
wife or husband). See Gouldman, 1970, p. 83.
156. See Association for Civil Rights in Israel, May 25, 1993. As mentioned earlier, there are
no official numbers regarding the number of requests for family unity based on marriage that were
refused or on the impact that the gender of the spouse had upon the refusal. The only occasion on
which the issue of sex-based discrimination was directly confronted in the context of immigration
policy was in 1993 in *Gabari'th v. Minister of Interior*, where the petitioner alleged discrimination

To sum up the question of acquisition of citizenship, Israeli citizenship can be established by way of return, residence, birth, or naturalization. Israeli citizenship is transmitted primarily through the *jus sanguinis* principle. Birthright entitlement to membership in the polity is equally guaranteed to all Israeli citizens, Arabs and Jews alike, regardless of the way in which they themselves established citizenship. Children born outside Israel to an Israeli parent acquire automatic citizenship at birth; however, their children are not entitled to Israeli citizenship by birth if the family has no effective ties to the country.

Rights and Obligations of Citizenship

Most of the civil, economic, and social entitlements guaranteed by law to Israeli citizens are equally applicable to permanent residents.[157] Citizenship makes a difference in two arenas, however: on the "rights" side, that is, the right to full political participation on the national level; and on the "obligations" side, that is, the duty to serve in the military.

Only citizens are entitled to vote for the Knesset (the Israeli Parliament) and for the prime minister (in direct elections).[158] Citizenship is also a precondition for employment in the civil service.[159] The right of Israeli citizens to enter the country, remain therein, and depart therefrom, is constitutionally protected.[160] In order to enter and depart Israel, a person must present a valid passport or a *laissez-passer* to an official at a frontier station.[161] "All persons are free to leave

---

by the minister of the interior against women from East Jerusalem who seek to establish residency status for their foreign husbands. The Court never reached a decision, however, because the petition was dismissed as moot after the minister of the interior granted permanent residency to the individual who brought the case, and also declared that "there would be no significance to the sex of the person requesting family unity from here thereafter." "Motion to Dismiss the Petition," H.C. 2797/93, *Gabari'th v. Minister of Interior.*

157. See Adalah, March 1998, p. 40. These benefits include, for example, entitlement to social security benefits, universal health care, and freedom of occupation. Individuals who enter Israeli on a temporary nonimmigrant visa (for example, tourists, foreign students, foreign workers) are granted a more limited set of rights and protections as specified by statute or case law. See Adalah, March 1998, p. 40. It is important to note that Basic Law: Human Dignity and Liberty (enacted in 1992) states that: "There shall be no violation of the life, body, or dignity *of any person as such.*" Israel, 1992, Basic Law: Human Dignity and Liberty, S.H. 1391, § 2 (emphasis added).

158. See Israel, 1958, Basic Law: The Knesset, S.H. 244, § 5. In March 1992, the proposal for direct election of the prime minister was adopted, although implementation was delayed until the 1996 election. Before this change, the prime minister was the head of ruling coalition in the Knesset.

159. Israel, 1959, Civil Service Law (Appointments), § 16.

160. See Israel, 1992, Basic Law: Human Dignity and Liberty, S.H. 1391, §§ 6(a), 6(b).

161. See Rubinstein, 1976, p. 184 [citing Entry into Israel Law, 1952, 6 L.S.I. 159 (1951-52) § 7 and Emergency Regulations (Departure from the State), 1948, 15 L.S.I. 179].

Israel";[162] however, Israeli citizens who have attained military age or are reserve soldiers can be prohibited from leaving Israel without a special travel permit from their military units.[163] Thus, in practice, all reserve soldiers must carry travel permits from their military units in order to leave the country lawfully.

By law, all Israeli citizens, male or female, are to be recruited at the age of eighteen for mandatory military service. The 1986 Defense Service Law (Consolidated Version) imposes a duty on every Israeli citizen, both men and women, to serve in the military.[164] Yet, as an administrative practice, the minister of defense has discretion to exempt certain persons from the obligation of mandatory military service.[165] This practice has been the case for many years for male ultra-Orthodox Jews who have attained the age of recruitment but are full-time students at a religious institution (*yeshiva*),[166] and for the majority of Palestinian Arab Israeli citizens.[167] Most Jewish Israeli citizens, however, do serve in the military. Male soldiers serve for a period of at least three years, while women soldiers usually serve for a period of two years.[168] These young men and women serve in the same units, but women are still largely barred from positions bearing the "direct combat" label.[169]

Unlike the United States and most other countries in the world, women in Israel have been admitted to the military service since the inception of the state in

162. See Israel, 1992, Basic Law: Human Dignity and Liberty, S.H. 1391, § 6(a).

163. See Rubinstein, 1976, pp. 184–85. Hence, any citizen must report to his or her military unit if called lawfully to service; failure to report is an offense for which a solider may be tried in a military court.

164. Israel, 1986, Defense Service Law (Consolidated Version), §§ 1, 13, 15.

165. See, generally, Kretzmer, 1989, pp. 98–107.

166. See Kretzmer, 1989, p. 106. The exemption of *yeshiva* students from military service by administrative practice rather than by law was struck down by the Supreme Court in December 1998. See Reinfeld, December 10, 1998; Ilan and Alon, December 10, 1998; H.C. 3267/97, *Rubinstein v. Minister of Defense*, decision given on Dec. 9, 1998 (unpublished).

167. Since the establishment of the state, recruiting officers, operating under the minister of defense, have refrained from recruiting the majority of Arab Israeli citizens for the draft. Male members of the Bedouin and Druze communities, however, have been recruited since the late 1950s. As Kretzmer notes, "there would appear to be two reasons for exempting the Arabs from military service. The official version is the wish not to present the Israeli Arabs with the conflict of having to take up arms against members of their own people (and possibly, even their own families). It would, however, be naive to believe that the fear that some Arabs might be tempted to use their arms against the Jewish state, rather than in defending it, was not an equally weighty reasons." See Kretzmer, 1989, p. 99 (citations omitted). These two reasons for not recruiting the majority of Palestinian Arab citizens to the Israeli military raise a host of questions (which go beyond the scope of this article) about how the Israeli government views Arab citizens, and how they view themselves in terms of identity and loyalty to the state.

168. See Kretzmer, 1989, p. 98.

169. The restriction on women holding direct combat positions is gradually being overturned. See, generally, Association for Civil Rights in Israel, 1996; H.C. 4541/94, *Miller v. Minister of Defense*, 49(4) P.D. 94.

1948. The hearing in the *Knesset* that preceded the enactment of the 1949 Defense Service Law, which established a mandatory duty for Israeli women (and men) to serve in the military, is full of references to women's contribution to statehood building (during the *Yishuv* period), and their *right*—as full and equal citizens of the newborn state—to serve in the military.[170] As David Ben Gurion, Israel's first prime minister, said:

> Our solider is first and foremost a citizen, in the fullest meaning of that term. A citizen belonging to his [or her] homeland, to the history of the nation, its culture and language. . . . [The military] is the state institution where all cleavages: ethnic, political, class-based or of any other sort, vanish. Each solider is equal to his companion in status.

Thus, "at the age of eighteen, immigrants and sons of the land, girls and boys, all are required . . . to know how to bear arms and use them."[171]

As previously mentioned, the emphasis on military service for the nation as the proof of inclusion in the body politic echoes a *republican* conception of citizenship, in which a connection is made between the commitment to make sacrifices for the nation and the right to fair share in governing.[172] The word "citizen" itself, as Linda Kerber observes, still carries "overtones inherited from antiquity and the Renaissance, when the citizen made the continued existence of the city possible by taking up arms on its behalf."[173] While much has changed since antiquity, political membership, especially in countries like Israel, still implies a profound connection between having full citizenship and the duty of military service.

This understanding of citizenship as a *practice* of active participation (not only as a mere bundle of rights) has had, however, an adverse effect of creating

170. See, for example, D.K. (1949) 1455, Statement of Knesset Member Y. Meridor.

171. D.K. (1949) 1336, Statement of Prime Minister and Minister of Defense David Ben Gurion. Ben Gurion's words were echoed by many of the other speakers. Some emphasized women's important contribution to the fight against the British Mandate authorities and the War of Independence, while others stressed the significance of military service in terms of full inclusion: "In creating a pioneer army in Israel, let the place of women not be neglected; we are equal participants in the building of the nation and in its protection." D.K. (1949) 1561. Even within this framework, however, women were always seen as "different" from men, as bearing a special responsibility the family and the home. The biblical image of the *eshet chayil* (or "woman of valor") who stands at the core of her family, home, and community, has, as Pnina Lahav observes, heavily influenced the political discourse regarding women's status in the early days of nation building in Israel. See Lahav, 1993, pp. 149, 125–53.

172. See, generally, Dahl, 1989, p. 246.

173. Kerber, 1993, pp. 95, 104.

in Israel what I label different "degrees of citizenship." By this term I refer to state practices and legal rules, as well as social practices and cultural conventions, that create a complex matrix of membership statuses that, explicitly or implicitly, differently allocate rights, duties, and ultimately powers among individuals who are all formally entitled to full and equal citizenship rights. While Jews and Palestinian Arab citizens of the Israeli State formally enjoy equal citizenship rights, for example, most Arab citizens are not recruited to the military (with the exception of male members of the Druze and Bedouin communities), and hence cannot "exercise their citizenship as *practice*, by attending to the common good."[174] In a country like Israel, where identity and group membership matter significantly and where wars and armed confrontations are still, for various exogenous and endogenous reasons, a real threat, military service has become an obvious demarcating tool for distinguishing between different members of the same polity—that is, between those who truly belong to the republic and those who are entitled to the rights of citizenship in the state but are conceived as less than full members of the political community because they do not partake in its most fundamental expressions of self-determination, that is, military service.[175]

In Israel, then, the clearest demarcation between different "degrees of citizenship" is the distinction between members of the Jewish majority and members of the Palestinian Arab citizen minority. Yet, every modern nation state has a potential tension between "citizenship in the state and membership of the nation. The former determines the criteria for formal participation in the political community. . . . The latter determines the criteria of substantive participation in the political community."[176] This potential tension between citizenship in the state and membership of the nation is aggravated in Israel, a state that is constitutionally defined as both *Jewish and democratic*.[177] The relationship be-

174. See Peled, 1992, p. 432 (emphasis added).
175. Some scholars consider the line of demarcation between these different degrees of citizenship as highly problematic. Peled, for example, suggests that Arab Israeli citizens cannot become full members because "Jewish ethnicity is a necessary condition for membership in the political community, while the contribution to the process of Jewish national redemption is a measure of one's civic virtue. This conception necessarily excludes the Arabs." Peled, 1992, p. 435. Smooha suggests that Israel is best categorized as a "democratic ethnic state" that combines an "extension of political and civil rights to individuals and certain collective rights to minorities with institutionalized dominance over the state by one of the ethnic groups." Smooha, 1990, pp. 389, 391.
176. Cohen, 1989, pp. 66, 67.
177. Israel has a set of Basic Laws that together serve as the formal core of the state's constitutional law. The definition of Israel as both a Jewish and democratic states appears, for example, in two Basic Laws enacted in 1992 (Basic Law: Freedom of Occupation, and Basic Law: Human Dignity and Liberty). This definition was already expressed in 1948, in Israel's Declaration of Inde-

tween the two terms of this definition is such that democracy usually takes priority, and it is extremely rare to explicitly use "Jew" and "non-Jew" as distinguishing factors among those already considered members of the body politic, that is, citizens. This is not the case, however, in determining who is *eligible* for membership in the state, as demonstrated by the Law of Return. The legislature sometimes uses the criterion of military service as a basis for providing supplemental social benefits to those who have participated in the highest obligation of citizenship, almost exclusively referring to members of the Jewish majority, thus discriminating between nominally equal Jewish and non-Jewish citizens. These social benefits include supplementary children allowances, tax credits, or assistance in mortgage payments, and go beyond the basic support provided to all other citizens.[178] While many countries provide discharged soldiers with benefits not available to others, the use of military service as criterion for entitlement in Israel may serve as a disguise for discrimination, because as a matter of administrative practice (not of law) most Israeli Arab citizens are not called up for military service and, thus, cannot enjoy those benefits that are provided exclusively to discharged soldiers.[179] In this respect, the republican ethos of active participation in the defense of the nation has the divisive effect of creating stratification between "first class" and "second class" Israeli citizens.[180]

Gender is another dividing line, which creates an even more complex matrix of "degrees of citizenship." By law, Israeli women are recruited to the military as an expression of their full membership in the state.[181] Even within this framework, however, women have always been "different" from men, bearing a special responsibility for the family and the home. Already in 1949, in presenting the Defense Service Law to the Knesset, David Ben Gurion noted, in analyzing the question of women's participation in the defense forces, that

> we must take into account two factors—and both of them together. The first factor—a woman has a special designation of motherhood ... the second factor—a woman is not only a woman, she also has a legal person-

---

pendence, and is commonly referred to by the Supreme Court. Various commentators have analyzed the legacy of this dual Jewish and democratic character of the State of Israel, and its political and legal consequences. See, generally, Kimmerling, 1985, p. 262.

178. See, generally, Kretzmer, 1989, pp. 98–107.

179. See Kretzmer, 1989, p. 99.

180. It is important to note that both the Jewish majority and the Palestinian Arab citizen minority are internally diverse communities. On certain issues, such as the peace process, for example, the ties that bind certain members across these two communities are deeper than the cleavages that divide among members within each community.

181. See Israel, 1986, Defense Service Law (Consolidated Version), §§ 13, 16.

ality [in her own right], in the same way as a man. As such, she must enjoy all the same rights and duties as a man.[182]

This understanding of motherhood as service to the nation, a duty that "women of the republic" bear toward the collective,[183] has found statutory expression in section 39 of the 1986 Defense Service Law (Consolidated Version), which states that "a mother to a child or a pregnant woman is exempted from the duty to military service upon informing [the military authorities] of her motherhood or pregnancy."[184] Similarly, a married woman at the age of recruitment may chose to volunteer for the military, although she is not bound to participate in this otherwise universal citizenship duty.[185] These exemptions illustrate that women's inclusion in the military, important as it may be in symbolic terms of equality, is still considered secondary—in the eyes of the Defense Service Law—to their "primary" contribution to the nation as wives and mothers. The duty of motherhood, it seems, takes precedence over women's other citizenship duties, namely military service, if these obligations are deemed to be in direct conflict with each other. Interestingly, the fact that male soldiers may also be husbands and fathers does not, in any way, affect their military status or duty as citizens.

Furthermore, while women in Israel have full citizenship rights, and are guaranteed equal treatment by law as wives and mothers, Israeli women are nevertheless subject to a system of gender-discriminatory religious codes that structurally relegate women to a "second class" citizenship status. For various historical reasons, Israel has preserved the ancient Ottoman Empire's *millet* system in the context of marriage and divorce regulation. Thus, no uniform state law applies over all citizens. Instead, each religious community governs its own members' marriage and divorce proceedings through a system of autonomous religious courts that have been vested with exclusive jurisdiction over these matters by the state. The communal autonomy granted to the various recognized religious communities in Israel is important in terms of permitting different citizens to preserve their cultural and religious group identity. Yet, it also gives Jewish and Muslim men certain privileges over their wives, instituted by religious authorities and sanctioned by state law, that would have never passed constitutional muster had they occurred outside the "protected" realm of religious family law.[186]

---

182. D.K. (1949) 1568-69, Statement of Prime Minister and Minister of Defense David Ben Gurion.
183. See, generally, Kerber, 1980.
184. See Israel, 1986, Defense Service Law (Consolidated Version), § 39(a).
185. See Israel, 1986, Defense Service Law (Consolidated Version), § 39(b).
186. I discuss this problem in detail in Shachar, 1998, pp. 285, 289–96.

Put in a broader comparative context, the Israeli case study shows that while citizenship as a legal concept is a crucial factor in determining who is inside or outside a given political community, significant differences may still be maintained *within* the polity *among* formally equal citizens. As my brief discussion of the differences in entitlement of Jews and Palestinian Arab Israeli citizens (and to a lesser extent, between male and female Israeli citizens) demonstrates, a complex interplay of legal rules, administrative practices, social factors, and cultural conventions determines the de facto status of formally equal members within the same political unit. Different "degrees of citizenship" are created among formally equal citizens of the same polity when access to certain obligations and goods is not equally distributed because of overt and covert discriminatory mechanisms. As mentioned above, the key obligation of citizenship (military service), under a republican conception of government, clearly imposes greater burdens upon Jewish Israeli citizens. At the same time, it also grants these individuals access to well-defined "extra" social benefits, for which Palestinian Arab citizens in the majority of cases cannot qualify because they are not generally recruited by the military.[187] Furthermore, even within the participatory Jewish community, men and women are not similarly situated, at least not in terms of their rights and duties at the intersection of family and military service duties in the public sphere. To complicate the picture even more, it is clear that Arab Israeli women are even more vulnerable to threats to their citizenship status, as they may be discriminated against both as Arabs and as women.[188] These different "degrees of citizenship," in short, stem not only from the bright-line laws of the government, but also from a multilayered social framework in which the mosaic of ethnicity and religion, as well as gender and class, determines to varying degrees and depending on the particular legal arena the first, second, or third class membership statuses of formally equal citizens.

Loss of Citizenship and Dual Citizenship

Israeli citizenship is hard to lose. An individual's voluntary renunciation of membership in the body politic is not sufficient to break the formal linkage to the state. Israeli citizenship may be renounced only with the expressed consent of the

187. See *supra* notes 177–78 and accompanying text. Note, however, that because of Israel's self-definition as a Jewish state, religious Orthodox Jews, who are exempted from military service as long as they continue their *yeshiva* (Jewish religious) studies, generally suffer little disability for their lack of military service—unlike their Arab citizens counterparts. See Kretzmer, 1989, pp. 106–107. This fact is due, in part, to the special status (or "cultural autonomy") granted in Israel to Orthodox Jews, but not to the Israel's Arab citizens. See, generally, Peled and Shafir, 1996.

188. See, generally, Crenshaw, 1989, p. 139 (discussing the intersection of race and gender in the lived experiences of women of color in the U.S. context, and critically analyzing the "single axis" legal framework that fails to address the multiplicity of different sources of discrimination).

minister of the interior to a person's request for expatriation.[189] Clearly, this approach to relinquishing citizenship is another facet of the republican conception encoded in Israeli citizenship law, which emphasizes the duties of membership and the ultimate loyalty to the nation expected of each person. In this view, citizenship is not an allegiance that an individual may freely and unilaterally sever; rather, it is a personal allegiance between the individual and the political community, the state, in which rights and obligations *for life* arise for each party. The state must provide minimum living conditions to all its citizens and assure their self-defense and protection. The individual is required to show loyalty and readiness to risk his or her life for the continued existence of the nation, hence the centrality and valorization of the obligation to serve in the military.

Contrary to the U.S. perception of expatriation as a voluntary relinquishment of citizenship, which involves a "natural" and "inherent" right of a person to depart from his or her country of origin, the Israeli understanding of expatriation echoes the common-law concept of perpetual allegiance to a person's native political community. Under the common-law approach, the right of expatriation is neither natural nor inherent in each citizen; rather, it is an expression of the state's authority to determine who is and who is not a member. Thus, under section 10 of the Citizenship Law, an Israeli citizen of full age may make a declaration to the effect that he or she desires to renounce his or her Israeli citizenship.[190] Such renunciation, however, will take effect only once the minister of the interior has expressed consent.[191]

Immigrants by return automatically establish Israeli citizenship upon settlement in Israel.[192] There is no legal requirement that an individual relinquish his or her previous citizenship affiliation before making *aliyah* to Israel.[193] Thus, Jewish Israeli citizens who are also citizens of other counties may continue to hold dual or multiple citizenship affiliations, regardless of why, when, and how these citizenship affiliations were established (that is, whether the foreign citizenship was acquired before immigration to Israel, by birth, or based on voluntary emigration from Israel).[194]

189. See Israel, 1980, Citizenship Law (Amendment No. 4), 34 L.S.I. 254, (1979–80), § 10A.
190. See Israel, 1980, Citizenship Law (Amendment No. 4), 34 L.S.I. 254, (1979–80).
191. See Israel, 1980, Citizenship Law (Amendment No. 4), 34 L.S.I. 254, (1979–80). Note that section 10A also states that only a citizen who is not a resident of Israel may seek to renounces his or her Israeli nationality.
192. See discussion *supra* Citizenship by Return.
193. See Israel, 1952, Citizenship Law, 6 L.S.I. 50, (1951–52), § 14(a).
194. The only case in which Israeli citizenship may be revoked because of a conflicting national loyalty is when an Israeli citizen has established residency or acquired citizenship in an country that is at a formal state of war with Israel. Such a person is presumed to have expatriated from Israel, and the minister of the interior has authority to denationalize the citizen. See Israel, 1980, Citizenship Law (Amendment No. 4), 34 L.S.I. 254, (1979–80), § 11(a). The minister of the interior, however, usually consents to expatriation requests made by persons who made *aliyah* to Israel

In the eyes of Israeli law, the Israeli citizenship status is presumed to have a lexical priority over all other national affiliations held by the individual. Accordingly, section 14(b) of the Citizenship Law states that a person who has dual or multiple citizenship is nevertheless legally "considered an Israel national."[195] This perception fits well with the understanding of Israeli citizenship as a special and almost inalienable bond between the individual and the political community. Yet this legal rule of membership may in practice have a negative effect on Israeli citizens who wish to sever their ties with the country. Even if Israeli citizens reside outside Israel for extended periods of time and are naturalized into their new political community, these individuals are still entitled to the rights and subject to the duties of Israeli citizenship according to Israeli law.[196] Thus, in order to enter and leave Israel, they must, like all other citizens, hold a valid Israeli passport. If they reside in Israel, they may be subject to Israeli taxation. Even if an Israeli national renounces his or her citizenship and the minister of the interior consents to the renunciation (as is often the case when the person emigrates from Israel), the loss of citizenship does not release a person from duties and responsibilities created *before* the loss of citizenship, hence a former Israeli citizen might still be obliged to serve in the Israeli military.[197]

Israeli citizenship is transmitted by descent.[198] Hence, the offspring of an Israeli parent automatically acquires Israeli citizenship at birth, regardless of the place of birth or the family's effective ties to Israel.[199] By the provisions of the

---

and were automatically granted Israeli citizenship, if they wish to maintain their previous citizenship in order to preserve certain rights in their native home country, such as the right to land ownership, inheritance, or pension payments. This issue is significant because a very high percentage of Israel's citizenry is not Israeli-born (as of 1996, for example, approximately 38 percent of the Israel's Jewish population was born outside the country). See *Statistical Abstract of Israel,* 1997. This type of expatriation of Israeli citizenship is relevant, then, only in those cases where in the eyes of the native home country, the establishment of Israeli citizenship status by the individual alongside her original citizenship status has detrimental effect on rights she would have been entitled to if she had maintained only her original citizenship status.

195. See Israel, 1952, Citizenship Law, 6 L.S.I. 50, (1951–52), § 14(b).
196. See Rubinstein, 1976, pp. 177–78.
197. This duty can be activated only when the person sets foot in Israel.
198. See discussion *supra* Citizenship by Birth.
199. To provide one well-known example: Samuel Sheinbein, a U.S. citizen accused of murder in the United States, fled to Israel after being named suspect in a brutal murder in a Washington suburb. A request for Sheinbein's extradition was made by the United States Justice Department and was supported by Israel's attorney general, Elyakim Rubinstein. According to Israel's Extradition Law, however, an Israeli citizen may not be extradited to another country to face trial for crimes he is alleged to have committed in that country. Judge Moshe Ravid of the Jerusalem District Court therefore had to determine whether Sheinbein, the son of an Israeli citizen, is an indeed an Israeli citizen by birth. On September 6, 1998, Judge Ravid determined that Sheinbein is an Israeli citizen but is nonetheless extraditable because he has no "affinity" to Israel. Yet, the Israel Supreme Court in a split three-to-two decision overturned the ruling of the Jerusalem District Court. On February 25, 1999, the majority decision found that "every Israeli citizens has immunity from extradition, ir-

Defense Service Law, this child, as an Israeli citizen, shall be called to military duty at the age of eighteen, even if he or she holds another citizenship or has resided for years outside Israel.[200]

Under the republican perception of membership expressed in Israeli citizenship law, such mandatory drafting was intended to preserve a special link between the Israeli state and the offspring of Israeli citizens who emigrated from the country, by providing these "lost" children access to the "heartland of citizenship practice" (military service).[201] The priorities of the polity can perhaps be seen by the way in which the obligations of citizenship are balanced against the right to vote—usually the most visible right of citizenship. Israelis who live abroad have no right to vote as "absentees" in national or municipal elections, but these Israelis and their children are formally subject to the obligation of military service. In reality, however, the result of this mandatory imposition of military duty upon children born outside the country has had an adverse effect, because "the bond that might have been created naturally by visits to Israel and intermingling with Israeli society is diminished by a law that converts the first visit to Israel into a potential recruitment trap."[202]

The perception of a birthright and of lifelong allegiance between the person born as an Israeli and the state is, as I have shown, clearly manifested in Israeli citizenship law and the various administrative practices governing the issue of loss of citizenship. The symbolic importance that the state attaches to this allegiance is best illustrated in the following particular case where the state stakes its right to a child's allegiance. The state reserves for itself the right *not* to renounce the citizenship status of a minor if the parents emigrated from Israel but have renounced their own Israeli citizenship status while still being residents of Israel. If one of the parents remains an Israeli citizen, the child does not lose his or her citizenship status. Furthermore, if the child remains a resident of Israel, his or her citizenship status will not be terminated, even if the parents renounced their own attachment to the state and the minister of the interior consented to their expatriation.[203]

---

respective of his affinity to Israel." The Supreme Court President, Aharon Barak, who was in the minority, "maintained that such immunity can be claimed only by a citizen for whom 'Israel is the center of his life and who participates in its life and joins his destiny to that of the country.'" Samuel Sheinbein was therefore not extradited to the United States. Instead his trial for murder took place in Israel. He pleaded guilty and was sentenced to twenty-four years in prison. He is now serving his term in an Israeli cell.

200. See Israel, 1986, Defense Service Law (Consolidated Version), § 13.

201. As an official publication of the Ministry of Immigrant Absorption puts this point, "army service is the 'entry card' to Israeli society and an important basis for social integration." See Ministry of Immigrant Absorption, June 1998, p. 29.

202. Rubinstein, 1976, p. 179.

203. See Israel, 1980, Citizenship Law (Amendment No. 4), 34 L.S.I. 254, (1979–80), § 10.

Note, however, that a citizen who has committed "an act consisting of a breach of allegiance to the State of Israel" may be unilaterally *denationalized* by the state.[204] This power has rarely, if ever, been used in Israel.[205] In recent years, however, citizenship has been revoked by way of *denaturalization*, that is, upon determination that citizenship status was wrongfully obtained based on false information.[206]

New Trends in Israeli Immigration Law

Similar to many other Western countries, Israel has been undergoing a sustained drive to "roll back" the state in recent years "from the formerly state-controlled public service arena, as well as an increasing 'recommodification' of formerly 'decommodified' services."[207] Examples of this process include the privatization of media and telecommunication services, the rise of private higher education institutions, and the liberalization of the foreign currency market. These changes, along with the steady rise in number since the late 1980s of foreign workers admitted to the country as temporary workers, are "indicators of Israel's movement toward a variant of neo-liberal market economy."[208]

It is estimated that approximately 200,000 foreign workers have entered Israel since the late 1980s. Of these foreign workers, fewer than 85,000 have entered the country lawfully.[209] Foreign workers in Israel are, in most cases, employed in low-skill, low-pay jobs, particularly in the areas of agriculture and construction. Until the 1980s (before the Palestinian *Intifada*), many of the jobs currently held by foreign workers were previously held by Palestinians Arabs from the West Bank and Gaza.[210] These Palestinian noncitizen workers were a cheap and flexible work force.[211] During the *Intifada*, rigid restrictions were imposed on Israeli employers who hired Palestinian noncitizen workers, and the frequent closures of the West Bank and Gaza for security reasons prevented the previous influx of Palestinian workers into Israel. These factors, along with the

---

204. Israel, 1980, Citizenship Law (Amendment No. 4), 34 L.S.I. 254, (1979–80), § 11(b).

205. There are no official figures regarding this practice. But of the known cases of Israelis who have been convicted of committing an act consisting a breach of allegiance to the State of Israel, none have been denationalized.

206. See Israel, 1980, Citizenship Law (Amendment No. 4), 34 L.S.I. 254, (1979–80), § 11(c).

207. Hirschl, 1997, pp. 136, 138.

208. Hirschl, 1997, pp. 136, 138.

209. See, generally, *Forty-Sixth Annual Report of the State's Comptroller 475-496,* 1996 (on the emerging problem of foreign workers in Israel); Israel Democracy Institute, 1998, p. 1.

210. See, generally, Bartram, 1998, pp. 303, 306–308.

211. See Bartram, 1998, p. 308. See, generally, Lewin-Epstein and Semyonov, 1993 (analyzing the status of citizen and noncitizen Arabs in the Israeli labor market).

gradual opening of the Israeli economy to global market forces, have worked to the detriment of Palestinian workers. Even when residents of the Palestinian Authority (established in Gaza and certain parts of the West Bank in 1993 based on the Oslo peace accords) now enter Israel for purposes of employment, they often find that many of the jobs they previously held have already been occupied by the new "army" of unprotected labor, the foreign workers.[212]

Foreign workers who enter the country lawfully receive temporary nonimmigrant work visas.[213] They must leave the country upon termination of their status, but there is no effective mechanism for enforcing this regulation. Children born in Israel to non-Israeli parents do not acquire citizenship at birth, since Israeli law does not follow the *jus soli* principle. If their parents were illegal residents, these children are not entitled to social benefits, such as state-underwritten health care coverage, to which all Israeli citizens and permanent residents are entitled. But municipal administrators, school principals, social workers, and health care providers who work in areas where many foreign workers live, such as poor neighborhoods in Southern Tel Aviv, have in most cases decided to overlook the status issue in order to ensure that children of illegal foreign workers are treated fairly and with human dignity.[214] As the principal of Bialik elementary school in Southern Tel Aviv (which received the prestigious Educational Award from Israel's president in 1998 on Israel's fiftieth anniversary) puts it, although many of the children attending her school are illegally residing in Israel, "I [and the Tel Aviv school district] have no interest in the question of whether their parents have documentation of legal residence or not. I only have interest in that these are children and [that regardless of their citizenship status] they are entitled to education. Good education."[215] Important and significant as this local effort is, it cannot resolve the need to establish a comprehensive governmental policy that will determine how to address the issue of long-term residence of foreign workers and of the legal status of their Israeli-born children.

Predictably, the large number of legal and illegal foreign workers who entered Israel since the late 1980s in a short period now pose new regulatory chal-

---

212. See Israel Democracy Institute, 1998, p. 1. Note that Israeli employment laws that regulate issues such as minimum payment, working hours, and workers compensation should, in theory, also be applicable to foreign workers (the law applies to any worker, regardless of his or her citizenship status). In practice, however, these employment laws have rarely been enforced in the case of foreign workers who are either dependent on their employer for their visa so the abuse of the law is never reported, or are illegally residing in Israel and would do whatever they can to avoid contact with state authorities. See Association for Civil Rights in Israel, 1996, pp. 227–28.

213. See Association for Civil Rights in Israel, 1996, p. 12.

214. Livine, June 26, 1998, p. 26.

215. Livine, June 26, 1998, p. 30.

lenges to Israel's citizenship law and immigration policy, which crystallized during the nation-building era of the 1950s and has since remained in place. Such new challenges are not unique to Israel and neither are the initial governmental reactions that have emerged in the 1990s.[216] More than ever before, the Israeli immigration policy of the past decade has been marked by a growing awareness of the problem of fraud.[217] Indeed, the gradual deregulation or "opening" of the Israeli market to international forces makes Israel a regional "magnet" for persons from poorer countries, as has been evidenced by the large numbers of foreign workers who have entered the country,[218] and the influx of Jewish and non-Jewish persons who established citizenship by way of return in the massive wave of immigration from the former Soviet Union in the 1990s.[219] Given these new trends, the Israeli media have sensationalized recent stories about people who entered into fictitious marriages in order to establish Israeli citizenship by way of return; people who falsified documents in order to claim their "Jewishness"; people who entered Israel on a nonimmigrant visitor visa with no intention to leave the country; and people who, while illegally residing and working in Israel, have been blackmailed or abused by persons who threatened to report their status to the police. Some human rights organizations in Israel have begun to address these issues by using due process and human dignity arguments in protection of foreign illegal workers.[220] On the whole, however, Israel has yet to establish a comprehensive policy toward these foreign workers who "temporarily" entered its borders (either legally or illegally) and—if anything can be learned from the related experiences of other countries—are likely to stay for good.[221]

Thus, the changing political relations with the Palestinian Authority and the emerging neoliberal economic order in Israel will inevitably bring to the forefront of Israeli public policy fundamental questions associated with the tension embedded between the rollback of the welfare state and increasing trends of globalization, such as the movement of goods, capitals, and persons across frontiers, on the one hand, and the republican, duty-bound and religious-based

---

216. See, generally, Cornelius, 1992, p. 3.

217. See, for example, Reinfeld, November 24, 1998.

218. Foreign workers who entered the country lawfully (that is, with work permits) were recruited primarily from Romania, Thailand, and the Philippines. See Bartram, 1998, p. 314.

219. See *supra* notes 62–67 and accompanying text.

220. These organizations include, among others, "Kav La'Oved," the Association for Civil Rights in Israel, and the Association of Doctors for Human Rights.

221. Israel, like other countries that place greater emphasis on the *jus sanguinis* principle, will eventually have to resolve the "second generation problem." Under current Israeli citizenship law, children born in Israel to noncitizens who reside in the country (whether legally or illegally) are not entitled to Israeli citizenship by birth, although they were born on its territory.

perceptions of membership with its more state-centrist understanding of identity, still encoded in Israeli citizenship law, on the other.[222]

Conclusion

As it now stands, the Law of Return still echoes the national Zionist goals written into law five decades ago with Israel's establishment as the sovereign modern Jewish state. The Law of Return upholds the right of every Jew to immigrate to Israel and to acquire Israeli citizenship automatically and immediately upon arrival in the country. There is no waiting period for this granting of citizenship because of the Zionist philosophy that regards the return of Jews to their ancestral homeland as an expression of the fundamental values upon which the state itself is based, namely, that Israel is to serve as a safe haven and homeland for the Jewish people.

As we have also seen, Israeli citizenship can also be acquired by way of residence, birth, or naturalization. Since 1980, all children born to an Israeli parent, regardless of the parent's religious, national, ethnic, or gender affinity, acquire automatic citizenship status by way of birthright. This equal birthright entitlement is devoid of any "differentiating" markers, thus ensuring that *all* Israelis have full formal and equal access to the basic rights associated with citizenship in a democratic state. Yet, as important and central as this formal entitlement to citizenship is to each individual, it cannot assure that the ethnocultural, republican conceptions of membership in the nation, which are still encoded in Israel's citizenship and immigration regime, will not systematically and adversely affect the distribution of power and social capital *among* different groups of Israeli citizens.[223]

Traditionally, Israel has been analyzed as representing an interesting and special case of a diverse society, where the tension between the Jewish and democratic principles upon which the state is founded creates what has been termed as an "ethnic democracy,"[224] whereby Israel's Arab citizens are guaranteed full civic and political rights but have no access to the "common good" foundations of the Jewish state.[225] In addition, according to the republican perceptions expressed in Israeli citizenship law, full membership in the polity requires *active* participation, reflected in the high value ascribed to military service. In this context, however, it is important to note that two groups—Pales-

222. See, generally, Hirschl, 1998, p. 427; Peled and Shafir, 1996.
223. See, generally, Cohen, 1989.
224. See, generally, Smooha, 1990.
225. See, generally, Peled, 1992.

tinian Arab Israeli citizens and certain Orthodox Jews—are generally excluded from the republican "active citizenship" conception, but with very different consequences. Palestinian Arab Israeli citizens are generally not called upon for national military service and are subject to various overt and covert discriminatory governmental policies. This fact should serve as a reminder that while Palestinian Arab Israelis are full members in the state, they are not necessarily full members in the nation.[226] The second group, comprising Orthodox Jews who are granted administrative exemption from military service because of their religious studies, has suffered far less injurious consequences from its systematic lack of participation in this key Zionist national expression of sovereignty. Since Orthodox Jews, unlike Israel's Palestinians citizens, are situated almost without question within the dominant Jewish community, their full membership in the nation is hardly ever challenged, even if they refrain from some of its crucial civic expressions.[227] In discussing the role of gender, in terms of affecting the de facto citizenship status of Israeli Jewish women, this article alluded to a more complex matrix of "degrees of citizenship," whereby religious and ethnic affiliation, *as well as* gender and class must be taken into account in analyzing one's membership status and entitlement to the full benefits and duties of equal citizenship.

There is no starker example than the combined provisions of the Law of Return and the Citizenship Law, with their built-in inclusionary-exclusionary dimensions, to express the particularistic nature of contemporary Israeli citizenship and immigration regime. Only time will tell whether the new challenges posed to this regime by a growing number of "temporary" foreign workers (and their Israeli-born noncitizen children), the transition of jurisdictional power over Palestinian "permanent residents" in the West Bank and Gaza Strip to the PA, and the growing constituency of non-Jewish immigrants by return who have arrived from the former Soviet Union and have settled in the country, will force a transformation in Israeli citizenship law, gradually making it more inclusive (for example, by giving greater weight to a *jus soli* principle).[228] Or, conversely, whether the challenges of the 1990s to the ethnocultural, republican narrative of the 1950s (still encoded in the Law of Return and the Citizenship Law) will only enhance the voices that are already calling for a more narrow,

226. See, generally, Kretzmer, 1989; Peled, 1992; Smooha, 1990.

227. Indeed, certain scholars claim that the "ethnocultural" aspects of Israeli citizenship, as encoded in the Law of Return, "guarantee the privileged position of the true keepers of the faith—religiously Orthodox Jews—in Israeli society." Shafir and Peled, 1998, pp. 408, 413.

228. In comparison, examine the planned changes in German citizenship law and naturalization procedures. See German Information Center, *German Citizenship & Naturalization*, April 4, 1999.

Halakhic definition of the right of return, and only give strength to the new voices that are calling for an imposition of tougher regulatory measures against illegal residents of the state (for example, deportation orders), thus making Israel's immigration policy even more restrictive and exclusionary than its current attitude toward non-Jews. With regard to such complex and troubling matters concerning the future of the Holy Land, one would do well to refrain from prophecy.

References

Adalah (the Legal Center for Arab Minority Rights in Israel). March 1998. *Legal Violations of Arab Minority Rights in Israel: A Report on Israel's Implementation of the International Convention on the Elimination of All Forms of Racial discrimination.*

Arian, Asher. 1998. *The Second Republic: Politics in Israel.* Chatham, N.J.: Chatham House Publishers.

Association for Civil Rights in Israel. 1996. "Israel Human Rights Focus." (In Hebrew, on file with author.)

Association for Civil Rights in Israel. (May 25, 1993.) "Petition to the Supreme Court: Gender Discrimination Against Residents of Jerusalem Who Marry Foreign Spouses." Press Release. (In Hebrew.)

Bartram, David V. 1998. "Foreign Workers in Israel: History and Theory." *International Migration Review,* no. 32.

Basic Law: Jerusalem, Capital of Israel. (January 3, 1999.) <http://www.mfa.gov.il/mfa/go.asp?MFAH00hf0>

Brubaker, Rogers. 1992. *Citizenship and Nationhood in France and Germany.* Cambridge, Mass.: Harvard University Press.

Canada. 1999. Citizenship Act, R.S.C., ch. C-29.

Cohen, Erik. 1989. "Citizenship, Nationality and Religion in Israel and Thailand." In *The Israeli State and Society: Boundaries and Frontiers,* ed. Baruch Kimmerling. Albany: SUNY Press.

Cohen, Robin. 1997. *Global Diasporas.* Seattle: University of Washington Press.

Committee on Feminism and International Law. 1998. "Women's Equality and Nationality in International Law." In *Preliminary Report: May 1998.* International Law Association. (On file with author.)

Cornelius, Wayne A. 1992. "The Ambivalent Quest for Immigration Control." In *Controlling Immigration.* Stanford, Calif.: Stanford University Press.

Crenshaw, Kimberle Williams. 1989. "Demarginalizing the Intersection of Race and Sex: A Black Feminist Critique of Antidiscrimination Doctrine, Feminist Theory, and Antiracist Politics." *1989 University of Chicago Legal Forum.*

Dahl, Robert A. 1989. *Democracy and Its Critics.* New Haven: Yale University Press.

"Declaration of Principles on Interim Self-Government Arrangements." (September 13, 1993.) <http://www.mfa.gov.il/mfa/go.asp?MFAH00q00>

D.K. 1949. "Statement of Foreign Minister Moshe Sharett." (In Hebrew, on file with author.)

D.K. 1949. "Statement of Knesset Member Y. Meridor." (In Hebrew, on file with author.)

D.K. 1949. "Statement of Prime Minister and Minister of Defense David Ben Gurion." (In Hebrew, on file with author.)

Economist Intelligence Unit. 1993–1994. *Country Profile: Israel, The Occupied Territories.*

Ehrlich, J. W. 1959. *Ehrlich's Blackstone.* Westport, Conn.: Greenwood Press.

Forty-Sixth Annual Report of the State's Comptroller 475-496. 1996. (In Hebrew, on file with author.)

Gaza-Jericho Agreement Annex II: Protocol Concerning Civil Affairs. (January 21, 1999.) <http://www.mfa.gov.il/mfa/go.asp?MFAH00q40>

German Information Center. *German Citizenship & Naturalization.* (April 4, 1999.) <http://www.germany-info.org/consular/cit.htm>

Goldscheider, Calvin. 1990. "Israel." In *Handbook on International Migration*, eds. William J. Serow et al. New York: Greenwood Press.

Gouldman, M. D. 1970. *Israel Nationality Law.* Jerusalem: Hebrew University Institute for Legislative Research and Comparative Law.

Hailbronner, Kay. 1989. "Citizenship and Nationhood in Germany." In *Immigration and the Politics of Citizenship in Europe and North America*, ed. William Rogers Brubaker. Lanham: University Press of America.

Hammar, Tomas. 1989. "State Nation, and Dual Citizenship." In *Immigration and the Politics of Citizenship in Europe and North America*, ed. William Rogers Brubaker. New York: University Press of America.

Herzl, Theodor. 1943. *Der Judenstaat*, trans. J. De Haas. New York: Scopus Publishers.

Hirschl, Ran. 1998. "Israel's 'Constitutional Revolution': The Legal Interpretation of Entrenched Civil Liberties in an Emerging Neo-Liberal Economic Order." *American Journal of Comparative Law*, no. 46.

Hirschl, Ran. 1997. "The 'Constitutional Revolution' and the Emergence of a New Economic Order in Israel." *Israel Studies*, no. 2.

Hofnung, Menachem. 1996. *Democracy, Law and National Security in Israel.* Aldershot: Dartmouth.

Hurewitz, J. C., ed. and trans. 1979. *The Middle East and North Africa in World Politics: A Documentary Record*, 2d ed., vol. 2. New Haven: Yale University Press.

Ilan, Shahar, and Gideon Alon. (December 10, 1998.) "Politicians on All Sides Accept Court Challenge." *Ha'aretz.* <http://www3.haaretz.co.il/eng/scripts/article.asp?id=35863&mador=1&datee=12/10/98>

Immigration and Marriage Fraud Amendments of 1986, Pub. L. No. 99-639, 11 Stat. 3537 (codified as amended in scattered sections of 8 U.S.C.).

Israel. 1998. Immigration and Nationality Act. 8 U.S.C.

Israel. 1992. Basic Law: Human Dignity and Liberty. S.H. 1391. <http://www.mfa.gov.il/mfa/go.asp?MFAH00hi0>

Israel. 1986. Defense Service Law (Consolidated Version). (On file with author.)

Israel. 1980. Citizenship Law (Amendment No. 4). 34 L.S.I. 254 (1979–80).

Israel. 1970. The Law of Return (Amendment No. 2). 24 L.S.I. 28. <http://www.mfa.gov.il/mfa/go.asp?MFAHOOkpO>

Israel, 1959. Civil Service Law (Appointments). (On file with author.)

Israel. 1958. Basic Law: The Knesset. S.H. 244. <http://www.mfa.gov.il/mfa/go. asp?MFAH00h80>

Israel. 1954. Prevention of Infiltration (Offenses and Jurisdiction) Law. 8 L.S.I. 133 (1953–54).

Israel. 1952. Citizenship Law. 6 L.S.I. 50 (1951–52).

Israel. 1952. Passports Law. 6 L.S.I 76 (1951–52).

Israel. 1950. The Law of Return. 4 L.S.I. 114. <http://www.mfa.gov.il/mfa/go. asp?MFAH00kp0>

Israel. 1948. Law and Administration Ordinance. 1 L.S.I. 7. (In Hebrew, on file with author.)

Israel at 50: A Statistical Glimpse. (Cited September 22, 1998.) <http://www.israel-mfa.gov.il/facts/israel50.html>

Israel Democracy Institute. 1998. *Policies for Renewed Growth: Foreign Workers in Israel.* (In Hebrew, on file with author.)

Kerber, Linda K. 1993. "'A Constitutional Right to be Treated Like . . . Ladies': Women, Civic Obligation, and Military Service." *1993 University of Chicago Law School Roundtable.*

Kerber, Linda K. 1980. *Women of the Republic: Intellect and Ideology in Revolutionary America.* Chapel Hill: University of North Carolina Press.

Kimmerling, Baruch, and Joel S. Migdal. 1993. *Palestinians: The Making of a People.* New York: Free Press.

Kimmerling, Baruch. 1985. "Between the Primordial and the Civil Definitions of the Collective Identity: Eretz Israel or the State of Israel." In *Comparative Social Dynamics,* eds. Erik Cohen et al. Boulder: Westview Press.

Klein, Claud. 1997. "The Right of Return in Israeli Law." *Tel Aviv Studies in Law,* no. 13.

Kook, Rebecca. 1996. "Between Uniqueness and Exclusion: The Politics of Identity in Israel in Comparative Perspective." In *Israel in Comparative Perspective: Challenging the Conventional Wisdom,* ed. Michael N. Barnett. Albany: SUNY Press.

Kretzmer, David. 1989. *The Legal Status of Arabs in Israel.* Boulder: Westview Press.

Kymlicka, Will. 1995. *Multicultural Citizenship: A Liberal Theory of Minority Rights.* Oxford: Oxford University Press.

Lahav, Pnina. 1997. *Judgement in Jerusalem.* Berkeley: University of California Press.

Lahav, Pnina. 1993. "When the Palliative Simply Impairs: The Debate in the Knesset on the Law for Women's Equality Rights." *Zmanim—A History Quarterly,* no. 12. (In Hebrew, on file with author.)

Lewin-Epstein, Noah, and Moshe Semyonov. 1993. *The Arab Minority in Israel's Economy: Patterns of Ethnic Inequality.* Boulder: Westview Press.

Livine, Neri. (June 26, 1998.) "Biyalik's Foreign Children." *Ha'aretz.* (In Hebrew.)

Lorch, Natanel, ed. 1993. *Major Knesset Debates, 1948–1981.* Lanham: University Press of America.

Lustick, Ian. 1980. *Arabs in the Jewish State: Israel's Control of a National Minority.* Austin: University of Texas Press.

Ministry of Immigrant Absorption. June 1998. *Immigration and Absorption 1989–1997: Annual Report.*

Ministry of Immigrant Absorption. 1996. *Aliyah Pocket Guide,* 6th ed.

Morris, Benny. 1990. *1948 and After: Israel and the Palestinians*. New York: Oxford University Press.

Morris, Benny. 1987. *The Birth of the Palestinian Refugee Problem: 1947–1949*. New York: Cambridge University Press.

Palestine History. (Cited January 19, 1999.) <http://www.arab.net/palestine/history/pe_israelstate.html>

Peled, Yoav, and Gershon Shafir. 1996. "The Roots of Peacemaking: The Dynamics of Citizenship in Israel, 1948–93." *International Journal of Middle Eastern Studies*, no. 28.

Peled, Yoav. 1992. "Ethnic Democracy and the Legal Construction of Citizenship: Arab Citizens of the Jewish State." *American Political Science Review*, no. 86, p. 432.

Peretz, Don, and Gideon Doron. 1997. *The Government and Politics of Israel*, 3rd ed. Boulder: Westview Press.

Portes, Alejandro, and József Böröcz. 1989. "Contemporary Immigration: Theoretical Perspectives on its Determinants and Modes of Incorporation." *International Migration Review*, no. 23, p. 606.

Reinfeld, Moshe. (February 26, 1999.) "Sheinbein Wins Appeal as Court Splits 3-2." *Ha'aretz*. <http://www3.haaretz.co.il/eng/htmls/6_4.htm>

Reinfeld, Moshe. (December 10, 1998.) "Yeshiva Draft Deferments Illegal, Court Rules." *Ha'aretz*. <http://www3.haaretz.co.il.eng/scripts/article.asp?id=35872&mador=1&datee=12/10/98>

Reinfeld, Moshe. (November 24, 1998.) "Mixed Couples Await Decision on Citizenship." *Ha'aretz*. <http://www3.haaretz.co.il/eng/htmls/16_4.htm>

Rubinstein, Amnon. 1994. *The Changing Status of the 'Territories' (West Bank and Gaza): From Escrow to Legal Mongrel*. In *Economic, Legal, and Demographic Dimensions of Arab-Israeli Relations*, ed. Ian Lustick. New York: Garland.

Rubinstein, Amnon. 1976. "Israel Nationality." *Tel Aviv University Studies Law*, no. 2.

Sapiro, Virginia. 1984. "Women, Citizenship, and Nationality: Immigration and Naturalization Policies in the United States." *Politics and Society*, no. 13.

Segal, Ze'ev. (September 7, 1998.) "Analysis: A New Definition of Citizenship." *Ha'aretz*. <http://www3.haaretz.co.il/eng/scripts/s. . .=Sheinbein&mador=1&se=true&date=9/9/98>

Shachar, Ayelet. 1998. "Group Identity and Women's Rights in Family Law: The Perils of Multicultural Accommodation." *Journal of Political Philosophy*, no. 6.

Shafir, Gershon, and Yoav Peled. 1998. "Citizenship and Stratification in an Ethnic Democracy." *Ethnic and Racial Studies*, no. 21.

Sharkansky, Ira. 1997. *Policy Making in Israel: Routines for Simple Problems and Coping with the Complex*. Pittsburgh: University of Pittsburgh Press.

Shlaim, Avi. 1995. "The Debate About 1948." *International Journal of Middle East Studies*, no. 27.

Smith, Rogers M. 1997. *Civic Ideals: Conflicting Visions of Citizenship in U.S. History*. New Haven: Yale University Press.

Smooha, Sammy. 1990. "Minority Status in an Ethnic Democracy: The Status of the Arab Minority in Israel." *Ethnic and Racial Studies*, no. 13.

Soffer, Arnon. 1994. "Demography and the Shaping of Israel's Borders." In *Economic, Legal, and Demographic Dimensions of Arab-Israel Relations*, ed. Ian S. Lustick. New York: Garland.

Somech, Alex. (June 12, 1998.) "Decline in Proportion of Jews among Soviet Immigrants." *Ha'aretz,* pp. 1–2. (In Hebrew.)

Statistical Abstract of Israel. 1997. No. 48. (On file with author.)

Stratton, Lisa C. 1992. "'The Right to Have Rights': Gender Discrimination in Nationality Laws." *Minnesota Law Review,* no. 77.

"The Declaration of the Establishment of the State of Israel." (May 14, 1948.) *Official Gazette,* no. 1. <http://www.knesset/docs/megilat_eng.htm>

UN General Assembly Resolution 181 (Partition Plan). (November 29, 1947.) <http://www.mfa.gov.il/mfa/go.asp?MFAH00ps0>

U.S. Census Bureau. (April 9, 1998.) "Foreign Born Population Reaches 25.8 Million, according to Census Bureau." <http://www.census.gov/Press-Release/cb98-57.html>

Weiner, Justus R. 1997. "The Palestinian Refugees' 'Right to Return' and the Peace Process." *Boston College International and Comparative Law Review,* no. 20.

Young, Iris Marion. 1989. "Polity and Group Difference: A Critique of the Ideal of Universal Citizenship." *Ethics,* no. 99.

Legal Cases

Cases listed below are all in Hebrew and, except for the last two, are on file with the author.

Afroyim v. Rusk, 387 U.S. 253 (1967).

H.C. 58/68, *Shalit v. Minister of Interior,* 23(2) P.D. 477.

H.C. 64/54, *Bader v. Minister of Police,* 8 P.D. 970.

H.C. 125/51, *Hassin v. Minister of Interior,* 5 P.D. 1386.

H.C. 125/80 *Angel v. Minister of the Interior,* 34(4) P.D. 329.

H.C. 157/51, *Abad v. Minister of Interior,* 5 P.D. 1680.

H.C. 264/87, *Sephardi Torah Guardians, Shas Movement v. Director of Population Registry,* 43(2) P.D. 723.

H.C. 328/60, *Mussa v. Minister of Interior,* 16 P.D. 1793, aff'd F.H. 3/63, *Minister of Interior v. Mussa,* 17 P.D. 2467.

H.C. 442/71, *Lansky v. Minister of the Interior,* 26(2) P.D. 337.

H.C. 1031/93, *Pessaro (Goldstein) v. Minister of Interior,* 49(4) P.D. 661.

H.C. 2797/93, *Gabari'th v. Minister of Interior,* "Motion to Dismiss the Petition."

H.C. 4541/94, *Miller v. Minister of Defense,* 49(4) P.D. 94.

H.C. 3648/97, *Stemka v. Minister of Interior* (decision pending).

H.C. 3648/97, *Stemka v. Minister of Interior,* "Petitioner's Brief."

H.C. 3497/97, *Kamella v. Minister of Interior,* decision given on Dec. 4, 1997 (unpublished).

H.C. 3267/97, *Rubinstein v. Minister of Defense,* decision given on Dec. 9, 1998 (unpublished).

CHAPTER FOURTEEN

Citizenship in Japan:
Legal Practice and
Contemporary Development

CHIKAKO KASHIWAZAKI

THE PURPOSE OF THIS paper is to discuss laws and practices concerning Japanese citizenship in comparative perspective and to draw out policy implications. The number of foreign residents registered in Japan increased from 884,000 in 1987 to 1,483,000, or 1.2 percent of the total population, in 1997.[1] The Japanese government reorganized visa categories in 1990 to cope with the growth of incoming foreigners, while maintaining the policy of not admitting "unskilled" labor. Rules regulating the attribution of nationality and naturalization have also remained strict. Increasing ethnic diversity in Japanese society raises questions about Japan citizenship, including the legal status of permanent resident aliens; policies concerning border control, on the one hand, and the integration of settled foreign residents, on the other; and criteria for attributing nationality. Together they pose a problem of how to construct and integrate a multiethnic society. Japan in this sense shares similar challenges with other immigrant-receiving countries.

Debates about citizenship and immigration in social sciences initially focused on immigrant-receiving countries in Western Europe, North America, and Australia, although the geographical scope is gradually broadening in recent years. The Japanese case also received some attention in the field of international migration studies when foreign migrant workers in the country increased in the 1980s. Nevertheless, the nature of the country's citizenship

---

1. *Zairyū Gaikokujin Tōkei*, 1998.

policies has only sparsely been documented in English.[2] Although Japan is often treated as a unique case, with its dominant image of ethnic homogeneity coupled with intolerance for outsiders, the uniqueness itself needs to be explored in comparative perspective.

Japan in Comparative Perspective

Comparative research suggests that citizenship policies might be effectively employed for the integration of immigrants in a democratic society.[3] Citizenship policies in a broad sense include rules for not only the attribution of full, formal citizenship but also the admission of legal migrants and the extension of "partial" citizenship for resident aliens.[4] The Japanese case is similar to other advanced industrial countries in that recent labor migration represents south-north migration, or migration from developing countries to developed countries. Experiences of Western European countries in particular provide useful points of comparison when studying the case of Japan, because Japan in its modern national state form was constructed by an indigenous majority group rather than by immigrants, as in the United States, Canada, and Australia.

Contemporary debates about citizenship policies in Western European countries have their roots in immigration in the post–World War II era. In response to sharp increases in the immigrant population, governments of these countries restricted admission and encouraged return migration in the 1970s. The result was the settlement of former "temporary" workers and an increase in family reunification. As immigrants were becoming a permanent feature of the society, host countries in Western Europe turned increasingly toward incorporation.[5] Over time, foreign workers and their families obtained a greater scope of citizenship rights. Referred to as "denizens," resident aliens with permanent resident status enjoy extensive civil and social citizenship rights, if not electoral rights on the national level.[6]

Denizens, however, do not possess full citizenship, notably full political rights. For fuller integration of immigrants into a democratic political community, it becomes important to give them the opportunity to obtain full citizen-

2. See Hanami, 1998, on legal dimensions. On the incorporation of foreigners into society and the issues of citizenship, see Kajita, 1998, and Miyajima, 1997.

3. Brubaker, 1989, *Immigration*; Hammar, 1985; Hammar, 1990; Layton-Henry, 1990; Castles and Miller, 1993.

4. By "partial citizenship" I mean any legal status to which a range of citizenship rights and duties are attached, but which falls short of full citizenship. Denizenship may be considered an advanced form of partial citizenship.

5. Soysal, 1994.

6. Hammar, 1990, pp. 12–15.

ship, not just denizenship. In the 1980s and 1990s, laws regulating nationality and citizenship were revised in immigrant-receiving countries such as Germany, the Netherlands, Sweden, and Switzerland, where nationality transmission was mainly based on *jus sanguinis* (by parentage). These revisions eased criteria for acquiring nationality by first-generation, long-term resident aliens as well as by the second and subsequent generations. Major types of legal and administrative changes include introduction or expansion of the as-of-right acquisition of citizenship; double *jus soli*, by which the third generation obtains citizenship automatically; and toleration for dual nationality.[7]

The development of the status of denizenship led to greater differentiation of status among noncitizens. As immigrant-receiving countries reinforced border control, undocumented aliens emerged as a significantly disadvantaged category in terms of legal protection. Lawful admission and access to permanent residence appear to play a major role in shaping one's life chances, perhaps even more than the possession of full citizenship.[8]

In sum, basic trends in Western European countries in the past three decades include the combination of tighter border control and efforts to incorporate immigrants into the host society, the emergence of denizens, and the lowering of barriers to acquiring nationality. The acquisition of nationality by immigrants is thus increasingly understood as a point on a continuum of legal status ranging from "aliens" to "denizens" and then to "full citizens."[9]

The Japanese Case

Japan is often cited as the only advanced industrial country that did not rely on foreign labor during the period of high economic growth. It is even asserted that ethnic and cultural homogeneity was in fact a key to postwar recovery and development.[10] This line of argument attaches importance to cultural factors that might be used to explain citizenship and immigration policies as well. The adoption of the principle of *jus sanguinis* and strict rules on naturalization would then be seen as a natural course of development given the characters of the Japanese. Reducing Japanese citizenship policies to "cultural" factors, how-

---

7. Bauböck, 1994, p. 33; Çinar, 1994; Soysal, 1994, pp. 26–27. Britain deviates from this general pattern. Migrants from Commonwealth countries used to acquire full citizenship upon settlement in Britain by virtue of being British subjects. Since the 1960s, however, they have been subject to increasingly restrictive admission rules. The unconditional *jus soli* was terminated in 1981, although full citizenship is still accessible to lawfully settled immigrants in Britain (Dummett and Nicol, 1990; Dummett, 1994).

8. Schuck, 1989; Brubaker, 1989. Yet, the United States has moved to reinforce the distinction between full citizenship and denizenship.

9. Çinar, 1994; van den Bedem, 1994.

10. Emphasis on homogeneity has downplayed internal cultural diversity and made minority populations in Japan "invisible." See Weiner, 1997, and Maher and Macdonald, 1995.

ever, only reinforces the notion of the "uniqueness" of Japan without much explanation. In what follows, I highlight historical factors, administrative
practices, and political choices that have been made concerning citizenship policies to show that the Japanese case can be fruitfully analyzed in comparative
perspective.

Because Japanese law follows *jus sanguinis*, the development of citizenship policies in Western European countries with similar legal traditions is
highly relevant to the country. To any state, the presence of a significant number of resident aliens poses potential problems if their marginalization leads to
social and political unrest. Like governments in European immigrant-receiving
societies, do policy makers in Japan also consider citizenship policies as a useful tool for promoting social and political integration? What are current policy
options? Before considering these questions, it would be useful to first examine
basic features of Japanese citizenship policies.

The Basic Features of Japanese Citizenship Policies

There is no unified, coherent policy that could be called the Japanese citizenship policy. Rather, a variety of laws, regulations, and administrative practices
together produce distinctive characteristics in the management of Japanese nationality and citizenship. Five basic features are discerned: *jus sanguinis* for nationality transmission, tight border control, strict naturalization rules, a close
relationship between nationality and family registry, and restrictive access to
the status of permanent residents. This section considers these five features in
historical perspective. Emphasis here is on the construction of nationality and
citizenship regulations in postwar Japan. New developments after 1980 will be
discussed in the next section.

The Principle of Jus Sanguinis

In cross-national comparisons of nationality law, it is customary to first
study the principle of nationality transmission, namely varied combinations of
jus soli (by birthplace) and *jus sanguinis* (by parentage) for attributing nationality at one's birth. Where the principle of *jus sanguinis* is dominant, second-generation immigrants do not automatically obtain citizenship and may remain
foreigners indefinitely unless they acquire citizenship later in life. Researchers
have related this role of *jus sanguinis* with the exclusion of immigrants and the
"ethnocultural conception of nationhood."[11]

11. Brubaker, 1992. It is unfortunate that Brubaker's thesis about the role of cultural idioms
had the effect of encouraging a simplistic understanding of nationality criteria based on a sharp dichotomy between *jus soli* and *jus sanguinis*.

Conventional understanding of *jus sanguinis* as a mechanism of exclusion based on ethnicity calls for a couple of qualifications, however. First, access to citizenship does not solely depend on the basic transmission rule. As discussed by Tomas Hammar, a potential immigrant faces three "entrance gates" before becoming a citizen, namely admission to the territory, permanent residence, and then acquisition of full citizenship.[12] Rules governing naturalization and dual nationality compose criteria for the third, final gate. A *jus sanguinis*–based system could potentially be just as open as a *jus soli*–based system when citizenship is highly accessible for immigrants whose parents are not citizens.[13]

Second, the legal principles of *jus soli* and *jus sanguinis* developed before the emergence of modern national states.[14] Although the rule emphasizing descent rather than birthplace appears to fit well with the image of the ethnically exclusive nature of contemporary Japanese society, the initial codification of the principle of *jus sanguinis* dates back to the late nineteenth century. The Meiji government codified nationality law in 1899 in response to the external pressure to modernize the regulation of nationality. The principle of *jus sanguinis* was a logical choice for two reasons. First, it was compatible with previous legal practices, in particular the family registration system that had been used to define the subject population. Second, the principle was prevalent in continental European countries, where many of the advisers to the Japanese government came from. Consequently, one cannot assume that the goal of ethnic homogeneity led to the descent-based attribution of nationality.[15]

The management of nationality under the Japanese colonial empire was also at odds with a simplistic association between *jus sanguinis* and ethnocultural conceptions of nationhood. Japan acquired Taiwan from China in 1895 as a re-

12. Hammar, 1990, pp. 16–18.

13. The principle of *jus soli* per se does not comprise an "open" or "inclusive" system. When it is combined with selective immigration control (the first gate), it could exhibit an exclusive character, such as in the pre-1965 U.S. system. "Openness" here also implies the notion of individual choice. Although unconditional *jus soli* is the most inclusive in terms of turning immigrants fully into citizens by the second generation, some immigrants may not wish to acquire nationality in the host country. A system that combines *jus sanguinis* with a well-developed denizenship and high accessibility to nationality is therefore considered no less satisfactory than *jus soli*, even from a normative point of view. Swedish law exemplifies accessible nationality with *jus sanguinis*.

14. *Jus soli* originated in the feudal era in England and was based on the allegiance of the subject to the lord (Dummett and Nicol, 1990, p. 24). In France, *parlements* between the sixteenth and eighteenth centuries developed a set of criteria for defining who belonged to France (Wells, 1995; Brubaker, 1992, pp. 37–38). Nationality regulations in France thereafter maintained the emphasis on one's birth and residence in the French territory. The adoption of *jus sanguinis* by German states was partly facilitated by concerns for the influx of the migrant poor (also Germans) from neighboring states (Brubaker, 1992, pp. 64–71). In all these cases, the initial adoption of particular rules about the attribution and transmission of membership had little ideological justification.

15. See Kashiwazaki, 1998, for the context in which the first nationality law was codified in Japan.

sult of the Sino-Japanese War. After defeating Russia in 1905, Japan gained influence over the Korean peninsula and formally annexed the territory in 1910. The Japanese colonial empire was thus multiethnic in its character, and yet the principle of *jus sanguinis* in nationality attribution remained intact. Taiwanese and Koreans possessed the common status of Japanese imperial subjects, even though it did not mean equality in citizenship rights and duties. In other words, the enlargement of the boundaries of "Japanese nationals" did not affect the rule of nationality *transmission*.

If the colonial period saw an enlargement of the boundaries of Japanese nationals, postwar reorganization of citizenship resulted in their shrinkage. With the defeat in World War II in 1945, Japan came under Allied occupation, which lasted until 1952. Koreans and Taiwanese were liberated from Japanese colonial rule. Yet, the question of nationality of those who continued to reside in Japan was not resolved immediately. The Japanese government associated former colonial subjects with social disorder and public security problems. On the Korean peninsula, two opposing states declared independence in 1948 under the influence of two superpowers, and a civil war erupted in 1950. U.S.-sponsored negotiations between Japan and South Korea failed to reach agreement on postwar settlement, including the issue of nationality. In the end, the Japanese government resorted to a unilateral measure and declared the uniform loss of Japanese nationality by former colonial subjects as of April 1952, when the San Francisco Peace Treaty went into effect.

In accordance with extensive democratization programs organized by the SCAP (Supreme Commander for the Allied Powers), the Japanese nationality law was revised during the occupation period. Revisions centered on the elimination of provisions that were based on the old patriarchal "family" ideas. For instance, the wife's nationality no longer automatically followed the husband's nationality. The reform, however, did not affect the principle of *jus sanguinis*. The nationality law of 1950, which retained the principle, is in effect to this day, with a few modifications. The law has exhibited an exclusive character in the postwar period partly because Koreans and Taiwanese were uniformly made foreigners in 1952, and thus the possession of Japanese nationality was confined to those who were "Japanese" by descent. Border control and the administration of naturalization further reinforced the restrictive nature of the regulation of nationality.

Border Control and Immigrant Policies

Japan is not a country of immigrants in the classic sense. Like most European countries, a dominant indigenous group initiated nation building. During the Tokugawa period (1603–1867), the government employed a seclusion policy, banning both emigration and immigration. Strict border control in contemporary Japan is often interpreted as a continuation from this policy in the past. It is wrong to assume, however, that modern Japan had not experienced labor migration before the influx of foreign workers in the 1980s.

In the late nineteenth century, European businesses brought with them Chinese workers, who worked as sales representatives, domestic servants, and longshoremen.[16] Several thousand mainland Chinese composed the majority of the foreign resident population. Increases in Chinese workers generated concerns about public morals and effects on wages, and anti-Chinese sentiments were expressed in the public debate. The government took measures to control and monitor unskilled labor. The "foreign worker problem" thus already existed a century ago.

Koreans formed an even larger migrant group in Japan during the colonial period. Because Koreans were technically Japanese nationals, their travel to Japan was *internal* migration, and the restriction by the Japanese government was limited.[17] As Japan entered total war in the late 1930s, more than 600,000 Koreans were brought to Japan as conscript labor.[18] The number of Koreans residing on Japanese home islands is estimated to have reached more than 2 million in 1945.[19]

After August 1945, the majority of Koreans in Japan rushed back to the Korean peninsula. More than half a million Koreans, however, could not or did not return immediately and remained in Japan. Some Korean migrants even came back to Japan after seeing the social and political turmoil in Korea. Those who stayed on in Japan eventually became the first generation of *zainichi*, or resident Koreans in Japan.

Because of concerns about the spread of communism, the SCAP was generally supportive of strict immigration control by the Japanese government.[20] The primary goal of the Japanese government was to monitor and control the activi-

16. Weiner, 1989, pp. 52–53; Yamawaki, 1994, p. 17ff; Kamachi, 1980.
17. The imperial Japanese state was not united regarding policies on controlling Korean migration. Whereas the Ministry of Interior was concerned about increases in Korean labor in Japan from the point of view of the maintenance of social order, the governor-general in Korea opposed restriction on Korean migration on the ground that Korea was part of the Japanese empire. The level of restriction also depended on changes in economic and labor market conditions. (Nishinarita, 1997, ch. 5; Yamawaki, 1994).
18. Weiner, 1994, ch. 6.
19. Morita, 1996, pp. 156–57.
20. Ōnuma, 1979–1980, and Kim T., 1997, analyze in detail the policies of the SCAP and the Japanese government between 1945 and 1952.

ties of Koreans in and out of Japan. The Alien Registration Order of 1947 stipulated that Koreans and certain Chinese residing in Japan were "regarded as aliens" for the purpose of this law, despite the fact that they still possessed Japanese nationality.[21] This law required non-Japanese persons to be registered with the authority and to carry their Certificates of Alien Registration at all times. The 1951 Immigration Control Order was based on the instruction by the SCAP to establish a comprehensive immigration control following the U.S. model. The U.S.-style immigration control system produced a different effect when it was accompanied by restrictive access to citizenship. With no avenues allowing immigrants for settlement, the system in Japan operated as nothing but strict border control.

The Japanese government in fact employed an explicit policy of not accepting immigrants for settlement. Existence of ethnic minority groups was deemed undesirable for the maintenance of social order and public security. The following statement in an official publication in the late 1950s shows how Justice Ministry officials understood immigration control and immigrant policy in light of national interests:

Since Japan is one of the most densely populated countries in the world, policies of controlling both population growth and immigration are strongly called for. It should therefore be a government policy to severely restrict the entry of foreigners into Japan. This is all the more so because there are undesirable foreigners who would threaten the lives of Japanese nationals by criminal activity and immoral conduct.[22]

The Japanese government thus perceived incoming foreign nationals primarily as a problem of public security and social order. Between 1952 and 1974, a total of more than 30,000 persons (of whom 97 percent were Koreans) were apprehended on account of illegal entry into Japan.[23] Foreign nationals already residing in Japan were also subject to a similar perception as potential criminals. The police intensely enforced the Alien Registration Law and apprehended resident aliens, mostly Koreans, on charges such as not carrying with them the Certificate of Alien Registration. Strict control of immigrants is also reflected in practices concerning naturalization.

21. Alien Registration Order, Article 11.
22. *Shutsunyūkoku Kanri*, 1959, p. 3.
23. *Shutsunyūkoku Kanri*, 1975, p. 118.

Administration of Naturalization

As discussed earlier, accessibility to citizenship may significantly vary because of rules concerning naturalization or the acquisition of nationality. For instance, the introduction of as-of-right acquisition of citizenship for the second generation and long-term resident aliens makes citizenship more accessible, even when the basic transmission principle remains *jus sanguinis*.

The Japanese system is characterized by restrictive access to citizenship for resident aliens. There is no category of aliens who enjoy as-of-right acquisition of Japanese nationality. In other words, any person who was not attributed Japanese nationality by birth has to go through the process of naturalization.[24] Rules concerning naturalization are codified in the nationality law. Applicants must satisfy the following conditions: five years of consecutive residence, an age of twenty years or more and of full capacity according to the law of his or her native country, good moral conduct, property or ability enough to lead a financially independent life, renunciation of previous nationality, and no current or previous membership in organizations that advocate the overthrow of the Constitution or of the government of Japan.[25]

The fact that final decision rests with the discretion by the Justice Ministry is often cited as the symbol of exclusive Japanese citizenship. It should be noted, however, that the use of discretion by the authority in naturalization is not unique to Japan. Rather, what makes the Japanese system exclusive is the strict administration of naturalization in practice combined with the lack of any alternative channel for obtaining citizenship.

Applicants for naturalization are required to submit extensive supporting documents.[26] Justice Ministry officials then carry out their own investigation to confirm that applicants satisfy criteria such as "good moral conduct." It may involve obtaining references from relevant offices such as the police and the tax office, and interviewing neighbors as well as supervisors and colleagues in the workplace to collect information on the reputation of the applicant.[27]

---

24. The 1984 revision to nationality law created a system of as-of-right acquisition. This system, however, is confined to specific cases such as where children born of a Japanese parent failed to obtain Japanese nationality at birth.

25. Nationality Law, Article 5. In the revised law of 1985, a person is eligible if he or she can make a living as a dependent of a family member.

26. The fee for naturalization is considered a major barrier discouraging potential applicants in some countries. It is interesting to note that naturalization itself is free of charge in Japan (*Kokuseki Kika no Jitsumu Sōdan,* 1993, p. 335). But it is, in practice, costly because applicants have to prepare a wide range of supporting documents.

27. Kim Y., 1990, pp. 64–66.

Potential applicants may be turned away even before submitting their applications, at the preliminary stage of "consultation" with officials. This happens when officials at local offices advise potential applicants against submitting an application because the chance of obtaining permission to naturalize is deemed low. A typical reason is the lack of supporting documents.

Cumbersome documentation is closely related to the Japanese family registry system, as discussed below. The administrative procedure requires that the applicant's family relationships be clearly known before naturalization is permitted. Applicants whose home countries have a system of family registry (South Korea and Taiwan) are required to obtain their family registry records from home. It is not always easy to locate applicants' records in their hometown, particularly for those who have already lived in Japan for decades. The process could be delayed further when records in official documents do not match actual relationships among family members and relatives.[28]

Supporting documents may also be considered insufficient in light of the criterion of "good moral conduct." This condition is adopted in naturalization laws of a number of other countries as well. In Japan, administrative practice is such that minor offenses have been considered problematic. Applicants who have a traffic violation record, for instance, may be advised to reapply a few years later.[29] Applicants have thus been rejected for technical or minor reasons even when naturalizing them would pose no apparent problem in light of national interests.

Another factor that has reduced the number of naturalizations is the practice of family-based naturalization. Administrative guidance of the Justice Ministry insisted on naturalizing household members as a group rather than just a specific individual within a family.[30] This policy was based on the legal norm of avoiding a situation where members of the same household hold different nationalities.

The system of naturalization is not designed to transform foreign nationals promptly into Japanese nationals. Restriction on naturalization corresponds to the government's stance on border control, namely that Japan does not admit immigration for the purpose of permanent settlement. More than half a million Koreans, however, have resided in Japan since before the end of the war. In

---

28. The information on family relationships is later entered into the new family registration record created for a naturalized person. Erroneous documentation is deemed unacceptable in light of the administrative norm of precise recording of actual relationships. If, for example, a father-child relationship on paper is found to be false, it has to be settled in court beforehand (*Kokuseki Kika no Jitsumu Sōdan,* 1993, pp. 462–63).

29. Kim Y., 1990, pp. 78–79.

30. Kim Y., 1990, pp. 74–75. This rule appears to be no longer enforced as strictly as before.

practice, then, the administration of naturalization up to the 1980s was primarily a question of how to deal with Koreans.

Given the cumbersome procedure, it appears that the Japanese government has been unwilling to give citizenship to Koreans. One cannot conclude, however, that the aim of the Japanese state has been to limit the number of naturalizations by Koreans to a minimum. In the mid-1960s, for instance, the Justice Ministry issued publications to explain the naturalization process in detail and to encourage application, although they maintained an emphasis on assimilation into Japanese society.[31] Naturalizations by Koreans were fewer than 2,500 per year in the mid-1950s, but increased to about 5,000 annually by the 1980s. Naturalization is on the rise further in recent years, as discussed in the next section.[32]

In response to Justice Ministry practices, dominant Korean organizations in Japan, Sōren and Mindan, have negatively viewed naturalization as humiliation.[33] They have in particular reacted against the notion of *dōka*, or assimilation into Japanese society. The Justice Ministry has explicitly employed assimilation as a condition for naturalization. In practice, it is measured by items such as the knowledge of Japanese language and lifestyle.[34] What is at issue, however, is the symbolic significance of the requirement of assimilation. The term *dōka* implies the loss of Korean identity, a reminder to Koreans of the assimilationist drive during the Japanese colonial period. Consequently, those who are naturalized and become Japanese could suffer from a sense of betrayal. Koreans in Japan, organizational leaders insisted, should retain Korean identity and live in Japan as overseas nationals of their home country.

In sum, administration of naturalization in Japan has been characterized by a complicated set of documentation with an emphasis on precise records, family-based naturalization, and criteria for assimilation and good conduct. The Korean community reacted against the system of naturalization with nationalistic sentiment. Once a foreign national is naturalized, a person's name is re-

---

31. Kim Y., 1990, p. 20–21.

32. The rate of permission was low in the 1950s, when one out of two applicants was likely to fail. In recent years, the rate of permission is said to have significantly increased, although statistics on details are not available to the author. An estimate of the chance of obtaining permission would have to take into consideration the number of potential applicants who are dissuaded by officials from applying (Kim Y., 1990, pp. 96–99).

33. Since the mid-1950s, Sōren and Mindan have been the two dominant organizations among Koreans residing in Japan, even though their influence has somewhat weakened after the 1980s. Sōren (Chongryun) is affiliated with North Korea, whereas Mindan has strong connections with South Korea. On the rivalry between the two organizations, see Lee and DeVos, 1981. See also Ryang, 1997, on Koreans affiliated with Sōren and North Korea.

34. Kim Y., 1990, p. 70.

corded into a family registry. A close relationship between the regulation of nationality and family registry is another major component of the administration of Japanese citizenship.

Family Registration System and Assimilation

Family registry in Japan is closely related to the management of nationality. On principle, every person who possesses Japanese nationality is registered in a family registry. Naturalization involves creating a new record in the Japanese family registration system.

Originally imported from China in the sixth century, the compilation of family registers has a long history in Japan.[35] Rulers in Japan used it in a variety of forms for the purpose of extracting resources from their subject population. Of particular relevance to contemporary citizenship policies are the ways in which the Meiji government renewed the use of family registry as a critical tool for consolidating its nationwide, centralized administration. As the Ainu to the north and the Okinawans to the south came under modern Japan's rule, their family registration records were also created. The standardization of family registry, a form of institutional assimilation, went hand in hand with cultural assimilation programs for these ethnic minority groups, including the enforcement of Japanese language use.

Just as in the cases vis-à-vis the Ainu and Okinawans, the Japanese colonial state gradually introduced Japanese-style family registry into Taiwan and Korea. The extreme assimilationist drive from the late 1930s involved further standardization of family registry. The policy of sōshikaimei, or forced adoption of Japanese-style names by colonial subjects, aimed at establishing Japanese family structure in the colonies while at the same time cultivating absolute loyalty to the Japanese emperor.[36]

In the postwar period, too, family registry retained its character as an assimilationist institution. Until 1984, a newly naturalized person was required to adopt a Japanese-style name. Koreans denounced this practice, calling it a denial of one's ethnic heritage through forced assimilation.

Permanent Resident Status

In Europe, settlement of foreign migrant workers and their families led to improvement in their legal protection and the development of the status of

35. Hisatake, 1991.
36. Miyata, Kim, and Yang, 1992.

denizenship, which then seems to have contributed to lowering barriers to the acquisition of full citizenship. In Japan, more than 75 percent of the total of 639,000 resident Koreans were Japanese-born in 1974.[37] If we focus only on the immigrants' length of stay, we should expect an even faster development of the status of permanent residents as well as greater access to full citizenship in Japan than in Europe. Yet, the incorporation of Koreans as Japanese nationals proceeded only slowly, as we have seen above, and so did the extension of partial citizenship rights for permanently settled resident aliens.

The 1952 immigration control system stipulated that every foreigner should obtain a visa status to reside in Japan. This requirement was waived for the Koreans and the Taiwanese who had continued to live in the country since before the end of war.[38] This arrangement was considered a tentative measure, until agreement would be reached between Japan and the relevant governments on the legal status of these people. The agreements were not forthcoming, however. Only in 1965 did Japan and South Korea open diplomatic relationships, whereas Japan has had no diplomatic ties with North Korea to this day. Consequently, North Korean nationality is not officially recognized in Japan. Resident Koreans who have obtained neither South Korean nor Japanese nationality, including those who identify with North Korea, have been practically stateless.

The waiver of the visa requirement in 1952 for Koreans and Taiwanese did not mean secure permanent residence for them. All resident aliens were subject to the Alien Registration Law with a risk of deportation. The Japanese government was interested in maintaining a wide discretion in repatriating "undesirable" foreigners and was unwilling to offer secure permanent resident status to de facto permanent residents. Continued residence of the former colonial subjects was therefore understood only as an exceptional measure because of the special conditions that originated in Japanese colonialism and war. Another exception was long-term resident Chinese from mainland China. In view of their prolonged stay in Japan, the government issued permanent resident permits to approximately 15,000 Chinese in 1952.[39] Otherwise, few people obtained the status of permanent resident stipulated in the immigration control law.[40]

---

37. *Shutsunyūkoku Kanri,* 1975, p. 105.
38. This category included roughly 600,000 persons, the vast majority of whom were Koreans.
39. *Shutsunyūkoku Kanri,* 1980, pp. 123–24.
40. Up to 1980, fewer than 200 persons annually obtained a permanent resident visa. The number of applicants was also small. The number of permissions increased to several thousand per year in the 1980s (*Shutsunyūkoku Kanri Tōkei Nempō*).

In pre-1980 Japan, then, resident aliens consisted of long-term residents (mostly Koreans, Taiwanese, and mainland Chinese) and just a small number of other foreign nationals holding visa statuses with time limits. The members of the latter group were not anticipated to become permanent residents, let alone Japanese nationals.

Summary and Comparative Perspective

In the course of the disintegration of their colonial empires, both Britain and France maintained political, economic, and cultural relationships with their former colonies. They continued to allow, at least initially, relatively free movement of people. In accordance with nationality and citizenship laws, lawfully settled Commonwealth immigrants possessed full citizenship in Britain. In France, too, former colonial subjects who settled in the "mother country" had access to French citizenship. In contrast, the collapse of the Japanese colonial empire resulted in a sharp demarcation between the Japanese and non-Japanese. Only the "Japanese proper" retained Japanese nationality and enjoyed full citizenship, whereas non-Japanese colonial subjects uniformly lost their Japanese nationality.

Reorganization of nationality and citizenship in the immediate postwar years consolidated the contemporary management of nationality and citizenship in Japan. Its restrictive nature is due to the combined effect of *jus sanguinis*, restrictive naturalization rules, and tight immigration control. The leaders of Koreans, the largest noncitizen group in Japan, on their part engaged in homeland politics. The situation on the Korean peninsula as well as their past experiences under Japanese colonialism fostered their nationalistic orientation. Both Justice Ministry officials and Korean leaders defined naturalization as giving up one's previous identity and becoming "Japanese" in terms of ethnicity, culture, and loyalty to the Japanese state. Nationality status was thus linked with ethnonational identity in the postwar period.

Despite the long-term settlement of Koreans and Taiwanese in Japan, legal rights for resident foreigners were slow to develop. Emphasis on security and social order by the Japanese government and nationalistic reactions by the Koreans were played out in the context of the cold war. The Japanese government maintained the explicit policy of avoiding settlement of immigrants, and foreigners entering Japan were admitted only as sojourners. Foreign nationals found no regular steps to follow for moving from being a temporary migrant to a denizen with secure permanent residence and then to a Japanese national. Problems and contradictions in postwar Japanese citizenship policies have been increasingly challenged since the 1980s.

Contemporary Development

The dominant portrayal of Japanese society in the post–World War II era has been that of ethnic and cultural homogeneity. The sense of homogeneity was reinforced by the small size of the foreign resident population, whose proportion to the total Japanese population just reached 1 percent in the early 1990s. In contrast, the proportion of resident aliens in countries such as Germany and France was more than 5 percent already in the mid-1970s. In these countries, the termination of active foreign labor recruitment was followed by family reunification and led to a greater recognition of the ethnically heterogeneous makeup of the society. The trend in Japan was almost the opposite. In the 1970s and 1980s the *nihonjinron* literature, or publications about the uniqueness of Japanese culture, society, and national character, popularized and reinforced the theme of homogeneity.[41]

Up to the early 1980s, the vast majority of "foreigners" in Japan were Korean and Chinese families who had resided in Japan since before 1945. Of the approximately 840,000 foreign residents in 1984, for instance, more than 640,000 Koreans and 22,000 Chinese fell into several categories of permanent residents.[42] Most Koreans used their Japanese names in social life, making ethnic diversity in society even less visible. The myth of ethnic homogeneity was not seriously disturbed.

In the 1980s, however, new groups of noncitizens arrived and settled in Japan in greater numbers than before, including Indochina refugees and foreign workers. The presence of these new groups in turn gave further impetus to the development of social movements by permanent resident Koreans, who demanded a greater scope of residence-based rights. As at the beginning of the 1990s, the legal status of resident Koreans in Japan was similar to the concept of denizenship, with secure residential rights. In this sense, recent citizenship trends in Japan to some extent parallel those in Western Europe. Nevertheless, criteria for the acquisition of full Japanese citizenship have changed little. This section considers these contemporary developments of Japanese citizenship.

International Legal Norms and Changes in International Context

Since the mid-1970s, Japan has come into prominence in the international arena as a major player in the world economy. Internationalization became a

---

41. On the *nihonjinron* literature, see Yoshino, 1992.
42. Nyūkan Tōkei Kenkyūkai, 1990, pp. 15, 76–79.

slogan for the new direction of the country, with demands from both within and abroad to open up, to take a leadership role, and to assume international responsibility. For the Japanese government, successful economic development provided the opportunity to assume a greater role in international cooperation and to increase its legitimacy as a competent, advanced Western democracy. To do so would require accepting an emerging set of international legal norms, including those in the area of citizenship.

Among international legal norms, the most relevant to the recent development of citizenship are the UN conventions on human rights and the rights of migrant workers and noncitizen residents. In Western Europe, international conventions on human rights have provided legal and normative underpinnings to the extension of partial citizenship rights to noncitizen residents. The goal of economic integration through free movement of people within the common market has also facilitated legislation regarding the legal rights and protection of migrants.[43]

Another major impetus for changing laws regarding citizenship and nationality is the principle of gender equality. The 1979 Convention on the Elimination of All Forms of Discrimination against Women required that signatory countries accord the same rights to women as they do to men in regard to their children's nationality. Consequently, a number of countries that had a patrilineal *jus sanguinis* system shifted to the bilineal system where children obtain both their father's and mother's nationality.[44]

In the absence of an equivalence of European integration, the role and the extent of international coordination are expected to be different for the Japanese case. Nevertheless, Japan has also been under the constraints of international legal norms. Admission of Indochinese refugees and the adoption of bilineal *jus sanguinis* are two examples that show the impact of international factors on nationality and citizenship regulations.

The end of the Vietnam War in 1975 generated refugees from Indochina. In the same year, the G7 Summit meeting was established. As the only Asian country admitted to membership in the G7 Summit, Japan was obliged to take some steps to accommodate refugees. In 1978, the Japanese government permitted the settlement of refugees within the set limit of the ceiling. The initial

---

43. Meehan, 1993.

44. The following countries changed from a patrilineal to bilineal system after 1960: East Germany (1967), the Philippines (1973), West Germany (1974), Denmark, Switzerland (1978), Sweden, Norway (1979), China, Israel (1980), Portugal, Turkey, Libya (1981), Spain (1982), Austria, Italy (1983), Greece, Japan (1984), Netherlands, Belgium, and Switzerland (1985) (Bauböck, 1994, p. 51, n. 24; Yamada and Tuchiya, 1985, p. 11). South Korea also changed to bilineal *jus sanguinis* in 1998.

quota was only for 500 refugees, although it was gradually expanded to 10,000 by 1985. At the end of 1997, 10,241 Indochina refugees had been accepted for settlement.[45]

Although the number of refugees settled in Japan was small, their arrival had a strong impact on the social rights of resident aliens. With the acceptance of refugees, the Japanese government was compelled to join relevant international conventions. Japan acceded to the International Covenant on Civil and Political Rights as well as the International Covenant on Economic, Social, and Cultural Rights in 1979, and then ratified the Convention relating to the Status of Refugees in 1981. Provisions in these conventions required that resident aliens be treated equally with citizens of the country in the areas of social security and welfare. Consequently, several legal changes removed eligibility restrictions based on nationality in such areas as national pension and public housing.[46] Furthermore, the creation of a new residential status for refugees in 1981 contributed to improvement in the legal status of preexisting long-term resident aliens.

Regarding nationality law, too, the Japanese government was compelled to adopt the principle of gender equality in nationality attribution.[47] In 1980, Japan signed the UN convention for eliminating discrimination against women. Accordingly, the principle of nationality attribution shifted from a patrilineal system to a bilineal system of *jus sanguinis* with the 1984 revision of nationality and family registration laws. The change did not represent a departure from *jus sanguinis*. Of interest, rather, is the way in which the Japanese government attempted to defend the principle of "one and only one nationality."

In the context of an ever-increasing number of international marriages by Japanese citizens, many of them with Koreans, the bilineal attribution of nationality was anticipated to generate a large number of potential dual nationals at birth. Government officials identified this as a serious problem and, in order to deal with the problem, instituted a "nationality selection" system.[48] Under this system, persons with two or more nationalities are advised to choose one nationality or another before reaching the age of twenty-two or, where applica-

---

45. *Shutsunyūkoku Kanri*, 1998.

46. The revision to the National Pension Plan in 1982, however, failed to cover a large number of elderly permanent resident aliens, who remained practically ineligible. This situation was partly rectified by the 1994 revision to the Pension Law that stipulated a lump-sum payment to persons who could not meet the condition on the minimum paid-up period (Tanaka, 1995, pp. 158–60; Tezuka, 1995, pp. 259–60).

47. In Japan, a particularly serious problem was that of statelessness among children born from an American father and a Japanese mother (Tanaka, 1995, pp. 167–68).

48. An official guidebook states: "Although the adoption of the bilineal system answers the demand for sexual equality, it at the same time gives rise to a very troublesome problem—that of dual nationality" (Yamada and Tuchiya, 1985, p. 36).

ble, within two years from the date on which they become dual nationals. Those who opt for Japanese nationality are required to make a "declaration of choice," which in practice means filling out family registration forms and submitting them to the local government office.[49]

The current international trend in coordinating nationalities is to have a greater degree of tolerance for the incidence of multiple nationality than for statelessness. The principle of "one nationality for everyone" is therefore increasingly understood to mean at least one nationality, rather than "only one," for each person. Furthermore, migrant-sending countries have tended to support dual nationality, which would allow their nationals to retain close relationships with their country of origin while enjoying full rights and protection in the host country.[50] Outside Europe, Mexico's recent move to allow dual nationality for those who become naturalized U.S. citizens is another example.[51] Insisting on the desirability of "only one" nationality, the official stance of the Japanese government therefore deviates from the current international legal norm.

In the same 1984 revision, however, the Justice Ministry made a significant concession on family registry. The new family registration law permitted the use of non-Japanese family names. The government abandoned the previous policy that strongly demanded Japanese-style names as well as the use of Chinese characters. Both the acceptance of non-Japanese names and the bilineal system indicate a limited liberalization in the regulation of nationality and family registry.

"Newcomers" and Revisions to Immigration Control Law

Migrant workers to Japan, mainly from other Asian countries, increased significantly from the 1980s.[52] The term "newcomers" was created to refer to them, to differentiate them from "old comers," or Koreans and Chinese families who had lived in Japan since the colonial period. The scale of migration, however, never came close to the levels experienced by Germany or France. The

49. Yamada and Tuchiya, 1985, p. 48. The declaration, however, in itself does not make a person a single-nationality holder. That is, since the Japanese government cannot unilaterally deprive a person of the other nationality, in practice the person could still retain dual nationality. Nevertheless, explicit official encouragement to renounce the other nationality is an expression of the government's desire to reduce dual nationality holders. Government officials summarizing the main points of the 1984 revision make it explicit that the nationality selection system was introduced in light of the principle of "one and only one nationality" (Hosokawa, 1985).

50. Hammar, 1990, pp. 112–13.

51. Aleinikoff, 1998, p. 30–31.

52. The literature on foreign workers written in Japanese is voluminous. English sources include Cornelius, 1994; Mori, 1997; Oka, 1994; Sellek, 1994; Shimada, 1994; Spencer, 1992; and Weiner and Hanami, 1998.

number of foreign workers, including both legal and illegal employees, was estimated at more than half a million in the early 1990s.[53]

Labor migration to Japan in the 1980s has some similarities with the
cases of Western European countries in the 1960s in that, because of demographic changes and labor shortages, foreign migrant workers came to fill
jobs at the lower strata in the labor market.[54] The demand for foreign workers
was particularly strong among small and medium-sized companies, which
found it increasingly difficult to recruit young Japanese into "3D" (dirty,
dangerous, and demanding) jobs. Brokers and other informal intermediaries
promoted migration to Japan, a destination made attractive by the strong
yen. Furthermore, many Asian labor migrants lost jobs in the Middle East
because of the decline of oil prices in the 1980s, and sought migration to Japan as an alternative.

Foreign workers (*gaikokujin rōdōsha*) in Japan include several categories of
people. In a broad sense it should even include Westerners working in Japan.
They, however, are predominantly employed in white-collar jobs, such as English language teachers and staff members in corporations. In the prevailing discourse about foreign workers, such Westerners are not considered *gaikokujin
rōdōsha* (literally "foreign national laborers"), and the term is strongly associated with migrants from less-developed, non-Western countries.

First, "foreign workers" typically refers to migrant workers who work on
construction sites, in metal processing, machine tool, and other manufacturing
companies, and in the service sector. In the absence of an official guest-worker
program, most migrant workers entered Japan as tourists and then overstayed
after the three-month limit. Consequently, the form of their employment is illegal, and those workers are always at the risk of apprehension and deportation.
The number of "overstayers," who compose the bulk of foreign workers, were
estimated at more than 100,000 in 1990 and then increased to nearly 300,000 by
1993.[55] Although their predominant image is that of male workers, foreign

---

53. Kajita, 1994, p. 14.

54. It is important to note, however, that the recruitment of foreign labor did not occur in Japan
earlier in the postwar era, such as during the high-growth period of the 1960s and 1970s. For one
thing, internal seasonal migrant workers served as a reservoir from which labor was drawn flexibly
on demand. Another difference from countries such as Germany and France is that large corporations in Japan pushed for automation in production instead of bringing in foreign workers. Furthermore, the government had confirmed its policy of not admitting foreign labor on the Cabinet level
and advocated greater participation of the elderly and women in the labor market (Kajita, 1994, pp.
19–20; Hachiya, 1992, p. 49).

55. Tezuka, 1995, p. 63.

workers also include a sizable number of women working without a valid visa, particularly in the sex industry.[56]

Second, ethnic Japanese from Latin American countries form a special category. After the 1990 revision to the immigration control law (discussed below), employers turned increasingly to the recruitment of ethnic Japanese, who were eligible for the long-term resident visa and were allowed to take up employment in any sector.[57] The number of Brazilians and Peruvians who reside in Japan with this visa increased from 67,000 in 1992 to more than 130,000 in 1997. The lawful nature of their stay and work therefore differentiates them from undocumented aliens.[58]

The next three groups enter Japan with a nontourist visa, but they share similar problems of precarious legal status with undocumented workers. Female workers recruited mainly from the Philippines by the "entertainment industry" often become victims of exploitation.[59] Trainees are another group, arriving under trainee programs that consist of classroom studies and practicum for acquiring technical skills. These programs, however, often serve as a channel to recruit unskilled labor. The third group consists of students enrolled in Japanese schools and colleges. Lacking sufficient financial means for living and studying, they seek part-time or full-time jobs. When their working hours exceed the prescribed limit, they fall into the category of illegal workers. These three groups of employees are not recognized as workers by law and hence are not covered by the standards of labor laws and health insurance systems.

Finally, with increases in international marriage, a significant proportion of newcomer resident foreigners hold a visa category called "spouse or child of Japanese nationals." Their number increased from 57,000 in 1988 to more than

---

56. The active recruitment of female migrants by the Japanese sex industry preceded the increase of male migrant workers. Until 1987, women had outnumbered men in the number of illegal workers apprehended (Ito, 1992; Sellek, 1994, pp. 171–72).

57. From the early 1980s, ethnic Japanese politicians in Brazil petitioned the Japanese government to improve the visa issuing method so that ethnic Japanese migrants from Brazil could more easily migrate and seek employment in Japan (Fujisaki, 1991). The admission of ethnic Japanese has been interpreted as a reflection of blood-based understanding of Japanese citizenship. It should be clarified, however, that ethnic Japanese from Latin American countries are not entitled to full citizenship. On this score, the legal arrangement in Japan differs significantly from both the Law of Return in Israel and the treatment of *Aussiedler* in Germany. The long-term resident visa issued to ethnic Japanese has a time limit of three years, although renewal is possible. Most ethnic Japanese migrants, on their part, come to Japan primarily to make money.

58. In terms of the total number of registered residents, there were approximately 233,000 Brazilians and 40,000 Peruvians at the end of 1997 (*Zairyū Gaikokujin Tōkei,* 1998).

59. The number of Filipino women who hold an "entertainer visa" increased from 874 in 1974 to more than 13,000 in 1988 (Nyūkan Tōkei Kenkyūkai, 1990, pp. 73, 82–83).

274,000 in 1997, contributing to the growth of the "settled" resident alien population as opposed to "temporary" residents.[60]

Heated debates on the issue of foreign workers took place toward the end of the 1980s. They centered on the choice between "opening up" the country and "staying closed."[61] Several rationales accompanied the argument for opening up. First, admitting foreign workers is inevitable because of structural changes in the economy. Second, greater personnel exchanges would contribute to the goal of internationalizing Japan from within. Third, accepting foreign workers can facilitate technological transfer, thereby fulfilling Japan's international responsibility as an economic power.

In contrast, proponents for staying closed made the following lines of argument. First, European experiences show that a guest-worker program would not work; the better way to cope with labor shortage is economic restructuring and the use of the elderly and women. Second, the employment of foreign workers at the lower strata of the labor market would lead to human rights problems and would severely damage the image of the country; Japan would be seen as exploiting people in less-developed countries not only overseas but also within the country. Third, the best way to fulfill the country's international responsibility is to assist developmental efforts in the form of financial aid, direct investment, and training, and not by importing labor for unskilled jobs.

What is most salient about the nature of this debate was a neglect of the history of labor importation under Japanese colonialism earlier in the twentieth century. Instead, a parallel was drawn from the mid-nineteenth century, as indicated by the use of *sakoku-kaikoku* (seclusion–open up the country) metaphors.[62] Both sides shared the prevailing conception of postwar Japanese nationhood as a homogeneous society.

At the same time, the changing international position of Japan decisively shaped the discourse among elites. Both sides expressed concerns about Japan's international image and how to fulfill its responsibility. They agreed on the need to internationalize Japan; the question was how. Both sides also raised the issue of human rights. Opponents of labor migration cited human rights problems as a rationale against carelessly admitting foreign workers, whereas grassroots activists and lawyers addressed the same issue as a basis for supporting the foreign workers who already resided in Japan. Yet, these debates offered few specific suggestions about long-term citizenship policies.

---

60. Nyūkan Tōkei Kenkyūkai, 1990, pp. 64–65; *Zairyū Gaikokujin Tōkei,* 1998. Brazilian nationals account for 41 percent of the 1997 figure.

61. See Oka, 1994, pp. 61–67, on the nature of the debate.

62. Lie, 1994, p. 10.

The Japanese government initially responded to increases in undocumented foreign migrant workers by reinforcing border control. The government temporarily abolished bilateral visa waiver agreements with Pakistan (1989), Bangladesh (1989), and Iran (1992) in order to reduce overstayers from these countries.[63] In light of the growth in the number of incoming foreign nationals, the government also reviewed and revised the immigration control law in 1989. The main thrust of the revision was twofold: to streamline immigration control processes by reorganizing visa categories, and to discourage the recruitment of illegal workers by introducing employer sanctions. In accordance with the need for internationalization, employment of foreign nationals with high or special skills was to be encouraged, and trainee programs for technical transfer were to be enhanced. But the ban on unskilled foreign labor was reaffirmed. The Ministry of Justice concluded that the question of unskilled labor would need to be studied cautiously from a variety of aspects.[64]

The revision to the immigration control law resulted in an influx of ethnic Japanese from South America, as discussed above. With the long-term resident status, they were not subject to restriction on the type of employment. Several cities and suburbs have seen the development of communities of Brazilians and Peruvians who took up blue-collar jobs in the manufacturing sector. The expanded trainee program also became a source of unskilled workers. The 1990 law reduced the requirement of classroom study and allowed greater allocation of time to on-the-job training. As at the end of 1997, the Chinese accounted for more than half of the total of 26,000 persons holding a trainee visa.[65] Since 1993, some 14,000 former trainees have obtained a special visa that allows them an additional period of stay in Japan for the purpose of gaining more working experiences.[66]

In 1991 another special law on immigration control went into effect and contributed to improvement in the permanent resident status of former colonial subjects. The contemporary situation of resident Koreans could be described as the "politics of denizenship," as discussed below.

"Old Comers" and the Politics of Denizenship

Throughout the 1970s, the residential status of long-term resident aliens remained insecure. The internal disparity within the Korean community was also

63. Tezuka, 1995, p. 29.
64. *Shutsunyūkoku Kanri,* 1992, pp. 3, 193–94.
65. *Zairyū Gaikokujin Tōkei,* 1998.
66. *Shutsunyūkoku Kanri,* 1998.

evident: South Korean nationals with the status of "permanent resident by treaty" were privileged compared with others regarding legal protection against deportation and social rights such as access to the national health care plan.[67]

The 1980s and early 1990s saw a gradual increase in the level of legal protection and the scope of partial citizenship rights for permanent resident aliens. Amendments to the Immigration Control Act (renamed the Immigration Control and Refugee Recognition Act) in 1981 created a new permanent resident status to cover the remaining long-term resident Koreans who did not have the status of "permanent resident by treaty." Thus, Koreans who identified with North Korea were also granted the status of permanent residence. The 1991 Immigration Control Special Law unified different categories of permanent resident status for former colonial subjects and their descendants into a common status called "special permanent residents." Persons holding this status may be deported only if they are sentenced to imprisonment longer than seven years, and if the Ministry of Justice finds a serious infringement of Japanese national interests by that crime.[68]

Access to social citizenship rights for long-term resident foreigners also improved over time, albeit gradually, in such areas as health insurance and social security.[69] In the early 1970s, Korean groups organized campaigns for removing the nationality barrier in the National Health Insurance program. By 1974, the vast majority of localities with a significant Korean population had issued ordinances allowing noncitizens to join the national plan.[70] The accomplishment on the local level, however, did not lead to any legal change on a national level. Only in 1986 did the central government extend the eligibility to all noncitizen residents residing in Japan for more than one year. The National Pension Plan also excluded resident foreigners based on the nationality clause. The clause was eliminated finally in 1982 as a measure to conform to the Refugee Convention.

With greater security in their permanent residence in Japan, resident Koreans became an equivalent of denizens. Their contemporary social movements

67. This status was a product of the 1965 ROK–Japan Treaty. By 1974, 342,000 persons had acquired it, whereas approximately 270,000 Koreans had not (Nyūkan Tōkei Kenkyūkai, 1990).
68. *Shutsunyūkoku Kanri,* 1992, pp. 118–19; Hanami, 1998, p. 222.
69. In Japan public programs for both health insurance and old-age pension consist of occupational (employees') plans and the national plan. Of these two, occupational plans do not have a nationality-based eligibility barrier. They are, however, applicable only to employees in medium-sized and large companies and hence were irrelevant for most Koreans who, excluded from large firms because of discrimination, were either self-employed or employed in small businesses. Their accessibility to social security therefore directly depended on national plans (Yoshioka, 1995).
70. Yoshioka, 1995, p. 53.

have focused on the improvement of the content of their denizenship. Contested areas include alien registration and fingerprinting, public sector employment, and voting rights.

In the 1980s, the permanent residence of Koreans was contested over the issue of fingerprinting on the alien registration certificate. The refusal of fingerprinting was addressed in the language of human rights and human dignity. The dissidents ran the risk of apprehension and the denial of a reentry permit when leaving Japan. The movement drew support among some Japanese citizens and also led to some international publicity about human rights problems in Japan. The question of fingerprinting was taken up in the Japan–South Korea negotiations on the legal status of resident Koreans that started in 1988. The 1991 memorandum issued by the two governments included a statement that the Japanese government would abolish fingerprinting for permanent resident Koreans and seek an alternative means for identity check. The revised Alien Registration Law of 1993 abolished the fingerprinting requirement for permanent residents.[71]

Public sector employment is another area to which resident aliens have had severely restricted access. The primary basis of exclusion was the official guideline set in 1953 by the Cabinet Legislation Bureau, according to which Japanese nationality was required of anyone occupying a position that involves "an exercise of public authority or the formation of public will."[72] Since state administration and courts applied this phrase broadly, noncitizens were virtually excluded from the public sector, including jobs in national and local governments, public corporations, national and public universities, and public schools. Although the validity of the practice was increasingly contested in the 1980s, the degree of accessibility to jobs remained low.[73] The movement for removing the nationality barrier from public sector employment continued in the 1990s, particularly concerning employment in local governments. Whereas several local governments opened up job opportunities for noncitizens, the central government reacted to limit the scope of those openings.

Demand for electoral rights has also gained strength in recent years. In 1990, eleven permanent resident Koreans (South Korean nationals) went to court, demanding voting rights in local elections. In 1995, the Supreme Court rejected the plaintiffs' claim, which confers electoral rights only on Japanese nationals.

71. *Shutsunyūkoku Kanri,* 1992; Tamura and Shigemi, 1993. In March 1999, the Cabinet meeting endorsed a bill that would abolish fingerprinting for all other resident aliens as well (*Asahi Shimbun,* March 9, 1999).

72. An official view expressed by the Cabinet Legislation Bureau in March 1953.

73. For instance, the total number of noncitizens formally employed as public school teachers was only about thirty as of 1985 (Tanaka, 1985, p. 40).

In the same ruling, however, the Court declared that the legislature could, under the Constitution, amend the law to permit voting by permanent residents. Consequently, it is now up to the Diet to take up the issue. Outside the court, Ri Yon fa, then a lecturer at Kansai University, organized a political party called Zainichitō (resident Koreans'–denizens' party) and "participated" in the upper house election in 1992.[74]

A growing number of scholars have also argued for the extension of voting rights for permanent resident aliens.[75] In response to the interests expressed by resident Koreans in local voting rights, South Korea has taken up the issue in diplomatic negotiations with Japan. In his latest visit to Japan in 1998, South Korean president Kim Dae-Jung requested the Japanese government to give local election rights to permanent resident Koreans. Among the dominant Korean ethnic organizations in Japan, Mindan now supports voting rights, whereas Sōren, connected with North Korea, has maintained the stance against obtaining voting rights in Japan, in accordance with its policy of not intervening in the politics of a foreign country.

The politics of citizenship in the 1980s and 1990s is thus characterized by a continued struggle by resident Koreans to improve their legal status. Their movements and demands have been informed by development of denizenship in Europe as well as by human rights discourse. Many Korean opinion leaders have retained a negative evaluation on acquiring Japanese nationality and focused exclusively on denizenship rather than *full* citizenship.[76] In their view, the challenge for the Korean community is to retain ethnic identity and cultural heritage while securing the equality of rights and opportunity as residents in Japanese society. Resident Koreans of the younger generation, however, are acquiring Japanese nationality in greater numbers.

Whereas the number of naturalizations by Koreans remained at the level of 5,000 to 6,000 per year in the 1970s and 1980s, it reached the 10,000 mark in 1995. The total number of naturalizations in Japan is also on the rise. Of some 15,000 naturalizations permitted in 1997, Koreans accounted for approximately 64 percent, followed by the Chinese.[77] The increase seems to indicate a

74. Since members of his party were noncitizens, they were not allowed to stand for election as official candidates. They were nevertheless able to hold an electoral campaign in the absence of legal provisions banning such activity (Ri, 1993).

75. Suh, 1995; Kondo, 1996; Hagino, 1996. While most proponents are for local voting rights, a few scholars support national-level electoral rights as well.

76. The orientation of second-generation Korean intellectuals is reflected in the following remarks by Kim Kyeung-duk, who won a legal battle and became the first noncitizen judicial trainee in 1978 and then the first noncitizen certified lawyer in Japan: "Even if a system of as-of-right nationality acquisition were instituted, it would only result in 'assimilationistic' acquisition just like current naturalization, in the absence of a secure legal and institutional framework that would enable us to live as Koreans" ("Teijyū Gaikokujin," 1990, p. 114).

77. *Hōmu Nenkan*, 1997.

weakened sense of betrayal that the Korean community attaches to naturalization. Most younger-generation resident Koreans today have little connection with their "home country." They are socialized in the Japanese environment, particularly through Japanese schooling. For these Koreans with high levels of cultural assimilation, the major concern is life chances within Japanese society rather than homeland affairs. Obtaining Japanese citizenship would mean the utmost residential security, greater legal protection, wider employment opportunities, as well as full rights for political participation in their country of permanent residence.

Younger-generation Korean groups have in recent years taken up the issue of naturalization, a topic that used to be a taboo in the prevailing discourse of dominant Korean organizations.[78] A few Korean opinion leaders now seek the possibility of retaining Korean ethnic identity while holding Japanese nationality, namely to construct the identity of "Korean-Japanese." The issue of full citizenship and ethnic-national identity is all the more important for the Korean community because intermarriages between Koreans and Japanese are generating children of dual nationality at birth because of the 1984 revision to the nationality law.[79] At the same time, other opinion leaders continue to warn of progressive assimilation into Japanese society as a result of the growing number of Japanese nationality holders among permanent resident Koreans.

Summary and Comparative Perspective

The development in the 1980s and 1990s is characterized by the gradual extension of partial citizenship rights for permanent residents, on the one hand, and the stability in criteria for full, formal citizenship, on the other. International dimensions and the interaction between the Japanese government and resident Koreans are important for understanding this development.

Korean social movements steadily challenged nationality-based discrimination with the aim of achieving a secure status as denizens. The principle of nationality transmission has been much less politicized than the issue of partial citizenship rights. The arrival of new groups had little impact on criteria for full citizenship. Indochinese refugees obtained long-term resident visas, whereas newcomer foreign workers have still been at the initial stage of settlement, their stay being widely regarded as temporary. Furthermore, the illegal nature of

---

78. An example of an active discussion on naturalization is found in Kanagawa Mintoren, et al., 1999.

79. These dual nationals at birth are now called *daburu* (the "double") instead of the previous *haafu* ("half") to attach a positive meaning. They are counted as Japanese nationals in official statistics.

many of the foreign workers' residence does not contribute to the active discussion of rules about the acquisition of nationality.

In comparative perspective, the Japanese case is marked by several characteristics. First, the Japanese state has consistently maintained the principle of not admitting unskilled labor, which in turn is an outgrowth of the basic policy of not admitting aliens for settlement.

The second point, and closely related to the above, has to do with permanent resident status. In Europe, settled long-term resident foreigners acquired permanent resident status as they continued to live in the host society. In Japan, permanent resident status holders had long been confined to former colonial subjects. Only in recent years have newcomers begun to apply and obtain the status.

Third, the recent developments of citizenship with regard to permanent residents are characterized by a sharp disjunction between the trend toward denizenship and easier access to full citizenship. Here, it is useful to employ Hammar's two models for the incorporation of permanent resident aliens.[80] One is the voting rights model, which aims at improving the status of denizenship. This approach allows resident aliens to enjoy legal status close to that of citizens, without obtaining formal citizenship in the host country. The other is the naturalization model, which increases access to citizenship. This approach emphasizes that fuller integration of immigrants into the political community requires the extension of full citizenship rather than denizenship. Policy tools include modifications to the nationality law and toleration of dual nationality. While recognizing the importance of seeking both approaches, most researchers, including Hammar, appear to lean toward the extension of full citizenship based on the norms of liberal democracy.

In Japan, debates over citizenship have had a sharp focus on denizenship. This is because the politics of legal status has been concerned mainly about Koreans, who have retained their organizational identity in part by *not* seeking full citizenship in Japan. The dominant strategy has therefore been to minimize the gap between citizenship and denizenship. Sections of the majority Japanese have also shared the same orientation. Advocating the acquisition of Japanese citizenship by Koreans could easily be seen as tolerating the Japanese state policy of assimilation. Thus, the issue of obtaining citizenship does not fall on the same continuum with the acquisition of permanent residence in Japan.

Finally, the role of the immigrants' countries of origin is also notable in the Japanese case. Recent discussions of immigration and citizenship have paid attention to the role of the sending country, mainly with regard to dual citizenship

80. Hammar, 1990, ch. 11.

and propensity for naturalization.[81] The case of Koreans in Japan calls for further analysis of this dimension. Even after most immigrants became second and third generations, the origin shaped both their identity and legal status. South Korea remains a major actor negotiating the legal status of Koreans permanently residing in Japan.[82] The rivaling North Korean government has also been keen on maintaining influence over the Korean community in Japan.[83]

Policy Implications

This section considers public policy implications on the basis of the previous discussion of citizenship in Japan. Laws regulating Japanese citizenship have been relatively stable over time, characterized by *jus sanguinis*, strict naturalization rules, and tight border control. Whereas some European immigrant-receiving countries have revised or modified criteria for acquiring citizenship for immigrants, Japan so far has not experienced much change except for a shift to the bilineal system. At the same time, "old comers," or permanently settled Koreans and Chinese, obtained the status of denizenship by the 1990s.

Given increases in the number of foreign residents and greater ethnic diversity in Japanese society, is the country also moving in a direction similar to other advanced industrial societies? What are the policy options? To draw out public policy implications, I will first consider factors shaping contemporary citizenship policies, including demographic, economic, social, political, and international dimensions.

Factors Shaping Contemporary Citizenship Policies

The initial impetus that fostered migration of foreign workers to Japan in the 1980s was a severe labor shortage. In the debates about importing labor, proponents argued that it was inevitable because of the structural problem of the labor market. This economic argument appeared to have weakened with the burst of the "bubble economy" in the early 1990s and the ensuing economic recession. Yet, although some foreign workers lost their jobs and returned home, others

81. Hammar, 1990, ch. 6; Freeman and Ögelman, 1998.

82. For instance, South Korea played a major role in the issue of fingerprinting as the government of immigrants' origin. It should be noted, however, that most resident Koreans affected by Japan–ROK agreements neither were born nor grew up in their "home country." Furthermore, Koreans in Japan who pledge allegiance to North Korea would not regard the South Korean government as *their* government.

83. Between 1959 and 1967, more than 80,000 Koreans in Japan repatriated to North Korea (*Hōmu Nenkan,* 1967). It is important to their families and relatives living in Japan to retain channels of communications and transportation with the country.

continued to live in Japan. The estimated number of overstayers has not decreased and stood at approximately 277,000 as at the beginning of 1998.[84] At the same time, the number of foreign nationals with a valid visa continue to rise, centering on Brazilians of ethnic Japanese origin who are free from employment restriction.

Some underlying conditions that generated demand for foreign labor in the 1980s still hold today, including the reluctance of young Japanese to take up "3D" jobs. Furthermore, Japanese society is rapidly aging while the decline in the birthrate continues.[85] It is not difficult to imagine that voices for importing labor will repeatedly rise with cyclic changes in economic conditions.

Despite the official policy of not admitting foreigners for settlement, a segment of resident aliens have de facto settled in Japan. With increases in foreign workers and their families in Japan, a number of problems arise regarding their rights as workers and residents in the local community. They include labor accidents, breaches of employment contracts, the infringement of human rights in the sex industry, medical care, housing discrimination, and education for children.

Initiatives for social and cultural integration have come mostly from the local levels of administration. Municipal governments in cities and towns with a high proportion of foreign residents have sought to provide them with necessary public services and to promote their integration into the local community. Accommodation of young foreign nationals in the educational system has been of particular concern to local governments. The number of pupils and junior high school students who need remedial Japanese language instruction increased from 5,500 in 1991 to 11,500 in 1995.[86] Schools have developed a variety of programs in order to manage ethnic and cultural diversity in the classroom.[87]

In contrast with local governments, the central government in Japan has so far taken few measures for the incorporation of resident foreigners into society. Given the basic policy of not admitting foreigners for settlement, the government is not likely to assume a major role in the integration of newcomer resi-

---

84. *Shutsunyūkoku Kanri,* 1998, p. 126.

85. On this score, *keizai senryaku kaigi* (the economic strategy conference), an advisory committee to the prime minister, touched on immigration and citizenship in its recent proposal issued in February 1999. As measures against a shrinking labor force, it proposes to consider the admission of foreign nationals as immigrants and to review the nationality law. <http://www.kantei.go.jp/jp/senryaku/990226tousin-ho.html>

86. Ministry of Education, 1997, p. 31. The figures include only pupils and students in the public school system.

87. Ōta, 1996.

dent aliens as members of the society. In Japan, the size of the foreign resident population is still small, which may also account for the lack of action for social integration on the part of the state.

The ideological climate has also shaped the ways in which citizenship rights of resident foreigners are taken up on the national level. During much of the postwar era, ideological conflict was at the center of politics in Japan. Issues of resident foreigners were subsumed in this conflict. Together with dominant Korean ethnic organizations in Japan, opposition political parties were concerned more with the rivalry between North and South Korea and with political development within South Korea, and less on the problems and challenges that long-term residents faced as they continued to live in Japanese society.

Since the 1980s, and in particular in the 1990s, political parties and media have shown greater interests in issues of resident aliens. The belief that Japanese society is monocultural and monoethnic is not as powerful as it used to be. The slogan *kyōsei*, or the idea of different people living together, is instead gaining currency. Voting rights for permanent residents also seem to be drawing support.

Changes in ideological climate cannot be overstated, however. Citizenship has not become a major political issue. "Foreigners" are still regarded primarily as targets of surveillance and control, and are frequently associated with incidence of crime. Media reports generate the image that aliens disturb a well-governed, relatively crime-free society.

Furthermore, international context to some extent differentiates Japan from Western European immigrant-receiving states. Despite the end of the cold war, relationships with North Korea have not normalized. Koreans in Japan who hold neither South Korean nor Japanese nationality find their legal status still closely tied to the political developments on the Korean peninsula. Instability in East Asia continues to shape Japanese state interests in international security. Officials are also concerned about a possible influx of refugees should there be some political turmoil in Korea.

Throughout the postwar period, the Japanese government has emphasized security and social order in its immigration control. One could argue that the conservative Japanese government has grossly exaggerated the international security threat. The point, however, is that the perceived threat from abroad provides the Japanese state with a rationale for maintaining strict regulation of immigration and citizenship. If the notion of threat is persuasive enough to the Japanese public, it will weaken voices for greater liberalization of the admission of foreign nationals and of criteria for obtaining citizenship.

Policy Options

I now consider policy options in several relevant areas.

ACCESS TO NATIONALITY: TRANSMISSION, NATURALIZATION, DUAL NA-
TIONALITY.   The principle of *jus sanguinis* has been criticized for its function
to exclude immigrants. It does not follow, however, that the adoption of *jus soli*
as the basic transmission principle could be the best solution. A more fruitful
approach would be to modify the current system to increase access to nationality by the immigrant population. In this sense, countries such as Sweden, Germany, Belgium, and the Netherlands should serve as models for Japan, rather
than the United States or Britain.

If the goal is to incorporate permanent residents into the polity, the basic direction would be to increase access to nationality by settled aliens. Several approaches can be considered: (1) modifying existing criteria for naturalization;
(2) toleration of dual nationality; (3) introduction of as-of-right nationality acquisition for those who are born or grew up in Japan; and (4) introduction of
double *jus soli*.

Because of sharp increases in the number of applications, the government
will be, to some extent, forced to employ the first option. Reform would include
streamlining and simplifying the screening process, in particular alleviating the
responsibility of applicants with regard to supporting documents. The last option, double *jus soli*, is not the most desirable option in the Japanese context.
Given the history of reaction against the acquisition of Japanese nationality
among Koreans, it is not realistic in the near future to adopt a system that involves unilateral attribution of Japanese nationality. Instead, toleration for dual
nationality and as-of-right acquisition would be effective as measures for the
incorporation of immigrants. They will particularly benefit dual nationals by
birth and those who currently hold permanent resident status.

LEGAL RIGHTS OF DENIZENS.   A segment of permanent resident aliens will
continue to hold on to their original citizenship, as in the case of long-term resident Koreans. Improvement in the status of denizenship is therefore of special
importance in the Japanese context. Basic civil and residential rights, including
protection against deportation and the right of reentry, have significantly improved over the years. Even in this area, further improvement is called for, concerning the law that makes it mandatory to carry the Alien Registration
Certificate at all times.

Another issue of importance is employment in the public sector. Current
practice in Japan significantly limits the job opportunities of noncitizens. With

a more developed form of denizenship, eligibility to public sector jobs could be made a rule rather than an exception. Since some local governments are willing to expand the scope of jobs available for noncitizens, the problem is also one of autonomy of local governments from the central government. The issue of local voting rights will be one of the major foci of the politics of denizenship in the years to come. With growing support from a variety of sectors, there is some chance that local voting rights will be granted to permanent residents. Yet, the initial phase might cover only the resident foreigners who hold "special permanent resident" status, namely long-term resident Koreans, Taiwanese, and mainland Chinese. The history of Japanese colonial rule provides greater impetus to the extension of electoral rights for these categories of people than for others. If and when this first step is achieved, the next task would be to generalize the system to other permanent residents, in a more institutionalized form rather than as mere compensation for past injustices.

ACCESS TO PERMANENT RESIDENT STATUS BY NEWCOMER RESIDENT ALIENS. Restrictive access to permanent resident status is likely to become a major barrier that hinders civic incorporation of newcomer resident foreigners into Japanese society. Under the current immigration control law, the status of permanent resident may be granted "only when the permanent residence of the person is considered to be beneficial to Japanese national interests," in addition to the fulfillment of other conditions, namely good moral conduct and the ability to maintain independent living.[88] A permanent resident visa is thus understood as if it were a highly exceptional type of legal status.[89] In light of anticipated increases in the number of de facto permanent residents, criteria for granting this status need to place greater emphasis on birth and residence in Japan. Introduction of an as-of-right component into conditions for the permanent resident visa will then contribute to laying a regular path from aliens to citizens.

ADMISSION CRITERIA FOR LEGAL ENTRY. A recent trend in the policies of advanced industrialized societies is characterized by border control efforts coupled with integration of lawfully settled foreigners. In Japan, in contrast, the integration component has been slow to develop, while strict border control has been central to immigration control policies. Unlike in some countries where

88. Immigration Control and Refugee Recognition Act, Article 22. The spouse or child of a permanent resident does not need to satisfy the latter conditions.
89. The number of permanent resident permits issued has sharply risen in the past couple of years. In 1997, more than 11,000 persons obtained permanent residence, including more than 3,300 Chinese, 2,100 Filipinos, and 1,900 Koreans (*Shutsunyūkoku Kanri Tōkei Nempō*, 1997). They likely include a large number of spouses of Japanese nationals (Miyajima and Kajita, 1996, p. 2).

undocumented immigrants are a by-product of authorized labor migration, in Japan unauthorized stay constituted *the* major form of labor migration. This situation has posed difficulty in forming public policies.

Current Japanese policies on admission consist mainly of a ban on unskilled labor migration and legal admission of ethnic Japanese from Latin America and trainees. In addition to these labor-related categories, spouses of Japanese citizens and family members of lawful residents may obtain a visa for lawful residence.

A major problem of the current approach is that it does not offer any specific policy measure vis-à-vis overstaying noncitizens, except for making greater effort to apprehend and deport them. From the point of view of the protection of human rights, it becomes increasingly problematic to apply these measures to immigrants more or less settled in Japanese society.

Amnesty is a possible policy tool, although a large-scale regularization program has not yet been seriously considered in Japan. Policy makers fear that such a measure would invite more migrants. As Hiroshi Komai argues, however, amnesty is primarily a question of human rights.[90] The Justice Ministry grants "special permission for residence" to overstayers case by case, but this has mostly been confined to persons having family ties to Japanese nationals.[91] Furthermore, as Takashi Miyajima points out, new visa categories would need to be created in accordance with regularization programs.[92]

Finally, a reform is required in the Japanese admission of refugees, which has remained at a low level. The Ministry of Justice recognized as refugees a total of 218 persons out of 1,654 applicants between 1982 and August 1998.[93] Those admitted are mostly Indochina refugees. Stringent criteria reflect the attitude on the part of the Japanese state that Japan has little room for accommodating extra burdens in this form. The number of applicants for refugee status is anticipated to increase, and the screening process requires greater transparency in the future.

Conclusion

More than half a million newcomer foreign workers and their families have already settled in Japan, and their number is expected to increase in the future.

90. Dialogue between Hiroshi Komai and Yasuo Kuwabara (Komai, 1994, pp. 71–74).

91. This permit was issued to 1,406 persons in 1997 (*Shustunyūkoku Kanri Tōkei Nenpō*, 1998).

92. Miyajima, 1993, pp. 69–72.

93. If we take the recent period between 1992 and August 1998, only twenty-one persons have been recognized as refugees (*Shutsunyūkoku Kanri*, 1998, p. 168).

They are increasingly incorporated into the labor market and local communities as members of the society. As far as legally settled foreign residents are concerned, their partial citizenship has gradually expanded in scope. Yet, the Japanese government still does not regard newcomers as future citizens.

To be sure, many of the newcomers harbor the idea of returning home. But experiences of international migrants in other regions of the world suggest that segments of resident aliens will remain in the host country. Citizenship policies in Japan need to discard the assumption that people of non-Japanese ethnic and national origin may become Japanese citizens only in exceptional instances. Instead, there is a need to create a path where one may move from a temporary foreign resident to a denizen and then to a citizen. In sum, what is needed is the perspective of conceptualizing resident aliens as future citizens of Japan.

References

Aleinikoff, T. Alexander. 1998. *Between Principles and Politics: The Direction of U.S. Citizenship Policy*. Washington, D.C.: Carnegie Endowment for International Peace.

Bauböck, Rainer. 1994. *Transnational Citizenship: Membership and Rights in International Migration*. Aldershot: Edward Elgar.

Brubaker, Rogers. 1992. *Citizenship and Nationhood in France and Germany*. Cambridge, Mass.: Harvard University Press.

Brubaker, William R., ed. 1989. *Immigration and the Politics of Citizenship in Europe and North America*. Lanham, Md.: University Press of America.

Brubaker, W. R. 1989. "Membership without Citizenship: The Economic and Social Rights of Noncitizens." In *Immigration and the Politics of Citizenship in Europe and North America*, ed. William R. Brubaker. Lanham, Md.: University Press of America, pp. 14–62.

Castles, Stephen, and Mark J. Miller. 1993. *The Age of Migration: International Population Movements in the Modern World*. New York: Guilford Press.

Çinar, Dilek. 1994. "From Aliens to Citizens. A Comparative Analysis of Rules of Transition." In *Transnational Citizenship: Membership and Rights in International Migration*, ed. Rainer Bauböck. Aldershot: Edward Elgar, pp. 49–72.

Cornelius, Wayne A. 1994. "Japan: The Illusion of Immigration Control." In *Controlling Immigration: A Global Perspective*, eds. Wayne A. Cornelius, Philip L. Martin, and James F. Hollifield. Stanford: Stanford University Press, pp. 375–410.

Dummett, Ann. 1994. "The Acquisition of British Citizenship: From Imperial Traditions to National Definitions." In *Transnational Citizenship: Membership and Rights in International Migration*, ed. Rainer Bauböck. Aldershot: Edward Elgar, pp. 75–84.

Dummett, Ann, and Andrew Nicol. 1990. *Subjects, Citizens, Aliens and Others: Nationality and Immigration Law*. London: Weidenfeld and Nicolson.

Freeman, Gary P., and Nedim Ögelman. 1998. "Homeland Citizenship Policies and the Status of Third Country Nationals in the EU." *Journal of Ethnic and Migration Studies*, vol. 24, no. 4, pp. 769–88.

Fujisaki, Yasuo. 1991. *Dekasegi Nikkei Gaikokujin Rōdōsha* (Ethnic Japanese foreign migrant workers). Tokyo: Akashi Shoten.

Hachiya, Takashi. 1992. "Gaikokujin Rōdōsha Mondai Ukeire to Seifu, Keizaikai no Tachiba" (The attitudes of the government and business on the issue of accepting foreign workers). *Kikan Rōdōhō*, no. 164, pp. 42–57.

Hagino, Yoshio. 1996. *Hanrei Kenkyū Gaikokujin no Jinken* (Case studies on human rights of aliens). Tokyo: Akashi Shoten.

Hammar, Tomas, ed. 1985. *European Immigration Policy: A Comparative Study*. Cambridge: Cambridge University Press.

Hammar, Tomas. 1990. *Democracy and the Nation-State: Aliens, Denizens and Citizens in a World of International Migration*. Aldershot: Avebury.

Hanami, Tadashi. 1998. "Japanese Policies on the Rights and Benefits Granted to Foreign Workers, Residents, Refugees and Illegals." In *Temporary Workers or Future Citizens: Japanese and U.S. Migration Policies*, eds. Myron Weiner and Tadashi Hanami. New York: New York University Press, pp. 211–37.

Hisatake, Ayako. 1991. "Kodai no Koseki: Nihon Kodai Koseki no Genryū wo Saguru" (The roots of the ancient Japanese family registration system). *Aichi Kyōiku Daigaku Kenkyū Hōkoku*, no. 40, pp. 135–52.

Hōmu Nenkan (Ministry of Justice annual). 1997. Tokyo: Ministry of Justice.

Hōmu Nenkan (Ministry of Justice annual). 1967. Tokyo: Ministry of Justice.

Hosokawa, Kiyoshi. 1985. "Kaisei Kokusekihō no Gaiyō" (Summary of the revised nationality law). In *Kaisei Kosekihō Kokusekihō no Kaisetsu*, ed. Hōmu Kenkyūkai. Tokyo: Kinyū Zaisei Jijō Kenkyūkai, pp. 1–40.

Ito, Ruri. 1992. "'Japayuki-san' Gensho Saikō" (Rethinking the 'Japayuki-san' Phenomenon). In *Gaikokujin Rōdōsha Ron*, eds. Toshio Iyotani and Takamichi Kajita. Tokyo: Kōbundo, pp. 293–332.

Kajita, Takamichi. 1998. "The Challenge of Incorporating Foreigners in Japan: 'Ethnic Japanese' and 'Sociological Japanese.'" In *Temporary Workers or Future Citizens: Japanese and U.S. Migration Policies*, eds. Myron Weiner and Tadashi Hanami. New York: New York University Press, pp.120–47.

Kajita, Takamichi. 1994. *Gaikokujin Rōdōsha to Nihon* (Foreign workers and Japan). Tokyo: Nihon Hōsō Shuppan Kyōkai.

Kamachi, Noriko. 1980. "The Chinese in Meiji Japan: Their Interaction with the Japanese before the Sino-Japanese War." In *The Chinese and the Japanese*, ed. Akira Iriye. Princeton: Princeton University Press, pp. 58–73.

Kanagawa, Mintōren, et al. 1999. *Korekara Zainichi o Dō Ikirunoka* (How we should live as "zainichi"). Meeting report.

Kashiwazaki, Chikako. 1998. "*Jus Sanguinis* in Japan: The Origin of Citizenship in a Comparative Perspective." *International Journal of Comparative Sociology*, vol. 39, no. 3, pp. 278–300.

Kim, Tai-ki. 1997. *Sengo Nihon Seiji to Zainichi Chōsenjin Mondai* (Postwar politics in Japan and the issue of resident Koreans). Tokyo: Keisō Shobō.

Kim, Yong-dal. 1990. *Zainichi Chōsenjin no Kika* (Naturalization of resident Koreans in Japan). Tokyo: Akashi Shoten.

Kokuseki Kika no Jitsumu Sōdan (A guidebook for the administration of nationality and naturalization). 1993. Tokyo: Nihon Kajo Shuppan.

Komai, Hiroshi. 1994. *Iminshakai Nihon no Kōsō* (Japan as a multiethnic society). Tokyo: Kokusai Shoin.

Kondo, Atsushi. 1996. *"Gaikokujin" no Sanseiken: Denizunshippu no Hikakukenkyū* (Voting rights of foreigners: a comparative study of denizenship). Tokyo: Akashi Shoten.

Layton-Henry, Zig, ed. 1990. *The Political Rights of Migrant Workers in Western Europe*. London: Sage.

Lee, Changsoo, and George De Vos. 1981. *Koreans in Japan: Ethnic Conflict and Accommodation*. Berkeley: University of California Press.

Lie, John. 1994. "The 'Problem' of Foreign Workers in Contemporary Japan." *Bulletin of Concerned Asian Scholars*, vol. 26, no. 3, pp. 3–11.

Maher, John C., and Gaynor Macdonald, eds. 1995. *Diversity in Japanese Culture and Language*. London and New York: Kegan Paul.

Meehan, Elizabeth. 1993. *Citizenship and the European Community*. London: Sage.

Miyajima, Takashi. 1997. "Immigration and the Redefinition of 'Citizenship' in Japan: 'One People-One Nation' in Question." In *Citizenship and National Identity: From Colonialism to Globalism*, ed. T. K. Oommen. New Delhi: Sage, pp. 121–41.

Miyajima, Takashi. 1993. *Gaikokujin Rōdōsha to Nihonshakai* (Foreign workers and Japanese society). Tokyo: Akashi Shoten.

Miyajima, Takashi, and Kajita Takamichi eds. 1996. *Gaikokujin Rōdōsha kara Shimin e* (From foreign workers to citizens). Tokyo: Yōhikaku.

Miyata, Setsuko, Yong-dal Kim, and T'ae-ho Yang. 1992. *Sōshikaimei*. Tokyo: Akashi Shoten.

Mombushō (Ministry of Education). 1997. "Gaikokujin Shijo Kyōiku nituite" (On the education of the children of foreign nationals). *Gaikokujin Tōroku*, vol. 466, pp. 29–39.

Mori, Hiromi. 1997. *Immigration Policy and Foreign Workers in Japan*. New York: St. Martin's Press.

Morita, Yoshio. 1996. *Sūji ga Kataru Zainichi Kankoku Chōsenjin no Rekishi* (The history of resident Koreans illustrated by statistics). Tokyo: Akashi Shoten.

Nishinarita, Yutaka. 1997. *Zainichi Chōsenjin no "Sekai" to "Teikoku" Kokka* (The "world" of resident Koreans and the "imperial" state). Tokyo: Tokyo University Press.

Nyūkan Tōkei Kenkyūkai, ed. 1990. *Wagakuni wo meguru Kokusai Jinryū no Hensen* (The transformation of international migration around our country). Immigration Bureau, Ministry of Justice.

Oka, Takashi. 1994. *Prying Open the Door: Foreign Workers in Japan*. Washington, D.C.: Carnegie Endowment for International Peace.

Ōnuma, Yasuaki. 1979–1980. "Zainichi Chōsenjin no Hōtekichii ni kansuru Ichikōsatsu" (Legal status of Koreans in Japan). *Hōgaku Kyōkai Zasshi*, vol. 96, no.3–vol. 97, no. 4.

Ōta, Haruo. 1996. "Nihongo Kyōiku to Bogo Kyōiku" (Japanese language and native language instructions). In *Gaikokujin Rōdōsha kara Shimin e* (From foreign workers to citizens), eds. T. Kajita and T. Miyajima. Tokyo: Yuhikaku, pp. 123–43.

Ri, Yon fa. 1993. *Zainichi Kankoku, Chōsenjin to Sanseiken* (Resident Koreans and electoral rights). Tokyo: Akashi Shoten.

Ryang, Sonia. 1997. *North Koreans in Japan: Language, Ideology, and Identity*. Boulder: Westview Press.

Schuck, Peter. 1989. "Membership in the Liberal Polity: The Devaluation of American Citizenship." In *Immigration and the Politics of Citizenship in Europe and North America*, ed. William R. Brubaker. Lanham, Md.: University Press of America, pp. 51–65.

Sellek, Yoko. 1994. "Illegal Foreign Migrant Workers in Japan: Change and Challenge in Japanese Society." In *Migration: The Asian Experience*, eds. Judith M. Brown and Rosemary Foot. New York: St. Martin's Press, pp. 169–201.

Shimada, Haruo. 1994. *Japan's Guest Workers: Issues in Public Policies*. Translated by R. Northridge. Tokyo: Tokyo University Press.

Shutsunyūkoku Kanri. 1998 edition. Tokyo: Ministry of Justice.

Shutsunyūkoku Kanri. 1992 edition. Tokyo: Ministry of Justice.

Shutsunyūkoku Kanri. 1975 edition. Tokyo: Ministry of Justice.

Shutsunyūkoku Kanri no Kaiko to Tembō. 1980 edition. Tokyo: Ministry of Justice.

Shutsunyūkoku Kanri to sono Jittai (Immigration control). 1959. Tokyo: Ministry of Justice.

Shutsunyūkoku Kanri Tōkei Nempō (Annual statistics on immigration control). 1997. Published annually. Tokyo: Ministry of Justice.

Soysal, Yasemin N. 1994. *Limits of Citizenship: Migrants and Postnational Membership in Europe*. Chicago: University of Chicago Press.

Spencer, Steven A. 1992. "Illegal Migrant Laborers in Japan." *International Migration Review*, vol. 26, no. 3, pp. 754–86.

Suh, Yong-dal, ed. 1995. *Kyōsei Shakai eno Chihō Sanseiken* (Local voting rights for a society of multiethnic coexistence). Tokyo: Shakai Hyōronsha.

Tamura, Mitsuru, supplemented by Kazutaka Shigemi. 1993. *Gaikokujin Tōrokuhō Chikujō Kaisetsu* (A commentary on the alien registration law), new edition. Tokyo: Nihon Kajo Shuppan.

Tanaka, Hiroshi. 1995. *Zainichi Gaikokujin* (Resident foreigners in Japan, new edition). Tokyo: Iwanami Shoten.

Tanaka, Hiroshi. 1985. "Gaikokujin no Kyoikukomuin Shikaku, sono Mondai to Haikei" (Eligibility of foreigners for public teaching positions: problems and background). *Hōritsu Jihō*, vol. 57, no. 5, pp. 37–42.

"Teijyū Gaikokujin: Nokosareta Mondai" (Resident foreigners: remaining problems), a roundtable discussion. 1990. *Sekai*, no. 544 (August), pp. 102–17.

Tezuka, Kazuaki. 1995. *Gaikokujin to Hō* (Noncitizens and law). Tokyo: Yūhikaku.

van den Bedem, Ruud. 1994. "Towards a System of Plural Nationality in the Netherlands. Changes in Regulations and Perceptions." In *Transnational Citizenship: Membership and Rights in International Migration*, ed. Rainer Bauböck. Aldershot: Edward Elgar, pp. 95–109.

Weiner, Michael, ed. 1997. *Japan's Minorities: The Illusion of Homogeneity*. London: Routledge.

Weiner, Michael. 1994. *Race and Migration in Imperial Japan*. London: Routledge.

Weiner, Michael. 1989. *The Origin of the Korean Community in Japan 1910–1923*. Atlantic Highlands, N.J.: Humanities Press International.

Wells, Charlotte C. 1995. *Law and Citizenship in Early Modern France*. Baltimore: Johns Hopkins University Press.

Yamada, Ryoichi, and Fumiaki Tuchiya. 1985. *An Easy Guide to the New Nationality Law*. Tokyo: Japan Times.

Yamawaki, Keizo. 1994. *Kindai-nihon to Gaikokujin Rōdōsha* (Modern Japan and foreign workers). Tokyo: Akashi Shoten.

Yoshino, Kosaku. 1992. *Cultural Nationalism in Contemporary Japan*. London: Routledge.

Yoshioka, Masuo. 1995. *Zainichi Gaikokujin to Shakaihoshō: Sengo Nihon no Mainoriti Jūmin no Jinken* (Social security for resident aliens: human rights of minority populations in postwar Japan). Tokyo: Shakai Hyōronsha.

Zairyū Gaikokujin Tōkei. 1998 edition. Tokyo: Nyūkan Kyōkai.

Conclusion

CHAPTER FIFTEEN

Managing Membership: New Trends in Citizenship and Nationality Policy

MIRIAM FELDBLUM

OVER THE PAST DECADES, changing citizenship practices and politics across different countries have provoked much popular commentary and critical analysis. The country and regional—in the case of the European Union—studies collected in this volume have highlighted numerous legislative, legal, and political changes. The previous chapters have addressed reforms affecting nationality attribution and acquisition, naturalization, and dual nationality. Some of the studies also analyzed changing benefits and rights accorded to noncitizens that enable the incorporation of immigrants as citizens, prospective citizens, or long-term foreign residents into the polity.[1] The aim of this final chapter is to draw from these varied national and cross-national policy trends some common themes on the ways that states are now managing the allocation and distribution of national membership.

What is meant by *citizenship* or *membership* here? As discussed in the introductory chapter of this volume, citizenship has been largely defined in this vol-

I would like to thank Yasemin Soysal, Bill Deverell, Stephanie Pincetl, Jennifer Tucker, and Chai Feldblum for their careful and close reading of an early version of this chapter. The chapter then benefited from the constructive comments and suggestions of Ari Zolberg, Rainer Bauböck, Joe Carens, Will Kymlicka, Alexander Aleinikoff, Demetri Papademetriou, Doug Klusmeyer, Christian Joppke, and Charles Tilly.

1. A few of the studies conducted for the comparative citizenship project focus primarily on formal state citizenship acquisition (for example, Baltic states and Mexico), while others include analyses of foreigners' rights in various policy areas, such as employment, welfare, social services, health care, politics, and education.

MIRIAM FELDBLUM

ume in terms of formal nationality and citizenship status. But substantive social-political membership is integral to our explanations as well. As amply demonstrated by the previous chapters, to fully understand the consequences of formal citizenship for foreigners and immigrants, we need to take into account their membership status and access in other policy domains, including social welfare, employment, and education. In practice, immigrants experience different apportionments of membership across policy domains, in terms of both their legal standing and substantive claims.

The trend of differentiated distributions of citizenship both within and across polities brings together many of the countries under discussion here. In Australia, Canada, the Western European member states of the EU, Israel, South Africa, Japan, and the United States, for example, rights traditionally associated with formal citizenship have been gradually extended to legal, permanent foreign residents over the past decades. Across these different states, legal foreign residents have access and rights to a large array of social, economic, education, and welfare benefits (and in certain cases political rights). Within this general convergence, important variations exist in the gradations of rights afforded to foreigners in different countries, in the ways in which the formal immigration status of the foreigner matters, and in contemporary trends to qualify rights and benefits already extended to immigrants.[2] Indeed, many national state authorities and agencies now appear to be rethinking how best to manage national membership.

This final chapter brings together three broad policy trends common to most of the countries under review within a perspective that examines the variations in the ways these states have sought to manage the distribution of national citizenship. The policy trends are the growing salience of dual nationality and other citizenship and nationality reforms; the changing rights, benefits, and claims-making of foreign residents; and the growing visibility of multiple levels of governance and participation. The chapter is then divided into three sections. In the first, I examine the proliferation of nationality and citizenship reforms across the different countries, which I suggest are indicators of how states seek to reprioritize citizenship as part of their efforts to manage membership distribution. The second section focuses on the extent to which states seek to qualify rights and benefits of immigrants. I discuss the issue that qualifying immigrants' access to rights and benefits stands in contrast to postwar trends of extending social, economic, and some political rights to foreigners, and the concurrent rise of claims-making and participation both for and by immigrants

---

2. For a comprehensive study of the rights of foreigners in Western European countries, see Çinar, Davy, and Waldrauch, 1999.

in these same policy domains. In the final section, I reflect on the emergent trend of multiplying governance, or, in other words, the extent to which multiple levels of governance appear to shape policy making and decisions about citizenship practices. While much of the chapter stresses the role of national state authorities and agencies and their efforts in structuring and managing different dimensions of formal and substantive citizenship, citizenship is no longer solely defined or informed by the national state level. As evidenced by the data collected for the different countries in the project, levels outside the national state—including international courts, organizations, and other entities—have assumed greater salience and consequence in citizenship policy making.

Reprioritizing Citizenship

What does the literature theorizing and studying citizenship and immigrants offer as way of insight into the actual policy making of citizenship acquisition or nationality reforms? On the one hand, scholarly studies often focus on changing historical or theoretical understandings of national membership or contemporary transformations in citizenship practices, ranging from the political and institutional to the ethnographic and sociological.[3] Policy conversations, on the other hand, usually grapple with pressing pragmatic concerns, such as how best to enable foreigner incorporation or on what grounds nationality criteria should be expanded or restricted. Yet, policy disputes over incorporation policies, dual nationality, citizenship promotion, and citizenship acquisition do rely on understandings and conceptions of national membership.[4] And, in recent years, the burgeoning literatures on citizenship and immigration have paid closer attention to actual nationality practices. Proliferating nationality reforms, the seeming convergence of nationality and citizenship acquisition policies across states, and the rise of dual nationality are some of the policy trends that now overlap with debates about immigrants, identity, and membership.[5]

---

3. The literature on citizenship and immigration in the United States, Europe, and elsewhere is vast and continually growing. See, for example, Bauböck, 1994, *Redefining*; Bauböck, 1994, *Transnational*; Soysal, 1994; Jacobson, 1996; Smith, 1997; Brubaker, 1989; Brubaker, 1996; Pickus, 1998, *Immigration*; Kymlicka, 1995, *Multicultural*; Feldblum, 1999; Favell, 1997.

4. Some of the chapters in this volume are very explicit in their inquiries about the relation between conceptions of citizenship and changing practices of citizenship. See, in particular, the chapters on South Africa, Israel, and Canada.

5. In fact, the interest in nationality and formal citizenship has generated a growth industry in scholarship and conferences. See, for example, Pickus, 1998, *Immigration*, and Hansen and Weil, 1999, for conference proceedings focusing on nationality and citizenship in the United States and Europe.

Scholarly debates that center on competing historical or contemporary understandings of national membership have needed to incorporate into their explanations current trends of nationality revisions and convergence, some of which belie past traditions.[6] Debates that center on immigrant incorporation and settlement have needed to assess the consequentiality of formal nationality status and access and the meaning of changing membership practices for different groups of foreigners and immigrants.[7] Debates about the relationship between the changing patterns of international migration and state sovereignty have explored the impact of changing citizenship policies and the increased incidence of dual nationality on state authority.[8] The following section takes up two national issues—dual nationality reforms and citizenship promotion practices—that were highlighted by the previous chapters, and offers insight into the ways different states may be rethinking their policy options.

Structuring Dual Nationality

Attention to the growing incidence of dual and multiple nationality has been increasing among both scholars and policy makers. Within many states, especially since the 1980s, long-held prohibitions against dual nationality have been loosened or formally rescinded. Many of the current analyses of dual nationality have focused on two dimensions. One has been the *de facto* incidence of dual nationals. The other has been the formal and informal bans or acceptances of dual nationality. The incidence of dual nationals is no doubt on the rise. Zappalà and Castles, for example, in this volume estimate that the number of dual nationals in Australia has increased to around 5 million Australian dual nationals today. Likewise, Aleinikoff notes that figures for dual nationals in the United States are in the millions.[9] In Western Europe, the number of dual nationals are believed to be at least several millions and rising. The increase in dual nationals in the postwar period has been due to a variety of factors, including increased migrations, gender equity reforms in nationality transmission and retention, reforms in nationality criteria, informal policy practices to ignore the ban of dual nationality, and actual legislation to lift the traditional ban on dual nationality. Immigrant "sending" countries, in particular, have realized the pragmatic usefulness of enabling dual nationality for their emigrants. Beyond domestic changes, international conventions on dual nationality have also

---

6. See, for example, Shafir, 1998; Tilly, 1996, *Citizenship*; Smith, 1997; Brubaker, 1996.

7. See Soysal, 1994; Jacobson, 1996; Bauböck, 1994, *Redefining*; Pickus, 1998, *Immigration*.

8. See Hollifield, forthcoming; Joppke, 1999; Sassen, 1996; Sassen, 1998, *Globalization* Zolberg, 1994.

9. See, also, Fritz, April 6, 1998, p. A1.

come under reconsideration. In 1997, the Council of Europe decided on the need to rescind parts of its 1963 Convention on Reduction of Cases of Multiple Nationality and Military Obligations in Cases of Multiple Nationality.

The informal or formal allowance of dual nationality can increase the availability of rights for immigrants. In the United States, a Dominican American politician has run for local office in both the United States and the Dominican Republic, despite the formal ban against dual nationality in the United States. The comparative literature on immigration also has shown that the transnational political participation of immigrants and dual nationals in numerous countries has grown.[10] Although the formal availability and implications of dual nationality still generate political controversy, as evidenced by conflict over nationality reform in Mexico in 1997–1998 and Germany in 1998–1999, many states (both sending and receiving countries of immigration) are now investigating ways to manage dual nationality rather than simply banning it.

Indeed, changes in dual nationality have long been framed simply as either-or trends. Either one has a singular nationality or one has access to multiple nationalities; a state either bans or allows dual nationality. But contemporary national practices point to the need for reassessment. The case of the Mexican nationality reform, for example, highlights the way in which a state can structure the practice of dual membership. In his analysis on Mexican nationality reforms, Becerra Ramírez argues that a central thrust of the reforms was "to prohibit dual citizenship, not dual nationality." The Mexican reforms were pragmatic in their recognition of multiple memberships on one level, mainly that of residence, but sought to ration access to membership on other levels, including political participation. The Mexican reforms specifically sought to bar dual nationals residing elsewhere from the right to vote and stand for office. Likewise, dual nationals in Mexico cannot hold public office or public employment (in areas that involve national security).

Other policy efforts also suggest attempts to qualify the status and rights of dual nationals. In Australia, the formalistic ban on dual nationality may affect the eligibility of dual nationals to hold public office. According to Zappalà and Castles, some sources estimate that up to forty members of Parliament could be affected by an adverse ruling in the matter. In his study of Canadian policies, Galloway analyzes the government's public reservations regarding dual nationality. The Parliamentary Standing Committee on Citizenship and Immigration recommended that the government explore the possibility of reintroducing a provision stipulating that those who take out a second citizenship lose their Ca-

---

10. See, for example, Levitt, 1998; Smith and Garunizo, 1998; Basch, Glick-Schiller, and Szanton Blanc, 1994; Kastoryano, 1994; Kastoryano, 1996; and Danese, 1998.

nadian status and that naturalized Canadians also have to declare "primacy" to their Canadian citizenship. In the 1999 German nationality reform, policy makers there retreated from a general embrace of dual nationality in the face of political opposition. Instead, the German reform permits second-generation youth, who would be automatically given German nationality under the new rules, to hold dual nationality until the age of twenty-three, at which point a choice would be required except when "unreasonable conditions" apply.[11]

Reforms that qualify certain components of citizenship even as they extend the possibility of dual nationality raise difficult questions. To what extent should states restrict certain kinds of citizenship access or dimensions of citizenship rights while granting qualified nationality access? What are the legal and social consequences of such policy making? In which domains (politics, public employment, and so on) are states seeking to qualify rights and benefits of national citizenship when coupled with dual nationality status? The studies presented here signal the need to pursue research on dual nationality reforms. Such research would address some of the debates now shaping policy making. Studies should also address the extent to which bans on dual nationality and renunciation of prior nationality have been deterrents to acquiring citizenship. Or to put it conversely, what is the extent to which lifting the ban on dual nationality actually increases the recovery of prior nationalities and the number of new naturalizations?

Research on dual nationality would necessarily include formal and informal policies, stated principles and actual practices, policy intentions and policy ramifications. In Australia, for example, the requirement of renunciation did not actually change until 1986, when it was removed from the allegiance oath in the Citizenship Act. But Zappalà and Castles note that other reforms after 1973 had the effect of raising naturalization rates. By 1991, according to the report, 70 percent of eligible overseas-born residents were Australian citizens. For certain groups of immigrants in Australia more than ten years, the rate was more than 95 percent. The new Mexican or German reforms provide excellent case studies to analyze the policy formation, implementation, and consequences of qualified dual nationality. The Mexican law came into effect in 1998, but there has been ongoing discussion about refining the voting and political rights of dual nationals. The clause on reacquiring Mexican nationality for those who lost it because of prohibitions against dual nationality is a transient one. One has to apply within five years after March 20, 1998. According to Becerra Ramírez, the Mexican Ministry of Foreign Affairs calculates there are 2 or 3 million people who will be able to recover their rights to Mexican nationality.

11. See Cohen, May 22, 1999, p. A3.

Citizenship Promotions

Even as policy makers debate the premises of dual nationality reforms, almost none question the premise of citizenship itself.[12] In fact, taking citizenship as a good has been fashioned into a formal policy response to the increased numbers of long-term foreign residents. Most of the countries discussed in this volume have not undertaken explicit and universalistic citizenship promotion campaigns.[13] At the same time, the larger theme of belonging—and of critically examining who is said to belong—runs through most of the country studies. Of course, the substance of this theme can vary greatly. The policy conversations regarding citizenship acquisition in the Baltic States, Russia, Israel, South Africa, and Mexico—none of which have undertaken general citizenship promotion campaigns—feature very different views of membership, rights, and belonging. What the different policy portraits have in common is the way in which state policy options are pursued in part based on implicit rationales or explicit argumentation about who belongs and what constitutes the national identity.

Deliberate citizenship promotion efforts bring these kinds of argumentation to the center of debate. To be sure, this is not a novel policy approach. But, in the past decades, citizenship promotion policies in Australia, Canada, and the United States also have incorporated presumptions or disputes about multicultural belonging in their policy conversations. In their study of Australian policy, Zappalà and Castles document the pendulum swings in policy between assimilationist and multicultural efforts. As discussed by Galloway, a similar debate has been under way in Canada, where "Who belongs?" is one of the most basic questions. In the United States, the report by the U.S. Commission on Immigration Reform arguing for the good of "Americanization" has generated a new debate among scholars, policy makers, and activists.[14] The chapters on Canadian, Australian, and U.S. policy underscore that citizenship promotion efforts have not only sought to enable and increase citizenship acquisition, but

12. See Schuck, 1998.

13. Some national governments have appointed commissions or councils specifically mandated to reflect on national citizenship, identity, and immigrants. See, for example, the report by the U.S. Commission on Immigration Reform, 1997; also Pickus, 1998, *Immigration*; Pickus, 1998, "Introduction." In Canada and Australia, commissions on multicultural rights and citizenship have also made policy recommendations; see Kymlicka, 1995, *Multicultural*; Kymlicka, 1995, *Rights*; and Kaplan, 1993. France, too, has appointed several national commissions and councils on citizenship and citizenship incorporation; see Feldblum, 1999.

14. There is a large literature on the history, theory, policy, and politics of multiculturalism and related policies. See, for example, Kymlicka, 1995, *Multicultural*; Kymlicka, 1995, *Rights*; Kaplan, 1993; Takaki, 1993; U.S. Commission on Immigration Reform, 1997; Pickus, 1998, *Immigration;* Pickus, 1998, "Introduction"; Joppke, 1997; and Favell, 1997.

also have been part of the political processes shaping the parameters and rationale of citizenship policy.

Is the discourse about the priority and value of citizenship more prevalent in
certain groups of policy measures (or when directed toward certain populations), while the stress on rights is predominant in other policy conversations?
Are these competing conversations? What is the policy impact of debates about
nationhood and identity? These questions could be usefully considered from a
cross-national perspective, taking into account the variation in citizenship criteria and citizenship promotion efforts. Today, state campaigns encouraging naturalization are often considered directly linked to rationales of prioritizing and
revaluing national citizenship. But, the examples of reform efforts and citizenship promotion campaigns in the United States, Australia, and Canada suggest
that empirical research that assesses the usefulness and ramifications of different incentives to naturalize is needed. Incentives may include citizenship promotion campaigns or a variety of other targeted policy measures: lifting the ban
on dual nationality, lifting requirements of renunciation of prior nationality,
easing naturalization processes or amnesty programs. At the same time, understandings of citizenship promotion have also been used to justify disincentives
and discrimination against foreigners. The disincentives may include discrimination against foreigners in jobs, harsher immigration control and deportation
measures, lack of entitlements and diminished access to social service benefits
for foreigners, difficulty in obtaining permanent residency status or diminished
citizenship birthrights for children born of foreign parents.[15]

States continue to rethink their policy options. In Canada, the governmental
decision to grant preferences to citizens had a dual purpose: to enhance the
meaning and value of citizenship and to provide an incentive to naturalize. Australia appears to limit public service jobs to citizens, in part to enhance the role
of citizenship as a social unifier in multicultural society.[16] The 1986 Australian
reform revised birthright citizenship so that children of illegal aliens would not
be granted citizenship at birth; children would be granted citizenship if they remained in Australia for ten years after birth. In Canada, a parliamentary committee on citizenship made a similar recommendation: the only children of

---

15. Numerous newspaper articles have documented the rising concerns among foreigners regarding the effects of federal welfare reform. In an article by Charisse Jones entitled "New Welfare
Law Sows Panic among Immigrants," the subtitle read, "Amid Rumors, a Flood of Citizenship Requests" (August 26, 1996, p. A1). Restrictive measures against foreigners are, of course, only one
cause (and perhaps not even the prime cause) of the rise in naturalization applications in the 1990s.
See the chapter by Aleinikoff in this volume.

16. Of course, such policies do not have a direct effect on naturalization rates.

foreigners granted birthright citizenship should be those born of parents who are permanent residents.

Qualifying Rights

Beyond their focus on formal nationality or citizenship acquisition, several of the previous chapters sought to trace the changing rights and benefits accorded to foreign residents. The array of recent policy efforts that entail the doling out of rights, access, and benefits for foreigners arguably constitutes another way in which national state policy makers and agencies seek to manage national membership. These policy efforts have come about through legislative reforms, administrative regulations, actual implementations, and legal decisions.

In their discussion of policy changes in Australia, Zappalà and Castles document the post-1996 government's turn from multicultural incorporation policies toward assimilationist principles, and note that fees for visas and English courses were increased and occupational English courses were cut. Shachar's study of Israeli policy and Klaaren's discussion of current South African policy efforts underscore that state barriers need not be formal legislation, but can include administrative decisions and other regulations. But, the focus on states rescinding rights and benefits to foreigners is not self-evident. In fact, it has been the reverse trend—the extension of rights and benefits to foreign residents in highly industrialized states—that has captured the attention of scholars. In this section, I briefly review the extension of rights and benefits to foreigners before turning to the trend of rescinding rights.

There has been much theorizing about the extension of rights in the latter part of the twentieth century. Scholars argue that states increasingly have given foreigners benefits and entitlements traditionally associated with the holding of formal state citizenship. These studies draw important distinctions among long-term, permanent foreign residents; short-term or more transient foreigners; and undocumented foreigners. With regard to many benefits and rights, residence rather than citizenship determined the kinds of rights and benefits to which foreigners were entitled. In her study of European policy, Soysal contended that the postwar expansion of benefits and access to foreign residents indicated that, in a more general sense, "personhood" was replacing nationality as a basis for rights and claims-making and that national identity was being decoupled from citizenship.[17] Soysal along with others seem to suggest that the extension of rights to foreigners is the product of ongoing forces, including the

17. Soysal, 1994.

continued progression of rights in democratic, industrialized polities; the continuing rise of human rights legislation and decisions; the growing influence of immigrants' rights groups; and the increasing internationalization of domestic policy.[18]

The previous chapters confirm the general trend. Within the member states of the European Union, permanent foreign residents have access to health care, education, social services, welfare, and other benefits. Some member states have granted local voting rights to permanent foreign residents. Kashiwazaki's study of foreigner rights in Japan traced how registered foreigners are covered by the National Pension law, health insurance, protective labor laws, and welfare provisions. Efforts to grant local suffrage to long-term foreign residents have also been under way in Japan. In Canada, permanent foreign residents are entitled access to the full range of benefits. In South Africa, noncitizens have been afforded constitutional protections, upheld by court decisions. In Israel, permanent residents have access to the universal health coverage and social security. In Australia, there is little difference between citizens and foreigners in most legal matters, including owning land; the right to family reunion; and the right to education, health care, and social services.

At the same time, the studies in this volume include instances where the rights and benefits of foreign residents have been taken away and qualified.[19] Australia and, to a far greater extent, the United States have aimed to qualify the rights of foreigners in terms of access to various programs and benefits. The Australian legislation delayed access to certain benefits by new foreign residents. In 1993, the government rescinded access to unemployment and sickness benefits for new immigrants (for the first six months). Later, the waiting period for foreigners to gain eligibility for most welfare benefits was increased from six months to two years. The U.S. 1996 welfare and immigration legislation sought to rescind rights from all groups of foreign residents. The legislation distinguished between all noncitizens and citizens, between foreign residents present in the United States before enactment of the law and legal immigrants arriving after its enactment, and among different groups of foreigners (for example, refugees, permanent residents, undocumented foreigners). While Australian and U.S. reforms may make a useful comparison, it should be noted that restrictive measures cannot be uniformly treated. Barrington's discussion of the

---

18. See, for example, Hammar, 1990; Bauböck, 1994, *Transnational*; Bauböck, 1994, *Redefining*; Soysal, 1994; Jacobson, 1996; Sassen, 1998, *Transnationalizing*.

19. Benefits can be and have been taken away from citizens as well as foreigners. This trend is not unique to foreigners. But I do not believe that foreigners and citizens as a whole are in analogous positions in this regard.

enactment of restrictive policies in the Baltic states takes place in domestic and regional contexts of contested democratization and regime change.

Legislative change is not the only means to rescinding or qualifying rights. Administrative efforts to enforce restrictions against foreigners (or decisions to deny or make more difficult the acquisition of permanent residency status) have become another counterpoint to the trend of extending benefits. The South African government appears to be pursuing a combination of executive restrictions and formal legislation to qualify the rights of noncitizens, both legal and undocumented residents. In Israel, a recent administrative reform qualified the rights (to a quick naturalization) of non-Israeli spouses married to Jewish citizens. Administrative decisions to enforce restrictions of access to education, health care, and other basic services to undocumented immigrants may not be a retraction of a *de jure* right, but they certainly implicate the loss of de facto membership rights. Court decisions limiting the rights of noncitizens to access and preference in public service employment and limiting foreigners' protection against deportation are arguably other cases in which rights are being qualified rather than protected or extended.

As Martiniello notes in his chapter on European Union (EU) citizenship, the creation, expansion, and continuing implementation of EU citizenship may qualify the rights and entitlements of non-European, long-term foreign residents. In the case of EU citizenship, rights are being granted to EU nationals who are foreign residents but not to third-country nationals, who could enjoy the same foreign residency status. In accordance with the logic and regulations entailed in European Union institutions, member states may seek to limit certain benefits and entitlements to their own nationals and other EU nationals. This logic now extends even to the far Right in these countries and, thus, encompasses a harsher exclusionary rhetoric. In 1998, the National Front in Vitrolles, France, attempted to limit the traditional French "childbirth allocation" to only French and EU nationals as part of their ongoing politics of "national preference."

By rescinding rights and entitlements of foreign residents, states (whether through legislation, administrative decisions, or court decisions) have reinforced the consequentiality of legal status among all categories of foreigners and between nationals and non-nationals. In this manner, the qualification of benefits and rights may be tied directly or indirectly to other trends managing formal citizenship rights and access. Consider the impact of different nationality reforms. Several countries have limited birthright citizenship. In 1986, Australia rescinded the birthright to citizenship for children born of illegal aliens or transients. In Canada, a parliamentary committee on citizenship made a similar recommendation, while politicians and scholars in the United States have also made such proposals. In France, noncitizen parents of minor children born in France can no longer claim citizenship for their children under the age of thirteen. In a different context, the citizenship legislation in the Baltic states also sought to restrict birthright citizenship and later citizenship acquisition.

On a pragmatic policy level, these changes in immigration laws or court and administrative rulings affect several different groups of foreigners and policy domains. Decisions, for example, that affect their parents may directly or indirectly shape the life chances and opportunities of minor children, both citizens and noncitizens. In Canada as elsewhere, the deportation of noncitizen parents of minor children who are citizens has caused the de facto loss of membership for those children. According to Australian law, minor children automatically lose their Australian citizenship when their parents acquire another citizenship. Not only is the children's access to nationality affected, but also changes in welfare, social service, and health coverage laws can limit these children's access to benefits and rights.[20] Another vulnerable group has been new immigrants. Sections of both the Australian and U.S. reforms rescinded access to certain programs according to the immigrants' date of entry.

Explanations of restrictive policy changes have often examined the outcomes as indicators of broader, anti-immigrant exclusionary politics. Certainly, the politics surrounding many of these changes have been part of nativist or anti-immigrant politics. But these policies also appear to be part of broader calls for a positive reinvigoration of state citizenship and an assertion of state sovereignty. In other words, these policy efforts are part of more general trends to better manage national membership. The question remains, do the policy measures complement the political intentions, principles, or rationales underlying them? In fact, the origins and consequences of the different kinds of new citizenship policies are understudied.

Consider the paradox of policy intentions and consequences of restrictive policy measures. In the aftermath of restrictive nationality reform politics in France (after 1987 and 1993) and the rescinding of benefits to foreigners in the United States (after 1995 and 1996), both countries experienced substantive increases in applications for citizenship acquisition. What exactly was the correlation between the political and concrete policy disincentives to "remaining foreign" and the increased rate of naturalizations? Was there an underlying intention to increase the rate of naturalization or other kinds of citizenship acquisition in both countries? If so, were these effective policy measures? The answers are mixed, even if we assume that restrictive measures were in part in-

---

20. Studies must take into account both legal changes and immigrant perceptions regarding the ramifications of those changes, which may affect their decision to seek benefits for their children.

tended to increase the value and appeal of the citizenship. In the case of the United States, anti-immigrant policies coincided with the period when many foreign residents became eligible for citizenship, and some scholars contend that enabling dual nationality would more effectively increase the naturalization rate. Debates also continue about whether the reinforcement or the diminishment of status distinctions are the best policy strategies to reinvigorate national citizenship (see the conflicting testimonies of law professor Schuck and political theorist Carens in the Canadian *Lavoie* case discussed in Galloway's chapter). Indeed, the pragmatic policy consequences of regulations, legislation, and rulings that are intended to promote assimilationist citizenship may paradoxically lay the groundwork for multicultural membership.

Clearly, further empirical research is needed to assess the consequences both of policies that reinforce status discriminations and of those that eliminate status distinctions. Studies of the theoretical and pragmatic implications of different policy options must grapple with policy intentions and citizenship conceptions. When immigrants embrace citizenship because of the disincentives of remaining foreigners, do such trends promote the conception or practice of citizenship envisioned by policy makers?[21] When third-county nationals within the European Union are encouraged to undergo member-state naturalization processes so that they, too, can partake in European Union citizenship, do such policy aims promote or erode the conceptions of national citizenship assumed by policy makers? Could such suggestions also lead policy makers to focus on implementing additional disincentives to retaining the legal status of third-country nationals in the EU? Addressing these questions would contribute important empirical evidence to the ongoing debates and literature regarding different forms and practices of citizenship.

The initial focus on citizenship may center on delineating changes in the access to formal citizenship status. Still, it is evident that questions of access as well as of rights, benefits, and entitlements are now decided on the basis of multiple kinds of claims.[22] Despite state attempts to qualify citizenship, the rights to gain access to citizenship as well as the rights and benefits traditionally associ-

---

21. Discussion of the debates regarding foreigners' motives for naturalization and the intended purpose of disincentives and incentives can be found in several of the papers in this volume. See, for example, the papers on Canada, Australia, Mexico, and Israel. With regard to Canada, also see Kaplan, 1993; and with regard to the United States, the report issued by the U.S. Commission on Immigration Reform, 1997; as well as Pickus, 1998, *Immigration*; and Pickus, 1998, "Introduction."

22. See, especially, the chapters in this volume on Israel, Canada, Australia, Japan, and the European Union. See, also, Hanami, 1998, pp. 211–37. For general arguments about claims-making by and for foreigners, immigrants, and other minority groups, see Soysal, 1994; Soysal, 1997; Jacobson, 1996; Kymlicka, 1995, *Multicultural*; Kymlicka, 1995, *Rights*.

ated with citizenship continue to be sought and obtained in numerous ways. Claims brought in order to ensure basic rights and entitlements for foreigners have relied on human rights rulings and conventions, entitlements granted to communities rather than individuals, and legislation granting protection on the basis of specific group claims.

The post-1996 efforts to roll back U.S. legislation restricting access to welfare, health care, and other social service benefits by legal foreign residents provided numerous examples of these different kinds of claims. Some efforts, for example, focused on facilitating disabled foreign residents' access to naturalization on the basis of federal legislation prohibiting discrimination against the disabled and mandating reasonable accommodations for the disabled. Other efforts focused on reinterpreting individual rights to welfare and health care as collective, community rights on the same level as fire and police protection. In their decision to restore food stamps to additional groups of legal foreign residents (those already legally resident in the United States at the time of the law's enactment in 1996), the U.S. Senate also heard arguments that human rights considerations called for such a restoration.[23]

Certainly, most of the opportunities for claims-making by immigrants are often confined to legal foreign residents. Undocumented foreigners have had fewer bases upon which to claim rights or access. In fact, even in cases where illegal foreign residents may be protected by law, their constrained and precarious lives as well as their fear of deportation may prevent them from seeking their rights.[24] Yet, the de facto membership and benefits of these foreigners raise important questions about future bases for claims. Often states extend benefits in practice to undocumented foreign residents. In her study of Israeli policy, Shachar, for example, distinguishes between principle and precedent when she notes that illegal foreign residents and their children born there are not entitled to health care or education. Many Israeli schools nonetheless provide schooling for such children. In the United States, current federal and state policy efforts seek to prevent almost all health care access to undocumented residents. Other state and federal policies, which intend to promote a healthy community, have mandated school-linked health care delivery programs, such as Healthy Start in California. These programs enable and facilitate participation by illegal foreign residents and their children. In fact, such programs seek

23. These efforts were detailed in conversations with Chai Feldblum, director of the Federal Legislation Clinic, Georgetown University Law Center, and with public health officials in Los Angeles County, and in memos compiled by the organization Catholic Charities. See, also, Alvarez, May 13, 1998, p. A1.

24. Undocumented workers, for example, are in principle covered by Japanese protective labor legislation but rarely seek its protection.

to increase all parents' participation and membership in the community. The competing policy priorities of restricting membership rights, on the one hand, and ensuring wider polity benefits, on the other, need to be better understood by policy makers and scholars alike.

What has been the impact of the different kinds of claims on citizenship and incorporation policy formation? The burgeoning claims reflect and contribute to an increase in the levels of governance through which appeals and policy are made. These levels range from local jurisdictions to supranational bodies, from international conventions and treaties to international courts. When a deportation appeal was rejected in the national courts in France, the appeal went onward to the European Court of Human Rights.[25] Numerous national courts, legislation, and administrative rulings have referenced international conventions and decisions, or have been informed by international bodies and mandates. The cross-national perspectives provided by the studies collected here underscore that levels of claims-making and governance can differ considerably. Within the European Union, Martiniello has shown that there are several different levels of claims-making in which non-EU immigrant groups (and EU nationals) may engage.[26] Barrington's study of the passage of citizenship legislation within the Baltic states highlighted not only the roles played by different international European bodies but also the potential possibilities for claims-making (regarding emigrants and citizens) by other states within the Russian Federation and Baltic states. This perspective is reinforced by Ginsburgs's thorough assessment of Russian efforts regarding citizenship status and rights that combine concerns for both its emigrants and immigrants.

Multiplying Governance

Though not a policy area, the trend toward multiple levels of governance has informed policy making in the areas of immigration control, citizenship, and immigrant incorporation. Many current analyses of immigration and citizenship frame their discussion within the context of the nation-state, the historic role national sovereignty has played in defining national membership and controlling migration, and the contemporary transformations of the state role. Control and implementation of migration, immigration, and citizenship policy implicate a certain level of national sovereignty, but the extent and substance of that authority have been contested and the rise of transnational factors in citi-

25. See, for example, European Court of Human Rights, *Mehemi v. France* (85/1996/704/896).
26. See, also, Marks and McAdam, 1996; Tarrow, 1995; Soysal, 1997.

zenship and immigration policy practices debated.[27] Scholars such as Sassen
have argued that contemporary

> immigration can be seen as a strategic research site for the examination of
> the relation—the distance, the tension—between the idea of sovereignty
> as control over who enters and the constraints states encounter in making
> actual policy on the matter. Immigration is thus a sort of wrench one can
> throw into theories about sovereignty.[28]

What is meant by *transnational phenomena* and *multiple levels of governance* varies. The term *transnational* has been used to describe emergent institutional settings where the locus in which authority resides or policy is
formulated or decisions are implemented goes beyond the national level. Many
of the institutions of the European Union and their associated policy, political,
or judicial settings are thus considered to be indicative of levels of governance
beyond the national states. Likewise, transnational actors or policy processes or
discourse have emerged in these institutional settings. *Transnational norms* refers to emergent norms, pressures, or rationales driving policy decisions or implementation that are decoupled from the sole logic of the national state and
territory. According to this perspective, institutional settings may remain domestic—as in national courts—while the decisions or practices emanating from
those settings are indicative of multiple levels of authority or influence.

The arguments elaborating the significance of transnational phenomena and
the associated multiple levels of authority and policy making have been advanced by scholars in different disciplines. Sassen, a political economist, contended that migration policy is becoming increasingly transnationalized.
According to her, the "relocation of various components of sovereignty . . .
brings with it a potential strengthening of alternative subjects of international
law and actors in international relations, for example, the growing voice of
nongovernmental organizations and minorities in international fora."[29] Legal
scholar Lung-Chu Chen argued more moderately that

> the sustained growth of international governmental organizations reflects
> not merely the increasing vigor of transnational interaction but also the
> shared participation of participants that many of their preferred values
> can be obtained only through or in conjunction with collaborative trans-

27. See, for example, Bosniak, 1998; Joppke, 1998; Hollifield, forthcoming.
28. Sassen, 1996, p. 63.
29. Sassen, 1998, *Globalization,* p. 92.

national action . . . such organizations dilute the importance of historic, somewhat arbitrary and unnatural, national boundaries. They may gradually provide alternatives to the overweening power of nation-state officials.[30]

Soysal, a sociologist, identified "postnational membership" configurations and described the emergence of transnational actors, discourses, and policy levels in immigration.[31] These scholars and others have tended to identify transnational configurations that have assumed a linear progression in the postwar period, including the cumulative effect of the conventions, growing global economy, increased transnational migration, and new discourses and memberships.[32]

Not surprisingly, the arguments regarding the emergence of transnational phenomena, the import of multiple levels of governance, and the extent of diminished national sovereignty have become quite controversial.[33] In response to such arguments, other scholars declare that regardless of the institutional setting, if the locus or basis of authority remains the national state, then those policy processes are indicative of the strength and adaptability of the nation-state. Or, they argue that regardless of the origin of norms and policy rationale, if the institutional settings in which these decisions and practices are taking place are domestic in nature, then those processes, too, are indicative of the continued predominance and adaptability of the national state.[34]

30. Chen, 1989, p. 58.

31. Soysal, 1994.

32. This tendency when identifying transnational discourses and norms (such as human rights) may also be linked to scholars' methodological and analytical frameworks. Martha Finnemore has noted that certain institutionalist models place their emphasis on "the mutually reinforcing and expansive nature of (Western cultural) norms. . . . Institutionalists specify no sources of instability, conflict, or opposition to the progressive expansion of world culture" (Finnemore, 1996, p. 343). While the institutionalist scholar Yasemin Soysal explicitly discusses a conflicted dialectic between national sovereignty and human rights norms, her conclusions still suggest a progressive and mostly linear expansion of transnational and postnational configurations (Soysal, 1996). See, also, Jacobson, 1996; Bauböck, 1994, *Transnational*; Hammar, 1990.

33. Debates continue in the literature over how to interpret the reassertions of sovereignty in such domains as immigration control and citizenship, on the one hand, and extension of rights to foreigners, on the other hand. The conflict is sometimes framed in terms of a dichotomy between globalization and nation-states, with "globalists"—who assert that nation-states are being diminished—on the one side and "nation-state defenders"—who assert that nation-states are firmly entrenched—on the other side (see Joppke, 1998). In fact, scholars who have advanced arguments about globalization explicitly refute the idea of a dichotomy and readily admit to state sovereignty actions in such areas as immigration control (see Sassen, 1996; Sassen, 1998, *Globalization*; Soysal, 1996).

34. See, for example, Joppke, 1997; Joppke, 1998; Joppke, 1999; Lahav, 1998; Lahav and Guiraudon, 1997; Freeman, 1998; Freeman, 1995.

Such arguments regarding ongoing national sovereignty are partly based on the assertion that domestic principles, agencies, and institutions weigh heavily against any rise of transnational actors, institutions, and norms. If some of these scholars acknowledge some level of transnational phenomena, such as that certain processes in which migration policies and practices take place have shifted beyond the national level, their focus is to downplay the significance of increasing levels of policy making and practices. In discussing the development of asylum policy in Germany, Britain, and the United States in the postwar period, Joppke argues that the "capacity of states to control immigration" is not declining and that there is "an increased willingness and insistence of states to maintain their sovereignty."[35] His arguments about asylum policy as well as other dimensions of immigration and citizenship policy rely on the contention that the processes and institutions engendering change in these countries, including the domestic courts, are wholly under state control.[36] Likewise, Lahav argues that services and operational practices delegated or "contracted out" by states counter arguments that states are "losing control" of migration flows and immigration policy.[37]

The data and analyses about citizenship policy formation, citizenship practices, and nationality reforms presented in this volume provide a rich source for understanding the ways in which numerous international and subnational forms of governance and sources of authority do shape policy options, strategies, and outcomes. Consider the varied examples of the Baltic states, the European Union, and South Africa. Barrington's analysis of citizenship reform in the Baltic states assessed the integral roles that international organizations—specifically the Organization for Security and Cooperation in Europe and the Council of Europe—played, both directly and indirectly through exerting pressure and providing resources, in different phases of the reform processes in Estonia and Latvia. Martiniello's study of European Union citizenship practices points out both interaction between the national and European practices and the potential consequences of EU citizenship on domestic citizenship-rights policies. New levels for engagement in citizenship politics and debate have also grown in importance and salience in Western Europe, and perhaps elsewhere as well.[38] Klaaren's reconstruction of the legislative history and impetus of the South African Citizenship Act of 1995 examines the influence of international norms and human rights discourse.

35. Joppke, 1997, pp. 260–61.
36. Joppke, 1997; Joppke, 1999.
37. Lahav, 1998, pp. 14–29.
38. See Wiener, 1998; Koslowski, 1999; Levitt, 1998; Holston and Appadurai, 1996.

Changes affecting citizenship policies and practices have taken place at all levels. These include the influence of decisions in various domestic and international courts and the logic drawn from international conventions. Regional bodies such as the European Council and the European Union as well as nongovernmental organizations and intergovernmental organizations have shaped national policy making in the past years.[39] General policy trends found in most of the countries and regions under review here have featured the privatization of programs, the devolution of policy, or the dispersal of policy formation and implementation to international levels.[40] While control over national citizenship criteria and immigration is being reasserted by national states, the evidence from the previous chapters demonstrates that policy may be initiated, authorized, qualified, implemented, and otherwise shaped by other levels of governance and sources of authority.

The multiplying modes of governance and sources of authority and implementation constitute a critical area of research for citizenship policy analysis. What are the specific historical and political contexts that encourage or enable the influence of non-national institutions or international human rights discourse? What are the pragmatic effects of pursuing policy strategies at different levels, such as appealing domestic deportation or criminal cases to international courts, making claims about immigrant rights (language, schools, religion, and so on) at the level of the European Union, or placing (direct or indirect) pressures on domestic citizenship legislation from international levels? Addressing these questions will also contribute to the contentious discussions regarding the extent to which national states today in effect are "governing by remote control," or whether other kinds of substantial transformations in sovereignty are taking place.[41]

Conclusion

This volume has provided in-depth portraits of citizenship and nationality policies in twelve countries and regions. Given the diversity of changes and contexts represented by the individual studies, it would be neither appropriate

39. Much research has focused on multiple levels of governance within the European Union (see, for example, Schmitter, 1996, and Shaw, 1997). The difficulties and importance of understanding which levels of competence decide policy for third-country nationals in the European Union is outlined in Guild, 1998.

40. It should also be noted that some of these changes are not novel; for example, Americanization efforts in the early twentieth century by the Progressives included citizenship classes, and regional associations have long existed in different forms in Europe.

41. The phrase "governing by remote control" comes from Lahav, 1998, who has cited Aristide Zolberg as the original source.

nor useful to presume to offer in this final chapter a forced synthetic summary of cross-national policy trends. Instead, I have sought to highlight some central policy trends—the growing salience of dual nationality and other formal citizenship reforms, the attention paid to the rights and benefits of foreign residents, and the visibility of multiple levels of governance and participation.

As explored by the diverse studies presented here, national state authorities and agencies appear to be rethinking how better to manage national membership. Taken together, these policy trends may be encapsulated by the term *rationing citizenship*. The patterns of rationing or allocating citizenship are significant because they point to ongoing and emergent state efforts to restructure the membership rights, benefits, and obligations of immigrants. Policy efforts to restrict immigrant rights have been visible in several of the polities discussed here. State policies in the United States and Australia sought to further qualify benefits and access based upon immigration status and length of residence. In the United States, in particular, the rationing of benefits and rights stressed anew divisions between citizens and all kinds of foreigners. Policy efforts to introduce gradations in membership have been successful as well. As explicated by Becerra Ramírez in his chapter on Mexico, the 1998 nationality reform there enabled dual nationality but placed restrictions on dual citizenship. In other words, the reform withheld some of the rights of national citizenship from dual nationals.

To be sure, the phrase *rationing citizenship* encompasses divergent policies featuring perhaps dissimilar political traditions and opposing political aims. But they arguably all underscore the simultaneous reality of national citizenships (and the rights and benefits traditionally associated with national citizenship) that are no longer solely shaped by national states, and new state measures to manage, allocate, and ration those memberships. One of the aims of this chapter has been to suggest that we pay close attention to these efforts to manage the allocation and distribution of what has become today both finite resource and fluid practice, that is, national citizenship.

The implications of the varied policy trends of rationing citizenship, especially once set in the context of reconfigurations of governance and forums for policy change, can be great. Reflecting on Hannah Arendt's contention that the nationalization of human rights laid the groundwork for totalitarianism, Zolberg has argued that the postwar trend toward a "globalization" of human rights constitutes a countertrend.[42] The studies presented here confirm that new participants and contributors have come to influence—or at least seek to engage in—the policies governing citizenship, including the broad array of what we

42. Zolberg, 1994.

define as citizenship matters and the more narrow domain of nationality reform. At the same time, policies qualifying the rights afforded to foreign residents—diminishing full access to all the rights of nationality when held by dual nationals and creating additional gradations of membership as in the case of the European Union citizenship—point to the ways in which a de facto renationalization of human rights need not take place primarily at the national level.

Taking the chapters in this volume as a point of departure, we may already identify several key factors to consider when examining policy changes and choices across national contexts. These include the dynamics among different levels of governance, the extent of institutional transformations (which could result from processes of democratic transitions or regional integration), and the structural and political opportunities for a wide array of participants to engage in citizenship politics. The experiences of immigration, immigrant incorporation, and citizenship transformations are not unique to any state nor confined within a single state. The dynamics between policies modifying nationality access and qualifying rights in the national domestic context and those policies and decisions taking place along different levels of governance have become increasingly complex and interdependent. The policy convergence across states, the contradictions of policy within and among states, and the unforeseen paradoxes of future policy directions will be best addressed by concrete, comparative, and analytical approaches.

References

Aleinikoff, T. Alexander. 1998. *Between Principles and Politics: The Direction of U.S. Citizenship Policy.* Washington, D.C.: Carnegie Endowment for International Peace.

Alvarez, Lizette. (May 13, 1998.) "In New Retreat, Senate Restores Food Stamps for Legal Immigrants." *New York Times*, p. A1.

Baldwin-Edards, Martin, and Martin Schain. 1994. *The Politics of Immigration in Western Europe.* London: Frank Cass.

Basch, Linda, Nina Glick-Schiller, and Cristina Szanton Blanc. 1994. *Nations Unbound: Transnational Projects, Postcolonial Predicaments, and Deterritorialized Nation-States.* New York: Gordon and Breach.

Bauböck, Rainer, ed. 1994. *Redefining the Status of Immigrants in Europe.* Aldershot: Avebury.

Bauböck, Rainer, ed. 1994. *Transnational Citizenship. Membership and Rights in International Migration.* Aldershot: Edward Elgar.

Beiner, Ronald, ed. 1993. *Theorizing Citizenship.* Albany: State University of New York Press.

Bissoondath, Neil. 1993. "A Question of Belonging: Multiculturalism and Citizenship." In *Belonging: The Meaning and Future of Canadian Citizenship*, ed. William Kaplan. Montreal and Kingston: McGill-Queen's University Press, pp. 368–87.

Bosniak, Linda. 1998. "The Citizenship of Aliens." *Social Text*, vol. 56.

Brubaker, W. Rogers. 1996. *Nationalism Reframed: Nationhood and the National Question in the New Europe*. Cambridge: Cambridge University Press.

Brubaker, W. Rogers. 1992. *Citizenship and Nationhood in France and Germany*. Cambridge, Mass.: Harvard University Press.

Brubaker, W. Rogers, ed. 1989. *Immigration and the Politics of Citizenship in Europe and North America*. Lanham, Md.: University Press of America.

Carens, Joseph. 1993. "Aliens and Citizens: The Case for Open Borders." In *Theorizing Citizenship*, ed. Ronald Beiner. Albany: State University of New York Press, pp. 229–53.

Carens, Joseph. 1989. "Membership and Morality: Admission to Citizenship in Liberal Democratic States." In *Immigration and the Politics of Citizenship in Europe and North America*, ed. W. Brubaker. Lanham, Md.: University Press of America, pp. 31–50.

Cesarani, David, and Mary Fulbrook, eds. 1996. *Citizenship, Nationality, and Migration in Europe*. London and New York: Routledge.

Chen, Lung-Chu. 1989. *An Introduction to International Law: A Policy-Oriented Perspective*. New Haven: Yale University Press.

Çinar, Dilek, Ulrike Davy, and Harald Waldrauch. 1999. "Comparing the Rights of Non-Citizens in Western Europe." *Research Perspectives on Migration*, vol. 2, no. 2.

Clarke, Paul Barry, ed. 1994. *Citizenship*. London: Pluto Press.

Cohen, Roger. (May 22, 1999.) "Germany Makes Citizenship Easier for Foreigners to Get." *New York Times*, p. A3

Council of Europe. 1997. *European Convention on Nationality: An Explanatory Report*. DIR/JUR (97) 6 (May). Strasbourg.

Danese, Gaia. 1998. "European Transcultural Collective Action of Migrants in Southern Mediterranean Countries: The Beginnings of Multi-level Organization in Italy and Spain." Paper presented at the Workshop on Migrants, Minorities and New Forms of Citizenship in the European Union, Florence, Italy, March 6–7.

Delbruck, Jost. 1994. "Global Migration—Immigration—Multiethnicity: Challenges to the Concept of the Nation-State." *Indiana Journal of Global Legal Studies*, vol. 2, issue 1 (Fall).

Favell, Adrian. 1997. *Philosophies of Integration: Immigration and the Idea of Citizenship in France and Britain*. London: Macmillan.

Feldblum, Miriam. 1999. *Reconstructing Citizenship: The Politics of Nationality Reform and Immigration in Contemporary France*. Albany: State University of New York Press.

Feldblum, Miriam. 1998. "Reconfiguring Citizenship in Western Europe." In *Challenge to the Nation-State: Immigration in Western Europe and the United States*, ed. C. Joppke. Oxford: Oxford University Press, pp. 231–71.

Finnemore, Martha. 1996. *National Interests in International Policy*. Ithaca and London: Cornell University Press.

Freeman, Gary. 1998. "The Decline of Sovereignty? Politics and Immigration Restriction in Liberal States." In *Challenge to the Nation-State: Immigration in Western Europe and the United States*, ed. C. Joppke. Oxford: Oxford University Press, pp. 86–108.

Freeman, Gary. 1995. "Modes of Immigration Politics in Liberal Democratic States." *International Migration Review,* vol. 29, no. 4, pp. 881–902.

Fritz, Mark. (April 6, 1998.) "Pledging Multiple Allegiances." *Los Angeles Times,* p. A1.

Guild, Elspeth. 1998. "From the Single European Act to the Amsterdam Treaty: In Search of Coherence in Law over Competence, Discretion, and Third Country Nationals." Paper presented at the Workshop on Migrants, Minorities and New Forms of Citizenship in the European Union, Florence, Italy, March 6–7.

Hammar, Tomas. 1990. *International Migration, Citizenship, and Democracy.* Aldershot: Gower.

Hanami, Tadishi. 1998. "Japanese Policies on the Rights and Benefits Granted to Foreign Workers, Residents, Refugees, and Illegals." In *Temporary Workers or Future Citizens: Japanese and US Migration Policies,* eds. Myron Weiner and Tadishi Hanami. New York: New York University Press.

Hansen, Randell, and Patrick Weil, eds. 1999. *Nationality Law in Europe.* London: MacMillan.

Hollinger, David. 1995. *Postethnic America.* New York: Basic Books.

Hollifield, James. 2000. "The Politics of International Migration: How Can We 'Bring the State Back In'?" In *Talking across Disciplines: Migration Theory in Social Science and Law,* eds. Caroline Brettell and James Hollifield. New York: Routledge.

Holston, James, and Arjun Appadurai. 1996. "Cities and Citizenship." *Public Culture,* vol. 8, pp. 187–204.

Jacobson, David. 1996. *Rights across Borders: Immigration and the Decline of Citizenship.* Baltimore and London: John Hopkins University Press.

Jones, Charisse. (August 26, 1996.) "New Welfare Law Sows Panic among Immigrants; Amid Rumors, a Flood of Citizenship Requests." *New York Times,* p. A1.

Joppke, Christian. 1999. *Immigration and the Nation-State: The United States, Germany, and Great Britain.* Oxford: Oxford University Press.

Joppke, Christian, ed. 1998. *Challenge to the Nation-State: Immigration in Western Europe and the United States.* Oxford: Oxford University Press.

Joppke, Christian. 1997. "Asylum and State Sovereignty: A Comparison of the United States, Germany, and Britain." *Comparative Political Studies,* vol. 30, no. 3, pp. 259–98.

Kaplan, William, ed. 1993. *Belonging: The Meaning and Future of Canadian Citizenship.* Montreal and Kingston: McGill-Queen's University Press.

Kastoryano, Riva. 1996. *La France, l'Allemagne et leurs immigrés: Négocier l'identité.* Paris: Armand Colin.

Kastoryano, Riva. 1994. "Mobilisation ethnique en Europe: Du national au transnational." *Revue européenne des migrations internationales,* vol. 10, no. 1, pp. 169–81.

Klusmeyer, Douglas B. 1993. "Aliens, Immigrants, and Citizens: The Politics of Inclusion in the Federal Republic of Germany." *Daedalus,* vol. 122, no. 3 (Summer), pp. 81–114.

Koslowski, Rey. Forthcoming. *Migration and Citizenship in World Politics: From Nation-States to European Polity.* Ithaca: Cornell University Press.

Kymlicka, Will. 1995. *Multicultural Citizenship: A Liberal Theory of Minority Rights.* Oxford: Clarendon Press.

Kymlicka, Will, ed. 1995. *The Rights of Minority Cultures.* Oxford: Oxford University Press.

Lahav, Gallya. 1998. "The Devolution and Privatization of Immigration Control: The State and Third Party Regulatory Agents." Paper presented at the Workshop on Migrants, Minorities and New Forms of Citizenship in the European Union, Florence, Italy, March 6–7.

Lahav, Gallya, and V. Guiraudon. 1997. "The Devolution of Immigration Regimes in Europe." Paper presented at the European Community Studies Association, Fifth Biennial International Conference, Seattle, Wash., May 29–June 1.

Levitt, Peggy. 1998. "Social Remittances: A Local-Level, Migration-Driven Form of Cultural Diffusion." *International Migration Review*, vol. 32, pp. 926–48.

Liebich, Andre, and Daniel Warner, with Jusna Dragovic, eds. 1995. *Citizenship East and West.* London and New York: Kegan Paul International.

Marks, Gary, and Doug McAdam. 1996. "Social Movements and the Changing Structure of Political Opportunity in the European Union." *West European Politics*, vol. 19, no. 2 (April), pp. 249–78.

Noiriel, Gerard, and Michel Offerle. 1997. "Citizenship and Nationality in Nineteenth Century France." In *European Integration in Social and Historical Perspective*, eds. J. Klaussen and L. Tilly. Lanham, Md.: Rowman and Littlefield.

Oommen, T. K. 1997. *Citizenship, Nationality and Ethnicity: Reconciling Competing Identities.* Cambridge: Polity Press.

Pickus, Noah, ed. 1998. *Immigration and Citizenship in the 21st Century.* Lanham, Md.: Rowman and Littlefield.

Pickus, Noah. 1998. "Introduction." In *Immigration and Citizenship in the 21st Century*, ed. Noah Pickus. Lanham, Md.: Rowman and Littlefield.

Sassen, Saskia. 1998. *Globalization and Its Discontents: Essays on the New Mobility of People and Money.* New York: New Press.

Sassen, Saskia. 1998. "The *de facto* Transnationalizing of Immigration Policy." In *Challenge to the Nation-State: Immigration in Western Europe and the United States*, ed. C. Joppke. Oxford: Oxford University Press, pp. 49–85.

Sassen, Saskia. 1996. *Losing Control? Sovereignty in an Age of Globalization.* 1995 Columbia University Leonard Hastings Schoff Memorial Lectures. New York: Columbia University Press.

Schmitter, Philippe C. 1996. "Examining the Present Euro-Polity with the Help of Past Theories." In *Governance in the European Union*, eds. Gary Marks, Fritz W. Scharpf, Philippe C. Schmitter, and Wolfgang Streck. London: Sage Publications.

Schuck, Peter H. 1998. *Citizens, Strangers and In-Betweens: Essays on Immigration and Citizenship.* Boulder: Westview Press.

Shafir, Gershon, ed. 1998. *The Citizenship Debates: A Reader.* Minneapolis: University of Minnesota Press.

Shaw, Jo. 1997. "Citizenship of the Union: Towards Post-National Membership." In *Collected Courses of the Academy of European Law 1995*, vol. VI, no. 1. The Hague: Kluwer Law International.

Shklar, Judith N. 1991. *American Citizenship: The Quest for Inclusion.* Cambridge, Mass.: Harvard University Press.

Smith, Michael Peter, and Luis Garunizo. 1998. "Transnationalism from Below." *Comparative Urban and Community Research*, vol. 6.

Smith, Rogers. 1997. *Civic Ideals: Conflicting Visions of Citizenship in U.S. History.* New Haven: Yale University Press.

Soysal, Yasemin N. 1997. "Changing Parameters of Citizenship and Claims-Making: Organized Islam in European Public Spheres." *Theory and Society*, vol. 26, no. 4, pp. 509–27.

Soysal, Yasemin N. 1996. "Changing Citizenship in Europe: Remarks on Postnational Membership and the National State." In *Citizenship, Nationality, and Migration in Europe*, eds. David Cesarani and Mary Fulbrook. London and New York: Routledge, pp. 17–29.

Soysal, Yasemin N. 1994. *Limits of Citizenship: Migrants and Postnational Membership in Europe.* Chicago: University of Chicago Press.

Spinner, Jeff. 1995. *The Boundaries of Citizenship: Race, Ethnicity, and Nationality in the Liberal State.* Baltimore and London: John Hopkins University Press.

Takaki, Ronald. 1993. *A Different Mirror: A History of Multicultural America.* Boston: Little, Brown.

Tarrow, Sidney. 1995. "The Europeanization of Conflict: Reflections from a Social Movement Perspective." *West European Politics*, vol. 18, no. 2.

Tilly, Charles, ed. 1996. *Citizenship, Identity and Social History.* International Review of Social History Supplement. London: Cambridge University Press.

Tilly, Charles. 1996. "Citizenship, Identity and Social History." In *Citizenship, Identity and Social History,* International Review of Social History Supplement, ed. Charles Tilly. London: Cambridge University Press.

Tilly, Charles. 1993. "National Self-Determination as a Problem for All of Us." *Daedalus*, vol. 122, no. 3 (Summer), pp. 29–36.

U.S. Commission on Immigration Reform. 1997. *Becoming an American: Immigration and Immigrant Policy.* Report to Congress. Washington, D.C.

Weil, Patrick. 1996. "Nationalities and Citizenships: The Lessons of the French Experience for Germany and Europe." In *Citizenship, Nationality, and Migration in Europe*, eds. David Cesarani and Mary Fulbrook. London and New York: Routledge, pp. 74–87.

Weiner, Antje. 1998. *"European" Citizenship Practice: Building Institutions of a Non-State.* Boulder: Westview Press.

Zolberg, Aristide. 1994. "Changing Sovereignty Games and International Relations." *Indiana Journal of Global Legal Studies*, vol. 2, issue 1 (Fall).

About the Authors

T. Alexander Aleinikoff is a Senior Associate with the Carnegie Endowment's International Migration Policy Program and Professor at the Georgetown University Law Center, teaching immigration and refugee law and constitutional law. From 1994 to 1997 he served first as General Counsel and then as Executive Associate Commissioner for the U.S. Immigration and Naturalization Service. He has written widely on immigration, citizenship, and refugee law and policy.

Lowell W. Barrington is Assistant Professor in the Department of Political Science at Marquette University. He is the principal investigator of a National Science Foundation–sponsored project surveying ethnic minorities in Kazakhstan, Kyrgyzstan, Belarus, and Ukraine. He is also Vice President for Publications of the Association for the Study of Nationalities, and the former Editor-in-Chief of *Analysis of Current Events*. His recent publications examine post-Soviet citizenship policy and post-Communist mass attitudes.

Rainer Bauböck is a Senior Researcher in the Research Unit on Institutional Change and European Integration at the Austrian Academy of Sciences, and Senior Lecturer at the Universities of Vienna and Innsbruck. His work focuses on normative political theory, comparative and theoretical research on citizenship, migration, ethnicity, and nationalism. Recent publications include *Transnational Citizenship: Membership and Rights in International Migration*

(Aldershot: Edward Elgar, 1994); and *Blurred Boundaries: Migration, Ethnicity, Citizenship* (Aldershot: Ashgate, 1998), edited with John Rundell.

Manuel Becerra Ramírez received Doctorates in Constitutional Law degree from the Universidad Nacional Autónoma de México (UNAM) and in International Law from the State University of Moscow, in Lomonosov. He is currently a full-time researcher at the Instituto de Investigaciones Jurídicas at UNAM, where he also teaches public international law.

Stephen Castles is Director of the Centre for Asia Pacific Social Transformation at the University of Wollongong. His publications include *Immigrant Workers and Class Structure in Western Europe* (London: Oxford University Press, 1973), with Godula Kosack; *The Age of Migration: International Migration in the Modern World* (London: MacMillan, 1993), with Mark Miller; and *Citizenship and Migration: Globalization and the Politics of Belonging* (London: MacMillan and New York: Routledge, 2000), with Alastair Davidson.

Miriam Feldblum is a Senior Research Associate in the Division of Humanities and Social Sciences at the California Institute of Technology. Her publications include *Reconstructing Citizenship* (New York: SUNY Press, 1999), on citizenship politics in France, and articles on comparative citizenship and immigration policies in Western Europe and the United States.

Donald Galloway is a Professor of Law at the University of Victoria, British Columbia, teaching Administrative Law, Immigration and Refugee Law, and Jurisprudence. He has recently published a book on Canadian immigration law, as well as a number of articles on related issues. Galloway is a member of Canada's Immigration and Refugee Board and is currently a member of the Board's Convention Refugee Determination Division.

George Ginsburgs earned his Doctorate in Political Science from the University of California, Los Angeles. He has been a Professor at the Rutgers University School of Law-Camden since 1973. He has published widely in such journals as the *American Slavic and East European Review* and *Political Science Quarterly* and is a member of the board of editors of both the *American Journal of Comparative Law* and the *Review of Central and East European Law*.

Chikako Kashiwazaki is Lecturer of Sociology at Sophia University, Tokyo. She received a Doctorate in Sociology from Brown University. Her research interests include ethnic relations, nationalism, and the historical dynamics of citizenship and nationality. She has published articles in *Research in Political Sociology* and *International Journal of Comparative Sociology*.

Jonathan Klaaren is Associate Professor at the Faculty of Law, University of the Witwatersrand, Johannesburg. He is an American citizen with South African permanent residence. With law degrees from both South Africa and the United States, he is currently working on a Doctorate on immigration law and racial and state formation in early twentieth-century South Africa through Yale University. He has published in the *South African Law Journal, South African Journal on Human Rights*, and *Columbia Human Rights Law Review*.

Douglas Klusmeyer is an Associate with the Carnegie Endowment's International Migration Policy Program, primarily working on comparative citizenship issues. He earned a B.A. from Northwestern University, and a Ph.D. in Modern European History and a J.D. from Stanford University. He has published a monograph, *Between Consent and Descent: Conceptions of Democratic Citizenship,* as well as articles in such journals as *Daedalus* and *SAIS Review*.

David A. Martin is Henry L. and Grace Doherty Professor of Law at the University of Virginia, teaching immigration, constitutional law, and international law. He is a graduate of Depauw University and Yale Law School, where he served as Editor-in-Chief of *Yale Law Journal*. From 1978 to 1980, he served as Special Assistant in the Human Rights Bureau of the U.S. Department of State. From August 1995 to January 1998, he served as General Counsel to the Immigration and Naturalization Service in Washington.

Marco Martiniello is Senior Research Fellow at the National Fund for Scientific Research (FNRS) and Lecturer in Politics at the University of Liège. He earned a B.A. in Sociology from the University of Liège and Ph.D. in Political Science from the European University Institute, Florence (Italy). He is the director of the Centre d'Etudes de l'Ethnicité et des Migrations (CEDEM). His latest books include *Migration, Citizenship and Ethno-National Identities in the European Union* (Aldershot: Avebury, 1995), as editor; *Sortir des ghettos culturels* (Paris: Presses de Sc. Po., 1997); *O9ù la la Belgique?* (Paris: L'Harmattan, 1998), co-edited; and *Multicultural Policies and the State* (Utrecht: ERCOMER, 1998).

Kathleen Newland is Co-director of the Carnegie Endowment's International Migration Policy Program. Her work focuses on refugee policy and international humanitarian response. Previously, she was a Lecturer in International Relations at the London School of Economics and a Consultant to the United Nations. Her numerous publications include *U.S. Refugee Policy: Dilemmas and Directions* (Washington, D.C.: Carnegie Endowment, 1995).

Ayelet Shachar is Assistant Professor of Law at the University of Toronto, teaching immigration law, multiculturalism, and civil procedure. She has a Doctorate from Yale University and degrees in Law and Political Science from Tel Aviv University. Her research addresses the intersection of contemporary political theory, family law, and immigration policy. She has recently published in the *Journal of Political Philosophy*, the *Canadian Journal of Women and the Law, Citizenship Studies*, and *Political Theory*, and is the author of *Multicultural Jurisdictions* (Cambridge University Press, forthcoming).

Gianni Zappalà has a Doctorate from the Faculty of Economics and Politics, University of Cambridge. He is currently the Research Coordinator for the Smith Family (a leading Australian welfare organization). He has held Research Fellow positions at the universities of Cambridge, Sydney, and Wollongong, and the Australian National University. In 1996 he was the Australian Parliamentary Fellow at Parliament House, Canberra. His publications include *Four Weddings, a Funeral and a Family Reunion: Ethnicity and Representation in Australian Federal Politics* (Canberra: AGPS, 1997).

Aristide R. Zolberg is University-in-Exile Professor of Political Science at the New School for Social Research; Director of the International Center for Migration, Ethnicity, and Citizenship; and Co-chair of the MacArthur Program on Global Change and Liberalism. He is a member of the Social Science Research Council's Committee on International Migration, the editorial boards of *International Migration Review* and *Journal of Refugee Studies*, and the advisory board of the Centre for Refugee Studies, York University, Canada. His recent books include *Escape from Violence: Conflict and the Refugee Crisis in the Developing World,* co-authored with Astri Suhrke and Sergio Aguayo.

Index

Afghans, 180, 214
Ainu, 445
Albania, 200
Aliyah (immigration, Hebrew), 389, 391, 394, 397, 421
Allies, 439
al-Nakaba, 403
Amnesty, 466
Apartheid, 222, 247; anti-apartheid, 235
Arab Palestinian. *See* Palestinian Arab
Arabic speakers in Australia, 34
Argentina, 140
Assimilation, 20, 30, 76, 115, 444, 445, 459
Australia, 3, 5, 7, 14, 24, 32, 139, 155, 476, 479, 481, 494; Australian Institute of Multicultural Affairs (AIMA), 51; Australian Labor Party, 50, 70, 72; Bureau of Immigration, Multicultural and Population Research, 53; Department of Immigration and Ethnic Affairs, 53, 150; Federal Department of Immigration, 49, 69; Humanitarian Program, 68; Joint Standing Committee on Migration, 57, 70; Liberal Party, 53, 57; Liberal-Country Party Coalition, 51; Liberal-National Party Coalition, 54; Migration Program, 68; national identity, 72; National Office of Overseas Skills Recognition, 53; National Party, 53; nativists, 72; Office of Multicultural Affairs, 51, 53, 72; primary citizenship, 61; regaining citizenship, 55;

Special Broadcasting Service, 51; White Australia Policy, 33, 50; Years of Citizenship, 53, 70
Australia, Defense Act, 67
Australia, National Agenda for a Multicultural Australia, 52
Australia, Nationality and Citizenship Act, 38, 45
Australia, Native Title Act, 42, 74
Australia, Naturalization Act, 45
Australia, Public Service Act, 67
Australia, Racial Discrimination Act, 42, 65, 77
Australian Citizenship Act, 43, 44, 54, 56, 60, 71
Austria, 75, 369
Azerbaijan, 179. *See also* Central Asian Republics; Commonwealth of Independent States; Soviet Union

Baltic States, 7, 8, 17, 175, 179, 253, 492; ethnic Russians, 256, 259, 267, 271, 274; minorities, 258. *See also* Soviet Union; *and individual states*
Bangladesh, 455
Bauböck, Rainer, 158
Beazley, Kim, 72
Becerra Ramírez, Manuel, 13, 479, 480, 494
Belarus, 179, 188; Belorussians, 181; Union Treaty with Russia, 188. *See also*

CARNEGIE ENDOWMENT FOR INTERNATIONAL PEACE

The Carnegie Endowment is a private, nonprofit organization dedicated to advancing cooperation between nations and promoting active international engagement by the United States. Founded in 1910, its work is nonpartisan and dedicated to achieving practical results. Through research, publishing, convening, and, on occasion, creating new institutions and international networks, Endowment associates shape fresh policy approaches. Their interests span geographic regions and the relations among governments, business, international organizations, and civil society, focusing on the economic, political, and technological forces driving global change. Through its Carnegie Moscow Center, the Endowment helps develop a tradition of public policy analysis in the states of the former Soviet Union and improve relations between Russia and the United States. The Endowment publishes *Foreign Policy*, one of the world's leading journals of international politics and economics, which reaches readers in more than 120 countries and in several languages

---